COMMON PUFFIN
Fratercula arctica

KING PENGUIN
Aptenodytes patagonicus

MOCKINGBIRD
Mimus polyglottos

CARACARA
Caracara cheriway

PIED WAGTAIL
Motacilla alba

COMMON GRACKLE
Quiscalus quiscula

CINEREOUS TINAMOU
Nothoprocta cinerascens

BOAT-TAILED GRACKLE
Cassidix mexicanus

GREY SEA EAGLE
Haliaeetus albicilla

SCISSOR-TAILED FLYCATCHER
Muscivora forficata

STORM PETREL
Hydrobates pelagicus

RAVEN
Corvus corax

SKYLARK
Alauda arvensis

GREAT TINAMOU
Tinamus major

MACGREGOR'S
BIRD OF PARADISE
Macgregoria pulchra

BLUE-GREY
GNATCATCHER
Polioptila caerulea

ARCTIC LOON
Gavia arctica

GOLDEN EAGLE
Aquila chrysaëtos

AMERICAN WOODCOCK
Philohela minor

COMMON CROW
Corvus brachyrhynchos

YELLOW-BILLED CUCKOO
Coccyzus americanus

ANHINGA
Anhinga anhinga

LIMPKIN
Aramus guarauna

SMALL-BILLED TINAMOU
Crypturellus parvirostris

EASTERN BLUEBIRD
Sialia sialis

SANDHILL CRANE
Grus canadensis

SAGE GROUSE
Centrocercus urophasianus

HOOPOE
Upupa epops

EUROPEAN BEE-EATER
Merops apiaster

BARN SWALLOW
Hirundo rustica

BROWN PELICAN
Pelecanus occidentalis

SPRUCE GROUSE
Canachites canadensis

RED-BREASTED PITTA
Pitta erythrogaster

SHARP-TAILED GROUSE
Pedioecetes phasianellus

MALLARD
Anas platyrhynchos

WHITE-WINGED TRILLER
Lalage sueurii

BROAD-BILLED HUMMINGBIRD
Cynanthus latirostris

OLIVE-SIDED FLYCATCHER
Nuttallornis borealis

BENNETT'S CASSOWARY
Casuarius bennetti

RATTLING CISTICOLA
Cisticola chiniana

GREAT ANTSHRIKE
Taraba major

GENTOO PENGUIN
Pygoscelis papua

SCARLET IBIS
Eudocimus ruber

AND
WHITE IBIS
Eudocimus albus

BIRDS
OF THE WORLD

A SURVEY OF THE TWENTY-SEVEN ORDERS
AND ONE HUNDRED AND FIFTY-FIVE FAMILIES

by OLIVER L. AUSTIN, JR.
Florida State Museum, University of Florida

Illustrated by ARTHUR SINGER

EDITED BY HERBERT S. ZIM
Consultant for this edition MAURICE BURTON

with a Foreword by PETER SCOTT

HAMLYN

LONDON / NEW YORK / SYDNEY / TORONTO

TABLE OF CONTENTS

FOREWORD *by Peter Scott* 8
   AUTHOR'S PREFACE 9
   INTRODUCTION 10
KIWIS—Apterygiformes 15
   KIWIS—*Apterygidae* 15
OSTRICHES—Struthioniformes 16
   OSTRICHES—*Struthionidae* 16
RHEAS—Rheiformes 18
   RHEAS—*Rheidae* 18
CASSOWARIES, EMUS—Casuariiformes . . . 18
   CASSOWARIES—*Casuariidae* 18
   EMUS—*Dromiceidae* 20
TINAMOUS—Tinamiformes 21
   TINAMOUS—*Tinamidae* 21
GREBES—Podicipediformes 22
   GREBES—*Podicipedidae* 22
DIVERS—Gaviiformes 24
   DIVERS—*Gaviidae* 24
PENGUINS—Sphenisciformes 26
   PENGUINS—*Spheniscidae* 26
TUBE-NOSED SWIMMERS—Procellariiformes 31
   ALBATROSSES—*Diomedeidae* 32
   SHEARWATERS—*Procellariidae* 34
   STORM PETRELS—*Hydrobatidae* 37
   DIVING PETRELS—*Pelecanoididae* 38
PELICANS AND ALLIES—Pelecaniformes . . 38
   TROPIC-BIRDS—*Phaëthontidae* 39
   PELICANS—*Pelecanidae* 40
   CORMORANTS—*Phalacrocoracidae* 43
   ANHINGAS (DARTERS) *Anhingidae* 45
   BOOBIES, GANNETS—*Sulidae* 46
   FRIGATE-BIRDS—*Fregatidae* 48
HERONS AND ALLIES—Ciconiiformes . . . 50
   HERONS AND BITTERNS—*Ardeidae* 50
   BOATBILL HERON—*Cochleariidae* 55
   WHALEHEAD STORK—*Balaenicipitidae* 55
   HAMMERHEAD—*Scopidae* 55
   STORKS—*Ciconiidae* 56
   IBISES AND SPOONBILLS—*Threskiornithidae* . . . 59
   FLAMINGOS—*Phoenicopteridae* 61
WATERFOWL—Anseriformes 63
   SCREAMERS—*Anhimidae* 63
   SWANS, GEESE, DUCKS—*Anatidae* 64
BIRDS OF PREY—Falconiformes 72
   AMERICAN VULTURES—*Cathartidae* 73

SECRETARY BIRDS—*Sagittariidae* 74
HAWKS, VULTURES, EAGLES—*Accipitridae* . . . 75
OSPREYS—*Pandionidae* 82
FALCONS AND CARACARAS—*Falconidae* 83
FOWL-LIKE BIRDS—Galliformes 85
   MEGAPODES-*Megapodiidae* 85
   CURASSOWS, GUANS, CHACHALACAS—*Cracidae* . 87
   GROUSE AND PTARMIGANS—*Tetraonidae* 88
   QUAILS, PARTRIDGES, PHEASANTS—*Phasianidae* . 92
   GUINEAFOWLS—*Numididae* 98
   TURKEYS—*Meleagrididae* 98
   HOATZIN—*Opisthocomidae* 100
CRANES, RAILS, AND ALLIES—Gruiformes . 101
   MESITAE—*Mesitornithidae* 101
   HEMIPODES—*Turnicidae* 102
   CRANES—*Gruidae* 102
   LIMPKIN—*Aramidae* 106
   TRUMPETERS—*Psophiidae* 106
   RAILS, GALLINULES, COOTS—*Rallidae* 107
   FINFOOTS—*Heliornithidae* 111
   KAGU—*Rhynochetidae* 111
   SERIEMAS—*Cariamidae* 112
   SUNBITTERN—*Eurypygidae* 112
   BUSTARDS—*Otidae* 113
WADERS, GULLS, AUKS—Charadriiformes . . 115
   JAÇANAS—*Jacanidae* 116
   PAINTED SNIPES—*Rostratulidae* 117
   OYSTERCATCHERS—*Haematopodidae* 118
   PLOVERS AND LAPWINGS—*Charadriidae* 118
   SANDPIPERS AND ALLIES—*Scolopacidae* 118
   STILTS AND AVOCETS—*Recurvirostridae* 123
   PHALAROPES—*Phalaropodidae* 124
   CRAB PLOVER—*Dromadidae* 125
   THICK-KNEES OR STONE CURLEWS—*Burhinidae* . . 125
   COURSERS, PRATINCOLES—*Glareolidae* 126
   SEEDSNIPES—*Thinocoridae* 127
   SHEATHBILLS—*Chionididae* 127
   SKUAS AND JAEGERS—*Stercorariidae* 128
   GULLS AND TERNS—*Laridae* 130
   SKIMMERS—*Rynchopidae* 137
   AUKS AND ALLIES—*Alcidae* 137
PIGEONS AND ALLIES—Columbiformes . . . 140
   SANDGROUSE—*Pteroclidae* 140
   DODOS AND SOLITAIRES—*Raphidae* 141
   PIGEONS AND DOVES—*Columbidae* 141
PARROTS AND ALLIES—Psittaciformes . . . 146
   PARROTS AND ALLIES—*Psittacidae* 146
CUCKOOS AND ALLIES—Cuculiformes . . . 150
   TOURACOS—*Musophagidae* 150

Published by THE HAMLYN PUBLISHING GROUP LIMITED - LONDON / NEW YORK / SYDNEY / TORONTO
Hamlyn House, Feltham, Middlesex, England, by arrangement with Golden Press.
© Copyright 1961 by Golden Press Inc. All rights reserved. This edition first published 1962. Tenth impression 1971.
ISBN 0 601 07055 0
Printed in Czechoslovakia by TSNP Martin
51637

CUCKOOS, ANIS, ROADRUNNERS, COUCALS—*Cuculidae* 151

OWLS—Strigiformes 154
  BARN OWLS—*Tytonidae* 154
  TYPICAL OWLS—*Strigidae* 155

GOATSUCKERS—Caprimulgiformes . . 159
  OILBIRD OR GUACHARO—*Steatornithidae* 160
  FROGMOUTHS—*Podargidae* 160
  POTOOS—*Nyctibiidae* 161
  OWLET-FROGMOUTHS—*Aegothelidae* 161
  NIGHTJARS—*Caprimulgidae* 162

SWIFTS, HUMMINGBIRDS—Apodiformes . . 164
  SWIFTS—*Apodidae* 165
  CRESTED SWIFTS—*Hemiprocnidae* 167
  HUMMINGBIRDS—*Trochilidae* 168

TROGONS—Trogoniformes 172
  TROGONS—*Trogonidae* 172

COLIES OR MOUSEBIRDS—Coliiformes . . . 174
  COLIES—*Coliidae* 174

KINGFISHERS AND ALLIES—Coraciiformes . 175
  KINGFISHERS—*Alcedinidae* 175
  TODIES—*Todidae* 178
  MOTMOTS—*Momotidae* 178
  BEE-EATERS—*Meropidae* 179
  ROLLERS—*Coraciidae* 179
  HOOPOES AND WOODHOOPOES—*Upupidae* . . . 182
  HORNBILLS—*Bucerotidae* 182

WOODPECKERS AND ALLIES—Piciformes . 184
  BARBETS—*Capitonidae* 185
  HONEYGUIDES—*Indicatoridae* 186
  JACAMARS—*Galbulidae* 187
  PUFFBIRDS—*Bucconidae* 187
  TOUCANS—*Ramphastidae* 188
  WOODPECKERS, WRYNECKS, PICULETS—*Picidae* . 191

PERCHING BIRDS—Passeriformes 195

BROADBILLS—Eurylaimi
  BROADBILLS—*Eurylaimidae* 195

TYRANT FLYCATCHERS AND ALLIES—Tyranni
  WOODCREEPERS—*Dendrocolaptidae* 196
  OVENBIRDS—*Furnariidae* 198
  ANTBIRDS—*Formicariidae* 199
  ANTPIPITS—*Conopophagidae* 201
  TAPACULOS—*Rhinocryptidae* 202
  COTINGAS—*Cotingidae* 203
  MANAKINS—*Pipridae* 205
  TYRANT FLYCATCHERS—*Tyrannidae* 207
  PLANTCUTTERS—*Phytotomidae* 210
  SHARPBILLS—*Oxyruncidae* 210

PITTAS—*Pittidae* 211
NEW ZEALAND WRENS—*Acanthisittidae* 212
ASITIES, FALSE SUNBIRDS—*Philepittidae* 212
LYREBIRDS AND SCRUB-BIRDS—Menurae
  LYREBIRDS—*Menuridae* 213
  SCRUB-BIRDS—*Atrichornithidae* 214
SONGBIRDS—Passeres
  LARKS—*Alaudidae* 215
  SWALLOWS AND MARTINS—*Hirundinidae* . . . 216
  CUCKOO-SHRIKES AND MINIVETS—*Campephagidae* 219
  DRONGOS—*Dicruridae* 220
  OLD WORLD ORIOLES—*Oriolidae* 221
  CROWS AND JAYS—*Corvidae* 223
  WATTLEBIRDS—*Callaeidae* 227
  MUDNEST BUILDERS—*Grallinidae* 227
  BUTCHERBIRDS AND BELLMAGPIES—*Cracticidae* . 228
  BOWERBIRDS—*Ptilonorhynchidae* 229
  BIRDS OF PARADISE—*Paradisaeidae* 232
  TITMICE—*Paridae* 235
  CREEPERS—*Certhiidae* 237
  NUTHATCHES AND ALLIES—*Sittidae* 237
  BABBLERS AND ALLIES—*Timaliidae* 240
  BULBULS—*Pycnonotidae* 243
  LEAFBIRDS AND ALLIES—*Chloropseidae* . . . 245
  DIPPERS—*Cinclidae* 246
  WRENS—*Troglodytidae* 247
  MOCKINGBIRDS AND THRASHERS—*Mimidae* . . 249
  THRUSHES—*Turdidae* 251
  OLD WORLD WARBLERS—*Sylviidae* 255
  OLD WORLD FLYCATCHERS—*Muscicapidae* . . . 259
  ACCENTORS—*Prunellidae* 262
  PIPITS AND WAGTAILS—*Motacillidae* 263
  WAXWINGS AND ALLIES—*Bombycillidae* 265
  WOOD-SWALLOWS—*Artamidae* 267
  VANGA-SHRIKES—*Vangidae* 268
  SHRIKES—*Laniidae* 269
  STARLINGS—*Sturnidae* 271
  HONEYEATERS—*Meliphagidae* 275
  SUNBIRDS—*Nectariniidae* 278
  FLOWERPECKERS—*Dicaeidae* 279
  WHITE-EYES—*Zosteropidae* 280
  VIREOS—*Vireonidae* 281
  HAWAIIAN HONEYCREEPERS—*Drepanidae* . . . 283
  WOOD WARBLERS AND BANANAQUITS—*Parulidae* 284
  ICTERIDS—*Icteridae* 287
  TANAGERS—*Thraupidae* 291
  NEW WORLD SEEDEATERS—*Fringillidae* 295
  OLD WORLD SEEDEATERS—*Ploceidae* 301
  BIBLIOGRAPHY 308
  INDEX 310

Archaeopteryx
(artist's reconstruction)

FOREWORD

by Peter Scott

In Britain we are proud of our reputation as a bird-conscious people. Our pride is well founded in history though our knowledge, and even our appreciation, often tends to be restricted to that odd assemblage of species labelled 'British Birds'. Yet these British birds, fascinating and various as they are, make up only a tiny part of the astonishing variety of the world's birds species. Our insularity is understandable, for wild birds that we can see and hear may be expected to have a much greater attraction than skins in cabinets or captive birds in zoos. But insularity in ornithology is regrettable at a time when there is so urgent a need to think of birds (and particularly of their conservation) on a world-wide scale. And there are additional reasons for fitting our British birds into a global context, for the study of evolution — the influence of different environments on different groups of birds, by which such variety came about — leads to one of the most majestic conceptions of the natural world.

I cannot imagine anyone with even the slightest interest in birds remaining unexcited as he turns the pages of this book. The plan is simple — a brief illustrated review of the birds of all the world, family by family; but this is no dusty catalogue. Thanks to Mr Singer's magnificent illustrations and Dr Austin's wide knowledge and skill in presenting it, a most impressive book has emerged. Every facet of bird biology, from morphology to breeding behaviour, and from parental care to mortality, is illuminated at some point or another. The author's unique knowledge of terns provides, as you would expect, an especially lively chapter, but he is just as successful in describing birds he has no business to know anything about. I am always glad to see wildfowl given a disproportionate share of space and am even more happy to find their chapter doing them so much credit.

Having established for ourselves Dr Austin's reliability, by seeing what he has to say about the birds we know, we can really let ourselves go among the birds we don't — Trumpeters, Trogons, Todies and Tapaculos, Seedsnipes, Seriemas and Sharpbills, Potoos and Plantcutters, Asities and False Sunbirds. If browsing amongst such riches fails to impress you with the diversity and exuberance of evolution, nothing will, except perhaps the fascinating diagram on pages 12 and 13. This colourful assortment of strange shapes summarizes in an ingenious way the course of evolution in the main groups of birds since birds began, well over 100 million years ago. How their fortunes have waxed and waned provokes the wildest but most delightful speculation. More usefully, the relative scarcity of species shown in many groups in recent times emphasizes once again the need for us to do all we can to conserve what now exists for the benefit of the future. A new effort to do just this is now in train and has led to the formation of The World Wildlife Fund, with headquarters in Switzerland and its London Office at 2 Caxton Street, S. W. 1. This covers the conservation of all wildlife and of the wild places it needs to live in, all over the world; and especially it covers the species which are threatened with extinction, among them many species of birds. We need all we can keep of the liveliest of living things.

Peter Scott.

Slimbridge, April, 1962

AUTHOR'S PREFACE

The following pages present a comprehensive survey of the world's birds to show them as they are, a natural living entity. I have tried to explain something of their origin and evolution, their distributions, life histories, behaviour, and their relationships to one another and to their environments. The accent in this treatment is on the major groups into which ornithologists subdivide the class Aves — the orders and families. These are based on the birds' anatomical similarities and differences, and reflect the evolutionary development and biological relationships of each group. The 27 orders and 155 families are presented in the customary lineal sequence, from the more primitive groups to the most specialized.

The classification used is basically that of Alexander Wetmore, which American ornithologists prefer to follow. A few changes have been made in the arrangement and sequence of Wetmore's latest revision (1960), particularly among the higher passerine or perching birds. These reflect my own review of recent researches and proposals, principally of Dean Amadon, W. J. Beecher, Pierce Brodkorb, Jean Delacour, E. T. Gilliard, Ernst Mayr, Charles Sibley, R. W. Storer, Erwin Stresemann, H. B. Tordoff, and Charles Vaurie.

Scientific names have been used sparingly in the text, though common names are not an adequate substitute. While they mean little to the non-professional, they are the very foundation of taxonomy and are universally understood. It is impossible to discuss birds in a treatise such as this without some recourse to them.

The scientific names used in the text and given for all birds illustrated are the standard binomials; the first name indicates the genus, the second the species. The minor geographical variations within species known as subspecies are referred to occasionally; they are beyond the scope of this book, and with a few exceptions the reader will not find the trinomials that identify them.

Many uncommon species and groups have no common names. Some scientific names have come into common use — trogon, junco, vireo, and phainopepla, to name some. Others used by ornithologists as more convenient and accurate appellations for certain groups, are rapidly coming into common use among amateurs—icterid, alcid, fringillid, and ploceid.

Fortunately reliable English common names are now available for most of the birds of the world. Lists of "accepted" common names have been published in most English-speaking countries for the birds that occur within their boundaries. For British ornithologists these are in the *Handbook of British Birds*, H. F. and G. Witherby, Ltd., London (5 vols). Similar lists are available for birds of many other parts of the world.

Classification and geographical distribution go hand in hand. Despite the great mobility which their powers of flight give birds, most species are restricted to definite ranges. The ranges of practically no two species are exactly alike, except perhaps for a few birds limited to certain small islands, yet those of many are closely similar. Zoologists divide the world into the regions shown on the map on page 10. The faunas of each region are comparatively uniform and self-contained. The ranges given for each species illustrated are as comprehensive as space limitations permit.

Where sexes of species illustrated differ significantly, they are indicated by the standard biologists' symbols, the arrow of Mars ♂ for male, and the mirror of Venus ♀ for female.

Sizes given for all birds illustrated or mentioned are the standard bird students' measure of length, from tip of bill to tip of tail of the bird laid flat on its back with neck extended normally. These measurements are of relative rather than exact significance. Sizes vary considerably with sex in some species. For a number of rare species no length measurements of the bird in the flesh have been recorded. These are taken from museum specimens and may be somewhat misleading. In some species the length measurement is deceptive because of the bird's extraordinarily long bill or tail, and others have feathers of the rump or wings greatly lengthened beyond the true tail, as in the two peafowl, the Quetzal, and the Pennant-winged Nightjar. Relatively few body weights, a far more significant (but more individually variable) measure of size, have been recorded except for game species.

The time when it was possible for one person to have a comprehensive knowledge of all the known animals and plants ended two centuries ago with Carl Gustav Linné, the great Linnaeus. The publication of the 10th edition of his "Systema Naturae," in 1758, which laid the foundation for modern taxonomy, also ushered in the age of the specialist. Today, the field of ornithology alone has become so vast that no one can aspire to see in a lifetime all the birds known to exist.

I have been fortunate in opportunities to travel and study exotic birds afield, but the species I have not seen are numerous. Hence much of the information set down in the following pages is secondhand, taken from the writings and reports of many other ornithologists. Were this a strictly scientific treatise, propriety would demand that I credit each author whose works I have consulted and whose researches and discoveries I have used. In a book of this scope such documentation would be of little help to the reader. In its place is a partial bibliography of the more important of the many works consulted in compiling this volume.

In place of a formal dedication, I wish to acknowledge a debt to my colleagues in ornithology, both living and dead, whose writings have made this compilation possible. For any errors in fact or interpretation, which I pray are minimal, I take full responsibility.

This book has been a truly co-operative venture, involving the artist, editor, and the staff of the publisher. Working with them has been a real pleasure. I thank particularly my friends and colleagues Herbert Friedmann and J. C. Dickinson Jr. for their suggestions, advice and critical reading of the text.

Arthur Singer, the artist, wishes to express his gratitude to those who have given him advice, information and encouragement.

Finally my thanks to Nita Rossman of the Florida State Museum staff, who typed and retyped my various drafts, and to a certain Elizabeth S. Austin, who helped and encouraged an often unreasonable husband while he completed his task.

Gainesville, Florida

March 15, 1961

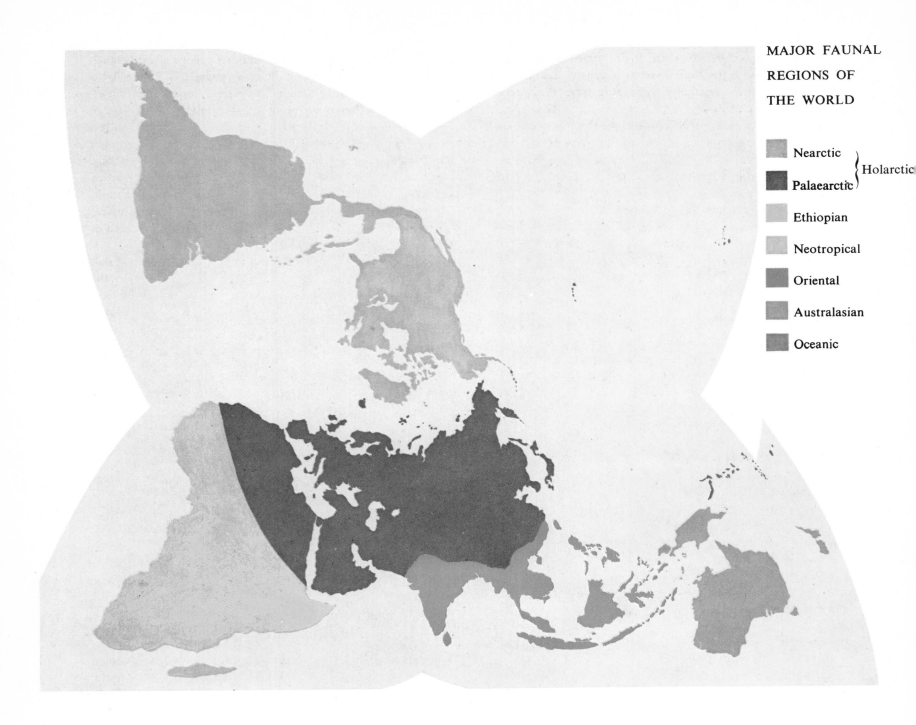

INTRODUCTION

The late Glover Morrill Allen, who guided my first serious work in ornithology, liked to point out that the study of birds is auspicious, and has been since Roman times. Auspicious comes from two Latin words, *avis* for bird and *spicere* to see. It derived from the ancient custom of foretelling the outcome of important undertakings by observing the flights or calls of birds or by examining their entrails. Though ornithology has advanced far beyond the simple delvings and probings of the Roman augurs, it is still basically the same practice of studying the habits, behaviour, and anatomy of birds. And it is still most auspicious to do so, for the destinies of both men and birds are by no means unrelated.

The Romans had no doubt of what they meant by *avis*, nor do we by bird, for birds alone have feathers. Their feathers make them one of the most distinctive of all classes of animals, and the easiest to recognize. To state it simply, if a creature has feathers, it's a bird; if it hasn't, it isn't.

Birds share their other salient characteristics with one or more of the other four classes of vertebrates—fishes, amphibians, reptiles, and mammals. With the mammals, which occupy the topmost rung of the evolutionary ladder, they share the feature of warm-bloodedness. Unlike the reptiles and all lower animals, birds and mammals maintain relatively constant body temperatures, usually higher than the surrounding atmosphere. This allows them to withstand colder climates than can cold-blooded creatures, and to maintain steadily a higher rate of body metabolism. The temperatures of birds, in fact, average about 10° F. above those of mammals, including man. Warm-bloodedness is accompanied in both birds and mammals by a four-part heart, which assures the body of a supply of oxygen-rich blood, uncontaminated by "used" blood as in reptiles, amphibians, and fishes.

The birds' nearest relatives are their immediate ancestors, the reptiles. Though the bird skeleton is greatly modified for flight, it most closely resembles the reptile type. Birds retain reptilian scales on their legs and feet, and their feathers are unquestionably modified reptilian scales—the two have the same chemical composition. Some prosaic zoologists have expressed the opinion that birds are merely "glorified reptiles." To this the ornithologist answers, "True, but how wonderfully glorified!"

Most glorious, fascinating, and intriguing to man, until so very recently earthbound, has always been the birds' supreme mastery of the air. Birds are neither nature's earliest nor latest venture in developing a flying animal. The power of gliding or flapping flight has been acquired independently by a few other vertebrates, by the flying fishes, by the extinct pterodactyls and the extant East Indian flying lizards among the reptiles, and in mammals by bats and a few marsupials and rodents. Man has finally accomplished the miracle of flight by that extension of himself, the machine.

Yet in all-round powers of individual flight, birds as a class remain supreme. They are rivalled only by the highest class of invertebrates, the insects, which, the fossil record shows, were flying long before the first vertebrate fought clear of the ground. And, against the insects, perhaps man's most serious rivals for dominance of the earth, birds remain his most effective and efficient ally.

We are not certain how birds first became fliers. It seems most likely that their early forebears ran on or climbed with their hind legs, which allowed them to spread their feathered forelimbs to act as planes or sails. From this simple beginning, as they glided from branch to branch or soared into the air from the ground, their skeletons gradually acquired modifications that increased their flying abilities. Their bones became lighter, and parts of their vertebrae and shoulder and pelvic girdles fused to form a light but strong body case. An essential adaptation to flight is the broad sternum or breastbone, with its strong keel for the attachment of the muscles needed to power the wings.

A number of flightless running birds, most of them of large size, lack a keel on their breastbone. These include the kiwis, ostriches, rheas, emus and cassowaries, and the extinct moas and elephant birds. At one time it was thought these keel-less birds, which show many primitive structural characteristics, perhaps represented a stage of development before birds learned to fly. They were believed closely related and were put in a separate subclass, the Ratitae (from Latin *ratis* a raft), as distinct from the Carinatae or keeled birds.

This formal distinction has now been discarded. Most students today believe the ratites' undeniably avian skeletal and other characteristics could have developed only for flight. For some reason these birds stopped flying, probably because they did not need to fly to escape enemies or obtain food. With disuse their wings and flying muscles atrophied, and their keels eventually disappeared. Another group of flightless birds, the penguins (page 26), simply substituted water for air and turned their wings into flippers. The penguins' forelimbs remain strongly functional, and their breastbone retains the keel to anchor the muscles that power them.

The ratites lost the ability to fly, and their keels, long in the past, some of them by early Tertiary time, 60 odd million years ago. Flightlessness has developed in other groups of birds much more recently, notably among the rails (page 107). Other flightless species exist today among the grebes, cormorants, ducks, and the parrots. Recently extinct forms include the Dodo (page 141) and the Great Auk (page 138). None of these flightless close relatives of flying birds has lost the keel completely, but in all it has degenerated noticeably, in some markedly. Hence the absence of the bony keel in the ratites is no longer regarded as indicating close relationship. Each order of them is thought to have developed independently in the part of the world where its members are found. The term ratite, however, is retained as a convenient label for them all.

Flight is so essential to birds that its loss is usually fatal. Flightless species are seldom able to survive changes in the environment that allowed this weakness to develop, particularly the appearance of predators. The surviving ratites compensated for loss of flight by the acquisition of other skills—superior abilities in fighting, running, or hiding. None, however, is very common today, and the percentage of recent extinction is far higher in all flightless species than in those that can take to the air to escape enemies.

The number of species of birds, both flying and flightless, living today or recently extinct (since the late 17th century, when the Dodo still lived) is about 8,650. My estimates of the numbers of birds for each family in the text total 8,635. This is close to the average of several recent counts made by others which range from a figure of 8,548 (Mayr and Amadon) to that of 8,809 (Brodkorb). The variations in these counts are not due to incomplete knowledge of the different kinds of birds, but to individual opinions of ornithologists on the specific status of certain forms. The slight 3 per cent difference between the low and high counts shows the close agreement among systematists on the classification of birds.

Though ornithologists are still discovering new species of birds at the rate of one or two a year, the world is now so well explored and the bird faunas so well known that it is doubtful if more than 100 species remain undiscovered in remote jungles, deserts, on mountain peaks, or oceanic islands. The percentage of unknown species in all other classes of animals is far higher, judging by the rate at which they are still being described. Balancing these few new discoveries in birds is the gradual reduction to subspecific rank of forms long considered as species. Hence it is unlikely that the round figure of 8,650 for the number of birds will change by more than 1 or 2 per cent in the near future.

Much of our knowledge of the evolutionary development of birds is based on study of their fossils. Fossilized remains of birds are not as plentiful as those of other vertebrates. Most birds are such frail creatures that they disintegrate rapidly after death and do not fossilize well. Few land birds die where their remains can be buried in waterlaid sediments, the richest source of fossils. Therefore they have not left as detailed a record of their development in the earth's upper layers as have, for instance, the mammals and the reptiles.

Nevertheless almost 1,700 bird species have been identified from fossil remains. About 800 of these are species living today, whose remains go back to late Pliocene time, about 2 million years ago. The other 900 are known only as fossils. Many of these are assigned to living orders and families, and were probably ancestral to modern types. Six orders and 41

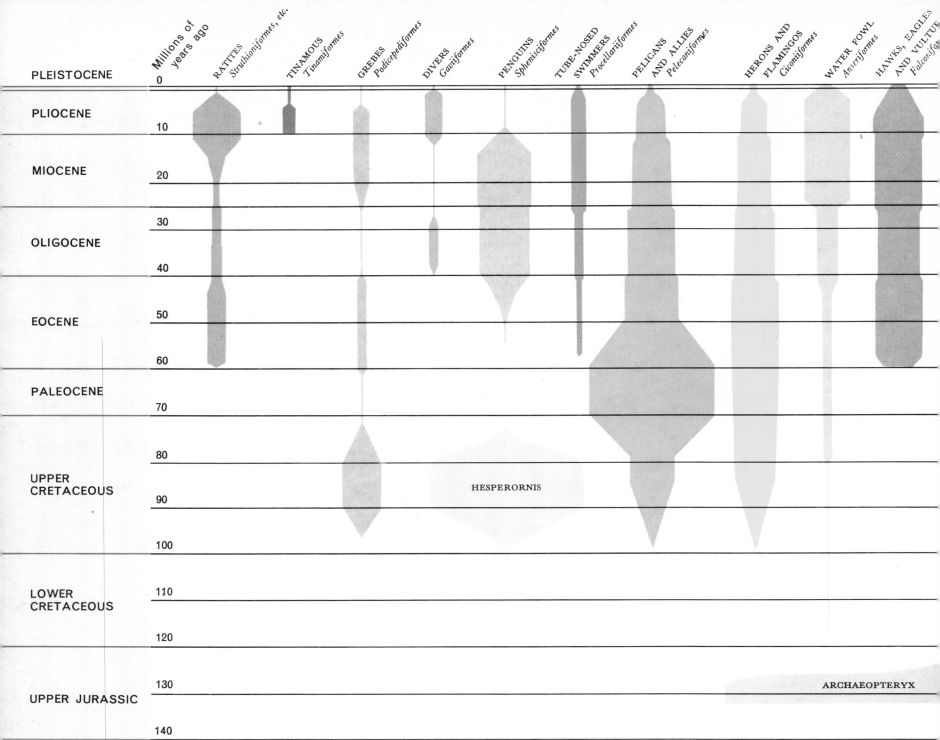

families are known only as fossils. Many of these represent "end of the line" developments, that, so far as we know, died out without descendants.

Birds evolved from reptilian stock during Mesozoic time, at least 150 million years ago, probably even earlier. From just what reptile stock they arose is hypothetical, but it is thought that small dinosaurs that ran about semi-upright on their hind legs may have been the birds' immediate ancestors. The earliest known bird is *Archaeopteryx* (ancient bird) from the upper Jurassic of Bavaria, believed to be about 130 million years old. *Archaeopteryx* was unquestionably a bird, as its feathers show plainly in the lithographic limestone in which the three known specimens are preserved. Apparently a land bird about the size of a crow, its wings had well-developed flight feathers, but its small breastbone indicates weak flying muscles. It differed from modern birds in having teeth in its bill, in retaining functional claws at the bend of the wing, and in having vertebrae extending into its tail instead of coalesced into a single small bone as in all living birds.

It would be interesting to know how many other avian species coexisted with *Archaeopteryx*, for it couldn't have been the only bird alive on the Jurassic earth. As yet we have no evidence of other land birds during the remainder of the Mesozoic Era. Two dozen species of Mesozoic water birds are known. All lived along the vast Cretaceous seas, where their chances of being fossilized and preserved were much better than they were for land birds. One of these was *Hesperornis* (western bird), a flightless diving bird, of which several species are known, about 6 feet long, that had teeth in its bill. Another was *Ichthyornis* (fish bird), a gull-like species with a strong keel. It was once thought to be toothed, but the jaw found close to its skeleton is now believed that of a reptile.

Bird fossils become increasingly plentiful from the Eocene onward. By then the toothed birds of the Mesozoic had disappeared, and their place was taken by forms closely resembling those living today. So many early Tertiary fossil birds are assignable to living groups that most, possibly all, living orders had probably arisen by or during Eocene time, and a good many living families as well, particularly among the non-passerine birds.

Other early Tertiary birds represent bizarre types, specialized for a particular mode of existence, many of them flight-

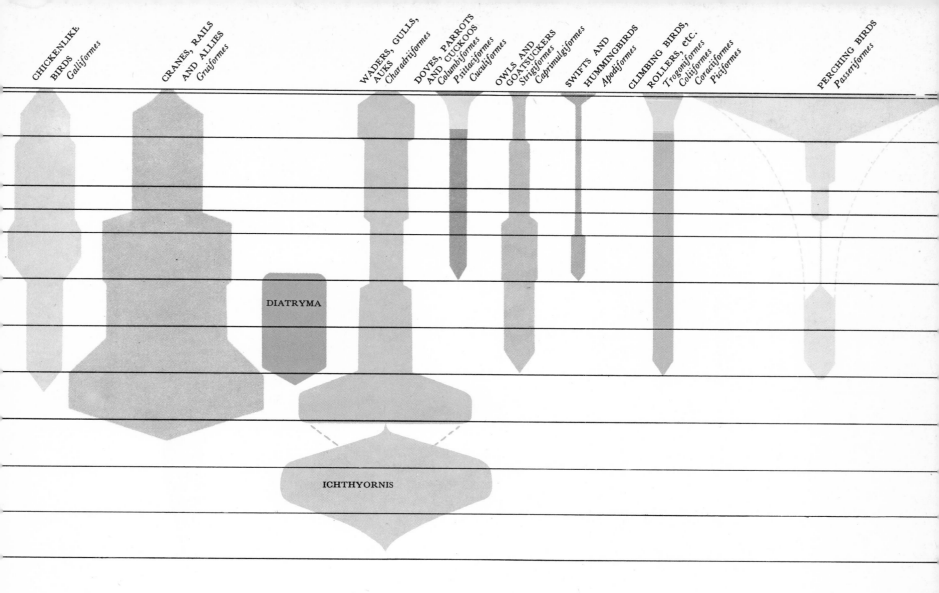

CHICKENLIKE BIRDS *Galliformes*
CRANES, RAILS AND ALLIES *Gruiformes*
WADERS, GULLS, AUKS *Charadriiformes*
DOVES, PARROTS AND CUCKOOS *Columbiformes* *Psittaciformes* *Cuculiformes*
OWLS AND GOATSUCKERS *Strigiformes* *Caprimulgiformes*
SWIFTS AND HUMMINGBIRDS *Apodiformes*
CLIMBING BIRDS, ROLLERS, etc. *Trogoniformes* *Coliiformes* *Coraciiformes* *Piciformes*
PERCHING BIRDS *Passeriformes*

DIATRYMA

ICHTHYORNIS

RELATIVE NUMBERS OF SPECIES IN THE MAIN GROUPS OF
BIRDS DURING PAST AGES AS SHOWN BY THE FOSSIL RECORD.

(From data compiled by Pierce Brodkorb)

less, that persisted for an epoch or two and vanished. One such was *Diatryma* (page 112) a large predacious relative of the cranes. Another was *Phororhacos*, a flightless ground bird about 5 feet tall that had a large head and an enormous hooked beak. Its long powerful legs show it was a good runner. Known from Oligocene and Miocene deposits in Brazil and Argentina, it must have been a fearsome carnivore.

By far the greatest number of bird fossils has been unearthed from Pliocene and Pleistocene deposits, all less than 10 million years old. Only recently have palaeontologists begun to sift these fossil-bearing sediments for tiny bones of birds and small mammals that fossil-hunters of former days, searching for larger, more dramatic finds, either ignored or overlooked. These finds are now beginning to give us a much more reliable picture of the immediate ancestry of living birds.

Though we have found fewer than 10 per cent of them as fossils (still a remarkable number, all things considered), all living bird species probably existed during the Pleistocene in much their present form. With them lived other species that vanished before or soon after the last ice sheets retreated. A recent count lists 248 species from North American ice age deposits, of which 185 are still extant today and 63 are extinct. At this ratio, the Pleistocene bird fauna of the world probably numbered about 11,500 species. This suggests birds as a class reached a peak from a quarter to a half million years ago, and have been in a gradual decline ever since.

According to these findings, the life of a bird species in the course of evolution has averaged perhaps a million years. On this basis my colleague, Pierce Brodkorb, has estimated that, between the time of *Archaeopteryx* and the present, somewhere between one and a half and two million species of birds have existed in the evolutionary process of developing the class Aves as we know it today. Of these we have specimen evidence for the existence of fewer than 10,000 species, or perhaps half of one per cent of the species that theory tells us have probably come and gone.

Relatively scant though the fossil record is for birds, it is now enough to give us some idea of the composition of the bird faunas of past geological ages. The accompanying graph shows the percentages of each order of birds known from each of the major epochs and periods. The figures are unquestionably biased in favour of the water birds and the larger

13

flightless ground birds because of their greater likelihood of being fossilized. Despite this bias, the graph shows the steady decline of the more primitive non-passerine orders. It also demonstrates that, numerically speaking, the perching birds are the heirs of the avian ages and should eventually inherit the birds' share of the earth, or whatever the dominant vertebrate, man, eventually leaves for them.

Evidence in the form of subfossil remains, mostly bones, and an occasional feather or egg, shows that a number of large extinct birds coexisted with modern man. Prominent among these are the 22 species of moas (Dinornithidae) of New Zealand, and the 11 species of elephant birds (Aepyornithidae) of Madagascar and South Africa. No man who saw these birds left a written or picture record of what they looked like, and our reconstructions of their appearance are based on their skeletal remains.

The moas were large, flightless ratite relatives of the kiwis and shared New Zealand with them until sometime after the first Maoris arrived there. The smallest of the 22 known species was about the size of a turkey. The largest, *Dinornis maximus*, towered about 13 feet above the ground. The cause of the moas' disappearance is not known. Archaeological evidence proves they lived contemporaneously with the early "pre-Maoris," often called the moa-hunters, who left remains of the moas they ate in their kitchen middens. The moas are believed to have disappeared shortly after the great immigration of Maori tribes into New Zealand about A.D. 1350. Legends of the moas still persist in Maori tribal lore.

The elephant birds were also flightless ratites. They are believed to have died out at about the same time as the moas, 500 to 700 years ago. Though the largest, *Aepyornis maximus*, stood only about 9 feet tall, it was the heaviest of all known birds and weighed almost half a ton. Its tremendous eggs, excellently preserved, are still found in swamps and among the boulders of stream beds in Madagascar. These thick-shelled 2-gallon eggs, about six times the size of an ostrich egg, are the largest single animal cell known. Their remarkable state of preservation and the freshness of skeletal elephant bird remains found in Madagascar suggest a possible basis for the legendary "roc" of the Arabian Nights. Sinbad the Sailor claimed this bird, of the mysterious lands he had visited to the southward, was so huge that it flew away with elephants to feed its young. However, *Aepyornis* was unquestionably flightless.

Man's impact on the birds, since his ascendency, has never been assessed in its entirety. History documents it reliably, though incompletely, only for about the past 350 years, roughly since the time of the Dodo. Starting with the Dodo, we have specimen evidence for the subsequent existence of at least 60 species that are certainly now extinct. A few of these, like the Labrador Duck and the Crested Shelduck (pages 68–69), were small relict populations of age-old, probably ultra-specialized, species that were apparently on their way out. They had so little contact with man he could hardly have influenced their destiny. For the disappearance of most of the rest, man has been responsible either directly or indirectly. He reduced some to the vanishing point by killing them for food—the Great Auk and the Passenger Pigeon (page 145) are examples. Others, most of them flightless, fell victims to predators he

introduced, as did the Dodo and some 15 species of flightless rails (page 110).

Man has affected bird population most adversely by altering or destroying the environments essential to their survival. The results of clearing forests and draining swamps for agriculture, and the many other changes man has made in the landscape as the human population has exploded during the past century, are most manifest on smaller land masses. In New Zealand at least four avian species have vanished within the past century, and another eight are reduced to such small populations that they are in grave danger of disappearing forever. Hawaii has also made major contributions to the list of gone and going species (see Hawaiian honeycreepers, page 283, and Nene, page 67).

Man's rapidly increasing occupation of the major continental land masses affects birds in many ways, not all as immediately dramatic, but all equally inexorable. In North America, in addition to the Great Auk, Labrador Duck, and Passenger Pigeon, we have lost the Carolina Parakeet (page 147), the Heath Hen (page 89), and probably the Ivory-billed Woodpecker (page 194). Hanging on precariously at best, are the few remaining Whooping Cranes (page 105). As forests and other wild covers shrink while cities and suburbs expand, there is less and less room for the birds that must have cover to survive.

The most recent threat to wild birds has been the mass and wholesale spreading of new insecticides. These are directly harmful to birds that eat the poisoned insects, worms, or fish (see Robin, page 252, and Common Tern, page 136). They are equally disastrous indirectly by eliminating all possible food for the many avian species that subsist on insects and little else—swallows and flycatchers, for instance. When the insects develop immunities to the toxins, they increase epidemically, for the birds that kept them in check are gone.

On the credit side of the ledger is rapidly increasing public awareness of these dangers. Conservation groups on both national and local levels are active in encouraging and assisting governments to adopt and enforce game laws to prevent killing beyond the quantities that wildife populations can withstand. Governments and private agencies the world over are setting aside wildlife reservations, sanctuaries, and parks where birds and other wildlife can exist with a minimum of disturbance. The prevention of stream pollution and the discharge of oil in coastal waters has reduced the danger to many coastal and other populations of water and shore birds.

There seems no way to avoid the shrinkage of forests, brushlands, and other cover in the face of human expansion. As public awareness of the importance of maintaining our wildlife increases, we are making a strong effort to preserve for posterity large segments of marginal lands and the wildlife they support. The chances of the thoughtlessness that destroyed the Great Auk and the Passenger Pigeon adding more species to the extinct list are rapidly decreasing.

From this uncertain present we can look at the living birds of the world scientifically arrayed into 27 orders and 155 families. The following pages show their similarities, affinities, differences and divergencies, and stress the habits, actions and life histories which make the world of birds so pleasurable and intriguing to explore.

STEWART ISLAND KIWI
Apteryx australis lawryi
Stewart Island, New Zealand 28 in.

NORTH ISLAND KIWI
Apteryx australis mantelli
North Island, New Zealand 26 in.

KIWIS

APTERYGIFORMES APTERYGIDAE

The visitor to New Zealand who sees kiwis wild in their native haunts today is fortunate. This is not because kiwis are rare, though they are no longer common, but because they are so shy and retiring. They live in thick, swampy forests, where they spend their days hidden in burrows or under spreading tree roots, and come out to forage only at night. But with luck, and in the "proper bush" as the New Zealanders call what little is left of the primeval kauri and tree-fern forests, one may still hear the shrill piping calls that long ago led the native Maoris to call them kiwis.

Roly-poly birds about the size of a large chicken, the kiwis are the smallest of the primitive flightless birds. They differ from the other four families of living ratites (birds with no keel on the breastbone) in so many anatomical features that their position on the avian family tree, other than close to its base, is uncertain. Their closest relatives seem to be the extinct moas that shared New Zealand with them until about 700 years ago.

The three living species of kiwis (two more are known from Pleistocene fossil deposits) are the only representatives of their family and order. They have dwindled in numbers over the past century. Part of their decline is attributable to the clearing of the New Zealand forests for agriculture, part to the introduction of stoats, weasels, opossums, dogs, and cats. Though early settlers hunted them for food, the kiwis have since earned a warm place in the hearts of the New Zealanders and are now rigidly protected.

In appearance kiwis are strangely unbird-like, and seem to be all body, bill, and feet. Their short, stout legs are spaced so far apart that they run with an awkward rolling gait, like an ungainly mechanical toy. Their long, coarse plumage completely hides their rudimentary 2-inch wings. They have neither wing nor tail plumes. Their contour feathers, whose lack of interlocking barbules gives them their hair-like effect, grow thickly all over the body except for a hidden bare patch on each side just under the ridiculous wings. Into this patch the kiwi tucks its head and bill when sleeping.

Kiwis are the only birds whose nostrils open at the very tip of the bill. They have a keen sense of smell, which most other birds lack, and apparently find the grubs and worms they eat mostly by scent. Their rather poor eyesight is compensated for in part by long, hairy bristles at the base of their 6-inch bill. These are believed to have a tactile function.

Kiwis nest in underground burrows and, as in most ratites, the male does all the incubating. The chalky white eggs are enormous, about 5 inches long. They weigh almost a pound, practically one fourth of the female's body weight. The clutch is one egg, rarely two, which takes 75 to 80 days to hatch.

Probably no bird or animal on earth has become more symbolic of its homeland than the kiwi. The chief motif on the Dominion seal, it also appears on New Zealand coins and postage stamps. It is used as a trademark for textiles, shoe polish, flour, and a score of other New Zealand products. New Zealand overseas troops proudly call themselves Kiwis. Such sentiment is the kiwi's best insurance for surviving the drastic changes still being made in its environment.

OSTRICHES

STRUTHIONIFORMES   STRUTHIONIDAE

The Ostrich is the largest of living birds. Adult males stand 8 feet tall and weigh more than 300 pounds; the hens are slightly smaller. Six geographical races differ from one another slightly in size, in skin colour of the bare thighs, head, and neck, and in the size and texture of their eggs. These are all members of a single species, the only representative of their order. Until recently Ostriches ranged from the Arabian and Sahara deserts southward throughout Africa.

The Ostrich family is an ancient one. Five fossil species are known, the oldest from the early Tertiary (about 50–60 million years ago). These ancient Ostriches occupied southern Europe and Asia as well as Africa, and lived as far north as the Mongolian deserts. Civilization has pushed their descendants into the wildest parts of their former range. The Arabian Ostrich has probably been wiped out — the last reported was one killed and eaten by Arabs in Saudi Arabia during World War II. Ostriches that formerly lived in the Egyptian, Nubian, and South African deserts have almost disappeared. Most wild birds survive in dry central Africa, where they still roam in the protected national parks.

Ostriches live in open, arid country and usually travel in bands of 10 to 50 birds. They congregate with gnus, zebras, antelopes, and other large grazing mammals in a sort of mutual alliance. The browsing animals stir up insects, small reptiles, and rodents for the Ostriches. The Ostriches, in turn, with their advantageous height, spot approaching danger. Ostriches also eat fruit, plants, and seeds.

Ostriches have managed to survive on a continent teeming with large predators partly by being alert and shy, partly by their fighting skill, but mainly by their speed. Tales of their running at 60 miles per hour are exaggerated. Pacing with cars shows about half that speed to be their maximum. Though they prefer to run from danger, Ostriches will fight when cornered and can be formidable antagonists. They fight with their feet, kicking out and down with vicious slashes of their heavy claws that can easily rip a lion or a man wide open.

The Ostrich is the only bird that has lost two of the four toes which most modern birds have. One of these two remaining toes is much smaller than the other, and it too may be disappearing in the evolutionary process of developing a single-toed hoof, as the horse did not so long ago.

As befits the largest of birds, the Ostrich lays the largest egg of any living bird. Oddly enough, the Ostrich egg is one of the smallest in relation to the size of the bird laying it. From 6 to 8 inches long and weighing up to 3 pounds, it is only one per cent of the female's weight. The eggs vary from white to yellowish, and their hard shiny surface is pitted with superficial pores of different sizes and shapes.

For a nest, the female Ostrich scrapes out a large depression in the sand in which she lays 10 to 12 eggs. Nests with 25 or 30 eggs result from several females laying in them. The frequency of such nests has given rise to the common belief that the Ostrich is polygamous, which has yet to be proved. As in most ratites the cock does most of the incubating and sits on the eggs faithfully each night. The Ostrich hen also incubates, always by day when her duller colour has a protective advantage. Often the eggs are left partly covered with sand in the daytime for the sun to keep warm.

The incubation period is 40 to 42 days. The sturdy, dappled chicks, after a short rest from their labours of pecking into the world, are soon able to travel with their parents. About a foot tall when hatched, they grow about a foot a month until they reach 5 or 6 feet, when the growth rate slows down. It takes an Ostrich 3 or 4 years to mature fully.

Though able to run vigorously soon after hatching, the chicks usually stretch out flat when danger threatens, necks extended, and "play 'possum." The chicks' well-known habit of feigning death probably was the origin of the oft-repeated canard that Ostriches bury their heads in the sand at the approach of danger. This, of course, just isn't so.

Ostriches were large and conspicuous residents of the lands that cradled our civilization, south and east of the Mediterranean. Here they have left their record since the dawn of history. Ostrich-egg cups have been found in Assyrian graves dated 3000 B.C. Ancient Egyptians, Chinese, and Greeks also found the strong shells made handy utensils.

In the Roman Empire, roast Ostrich was considered a fitting main course for the Emperor's feasts. Roman physicians used Ostrich fat as a drug and prescribed the gizzard stones as a remedy for eye diseases. One ancient and enduring folktale, recorded in the medieval herbals and even mentioned by Shakespeare, is the belief that Ostriches can digest metal. This, like the head-burying legend, has some basis in fact. Captive Ostriches are attracted by shining objects and will swallow watches, brooches, bottle tops, and small pieces of metal or glass left within reach. Unless these have sharp points, such items in their diet probably do the birds little harm. They remain in the gizzard to be slowly ground down with the stones the birds swallow to aid their digestion.

Ostriches domesticate readily and do well in captivity, where they have been found to live about 50 years. They have been trained for riding and to pull carts, but do not make good draft animals because they tire easily and then squat down and quit. Inclined to be bad tempered, they make untrustworthy as well as ungainly pets. The voice of the Ostrich is a loud hiss and a booming roar.

Ostrich plumes have found a ready market since the days of the Crusades, when knights used them to decorate their helmets. (This was probably the origin of their use as an heraldic symbol.) The plumes reached their height of fashion in the late 19th century, when they brought from £50 to £100 per pound. As the supply of wild plumes dwindled, it became profitable to raise Ostriches in captivity, for a full-grown male bird produces about a pound of plumes annually.

The plumes of commerce grow only on the wings and tail. The 16 plumes on each wing are purely decorative, and dangle and flap crazily in the wind as the bird runs. The 50 to 60 tail plumes grow in layers above the 14 or so true tail feathers. When mature, the feathers are harvested without harm to the bird, which grows a new set each year.

Ostrich farms were first established in Africa in the 1860's. Ostriches were first taken to America in the 1880's, where they were raised first in California, then in Arizona, Oklahoma, Texas, Arkansas, and Florida. The market is no longer as lucrative for plumes as it was 70 years ago, and today the birds are kept mainly in zoos. Their skin makes a fine, soft leather in some demand for gloves and purses.

OSTRICH ♂ ♀
Struthio camelus
Plainslands of Africa 72 in.

female

male

RHEAS

RHEIFORMES   RHEIDAE

The rheas, sometimes called South American ostriches, bear only a superficial resemblance to the African ratites, and are much smaller. Standing 4 to 5 feet tall and weighing up to 50 pounds, they are still the largest New World birds. Like the Ostrich they are shy inhabitants of treeless, open country. They travel in small flocks, often in company with herds of deer, and depend on running speed to escape their enemies. Rheas differ from the unrelated Ostrich in foot, pelvic, and palate structure; their thighs, head, and neck are feathered, their equally useless wings are longer, they lack tail plumes, and their body plumage is softer.

The Common Rhea formerly roamed the Brazilian and Argentine pampas in large numbers, but the great flocks of a century ago have retreated before the pitiless advances of agriculture. The only other species, the Long-billed, or Darwin's, Rhea is a smaller, browner bird with white-tipped wing feathers. It roams the wild eastern foothills of the Andes from Peru and Bolivia south to the Straits of Magellan. Each species has three geographical races.

Rheas are polygamous and the larger, darker males assume most of the domestic chores. Each cock takes a harem of up to 5 or 6 hens and scrapes out for them a large nest a yard or more in diameter and lined thinly with grass. In this his mates lay 20 to 30, sometimes 50, yellow to greenish eggs, each about 5 inches long. Once the male starts incubating he is so diligent he drives the hens away from the nest and forces those with more eggs to lay to deposit them out in the open. The chicks hatch after a 6-week incubation period, and soon run about uttering shrill whistles. The cock may shepherd them for another 6 weeks before they take off on their own. The cocks have a loud, booming, far-carrying call, but the hens are voiceless.

Rheas were hunted for both food and sport and, until recently, for their wing feathers which, being neither as choice nor attractive as Ostrich plumes, were used mostly for feather dusters. In the early days those pampas cowboys, the gauchos, pursued rheas on horseback with bolas. Bolas are 2- or 3-thonged leather slings weighted with stones which, when thrown skilfully, wrap around the legs and trip the fleeing birds. From a fresh start a rhea can outdistance the fleetest horse, but the birds hide in the tall grass and double back on their tracks, which makes them an easy quarry.

Rheas have never been raised commercially, but they tame easily and, except for a fondness for houseplants and garden produce, reportedly make good pets. They share the Ostrich's curiosity for bright and shining objects, and are equally good zoo denizens. They have a wide range of diet, mainly vegetable but including some insects and small animals.

CASSOWARIES

CASUARIIFORMES   CASUARIIDAE

These large, powerful ratites are native to northern Australia, New Guinea, and adjacent islands. The cassowary populations differ slightly on each of the many islands they inhabit, and some 30 kinds have been described. Students now unite these into three species, each with many subspecies.

Heavy-bodied birds with short, stout legs, cassowaries are forest dwellers, at home in the dense Papuan jungles. Their long, drooping plumage is coarse, hard, and hair-like, and makes a thick mat to protect the birds from the thorny underbrush they inhabit. Cassowaries have no tail feathers, but their rudimentary wings, hidden beneath the body plumage, bear 3 to 5 long, wiry, vaneless quills which curve along the body as added buffers against prickly vines and branches.

A distinctive feature is their large casque, a bony helmet on the forehead, which they use to fend off obstructions as they run through the thick undergrowth. The skin of their featherless heads and necks combines vivid reds, blues, purples, and yellows, and two species have decorative wattles hanging from their throats. The sexes are alike in colour, the adults black, the immature birds brownish, but the females are distinctly larger than the males, a reversal occurring in no other ratite and in few other groups of birds.

Despite their size and conspicuous colouring, cassowaries are hard to observe, for they are shy, wary, and somewhat nocturnal. They are notoriously bad tempered and pugnacious. When a cassowary attacks, the prudent observer takes to the nearest tree, for the birds have killed many a Papuan. They fight by leaping feet first at an enemy and slashing with their powerful claws. Their middle and outer toes are strongly clawed, and the inner one bears a long, sharp spike that is a particularly vicious and fearsome weapon.

Cassowaries are not known to be polygamous. Their nest is a shallow platform of leaves on the forest floor, in which the female lays 3 to 6 large, dark green eggs. The male alone incubates. The young at hatching are striped lengthwise in a dazzle pattern that hides them effectively in the underbrush. Both parents care for the young.

The cassowary diet is mainly berries and fruits. They also eat some plants, insects, and an occasional small animal. They can run at prodigious speeds, reportedly up to 30 miles an hour even through thick brush, and they swim across jungle rivers when they want to. Their voice is variously described as a hoarse, harsh croaking, squeaking, howling, grunting, snorting, or bellowing.

COMMON RHEA (white phase)
Rhea americana
Argentina 52 in.

COMMON RHEA
Rhea americana
Brazil, Uruguay, Argentina 52 in.

AUSTRALIAN CASSOWARY
Casuarius casuarius
Northern Australia and
New Guinea 65 in.

BENNETT'S CASSOWARY
Casuarius bennetti
New Guinea and adjacent islands 52 in.

male

female

EMU ♂, ♀
Dromiceius novae-hollandiae
Grasslands of Australia 75 in.

young

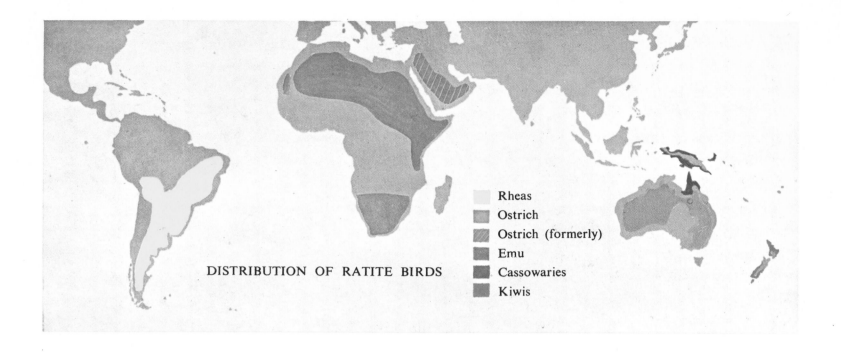

DISTRIBUTION OF RATITE BIRDS

Rheas
Ostrich
Ostrich (formerly)
Emu
Cassowaries
Kiwis

EMUS

CASUARIIFORMES   DROMICEIDAE

Though Emus still occur in much of their former range, the open, semi-arid plains of Australia, they are reduced in numbers and only one species is still extant. Three emus, those of Tasmania and of two smaller islands off the south coast, vanished a century ago, early casualties in the settlement of Australia. Three more species known only from fossil remains show the family was more diversified there in Pleistocene times—15,000 to 100,000 years ago.

The surviving Emu, standing 5 to 6 feet tall and weighing up to 120 pounds, is second in size only to the Ostrich among living birds. Closely related to the neighbouring cassowaries (both are placed in the same order), the Emu has the same coarse, drooping, hairy plumage, lacks tail quills, and has even more rudimentary wings. As in the cassowaries, the Emu's feathers are double, each having an aftershaft almost equal in length to the main feather. The Emu lacks the cassowaries' casque, dagger-like inner claw, and hard, vaneless wing quills. Its back is broader and flatter, and its head and neck are feathered except for two bare spots on each side. Emu sexes are alike, but the males are usually larger. The sexes can be told apart by their voices: both hiss and grunt, but the males utter series of guttural notes; the females' calls are resonant and booming.

Emus are fast runners, credited with speeds up to 30 miles an hour. They also can swim well. They usually travel in small flocks, except during the breeding season when they go about in pairs. They are friendly and inquisitive when undisturbed, and sometimes follow men apparently to look at them. Emus live largely on plant food, mainly fruit and berries. They also eat insects and are fond of caterpillars.

Emus start to breed in their second year and lay their eggs in the autumn—February and March "down under." For a nest the Emu makes a flat bed of grasses, bark, and leaves, always in open country but usually at the base of a tree or bush. Despite their large size, the nests are well hidden and hard to find. The usual clutch is 7 to 10 eggs, though as many as 16 are reported. The eggs are dark green in colour, average 5½ inches in length, and weigh about 1½ pounds. When fresh their surface is rough and granulated, but they wear smooth during incubation and become darker. Incubation is completely by the male and takes from 59 to 61 days. He also broods the chicks for the first few days after they hatch. The chicks are a sooty white, strikingly marked with longitudinal black and yellow stripes.

In colonial days the Australian settlers hunted Emus for their meat, which is said to taste much like beef, and for their oil, which they used in lamps. Frontier housewives made omelettes of their eggs, which they first broke into a basin and let stand overnight so that they could skim off the oil which rose to the top. One Emu egg made enough omelette for a whole hungry family.

Though human progress has long worked against them, these large ratites are reported to be still fairly plentiful in parts of Australia. They make nuisances of themselves in farming country by knocking down fences, trampling and eating crops. In the 1930's wheat farmers in western Australia raised such a fuss about Emus damaging their grain that the Government sent a military detachment of machine gunners to destroy the birds. After a month of costly chasing about the hinterland and raising lots of dust, the detachment returned sheepishly to barracks. Though the "Emu War" was a fiasco, Emus are still killed in numbers, and rural districts still offer bounties for their beaks and eggs.

To assure them a place as agriculture advances, a movement is now afoot in Australia to establish sanctuaries where Emus can continue their existence unhampered in the wild. The species breeds readily in captivity, and live specimens are scattered among the world's zoos.

TINAMOUS

TINAMIFORMES   TINAMIDAE

The tinamous are primitive ground birds found from southern Mexico through Central and South America to Patagonia. The 45 or so species (some students lump them into 33 species, others split them into 51) range from the size of a small bantam to that of a large rooster. They have rather slender, slightly down-curved bills and very short tails, so short that the body feathers hide them in some species. All tinamous are protectively coloured in tawny browns and greys, often attractively barred, streaked, or mottled. The sexes are similar in form and colour, but the females are often slightly larger than the males.

In structure and behaviour the tinamous present anomalies that have long baffled ornithologists. Though they have a strongly keeled breastbone, other skeletal characters, particularly their palate structure, show them related to the ratite birds. The females are aggressive and do much of the courting. Like most ratites, male tinamous do most of the incubating and rearing of the young. Another anomaly is their possession of powder-down feathers, which are absent in all ratites, but found haphazardly in other groups, notably the herons, mesitae, and parrots.

Tinamous are not even distantly related to the partridges and quails which they resemble superficially. Their nearest relatives are thought to be the rheas. Students today tend to regard them as a unique group of relatively unspecialized birds, probably nearer the ancestral stock from which all modern birds have descended than any other living bird.

CRESTED TINAMOU
Eudromia elegans
Pampas of Argentina 14 in.

VARIEGATED TINAMOU
Crypturellus variegatus
Northern South America, south to
Ecuador and the Guianas 9 in.

Therefore, tinamous are pictured as originating close to the base of the avian family tree.

The tinamous have adapted themselves to a wide range of habitats, from dense lowland jungle to sparse upland scrub country. Several species live on the grassy slopes of the high Andes 10,000 to 14,000 feet above sea level. Others, the handsome Crested Tinamou among them, range widely over the open pampas. Still others, like the smaller Variegated Tinamou, live only in damp lowland rainforests. None of them is migratory.

The tinamous' calls are flutey, mellow whistles and trills. Their food is largely seeds, berries, and small fruits. They also eat some insects and other animal food. They forage entirely on the ground, run rapidly, and crouch for concealment in the presence of danger. When flushed they fly strongly with rapidly whirring wings, but seldom for more than a few hundred yards, before dropping again into cover.

Throughout their range, tinamous are hunted widely for both sport and food. I consider them one of the finest eating of all birds. Their breast meat is light in colour like a chicken's but much more tender, sweeter, and full of flavour. A number of attempts have been made to introduce tinamous into North America for sporting purposes. So far these efforts have met with no success.

The tinamous are ground nesters and lay from 1 to 10 or 12 eggs in a simple nest well concealed under vegetation. Their eggs are outstanding among those of all birds for their hard, porcelain-like gloss and for their vivid clear colouring, which ranges from a wine red in one species to yellow, green, blue, and even purple in others. The male usually builds the nest and always does the incubating, which lasts about 3 weeks in most species, slightly longer in the larger ones. The downy chicks are buff coloured with darker stripings and mottlings. They are highly precocious and run about soon after hatching. Most are able to fly short distances before they are half grown.

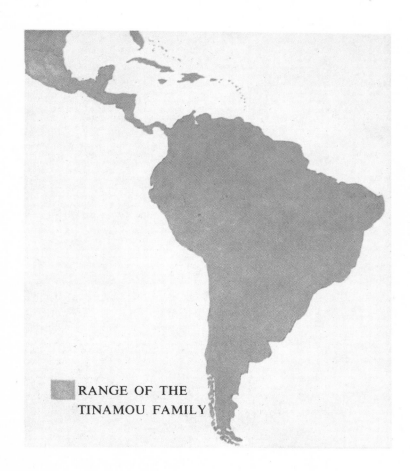

RANGE OF THE
TINAMOU FAMILY

21

GREBES

PODICIPEDIFORMES   PODICIPEDIDAE

The grebes are sleek, dapper water birds of rather primitive appearance found practically throughout the world. Most are smallish birds that look somewhat like ducks at a distance, but they usually ride higher in the water and their long, thin necks and short, slender, more pointed bills are good distinguishing marks. Grebes are not highly gregarious, but often travel in small flocks, and several species nest in loose colonies. All of them breed on fresh water; a few species migrate to coastal waters in winter.

Grebes were formerly classified with divers to which they are totally unrelated. Like divers, grebes are foot-propelled swimmers with legs placed far back on their bodies (their ordinal name, Podicipediformes, means "the rump-foots"), but their feet are webbed very differently. Instead of being connected by leathery skin as in most water birds, each of the grebe's toes is separately fringed with stiff, horny flaps. This condition, called lobate webbing, occurs in only three other bird families, in the phalaropes, in the coots, and in the finfoots. The development of lobate webbing in these distant families is a case of parallel evolution in response to the same needs. It does not signify any phylogenetic relationship.

Structurally grebes are distinct from other swimming birds in a number of ways. One outstanding characteristic is their soft, thick, lustrous plumage, formerly much in demand for decorating women's hats. Another is their lack of a functional tail. Their few tail feathers are short and soft, have only rudimentary quills, and are useless for steering. Both in the water and in the air grebes steer with their feet, which trail behind them conspicuously in flight.

Though grebes are weak fliers (several species are practically flightless), some northern species migrate long distances overland. Their short wings are cupped in a graceful camber and fit closely to the body when not in use. They fly with rapid, whirring wingbeats and have trouble taking off even from water, so they usually dive to escape danger.

Grebes feed on small fish, insect larvae, crustaceans, and other aquatic life. They do not dive as deeply as do the divers, seldom more than 20 feet or so, nor do they stay under as long. When feeding undisturbed their dives average 30 seconds or less. Nor can they swim as fast or as far underwater. One of the grebes' outstanding traits is their marvellous agility and quickness in the water, which has earned them such vernacular names as water-witch and hell-diver.

Though they usually ride cork-like high in the water, grebes share with the divers the ability to increase their specific gravity by expelling air from within their bodies and from under their feathers. When suspicious of approaching danger, they sink slowly down until only their eyes and bill are level with the surface, and they often swim about at periscope depth with just the head exposed. Again, like divers, they have been credited by hunters with being able to dive at the flash of a gun quickly enough to dodge the shot. Grebes are no longer killed for their feathers or for their rather fishy flesh, except by primitive peoples.

The grebe family is composed of 18 living species divided among 4 genera. Ten of these species and three of the genera are confined to the New World. The largest genus, *Podiceps* with 13 species, has representatives on all the major land masses of the world except Antarctica. Three of its species, the Red-necked, Horned, and Eared grebes, breed in the circumpolar areas of the Northern Hemisphere and winter southward in temperate latitudes of both northern

RED-NECKED GREBE
Podiceps grisegena
Northern Hemisphere: Eurasia,
North America 13 in.

HORNED GREBE
Podiceps auritus
Northen Hemisphere: Eurasia,
North America 13 in.

GREAT CRESTED GREBE
Podiceps cristatus
Eastern Hemisphere: Eurasia, Africa,
Australia, New Zealand 19 in.

continents. Another, the large 19-inch Great Crested Grebe, lives throughout Eurasia, Africa, and the East Indies, and also in Australia and New Zealand. Its small 10-inch relative, the familiar Little Grebe of Europe, has a similarly widespread distribution throughout the Old World. The common Pied-billed Grebe, found widely throughout the Americas, resembles the Little Grebe in size and general appearance and habits, but has a distinctive black band around its beak.

Other grebes have singularly limited ranges. One species occurs only in Madagascar, another is limited to New Zealand, a third to Australia, a fourth to the Falkland Islands. Three more species are each restricted to large alpine lakes in the New World. The most aberrant of these is the flightless Titicaca Grebe, isolated on that loftiest of navigable lakes two miles high in the Bolivian Andes. Another distinct species lives on Lake Junin, at a 13,000-foot altitude in Peru. Lake Atitlan, a mile above sea level in the Guatemala highlands, is the home of a giant relative of the Pied-billed Grebe, similar to it in markings but almost half as large again.

We know little of the remote ancestry of the grebes, though obviously they evolved from a distinctive parent stock that must have been well established all over the world before Tertiary time. In addition to the nine living species whose remains have been found in Ice Age strata, eight fossil grebes have been described, each from only a few bones, and all but two of them assigned to living genera. The earliest of the fossil grebes is *Neogaeornis*, known only from its leg bones found in Chilean Upper Cretaceous deposits laid down more than 80 million years ago.

Grebes are not noisy birds, but they have a variety of trumpeting calls, shrill whistles, and piercing wails, and they often chatter conversationally in strange croaks, chuckles, and whinnies. They are famous for their elaborate courtships, in which the females take almost as active a part as the males. Both sexes of some species have decorative nuptial plumes, "horns," "ears," or "collars" which they display to each other,

and their matings are frequently preceded by intricate, spectacular dances in and on the water.

Mutual nest building is an integral part of their courtship. Both birds gather pieces of reed, rushes, and other water plants and mat them into a soggy platform floating in shallow water and anchored to a convenient clump of reeds, with little attempt at concealment. In a depression in this damp foundation, often below water level, they lay from 3 to 10 chalky eggs. The eggs are white or faintly tinged with blue or green when fresh, but they soon become stained a dirty brown by the rotting wet vegetation pulled over them by the incubating birds when they leave the nest. This seems more to keep the eggs warm than to hide them, for the eggs are never covered until the clutch is complete. Incubation varies from 20 days in the smallest species to 28 to 30 days in the larger grebes.

Grebes carry the downy chicks about on their backs, sometimes out in the open, more often concealed under their wings or among their back feathers, with just the dappled heads sticking out. Adults dive with the young aboard, and sometimes the youngsters are dislodged and come bouncing to the surface. The chicks do not dive well until they are several weeks old. Both parents share the duties of riding the chicks around and feeding them. When, as happens in some species, a second brood is started before the first young are mature, the male takes charge of the first one while the female starts incubating her second clutch.

Grebes have one peculiar and unique habit which has yet to be explained satisfactorily. They eat quantities of their own body feathers, and even the stomachs of chicks a few days old contain wads of their parents' feathers. As feathers have little or no nutritive value, they may be swallowed to aid digestion in some way, perhaps by trapping and holding sharp fish bones in the stomach until they have softened enough to pass through the rest of the digestive tract without puncturing the walls. Nobody knows for certain.

DIVERS

GAVIIFORMES   GAVIIDAE

To those who know the northlands, the divers are living symbols of that wild, enchanting country. No one who has ever heard the divers' music—the mournful far-carrying call-notes and the uninhibited, cacophonous, crazy laughter—ever forgets it. It embodies the very spirit of far places, of forest-clad lakes where the clear air is scented with balsam and fir, of the canoe country of the voyageur and the long portage, of lonely pools in the thawing tundra girt with nodding cotton grass where lemmings play.

To the prosaic scientist the divers are a small, discrete group of somewhat primitive northern water birds that show no close affinities to any other avian order. Bones of three of the four living species have been found in Ice Age deposits. Seven more species are known only as fossils, the earliest of Eocene age, about 50 million years old. The group probably developed into much its present form in late Mesozoic time, 100 million or more years ago, in the land masses surrounding the Arctic Ocean, where its descendants have lived ever since.

The four living divers are large, handsome birds so similar in structure they are united (with five of the fossil forms) into the single genus *Gavia*. They all have sleek, torpedo-shaped bodies, fairly long, stout necks, straight, pointed beaks, and short, almost insignificant tails. Their narrow, tapering wings are set well back amidships, and hardly seem large enough to lift their heavy bodies into the air.

The divers are the only birds whose legs are encased within the body down to the ankle joint. Their webbed feet and flattened tarsi jut out behind their sterns like twin propellers, and are powered by strong muscles hidden within the body. This design is fine for swimming, but makes divers almost helpless on land, where they can barely hold their bodies half erect and shuffle along a few clumsy paces at a time. This weakness may be responsible for their North American name of "loon" which is supposedly a corruption of the Old Scandinavian word *lómr*, meaning an awkward person.

In the water divers are anything but awkward. They rank with the finest of swimmers and are noted especially for their diving ability—hence their British common name. Unlike the penguins, which "fly" through the water with their stubby flippers and use their feet only for steering, the divers propel themselves with their feet and use their wings solely in balancing and in turning. Divers dive from the surface with a perceptible effort, arching the neck, pointing the beak downward, and plunging under with a powerful thrust from their strong feet. This they can do in a proverbial flash, when they are alarmed.

Divers are among the very few birds whose bones are solid and heavy instead of pneumatic. Their specific gravity is close to that of water, and they can increase it enough, by expelling air from within their bodies and from under their feathers, to sink themselves slowly and quietly beneath the water, leaving scarcely a ripple. With other diving birds they also enjoy a special blood and muscle chemistry that helps them stay under water. This involves both a resistance to the toxic effects of carbon dioxide and the facility to store extra oxygen in the blood.

That divers can dive to great depths is proved by one taken in a fisherman's net set 240 feet below the surface. They usually pursue the fish which are their principal food in much shallower water, and seldom stay under more than a minute. When feeding undisturbed, their dives average from 30 to 45 seconds. When forced to escape enemies they can stay under for several minutes, and swim perhaps three or four hundred yards in that time. Dives of three to five minutes have been reported. Tales of divers remaining underwater longer than five minutes and swimming a half mile or more while submerged must be regarded with suspicion, for the birds are physically incapable of doing so.

Despite the fact that divers have the least wing surface in proportion to their weight of any flying bird, they are strong fliers. They have trouble getting airborne, and cannot rise from land. When fooled, as they sometimes are, into alighting on new smooth black ice or on glossy wet pavements at night, they stay grounded unless they can reach open water, where they have to spatter along the surface, half running, half flying, anywhere from 25 yards to a quarter mile, depending on wind conditions, to take flight.

Once aloft, however, their flight is swift, powerful, and direct. Their air speed has been estimated up to 60 miles an hour. Like all heavy-bodied, short-winged birds, they fly with rapid wingbeats. In flight they present an unmistakable hunchbacked appearance, the neck extended first downward and then straight out in front, the feet trailing behind the short, stiff tail. Some divers make overland flights of a thousand miles and more from their nesting grounds in arctic or subarctic lakes to the salt waters where they winter.

All the divers are extremely vocal, especially during the breeding season and at night. They have a variety of loud calls, yodels, tremolos, and wails that they use in courtship. The Great Northern Diver's drawn-out call note—ah-ooooooooo'-aah—rising in the middle and falling at the end, is one of the loveliest sounds in nature. The uninitiated sometimes mistakes this wail for the howl of a wolf, which it strongly resembles. To others, the divers' weird calls are frightening, especially the eerie maniacal "laughter" that is doubtless responsible for the expression "crazy as a loon."

Divers normally come to land only to nest, usually on islets or lonely promontories along the wild shores of northern fresh-water lakes and ponds. They lay two large, dark-brown eggs heavily spotted with black in a crude depression only a foot or two from the water which they line with whatever vegetation is at hand. After an incubation period of about 29 days the chicks appear as fluffy balls of coal-black down, which fades to grey on the sides and white on the belly.

As soon as their down dries the chicks take to the water with their parents. They swim feebly at first, and need quite a bit of coddling for the first two weeks. They frequently scramble up on to their parents' backs for a ride, and it takes them a fortnight to learn to dive well. They grow rapidly and are usually able to fly in about 10 to 11 weeks.

Divers are long-lived. One Red-throated Diver ringed at Goteborg, Sweden, was recovered after 23 years. A Black-throated Diver banded at Rositten, Germany, lived 18 years. Their natural enemies are few. Mink and otter eat some eggs, and large pike or muskellunge get an occasional chick. Eskimos and Indians used to make garments of diver skins, and still use the breasts and neck patches to decorate tobacco pouches and ditty bags. Primitive peoples relish their meat, which is good eating, but it is too tough and fishy to suit modern palates. Large numbers of divers now perish from the effects of the waste oil from ships in the coastal waters where they winter.

In one place in the world divers are a material help to man. On the Inland Sea of Japan near Seto, the fishermen depend on Red-throated and Black-throated Divers to drive the fish into schools so that they can be netted easily. These Japanese fishermen take pains to avoid frightening the birds or hurting them in their nets, and the divers have become so tame they swim among the schooling fish right next to the fishing boats.

Fishermen elsewhere in the world usually regard divers with disfavour as unwelcome competitors. Fisheries experts who have investigated their complaints find the birds do some damage to set lines and nets, especially when concentrated in flocks on the wintering grounds and during migration. Their studies showed that divers feed mainly on fish species of minor economic importance, and during most of the year the birds are far too scattered to have any measurable effect on fish populations. The experts concluded that the divers' aesthetic value more than compensates for the fish they eat, and so the birds remain on the protected list in Britain and North America as well as in Japan.

Diver sexes are alike and they cannot be told apart by size or colour. In late summer the adults moult into a drab winter plumage, grey above and white below. In the winter garb all four species are so alike that experts sometimes have trouble telling them apart. The best identifying marks in winter are size, shape, and carriage.

In their breeding plumage, which they acquire by a moult in March or April while still on the wintering grounds, each of the four divers is easy to recognize. The best known is the Great Northern Diver, a 36-inch bird with a glossy black head and neck marked with a white-striped collar and throat patch,

and a black back strikingly barred and dotted with white. Largest of the divers is the 40-inch White-billed Diver, patterned much like the Great Northern Diver, but with a large whitish bill that can be distinguished as far as the bird can be seen. All the other divers have black bills.

The White-billed Diver is the most restricted in range and the least known of the group. It breeds in the far north from northernmost Russia eastward across northern Siberia and Alaska to the Mackenzie Delta. It winters farther north than any of the other divers, seldom coming south of Norway and Sweden, northern Japan, and southeastern Alaska.

The smallest of the divers is the circumpolar Red-throated, only 24 inches long, and the Black-throated Diver is only slightly larger. The Black-throated Diver's back is patterned black and white like the Great Northern Diver's, but its throat is black and its head and nape are soft grey. The red bib of the Red-throated Diver looks black at a distance and is hard to see in the field, but the species always has a grey instead of a mottled black and white back.

The Red-throated is the most widely distributed of the divers. It breeds in small pools in the arctic and subarctic tundra completely around the world, and winters southward along the coasts of North America to California and Florida, in Asia to China and Formosa, and in Europe to the Mediterranean, Black, and Caspian seas.

The Great Northern Diver breeds across northern North America, into Greenland and Iceland. A few winter in the Great Lakes, but most of them move to salt water, south to northern Mexico on the Pacific coast, to Florida on the Atlantic, and around the Gulf of Mexico to Texas. One population, probably those nesting in Greenland and Iceland, winters in Europe from Great Britain to the Mediterranean. In North America the Great Northern Diver is known as the Common Loon.

The Black-throated Diver nests across northern Eurasia from Scotland to the Bering Sea and on across northern North America to the west side of Hudson Bay. It winters south along both coasts of the Pacific to California, China, and Japan. In Europe it reaches the Mediterranean and Black seas but occurs only accidentally on the Atlantic Coast of North America.

BLACK-THROATED DIVER
Gavia arctica
Northern Eurasia; Alaska to
Hudson Bay and Baffin Island 25 in.

GREAT NORTHERN DIVER
Gavia immer
Northern North America, Greenland,
and Iceland 35 in.

RED-THROATED DIVER
Gavia stellata
Northern Eurasia; northern
and coastal North America 24 in.

EMPEROR PENGUIN
Aptenodytes forsteri
Shores of Antarctica 48 in.

KING PENGUIN
Aptenodytes patagonicus
Falklands and other
subantarctic islands 38 in.

PENGUINS

SPHENISCIFORMES   SPHENISCIDAE

The frock-coated penguins, whose lovable caricaturing of human mannerisms is familiar to everyone, form one of the most compact and distinctive of all avian orders. Most authorities today recognize 15 (some only 14) species divided among 6 genera, and all united into a single family.

The name penguin, from two old Welsh words meaning "white head," referred originally to the now extinct Great Auk of the North Atlantic, and was transferred to the totally unrelated, though vaguely similar, southern birds by seafarers a century and a half ago. Their scientific name comes from the Greek *spheniskos*, meaning "a small wedge," and refers to the penguins' narrow, flipper-like wings, which are useless for flying but marvellous for swimming—and quite effective for battering the shins of human visitors to their nesting grounds.

Penguins occur only in the Southern Hemisphere, and their centre of abundance is the forbidding seas separating Cape Horn, the Cape of Good Hope, Australia, and New Zealand from the antarctic ice pack. Publicity for the Byrd and other antarctic expeditions, and more recently for the International Geophysical Year of 1957–1958, has made the penguins almost synonymous with Antarctica in the public's mind, yet only two species are restricted to that area, the Emperor and the Adélie.

The penguins are an ancient, primitive group, highly specialized for a marine existence, and their relationship to other birds is still the subject of considerable debate. Their lack of flight feathers on the wings is unique among the birds with keeled breastbones. The presence of this strong keel and the brief appearance of wing quills early in their embryonic life show that penguins undoubtedly developed from flying ancestors in the remote past. The lack of a flexible "elbow" joint is also unique. The flipper is stiff and moves only at the shoulder. The peculiar structure of the penguin's beak, formed of several coalesced horny plates instead of a single sheath as in most other birds, suggests a possible distant kinship with the one other predominantly southern oceanic group, the albatrosses. Other anatomical characters suggest remote affinities to the divers and to the cormorants and pelicans.

The fossil record shows penguins were well established over much of their present range early in Tertiary time (about 50 million years ago). Eocene and Oligocene deposits in New Zealand and the South Orkneys and Miocene strata in Patagonia have yielded the bones of a score or more ancient penguins. Even at that early age, when modern birds were just beginning to develop, the order was sharply defined and the fossil penguins had already differentiated into groups with much the same characteristics that their descendants show today. They seem to have been close facsimiles of living forms, except that their wings and legs were longer in proportion to their bodies, and some of them were much larger. *Anthropornis* of the South Orkneys and *Palaeudyptes* of New Zealand stood more than 5 feet tall. The plant and invertebrate fossils found with them indicate that these ancestral penguins lived under warm, perhaps subtropical, conditions.

Though the penguins' ancestors lost the power of flight 100 million or so years ago, they have amply compensated for it by their superb swimming skill, which rivals that of the seals and porpoises. They are indeed the most truly marine of all birds, and ideally adapted for pelagic life. Their chunky bodies are streamlined for ease of passage through the water, patterned much like the blimp-like hull of the advanced submarine *Albacore*. Their stiff, close-packed feathers grow thickly all over the body instead of in discrete tracts as in most other birds. They form a thick insulating mat with a smooth, shiny surface that is impervious to water and offers little if any resistance to the bird's passage through it. Penguins are "side-wheelers" and get all their motive power from their short, powerful flippers, with which they literally fly through the water. Their heavy, webbed feet, placed well aft on short, thick legs, act as rudders. Their necks are short but flexible, their beaks are stout and sharp-pointed.

Penguins are more at home under than on the sea surface, where they swim with just their heads and sometimes the top of their backs visible. This keeps their flippers down where they are more effective. When going places they make their best time completely submerged, and often travel like a school of porpoises, leaping out of the water intermittently in short, graceful arcs to breathe as they go. I have watched migrating Adélies outdistance our ship with ease in this fashion when she was doing 16 knots. Penguins' underwater speed has been estimated well in excess of 25 miles per hour. They can propel themselves fast enough to "dive" upward 6 feet or more into the air to land on an otherwise inaccessible ice pan or rock. When feeding they dart about amid schools of shrimp and fish with bat-like agility and irregularity.

On land, penguins are handicapped by the position of their short legs, set far back on their bodies. This forces them to stand upright and to hop as do the crested penguins, or to waddle along clumsily with short steps as do most other species. Their comparative clumsiness and helplessness out of water are of little importance in lands where there are no carnivorous animals. Even so, they are harassed on their breeding grounds by several species of predatory birds. Sheathbills and Giant Petrels stand around all the subantarctic colonies waiting for a chance to take an unguarded egg or chick, and the Skua takes a measurable toll of the eggs and young of the Adélies every year. At sea the main enemies of penguins are the Leopard Seal and the Killer Whale, about the only sea

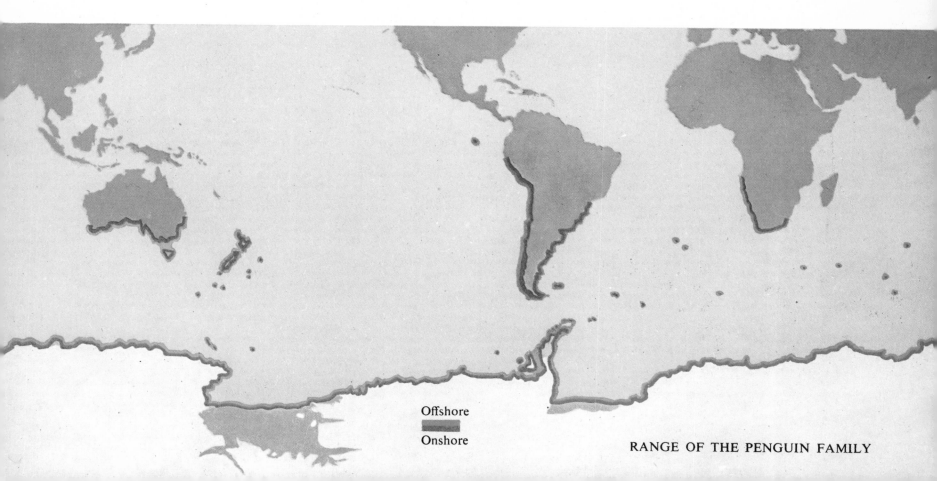

Offshore

Onshore

RANGE OF THE PENGUIN FAMILY

CHINSTRAP PENGUIN
Pygoscelis antarctica
South Orkneys and other small
antarctic islands   30 in.

creatures large enough and agile enough to prey on them successfully in their element.

The Emperor and the Adélie penguins migrate long distances over the antarctic ice to reach their nesting grounds. After shuffling along upright for a few steps they flop on to their bellies and propel themselves over the smooth ice in snow-toboggan fashion, using their flippers as paddles, helped along by piston-like thrusts of their feet. When the going is good they can travel in this manner faster than a man can ski.

Fish, squid, and shrimp are penguins' principal food, all of which they catch under water. They do not know how to eat on land, and penguins captured for zoos have to be force-fed

for weeks before they learn to pick up the fish thrown to them. Penguins leave the sea only to breed and to moult and, of course, have to fast all the time they are away from the water. Their unique ability to go long periods without food, living on the layer of fat stored under their skins, allows them to nest long distances from open water in the forbidding icy antarctic wastes and to carry out their breeding cycles on equally cheerless and foodless rocky islands.

The Emperor and its close relative the King Penguin are the largest of living penguins, the Emperor reaching 4 feet tall, the King about 3½ feet. Next in size, standing slightly over 2 feet, are the Adélie (named after Adélie Land where it was first found) and its two closest relatives, the circumpolar Gentoo and the Chinstrap penguins of the extreme South Atlantic and adjoining seas. Only slightly smaller is the group of so-called "short-tailed" penguins of the genus *Spheniscus* which, as the earliest to be named, also named both the order and family. These include the northernmost of the penguins, the Jackass Penguin of South African waters, named for its donkey-like braying, the Magellan Penguin of the Cape Horn region, and the Humboldt Penguin which nests from the Falklands along the west coast of South America northward to Peru. Most northerly of all is the much smaller (20 inches) Galapagos Penguin which inhabits the northern end of the cool Humboldt Current only 6° south of the Equator, and apparently breeds on the lonely Galapagos Islands, though nothing is known of its nesting habits.

Another well-marked group is the three *Eudyptes*, or "crested" penguins, all about 2 feet tall, each with a distinctive plume of golden-yellow feathers on either side of the head. This genus includes the circumpolar Rockhopper and Macaroni penguins, and the true Crested Penguin of New Zealand waters.

Restricted to New Zealand is the slightly larger Yellow-eyed Penguin which has a pale yellow band of slightly elongated feathers extending from the eyes around the back of the head. The biology and behaviour of this penguin have been

MAGELLAN PENGUIN
Spheniscus magellanicus
Chile, Tierra del Fuego,
Falkland Islands   25 in.

JACKASS PENGUIN
Spheniscus demersus
Islets off west coast of
South Africa   28 in.

LITTLE PENGUIN
Eudyptula minor
Australia,
New Zealand   13 in.

GENTOO PENGUIN
Pygoscelis papua
South Shetlands and other sm
antarctic islands   30 in.

studied intensively. In New Zealand and Australia also lives the smallest of the group, the foot-high Little (or Blue) Penguin. The Yellow-eyed and Little penguins nest underground, in burrows or rock crevices.

Most penguins are highly gregarious and breed in colonies, often of tremendous size. I estimated at least a half-million birds crammed into one 500-acre Adélie colony on Ross Island, McMurdo Sound. Some 30,000 pairs occupied the 40-acre foreland at Cape Hallett in Victoria Land before most of them were evicted to make way for an IGY substation and an emergency landing strip for aircraft. Carbon dating of mummified remains found only eight inches below the frozen surface at this site showed them to be about 650 years old. Recent ringing work has proved the Adélie, and doubtless all penguins as well, exhibits "site-tenacity" to a remarkable degree. The birds return to the same colony to breed year after year, and select almost the same spot for their nests.

The two largest penguins, the King and the Emperor, make no nest but incubate standing upright with their single egg held on top of their feet and huddled under a fold of the belly skin. All the other species incubate in more normal avian fashion, lying horizontally over their (usually two) eggs in some sort of a nest built of whatever materials are available. The Yellow-eyed, Little, and most *Spheniscus* penguins nest in burrows, practically all other species on the surface. Penguins like the Macaroni, Gentoo and Crested make crude nests of mud and whatever vegetation is present. The Adélie uses small pebbles, the only movable material available in its home.

The Emperor Penguin is probably the only bird on earth that almost never sets foot on bare land. It spends its life off the cold coast of Antarctica, living much of the year in the broken offshore icepack and feeding in its krill-rich waters. It is one of the few birds that start their reproduction cycle in autumn instead of spring. Its most amazing breeding cycle starts when the old birds come ashore to breed late in March—autumn in the Southern Hemisphere. They return unerringly over the ice to the spot on the shore-ice near the coast where they bred

the year before. Here the Emperors go through their courtship and, in May, just as the sun is setting for the long antarctic winter, the female lays her single egg, which is almost immediately taken in charge by her mate. She then heads for parts unknown, presumably to open water to break her fast, for she has not eaten for some seven or eight weeks — since she first came on the ice. The males, left alone, gather together in large "pods" for protection against the icy blasts of winter, milling in and out to share the warmest spot in the centre of the group. Each carefully holds his egg in place on his feet every minute of the time.

The temperatures during June and July fall to 40° below zero F., and the cold is intensified by 100-mile winds. Throughout the long, dark antarctic night the male Emperor bears the hope for the future of his race. To drop the egg or expose it momentarily in such temperatures means death to the embryo, and the mortality is indeed tremendous from this cause alone. The incubation period of the Emperor Penguin is 62 to 64 days, and the male accomplishes the entire stint without relief, losing in the process a third of its weight—dropping roughly from 75 to 50 pounds. When the egg hatches, he still has an exudate in his crop to feed the chick for the first day or two. Then the females, sleek, glossy, fat and full of food, come tobogganing in over the ice to relieve their mates and care for their chicks, while the males head for open water to regain their lost weight. This takes them only a few weeks, and by the end of August they come back in turn to help feed the chick for the next three months.

Several explanations have been advanced to account for this amazing reversal of the normal avian sex cycle. The physiology of it is still imperfectly understood, but the timing probably developed in response to the two-month incubation of the egg and the four-month growth period for the young. In this cycle the young Emperor Penguin reaches the point when it must fend for itself at the most favourable time of the year—in early December when the shore ice is melting and the antarctic summer is just starting.

ADÉLIE PENGUIN
Pygoscelis adeliae
Shores of Antarctica   30 in.

ROCKHOPPER PENGUIN
Eudyptes crestatus
Falklands and other
subantarctic islands   25 in.

BLACK-FOOTED ALBATROSS
Diomedea nigripes
North Pacific Ocean 28 in.

WANDERING ALBATROSS
Diomedea exulans
Southern oceans from 30° to
60° S. lat. 48 in.

LAYSAN ALBATROSS
Diomedea immutabilis
North Pacific Ocean 32 in.

TUBE-NOSED SWIMMERS

PROCELLARIIFORMES

The next four families, albatrosses, shearwaters, storm petrels, and diving petrels, are so closely related that they are put together into one order — Procellariiformes. However, the group is often called by an older name, Tubinares, or tube-noses, because of their outstanding physical characteristic. In each of the order's 92 species the nostrils extend on to the bill in short tubes, sometimes opening on each side, more often united on top of the upper bill, or culmen.

All Tubinares are highly pelagic and spend most of their lives wandering over the trackless seas, coming to land only to nest. All lay a single white egg, usually in an underground burrow—only albatrosses habitually make open nests. Most

are active on the breeding grounds only at night, and their incubation and fledging periods are relatively long. Tubinares have a clear yellow stomach oil which they feed their newly hatched young, and which they discharge from mouth and nostrils when disturbed. All have a distinctive musty body odour that is so persistent that it clings to preserved museum specimens for decades.

These and other features of anatomy and behaviour set the Tubinares apart from all other bird groups, and they have no near relatives. Three fourths of them (70 species) breed and spend most, if not all, their lives south of the equator. Their fossil record goes back some 60 million years to Eocene time. They doubtless evolved from some yet undiscovered ancestor in the lands around the southern oceans in Cretaceous time, 100 million or more years ago.

Each of the four families of Tubinares is fairly distinctive in its own right and, with minor exceptions, the easiest way to differentiate between them is by size. The albatrosses are the largest of the order; all of them are about the size of a goose—large, stout-bodied birds with long, narrow wings. The shearwater family is rather heterogeneous, but its typical members are medium sized, about the size of small gulls or large terns. Their bodies are slenderer than those of albatrosses, and they too have long, slim, tapering wings. The storm petrels are all small, darkish birds, none over 10 inches long, the size of our blackbirds, and with relatively shorter, broader wings than their larger relatives. The diving petrels are a unique group of fat-bodied, short-winged Tubinares adapted to a life in rather than over the water.

PINTADO PETREL (CAPE PIGEON)
Daption capensis
Southern oceans 14 in.

GOULD
(WHITE-WINGED) PETREL
Pterodroma leucoptera
North and
South Pacific oceans 12 in.

WILSON'S PETREL
Oceanites oceanicus
Coastal Antarctica and antarctic islands
north to North Atlantic, South Pacific,
and Indian oceans 7 in.

LEACH'S PETREL
Oceanodroma leucorhoa
North Atlantic and
North Pacific oceans 8 in.

STORM PETREL
Hydrobates pelagicus
Eastern North Atlantic and
Mediterranean waters 6 in.

FULMAR
Fulmarus glacialis
Arctic and northern Atlantic and
Pacific oceans 18 in.

ALBATROSSES

PROCELLARIIFORMES   DIOMEDEIDAE

When 15th-century Portuguese navigators first ventured down the coast of Africa into the windy South Atlantic they encountered large black-and-white sea birds with stout bodies and long pointed wings. They called these strange birds "alcatraz," the Portuguese word for large sea birds, particularly the pelicans familiar to them in Mediterranean waters. English sailors corrupted alcatraz into albatross, the name we have used ever since for these monarchs of the ocean winds.

Albatrosses are familiar to all blue-water seamen, whose ships they have followed since the days of Magellan. Their distribution is world-wide except for the North Atlantic and the frozen Arctic oceans. Albatrosses were part of the legends and lore of the sea long before Coleridge made them famous in literature. Superstitious sailors thought them the spirits of seamen swept overboard in gales, and regarded them as the harbingers of winds, mists, and fogs. The Ancient Mariner, you may remember, was first condemned for killing the bird that brought the storm winds, and later praised for destroying the bird that brought the fog. That the mariners of old should associate albatrosses with storms and wind is not surprising, for wind is the element of these birds. They are complete masters of it, and without it they are almost helpless.

Few sailors can tell more than one or two of the 13 species of albatross apart. They lump them by colour into white ones and dark ones. Just as few ever refer to the birds as albatrosses. In sea vernacular they are gooneys and mollymawks. "Gooney" was originally "goney," the Old English word for a stupid person, and the source of our slang "goon." "Mollymawk," also "mollyhawk," or just plain "molly," comes from the Dutch "mallemok," meaning a stupid gull. Sailors have always regarded albatrosses as dumb, which they doubtless are by human standards. Japanese fishermen have known them for centuries as "bakadori," or fool-birds.

These names may be based on the birds' apparent lack of fear at sea, for ship-following albatrosses often swoop over the taffrail. Perhaps it is because of their helplessness when they land on a vessel's deck and, unable to rise over the bulwarks, vomit their stomach oil in annoyance. More likely they are so named because of their solemn, inexpressive facial mien. On their nesting grounds there is no doubt of their stupidity, for no amount of contact seems to teach them to fear man. They resent his intrusion, and when disturbed on the nest or with a chick they will try to ward off the intruder with vicious stabs of the beak. But they have never learned to get out of man's way, and it looks as though they never will. On Midway Island birds nest on the lawns next to houses, and incubate serenely alongside roads, paying no attention to the jeeps and trucks rumbling past.

Albatrosses are the unquestioned champions of gliding flight. Their long, narrow, tapered wings are so perfectly designed to take advantage of the updrafts from the waves that, given wind enough, they travel effortlessly in any direction, upwind as well as down, with hardly a wingstroke. I have watched these birds keep up all day with fast ocean vessels, coursing up alongside on almost motionless wings, then playing back and forth, up and back over the wake in irregular circles,

figure eights, and letter S's, waiting for the screw to bring a squid to the surface, or for the garbage detail to drop galley scraps overboard.

The perfect gliding aerofoil of the albatross wing is inefficient for flapping flight, so when the wind drops to a flat calm the albatrosses are practically "grounded." That is why most of them live in the windiest, roughest seas in the world, and why, as the oldtime sailormen were aware, the harder it blows, within reason, the more albatrosses you see. This also helps to explain their distribution, which is largely governed by the prevailing wind patterns over the world's oceans.

The centre of albatross distribution today is the southern seas between the Tropic of Capricorn and the Antarctic Circle. Here 9 of the 13 living forms occur. In the "Roaring Forties" and "Furious Fifties," the belt of high winds that blow continuously from west to east between the continents' southern tips and the antarctic ice, the albatrosses are most at home. Several species live at its northern edge in one segment of ocean—Buller's Albatross, for instance, seems largely confined to New Zealand waters. Others, like the Wandering, the Black-browed, and the two Sooty albatrosses, are found completely around the world. With winds of from 10 to 50 knots in those latitudes, it is a simple matter for these great gliders to circle the globe at will. The distance around the world at 40° south latitude is roughly 19,000 miles. Riding a wind of only 10 knots—a light one for these latitudes—will carry the bird 250 miles per day. So it should not strain an albatross to travel around the world in 80 days, with much less effort than Jules Verne's hero. Recent recoveries of ringed birds suggest some individuals do just that.

The windless doldrums that stretch across both the Atlantic and the Pacific at the equator are effective natural barriers to these large gliders, and few succeed in crossing them. Fossilized bones of a Pliocene albatross found in England show these birds soared on North Atlantic winds before the ice age. In historic times too few albatrosses straggled into the North Atlantic for any species of the family to establish itself there. Fewer than a dozen individuals of four species have been reliably reported in the North Atlantic during the past century. One of the most famous of these was a lone Black-browed Albatross that probably followed a sailing ship north to Europe on favourable winds, and was first noticed in the Faroe Islands in 1860. There it hobnobbed with a colony of gannets, and accompanied them southward every winter to the British Isles and back to the Faroes every spring. An overzealous and misguided hunter shot it in 1894. Its remains are in a Copenhagen museum.

No southern albatross has ever been taken in the North Pacific in Recent times, but long before the last ice age the ancestors of the three species that occur there today managed to cross the doldrum barrier. Two of these, the slate-coloured Black-footed Albatross and the white-bodied, black-winged, and black-backed Laysan Albatross, nest in the Leeward Islands west of Hawaii and on other isolated islets in the western Pacific. These North Pacific albatrosses retain their ancestors' habit of nesting in the Southern Hemisphere spring and summer from October to April. When not nesting they cruise over the entire North Pacific from California to China and north into the Bering Sea, generally following the circular wind pattern of the Pacific which mariners took advantage of in the days of sail.

The third North Pacific species is the Short-tailed, or Steller's, Albatross, discovered by the indefatigable naturalist who accompanied Vitus Bering on his great trek across Siberia to the Pacific in 1740. Steller's Albatross is similar to the Laysan, but is much larger, has a white instead of a black back, and a yellow instead of a dark bill. It once nested in numbers in the Bonins and other small islands south of Japan, and followed the Pacific trade winds northward to the Bering Sea, east and south past California, then back westward to its home. Steller's Albatross was almost wiped out by Japanese plume hunters early in this century, and for a time it was feared extinct. In 1953, 20 years after the last one had been reported, a few birds appeared miraculously from the ocean wastes to nest again on Torishima, a lonely volcanic islet 400 miles south of Tokyo. This was formerly the site of the largest colony of these birds, and is now a Japanese weather station. The Japanese have made the bird a "natural monument" and give it rigid protection. At last reports (1959) the colony numbered about 50 individuals. It is hoped that this nucleus may expand to the species' former numbers.

South of the equator in the Pacific are the great windy stretches where albatrosses are most numerous. Closest to the equator is the Waved Albatross, which breeds in the Galapagos Islands and "winters" over the rich waters of the Humboldt Current off Ecuador and Peru.

The best-known albatross of the southern oceans is the great Wandering Albatross, whose 11-foot wingspan is the largest of all living birds. Adults are pure white with black wingtips. They take several years to attain this plumage. The first year they are brownish slate; then gradually the adult plumage develops during successive moults, and many birds seen at sea are in pied intermediate plumages. Other southern species of the same general aspect are the slightly smaller Royal Albatross (9-foot wingspread), and the still smaller Yellow-nosed, Grey-headed, and Black-browed species with 6- to 8-foot spreads. Two species, the Sooty and the Light-mantled Sooty albatrosses, are soft grey-brown.

Most albatrosses breed in colonies on offshore or oceanic islands. The nest is sometimes a mere scrape on the ground. More often the birds build a concave mound of mud or soil lined crudely with feathers and grasses. Both parents share incubating the single white egg. This takes about 65 days in the smaller species such as the Laysan and Black-footed, and from 77 to 81 days in the largest ones, the Royal and Wandering albatrosses. Both parents feed the young by regurgitation. It takes the young of smaller species from 2½ to 3 months to fledge. The young of larger species remain in the rookery 8 to 9 months. The nesting cycle of the Wandering Albatross is so long that the adults breed every other year instead of annually. Recent ringing studies show the Laysan Albatross does not nest until it is at least 7 years old. The maturation period may be even longer in the larger birds.

Albatrosses are famous for the courtship antics they carry on throughout the breeding season. These involve grotesque, awkward dancing, accompanied by bowing, scraping, snapping of bills, and "prolonged nasal groans." This latter is usually a duet by the mated pair, but occasionally more individuals join in before actual pairing is settled.

Before man invaded their domain, albatrosses had few enemies, and, until the 19th century, man's impact on albatross populations was not serious. In sailing-ship days, sailors caught them on baited hooks trailed over the stern. The maritime tradition of bad luck attending those who killed the ship-followers never prevented bored or hungry seamen from killing albatrosses. Fresh meat, regardless of flavour, was a welcome change from the monotonous diet of "salt horse and hardtack." Ships that reached large rookeries on isolated islands took both birds and eggs for the ship's stores.

The slaughter of albatrosses began in earnest in the late 19th century, when a market developed for their plumage. Wings were used in millinery and body feathers were sold for mattress- and pillow-stuffing as "swans' down." The North Pacific rookeries bore the brunt of this exploitation, much of which was carried on by the Japanese, though Americans, Canadians, French, and others were also in the business. The largest and most famous albatross rookery of those days was on Laysan Island, about 1,000 miles west of Hawaii. Graphic reports of the almost unbelievable slaughter there led President Theodore Roosevelt to set this and other islands in the

WANDERING ALBATROSS
Diomedea exulans

Leeward chain aside as a wildlife reservation, in 1909. Even this did not stop raiding by poachers, and the North Pacific albatross population declined markedly before lessening demand, falling prices, and rising public sentiment put an end to the practice.

World War II brought an unprecedented influx of humans to the lonely Pacific islands where albatrosses nest. When the Japanese were finally dislodged from Wake Island, all the birds were gone from that famous rookery. The starving garrison had used them for food. The birds have not yet returned, after 15 years. The albatrosses on Midway were more fortunate, and at the end of hostilities a sizable colony was still breeding there.

The Midway Islands have been occupied by Americans for half a century. It is one of the few places shared by albatrosses and by humans. Until recently birds and people have got along together very well. In 1935 Midway became an air base for trans-Pacific planes, and hundreds of passengers have been amused by the gooneys' antics. During World War II, aircraft activities on Midway increased enormously. After the war the United States Navy took over the islands. In spite of the changes, birds and sailors got along famously.

Albatrosses have been a minor hazard to aircraft ever since the building of the Midway runway. Aircraft have collided with birds there in as many as one in every six landings or takeoffs during daylight hours in the nesting season. While usually fatal to the birds, these collisions did comparatively little damage to the aircraft, and caused no crashes. The advent of high-speed jets, however, increased the danger seriously, for a bird sucked into a jet intake can explode the plane. The U. S. Fish and Wildlife Service has been studying the problem for 10 years. Attempts to transplant the birds to other islands have been unsuccessful because of the species' territorial fidelity. They insist on coming back to nest in the same place every year. The Navy even went so far as to kill 30,000 birds in the neighbourhood of the runway, but this had no immediate effect on the number of strikes. The prospect of wiping out the entire huge Midway albatross colony, even in the interest of air (and national) safety, is not pleasant to contemplate, for here nest at least one-third of the world's population of Laysan Albatrosses. Bulldozers have levelled the dunes near the runway that produce the updrafts the birds insist on riding into the paths of the planes. This has been a major factor in reducing the strikes by 70 per cent.

SHEARWATERS

PROCELLARIIFORMES   PROCELLARIIDAE

This is by far the largest family of the Tubinares. Its 53 members, united by similarities in the nasal tubes, and by other anatomical characteristics, are found on all the unfrozen salt waters of the world. All are migratory, and several have a good claim to the title of the world's greatest travellers. Shearwaters get their name from their habit of skimming over the sea barely above the water, swooping along the troughs of giant waves on almost motionless wings. Many members of the shearwater family are commonly called petrels. Shearwaters are not as familiar to sailors as are albatrosses because they do not habitually follow ships.

Most shearwaters are medium-sized birds, from 15 to 25 inches long, with slender, streamlined bodies and long, thin, pointed wings, 2 to 2½ feet from tip to tip. The bulk of the family is made up of members of two genera, the 23 species of *Pterodroma*, sometimes called the "gadfly petrels," and the 17 true shearwaters of the genus *Puffinus*, so named in the mistaken idea that they were puffins. These are rather drab birds—several are black, dark brown, or dark grey; one is pure white. Most are greyish above and lighter below.

Typical of the *Puffinus* group is the Manx Shearwater of European North Atlantic waters. This 14-inch bird with a 2-foot wingspread, dark above and white below, nests widely on islands off western Europe and in the Mediterranean—the Azores, Canaries, and the British Isles; the Faroes, Iceland, and Bermuda. Oddly it has not bred at the Isle of Man, after

MANX SHEARWATER
Puffinus puffinus
Eastern North Atlantic and
Mediterranean waters 14 in.

which it is named, since about 1800. It winters south to Brazil and Argentina. Ringing studies in England show these birds to be remarkably faithful to their breeding sites, and to have an uncanny ability to return, even from strange seas. One Manx Shearwater, taken from its nest off the coast of Wales, was carried across the Atlantic to Boston by an air passenger and released near Boston International Airport over unfamiliar waters. It was back at its nest, 3,400 miles to the east, 12½ days later.

No less amazing are the travels of the Slender-billed, or Short-tailed, Shearwater that nests in huge colonies on islands in Bass Strait between Australia and Tasmania. This shearwater migrates clockwise each year around the entire Pacific Basin (see map). The Slender-billed Shearwater is slightly smaller than the Manx, and is entirely sooty brown, slightly lighter on the belly. This is one of several species known in Australia and New Zealand as "mutton-birds" because they were widely used for food by the early settlers. Even today a thriving industry exists on its breeding grounds. The young are taken from the nest, canned, and sold as "Tasmanian Squab." In recent years, thanks to the intervention of the Australian government, scientists have made intensive studies of these shearwaters and regulate the annual harvest of young birds to maintain the annual yield.

Because of these Australian studies, more is known about the habits, life history, and distribution of this bird than of other shearwaters. Ringing studies, now in their 16th year, show the bird must be comparatively long-lived, for it has an unusually long period of sexual immaturity. Apparently females do not begin to breed until they are five years old; males begin at seven. Like most other shearwaters, the birds lay their single egg in burrows in November. Both parents incubate in long alternate shifts, the male taking the first 12- to 14-day stint, the female the second, through the 52 to 55 days it takes the egg to hatch. Each bird remains on the nest throughout its shift without food or water.

The young are fed by both parents, who regurgitate half-digested shrimp. Despite a 2- to 3-day interval between feedings, the young grow so rapidly they often exceed their parents in weight in 4 to 6 weeks. As they begin to sprout their flight feathers the feedings taper off, until at last, after some 14 weeks of feeding, the parents desert the fat, oily chicks. After about a week alone in their burrows, slowly absorbing their fat, growing their feathers, and getting down to size, the chicks emerge at night of their own accord, exercise their wings, and take their departure from the nesting grounds unattended. They fly northward on the traditional migration route, and do not return for 3 to 4 years. Then they may appear as nonbreeding adults, usually on the same islet where they were reared, and where they will eventually nest and raise their young.

It is at the end of the fledgling period, just as the fat, oily young are deserted by their parents, that the young birds are harvested. Tasmanians haul them from their burrows, kill them quickly, hang them to drain out their valuable stomach oil, and then process them for canning. In the old days they were salted down. "Tasmanian Squab" is a delicacy, as troops who got them in their rations during World War II soon discovered. They are succulent, and to my surprise not a bit fishy. The take of "Squab" is so regulated that enough young are allowed to fly away each year to balance the estimated adult

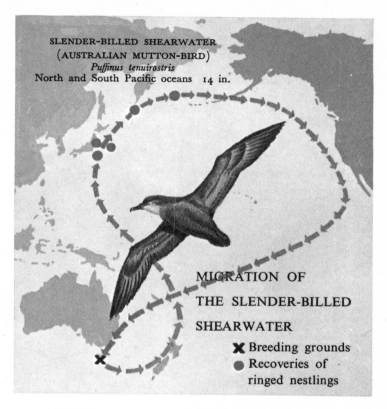

SLENDER-BILLED SHEARWATER
(AUSTRALIAN MUTTON-BIRD)
Puffinus tenuirostris
North and South Pacific oceans 14 in.

MIGRATION OF
THE SLENDER-BILLED
SHEARWATER
✘ Breeding grounds
● Recoveries of ringed nestlings

annual mortality rate. So despite the killing of hundreds of thousands of mutton-bird chicks annually, immense flocks still fly their clockwise courses around the Pacific and blacken the water of Bass Strait every October before they go ashore to nest.

One of the commonest shearwaters of the Atlantic is the Greater Shearwater, the "hagdon" of the Newfoundland fisherman, which concentrates in immense numbers every spring on the Grand Banks and in the Straits of Belle Isle. This 20-inch bird, grey above and white below, was a bird of mystery for years until its nesting ground was finally located in the 1920's on remote Tristan da Cunha, a small island in the South Atlantic. Greater Shearwaters apparently follow the wind pattern around the Atlantic basin the same way their antipodean relatives do in the Pacific. They nest during the southern summer and "winter" in the north during the northern summer.

One of the most widespread of the shearwaters is the 16-inch Sooty Shearwater, which breeds circumpolarly around the southern lands of the Southern Hemisphere. Annually one population in the Pacific and another in the Atlantic migrate northward to subarctic waters. They are there during the northern spring and summer, and return every autumn to the ancestral breeding grounds below the Tropic of Capricorn.

Classified with the shearwaters are the two fulmars (originally "foul-gull"), whose name derives from their characteristic musty smell and their habit of spitting an equally smelly stomach oil at intruders on the nesting grounds. The northern Fulmar is a sleek though chunky bird with the typical narrow, pointed shearwater wings. It has the same habit of swooping down between wave crests like "two wings on a mackerel." It breeds circumpolarly around the northern parts of the Northern Hemisphere. The Fulmar of the North Atlantic is silver grey above, white below. The northern Pacific birds have two colour phases, one identical to the Atlantic, the other a sooty brown, lighter below. The Atlantic birds accompany fishing vessels and scavenge scraps and waste fish. The population has increased markedly during the last century, and the Fulmar is now one of the commonest pelagic birds, coming as far south in winter as Massachusetts and France. The Pacific birds winter south to southern California and Japan.

At the other end of the world, breeding circumpolarly around the continent of Antarctica and on antarctic islands, is the Silver-grey Fulmar, slightly smaller than its arctic cousin, but practically identical to it otherwise. This bird migrates northward in the Southern Hemisphere winter to St. Helena, Cape Frio in Africa, Peru, Australia, and New Zealand.

Largest member of the shearwater family is the Giant Petrel of subantarctic waters, sometimes called Giant Fulmar, but known widely to sailors and southern fishermen as the "Nelly," or "Stinker." Despite its grace as a flier, this species is unattractive and unlovely in its appearance and habits. Though it feeds at sea on shrimp, squid, and fish, it is predatory in summer on the colonies of penguins and other antarctic birds. The Giant Petrel is 3 feet long with a wingspan of about 8 feet. Its wings are a trifle broader than those of the albatrosses it so strongly resembles. Most are a solid blackish brown, which sets off the large, yellow bill. At the southern fringe of its range along the antarctic continent a pure white colour phase occurs.

The Giant Petrel breeds on subantarctic islands completely around the world, and is one of the few above-ground nesters among the shearwaters. Large numbers ringed in the Falkland Dependencies by the British, and on Heard and Macquarie islands by the Australians, have been recovered on the opposite side of the world from where they were ringed. Like so many of the sea birds of those latitudes, the Giant Petrels apparently take advantage of the steady west wind drift to circle around the world during their nonbreeding season.

Another common and wide-ranging southern seas species is the Cape Pigeon, or Pintado Petrel, unmistakable in its checkered black and white. The Cape Pigeon frequently follows ships, and is familiar to all sailors who have rounded the southern capes. It breeds circumpolarly on subantarctic islands, and occasionally strays northward beyond the equator. Large flocks gather near the antarctic whale factory ships to feed on their oily refuse.

Among other members of this large, diverse family that deserve mention is the lovely dove-like Snowy Petrel of antarctic waters, a pure white bird 16 inches long with black bill and eyes. It nests all around Antarctica and seldom moves northward of the limits of antarctic pack ice, and therefore has one of the southernmost distributions of all flying birds. Found with it is the 17-inch Antarctic Petrel, brown above and white below, with broad patches of white on the wings and tail.

A compact and little-known group is the prions, or whalebirds, a genus of four species of small, pearly-grey birds, 11 to 12 inches long, that fly across the cold antarctic seas in large flocks. They stay close to the water like storm petrels, suddenly appearing out of nowhere like wraiths around the ship and disappearing into the ocean vastnesses as suddenly as they came. They are hole-nesters and breed on many subantarctic islands.

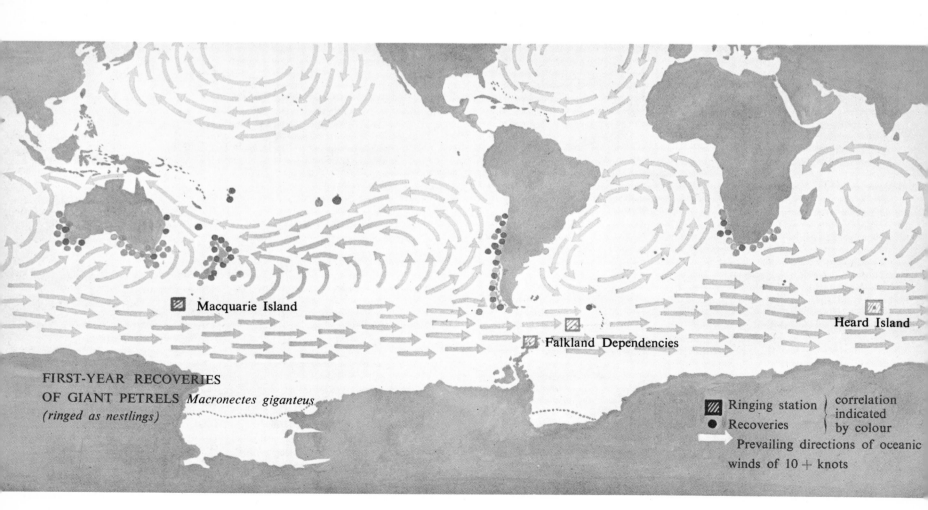

FIRST-YEAR RECOVERIES
OF GIANT PETRELS *Macronectes giganteus*
(ringed as nestlings)

Macquarie Island

Falkland Dependencies

Heard Island

Ringing station ⎫ correlation
Recoveries ⎬ indicated
→ Prevailing directions of oceanic ⎭ by colour
winds of 10 + knots

STORM PETRELS

PROCELLARIIFORMES   HYDROBATIDAE

Probably no sea birds are the subject of more folklore, legends, and myths than the little storm petrels, so-called from the old sailors' superstition that their presence presages a storm. This is not exactly true, but they often do appear suddenly at sea at the onset of windy weather, seemingly out of nowhere. The name petrel is thought to be a diminutive of St. Peter, who walked on water with the Saviour's help. It could just as well have come from the birds' twittering cries, heard over the water during the still watches of the night. Sailors call these birds "Mother Carey's chickens," and there is little question that this name comes from "Mater Cara," the Divine Virgin, who is guardian of all seamen.

To deepwater sailors the storm petrels are among the most familiar of oceanic birds, for they commonly follow ships, and they are so distinctive they are easily recognized as such. There is no mistaking the little dark-coloured birds, the size of a blackbird or a large swallow, seen fluttering over the wake. The largest of the 22 species is only 10 inches in length, and they are the smallest of the pelagic birds.

Most of the storm petrels are solid black or dark brown above and below, and usually have a conspicuous white rump patch (see page 31). Many of these dark, white-rumped species are so similar they are exceedingly difficult to tell apart at sea. The slight distinguishing marks between them are hard to discern at any distance, especially as the birds keep moving and are seldom still. The three species of frigate-petrels, limited to the southern oceans, show white on their underparts. The Fork-tailed Petrel of the North Pacific is pearly grey above and below.

In common with all the tube-nosed swimmers, the storm petrels spend most of their lives at sea and come to land only to breed. They occur in practically all the open oceans of the world. At sea they are apparently as active at night as they are during the day. In waters where they are common they occasionally "rain" aboard vessels in the darkness, apparently confused by the lights, especially in thick weather.

Typically, storm petrels are seen flying close to the water with erratic, fluttering wingbeats, sometimes singly, more often in small scattered flocks. Occasionally they appear in tremendous numbers where food is plentiful, especially near their breeding grounds. They course back and forth over a ship's wake in search of small marine life brought to the surface by the propeller, and will peck at galley scraps thrown overboard, especially if these are fatty. Their normal diet is the small organisms, tiny shrimp, squid, and other crustaceans and molluscs that drift near the sea surface as plankton.

Storm petrels usually snatch their food from the water without alighting. When feeding they hover close to the surface on fluttering wings and pat the water with their feet, sometimes with both feet together, more often alternately, giving the illusion they are walking. Infrequently but occasionally they alight and dip under the surface for a morsel. On the water they float buoyantly high on the surface, but they are not strong swimmers. Unless the wind is strong, they may patter some distance over the water before getting up enough speed to become airborne. Their legs are too weak to support them on land, and at their nests they shuffle along on their entire tarsus, aided by their wings.

The various storm petrels breed from the subarctic to the antarctic, most of them in colonies on offshore islands. A few nest high in coastal mountains at some distance from the sea. All lay their single oval white egg in a burrow they dig with their beak and feet 2 or 3 feet into soft soil under matted grass, or in crevices or crannies under loose rocks. On their nesting grounds the storm petrels are completely nocturnal. A colony with thousands of nests seems quiet and deserted by day, for the birds never leave their burrows except in darkness. After nightfall when the birds come in from the sea to relieve their incubating mates or to feed the young, the air is filled with their twittering cries and the rustling of their wings. Just before dawn they vanish, either into their burrows or over the distant horizon of the sea.

The incubation period is amazingly long in these small birds, from 5½ to 7 weeks. Throughout it both parents brood alternately for from 2 to 4 days at a stretch, each remaining in the burrow without food until relieved, which always takes place at night. The young hatch covered with a dense coat of greyish or brownish down. The parents feed them at first on their clear, musty-smelling stomach oil, later with half-digested regurgitated shrimp or squid. It takes them from 7 to 9 weeks to mature, and they remain in the burrow until fully fledged. The parents then desert them and, when ready, the young make their own way to the sea at night.

Best known of the northern storm petrels, though not a chronic ship-follower, is Leach's Petrel, identifiable by its forked tail (page 31) and light, bouncing flight. Leach's Petrel breeds around the northern North Atlantic from Maine, Greenland, Iceland, and the Faroe Islands to Great Britain, and similarly around the North Pacific from Lower California northward to Alaska and down the Asiatic side to Japan and Korea. The Atlantic population winters below the equator on both sides of the South Atlantic. The Pacific birds do not cross the line, and apparently winter at sea fairly near their breeding grounds.

A more habitual ship-follower is the Storm Petrel of eastern North Atlantic and Mediterranean waters. Smaller than Leach's, the Storm Petrel has a square tail, short black legs and feet, and a more fluttery and bat-like flight. It nests on islets from Iceland to Norway and along the European coasts of the Atlantic and Mediterranean, and winters southward to the Red Sea and the southwest coast of Africa.

Another common ship-follower in the North Atlantic during the summer is Wilson's Petrel, also square-tailed, but distinguishable from the other species by its longer legs, which project beyond the tail in flight. Wilson's Petrel nests circumpolarly on the antarctic continent and on many sub-antarctic islands. So large are some of its colonies one author credits it as perhaps the most numerous bird in the world. Though it "winters" north in the Atlantic to the British Isles and Labrador, and in the Indian Ocean to the Red Sea, Wilson's Petrel does not move northward in the Pacific beyond the southernmost of the oceanic islands.

DIVING PETRELS

PROCELLARIIFORMES   PELECANOIDIDAE

COMMON DIVING PETREL
Pelecanoides urinatrix
Subantarctic coasts and islands 8 in.

The four diving petrels of the colder southern oceans form the most aberrant family of the Tubinares. They are apparently the descendants of Southern Hemisphere petrel stock that long ago adopted a different method of obtaining their living. Instead of flying over sea to find food on the surface, they dive for fish and other marine organisms in the manner of the unrelated auks of the northern seas. Their striking superficial resemblance to the smaller auks is a fine example of parallel evolution. Like the auks they are excellent divers, and swim underwater with their wings. Unlike other Tubinares they fly with rapid, whirring wingbeats. Flying close to the sea surface, they frequently dive into a wave top and emerge, still flying, from the other side.

The four species are so alike one almost has to have them in hand to tell them apart. All are small, chunky birds, from 7 to 10 inches in length, blackish above and white below. Their short bills are broad at the base, hooked at the tip, and surmounted by tubular nostrils which open upward. Their neck, wings, and tail are short, and their stout legs placed well back on the body accentuate their resemblance to the auklets.

Diving petrels are usually most plentiful in the waters near the coasts and islands where they breed. They show no pronounced migratory movements, but single birds and scattered small flocks are occasionally found far at sea. The Common Diving Petrel, the most widespread member of the group, occurs from the Atlantic coast of Argentina eastward across the South Atlantic and Indian oceans to Australia and New Zealand. The Magellan Diving Petrel is limited to the Cape Horn region. The Georgian Diving Petrel breeds on South Georgia and on Macquarie and Auckland islands. The northernmost and largest species, the Peruvian Diving Petrel, nests on islands off the west coast of South America from Chile to Peru.

The breeding habits of the diving petrels closely parallel those of the storm petrels. They lay their single white egg in a burrow they dig in the soft soil, and are nocturnal on the nesting grounds. Both parents incubate alternately, and the incubation and fledging period are abnormally long, reportedly from 6 to 8 weeks each. Their cries on the nesting grounds have been likened to the mewing of a cat or the croaking of frogs.

PELICANS AND
THEIR ALLIES

PELECANIFORMES

United in this order are six families of large, acquatic, fish-eating birds often called the Steganopodes, or totipalmate swimmers. While each family is strongly distinctive and well marked in its own right, all share characteristics of anatomy and behaviour that unite them into a natural group. Chief among these is their foot structure. They are the only birds that have all four toes connected by webs. The hind toe is turned partly forward and webbed to the innermost front toe.

All members of the order have short legs and large wings with 11 primary feathers, the outermost usually greatly reduced. All are strong fliers, and most of them swim well but walk poorly. All have long beaks, as long or longer than the head. All but the tropic-birds have very small nostrils that sometimes lack external openings. All have a gular or throat pouch, which is often unfeathered and reaches its greatest development in the pelicans. All but the cormorants and anhingas have highly pneumatic skeletons, and many have subcutaneous air sacs as well.

The Pelecaniformes are altricial; the young hatch blind, frequently naked, and are fed in the nest by regurgitation by both parents. They build crude, flimsy nests (the tropic-birds make none) and usually lay a small clutch (1 to 6) of chalky white eggs which both sexes incubate. Incubation periods vary from 3 to 6 weeks, fledging times from 5 to 8 weeks.

An ancient group, the Pelecaniformes have one of the oldest fossil records of any living order. Classified here is *Elopteryx*, a cormorant-like bird known from leg bones found in Hungarian Cretaceous deposits 100 million or so years old. Fossils of several modern genera are known from Oligocene time, 40 million years ago. Their nearest relatives seem to be the tube-nosed swimmers.

Always found on or near water, the distribution of the order is world wide in temperate and tropical regions.

1 RED-TAILED TROPIC-BIRD
Phaëthon rubricauda
Tropical Pacific and
Indian oceans 19-35 in.

2 WHITE-TAILED (YELLOW-BILLED)
TROPIC-BIRD
Phaëthon lepturus
Tropical Pacific, Atlantic,
and Indian oceans 16-32 in.

3 RED-BILLED TROPIC-BIRD
Phaëthon aethereus
Tropical Pacific, Atlantic,
and Indian oceans 24-40 in.

TROPIC-BIRDS

PELECANIFORMES   PHAËTHONTIDAE

Tropic-birds are aptly named, for they rarely stray beyond the tropic seas. The most pelagic birds of their order, they range throughout the warmer parts of the Atlantic, Pacific, and Indian oceans, and are often encountered hundreds of miles from the nearest land, over waters inhabited by few other birds. They are not ship-followers, but show a curiosity in passing vessels which is easily satisfied. They appear out of the blue, flying 50 to 100 feet above the water, with graceful, steady wingbeats, like large white doves. They fly over the vessel, announce their presence with shrill screams, circle it once or twice, then disappear as suddenly as they came.

The family contains only three species, all united in the single genus *Phaëthon*. All are white with a few black markings on the head and wings. Occasionally they show a faint pink or salmon sheen, noticeable only with the bird in the hand. Tropic-birds are from 16 to 20 inches long, not counting the two central tail feathers which stream out an additional foot like a marlin spike, which is why sailors call them "bo's'n-birds." The young of the year lack the elongated tail feathers, and have their backs finely barred with black.

The Red-billed Tropic-bird of the tropical western Pacific, the central Atlantic, the Red Sea, and the Persian Gulf is the only one in which the juvenile back-barring persists in the adult. Its bill is a strong red, its tail feathers white. The White-tailed Tropic-bird, with white tail and a bright yellow bill, is the most wide-ranging of the three species, nesting on oceanic islands completely around the world. The Red-tailed Tropic-bird, its central tail feathers a bright vermilion, nests on islands from the Indian Ocean to the central Pacific.

Tropic-birds seldom rest on the water and are poor swim-

mers. However, they float buoyantly when they do alight. They feed mostly on fish and squid. The fishing bird hovers a moment on rapid wings, as if taking aim, 50 feet or more in the air, then plummets down with half-closed wings, sometimes spiralling slightly. Plunging in with a slight splash, it reappears in a second or two with its prey in its beak, shakes the water from its plumage, and takes wing again.

Tropic-birds make no nest, but lay their single egg on a ledge in a sea cliff, or on the ground under a shrub on low-lying islands. Their nesting cycle takes about 3 months, 28 days of incubation by both parents and another 60 to 65 days for the chick to fledge. As in petrels, when fledging time comes the adults desert the young, which set out to face the world on their own. In some parts of their range they rear two broods each year.

Tropic-birds are not gregarious, and are found in numbers only near their breeding grounds, where they gather to take advantage of suitable terrain. At sea seldom are more than a single pair encountered together. On their nesting grounds, they are amazingly indifferent to humans. Though they squawk and peck at the intruder, they remain on their single egg until lifted off. Native tribes of the South Sea islands value the tail plumes of the Red-tailed Tropic-bird for ornamental use, and gather them by pulling them out of the nesting birds, without otherwise harming them.

The chief enemy of tropic-birds is man. In Bermuda the White-tailed Tropic-bird was badly decimated by egg gatherers. With protection these birds have made a comeback and now nest in abundance on the Bermuda cliffs. Rats do them some damage on West Indies nesting grounds.

PELICANS

PELECANIFORMES   PELECANIDAE

Its renown as the bird "whose bill holds more than its belly can," overshadows the pelican's claim to fame as a bird of great antiquity. Pelican bones found in Oligocene deposits 30 to 40 million years old are so similar to those of living pelicans that the ancient birds are placed in the same genus, *Pelecanus*. Remains of living species are plentiful in Pleistocene deposits.

Pelicans have been known for so long that the very derivation of their name is lost in antiquity. Greeks and Romans called them pelicans or pelecans, and so have all Europeans since, except the Spanish and Portuguese, who call them "alcatraz." (Pelicans once lived on the rocky island in San Francisco Bay that bears this Spanish name.) Strangest of all the ancient beliefs about these large, grotesque birds was one, common in the Middle Ages, that pelicans fed their young on their own blood, obtained by puncturing their breasts with their beaks. This led to an identification with Christ's suffering, and to the use of the pelican to symbolize charity and piety in medieval heraldry.

The famous limerick's claim about the pelican's pouch has some basis in fact. The White Pelican's gular pouch can hold almost 3 gallons, two to three times the capacity of its stomach. There fact ends, however, for the bird cannot "hold in its beak enough food for a week." The bare, distensible skin of the throat may have some value as a cooling device, used the way a panting dog does his tongue. But pelicans use the pouch mainly as a dip net for catching fish.

WHITE PELICAN
Pelecanus onocrotalus
Southeastern Europe, Asia, Africa 65 in.

COMMON (GREAT) CORMORANT
Phalacrocorax carbo
Eurasia 36 in.

DOUBLE-CRESTED CORMORANT
Phalacrocorax auritus
Coastal North America 35 in.

KING SHAG
*Phalacrocorax
carunculatus*
New Zealand
20 in.

GUANAY CORMORANT
Phalacrocorax bougainvillei
Peru and Chile 30 in.

They keep food in it just long enough to drain out the water; then they swallow their prey.

There are 6 living species of pelican, 2 in the New World, 4 in the Old. Another 10 species are known as fossils. The Brown Pelican of the New World is a coastal and marine bird. It breeds on the South Atlantic and Gulf coasts of America (it is the state bird of Louisiana), through the West Indies to Venezuela. Along the Pacific it ranges from central California to Chile, with one population on the Galapagos Islands.

The other five species are chiefly white birds with black wingtips, some with shades of pinks and greys. All are inland species that breed on large lakes. Some move to coastal salt waters in winter. The American White Pelican nests along lakes from British Columbia and Ontario south to Texas. The four Old World species are found in southern Europe, Africa, southern Asia, and south to Australia.

BROWN PELICAN
Pelecanus occidentalis
Southern United States, Central and South America 50 in.

ANHINGA ♂
Anhinga anhinga
Southeastern United States, Central and South America 36 in.

The Brown Pelican has a wingspan of about 6½ feet, some of the larger white species more than 9 feet. An amazing network of air sacs runs through their bones and under their skin. Yet despite these advantages pelicans have trouble taking flight. When they have no helping wind they patter awkwardly for some distance to get up flight speed. Once airborne their flight is strong, skilful, buoyant, and graceful. With the wind astern, they fly along from 50 to 100 feet up. When bucking headwinds they skim the wave tops, where water friction reduces the wind force and the small updrafts from the waves give them enough lift to glide steadily, with an occasional flap or two of their wings to keep up momentum.

BROWN PELICAN
Pelecanus occidentalis
Southern United States, Central
and South America 50 in.

Pelicans are noted for their sociability and for their almost military regimentation. They nest in colonies and usually remain in flocks when away from the breeding grounds. They forage together and rest together, and what one does they all do. When resting either on land or on water they all face the same way, with the head held high and the beak pointed down along the upright neck. In flight pelicans carry their heads well back on their shoulders, with the long beak resting partly on the folded neck.

Pelicans fly in long lines, sometimes in a V formation, sometimes abreast, sometimes in single file directly behind one another. Most often they form a wide echelon, each bird slightly behind and to one side of the next. Their flight formations are perfectly spaced and their wingstrokes are synchronized, sometimes beating and gliding in unison, more often in regular succession.

One of the White Pelican's communal activities is co-operative fishing. The birds form a crescent on the water some distance off shore. As if on signal, all start swimming shoreward together, beating the water furiously with their wings and feet to drive the fish into the shallows, gradually closing the arc at the same time. Once the fish are schooled, each bird swoops his beak and pouch back and forth like an animated dip net.

The Brown Pelican fishes by diving on its prey in a most awkward and ungraceful manner. The birds cruise 10 to 30 feet above the water and plunge down on half-spread wings. They always dive downwind and hit the water with a tremendous splash. They seldom go completely under, for their subcutaneous air sacs, which may help cushion their landing, make them so buoyant that they pop to the surface immediately, tail and back first. Shaking the water from their wings, they lift their heads to drain the water from their down-pointed beaks, and swallow their catch. At this rewarding moment they are often robbed by waiting gulls.

Pelicans usually nest on islands or in marshes, but show no specific site preferences. Most often they nest on the ground and lay their eggs in a crude hollow lined with sticks and vegetation. When they nest off the ground they build a loose platform of sticks and reeds in low trees, bushes or mangroves. They lay from 1 to 4 chalky white eggs, which both sexes incubate alternately for 4 to 5 weeks. Young pelicans, naked at hatching, are ugly, unattractive, and reptile-like, but in a day or two tufts of white down appear and they soon look more like birds.

The newly hatched, feeble, and unco-ordinated chicks can hardly hold up their heads. For the adult pelican to feed the blind, helpless, 3-inch chick from its huge bill is no simple matter. The parent manages to regurgitate half-digested food into the bill and dribble it into the youngster's crop. The chick grows rapidly, and after a week is able to poke its head into the parent's pouch. The young are able to fly in about 2 months.

Birds the size of pelicans require large quantities of food. The daily ration of an adult has been estimated at about 4 pounds. It takes about 150 pounds of fish to rear a young pelican to the flying stage. Fortunately, pelicans feed mostly on fish which have no commercial or sporting value. The amount of food needed by even a moderate-sized pelican colony is so great that food supply is often a limiting factor in pelican distribution. In the large, partly saline lakes of east central Africa, where food is abundant, White Pelicans nest by the countless thousands. Those that nest on islets in the Great Salt Lake, Utah, which is fishless, have to fly 30 to 100 miles daily to and from Utah Lake and other bodies of fresh water, returning with their gullets full of food for their ever-hungry young.

Once fledged, pelicans mature slowly. It takes them 3 years to attain their full adult plumage. They probably do not breed before their third or fourth summer. Too few have been ringed to provide sound information on their longevity, but this may be 30 years and upwards.

CORMORANTS

PELECANIFORMES   PHALACROCORACIDAE

The largest family among the totipalmate swimmers is the 30 species of cormorants. With the exception of their close relatives the anhingas, they are the least marine birds of the order. Their habitat is coastal waters, inland lakes, and rivers. They are seldom found out of sight of land. Cormorants are an ancient group, for some 21 species are known as fossils, the oldest from early Tertiary time some 50 million years ago. The modern genus *Phalacrocorax*, to which most of the living species are assigned, dates back 40 million years to Oligocene time. Today they are found the world around, except on islands in the central Pacific and in the north-central portions of Canada and Siberia.

Cormorants, when flying, vaguely resemble geese, and when in the water, divers. Outstanding characteristics of the Northern Hemisphere species are the uniform dark colour, the long, thin, sharply hooked bill, and the bare patches about the face and throat, frequently brightly coloured in yellows, oranges, and blues. The dark colour of these cormorants is responsible for their common name, which is an English corruption of the Latin *corvus marinus*, or "sea crow." The bare facial patches are responsible for their scientific name, which means bald raven. Cormorants are also known as shags, perhaps from the shaggy plumes several species sport on their heads during the breeding season. In Britain the term shag is restricted to the common coastal cormorant of western Europe as a means of differentiating it from the only other native species, the Common, or Great, Cormorant, which is a more inland species. Elsewhere in the English-speaking world the terms cormorant and shag are used more or less interchangeably, unless replaced by some less lovely local appellation.

All the cormorants catch fish by diving from the surface and chasing them under water. Cormorants' bodies lack the subcutaneous air sacs of the gannets, tropic-birds, and pelicans, and their bones are much less pneumatic. Hence they float lower on the surface of the water. They share with divers and grebes the ability to change their specific gravity so they sink gradually under the surface, and they frequently swim about with just the head or the top of the back exposed. Underwater they propel themselves mainly with their feet, assisted to some extent by their half-opened wings. They are credited with being able to dive to great depths. Marine species have been caught in nets 70 to 100 feet below the surface. Usually cormorants feed in shallower water, less than 25 feet deep, and rarely stay under more than a minute. They seldom eat the fish they catch under water, but come to the surface and juggle it around in their beaks to get it facing the right way before swallowing it.

The large quantity of fish they consume does not endear cormorants to fishermen, though investigations have proved that most of the species they eat are of minor economic importance. Small eels are a favourite food in bays. Rock cod, carp, and other slow-swimming fishes form the bulk of their diet. The faster food fishes escape them.

At the same time, in several parts of the world, cormorants are of considerable value to man. On the west coast of South America the Guanay is one of the chief sources of nitrogen-rich guano, mined on the Peruvian islands since the early 19th century and shipped the world around for fertilizer. The Cape Cormorant of South Africa is another rich guano producer, and commercial firms there have encouraged the birds by building offshore platforms on which they roost and breed. This was also done on the west coast of Florida. The Japanese have used the droppings accumulated on offshore roosting islands for years, and customarily spread straw under the trees where the colonies breed inland to catch the precious excreta to fertilize the rice paddies.

In China and Japan cormorants have been used in fishing for centuries. The technique varies in different parts of the Orient. In Japan each cormorant fisherman customarily uses a team of about a dozen birds, each on a leather tether. The birds perch on the bow of the boat, which has hanging over it an open metal basket in which faggots are burned for light. The fisherman usually works at dusk, floating downstream, and handles his birds on their tethers. Birds are prevented from swallowing the fish by a thong tied around the base of the neck. As each bird fills its throat, the fisherman pulls it aboard, strips the fish from its gullet, and tosses it back again into the water. At the end of the voyage the fisherman feeds each bird a throat-full of fish as its share of the catch, and removes the constricting thong from the base of the neck so the bird can swallow. After packing the bird's throat with fish, he has to retie the thong around the neck *above* the fish; otherwise the birds throw them up, so conditioned are they to vomiting their catch.

Modern fishing methods made cormorant fishing uneconomical in Japan years ago, but the practice is kept alive by the Japanese Imperial Household for its cultural interest and as a tourist attraction. The Household subsidizes an ancient guild of cormorant fishermen on the Nagara River at Gifu, who still carry on the art in all its medieval trappings. The Gifu fishermen spurn the Common Cormorant, which nests throughout Honshu, and which rival fishermen on the Tamagawa River use. Gifu fishermen prefer the larger Sea Cormorant of Japan, which a guild of bird-limers catches for them on the sea cliffs of northeastern Honshu. As a reason for this preference, the Gifu fishermen claim the Sea Cormorant is a larger bird, and its throat holds more and larger fish.

Cormorants vary in size from that of a small duck to a large goose. Lengths, which vary from 18 to 40 inches, are deceptive, for the smaller species have much longer tails than the larger ones. Northern Hemisphere species are dark brown and black, with bronze to purplish sheens on their feathers. At nesting time most grow long white plumes on the head, neck, and thighs, which are shed soon after the young hatch.

Largest of the cormorants is the Common, or Great, Cormorant, which nests from Nova Scotia and Labrador through Greenland, Iceland, across Eurasia, south to central Africa, and in Australia and New Zealand. The commonest species

RED-FACED CORMORANT
Phalacrocorax urile
Bering Sea and northern
North Pacific Ocean   28 in.

in North America is the Double-crested Cormorant, a slightly smaller bird, similar in colour but with the throat skin bright orange and two tufts of curly white and black feathers on the head at breeding time. It nests both on coasts and inland from southern Alaska and Newfoundland south to Florida and Baja California. About the same size, and commoner on the Pacific Coast is Brandt's Cormorant.

Slightly more than half of the known species of cormorants are residents of the Southern Hemisphere, and many of these, instead of being solidly dark, have white bellies. Typical are the Guanay of western South America, and the King Cormorant of the Falklands, South Georgia, and the Crozet Islands. Other white-bellied southern birds include the Spotted, Pied, and White-breasted cormorants of New Zealand and Australia. One of the smallest is the 18- to 20-inch Pygmy Cormorant that breeds from southeastern Europe across southern Asia to Malaya.

One species, evidently from northern dark stock, has been isolated on the Galapagos Islands long enough to become flightless. It is a large bird, one of the largest of the group, but its wings have shrunk to the point where they are about the size of a penguin's flippers, and just as useless for flying. The Flightless Cormorant nests along the shores of two of the main Galapagos Islands, and the population is so small that the introduction of predators could easily wipe it out.

One recent species of cormorant is now extinct. The only naturalist who ever saw the Spectacled, or Pallas's, Cormorant alive was George Wilhelm Steller, who collected the first ones known to science when he was marooned on the Komandorski Islands with Vitus Bering in 1741. This was a large cormorant, probably a poor flier, tame, and restricted in its range to that one little group of islands. A century later it had disappeared, doubtless killed for food by the Aleuts. Only five specimens exist, all in European museums.

Most cormorants are fairly strong fliers, and the northern species are migratory. They fly with necks outstretched, and with a steady beat of their wings, interrupted by occasional short stretches of soaring. On long flights the bill is often held slightly open, probably to facilitate the intake of air, for in adult cormorants the external nostrils, open at hatching, are completely closed, and the bird must take in air through its mouth.

Another noteworthy characteristic of the cormorants is their habit of spreading their wings to dry. For some reason their flight feathers do not seem to be as water-repellent as those of other water birds. After a period in the water cormorants

come ashore, perch on the beach, on a convenient rock or tree (or else find a buoy or a channel marker alongshore) and roost with their wings half spread to the sun and the breeze. This accounts in part for the fact that cormorants, unlike ducks, divers, grebes, penguins, pelicans, and other swimming birds, almost never rest in the water, but come ashore for their siestas.

One recent investigator, after examining the mechanics of the cormorant's skeleton and the bird's centre of gravity, suggests that the bird is somewhat off balance in its customary upright position with its wings folded in place, and that spreading its wings distributes its weight more evenly and helps the bird keep its balance. But I still prefer the fishermen's metaphor of the cormorants drying their sails.

Most cormorants nest colonially; sometimes, as in the Guanay, in tremendous aggregations of thousands. The littoral species are mostly ground nesters, and breed on offshore skerries and rocky islets or on steep sea cliffs. The Great Cormorant frequently nests in this fashion, but just as often nests high up in trees. Ground nesters build a lump of a nest, using sticks and vegetation, which is soon plastered together with their droppings and offal. In this they lay 2 to 4, occasionally 6, pale bluish or greenish eggs with a chalky surface. Both sexes incubate, and the incubation period varies from 3 to 5 weeks. Like the rest of the order, the young are born blind .and naked, and at first seem more reptilian than avian. The rearing period is from 5 to 8 weeks. Most species are single-brooded, but a few may nest twice each year. The young are fed by regurgitation. Parents feed the newly hatched helpless chick by dropping bits of half-digested food into its mouth from the hooked tips of their own bills, but as the young grow they are soon able to push forward as an adult lands on the nest and poke their heads down their parents' gullets for their meals.

Cormorant roosts and rookeries are no places for the fastidious to visit, for the stench of their droppings and of regurgitated fish and offal is not pleasant, and flies usually swarm to the feast. They can hardly be considered dainty birds, either in aspect or in manner.

Cormorants are long-lived, and once past the dangerous first year when the mortality in almost all birds is highest, their annual mortality rate is fairly low. The oldest ringed cormorant known is a Great Cormorant ringed in England and recovered after 18 years. Studies of the survival rate of adults suggest the potential life span in the species may be twice that long.

44

ANHINGAS (DARTERS)

PELECANIFORMES ANHINGIDAE

The anhingas are so closely allied to the cormorants that some students accord them only subfamily rank under the cormorants. But despite a superficial resemblance to cormorants in appearance and habits, they differ strongly. Anhingas are long, slim water birds that inhabit the wooded borders of fresh-water lakes, rivers, and swamps in warm temperate and tropical latitudes. They are the least marine of all the toti-palmate swimmers, and only rarely visit brackish waters in a few parts of their extensive range. In America they nest from Oklahoma, Tennessee, and North Carolina southward through Cuba and Central and South America, to Argentina.

Other anhinga populations live in Africa south of the Sahara and in Madagascar; in southern Asia and from the northern East Indies to the Philippines; in New Guinea and Australia. Each of these four populations, which are known in the Old World as darters, differs considerably from the others in colour, but all are so alike in size (32 to 36 inches), general colour pattern, structure, habits, and behaviour that some ornithologists regard them as geographical representatives of a single species. Others divide them into two species, but until better biological evidence of their interrelationships is available it is more convenient to regard them as four.

The distinctive name anhinga comes from the language of the Amazonian Indians. A common name for them in the United States is water turkey, though they do not bear the slightest resemblance to a turkey. Their heads are slimmer than cormorants', their bills longer, thinner, and sharp-pointed instead of hooked; their necks are longer, more slender, and differently jointed; their body feathers are thicker and more compact; and the sexes are unlike in colour. They share the characteristics of the order and other superficial similarities with cormorants, including the relative permeability of their flight feathers to water which forces them to spread their wings to dry after swimming. Like the other families in this order they are a very ancient group. Eocene fossils suggest that anhingas developed their familiar distinctions before Tertiary time, in the region of 80 million years ago.

Anhingas nest in small colonies, often in company with herons and ibises. They build a bulky nest of sticks lined with green leaves in bushes or trees from 3 to 30 feet above the water. Their chalky, bluish-white eggs are noticeably pointed at one end, and take from 25 to 28 days to hatch. Both parents incubate and feed the young by regurgitation. The chicks, born blind and naked, soon sprout their first coat of white down and mature rapidly. At the age of 2 weeks, if danger threatens, they scramble from the nest into the water and dive out of sight with impunity. Unless a lurking alligator grabs them in the meantime, they work their way back up into the nest when the danger is past, using their neck and wings as well as feet for climbing. The young stay in or near the nest until they are fledged, which usually takes from 6 to 8 weeks.

Anhingas are strong fliers, and those in the northern part of the North American range migrate southward in winter.

At that time they are occasionally found feeding in brackish waters. They fly with steady, rapid wingbeats, much like cormorants, but glide and climb more. On sunny days when the air currents are favourable they often climb in circles several hundred feet in the air and soar on motionless wings above their nesting or roosting grounds. Their slim necks are held straight in front and their long tails stream behind making a perfect cross in the sky. When done with playing and soaring, they close their wings and plummet downward to their roosts.

Anhingas enter the water only to escape danger and to feed. They propel themselves under water with their powerful feet, their wings usually held close to their bodies. They frequently swim along with their bodies submerged and just their snake-like head and neck exposed—hence the name snake bird, an alternate vernacular name that is widely used. Their equally fitting name, darter, comes from the way they dart their rapier-like beak at their prey. They hunt with their necks folded in an S against their shoulders and, when within striking range, shoot it out as though it were a coiled spring to impale the luckless fish with their beak. They then come to the surface, toss the fish off their beaks into the air, catch it and juggle it to get it headed right, and swallow it whole. Several observers have pointed out that anhingas are thus the original underwater spear fishermen.

While fish are the mainstay of the anhinga diet, they also eat crayfish, frogs, salamanders, and water insects. They treat most of their prey the same way, first impaling it on their bills, and frequently beating it and pounding it to stop its struggling before swallowing it.

Like cormorants, anhingas have no air sacs under the skin and their bones are quite heavy, doubtless an adaptation to increase their specific gravity for diving. The external nostrils are completely closed in the adults, and this also helps. The anhinga stomach has a peculiar hairy lining, whose function is unknown, but it is thought that it may be of use in straining out fish bones.

ANHINGA ♂
Anhinga anhinga
Southeastern United States,
Central and South America 36 in.

BOOBIES AND GANNETS

PELECANIFORMES   SULIDAE

The nine species in this family are goose-sized sea birds with heavy streamlined bodies. They have long pointed wings, straight sharp beaks, long wedge-shaped tails, and short stout legs. All fish by diving on their prey from a spectacular height and pursuing it underwater. Like the pelicans, gannets and boobies have a network of air sacs under the skin that helps cushion their impact with the water and gives them greater buoyancy.

The family falls into two natural groups, the gannets of northern and southern temperate waters, and the boobies of tropical seas. The Northern Gannet, which nests around the northern North Atlantic from the Gulf of St. Lawrence through Iceland and the Faroes to the British Isles, was the first of the family known to Europeans. The name they gave it comes from the same root as gander, a male goose, and the names sea goose and solan goose still persists for it, the latter from "sula," the old Scandinavian name for the bird, which was appropriated for the scientific name of the family.

Similar to the Northern Gannet are the Cape Gannet of South Africa and the Australian Gannet of New Zealand and Australia. Adults of all three are pure white with black wingtips and yellowish heads; immature birds are brownish grey above, mottled with small white spots, and white below. The three differ from one another mainly in size, colour of soft parts, and in shade and amount of black in wings and tail. Because these differences are so slight, some students regard the gannets as races of a single species, despite the wide gaps between their ranges and the lack of intergradation among them.

The gannets are the only strongly migratory birds in the family. The Northern Gannet winters from the Virginia Capes to the Gulf of Mexico and from Britain to the Canary Islands and North Africa. The Cape Gannet moves northward in the southern winter into warmer waters along both coasts of Africa. The New Zealand population of the Australian Gannet migrates westward across the Tasman Sea to winter with its Australian kin off the coasts of eastern and southern Australia.

The urge to migrate is strongest in young birds, and seems to decrease gradually with age. Ringing recoveries show the longest flights, up to 4,000 miles, are made by young gannets in their first year. The older birds tend to disperse through waters nearer their breeding grounds, as do most of the boobies, rather than to migrate in the full sense of the term. Young gannets sometimes remain on the wintering grounds for two or more years, and do not return to the gannetries until they are three years old. They may not breed until they are four or more. The oldest ringed gannet recovered to date was 16 years old, but the species is doubtless much longer lived.

Gannets are colonial breeders, and often nest on narrow ledges in seaward-facing precipices where they may cram into every available foot of space. When Audubon visited the famous gannetry on Bird Rock in the Gulf of St. Lawrence

in 1833, he saw the precipitous spire rising above the horizon in the distance. He first thought it was covered with several feet of snow, but as his vessel came nearer, the snow proved to be the countless thousands of gannets that then nested there. The flat top of the rock was occupied by at least 100,000 pairs of birds, and another 50,000 jammed every cranny of the ledges around the sides. In 1869 the Canadian government built a lighthouse on Bird Rock, which made the top accessible to passing fishermen, who made it a practice to visit the island and club the defenceless nesting birds for bait. By the turn of the century they had wiped out all the birds from the top, and reduced those on the ledges to a few thousand, nesting in the most inaccessible shelves. Protection by the Canadian government shortly thereafter turned the tide, and the population of the St. Lawrence gannetries is now on the rise.

Gannets build a crude nest of mud, kelp, or rockweed, which they add to year after year until it is quite large. In this they lay their single chalky-white egg, which soon becomes badly stained and discoloured by dirt and excrement. In common with the rest of their order, gannets have no brood patch. Instead they have developed the unique habit of covering their eggs with their feet. The incubating bird places one foot carefully over one side of the egg, the other over the other side, overlapping slightly in the centre, and then lowers its body over its feet until the breast feathers barely cover them.

Incubation is by both sexes, who relieve each other at the nest each day through the 42-day incubation period. At hatching the chick is blind and naked, but soon grows its first coat of white down. It is fed by regurgitation for some 10 to 12 weeks until its flight feathers are well developed. Then it is suddenly deserted by its parents. It may remain in or near the nest for another week, flexing its wing muscles and living on its accumulated fat. Some young are able to fly from the gannetry if the wind is strong, but usually they swim out to sea. They may swim about for another week or two until they thin down and toughen up enough for their wings to support them.

Away from the nesting grounds gannets are occasionally encountered singly, more often in small flocks of 10 to 100 or more birds. They usually cruise along the coasts a mile or more off shore, though schooling fish may lure them almost in to the breakers. The gannets' main food is fish of the herring family, and a flock gathers over the schooling fish to feed in a mad scramble, diving from a height of 50 to 100 feet on to their prey. A flock of feeding gannets is a thrilling sight. Wheeling above the schooling fish, they plummet down in a continuous rain of birds, each hitting the water with a resounding splash that sends spray 10 feet or more in the air. Each swallows its fish underwater, coming up a moment later to take off for the next dive. Gannets swim underwater, using their feet and half-opened wings, and are able to dive to considerable depths, as birds caught in fishermen's nets 90 feet below the surface attest. Usually they stay underwater only a few seconds.

The six species of boobies are all birds of tropic and subtropic waters. Three, the Masked, Red-footed, and Brown, are found practically the world around. Two, the Peruvian and Blue-footed, live only off the west coasts of the Americas, and the little-known Abbott's Booby is limited to the Indian Ocean. Abbott's Booby is a white and black bird, smallest of the whitish boobies. It is believed to nest in trees on Assumption Island near Madagascar and on Christmas Island near Java.

Boobies are so named because some people feel they look stupid and act stupid. They cannot seem to learn that man is their enemy. They earned their name years ago, partly from their appearance, partly from their habit of landing on sailing ships and sitting quietly in the rigging for a hungry sailor to grab. They show just as little apprehension of man on the nesting grounds, and owe their survival in this hard, cruel world to their penchant for nesting on islands little visited by man, or on inaccessible cliffs where he can't reach them.

Largest of the boobies is the Masked Booby, sometimes called the Blue-faced. It is the size of a gannet, which it strongly resembles, being a white bird with black wings, but its head is pure white, and the naked skin of its face and throat is blue-black. Its feet vary in colour in different populations from orangey yellow to a bluish slate, but they are never red as in the very similar though smaller Red-footed Booby, which is considerably limited in its distribution by being a tree nester.

The Brown Booby is perhaps the commonest species in the tropics. In adult plumage its wholly dark-brown upper parts and breast with a contrasting white belly are distinctive. The nondescript immature birds resemble other immature boobies. It nests on islands in the Gulf of Mexico, the Caribbean, the central Atlantic, the Indian and Pacific oceans and on the west coast of America from Baja California south to Panama and the Cocos Islands.

The Blue-footed Booby is a grey-headed, brown-backed, white-bellied bird with bright blue feet that nests from Baja California south to Peru, and in the Galapagos Islands. The Peruvian Booby, the *piquero* of the Latin Americans, is a slightly smaller bird that nests on islands off Peru and south to Chile, and is one of the commonest birds in the cold, rich waters of the Humboldt Current. It is one of the several sea birds that contribute their excrement and carcasses to build up the guano deposits of those islands. Its white head, neck, and breast, as well as its blackish feet, distinguish it from the Blue-footed Booby.

Boobies are very fond of flying fish, and have learned that ships will stir them up, much as cowbirds and Cattle Egrets have learned that cattle will flush insects out of the grass. Hungry boobies frequently accompany ships, never trailing them as do the albatrosses, petrels, or gulls, but coasting back and forth over the bow waiting for flying fish to break cover. Then down they plunge on a long slant, hitting the water just at the right moment as the flying fish ducks in. They reappear in a moment with the fish in their beak, juggle with it for a jiffy, swallow it, and then take up the vigil again.

NORTHERN GANNET
Morus bassanus
Coastal North Atlantic Ocean 40 in.

adult

immature

BLUE-FACED BOOBY
Sula dactylatra
Tropical Atlantic, Pacific, and
Indian oceans 32 in.

BLUE-FOOTED BOOBY
Sula nebouxii
Tropical eastern Pacific; Mexico to
Peru and the Galapagos Islands 32 in.

BROWN BOOBY
Sula leucogaster
Tropic and subtropic coasts and
islands of the world 30 in.

RED-FOOTED BOOBY
Sula sula
Tropical Atlantic, Pacific, and
Indian oceans 29 in.

FRIGATE-BIRDS

PELECANIFORMES   FREGATIDAE

GREAT FRIGATE-BIRD
Fregata minor
Coasts and islands of tropical Indian,
central and western Pacific,
and South Atlantic oceans 40 in.

BROWN BOOBY
Sula leucogaster
Tropic and subtropic coasts and
islands of the world 30 in.

**MAGNIFICENT
FRIGATE-BIRD** ♂ ♀
Fregata magnificens
Coasts and islands of
tropical Atlantic and
eastern Pacific oceans
40 in.

male

These feathered buccaneers of the tropic seas are unquestionably the most aerial of all water birds. Despite their fully
webbed feet, the swimming abilities of all their close relatives,
and the fact that they spend all their lives over the water
and get most of their food from the sea, frigate-birds seldom
enter the ocean of their own accord. If they do land in it
accidentally, their feathers soon become water-logged, and
they have difficulty taking flight again.

The frigate-birds, or "man-o'-war birds" as the sailors call
them, are equally inept on land. They can only shuffle along
clumsily, or climb to a high enough place to take off. Without

a strong wind to help them they have trouble taking flight. Therefore they always roost on trees or bushes, or on buoys where their long, pointed wings can have free play and they can quickly gain airspeed. Frigate-birds spend most of their time soaring out over the ocean, usually, however, within sight of land. Once airborne, however, their flight is little short of miraculous. They soar motionless by the hour hanging steadily, quietly in the sky. With only a 3- to 4-pound body to support, their 7-foot wingspan has the greatest plane surface in proportion to weight of any bird. Frigate-birds can fly rings around all the other sea birds, and do so to harass them into giving up their food.

Frigate-birds have a well-known propensity for preying on boobies, pelicans, cormorants, and gulls, chasing them and pecking at them until they drop or disgorge their load to lighten ship and escape their tormentors. Then the frigate-

female

bird swoops down and scoops the morsel out of mid-air before it reaches the water. But frigate-birds are also quite capable of catching their own food from the sea surface, and depend mainly on this skill for their livelihood, rather than on their piracy. Fish are, of course, their mainstay. Flying fish are a common prey. As these skitter along when flushed by dolphins, albacores, and other large fish from below, the frigate-birds snatch them out of the air. But the range of the frigate-birds' diet is wide, and they pick up almost anything floating on the surface that strikes their fancy—jellyfish, squid, young turtles, and other creatures. They pick these neatly out of the water with their long hooked beaks without making a ripple or getting a drop of water on their feathers.

The frigate-bird habitually preys on the young of colonial-nesting sea birds. Few tropical colonies of terns, boobies, cormorants, or pelicans are without attendant frigate-birds hanging overhead, waiting for a chick to be exposed or unattended for just the second it takes the marauder to swoop down and snatch it from its nest. Nor are the frigates' own young immune from attack, and if left exposed may be devoured by a hungry cannibalistic neighbour.

Frigate-birds nest on oceanic islands, often in the colonies of other species that they harass and prey upon. They build a frail nest of sticks, sometimes on the ground, more often on a boulder or in the top of a bush or tree. The male picks the site, stakes it out with a few twigs, and sits there inflating his throat pouch to attract his mate. The male's gular pouch is normally orange in colour, but it turns bright red during the courtship season. He inflates it like a toy balloon, and keeps it so for hours while he sits on the empty nest, adding to it the sticks brought by the female, and protecting it from stick-filching by nearby pairs. Soon after the single, oval chalky-white egg is laid, the male no longer inflates his pouch and it fades to dull orange again. Both parents share the brooding duties through the 6-week incubation period, feeding and guarding the young. The male is believed to assume most of these chores, but neither egg nor chick are left unattended for fear of marauding by neighbours. The chicks hatch blind and naked, but are soon covered with white down. In their immature plumage all are white-headed, and it takes them 2 to 3 years to assume full black adult dress. Sexes differ in plumage; females are slightly larger and lighter in colour.

The Magnificent Frigate-bird of New World waters ranges from the Bahamas, the Gulf Coast, and Baja California south to Brazil and Ecuador. The male is a solid metallic purplish black. The female is marked with white on the neck and throat. The Great Frigate-bird (40 inches from tip of bill to tip of tail) of the Indian Ocean, the central and western Pacific, and the southwestern Atlantic, is similarly coloured but has a distinctive brown band across its wings. The Ascension Frigate-bird is limited to the waters about that lonely island in the tropical South Atlantic. Adults of both sexes are black. In the Christmas Island Frigate-bird, limited to the Indian Ocean, both sexes are white below. The Lesser Frigate-bird, the smallest of the group, is only some 32 inches in length. The adults are black with distinctive white patches on the sides under the wings. This species breeds at South Trinidad Island off Brazil, on islands off Madagascar, and in the South Pacific from New Caledonia to Australia.

HERONS AND THEIR ALLIES

CICONIIFORMES

This order consists of 114 species united into seven families. All are wading birds adapted to a life in marshes or shallow waters, though a few have become accustomed to living on dry uplands. They range in size from the Little Bittern, that stands barely 10 inches high with neck outstretched, to the great Adjutant and Saddle-billed storks that tower over 5 feet. All are long-legged, long-necked, long-billed birds with broad, rounded wings and comparatively short tails. All have four long spreading toes, the three front ones slightly webbed at the base in some families, the lower part of the tibia bare of feathers, and similar palatine, cranial, and other anatomical features. Their plumage is variable, but usually simple in pattern and colour. The sexes are alike or closely similar.

Cosmopolitan in distribution, birds of this order are found in almost all ice-free lands of the world except a few oceanic islands. They live on animal food, most of it aquatic – fishes, crustaceans, amphibians, and also insects and reptiles. A few have become carrion eaters. Flight is strong throughout the order, and most temperate zone species are migratory.

The Ciconiiformes are an ancient group dating back some 100 million years to Cretaceous times. Their antiquity is further attested by their diversity and by their discontinuous distributions. Three of the families in this order are monotypic, each with a single species whose structural features are common to those of the order, but are different enough to exclude the birds from the other three larger families.

HERONS AND BITTERNS

CICONIIFORMES ARDEIDAE

This family with some 62 species is the largest as well as the most widespread of the order. In addition to features shared with the other six families, the herons are distinct in having the head completely feathered except for the naked lores, and in having neck vertebrae of unequal length. This forces them to carry their necks kinked into an S-shape when flying, and frequently when at rest. The tip of the bill is usually straight, sometimes slightly curved, and the claw of the middle toe has small serrations on its side like the teeth of a comb. The hind toe is level with the three front ones so the bird stands on all four toes.

Though ornithologists differ on the relationships within the heron family, they usually divide these birds into five fairly distinct groups. A feature widely used in the classification of herons is their powder-downs. These are a peculiar type of feather that is never shed and continues to grow from the base throughout the life of the bird. They fray continually at the tip into a powder that is used for dressing the other feathers. Powder-downs occur widely in several bird groups. They reach their peak of development in the herons, where they grow in well-marked paired patches in the bare spaces of the breast, rump, and flanks.

GREAT BLUE HERON
Ardea herodias
North America 52 in.

LEAST BITTERN
Ixobrychus exilis
Western Hemisphere: southern Canada to Brazil and Paraguay 14 in.

GREEN HERON
Butorides virescens
North and Central America 20 in.

REDDISH EGRET
Dichromanassa rufescens
Southeastern United States,
West Indies, Central America 29 in.

BLACK HERON
Melanophoyx ardesiaca
Tropical East Africa 24 in.

SNOWY EGRET
Egretta thula
Central United States
to Argentina 25 in.

CATTLE EGRET
Bubulcus ibis
Eurasia, Africa, Australia,
northeastern South America,
southern and central United States 20 in.

YELLOW-CROWNED NIGHT-HERON
Nyctanassa violacea
United States to Peru and Brazil 28 in.

BLACK-CROWNED
NIGHT-HERON
Nycticorax nycticorax
Almost cosmopolitan in
temperate and
tropical regions 28 in.

COMMON
(LARGE) EGRET
Casmerodius alba
Central U.S. to Argentina;
Eurasia, Africa, Australia
1. *EUROPEAN SUBSPECIES,*
C. a. alba 38 in.
2. *AMERICAN SUBSPECIES,*
C. a. egretta 40 in.

PURPLE HERON
Ardea purpurea
Eurasia, Africa 31 in.

LITTLE BLUE HERON
Hydranassa caerulea
Eastern United States to Peru and Uruguay 25 in.

1 LITTLE BITTERN
Ixobrychus minutus
Eastern Hemisphere: Eurasia, Africa,
Australia, New Zealand 14 in.

2 LINED TIGER HERON
Tigrisoma lineatum
Central and northern South America 30 in.

3 AMERICAN BITTERN
Botaurus lentiginosus
North America 34 in.

Herons use their powder-down powder for removing oil, grease, and slime from their feathers. Some herons apply it with their beaks. The bitterns, who are great eel eaters, rub their heads in the breast powder-down patches after a meal until their head feathers take on a powdery appearance. They leave the powder on for a while to soak up the slime and dirt, and then comb it out by vigorous scratching, mainly with the serrated nail of the middle toe. When the feathers are clean again they add waterproofing with their own oil from the preen gland.

The 12 species of bitterns, each of which has but two pairs of powder-down patches, form one of the most distinctive and uniform of the five heron tribes. They have relatively shorter legs and bills than the other herons, all are exclusively inhabitants of reedy marshes, and all nest on or near the ground, always in solitary pairs and never in colonies. All of them are tawny brownish birds, their soft body feathers richly streaked and speckled to resemble the reeds in which they live.

Unlike most of their relatives, bitterns depend on their camouflage instead of flight when danger threatens. They

have an uncanny knack of freezing into a reed-like pose with body, neck, and bill pointed skyward. This so blends them into their surroundings that it takes sharp eyes indeed to spot them if they do not move. The bittern seems to know which side is most concealingly coloured, and it will turn slowly to keep its striped front facing the intruder. On a windy day they will even sway slightly as if with the breeze.

Four of the bitterns, members of the genus *Botaurus*, are fairly large birds, 26 to 30 inches in length and standing about 2 to 2½ feet tall. One species nests widely throughout temperate North America, another from Mexico southward through Brazil, a third across Eurasia and into South Africa, and the fourth in Australia and New Zealand. Their ranges do not overlap, and all four are so similar in appearance and habits that some students regard them as a single species.

Bitterns are famed for the males' weird mating calls, variously described as a guttural gulping, belching, braying, or booming. Their cries have given the bitterns such vernacular names as "thunder pumper" and "stake driver." The three-syllable notes of the mating call are not very loud, but have considerable carrying power. The male's esophagus becomes thickened in the spring to facilitate their utterance, which is accompanied by a series of violent, convulsive movements. The noise is almost impossible for a human larynx to imitate. In medieval times bitterns were often hunted with falcons. They were reportedly a favourite dish of Henry VIII of England.

The large bitterns nest on the ground in marshy reed beds or along the shores of large lakes and rivers. The female alone builds the nest, a haphazard structure of reeds and sedges in which she lays her 3 to 6 brownish eggs. Both sexes incubate the eggs for 25 to 28 days; then the female feeds the young for the 2 to 3 weeks they remain in the nest, regurgitating half-digested food into her bill, where the fledglings soon learn to reach for it. It takes them about 8 weeks to grow full flight feathers.

The eight small bitterns of the genus *Ixobrychus* are a more varied group than their larger relatives. Most of them have bodies the size of a small dove and stand less than a foot high. They are the smallest birds of the order as well as of the family. They have the concealing coloration of the large bitterns, but are more solidly patterned with dark and light patches. The females are lighter, duller, and more heavily streaked than the males. While the differences are minor, they are the only herons in which the sexes differ in colour. These shy, skulking, retiring birds are seldom seen and are difficult to flush from the marshes they inhabit. Both sexes are fairly vocal throughout the year, but their notes are neither loud nor distinctive. The spring call of the male is a low, unimpressive croaking.

The small bitterns range widely throughout the tropic and temperate zones. The Little Bittern of Europe breeds across Eurasia, southward through Africa, and in Madagascar, Australia, and New Zealand. The Least Bittern of North America is a very similar bird, nesting from southern Canada into Central America and migrating southward throughout its range. Other species live in South America, eastern Asia, and in the East Indies. One species, the Black Mangrove Bittern of southeastern Asia and Australia, is about half as large again as the others, and is usually put in another genus, *Dupetor*.

Little Bitterns nest slightly off the ground, usually in a flimsy basket of reeds and marsh vegetation a foot or two up amongst marsh or swamp plants. They lay 4 to 6 chalky white eggs, which take 16 to 19 days to hatch. Both parents incubate and feed the young by regurgitation. The young remain in the nest only about a week before they start exploring in its vicinity. They start to fly when about a month old. The Little Bitterns' food consists largely of aquatic insects and a wide variety of other marsh life; small minnows make up about one quarter of their diet, crustaceans, amphibians, and even an occasional shrew or small marsh bird, the remainder.

The most primitive and least specialized of the herons is the small relict group of six species in four genera that make up the tiger herons, or tiger bitterns. They are bittern-like in many ways. They have cryptic concealing coloration, solitary habits, mimic their surroundings when in danger, and have a loud booming mating call. But as all of them have three pairs of powder-down patches, and two of them vestiges of a fourth, they are more fittingly called herons. The tiger herons are widely scattered; one in New Guinea, one in central Africa, and four in Central and South America. This suggests they are probably the survivors of much more cosmopolitan ancestors which have disappeared from the intervening areas. Typical of the group is the Lined Tiger Heron of Central and South America, a fairly widespread bird of wooded streams and marshes.

The third tribe of herons, the night herons, are aptly named, for they are most active and do most of their feeding at night, though they are seen abroad during the day. The night herons are divisible into two distantly related groups, the older and more primitive of which are the four oriental night herons of the genus *Gorsachius*. Three of these live in eastern Asia from Japan south through Malaya and the Philippines into the East Indies; the fourth lives in central Africa. The Japanese Night Heron, representative of the group, is a bittern-like bird in size and appearance, largely brown in colour, prettily streaked and vermiculated with dark brown and black, and with a slightly elongated nuchal crest. It is a shy and retiring forest dweller. Its low, simple croaking echoes monotonously through the night.

The Japanese Night Heron eats crabs and other crustaceans, insects, and small fish. By day it remains quietly high in the trees, but in cloudy or rainy weather it ventures out in daytime to forage along wooded streams. For a nest it builds a crude, rickety platform of sticks, from 20 to 50 feet up in an evergreen tree. It does not nest colonially, but up to a dozen pairs may be found nesting fairly near one another in a favoured locality. The female lays 3 to 4 white eggs, which are incubated 17 to 20 days. The young remain 35 to 37 days in the nest before flying. Incubating birds have the bittern-like habit of holding their heads and necks rigidly erect in imitation of an upright branch.

Far better known are the five night herons of the *Nycticorax* group, of which the Black-crowned Night Heron is the most widely distributed. It breeds throughout North and South America, across Eurasia, and south into Africa and the East Indies. This pale-grey and white bird has a black crown and mantle, bright red eyes, and two long, narrow, white nuchal plumes. Like the oriental night herons it has comparatively short legs and neck, and a rather thick bill. The Rufous Night Heron of the western Pacific Islands and Australia is slightly larger, chestnut above and light buffy below. Three other species, including the Yellow-crowned Night Heron of North and South America, are found only in the New World.

The Black-crowned Night Heron flies with its head set well back on its shoulders. One hears its monosyllabic guttural "wock, wock" as it flies from its daytime roosts to feed on the tidal flats through the night. In New England its call has caused it to be known widely as the "qwauk" or "qwa bird." In Japan, where it is quite common, the Black-crowned Night Heron occupies a unique position as the only bird ever raised to the Japanese peerage. According to legend, the 10th-century Emperor Daigo was so pleased with the beauty and tameness of a heron gracing his new gardens in the Kyoto capital that he appointed it to the fifth court rank of "go-i," and to this day the Black-crowned Night Heron bears the title "goi heron" as its common name everywhere in Japan.

The Black-crowned Night Heron breeds colonially, sometimes in small bands of a dozen or so pairs. Frequently hundreds of pairs nest together over several acres of woodlands, often in company with other herons and ibises. They build stick nests in trees or high limbs, and lay 3 to 5 bluish-green eggs, which both sexes incubate. As the eggs are laid at 48-hour intervals and incubation begins with the first one laid, the 21-day incubation period may be extended another 6 to 8 days for the whole clutch to hatch. The young are fed mostly on fish. They leave the nest a month after hatching, but do not fly well until they are about 6 weeks old.

Night herons are highly migratory throughout most of their range, the northernmost nesters flying the farthest south. Banding has shown that instead of migrating southward immediately on leaving the nesting grounds, young night herons first spread out in all directions like fragments of an exploding bomb, evidently in search of new territory. This phenomenon is aptly called the "grenade effect." A number of other herons show it as well. The young move some distance north, east, or west after nesting before heading south.

The largest tribe of herons are the so-called typical or day herons, a group of 35 species which systematists place in from 6 to 10 or more genera. The tribe includes the largest, most ornate, as well as the most highly developed of all the herons.

Simplest and least ornamented of the tribe are the three small green herons of the genus *Butorides* and the seven pond, or squacco, herons of the genus *Ardeola*. Two of the green herons between them occupy almost all the temperate and tropic parts of the world except Europe and central and western Asia. The main difference between the two is the colour of the nape of the neck and they may eventually prove to be geographical forms of a single species. The third is a melanistic or dark species of otherwise similar aspect and habits, found only in the Galapagos Islands.

The Green Heron is a familiar bird along the edges of ponds and streams throughout temperate America. Its peculiar "skeow" note sounds all along U.S. waterways. It nests sometimes alone, more often in small colonies, building a nest of sticks from 5 to 20 feet up in trees or tall shrubs, usually near the water. Mangroves are favoured in the tropics and subtropics. The 3 to 5 greenish eggs hatch in 20 days.

Pond herons are an Old World group of smallish, light-coloured herons (some are pure white) with comparatively short legs, necks, and bills, and comparatively heavy bodies. Ranging throughout southern Eurasia and Africa, they are rather tame, sociable birds found frequently around villages and pastures. Colonial nesters, they often breed in tremendous colonies in company with other herons and ibises.

Best known of this group is the Buff-backed Heron, commonly called the Cattle Egret. A native of southern Eurasia and northern Africa, this species has been expanding its range explosively during the past half century. It appeared in British Guiana sometime between World Wars I and II apparently of its own efforts. Enough individuals wandered or were blown across the South Atlantic to establish a population there in the coastal mangroves, which thrived and is still expanding. Wandering northward through the West Indies, a small colony established itself in Florida in the early 1950's and nested successfully on islets in Lake Okeechobee.

The Cattle Egret now breeds northward as far as New Jersey and westward to Texas. Wandering individuals have been reported from most eastern states northward to Maine and westward to Minnesota, and Kansas. The species has recently invaded Australia in much the same fashion.

Wherever it goes the Cattle Egret takes with it its habit of consorting with large ruminants, wherefore its name. It forages fearlessly around their feet on the insects the animals dislodge and, at times, perches on the animals' backs. It is readily recognizable in breeding plumage by the brownish patches on its head, breast, and back, otherwise by its slightly curved, shortish yellow bill and dark yellow legs.

The five herons of the *Hydranassa* complex are a varied group of small to medium-sized birds, distinctive mainly in being intermediate between the non-plumed green and pond herons and the egrets. Among them are the American Little Blue Heron and Louisiana Heron and Reddish Egret. Other members of the group are the Pied Heron of Australia and the Black Heron of Africa, aberrant forms often assigned to different genera.

The eight egrets are an important group of tropical and temperate climes. All are pure white or have a white phase and are famous for the beautiful feathery plumes, or aigrettes, they grow during the breeding season. This fancy nuptial dress was nearly their downfall, for the birds were slaughtered on their nests by the hundreds of thousands to satisfy the demands of fashion at the turn of the century. It took a long campaign by conservationists to arouse public sentiment enough to put an end to the practice. Thanks to the active protection now afforded in the United States, and the nesting reservations set aside by the Audubon societies and by federal and state agencies, the Snowy Egret and the larger Common Egret are plentiful once more, not only in the southland, but, at the close of the breeding season, as

wanderers north to southern Canada. Unfortunately, a black market still exists for aigrettes in lands where little attention is paid to the principles of conservation. In northern South America egrets are still slaughtered for their plumes. Very similar to the American Snowy Egret is the Little Egret of southern Eurasia, Africa, and Australia. The Common Egret is almost cosmopolitan in distribution, and is often called the great white heron.

Classed with the egrets are the two reef herons that occupy the lands bordering the Indian Ocean, the western Pacific, and the islands therein. Their plumes are neither as long nor as showy as those of the true egrets. These birds of coastal salt waters have two colour phases, a white and a blue. Some populations are all white, while those of high latitudes tend to be all blue. In parts of their range intermediates occur whose colour and relative frequency follow the Mendelian laws of inheritance.

Kings of the heron family are the 11 large herons of the genus *Ardea*, typical of which are the Great Blue Heron of North and Middle America and the West Indies, and the very similar Grey Heron of Eurasia, Africa, and Madagascar. Other large members of the genus are the Imperial and Goliath herons of India and Africa, and the Sumatra, or Giant, Heron of southeastern Asia and the East Indies. All are large birds, standing 4 to 5 feet tall. Only slightly smaller is the handsome Purple Heron of Eurasia, Africa, and Madagascar.

The stately Great Blue Heron is a distinctive and well-known bird, so large that one can't help noticing it. It nests in colonies, occasionally with other species, usually building its large stick nests in trees, 50 to 100 feet above the ground. The Great Blue lays 4 to 6 pale-greenish eggs which both sexes incubate for about 25 to 28 days. Both parents feed the young, at first by regurgitation, later on whole fish.

Large heronries, particularly those of white species, are a beautiful sight from a distance, the birds contrasting against the green of the trees. It is not unusual to find five or more species nesting together in one favoured spot. Some of the large heronries in Japan cover acres in which every tree has at least one nest and some have dozens. Breeding close to one another will be Night Herons, Common, Intermediate, and Little Egrets, Grey Herons, and often several species of cormorants, anhingas, and ibises as well.

Mortality in young herons is highest on the nesting grounds, and remains fairly high during their first ventures into the world. Ringing figures show first-year mortality averages 70 per cent. But those that survive the first 6 months on their own can look forward to a long life, for adult mortality is only about 30 per cent each year. The heron record for longevity is held by a Grey Heron ringed at Rossiten, Germany, which lived 24½ years.

Only one heron remains—the Agami, or Chestnut-backed, Heron of Central and northern South America. This is one of the handsomest of all the herons. It shows affinities to the ardeids, the egrets, and the bitterns, but fits into none of these tribes. Though definitely of the family Ardeidae, it is one of those odd offshoots of this ancient group that has survived just to puzzle ornithologists. As it has three powder-down patches, it is by definition a heron, and a handsome and intriguing one well worthy of further study.

AGAMI HERON
Agamia agami
Mexico to Peru and Brazil 30 in.

BOATBILL, WHALEHEAD,
AND HAMMERHEAD

CICONIIFORMES { COCHLEARIIDAE
BALAENICIPITIDAE
SCOPIDAE

BOATBILL HERON
Cochlearius cochlearius
Southern Mexico to Peru and southern Brazil 22 in.

Each of these three ciconiids possesses distinctive combinations of features that do not coincide with those of the other four families of the order. The Boatbill shows its closest affinities to the herons, the Whalehead seems nearest to the storks, and the Hammerhead shows similarities to both families. All three are so aberrant, however, that until more knowledge is available, particularly on their habits and behaviour, that may give additional clues to their ancestry and relationships, they are each accorded family rank.

Perhaps least aberrant of the three is the Boatbill Heron, a rather lethargic bird that lives in fresh-water mangrove swamps from central Mexico southward through Brazil. It bears a strong resemblance to the *Nycticorax* night herons in size and colour pattern. Its upper parts are largely grey with black patches on the head, back, and flanks. Its underparts, however, are brownish, and its nuchal crest, instead of being two long, thin, white plumes, is made of shorter, broader, black feathers. The Boatbill shows its relationship to the herons in its combed central toenail and in its powder-down patches, of which it has four pairs. Its partly bare throat and somewhat distensible gular pouch are more stork- or ibis-like.

The Boatbill's outstanding feature is its broad, scoop-like bill, which is 3 inches long and 2 inches wide, and totally unlike that of any other bird in the order. Perhaps associated with the development of the unique bill are the wide flaring palate bones, so different from the narrow ones of all other herons. The few reports available on how the bird uses this strange bill are conflicting. It is reported to eat worms, crustaceans, fish, amphibians, and even small mammals. It is difficult to see how such a bill would be useful in catching active prey like fish and mice, and it seems more fitted to puddling in the muck and mud of its mangrove habitat for less elusive food.

The Boatbill's habits are imperfectly known, for it spends its days hidden in the mangrove thickets and comes out to feed chiefly at night. Reflecting its nocturnal habits, its eyes are comparatively large. Its voice is described as a harsh, frog-like croaking, squawking, or barking, and it is also reported to have the stork habit of clapping and rattling its bill. It nests sometimes alone, sometimes in small colonies, occasionally in company with night herons. Like them it builds a shallow stick nest in the mangrove trees. It lays 2 to 4 blue-white eggs which both sexes incubate. Very little else is known about it.

The grotesque Whalehead, often called the Shoebill Stork from its ungainly 8-inch beak which is almost as wide as it is long, is restricted to the papyrus swamps of the upper White Nile and its tributaries in central East Africa. It is a morose-looking, shy bird, 3½ to 4 feet tall, that usually keeps its distance from man. It is often seen singly or in pairs wading in the shallows, or standing quietly with its bill resting on its chest. It occasionally soars high over the tropical marshlands of the Sudan, Uganda, and the Congo It flies with its neck and head folded back heron-fashion. It also resembles the herons in having a slight comb on its central claw, and in having its hind toe level with the three unwebbed front ones. It also has a single pair of powder-down patches on its rump, though how it is able to distribute the powder with its awkward, ungainly bill is unknown. Other anatomical features are more stork-like than heron-like. According to native reports it utters a loud, shrill call when flying, but this is not substantiated, and it is known to have the stork habit of rattling its bill to express emotion.

The Whalehead's boot-like bill is apparently adapted to probing in the muddy waters for lungfish and gars, its favourite foods, though it also eats frogs and perhaps young turtles, crocodiles, and small mammals, and is reportedly not above feeding on floating carrion. The Whalehead is a ground nester, and lays its two eggs on the flattened grasses on a high dry spot in the marshes. Its eggs are chalky white when fresh but like those of many marsh birds soon become stained a dirty brown.

The Hammerhead, or Hamerkop as it is called in its African home, is a queer-looking bird that resists all efforts to classify it satisfactorily. It lacks powder-downs and flies with its neck extended like a stork or ibis, yet it has heron-like voice organs and a variety of calls. Its hind toe is level with the others and it has heron-like teeth on the outer edge of its middle claw. Its wide, flat bill is unlike that of any other species in the order, and the bird lice that infest it are most closely allied to those found on certain plovers.

This heron-like bird about 20 inches long is brownish in colour with glossy purplish tinges on the back and wings. Its legs are comparatively short, and its large head is set on a rather short, thick neck. It gets its name from its long crest, which it carries horizontally like the nail-pulling end of a claw hammer.

Widely distributed over tropical Africa, Madagascar, and ranging northward into southwest Arabia, the Hammerhead is the subject of native legends and superstitions wherever it is found. They are largely regarded as birds of ill omen, and the belief that molesting them brings bad luck has helped to

SHOEBILL STORK
(WHALEHEAD)
Balaeniceps rex
Africa, Upper White Nile south to
Katanga and Uganda   47 in.

HAMMERHEAD
Scopus umbretta
Southwest Arabia, Africa, and Madagascar   20 in.

protect Hammerheads. They may be found singly, in pairs, or in small flocks wherever there is water, such as irrigation ditches, roadside pools, or along the banks of streams. They are given to strange, awkward gambolling, and when two or three are together they jump in the air and dance around one another for no apparent reason. Then suddenly they bow to each other, pull their heads back on their shoulders, and retire to solemn stolidity. Their food is varied, mostly water insects, worms, snails, grasshoppers, small fish, and amphibians. They are most active in the evening, and are somewhat nocturnal.

The Hammerhead builds a huge, remarkably intricate nest, a flattened, dome-shaped structure sometimes 6 feet or more in diameter with a compartmented interior and a rather small entrance hidden on the least accessible side. The nests are built mostly of sticks plastered in place with mud, and decorated on the outside with bright-coloured objects such as pieces of cloth, crockery, bones, and similar unusual materials. The nests are sometimes built among rock ledges, more often in large trees, and sometimes five or six may be found close to each other. Though native legend has it that other kinds of birds help the Hammerkop by bringing up nesting materials, each nest is the work of a single pair, which may spend several months building it, and then use it for years, adding to it and repairing it as necessary. In an innermost compartment of this complex nest are laid the 3 to 6 smallish white eggs, which both sexes incubate.

STORKS

CICONIIFORMES   CICONIIDAE

The 17 species of storks are nearly cosmopolitan, occurring throughout the warmer parts of the world except in New Zealand, Oceania, and northern North America. They differ from other families in the order by lacking powder-downs and the serrated middle claw, in having rather short toes which are partially webbed at the base, and in lacking muscles to their syrinx, or voice box. Adult storks are mute and express themselves only by rattling their bills. Their hind toe is elevated above the other three.

The antiquity of storks is shown by the score or more of fossil species dating back some 50 million years to Oligo-

cene time. All are strong-winged and fly with alternate periods of flapping and soaring. They hold their necks straight out in flight and their long legs trail behind. The northern storks that are migratory usually travel in large flocks.

The stork's legendary role in human obstetrics is one of the happiest and most persistent, though least justified, myths in our cultural history. The stork of the legend is the White Stork of Europe, which has been regarded as a bird of good omen since the early Middle Ages, especially among the Teutonic peoples. That so large and striking a bird is still common today in the heavily populated regions from Holland eastward to the Balkans is due entirely to the protection afforded it by this superstition.

Absence of such tradition has driven the White Stork from France as a breeding species, though it once nested there as commonly as it still does in Germany and Poland where, in some rural villages, almost every house boasts a stork nest on its roof. The White Stork at one time doubtless nested in rocky cliffs and in trees, as its close relatives in other parts of the world do today. But for generations the European populations of storks have bred on the roofs of human habitations, and their presence is regarded as such a sign of good luck that house owners frequently put platforms and baskets on their roofs in the hope that storks will make use of them.

The White Stork breeds from western Europe eastward across Asia to China and Japan. Except for the central European population, which sentiment protects on its breeding grounds, the species has become comparatively rare. Its long migratory flights southward into Africa have been common knowledge since biblical times, but only in the last few decades have ringing activities allowed the routes to be traced with any accuracy. Hundreds of young storks ringed in their rooftop nests in northern Europe show the population divides

WHITE STORK
Ciconia ciconia
Eurasia 40 in.

BLACK STORK
Ciconia nigra
Eurasia 38 in.

SADDLE-BILLED STORK
Ephippiorhynchus senegalensis
Tropical Africa 52 in.

JABIRU
Jabiru mycteria
Southern Mexico to Argentina 55 in.

MARABOU
(ADJUTANT) STORK
Leptoptilos crumeniferus
Tropical Africa 60 in.

WOOD STORK
Mycteria americana
Southeastern United States
to Peru and Argentina 47 in.

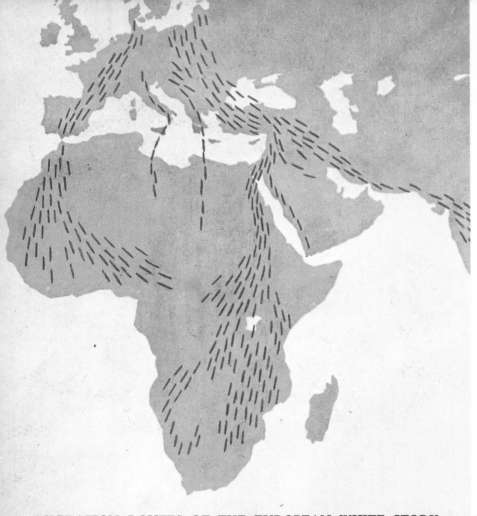

MIGRATION ROUTES OF THE EUROPEAN WHITE STORK

into two main groups: the western population migrates down through the Iberian peninsula and across from Gibraltar into Africa, while the eastern population skirts the eastern end of the Mediterranean down through Israel and across Egypt. A smaller population follows southward along the Italian boot and crosses the short water hop over the Mediterranean from Sicily to North Africa.

Storks show considerable faithfulness to their natal site. Individual storks return to the same rooftop to nest year after year and young birds tend to come back to the same area to find a nesting place. So far, ringing records show the oldest wild storks live about 20 years, but the ringing programme is still young and doubtless older records will soon be forthcoming. Captive birds have lived longer in zoos.

On their nesting grounds White Storks forage widely, mostly on the shores of lakes, streams, and in marshes but also over cultivated lands. Both sexes work at repairing the old nest or building a new one. The male usually brings the material, which can be grass, sticks, twigs, lumps of earth, or even rags and paper. The female arranges the materials to form a rough platform. On this she lays from 3 to 5 eggs which the male helps incubate by day; the female generally sits during the night. It takes from 29 to 30 days for each egg to hatch. Both parents feed the newly hatched young, at first by shaking half-digested food out of their bills into the nest where the young pick up the small pieces. As the young grow larger they are given frogs, fishes, birds, snakes, large insects, and small mammals. They remain in the nest about 8 weeks before taking flight. When taking flight from the ground, the stork gives a few short jumps before rising into the air. In the spring the mated pairs often soar

high on almost motionless wings, flying in spirals until nearly out of sight. They migrate in large flocks, often numbering several thousands strong.

The Black Stork is a slightly smaller bird than the White and has approximately the same distribution, nesting from central Europe eastward to China and Korea. It is a much wilder bird and is seldom seen near dwellings. It usually breeds on rocky cliffs or builds its large nest in the tops of tall trees. The sentiment connected with the White Stork does not seem to extend to the Black, which has not been so fortunate and in some parts of its range, particularly in the East, is becoming very rare. In fact it is feared that the northeastern population in China and Korea has been extirpated during the recent wars.

One of the tallest storks and certainly one of the handsomest is the Saddle-billed Stork of central Africa, so called because of the saddle-like shield on the top of its tremendous pointed bill. Largest of the storks are the three species of Marabou found in southern Asia and in tropical Africa. The appearance of these unattractive birds is hardly enhanced by the naked pouch hanging a foot or more below their throats. This appendage is apparently part of the respiratory system, though its function is poorly understood. The Marabou Storks are commonly known as Adjutants because their pompous, measured gait reminded the British colonial troops of those seldom-loved officers.

The Adjutants are largely scavengers and sometimes may be found in dry areas far from water. Despite their size, their eating habits so discourage people from molesting them that they have been able to survive in populated countries. They are powerful birds and their tremendous, heavy bills are a fearsome weapon that no other scavengers care to dispute, so Adjutants walk away with choice morsels with little disturbance from the vultures. They are protected by laws in many places, particularly in India, where even the dogs won't dispute the right of way with them.

The largest stork in the New World and one of the largest American flying birds is the Jabiru, found from Mexico south to Argentina. Jabiru is the Amazonian Indian name for this bird which has a white and black body and naked black head. Unlike the Adjutant, which it strongly resembles, it is not a scavenger, but forages for fish, amphibians, and other animal life through shallow tropical swamps—mainly in fresh water, occasionally in brackish.

Best known of the American storks is the Wood Stork, formerly called the wood ibis, a common bird in South Florida, where its nesting grounds have been protected for many years by the Audubon societies. The Wood Stork breeds in great colonies, building its huge nests in the Big Cypress and other Florida swamps. Sometimes as many as four to five thousand birds occupy a few acres of land. Their nests are usually in large cypresses and sometimes every tree over a space of many acres will have from a dozen to as many as 50 nests. The Wood Stork is largely a fresh-water feeder, though occasionally it goes into tidewaters when the fishing is good. Usually they feed in small flocks through the wet grassy Everglades in water up to a foot deep. They have a peculiar habit of feeding in echelons in a more or less co-operative pattern. Each bird stirs and muddles the water ahead of him with one foot to rouse animal life into action, and then grabs the fleeing prey with its bill.

IBISES AND SPOONBILLS

CICONIIFORMES   THRESKIORNITHIDAE

This family contains 28 species of medium-sized wading birds 20 to 40 inches long. They range throughout the world's warm-temperate and tropical regions except in Oceania. A characteristic of the family is a face bare of feathers. In one group the entire head and neck is naked. Like the storks they have no powder-down patches and most have no voice box. The few that do have a voice only croak or crackle harshly. But their toes are longer than the stork's, the hind toe is slightly elevated, and the middle claw is slightly scalloped like that of the herons.

The family is divided into two natural groups, the ibises with long, thin, and strongly down-curved bills and the spoonbills whose bills are broad and flat, as their name implies. All are gregarious birds, travelling and breeding in flocks. They fly with their necks straight out in front, their long legs trailing behind. The spoonbills fly with a steady wingbeat, but the ibises frequently alternate flapping and soaring, which the large flocks in flight frequently perform in unison.

That the ibises are an ancient group is indicated by their fossil record which goes back some 60 million years to Eocene time. Their record in human history goes back some 5,000 years. The ancient Egyptians venerated the Sacred Ibis and made it an integral part of their religion and of their written hieroglyphics. To them the Sacred Ibis was the god Thoth, the scribe of the gods, whose duty it was to record the story of every human being. Thoth is pictured in the old Egyptian friezes as having the head of an ibis. Carvings of the Sacred Ibis are found in many Egyptian monuments and the birds themselves were mummified and buried in the temples and with the pharaohs. In Egypt today the Sacred Ibis is a rare bird indeed, for it is common only in Africa south of the Sahara. Closely related species occur across southern Asia, in the East Indies, on Madagascar, and in Australia. All are birds of shores and marshes and feed on amphibians, insects, insect larvae, and other small aquatic animals.

One of the most widely distributed of the ibises is the handsome Glossy Ibis. It is small for an ibis, only about 20 inches in length, but its dark plumage shines in bronzes and purples. The Glossy Ibis breeds across southern Eurasia, in Africa, Madagascar, the East Indies, and Australia, also in North America from Florida northward along the Atlantic Coast to New Jersey and from the Gulf Coast southward into the West Indies and Mexico. A closely related form, the White-faced Glossy Ibis, breeds from the western United States south through Central America and western South America to Chile and Argentina. Another species lives in the highlands of Peru and Bolivia.

The best known ibis in the New World is the White Ibis, slightly larger than the Glossy, which breeds in large colonies in the forested lowlands along the Gulf Coast and southward to northern South America. Colonies of White Ibis nest in wet woodlands, usually in brackish coastal swamps or on the shores of fresh-water lakes. They build a flimsy circular nest of sticks about 2 feet in diameter, in which they lay 3 to 5 eggs, white and irregularly spotted and blotched with brown. Both sexes incubate for about 21 days. The young are fed a

1 SACRED IBIS
Threskiornis aethiopica
Africa and Madagascar   30 in.

2 GLOSSY IBIS
Plegadis falcinellus
Southern Eurasia, Africa, Madagascar, Australia, United States Gulf Coast, Cuba, Hispaniola, Puerto Rico   22 in.

3 SCARLET IBIS
Eudocimus ruber
Tropical South America;
northwestern Venezuela to Brazil   24 in.

4 WHITE IBIS
Eudocimus albus
Southern United States, West Indies, Central and northern South America   27 in.

variety of food. Crayfish is a staple when obtainable, otherwise they get insects, grasshoppers, cutworms, and even small snakes, slugs, and snails. A week or two after hatching, the young birds leave the nest and crawl around on the nearby branches of the trees. When they fall into the water, which they frequently do, they are able to swim well enough to get back to the tree trunk and clamber up. Their first juvenile plumage is quite different from the adult, being a striking dark grey-brown and white. They do not assume the pure white adult plumage with black wingtips until they reach their second year.

One of the handsomest of all birds is the vivid Scarlet Ibis (*see* Title Page), which lives from Venezuela south to Brazil and which strays accidentally northward into the West Indies and, rarely, to United States shores. Because of its great beauty it has been slaughtered mercilessly for its feathers. But it is also killed for its meat, which, though rather rank and oily, is relished by the natives in the areas it inhabits. Like the other ibises, it breeds in large colonies in the coastal mangrove swamps, but the flocks of thousands seen half a century ago are no more. Unless some way of protecting these birds is found, they are likely to go the way of most large, edible birds that come in contact with man.

Four of the species of spoonbills are predominantly white birds of Old World distribution. The best known of these is the Common Spoonbill, which breeds from western Europe eastward to India. Closely related forms replace it eastward in Asia to China and Japan and southward to Australia and New Zealand. The European Common Spoonbill migrates south to winter in Africa. These birds nest in colonies, usually on the ground in marshes or on islands in coastal lagoons. Like the ibises they lay from 3 to 5 (usually 4) eggs, which are dull white and blotched with brown. Both sexes incubate for an estimated 21 days. The young are fed by regurgitation and, as they grow, the young birds shove their wide bills down the throats of the adults for their food. The other white spoonbills are tree nesters.

Spoonbills fly rather quickly with the neck straight out in front and with steady, regular, rapid wingbeats, gliding only occasionally. Like the storks and some herons, they sometimes soar to considerable heights. They feed in shallow waters in the open and in marshes. Wading along with their half-open bills partly immersed, they swing their heads from side to side in a characteristic manner as they walk and close their bills on anything edible they encounter. Their food is primarily small crustaceans, insects, fishes, amphibians, and worms, with some vegetable matter.

The lovely Roseate Spoonbill, which formerly nested in thousands from the Gulf Coast of the United States southward to Argentina and Chile, is another bird that man has almost wiped out. Protective legislation and the establishment of refuges on its last remaining breeding grounds in Florida came only just in time to save the last pitiful remnants of the former thousands that at one time thronged Florida. While no longer persecuted in the United States, this spoonbill migrates southward in winter to lands where fewer conservation measures have been taken; hence the species has not made the comeback that other similarly threatened birds have made. Unlike the white spoonbills of the Old World, which seldom nest in company with other species, the Roseate Spoonbill in America usually nests in mixed colonies with Wood Storks and egrets. They lay from 3 to 5 eggs coloured a dirty white, splotched with various shades of brown. So far as is known, their nesting procedures and rearing of the young are identical to those of the white species.

In flight, the flocks of ibises and spoonbills form diagonal lines, occasionally V-shaped, with each bird in echelon a little behind and to one side of the bird ahead. Both ibises and spoonbills are rather quiet birds, and the only notes ever heard from them are a low grunting or a croaking on the breeding grounds. The spoonbills are now threatened in Florida by the rapid development of coastal real estate which is destroying, with bulldozers and draglines, the last remaining sloughs where these lovely birds feed.

ROSEATE SPOONBILL
Ajaia ajaja
Southeastern United States and
West Indies to Argentina and Chile 34 in.

EURASIAN
SPOONBILL
Platalea leucorodia
Eurasia and
northern Africa 34

FLAMINGOS

CICONIIFORMES   PHOENICOPTERIDAE

Certainly one of the most picturesque and beautiful of the world's birds, the flamingo has long puzzled those concerned with avian classification. Flamingos have been grouped variously with the ducks and geese, and even with the gallinaceous birds, to both of which they show resemblances, but they seem most closely related to the storks and ibises.

Flamingos' necks and legs are longer in proportion to their bodies than those of any other species of bird. The three front toes are fully webbed; the hind toe is elevated in two species of flamingo but absent in the other two. The downy young

are distinctly goose-like. Flamingos fly in long skeins, with necks straight out in front, their feet trailing behind. They are vocal in flight, honking much like geese. Additional evidence of their possible ancient relationships is found in their external parasites, the biting bird lice called mallophaga, which are vastly different from those of any other group but strongly resemble those of the waterfowl. The flamingos branched off into much their present form fairly early in geological time, before the dawn of the Tertiary. *Scaniornis* from the upper Cretaceous of Sweden is considered to be a

61

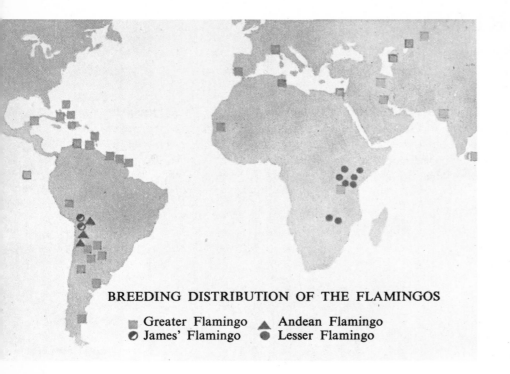

BREEDING DISTRIBUTION OF THE FLAMINGOS

■ Greater Flamingo   ▲ Andean Flamingo
◑ James' Flamingo   ● Lesser Flamingo

primitive flamingo. Fossil flamingos referable to present genera have been found in European Oligocene deposits.

The distribution of the four living species of flamingo is discontinuous, with populations in southern Eurasia, Africa, Madagascar, the Caribbean area, and in southern South America. Best known and most widespread is the Greater Flamingo, a whitish bird with pink wings, which nests in eastern Africa (Kenya) and from the shores of the Mediterranean eastward to the Kirghiz steppes, western India, and (formerly) Ceylon. Another population of the Greater Flamingo, and the reddest of all the flamingos, breeds in the West Indies and on the Galapagos Islands. This group is much reduced in numbers. A third race of the Greater Flamingo is a smaller, lighter-coloured bird, sometimes called the Chilean Flamingo, found in temperate South America from Peru southward through Uruguay to Tierra del Fuego. The Lesser Flamingo is a distinct species that nests only in the great rift valleys of Africa. Two other small species, the Andean Flamingo and James's Flamingo, are found only in the Andean highlands of southern Peru, Bolivia, and Chile.

Flamingos seem to prefer brackish or salt waters. Even the inland species of Africa and the Andes breed in muddy, shallow alkaline lakes. All flamingos usually nest in the same way and build a mud nest much like the pedestal for a soup tureen or punch bowl. These flattened cones vary from 5 to 18 inches in height, and from 15 to 30 inches in diameter at the base. They are about a foot in diameter at the top, which is faintly hollowed out like a saucer. The nest is built up of soft mud which soon hardens. In the saucer-like top, the female lays her single white egg, which both sexes incubate alternately for 28 to 32 days. The incubating flamingo sits on top of the mound with its long legs folded at the "heel," which projects out from under the tail.

Three or four days after hatching, the young flamingos are strong and steady enough to leave the nest and hop off into the mud or the water and herd with other young of their own age. They swim strongly and they can run fast enough to be hard to catch, as scientists who have tried to ring them can attest. Within three weeks the young are able to forage for themselves, though a few parents usually tend the creches until the young are able to fly.

The bill of the flamingo is unique among birds, as is its feeding method. The birds feed with their top bill bottommost and the lower bill above it pumping against it to sieve the water and mud through the slits on the top bill and the similar tooth-like projections on the tongue which act as a sieve. The flamingos' food covers a wide range of small animals and plants. In some areas their main food is actually the highly nitrogenous muck in which they live. It contains a rich mixture of algae and diatoms, protozoans, small worms, aquatic plants, insect larvae, even some small molluscs and crustaceans. This rich soup is strained by the pumping action of the throat through the bill and tongue. The tongue of the flamingo is very large in comparison to those of the waterfowl and the herons, and prevents them from swallowing large pieces of food.

The tongue of the flamingo was reportedly a great delicacy in Roman days and was served frequently at emperors' banquets. Since those days, however, few peoples have regarded flamingo meat as tasty and the bird has been persecuted largely for its beautiful plumage rather than for food, though it is still eaten in some places in the world by people who live a marginal existence.

Large numbers of flamingos have recently been ringed in the famous colonies in the Camargue in southern France. Recaptures from these ringings show that the European populations of the Greater Flamingo migrate across the Mediterranean to their wintering grounds in Africa, where they join the tremendous colonies of the Lesser Flamingo to feed in the brackish lakes of the rift valleys.

The New World colonies of the Greater Flamingo in the West Indies have led a precarious existence for the past century. The birds have been killed as food, for sport, and for their plumage. Only the vigilant action of conservationists has been able to preserve a small remnant of the large colonies that formerly nested in the Bahamas. Efforts to preserve these colonies were fairly successful until World War II when a new enemy, the aeroplane, threatened. Flamingos are so skittish of aircraft that they panic when one appears. If a plane flies near a breeding colony the birds desert it in a frenzy with disastrous loss of eggs and young. Steps are now being taken to remedy this situation, which becomes more critical as new and larger resorts are opened in the Bahamas.

The most prosperous flamingo colonies today are those of the East African alkaline lakes, where the Lesser Flamingo nests in almost countless thousands, joined by some Greater Flamingos as well. There is no lovelier sight in nature than a large flight of flamingos on the wing, and it would be a blot against mankind were this lovely and curious bird to disappear. It does well in captivity, however, and the West Indies birds brought to the racetracks at Hialeah in southern Florida have prospered and are now breeding within the racecourse—the only breeding colony of flamingos in the United States. Some of these birds occasionally escape, and when seen, give rise to reports of flamingos in the Everglades.

WATERFOWL

ANSERIFORMES

This ancient and well-differentiated group of birds is divided into two suborders, each of a single, strongly marked family. One contains only the three South American screamers, the other the 145 "true" waterfowl found practically the world over. Although quite dissimilar in appearance, the two groups show strong anatomical affinities.

Members of the order are relatively full-bodied, long-necked, short-legged swimming or semi-aquatic birds. Among their structural features are their 11 primary wing feathers (the first always reduced in size), a feathered oil gland, rounded open nostrils, and sundry skeletal and muscular similarities of a highly technical nature. Most are strong fliers. Adults have an undercoat of down feathers and lack an incubation patch (as do ratites and totipalmate swimmers). Their eggs are never spotted, and their downy young are able to leave the nest shortly after hatching.

SCREAMERS

ANSERIFORMES ANHIMIDAE

The three South American screamers are fairly long-legged wading and swimming birds the size of small turkeys. Though unquestionably allied to the waterfowl, they are not at all duck-like in appearance. The bill is short and curved as in game-birds. The head is rather small and slender, the neck rather short. The feathers of the head and neck are short, soft, and downy. The feet and legs are fleshy, the lower half of the tibia is bare, and the three long front toes show just a trace of webbing between them. The strong wings are armed with two large, sharp spurs on their forward edge.

The screamers boast several unique anatomical features. First, their feathers grow continuously over their bodies without the bare spaces (apteria) between tracts most other birds have. This condition is shared only by the ostrich, the penguins, and the colies. Also peculiar is their lack of the small bony straps called uncinate processes that strengthen the rib-cages in all other birds except the primitive and long extinct *Archaeopteryx*. Furthermore they have developed pneumaticity to a higher degree than any other bird. Almost all their bones are hollow, even the end of the spine and the outer digits of the wings and toes. Like the pelicans, they have an intricate series of air sacs under the skin which crackle audibly when pressed.

Screamers are birds of marshes, wet grasslands, and forest lagoons; they are often seen walking on the floating masses of vegetation in jungle lakes where their long toes support them. They are strong fliers, but rise from the ground or water heavily, their wings making an audible swishing sound as they beat the air. They often fly to considerable heights and soar for hours. When disturbed, screamers fly up to treetops where they can see approaching danger. They annoy hunters by giving the alarm to all game in the vicinity with their loud, goose-like calls. With voices powerful and far-carrying, they trumpet day and night throughout the year. Breeding pairs call back and forth to one another, and when the birds flock together after the breeding season they sing in concert.

Screamers are vegetable feeders, and live largely on succulent grasses and seeds, mostly of water plants. In some farming areas they show a fondness for forage plants.

They build a shallow nest of rushes and reeds on the ground, usually in grassy marshes. They lay from 2 to 6 large white eggs, which take from 42 to 44 days to hatch, both sexes sharing the incubation. The chicks at hatching are covered with buffy down and look something like baby swans. They soon desert the nest and follow their parents about as do waterfowl.

The Horned Screamer ranges over most of northern tropical South America. Its peculiar 6-inch frontal spike curves forward from its forehead toward its bill. The Crested and Black-necked screamers have crests of feathers instead of the spike. The Crested Screamer is widely distributed over the pampas regions of southern Brazil, Argentina, Paraguay, and Uruguay, where the natives call it "chajá" from its oft-reiterated cry. The Black-necked Screamer, smallest of the three species, is restricted to northern Colombia and Venezuela. All three screamers do well in captivity and are seen commonly in zoos. Also they tame readily and have bred successfully in captivity.

BLACK-NECKED SCREAMER
Chauna chavaria
Northern Colombia and Venezuela 28 in.

HORNED SCREAMER
Anhima cornuta
Northern tropical
South America 33 in.

SWANS, GEESE, AND DUCKS

ANSERIFORMES   ANATIDAE

The waterfowl have intrigued man for centuries. Perhaps no other group of birds has been more intimately connected with the human race. Waterfowl were among the first birds to be domesticated. Man has used them for food, for sport, and as a source of aesthetic pleasure. He has harvested them, eaten them, bred them, painted them, studied them, and written about them. The literature on waterfowl today is probably the most extensive for any group of birds.

Roughly 145 species are classed as waterfowl. They are diversified, yet as a group they are so homogenous that few have trouble recognizing any of them as members of the family. All the members of this family are swimming birds with comparatively short legs and webbed front toes. They have rather long necks and broad "duck" bills. All are heavily feathered and, with a few notable exceptions, are strong fliers. Though a few are solitary, most are highly gregarious; flocking is instinctive to them. They migrate in flocks; they feed in flocks; a few are even colonial in their breeding.

Despite their typical sameness, their great diversity has given the taxonomists no little trouble arranging them in natural groups that show their relationships. These birds are, of course, of ancient lineage. Their fossil record goes back into Mesozoic time, about 80 million years ago.

Present thinking, based not only on their anatomy and distribution but equally on the habits and behaviour of these birds, tends to group them all into the single family Anatidae. This is further divided into three subfamilies, two of which are broken into a number of tribes. Agreement on the exact arrangement and sequence of these various groups is not unanimous. The problems of their inter-relationships are so fascinating, however, that more active work is now being done to ferret them out than on almost any other group of birds. New evidence is constantly being discovered, linking forms previously thought to be quite distinct.

Waterfowl are so familiar that fairly definite ideas of the various groups are fixed in the popular mind. Most people know the swans as great white birds. Some know that there is also a black swan and a black-necked one. But the main point is that they are the biggest of the waterfowl and their necks are longer than their bodies. The term goose, likewise, has a definite connotation to most people. In general, geese are smaller than swans but bigger than ducks, and have long necks which are shorter than the swans' in comparison to their bodies. Smaller waterfowl, to most of us, are just ducks. Those who have looked further into the subject recognize differences between fresh-water ducks and sea ducks, between dipping ducks and diving ducks, between ducks that live on nothing but fish and those that eat grain and other vegetable matter as well.

To a certain extent these distinctions hold true when experts arrange the ducks into their natural classifications on the basis of morphology and habits. The swans are a fairly distinct group. So are all the smaller birds generally called ducks. The geese are intermediate between them. When we examine these groups closely, we find many birds called geese are actually members of duck tribes, and vice versa. In spite of recent research, many waterfowl refuse to fall into the categories set up to make it easier for us to understand their relationships. The waterfowl are such an ancient and diversified group, and number so many relict species of indeterminate ancestry, that much remains to be learned before ornithologists agree on how to classify them. Students do agree on the subfamily Anserinae, which contains the

CAPE BARREN GOOSE
Cereopsis novae-hollandiae
Islands off southern Australia 30 in.

SPUR-WING GOOSE
Plectropterus gambensis
Tropical Africa 30-32 in.

WHITE-FRONTED GOO
Anser albifrons
Northern Eurasia,
North America
Greenland 26 in.

AMERICAN VULTURES

FALCONIFORMES   CATHARTIDAE

Despite their superficial similarities in being large, soaring carrion eaters with unattractive, bare heads, the New World and the Old World vultures are some distance apart systematically. The Old World vultures are allied to the eagles and are included as a subfamily of the accipitrine hawks. The American vultures are of more ancient lineage and show distant affinities to the storks and to the cormorants. Their rather long toes are not strongly hooked for grasping as are those of all the other raptors. The hind toe is somewhat elevated and the three front toes have rudimentary webs at the base. The nostril openings are longitudinal instead of round, and the nasal passages within the bill are only partly divided. As they have no syrinx, American vultures are voiceless and can utter only weak hissing sounds.

The American vultures are unquestionably the best of the soaring land birds. Voracious and indiscriminate consumers of carrion and animal refuse, they are anything but finicky in their eating habits. They lack the dash and the strength of the typical raptors, and seldom attack any prey able to offer resistance. Their beaks are so weak that they are unable to tear flesh until it has partly rotted. Though they occasionally attack the helpless young of some mammals, their usual food is from carcasses.

The family boasts two of the largest living flying birds, the California Condor and the Andean Condor, each of which has a wingspan of almost 10 feet and weighs from 20 to 25 pounds. The breadth of the condors' wings gives them a far greater wing surface area than those of the pelagic albatrosses, which equal them in span but not nearly in wing surface or body weight. The family also boasts the largest flying bird that ever lived. *Teratornis incredibilis*, a vulture found in Pleistocene deposits in Nevada, had a wingspread estimated at 16 to 17 feet. The smaller *Teratornis merriami*, with a wingspread of only 11 to 12 feet, ranged across southern North America from Florida to California in the glacial period.

The antiquity of the New World vultures is shown by their rich fossil record. The six living species and a score or more fossil species are all of New World distribution. Cathartid fossil fragments found in Oligocene deposits in France and in Eocene strata in Germany show the family present 40 to 50 million years ago in the Old World where none has since been recorded. In North America some eight fossil genera have been described, the oldest going back 55 million years to the middle Eocene. Remains of the three living North American species are so plentiful in Pleistocene deposits that all three species must have been more abundant then than they are now, particularly the now-vanishing California Condor.

The California Condor, the largest North American bird, is unfortunately one of the rarest today. After the Ice Age it apparently retreated to the western highlands. When the '49ers first went West, the California Condor was still fairly plentiful in the California mountains, but the population is now reduced to a few pairs breeding in the coastal ranges of south central California southward to northern Lower California. Careful estimates in 1940 and 1950 showed the total population to number perhaps 60 birds, and there seems to have been no trend upward since.

Man has always been the California Condor's chief enemy, for little else is able to prey upon it. Though the bird was never hunted for sport, so large a target coming within range of any hunter is almost too tempting to resist. Shooting alone does not account entirely for its rapid disappearance, for it is comparatively shy and not easily approached within gunshot range. Many were poisoned by strychnine which ranchers inserted into dead cattle to kill wolves and coyotes. Two other factors were the decline of its usual food as the settling of the West reduced the population of wild animals, and the species' very slow rate of reproduction. The California Condor lays but a single egg and the birds do not breed until they are at least 6 years old. Compensating for this in part is the long life expectancy that the adult birds enjoy, barring accidents. Vultures have lived for 50 years in zoos. As yet we have no ringing information on which to base vital statistics.

The great Andean Condor, while rare, is apparently not in such grave danger of extermination as its northern cousin. It lives in the high Andes from Venezuela and Colombia to Patagonia, and its range covers such a wide expanse of sparsely settled territory that its chances of survival are better.

The third largest of the New World vultures, and certainly the most strikingly handsome, if that adjective can be applied to these birds, is the black and white King Vulture that ranges from southern Mexico through the tropical rain forests to Argentina. The naked head of this bird is brilliantly coloured in a variety of purples, greens, and yellows, which the bird does not assume until it reaches adult plumage in its third or fourth year. Its wattled and warted mien appears frequently in aboriginal Indian art.

Best known and most widely distributed of the family are the Black Vulture and the Turkey Vulture, both of which are widely distributed from northern United States southward to southern South America. Soaring over the countryside on motionless wings, they are a common sight in the southern states where they are widely and incorrectly called "buzzards." (Properly, "buzzard" refers to broad-winged hawks of the genus *Buteo*, typified by the Red-tailed and Red-shouldered hawks.) Each species breaks into several geographical races, and the peripheral populations, both north and south, are migratory.

Vultures are famed for their keen eyesight. They seek their food by soaring on steady wings anywhere from just above tree-top level to hundreds of feet up in the air. Their soaring depends much on the weather conditions, for they ride the thermal updrafts round and round. While vultures are not gregarious birds in the strict sense, they often roost together at night, and large numbers gather where food is available. A circling vulture sees another a mile or more away suddenly swoop down and knows, perhaps by some telepathic sense, that it has found food. As it soars thither to investigate, it is followed by the next bird, and the next.

There has been much debate over the vultures' sense of smell. They are so keen in finding food that it was thought that the olfactory sense, notoriously weak in all birds, must help them out. Long series of experiments have shown that they possibly do have a better sense of smell than other birds and are occasionally able to find food that way, but eyesight is far more important to them. It hasn't taken these birds long to find that highways, where small animals are constantly being killed by speeding cars, are a rich source of food. Vultures now patrol the main southern routes almost as regularly as the highway police, and frequently become victims themselves of the same cars that provide them an easy living.

The Turkey and Black vultures are both ground nesters, sometimes nesting under overhanging rocks, occasionally in holes and hollow stumps. They lay two, rarely three, eggs. The incubation period is about 6 weeks, and it takes the young another 10 weeks to mature. The young are born with down feathers covering the head; these disappear when the adult plumage is assumed. It is believed that the bareheadedness of vultures is a feeding adaptation. The carrion they eat would soon stain and mat down their head feathers.

Because of their unsavoury food habits, vultures are smelly birds and not at all pleasant to handle. Relatively few have been ringed. They have recently been suspected of carrying cattle diseases, and because of this have been persecuted by some cattle raisers. By and large, however, their scavenging habits are of such value in removing sources of infection that in most of the United States they are protected by law.

The sixth species of the family, the Yellow-headed Vulture, is congeneric with the Turkey Vulture and has much the same habits. It ranges from Vera Cruz, Mexico, southward to northern Argentina and Uruguay.

SECRETARY BIRD

FALCONIFORMES   SAGITTARIIDAE

Its crest of long plumes, which suggest a bunch of quill pens stuck behind the ear of an old-time lawyer's clerk, are responsible for the Secretary Bird's name. This long-legged, cursorial African hawk is so unlike all other members of the order, it is placed in a family by itself.

Well known as a snake-killer, the Secretary Bird also preys on other reptiles, small mammals, large insects, especially locusts, and is fond of young birds and eggs. Widely regarded as a beneficial species, the Secretary Bird is protected by game laws wherever they exist in Africa. Farmers in agricultural South Africa sometimes keep domesticated ones to help clear farms of snakes and rats, though they have to be kept away from young chickens and other farmyard fowl.

Unlike all other hawks, the Secretary Bird hunts on foot and runs after its prey in zigzag fashion, frequently flapping its wings, more to dazzle and confuse its victim than to help its own progress. Its generic name, *Sagittarius*, refers to its stalking its prey afoot, like an archer. When a snake strikes, the bird usually takes the blow on its wing feathers, where the snake can do no harm. It kills snakes by striking them down with one foot, usually behind the head, and then battering the victims with its wings. Snakes too large or tough to kill in this fashion, it carries aloft and drops on the hard ground, just as a gull breaks open a clam.

The Secretary Bird ranges throughout Africa south of the Sahara, except for the equatorial forested regions. An inhabitant of open plains and the brush-covered veldt, it wanders widely in search of food and is believed to be partly migratory. Though not gregarious, numbers gather when brush fires sweeping the veldt drive out and cripple small animals, making them easy prey. They are most frequently encountered in pairs, which forage at some distance apart—perhaps a half mile or more—but keep in vocal contact with full-throated, triple-syllabled, reedy calls that carry far.

Secretary Birds are believed to mate for life. Contrary to the usual raptorine pattern, the female is slightly smaller than the male. Each pair builds a crude nest of sticks in a low bush or tree, seldom more than 20 feet above the ground, and if not disturbed will use the same nest year after year until it gets quite large, perhaps 6 feet across. On this platform, they usually lay two eggs, which take about 7 weeks to hatch. Both sexes incubate and help feed the young by regurgitation of half-digested food. They seem to prefer to feed their young on small mammals. As in most raptors, the newly hatched chicks, covered with white down, are very helpless. It is several weeks before they can stand, and about 2 months before they fledge fully.

SECRETARY BIRD
Sagittarius serpentarius
Africa south
of the Sahara   46 in.

OLD WORLD VULTURES, HAWKS, EAGLES, KITES, HARRIERS

FALCONIFORMES   ACCIPITRIDAE

The family Accipitridae is the most heterogeneous as well as the largest family among the raptors. Its 205 species divided among 70 or more genera comprise an exceedingly varied assemblage of predators. They range in size from the dashing little Sharp-shinned Hawk, scarcely larger than the quail and doves it occasionally preys upon, to the giant sloth-killing Harpy Eagle of the Amazon jungles. Here are united such improbable close relatives as the huge carrion-eaters of the Old World and the sleek, graceful, insect-hawking Swallow-tailed Kite of the New.

The accipitrine raptors are generally distinguished from falcons by their unnotched upper bill and their broader wings, usually rounded at the tips. These external characteristics are not infallible, and their classification is based largely on highly technical comparisons of their internal anatomy. The nine subfamilies into which the family is divided are each fairly distinct, but several tend to merge into one another through intermediate forms that are difficult to assign definitely. As yet no completely satisfactory arrangement of the family has been proposed.

A further obstacle to any non-technical discussion of the family is the failure of the common names used to designate familiar species to conform to the accepted technical classification. Large raptors commonly called eagles are assigned to two different subfamilies; dissimilar birds of three subfamilies are called kites. The best and original term for the broad-winged soaring hawks as a group is the appellation buzzard, which many Americans apply to the vultures.

One of the most distinctive of the subfamilies of this perplexing family is the Aegypiinae, the Old World vultures. Though they bear a strong superficial resemblance to the American vultures, their strongly hooked feet, round nostrils, and syrinx show they developed more recently, probably from an eagle-like ancestor. They doubtless acquired their bare heads in response to their carrion-feeding habits, as did the New World cathartids before them. The smallest and least specialized of them, the dirty-white Egyptian Vulture, has only the face bare. The rest of its head and neck is completely feathered.

Ranging throughout Africa and eastward through Arabia to India, the Egyptian Vulture has had a long association with mankind, as its vernacular name, "Pharaoh's chicken," implies. Accurate drawings of it have been found on the walls of Egyptian tombs. It eats any kind of carrion and excrement. It cleans up the carcasses of dead animals after the larger vultures have finished. Though exceedingly valuable as a scavenger, the Egyptian Vulture has suffered considerably from indiscriminate poisoning campaigns in many parts of its range, and is no longer as common as it once was. It usually nests on cliffs or in small caves, and sometimes uses old nests of other species in trees. It usually lays two eggs, which both parents incubate for 43 days.

More typical of the Old World vultures is the immense Griffon Vulture, which can withdraw almost all of its ugly head into the large white ruff around its neck. Found from southern Europe and North Africa eastward to India, it is a bird of mountainous country, usually seen soaring at great heights watching ceaselessly for carrion. Despite its great size and power, it seldom kills its food and usually will not touch prey that shows a sign of life. It is one of the birds that are seen around the burning ghats of India waiting for a corpse not completely consumed by fire to fall into the river.

EARED VULTURE
Torgos tracheliotus
Temperate and
tropical Africa   43 in.

GRIFFON VULTURE
Gyps fulvus
Southern Europe, southwestern Asia,
South Africa   41 in.

WHITE-HEADED VULTURE
Trigonoceps occipitalis
Unforested central Africa   33 in.

EGYPTIAN VULTURE
Neophron percnopterus
Southern Europe, southwestern Asia,
Africa   6 in.

The Griffon is one of the few raptors that at times nests colonially, usually on cliff ledges, in caves, or in recesses among rock slides. Each pair lays but a single egg, which takes from 48 to 52 days to hatch. The parents alternate incubation duties every other day. They feed the chick on half-digested carrion they disgorge at the nest. The fledgling remains in the nest about 3 months before taking flight.

Although darker than the Griffon, the Hooded Vulture is somewhat similar in appearance. One of the commonest vultures of eastern Africa, its range extends from southern Egypt southward to Natal. Like its relatives, it is an omnivorous feeder, frequently hanging around towns and native villages, often roosting in fairly large companies near its source of food. The Hooded Vulture also scavenges for dead fish along sea shores.

The White-headed Vulture, widely distributed throughout central Africa, is a more aggressive species than the other vultures and seems to retain some of the habits of the eagles from which this group of birds supposedly descended. While its principal diet is carrion and it will come to a kill of dead animals like all the other vultures, it occasionally attacks and kills other birds, small antelope, and other game for itself.

While the vultures are an interesting group of birds scientifically and perform an exceedingly useful function in scavenging, particularly in backward places where sanitation is not good, they have little aesthetic appeal. They strike most of us as practical but not very pleasant creatures.

The seven species of white-tailed kites of the subfamily Elaninae are rather primitive and comparatively unspecialized birds. They occur around the world from extreme southern United States, southern Europe, and Asia south of the Himalayas, southward throughout South America, Africa, and Australia. Most of them are light-coloured birds, attractive in appearance, with an airy, graceful flight. All are tree nesters, laying from 2 to 5 white eggs richly mottled with browns and reds. As in most hawks the incubation period is long,

GOSHAWK
Accipiter gentilis
Temperate Northern Hemisphere,
circumpolar 22 in.

4 weeks or more. All kites are excellent fliers. They sometimes hover with the fluttering wings held gull-fashion well above the body, and frequently they dangle their legs while flying. They live on animals, mostly small rodents, snakes, lizards, frogs, grasshoppers, beetles and other insects, and a few small birds. One African species, the Bat-eating Kite, spends its days hidden in the heavy forest foliage and comes out at evening to feed on bats and late-flying small birds which it catches on the wing and eats from its claws while still flying. The White-tailed Kite is now very rare in the southern parts of the United States, but still fairly common in parts of Central and South America.

SWALLOW-TAILED KITE
Elanoides forficatus
Southern United States to
northern Argentina 24 in.

EVERGLADE KITE ♂
Rostrhamus sociabilis
Florida, Cuba, and southern Mexico to
eastern Argentina 18 in.

BRAHMINY KITE
Haliastur indus
India to the Solomon Islands
and Australia 18 in.

The Swallow-tailed and Hook-billed kites of the New World are members of the subfamily Perninae, typified by the Honey Buzzard of the Old World, which breeds across temperate Eurasia and migrates southward throughout its range. A fairly strong flier, the Honey Buzzard soars quite often and perches both on trees and on the ground, where it walks about with ease and agility. It gets its name from its habit of attacking the nests of wasps and bees, not for the honey they contain but for the insects and their larvae which it digs out of the ground using its feet alternately. As it picks up a stinging insect, it nips off the business end of the thorax with its bill before eating it.

The Swallow-tailed Kite is one of the loveliest and daintiest American hawks. It feeds mainly on insects, small reptiles, and various amphibians. At one time it bred rather widely through most of the United States, but it is now restricted to the extreme southern states around the Gulf of Mexico from Florida to Texas. The species migrates southward in winter as far as northern South America. In flight the Swallow-tailed Kite is graceful and buoyant. It courses over open land in search of food like a glorified swallow, swooping in circles high overhead, then scaling down close to the ground. Just why it has disappeared is difficult to understand. It lays two eggs, occasionally three, in a nest high in a tree. Both parents incubate and care for the young. Owing to its rarity and the difficulty of finding and reaching nests, its breeding habits have not been well studied. It is obvious, however, that its rate of reproduction is not high enough to balance the mortality in the adult population.

The fourth subfamily of the Accipitridae is the Milvinae, the true kites, a poorly marked group with close affinities to the previous two groups and forming something of a link between them and the following groups. In North and Central America the true kites are represented by the Mississippi Kite, the Plumbeous Kite, and one of the rarest, the Everglade Kite, found in North America only in the depths of the Florida Everglades, where it lives almost entirely on a single species of fresh-water snail (*Pomacea*, the apple snail). This selectivity in its diet undoubtedly has something to do with its limited distribution. The extremely long hook on its bill is especially adapted for eating snails; it holds the snail until the animal comes partly out of its shell and then spears it with the tip of the bill and pulls it the rest of the way out.

Closely related Old World species include the common Black Kite of Eurasia, found from the Mediterranean eastward to Japan. Another is the comely Brahminy Kite, with a red-brown back and white head, which ranges from India eastward to the Solomons and southward to Australia. These kites are to some extent scavengers. They are found occasionally inland near villages where they scrounge around rubbish dumps looking for mice and rats, lizards, and grasshoppers. A large part of their food is carrion. In the warm-temperate regions of Asia they are common birds around harbours, where they take the place of gulls scavenging for scraps. All kites pick their food up with their feet and frequently eat it from their claws while in flight.

Largest of the kites is the 4-foot Lammergeyer, whose pointed wings span 8 to 10 feet. A resident of high mountain ranges in Africa, southern Europe, and central Asia, it is commonly called the Bearded Vulture, from the prominent patch of black bristles below the bill and its carrion-eating

RED-TAILED HAWK
Buteo jamaicensis
North America, Central America,
West Indies 25 in.

habits. A favourite food of the Lammergeyer is bones. After vultures have cleaned a carcass—and they do a thorough job—it moves in for the bare skeleton. Small bones it swallows whole, and larger ones it drops from a height to shatter them on the rocks below.

The nominate family Accipitrinae is one of the larger and more compact of the subfamilies of the Accipitridae. Some 40 species belong to the single genus *Accipiter*, one of the largest and most widely distributed of all the raptorine genera, occurring throughout the temperate and tropical areas of the world except Oceania and New Zealand. The accipiters are hunting hawks that live largely on small mammals and birds. They are sharp-clawed, long-shanked, and quick, dashing fliers with noticeably rounded wings. Their broad wings and long tail give them the speed and control of movement necessary to fly swiftly through wooded growth, to check their movements quickly, and to make the abrupt turns needed in their hunting.

Typical of the group is the sturdy Goshawk, a 20- to 24-inch bird that breeds circumpolarly in the northern parts of the temperate regions and winters somewhat southward. It is still common in parts of Europe, Siberia, and eastern Asia, but unfortunately is becoming quite rare in North America, and is now one of the least plentiful Western Hemisphere hawks. The Goshawk was widely used in falconry, and in Japan was a great favourite for hunting rabbits and marsh birds. Instead of striking its prey and disabling it in passing with a blow of its talons, the Goshawk usually strikes and stays with its victim, riding birds to the ground. In feudal days the Japanese falconers used the Goshawk to hunt cranes. No hunting Goshawk was entitled to wear royal purple jesses until it had killed the most noble of all game, the great Japanese, or Manchurian, Crane. Though this crane is several times the Goshawk's size it is no match for the accipiter in a flying fight.

Besides the Goshawk, the genus *Accipiter* includes several smaller and more plentiful members. Among these are Cooper's Hawk, the Sharp-shinned Hawk (one of the smallest of the family), and the very similar European Sparrow Hawk. In these species the male is about 11 inches long, the female 14 to 15 inches. Throughout the *Accipiter* group the females are considerably larger than the males.

GOLDEN EAGLE
Aquila chrysaëtos
Northern Hemisphere, circumpolar 33 in.

The accipiters build fairly substantial nests of sticks and twigs in trees, usually with a cup in the centre lined with small twigs or bark, occasionally with evergreen shoots. The typical eggs are white, heavily marked with brownish spots and blotches. Three to five eggs is the normal clutch and the incubation period is comparatively long, from 4 to 5 weeks. Incubation is usually by the female alone, but the male brings her food while she is on the nest. The period of fledging takes another 5 to 6 weeks.

The largest and most diverse and heterogeneous subfamily is the Buteoninae, another cosmopolitan group containing some 90 species divided among 29 genera. These are mostly medium- to large-sized hawks and eagles with shorter legs and tails than the accipiters, and slightly longer, broad, rounded wings. The largest genus, *Buteo,* with some 26 species, is typical of the group. It is this group of hawks that the term "buzzard" most correctly designates, for this is what they have been called in Britain for four centuries. Here are some of the most familiar of all the large hawks. The American Red-tailed Hawk, at once identifiable by the broad rufous tail, is very similar to the common English Buzzard and frequently seen circling high up over American woodlands, usually in pairs.

Other common North American buteos are the Red-shouldered, Swainson's, and Broad-winged Hawks. All the buteos are hunting hawks, but they are neither as dashing nor such skilful hunters as the accipiters or the falcons. They live largely on reptiles, amphibians, and small mammals up to the size of rabbits rather than on small birds. Because of their tremendous rat-catching abilities, they are definitely beneficial to farmers. Nevertheless, they are hawks and as such are persecuted by uninformed hunters, who regard them as competitors for game. Buteonine hawks often migrate with accipiters in large companies following the same flight lines year after year, usually along mountain ridges where the updrafts help them soar southward with the least effort. Well-meaning but misguided hunters once slaughtered hawks as they flew these flight lines. Local protection and educational programmes have now helped eliminate needless killing.

BALD EAGLE
Haliaeetus leucocephalus
North America, northeastern Siberia 34 in.

BATELEUR EAGLE
Terathopius ecaudatus
Arabia and Africa southward from Senegal and the Sudan, except for forested West Africa 24 in.

HARPY EAGLE
Harpia harpyja
Southern Mexico to northern Argentina 38 in.

ORNATE HAWK-EAGLE
Spizaëtus ornatus
Southern Mexico to northern Argentina
24 in.

Most of the large raptorine birds we call eagles are classified in this subfamily. Most regal of them is the Golden Eagle, holarctic in distribution and at one time found completely across Eurasia and North America, mostly in mountainous areas. Its present rarity through most of its range is largely due to shooting by "sportsmen." The Golden Eagle is indeed a great hunter, and feeds largely on animals which it kills with its powerful talons: rabbits, marmots, woodchucks, and ground squirrels. It has been trained for hunting in Asia and is used for larger game than other hawks. The Golden Eagle was symbolic of Rome's power, and its image surmounted the staffs borne in front of every Roman legion. The Romans called it *Aquila,* the generic name it bears today.

80

Golden Eagles are long-lived birds and once having established a nesting spot come back to it year after year. Though they sometimes nest in trees, their favourite aerie is an inaccessible ledge on a cliff. They build a huge, bulky nest of sticks and they add to it yearly. The usual clutch is two eggs, sometimes only one. Like those of other hawks, the eggs are usually white, flecked and spotted with various shades of brown. The female does most of the incubating, but the male occasionally helps her for short periods. The incubation lasts about 6 weeks. Both parents feed the young, though the male seems to bring more food than the female. He occasionally helps to brood the young ones. Young eagles remain in the nest for at least 11 weeks before they are able to fly.

The United States' national bird, the Bald Eagle, is less noble than the Golden Eagle, in habits if not in appearance. It does some hunting for itself and is able to catch a few waterfowl and marsh rabbits. Like the Golden Eagle, it is not above taking the young of large animals, when it can catch them, and has been known to take spotted fawns. By far the greater part of its food is fish. It catches a few fish for itself but picks most of them up dead along the shore. A favourite Bald Eagle gambit is harassing that expert fisherman, the Osprey, and forcing it to drop its catch, which the eagle often retrieves before the fish hits the water.

While the Bald Eagle breeds throughout North America, it has become quite rare in most of its range and is plentiful today only in Alaska and in Florida. In Florida its numbers have declined markedly in the last two decades; just why is not certain, for the species is protected and is seldom shot. Though it is long-lived and lays two eggs, it is not rearing enough young to replace the annual mortality. It builds a bulky nest in a treetop, and established pairs return to the same site year after year. Destruction of nesting trees as the human population expands is partly blamed for its decline. Suspected, but not as yet proved, is poisoning by air-sprayed DDT ingested with poisoned fish the eagle eats. Young eagles ringed in Florida have been found to wander northward to Canada after leaving the nest.

In the same genus, *Haliaeetus*, with the Bald Eagle are a number of other large eagles generally known as the sea eagles. All are of similar aspect, and vary mainly in their possession of a white head or tail. Some species lack both the white head and white tail; some have only the tail white. One occurs in Africa, another in Madagascar, a third in the Malayan region and in the Solomon Islands. A fourth, the White-tailed Sea Eagle, which nests from Greenland and Iceland eastward across northern Siberia, is known to crossword puzzle fans as the erne, a term long ago gone into disuse and never used elsewhere, even by ornithologists.

Well worthy of the noble designation of eagle is the Harpy Eagle, a jungle-inhabiting raptor living from southern Mexico southward through the Amazon forests to southern Brazil. This large, powerful, crested bird has one of the strongest sets of talons in the whole tribe. It eats macaws and one of its favourite foods is also a crossword puzzle inhabitant, the ai, or three-toed sloth.

The eighth subfamily of the Accipitridae, the Circinae, contains the harriers or marsh hawks. Most of its 17 species are placed in the genus *Circus*. They are fairly long-legged raptors with long, square tails and long, slightly rounded wings. All have distinctly owl-like facial discs. They are birds of open

HEN HARRIER (MARSH HAWK) ♂
Circus cyaneus
Temperate Northern Hemisphere,
circumpolar 24 in.

lands, marshes, and prairies, given to harrying—that is, coursing up and down, back and forth over open grassy fields and marshes in search of small mammals, birds, reptiles, and frogs. The harriers are almost cosmopolitan in distribution, absent only from the polar regions, Oceania, and New Zealand. The Hen Harrier, a circumpolar species called the Marsh Hawk in North America, is typical of the group. This well-known hawk, recognizable immediately by its distinctive white rump patch, shows strong sexual dichromatism, which occurs in few other raptors. The female is brown, the male grey. Young males resemble the female until they develop their full adult plumage.

Most harriers are ground nesters. The Hen Harrier nests in marshes where it builds a low platform of grasses and weeds—mostly the work of the female. She lays anything from 3 to 6 eggs and does all the incubating. The male occasionally feeds her on the nest. The incubation period is from 4 to 5 weeks and it takes another 5 to 6 weeks for the young to mature. The male brings all their food at first, but later the female helps.

The last subfamily of the Accipitridae is the Circaetinae, often called the serpent eagles. These fairly large, broad-winged birds are fond of soaring over marshy areas. They live primarily on reptiles and amphibians. Typical of the group is the Bateleur Eagle, a striking eastern African species with long, broad wings and a rather short tail. Its bare face may reflect its occasional lapses into carrion eating, but it usually does its own killing. It preys on almost all kinds of small game but, like the rest of its group, it is particularly fond of snakes. Almost always seen soaring and sailing at considerable speed, the Bateleur frequently rocks in flight. It also has earned an unusual reputation as an aerial acrobat and sometimes turns somersaults playfully in the air, much like a Tumbler Pigeon. One observer says its downward swoop "when it means serious business, is magnificent with a noise like a six-inch shell."

OSPREY OR FISH HAWK

FALCONIFORMES   PANDIONIDAE

Though never found far from water, the Osprey is one of the most widely distributed of all birds. It ranges along all coasts and along the larger lakes and rivers of the continental land masses of the world. It has successfully colonized oceanic islands where no other hawks have been able to survive. The only non-frozen lands it has not occupied successfully are New Zealand, where it has never occurred, and the Hawaiian Islands, where it appears sporadically. The widely scattered Osprey population of the world is divided into five subspecies that differ only slightly in colour and size.

In appearance the Osprey closely resembles the large accipitrine hawks and eagles. It is a large, powerful, soaring and flapping hawk 20-24 inches long, with broad, somewhat pointed wings. Females average slightly larger than the males. Its internal anatomy resembles that of the Accipitridae most closely, but the arrangement of its feather tracts closely approximates that of the New World vultures. Its distinctive leg and foot structures, however, warrant placing it in a family of its own. Its thighs are heavily feathered and its legs are bare. Its four toes are of equal length instead of unequal as in all other raptors. Its outer toe is reversible as in the owls, so that it can grasp its prey with two toes in front and two behind. Each toe is tipped with a long, sharp, down-curved claw, and the pads of the under-surface of the foot have short, stiff spicules to help hold slippery prey.

Though it has been known to take other food when pressed by hunger, the Osprey usually lives entirely on fish which it catches alive. It soars in circles over the water anywhere from 50 to 200 feet up until it sights its prey. It hovers a moment, then plunges down feet first with wings half closed, and often goes under water completely with a great splash, to re-emerge in a few seconds with a fish grasped tightly in both talons. Labouring clear of the surface with its burden, it shakes itself momentarily to throw the water out of its plumage and flies off, with the fish held head foremost in its talons, to a convenient tree, high rock, or to its nest to eat. It is frequently harassed by larger, less skilful fishermen among the hawks and eagles. The Bald Eagle worries the Osprey considerably and takes its catch away from it. While the Osprey prefers to catch fish alive, it is not above picking up a dead fish which is still fresh. Unlike the Bald Eagle, it will not touch a fish that has started to go bad.

The Osprey builds a tremendous nest of sticks, sometimes using branches 5 feet long, and pads the centre with bits of seaweed or other vegetation. In America the nests are usually placed high in a tall, dead tree; in coastal regions where trees are scarce, the tops of telegraph poles are welcome substitutes. The bulky nests so disrupt electric power and telephone service by short circuiting the wires that it is often found expedient to erect special platforms for the Ospreys to use—usually old wagon wheels supported horizontally on an added length of pole. In Europe the Osprey prefers to nest in pine trees, sometimes on sea cliffs. It occasionally nests on the ground, mainly on small islands where no elevations are available and where predators are absent. The nests are occupied

OSPREY
Pandion haliaetus
Almost cosmopolitan. Absent from
polar regions, New Zealand, and
southern South America 24 in.

young

year after year and are added to each year. Records show single nests occupied annually for more than 40 years, quite possibly by the same birds. For a long time the Osprey held the age record for a ringed bird at 21 years: one ringed in 1914 was recovered in 1934.

Each pair of Ospreys usually lays three eggs, which vary greatly in pattern. Strikingly marked with blotches and spots of red, brown, and chocolate on a white ground, they were once coveted by egg collectors. Incubation is chiefly by the female, relieved occasionally by the male when she is off feeding. The period lasts 5 weeks, and it takes the young another 8 to 10 weeks to fledge.

In North America the Osprey breeds commonly along the coasts from Labrador to Florida and from Alaska to Mexico. Its nests can also be seen around many large interior lakes. The population migrates southward in winter as far as northern South America.

The Osprey has no real natural enemies other than man. The Bald Eagles, frigate-birds, and other predators that chase it and make it drop its food are merely annoyances. The fish it eats are mainly coarse fish of little economic importance, and it is nowhere abundant enough to make serious inroads on fish populations. Yet gamekeepers in Scotland, at about the turn of the century, succeeded in driving out the last Ospreys from the British Isles, where it was formerly a common summer resident. Every subsequent attempt the species made to nest in Britain was broken up by the iniquitous egg collectors. However, in 1958, bird lovers set up a round-the-clock guard on a pair that ventured to breed in Scotland. Their protection allowed the young to hatch and fledge successfully. The success was repeated the following year. It is hoped, from this start and with increased protection that the species will once again become a breeding bird in the northern British Isles.

FALCONS AND CARACARAS

FALCONIFORMES   FALCONIDAE

The family Falconidae is another heterogeneous group, varying from the swiftly darting little falconets 6½ inches in length to the 24-inch Gyrfalcon of the arctic tundras and from the swift-flying predatory Peregrine, Hobby, and Merlin to the comparatively sluggish, scavenging caracaras. In addition to the internal anatomical characters that distinguish them from the other raptorine families, the falcons have comparatively long pointed wings, bare tarsi and feet, thighs covered with loose feathers that look like pantaloons, and usually a notch, or "tooth," in the upper bill. The 58 species are grouped into four fairly well-marked subfamilies.

The subfamily Herpetotherinae contains the rather primitive Laughing Falcon and the four forest falcons of continental Central and South America. The Laughing Falcon lives almost entirely on snakes. The dashing, soft-feathered forest falcons prey on small birds and mammals.

The nine caracaras of the subfamily Polyborinae find their greatest development in South America. One species, the Caracara, ranges northward through Central America to the Gulf states and is a common resident in the prairie region of Florida. A striking bird with a well-marked black cap, it is the national bird of Mexico. It nests in the prairie regions of central Florida centred around Kissimmee prairie and Lake Okeechobee, where it often builds its nest in the centre of a cabbage palm. Its two eggs take from 4 to 5 weeks to hatch after incubation by both parents. The young remain in the nest some 10 weeks before they learn to fly.

The caracaras have long, strong legs and walk with agility. They spend quite a bit of time on the ground and feed largely on carrion. Frequently seen with vultures around a carcass, they are boldly aggressive and stand at the top of the pecking order among the New World scavengers. They will drive vultures away from a meal and walk right in and take whatever titbits they want. Like the vultures, they have learned that highways are a good source of food and patrol them watching for animals killed by vehicles.

The falconets, or pygmy falcons, of the subfamily Poliohieracinae occur in South America, Malaya, the Philippines, and Africa. Some nine species are recognized, all of them very small birds. The smallest is the Pygmy Falconet of the Philippines which is only 6 ½ inches in length. Most of these diminutive falcons live on insects; a few of them eat small reptiles. They hunt insects much like flycatchers, sitting on the top of a dead tree and dashing out in short forays after their prey. They usually nest in old woodpecker holes.

The nominate subfamily Falconinae contains the true falcons. It is composed of 35 species all assigned to the genus *Falco*. Typical of these, and one of the most noble, is the Peregrine, for centuries the falconers' favourite bird. The Peregrine shares with the Osprey the distinction of being one of

CARACARA
Caracara cheriway
Extreme southern United States to
Venezuela, Colombia, and Peru   24 in.

PEREGRINE FALCON ♂
Falco peregrinus
Entire Northern Hemisphere,
Australia, South Africa,
Patagonia, Falkland Islands 18 in.

AMERICAN SPARROW HAWK ♂
Falco sparverius
Western Hemisphere, from tree line
south to Tierra del Fuego 12 in.

the most widely distributed of all bird species. It breeds on all the major land masses from the arctic tundras southward through South America, Africa, and Australia. It is absent from New Zealand but has colonized a number of the oceanic outposts as far at sea as the Bonin and Volcano islands. Some 16 geographical races are recognized. The North American population are generally called Duck Hawks.

The swoop of the hunting Peregrine is one of the most thrilling sights in nature. The bird is a fast, strong flier and usually hunts from several hundred feet up in the air, swooping down at tremendous speeds upon its prey. Its dives have been clocked at 175 miles an hour by a pursuing aeroplane. The Peregrine is a clean killer. It strikes its prey once with its feet in passing, usually breaking the prey's back or crippling it so that it falls helplessly to earth. The falcon circles up and around in an Immelmann turn, and comes back to feast at its leisure.

The largest of the hunting falcons is the Gyrfalcon of the arctic tundras, a circumpolar species divided into a number of races varying in colour from pure white to a very dark grey. These large, powerful birds have always been prized by falconers. In medieval times the use of the Gyrfalcon was restricted to royalty. Under the same feudal system, only earls were allowed to use the Peregrine, and only the hunting clergy could fly the small Hobby and Merlin. Common folk were not allowed to hunt with falcons.

Much the same hierarchy prevailed in Japan, where trained hawks were first introduced from Korea in A.D. 355 and presented to the reigning emperor. Shortly thereafter falconry became such a popular sport among the aristocracy that they created and maintained vast game preserves to assure its perpetuation. Hawking remained one of the dominant factors in all wildlife conservation in Japan until the close of the

Tokugawa period less than 100 years ago. Even in modern Japan, long after the scarcity of both hawks and game made hawking impractical, the ancient art has been kept alive for its cultural value and interest by the Imperial Household. Until World War II the Imperial hunting grounds at Saitama maintained a stable of 20 birds.

In Shogunate days, falconry assumed ceremonial aspects. These involved the wearing of traditional costumes and rigid adherence to ritualistic procedures. The leg jesses of the Imperial falcons were coloured according to the bird's rank, based on what it had killed. To obtain the royal purple, the falcon had to have killed the large white Japanese crane, several times its size. Other birds wore red, blue, yellow, and brown jesses, signifying their hunting prowess and accomplishments.

One of the commonest falcons in North America is the wide-ranging Sparrow Hawk, frequently seen perched on telephone wires alongside country roads. Closely related to the European Kestrel, it hunts in much the same fashion, hovering into the wind over meadows and grasslands looking for a mouse or grasshopper on which to pounce. Sparrow Hawk is an unfortunate misnomer for this bird, for while it does occasionally kill small birds, its food is mainly large insects and small rodents, and it is a highly beneficial species. Like its larger relatives, the little Sparrow Hawk can be trained to the wrist and to hunt small birds, mice, or grasshoppers, if you wish. The birds tame easily and make excellent and interesting pets.

Falcons build no nests of their own. Some nest on the ground; more often they nest on cliff ledges the way the Gyrfalcon and the Peregrine usually do, laying their eggs out in the open. Frequently these falcons will appropriate the abandoned tree nests of other species—usually those of another hawk or of a crow. The Merlin is a ground nester, and makes a bare scrape in open moorlands for its eggs. The American Sparrow Hawk nests in holes in trees and will use bird boxes. The larger falcons usually lay from 2 to 4 eggs, the smaller ones from 3 to 5. All need an incubation period of about 4 weeks. Usually the female takes the responsibility for incubation, though the male occasionally may sit on the eggs for a short period during the day while his mate is out hunting. It takes the young from 4 to 6 weeks to fledge and frequently, even after fledging, the young apparently have to be fed by their parents until they develop hunting skills of their own.

RED-THIGHED FALCONET
Microhierax caerulescens
Southeastern Asia, India to Indochina 6-7 in.

FOWL-LIKE BIRDS

GALLIFORMES

The order of fowl-like birds (*gallus* is Latin for cock) is a large one of some 240 species divided among six fairly well-marked families. All have the characteristics of domestic fowl. Most are ground birds with short, stout, down-curved bills and large, heavy feet with three toes in front and a shorter one behind; they are good runners, fly well for short distances, but cannot swim. Their wings are short, rounded, and curved to fit the body. They tend to be permanent residents wherever they occur. Only four species are migratory.

The order is almost cosmopolitan in its distribution, and absent only from Polynesia and Antarctica. The fossil record shows that fowl-like birds were differentiated and were well established as a group early in Tertiary time, 75 million or more years ago. Their relationship to other bird orders is not clear cut. Most of the Galliformes are not overly specialized and the order should appear low on the family tree. Its roots are certainly close to the basic stock from which most birds developed in Mesozoic time.

The recent history of the order is closely tied to that of the development of man. Various Galliformes were among the earliest, if not the first, wild birds to be domesticated. All of them have light, succulent breast meat of pleasing flavour. Many of them are breathlessly beautiful and their only rivals among the sporting birds are the waterfowl. Because of their appeal and attractiveness from all these standpoints, man has captured and bred in captivity members of almost every family, and has been instrumental in expanding the ranges of the more adaptable species.

MEGAPODES OR MOUND BUILDERS

GALLIFORMES   MEGAPODIIDAE

The megapodes, a group of queer Australian and Malayan fowl, are the only animals above the reptiles in the evolutionary scale that do not depend on their own body heat to incubate their eggs or young. They are typical gallinaceous birds ranging in size from that of a bantam chicken to that of a small turkey. The ten known species divided among six genera range from Australia to the Philippines, eastward to Samoa, and westward to the Nicobar Islands.

All are shy ground birds, with a not ungraceful walk. They fly only when hard-pressed, and then only to the lower branches of nearby trees. Yet some make considerable flights over water to roost on offshore islands. Some have the head and neck partly or wholly bare, a few have wattles on the foreneck, one has a casque, and one is crested. All have very large and strong feet, legs, and claws—in fact, *megapod* is a Greek word which means "large foot." The sexes are similar, the males sometimes slightly larger and darker than the females. Their usual voice is a hoarse clucking; at night they are given to mewing notes or noisy cackles. They feed largely on fallen fruit and seeds, but eat some small animals, including crabs. Most megapodes are forest birds that live in valleys or among thickets near rivers or the sea. Some live in dry scrub country. None is migratory.

The most wide-ranging and perhaps the best known of the megapode family are the three scrub fowl of the genus *Megapodius*. These chicken-sized birds are distributed from the

BRUSH TURKEY
Alectura lathami
Eastern Australia   30 in.

MALLEE FOWL
Leipoa ocellata
Central and southern Australia   24 in.

GREAT CURASSOW ♂ ♀
Crax rubra
Southern Mexico to Ecuador 38 in.

female

male

GREAT RAZOR-BILLED CURASSOW ♂
Mitu mitu
Amazon forests from Peru
to the Guianas 35 in.

Philippines, Marianas, and Nicobar islands on the north, east to Samoa, and south into New Guinea and the New Hebrides. The scrub fowl let the heat generated by rotting vegetation incubate their eggs for them. Standing on one foot and scratching backward with the other, they rake together a huge heap of vegetation on the forest floor, piling up a roughly conical mound from 5 to 7 feet high and about 20 feet, sometimes more, in diameter. This may take all the litter from the forest floor for a hundred yards around. Usually a mound is built by a single pair of birds; occasionally they are communal affairs shared by a number of pairs. After the vegetation mixed with soil has started to rot and to generate heat up to around 95° or 96° F, the nest is ready. The female then climbs on the mound, digs a hole several feet deep, and deposits a single egg. She covers the hole up again and returns the next day or the day after to deposit another one. Each female lays from 5 to 8 whitish to salmon-coloured eggs, which soon become stained to a dark brown.

The incubation period is 8 to 9 weeks, which is long indeed for a gallinaceous bird and is exceeded only by the long incubation periods of the largest albatrosses, the Emperor Penguin, and the Kiwi. Throughout the incubation period, the parent birds stay close to the mounds and visit them daily. They are sensitive to the amount of heat generated within, and dig down to the eggs quite frequently, to make sure the temperature is right and perhaps to air them. The young hatch unassisted and work their way up from beneath the soil of their own accord. Well feathered and able to fly immediately, they are on their own from the very start.

Another megapode whose nesting habits have been carefully studied is the Mallee Fowl of Australia, a species confined to the dry growth eucalyptus or "mallee" scrub of south-

ern Australia, a semidesert region of low rainfall and wide extremes of temperatures. The Mallee Fowl go to a great deal of trouble in building their nesting mounds. First they excavate a hole up to 10 feet in diameter and 3 feet deep, which they fill with a combination of vegetation and sand, gradually building it up until it may be 2 to 3 feet above the ground level and from 6 to 18 feet in diameter. In this dry region the eggs are laid early in the spring when there is enough rain to start the vegetation rotting and to provide some heat. As things dry out toward the latter part of the incubation period, the heat of the sun also plays a part. The parent birds watch the mound carefully and open it daily to regulate the amount of heat inside by covering the eggs with sand as needed. The male Mallee Fowl is more assiduous in his care of the mound than is the female and is believed to test the temperature within it with his tongue. The principal activity during the earlier part of the season seems to be to keep the mound from overheating. Later, when the sun becomes the principal source of heat, they increase the temperature reaching the eggs by scratching sand away.

The Maleo Fowl of the Celebes usually deposits its eggs in the black volcanic sand along certain beaches that absorb the rays of the sun's heat best, and some of these birds lay their eggs on the sides of active volcanoes where steam from hot springs does the work for them. The large Brush Turkey of northern Australia, often called the Talegallus, is one of the largest of the megapodes. It builds the largest mounds known, sometimes 50 feet in diameter and 8 to 10 feet high, in which the eggs are incubated entirely by rotting vegetation.

Megapodes frequently use the same mounds year after year, throwing fresh vegetation in them, but the Mallee Fowl often builds its mound from scratch every spring.

86

CURASSOWS, GUANS, AND CHACHALACAS

GALLIFORMES   CRACIDAE

The 38 species of gallinaceous birds comprising this family are found throughout tropical and semitropical America from Texas southward to Argentina. In past ages the family was more widespread in North America. Fossil cracids have been found in Miocene deposits in Florida and in Oligocene deposits in South Dakota.

These fair-sized birds, 20 to 40 inches in length, are notable for their arboreal habits. While they are to a great extent ground feeders, living on vegetation, fruits, insects, and worms, they take refuge in trees when disturbed. They roost in trees at night, and are one of the few members of the order that habitually nest in trees. While their legs and feet are smaller than those of the megapodes of Australia and the East Indies, they share with those weird birds the possession of a large hind toe on the same level with the three front toes. In this respect both differ from all the other Galliformes. Cracids also differ in laying only two or three eggs, which are very large in proportion to the size of the bird, always dull white, peculiarly shaped, and have a roughly granulated shell.

The largest and handsomest birds of the family are the curassows. The seven species are all forest-inhabiting birds the size of turkeys, though not as heavy. They have a crest of strongly recurved erectile feathers and a bright yellow or orange bill frequently with a fleshy cere or a frontal protuberance. The males are usually black, often with white underparts, and the females are usually brown and duller in colour. Their meat is delicious, much like turkey but richer and more flavoured.

WHITE-CRESTED GUAN
Pipile cumanensis
Venezuela and Ecuador to Paraguay
and Argentina   35 in.

RUFOUS-BELLIED CHACHALACA
Ortalis wagleri
Western Mexico   25 in.

The curassows for some strange reason take their name from the island of Curaçao in the Dutch West Indies, where none of them occurs. The Spanish-speaking South and Central Americans always call them *pavo del monte*, or mountain peacock, a not unfitting name. They are gentle birds that tame easily. Though they do not breed well in captivity, they domesticate with no trouble and will consort freely with the farmyard flock.

The guans (the name is of Carib Indian origin), though smaller than the curassows, are also fairly large birds, brownish to olive green in colour; the sexes are alike. They usually have the face, and sometimes part of the throat, bare of feathers. The back feathers frequently give a bronze or coppery reflection. Some of the guans have wattles on the throat. Most of them belong to the genus *Penelope*, of which 11 species are recognized. Guans live mostly in the tops of forest trees and feed on fruit. They are quite gregarious and outside the breeding season may be encountered in sizable flocks.

The chachalacas are the smallest birds of the family, ranging up to 2 feet in length. Thirteen species are placed in the genus *Ortalis*. They are slender, long-tailed, rather graceful birds of the smaller forests, often found along the jungle edges and in open clearings and grassland. Most are rather plain brownish-green to olive in colour, with the naked skin of the throat bright red in most species. Frequently they have a bare greyish space of skin around the eyes. Chachalacas are noisy birds, and flocks cackling together at dawn and dusk produce quite a racket. Their call notes are suggested by their onomatopoeic name which is, of course, taken from their cries and is of native Caribbean origin.

CAPERCAILLIE ♂
Tetrao urogallus
Forested Europe to central Siberia   34 in.

RUFFED GROUSE ♂
Bonasa umbellus
North temperate
North America   18 in.

SAGE GROUSE ♂
Centrocercus urophasianus
West-central North America   28 in.

BLACK GROUSE ♂
Lyrurus tetrix
Forested central Eurasia   21 in.

GROUSE AND PTARMIGANS

GALLIFORMES   TETRAONIDAE

The 18 species of fine game birds this family comprises are all of Northern Hemisphere distribution. Among the grouse, six species of four genera range across temperate and north temperate Eurasia; eight species of six genera are peculiar to the north temperate regions of the New World. The ptarmigan genus, *Lagopus*, is circumpolar in distribution, and two of its four species are also completely circumpolar.

The grouse and ptarmigans are distinctive among the Galliformes in having the tarsus at least partly feathered (often completely so, and the feet as well), in having a short, down-curved bill, the nostrils feathered, and often a patch of brightly coloured bare skin over the eye. All have the hind toe markedly shorter than the front three and slightly elevated above them. Most genera grow fringe-like processes like the teeth of a comb on the sides of the toes in winter. These are shed in summer. Their rather short necks usually sport either an inflatable bare spot or tufts of erectile feathers. The sexes may be alike in colour or different. The males are usually larger than the females, markedly so in some species.

The largest of the grouse is the turkey-sized Capercaillie of Eurasian evergreen forests. The male is a striking black bird about 3 feet in length with a large rounded tail which it extends in a fan when displaying. The hen is fully a third smaller, brownish and dull coloured. Its principal foods throughout the year are the shoots and buds of conifers, augmented by other vegetable matter and berries in season. At breeding time the female and the young boost their protein intake with insects and insect larvae. As it lives only in mature stands of large spruce and pine with some undergrowth of berry-bearing shrubs, the advances of human civilization have driven the Capercaillie farther and farther back as the forests have retreated. While still fairly plentiful in parts of Scandinavia and in the Siberian taiga, it is restricted in most of Europe to mountain forests and private preserves. Because of its size and delicious flesh it is widely hunted. Only its shyness and elusiveness have enabled it to survive this long against mounting hunting pressure.

Capercaillies are usually solitary birds, seldom found in flocks. They are highly polygamous. Each cock takes a harem of from two or three to a dozen or more hens, depending on his virility, and establishes a breeding territory of his own. Old cocks often return to the same place year after year. In early spring the cock repairs to his breeding site, usually an elevated evergreen woodland which affords a view of the surrounding country. Here he perches in a pine tree and starts his long and involved love song. Strutting back and forth on a branch, he crows and calls, spreading his tail turkey fashion. He drives all other males away from his chosen site and fights viciously to guard his domain and his harem.

The females nest within the territory established by the cock in the vicinity of his central lookout and courting post. They usually scrape a crude hollow in the ground with very little lining, often at the base of a tree. The normal clutch is from 5 to 8 eggs which the female incubates alone for the 27 to 29 days it takes them to hatch. The young are reared entirely by the female and they frequently remain in family groups throughout the summer.

Very similar to the Capercaillie in habits and polygamous behaviour is the Black Grouse of Eurasia, which sportsmen call "black game," the male being the "black cock" and the female the "grey hen." A bird of the open mixed woodlands and brushlands, it prefers birch woods fringing open moors, rushy pastures, and marshes. The cock is unmistakable—a black bird the size of a large rooster with lyre-shaped outer tail feathers and a conspicuous white wing bar. In breeding season the cock has red wattles over the eye. The hen is some 5 inches shorter, brownish in colour barred with black.

The Black Grouse is considerably more sociable and gregarious than the Capercaillie. In the spring the males establish communal display grounds called "leks" where each cock establishes a territory of his own on which he goes through elaborate courtship antics to attract the hens. This involves bowing and scraping with tail spread, wings half opened, and the red wattles above the eye distended. The display is accompanied by crowing and a rather musical bubbling song uttered both from the ground and from trees. As in the Capercaillie, the nesting of the Black Grouse is entirely by the female. The species usually nests in open woodlands or on grassy heaths and moors, scraping a hollow in the ground, usually in the shelter of a clump of grass or heather. In this the hen lays 6 to 10 eggs which take from 24 to 26 days to hatch. The young remain with the attending hen for some 3 weeks before they branch out on their own, but they tend to remain, like the Capercaillie, in family groups into the summer and in small flocks of from 10 to 25 birds through the autumn. The sexes usually remain together until the males repair to the leks in spring.

Three North American grouse, the Sage Grouse, the Prairie Chicken, and the Sharp-tailed Grouse, are also polygamous and similar in behaviour and habits to the Capercaillie and Black Grouse. All three have bare air sacs in the sides of the neck that they inflate and puff out to look like small oranges during courtship and which add resonance to their "booming" calls. The most imposing of these is the Sage Grouse, whose distribution coincides almost exactly with that of the sage-brush of the western plains. The largest of the New World grouse, it is second in size only to the Capercaillie. Adult males reach 2½ feet in length and weigh up to 8 pounds; females may be several pounds lighter. When displaying the male puffs out an ornamental ruff of white feathers on the loose skin around its neck and breast like a white feather boa.

The Prairie Chicken and the Sharp-tailed Grouse, in addi-

SPRUCE GROUSE ♂
Canachites canadensis
Conifer forests, Alaska to Labrador,
Oregon to Maine   16 in.

tion to their air sacs, have tufts of erectile feathers on the sides of the neck which stand up straight during their dancing antics. The Prairie Chicken was formerly widespread across all the plainslands of North America, east as far as New England and south to Washington, D. C. The Atlantic seaboard variety, known as the Heath Hen, disappeared from the mainland about 1835 and from then on was confined to Martha's Vineyard in Buzzard's Bay where a small population managed to persist until 1932.

In the early spring, the Prairie Chicken males repair to their booming grounds, usually on slight rises or open ridges in the prairie and will use the same ones every year, unless the character of the land is altered. Here at dawn, and again at dusk, the males go through their elaborate courtship antics, bowing and scraping and posturing with their wings half down, each male on its own particular territory. At the same time they utter a rising three-syllable booming note. Fifty or more birds booming together make a steady, continuous, almost humming sound. The dance that accompanies the booming is spectacular. The cock runs a few steps, stamping his feet rapidly and so hard that the steps can be heard 100 feet or more away, and pivots around in circles with his brilliant orange air sacs inflated, the long neck feathers erected over the head and fleshy orange eyebrows prominently displayed. He then spreads his tail fan-wise, snaps it together with a sharp click, and starts to boom.

The males keep up this performance morning after morning for several weeks until the females appear in late March or early April. Then the tempo and crescendo of the dance and booming increase. Mating takes place rather indiscriminately on the booming grounds, after which each hen selects her nest site and builds a flimsy nest of dead grasses on the ground, usually in the open prairie, sometimes hidden under brush or briar. The usual clutch is from 12 to 16 tan eggs flecked with small brown and red spots. The incubation period is 23 days and the highly precocial chicks leave the nest with the mother bird a few hours after hatching.

The Sharp-tailed Grouse is similar in size and colour to the Prairie Chicken, but slightly more northern in distribution. It also inhabits prairie country, but prefers brushlands and clearings of open forests. Two pointed central tail feathers extend beyond the rest of the tail.

One of the best-loved of North American sporting birds is the Ruffed Grouse, so-called for the ruff-like patches of feath-

WILLOW GROUSE
(winter plumage, summer plumage)
Lagopus lagopus
Northern Northern Hemisphere,
circumpolar 15 in.

PRAIRIE CHICKEN ♂ ♀
Tympanuchus cupido
West-central North America 17 in.

ers on either side of the neck. Sportsmen in North America often call it a "partridge," which it isn't. The Ruffed Grouse is an inhabitant of open deciduous woodlands, mixed forests, and broken scrub country—the pleasantest of all surroundings for a hunter on a crisp October day when the leaves have turned and the land is bright with colour.

Unlike the Prairie Chicken group, the Ruffed Grouse is monogamous. The male's courtship is characterized by his springtime drumming. The sound is familiar to everyone who has been in grouse country in spring—a dull, hollow thumping that starts slowly and increases in tempo until it finishes in a rapid roll like mild thunder. For many years the exact way in which the bird produced the sound was in doubt. Some observers claimed that the birds beat their wings against their drumming log, others that the birds produced the sound by striking their wings against their sides. Some postulated that the wings were struck together behind the back or in front of the breast. Slow-motion pictures of the performance prove that the bird strikes nothing whatever with its wings, and that the sound is produced by the cupped wing brought downward, forward, and then upward in the air as the bird stands motionless on its drumming log, braced back against its tail.

Like most grouse, the Ruffed Grouse raises but one brood a year. The nest is usually built on the ground near the base of a tree. The normal clutch is anywhere from 9 to 14 eggs, with 12 the usual number. The incubation period is about

24 days. The female does all the incubating and caring for the precocial young.

In the evergreen belt that spans North America from the northern United States across Canada to the tree line lives the darker, greyer Spruce Grouse, widely known as the "fool hen" because of its tameness and reluctance to recognize man as a potential enemy. This weakness has proved its undoing near human settlements and, except where rigidly protected in national parks and wildlife reservations, it is now found only in remote north woods where men seldom penetrate. The Spruce Grouse shares with the porcupine the distinction of being one of the few animals that a starving traveller can kill for food without a firearm. When flushed from the ground the birds fly to the nearest tree and perch stolidly on a low branch. They can be pulled down one by one with a wire or stiff string snare on the end of a stick. In summer and autumn, when they feed largely on berries, their flesh is delicious, but in winter and early spring, when their diet is mainly spruce buds, it takes on a turpentine flavour.

Like the Ruffed Grouse, the Spruce Grouse is monogamous. Its courtship also involves drumming, but not as perfect as that of the Ruffed Grouse and often performed in a circular flight above the female. The nesting habits are also similar. The Spruce Grouse nests on the ground, and the incubating and rearing of the young are entirely by the hen.

Quite similar in appearance and habits to the Spruce Grouse is the Blue Grouse of the western mountains, whose various geographical populations are also known as dusky grouse or sooty grouse. Many of these grouse perform a short seasonal migration, nesting in the scrubby evergreen growth near the tree line in spring and summer and retreating down the mountains as winter snows cover the usual food. In remote areas where it is seldom bothered, the Blue Grouse is almost as tame as the Spruce Grouse, but it becomes wary upon contact with man and is a popular sporting bird in western United States and Canada.

A Eurasian counterpart of these grouse is the Hazel Grouse, found in the mixed forests across northern and central Europe and Siberia. It is also tame where undisturbed and an unsatisfactory game bird because it flies poorly, and usually perches in a tree within easy range when flushed. It, likewise, is monogamous and its nesting habits are similar to those of the Spruce Grouse.

The four species of ptarmigans are smallish, rather primitive grouse of boreal distribution. Two species, the Willow Grouse and the Rock Ptarmigan, are completely circumpolar. The White-tailed Ptarmigan is limited to the high western Cordilleras from Alaska south to the northern United States. The fourth is the Red Grouse, a well-known game bird found in the northern parts of the British Isles.

Most northerly of the four is the Willow Grouse, which is widely distributed around the arctic barren lands of both continents and the arctic islands southward into the willow scrub of the subarctic. The Rock Ptarmigan is very similar in size and appearance, differing only in having a slightly smaller bill and a black loral patch that persists even in the otherwise pure white winter plumage. The range of the Rock Ptarmigan extends considerably farther south, and isolated populations survive on mountain tops south as far as the Pyrenees, the Alps, central Asia, and the main island of Japan. The Rock Ptarmigan comes south in the New World as far as Labrador and Newfoundland in the east and to northern British Columbia in the Rocky Mountains.

Ptarmigans are unique in having the toes, as well as the tarsus, completely feathered, supposedly an adaptation to walking in soft snow. They are the most thoroughly monogamous of all the grouse. While the female does all the incubating, the male usually remains nearby and lends a hand with the rearing of the chicks. The young are notoriously precocial and are able to run and hide an hour or two after hatching. The old tale that they can fly with bits of the eggshell still clinging to them is a bit exaggerated, but their wing quills do grow fast and they are usually able to take flight at about the 10th or 12th day.

The most interesting adaptation of the ptarmigans to their arctic and subarctic environment is their two completely different plumages. The exception is the Red Grouse, which lives in the moorlands of Great Britain and Ireland where snow is seldom if ever a problem. It retains its colourful red-brown plumage the year round. Other ptarmigans are protectively coloured pure white in winter. This plumage is assumed during their post-nuptial moult in the autumn. As the snow starts to melt in the spring and patches of brown earth and tundra appear, the ptarmigan starts to moult again into a brownish, more grouse-like plumage. The Rock Ptarmigan retains its white wing feathers throughout all plumages and is unique in having a third greyish plumage stage in the late

autumn, which harmonizes better with the dry grey of the rocky tundra where they live. During the spring and autumn moults ptarmigans take on a patchwork appearance, partly white and partly brown, which harmonizes with the patches of snow in their habitat. Often females moult a little earlier in spring than the males and lose their white plumage sooner, which gives them more protection while incubating.

One of the most intriguing phenomena exhibited by all the grouse is their marked fluctuations in abundance. This is shown to some extent by all species and has been studied intensively in a number, particularly in the Ruffed Grouse. As yet there is no clear picture of the causes. The cycle of peak abundance followed by a rapid dying-off, much as occurs in the famous lemmings, seems to occur regularly at anywhere from 7- to 10-year intervals. The course of the cycle seems to lie in the combination of many factors which are so closely inter-related that it is impossible to separate them out and to lay the blame on any single one. Fortunately, all the grouse have fairly high reproductive potentialities and are able to recover after the cataclysms of one sort or another that periodically cut down their populations to low levels.

RED-LEGGED PARTRIDGE ♂
Alectoris rufa
Western Europe, England to Spain,
Canary Islands 13 in.

BOBWHITE QUAIL ♂
Colinus virginianus
Eastern and central United States
to southern Mexico 10 in.

CALIFORNIA QUAIL ♂
Lophortyx californicus
Oregon to Lower California 9 in.

PAINTED QUAIL ♂
Francolinus pintadeanus
Southeastern Asia, East Indies,
northern Australia 6 in.

CHINESE FRANCOLIN ♂
Excalfactoria chinensis
Southeastern Asia 13 in.

MOUNTAIN QUAIL ♂
Oreortyx pictus
Washington and Idaho to Lower California 11 in.

QUAILS, PARTRIDGES, AND PHEASANTS

GALLIFORMES   PHASIANIDAE

The family Phasianidae is by far the largest and most varied of the gallinaceous birds. Its 178 species range in size from the tiny Painted Quail, scarcely larger than a sparrow, to the giant Argus Pheasant and the peafowl, the monarchs of the order. Many of the smaller quails and partridges are dull-coloured and drab. The pheasants include some of the most incredibly beautiful birds in the avian kingdom, whose breathtaking colours are rivalled only by those of the humming-birds and birds of paradise. The hummingbirds are small avian jewels, but the pheasants display their gaudy brilliance in a spectacular array to delight an advertising man's heart.

The family characteristics are unfeathered nostrils, absence of inflatable air sacs in the neck, feet naked and clean, and the tarsus usually so (partly feathered at the top in only a few species). Many species have heavy spurs on the back of the tarsus above the hind toe. Essentially of temperate and tropical distribution, the family is absent from the polar regions, Oceania, northern North America, southern South America, and northeastern Asia.

The family is so diverse that it is difficult to divide into natural groups, but three fairly well marked subfamilies are generally recognized: the Odontophorinae (the New World

RING-NECKED PHEASANT ♂
Phasianus colchicus
Temperate Asia 35 in.

GOLDEN PHEASANT ♂
Chrysolophus pictus
Highlands of central China 36 in.

LADY AMHERST PHEASANT ♂
Chrysolophus amherstiae
Southeastern Tibet to Upper Burma 50 in.

SILVER PHEASANT ♂
Gennaeus nycthemerus
Highlands of southeastern Asia 39 in.

IMPEYAN PHEASANT ♂
Lophophorus impejanus
Himalayas 23 in.

TEMMINCK'S TRAGOPAN ♂
Tragopan temmincki
Southeastern Tibet to Tonkin 23 in.

quails), the Perdicinae (the Old World quails and partridges), and the Phasianinae (the true pheasants and peafowls).

The New World quails are a fairly homogenous group of small to medium-sized birds, seldom larger than a bantam hen. They lack the spurs sported by the pheasants and most Old World partridges, and have a single serration, or "tooth," in the cutting edge of the upper bill which the other two subfamilies lack. Its 33 species, divided among 10 genera, range from southern Canada to northern Argentina.

Typical of the New World quails, and certainly among the best known, are the Bobwhites, familiar in eastern and southern fields and scrublands, and the plumed California Quail of the lowlands and valleys of the Pacific Coast. Both these species, like all quail, are popular sporting birds. They lie well to dogs, fly fast and straight, and offer a fairly difficult target. They live in good upland hunting country and, of course, are excellent eating.

With the urbanization of much of their range, both species

have happily managed to adapt themselves to man's presence. They have become familiar in the less built-up suburbs, where they have practically attained songbird status, and may even be seen in urban parks. The Bobwhite's cheerily whistled announcement of its name is becoming increasingly familiar around eastern and southern cities of the U.S.A. where the birds have found havens within townships so thickly settled that hunting cannot be permitted. Similarly, large flocks of semi-tame California Quail are one of the most attractive sights in the parks of San Francisco and other West Coast cities.

Both the California Quail and the Bobwhite were introduced to New Zealand with strangely contrasting results. The first California Quail were introduced to North Island in 1865 and successive plantings were made during the next few years. The birds prospered, spread rapidly, and by the turn of the century became so plentiful in some regions that they were hunted for market, and even exported frozen to England. Still one of the commonest New Zealand ground birds, Cali-

REEVES PHEASANT ♂
Syrmaticus reevesii
Highlands of north and
central China 60 in.

FIREBACK PHEASANT ♂
Lophura diardi
Thailand and Indochina 26 in.

COPPER PHEASANT ♂
Syrmaticus soemmerringii
Highlands of Japan 42 in.

SWINHOE'S PHEASANT ♂
Gennaeus swinhoii
Highlands of Formosa 29 in

BROWN EARED PHEASANT ♂
Crossoptilon mantchuricum
Mountains of northeastern China 38 in.

fornia Quail are widespread today over the sheep fields and gorse country of the North Island. Flocks of them roam through the lovely Auckland parks just as they do at Golden Gate Park in San Francisco. Large numbers of Bobwhite were introduced to North Island between 1898 and about 1905. These birds never prospered and the next decade saw them gradually decline. Small numbers are still reported in a few isolated spots, barely managing to hold their own.

None of the New World quails is migratory and all of them tend to be resident wherever they are found, except in the West where some of the mountain species move altitudinally with the changing seasons. As few individual quail move more than a few miles from their birthplace during their lifetimes the resultant lack of gene flow encourages the perpetuation of local variations in size and colour. When these variations are sufficiently marked and stable, the population is distinguished as a subspecies or geographical race. Five subspecies of the Bobwhite are currently recognized in the United States, and 14 more have been described from Cuba, Mexico, and Guatemala. All of them are characterized by differences in shade of colour and in size.

Three other species of bobwhite quail occur from Mexico through Central and South America to Argentina. One, the Black-throated Bobwhite, has a black instead of a white throat. The Crested Bobwhite has a more distinct crest than the other species. The White-breasted, or White-faced, Bobwhite has the entire chin, upper throat, and face white.

The varied habitats of western plains and mountains support the greyish California Quail, and its several relatives with plumed heads and black facial markings. The largest and one of the handsomest of these is the Mountain Quail, sometimes called the Plumed Quail, found widely at medium elevations through the southern Rocky Mountains. Other similar species are Gambel's Quail of the dry arroyos of the Rockies' eastern foothills and the plains of Colorado and Nevada, and the Harlequin Quail, boldly marked with chestnut, black, and white about the face and flanks. It lives at elevations of from 4,000 to 9,000 feet from Arizona to central Texas and south into central Mexico.

Quails are monogamous and all are ground nesters. Most species are highly prolific, laying from 12 to 15 eggs per clutch. In the warmer parts of their range, some multi-brooded species raise as many as three broods in a year. A single brood is the norm for more northern populations. All quail build a sturdy nest on the ground, usually hidden under vegetation. The female does most of the nest building and incubating, but the cock may assist and often takes charge of the young. The incubation period varies among the species from 21 to 25 days. The extremely precocial young run strongly soon after hatching, and shortly are able to catch food for themselves. Their wing quills grow so rapidly they can usually fly short distances at the age of a week.

Quails usually remain in family groups and, as the young mature, families mingle together, sometimes in sizeable coveys of 100 or more birds. They remain in flocks throughout the autumn and into the winter. The Bobwhite is well known for its habit of roosting in coveys at night in a small tight circle, the birds huddled together on the ground with their tails inward and their heads out. Most of the western quail roost at night in bushes or low trees instead of on the ground. These western species are not as satisfactory sporting birds, for they seldom lie closely to the dog and tend to run at the approach of danger rather than lying close and then flying. Many were formerly baited and trapped for market until conservation legislation put a stop to it.

The Old World quail, partridges, and related species of the subfamily Perdicinae total perhaps 95 species of 30 genera. They are so varied a group that it is difficult to characterize them. For the most part they are relatively plain-coloured, small to medium-sized birds, shorter, stouter, and with a deeper build than the New World quail. They lack the toothed serration on the cutting edge of the upper mandible. Most, but not all of them, have spurs on the rear of the tarsus. Widespread over most of Eurasia, Africa, and the Australo-Malayan region, they also include the francolins and the spurfowls.

The smallest of the "true" quails are the little painted quails of the genus *Excalfactoria*, sometimes called the "blue quails." One species is found throughout South Africa, another across southern Asia from India to China, Okinawa, the Philippines, and southward through Indonesia to Australia. Little birds scarcely larger than sparrows, painted quails live in open plains and grasslands where they scurry through the grass and underbrush in small coveys like so many small rodents, and they are about as difficult to flush. Nevertheless

COMMON PEAFOWL ♂
Pavo cristatus
India and Ceylon
80-92 in., including train

94

when once a-wing they fly strongly with a deceptively fast and swerving flight. Most of them are local wanderers, moving considerable distances in search of food.

The only truly migratory members of the order Galliformes are the four species of the widespread genus *Coturnix*. Typical and best known of this group is the migratory Quail of Eurasia, a small mottled brownish bird considerably smaller than the Bobwhite. Birds that breed in Europe and western Asia migrate southward across the Mediterranean into northern Africa. Formerly they migrated in phenomenal, almost unbelievable numbers. The Bible is the authority (Exodus xvi: 13 et seq.) for one such flight in the Sinai Desert, where the Children of Israel gathered them for two days and one night. One researcher has estimated from the Biblical account that the Children of Israel killed some 9 million Quail.

Large flights of Quail continued through the 19th and into the 20th century, when over-exploitation for the market and lack of conservation measures finally decimated the *Coturnix* populations. At the turn of the century the Egyptians were exporting over 2 million each year. This reached a peak of over 3 million in 1920. By the 1930's the big flocks were gone. Similar migrations formerly occurred elsewhere in the species' range. In eastern Asia in the early 1920's Quail were killed and marketed by the millions as they gathered near Port Arthur to cross the Yellow Sea.

The Japanese have successfully domesticated the *Coturnix* Quail and now raise them in large numbers as egg producers. The Japanese keep the hen birds individually in small cages not much larger than the bird itself. Individual birds so confined will lay up to 200 eggs per year. These dainty little eggs, prettily spotted with dark red-brown, are often more plentiful in the Tokyo markets than hens' eggs.

Because of the ease with which they are obtained abroad and raised in captivity, a number of attempts have been made to introduce the *Coturnix* Quail to North America as a game bird. The most recent effort was in the mid-1950's when thousands were released throughout our southern states. Though a few birds bred successfully in the wild the year of release, every such attempt has met with failure. The birds migrated in the autumn and never returned. Those released in the Gulf states probably vanished into the Gulf of Mexico.

A close relative of the Eurasian migratory Quail is the Harlequin Quail of South Africa whose head, throat, and breast are gaily striped with black, white, and chocolate-tan. These birds are very erratic in their seasonal movements. They sometimes descend on a district in large numbers, breed almost everywhere, and disappear in a few weeks.

Their movements seem to be governed largely by the amount of rainfall. Another related species is fairly common in Australia. Still another formerly occurred in New Zealand, but has been extinct since about 1870.

The partridges and francolins are slightly larger birds, none of them migratory and all of them highly regarded as sporting birds. Two of the European species, the Grey Partridge and the Red-legged Partridge, have been introduced into North America with some local success. The Grey Partridge is known in the U.S.A. as the Hungarian or Hun, and is a popular game bird where it has succeeded, mostly in the Middle West.

The francolins and spurfowl are the largest of the subfamily, some reaching 18 inches in length and weighing up to 3½ pounds. Very similar to the partridges in habits and appearance, most are dull-coloured inhabitants of brush and open grasslands. They are difficult to flush but when once a-wing they fly fast and straight.

The 50-odd species of true pheasants include some of the showiest birds in the entire avian kingdom. The fine feathers here all belong to the males; their consorts are invariably drab. The true pheasants are all clean-legged birds, usually spurred (a few genera lack spurs), and are characterized by a long ornate tail which is always arched or "vaulted" into an inverted V-shape in cross section.

The native home of the pheasants is central and southern Asia south into the Malay Archipelago. One single species, the Congo Peacock, managed to remain hidden in that West African river rainforest until very recently, when its discovery far from the range of any other known pheasant electrified the ornithological world. So attracted has man always been by the beauty and the utility of these wonderful birds that he has interfered greatly with their natural distribution. Thanks to this, pheasants are, without question, the most widely distributed of all birds in the world, for to this family belong all the domestic fowl.

The "typical" pheasant and certainly one of the most widespread and best known today is the Ring-necked, or English, or Mongolian, Pheasant which Linnaeus, the father of modern taxonomy, named *Phasianus colchicus,* the Pheasant of Colchis. Before man interfered with its distribution it ranged from Asia Minor across southern and central Asia to eastern

China and Korea. According to fairly well substantiated legend, some birds of the western population which lack the white neck-ring, were brought from Colchis to Greece by the Argonauts, and could well have been the Golden Fleece that Jason sought.

The name pheasant is an English corruption of the Latin *Phasianus,* which in turn was derived from the Greek *Phasianornis,* which means "the bird of Phasis." Phasis was the old name of a river in the ancient province of Colchis, which lay just eastward of the Black Sea, where the Greek Argonauts may have found the original stock they brought home with them. The present distribution of the subspecies seems to bear this out or, at least, casts no doubt on it. The Romans are credited with carrying this stock to England.

Some 40 different racial populations of the Common Pheasant have been described. It was the dark-necked form, without the white neck-ring, that was first introduced into the United States from England about 1790, first into New Hampshire and then into New Jersey, and which soon established itself along the Atlantic seaboard. Stock of the same species, but of eastern races from China and Mongolia with white neck-rings, was first introduced into California in 1857. Large numbers were released in Oregon in the 1880's. Since then the bird has gradually acclimatized itself in a broad belt across southern Canada and the northern United States and is now listed as a game bird in all but three states.

The present game pheasant of the continental United States is a hybrid bird, a mixture of many wild populations. The white neck-ring has persisted over the dark-necked form, which has practically disappeared. In Europe, the black-necked bird is still by far the commoner. The species has also been introduced successfully into New Zealand, the Hawaiian Islands, Samoa, and St. Helena.

High in the mountains from the Himalayas eastward across China to Japan, Formosa, and Indochina live a number of breathtakingly beautiful pheasants which are frequently seen in zoos. Among the most popular and startling of these are the Golden Pheasant, the Silver Pheasant, and the graceful Lady Amherst Pheasant. The magnificent male Reeves Pheasant

QUAIL ♂
Coturnix coturnix
Temperate Eurasia,
Africa, Madagascar   8 in.

has an incredibly long tail which makes it one of the longest birds alive today, measuring a full 5 feet from the tip of the tail to the tip of the beak.

Seldom found in captivity is the wild and wary Copper Pheasant of the highlands of Japan, one of the finest sporting birds in the world. It lives in rugged, mountainous country, usually on the edges of cryptomeria or cypress forests. When it flushes it dives down the mountainside over the heads of puffing hunters with deceptive speed. The Copper Pheasant is still fairly plentiful in its native haunts. It does not tame easily and has only recently been bred successfully in captivity.

Several pheasants are so shy, or else live in such difficult country, that they escaped discovery until fairly recently. About 1900 a British collector obtained two strange long black feathers from aborigines in the Formosa mountains. Several years later a complete specimen was obtained, and shortly live birds were caught and taken into captivity. This was the distinctive Mikado Pheasant—shiny black and boldly marked with white—a striking pheasant, unlike any other known.

Even more startling was the discovery in the Congo rainforests in the 1930's of a shy jungle peafowl, the first of the true pheasants known from Africa. For over 20 years only a single feather of this bird was known. Then, by some of the most persistent detective work ever done, Dr. James Chapin found the handsome bronze and green Congo Peacock in the depths of swampy wet jungles of the Congo where it had survived until then unknown in science.

High in the Himalayas and in the adjoining mountains of India and China live heavy-bodied, short-tailed pheasants known as the impeyan pheasants or monals, and the tragopans or horned pheasants. The tragopans have rather short rounded tails, the feathers of which, unlike those of the rest of the pheasants, all lie in one plane instead of being arched. They are beautifully patterned rather than brightly coloured. This group is unique among the pheasants in being tree-dwellers, and the tragopans are tree nesters. Most of them have horn-like protuberances and fleshy wattles about the head. The impeyan pheasants live in the highest mountains, usually near the snowline, and are the most iridescent and brilliantly coloured of all the pheasants.

Deep in the jungles of the Malayan Peninsula, Sumatra, and Borneo lives the Great Argus Pheasant, 6 to 7 feet in length including the long tail. The secondary flight feathers of this species are greatly elongated, broadened, and patterned down the centre with a chain of eye-spots which are, of course, responsible for its name. Unlike most other pheasants, the argus pheasants are not brilliantly coloured, being mainly brown and grey, but they are exquisitely marked with black. They are so shy and timid that very little is known of their habits in the wild. Some students believe that the Great Argus, or its relative, Reinhart's Argus Pheasant, may have been the origin of the ancient Egyptian and oriental legends of the Phoenix. Most, however, believe it was the Golden Pheasant or a bird of paradise.

The ancient history of the peafowl and its early contacts with man is more adequately documented. The Common Peafowl, a familiar resident of most zoos, has been semi-domesticated for ages. A native of southern India and Ceylon, it was apparently well known to the ancient Greeks and Romans who made it part of their mythologies as a favourite

JUNGLE FOWL ♂ ♀
Gallus gallus
Southeastern Asia 30 in.

bird of the goddess Juno or Hera. In several places the Bible mentions that King Solomon, who built his fabulous temple about 1000 B.C., imported peafowl to the Holy Land.

Though they have been widely kept as ornamental birds on estates in this country, and America, peafowl are quarrelsome and do not mix well with other domestic animals. The long ornamental feathers, which the peacock displays so magnificently before the peahen, are not its true tail feathers but are elongated upper tail coverts.

A second species of peafowl, the Javanese Peafowl, which ranges through the wet jungles from Burma south through the Malayan Peninsula and Indochina to Java, is very similar to the Common Peafowl in size, form, and colour, but its head, neck, and underparts are green instead of blue, and its crest feathers are fully webbed and come to a point behind the forehead. Wild peafowl inhabit open dry forest country and travel in small flocks, feeding on the ground. They fly strongly but lumberingly and roost in trees at night. Their voice is a harsh, unpleasant screech not at all in keeping with the beauty of their plumage.

By far the most important bird to man and, thanks to his influence and interference, certainly the most plentiful and the most widespread of all avian species, is the common domestic fowl. Of all wild birds, this one has proved to be the most amenable and tractable to domestication. So many strains have been developed through breeding that many modern forms bear little resemblance to their wild ancestors.

Nevertheless, domestic fowl are pheasants. Their ancestors are probably one of the four species of jungle fowls that range from India and Ceylon eastward to Indochina and Java.

These wild jungle fowl differ from the other pheasants in having a comb and wattles about the head and in having the tail more arched and curved. Anthropologists believe they were first domesticated by Bronze Age peoples about 4000 B.C. There is clear evidence of their being in domestication in India in 3200 B.C. Domesticated birds were raised all around the Mediterranean, and the Romans, as we well know, used them for sacrifices and for auguries.

Our Indo-European ancestors were not the only ones to domesticate the jungle fowl, for Asiatic seafarers carried them to the Philippines and to many Polynesian islands. Until recently the first poultry were thought to have been taken to the New World by Europeans after its discovery by Columbus. Recent evidence that Central and South American Indian tribes had domesticated poultry when the Spaniards first made contact with them suggests that poultry may have reached South America in pre-Columbian days from eastern Asia, carried by Polynesian seafarers.

The keeping of game-cocks for cock fighting by primitive peoples is believed more responsible for the birds' early spread and domestication than its food-producing potentialities either for meat or for eggs. The fighting cocks of today bear the strongest resemblance to the wild ancestral stock. The greatest divergencies from the wild stock have been made for food production or for ornament. The most ornamental domestic birds are the long-tailed fowls developed by the Japanese. In this strain the central tail feathers are not moulted as in all other pheasants, but continue to grow through the bird's life. Fanciers take great pride in raising birds whose tail feathers extend 20 feet and more in length.

GUINEAFOWLS

GALLIFORMES   NUMIDIDAE

Guineafowls are found in the wild only in Africa south of the Sahara, and in Madagascar. Seven species are known, assigned to five genera. All seven are unmistakably similar, typified by the familiar domestic guineafowl with its bare head and neck, sleekly curved body of smooth dark feathers spangled with white, and short tail almost completely hidden by the tail coverts.

Largest and most striking of the family is the Vulturine Guineafowl, so called from the resemblance of its head to that of an Old World vulture. An inhabitant of the thorn-covered plains of East Africa, it is the only species in which the tail feathers project beyond the tail coverts. In the wooded valleys of the brush country of South Africa live three species of crested guineafowls whose otherwise bare crowns sport tufts of bristly feathers. The somewhat different bony-crested guineafowls are birds of open forests and grasslands of West Africa. One of these, the Helmeted Guineafowl, is the ancestor of the domestic guineafowl. The other two are the rather rare and little-known Black Guineafowl and the Turkey, or White-breasted, Guineafowl. Both of these species have rudimentary spurs on their tarsi, evidence of the family's distant relationship to the pheasants.

Guineafowls were apparently domesticated by the ancient Greeks and Romans who brought them from Africa and called them Numidian birds—hence the scientific name of the family. This domestic stock disappeared early in the Christian era. The bird was apparently unknown to medieval Europeans until the intrepid Portuguese navigators of the 15th century ventured down the west coast of Africa and brought stock of Helmeted Guineafowl back from the Guinea coast.

Though the horny helmet tends to increase in size in captivity, domestication and selective breeding have wrought relatively few changes in the Helmeted Guineafowl. Some pure white strains and other colour variants have been produced, but the birds' basic structure and habits remain unchanged.

This may reflect a sturdy, innate lack of plasticity in the species, but more likely is because the birds have not received the same kind of attention we have given to the domestic fowl.

From the poultryman's viewpoint, guineafowl are neither productive nor profitable. Their egg production is low and the birds are a bit tricky to raise. Their flesh, however, is exceedingly tasty and those raised commercially today are produced mainly for the high-priced gourmet's market. Besides its gastronomic value, the domestic guineafowl has traditionally won its keep by being the watchdog of the farmer's flock. At the first hint of danger the guineafowl's harsh, strident clamour alerts the farmer to the presence of a possible predator, be it a human thief, a threatening hawk, or a slinking cat or weasel. Their ear-splitting cackling, released at the slightest provocation, can be a nuisance around the farmyard. Probably another reason for their lack of popularity today is that guineafowl are particularly noisy when they go to roost at night. Like a bunch of teenage girls in a dormitory, it takes them a good while to settle down and get to sleep.

In the wild all guineafowl are gregarious. They travel in flocks of anywhere from a dozen up to several hundred birds. The flocks disperse only when the birds pair off during the breeding season, and re-form again as soon as the young are able to fend for themselves. They are great runners and usually elude their enemies by running rather than flying. Flocks are known to move as much as 20 miles in a day, entirely on foot.

Though essentially ground birds, guineafowl can fly strongly when necessary. They always fly up into trees to roost at night, a habit retained by the domestic birds. Domesticated guineafowl have gone wild in eastern Cuba and Hispaniola in the West Indies. There have been many attempts to introduce the guineafowl into New World prairies and brushlands as a game bird, but its habit of running from danger rather than flying does not make for good shooting and discourages these efforts.

TURKEYS

GALLIFORMES   MELEAGRIDIDAE

The turkeys show many similarities to the pheasants but enough differences to warrant giving them separate family status. While male turkeys have spurs, they have rudimentary webs between their toes, and their tails are not vaulted. Their naked heads and necks give them a superficial resemblance to the guineafowl, with which early writers confused them. Their generic name, *Meleagris* (from Meleager, the mythical hero of the Calydonian boar hunt), was already fittingly in use for the Helmeted Guineafowl when the great Linnaeus misapplied it to the turkey.

Just how they received the highly inappropriate English name "turkey" has never been satisfactorily explained. Con-

fusion with the guineafowl (Turkey was a general name for all Moslem countries, including those in Africa, in the 15th and 16th centuries) is doubtless partly responsible, possibly encouraged by the bird's clucking "turk-turk-turk." At any rate, they were widely known as "turkie-fowle" in 16th-century England, when they reportedly were first served as a table delicacy to Henry VII. They were in common use for holiday feasting by the time of James I.

Despite their name, the turkeys are entirely indigenous to the New World, and were first brought to Europe by the Spanish conquistadors who found them domesticated by the Indians in Mexico early in the 16th century. The ancestral home of the two species in the family formerly extended from Maine to South Dakota and southward through Mexico to Guatemala. As the seven species known as fossils date back 40 million or more years to Oligocene time and are all from American deposits, there is no question of the American ancestry of these birds. Benjamin Franklin had good grounds for preferring the adoption of the turkey, a thoroughly native, useful, and handsome bird, as the national symbol of the U.S.A. in preference to the Bald Eagle, a fish-eating scavenger native also to Canada and northeastern Asia.

The Common Turkey ranges today from the eastern United States to southern Mexico. The birds vary somewhat in colour and size throughout their wide range, and seven geographical races are currently recognized. The population of eastern and northern Mexico, some of which the conquistadors took to Europe, is the ancestor of the domestic turkey. These birds differ from the wild turkeys of the eastern United States mainly in having lighter tips to the tail feathers.

Less familiar is the Ocellated Turkey of the Yucatan peninsula, British Honduras, and Guatemala. This bird of the subtropical lowlands is strikingly similar to the Common Turkey but is smaller and lacks a beard-like chest tuft. It has the bare skin of its head blue instead of red, and is ornamented with different types of wattles and protuberances. Most distinctive are the long, rounded tail feathers, each marked near the end with the prominent staring eyespot responsible for its vernacular name.

Turkeys are woodland birds that like open mixed forests. They roam about in small flocks feeding on the ground and roost at night in the trees. They are strong fliers but never fly long distances and are not migratory. They are as polyg-

amous in the wild as they are in the barnyard, and the strutting, gobbling courtship display of the Common Turkey is too familiar to need description. After mating the turkey hens go off by themselves to build their nests on the ground. A hen lays from 8 to 15 eggs which require 28 days of incubation, and each hen rears her own brood of young.

The wild turkeys that the Pilgrim Fathers found on their arrival in New England remained so plentiful until Washington's time that they were sold in the markets for a cent or two a pound. Then, as is so often the case, man pushed forward, the forests disappeared, and hunting pressure increased. The last wild bird vanished from New England woods more than a century ago. Thanks to the regulation of hunting and to good game management, turkeys are still common enough in woodlands from Pennsylvania southward into Florida to justify a short open hunting season each year.

Though the turkey has been domesticated for more than four centuries, only within the past decades have poultrymen attempted to improve the strain by selective breeding. The most popular result of their efforts is the smaller white turkey which plucks more easily than the bronze type, matures more quickly, and has a larger breast of white meat. Few ovens in apartment kitchens are large enough to hold a noble 30-pound gobbler, and in truth the smaller birds seem to be more tender if not as tasty.

OCELLATED TURKEY ♂
Agriocharis ocellata
Yucatan, British Honduras, Guatemala 36 in.

WILD TURKEY ♂
Meleagris gallopavo
Southeastern United States
and Mexico 48 in.

VULTURINE
GUINEAFOWL ♂
Acryllium vulturinum
Tropical East Africa 24 in.

HOATZIN

GALLIFORMES   OPISTHOCOMIDAE

The Hoatzin is an avian anachronism that has given bird classifiers trouble ever since its peculiarities became known in the early 19th century. It has so many unique features, of both anatomy and behaviour that some systematists feel it deserves separate ordinal rank by itself. It shows some structural affinities to the cuckoos, but most students now agree that it is most closely allied to the Galliformes. This is confirmed by recent studies of the composition of its egg-white proteins.

The Hoatzin's peculiar name is of Nahuatl (Aztec) Indian origin. It is a slender, somewhat pheasant-like, brownish bird 2 feet in length, with a long, loose crest of rather stiffly shafted feathers. Its bill is short and stout, its neck long and slender, and its head rather small for its size. Its strong legs are of medium length, its toes long and strong, and its wings and tail long and rounded. Its voice is limited to a harsh screeching and a monotonous throaty chattering.

The Hoatzin lives only in the shrubby trees bordering tropical streams in northeastern South America from the Amazon region northward through the Guianas and Venezuela to eastern Colombia. Small colonies of 10 to 50 birds live together. A pair builds a platform of sticks for a nest in the river shrubbery, anywhere from 5 to 20 feet above the water. The female lays 2 to 3 white eggs spotted with brown, which strongly resemble those of a rail.

Little is known of the sharing of parental duties, but incubation takes 28 days. At hatching the almost naked chick shows the species' most interesting primitive peculiarity. At the tip of each wing are two well-developed, functional claws. Soon after hatching the chick starts to creep, using all four limbs in reptile fashion and using the wing claws to cling to branches as it crawls from its nest. The claws disappear after the first 2 or 3 weeks and no vestige of them remains in the adult bird. Their presence in the chick suggests their presence in a long-vanished and unknown ancestor. An adult bird with functional wing claws could be one of the many missing links in the evolution of birds from reptiles.

Another peculiarity of the chick is its ability to swim well should it fall into the water. It can get back to its tree and clamber up again. This ability is lacking in the young of all other gallinaceous birds. Hoatzins also have a peculiar musty body odour which is so strong that British residents of the Guianas call them "stink birds."

The other unique characteristic of the Hoatzin is its immense, well-developed, heavily muscled, two-part crop, which seems to work as a sort of gizzard. The crop is used both for storage and for starting digestion of the rubbery leaves of the arum plants that are the species' main food. So enormous is the crop that it occupies fully a third of the forward part of the body and has displaced the shoulder girdle and sternum. It has reduced the size of the keel and the flying muscles. The short keel occupies only the posterior third of the Hoatzin's sternum, and the flying muscles are so weak that the bird flies poorly. It can do little more than glide from the top of the bushes on one side of a stream to the bottom branches of those on the other side. Naturally this makes the species quite sedentary, and small populations have remained isolated in their little river valleys for generation after generation.

It is interesting to speculate on the Hoatzin's history through the distant past. It shows such a peculiar combination of primitive yet highly specialized characteristics that its placement in any lineal scheme of classification is doubly difficult. It is one of those peculiar relics that has remained relatively unchanged for ages in a narrow, restricted range, while its farther-ranging relatives moved away and disappeared in the process of evolution. The Hoatzin remains behind as a vague clue to possible characteristics of the pre-avian ancestors of modern birds.

RANGE OF HOATZIN

HOATZIN
Opisthocomus hoazin
Amazon forest region   24 in.

CRANES, RAILS, AND ALLIES

GRUIFORMES

This order is a conglomeration of 11 rather diversified living families, 7 of which contain 3 species or less, and 10 families that are known only as fossils. Its members are united mainly on the basis of their internal anatomy, particularly similarities in skeletal and muscular structures. These show the 199 living (or recently extinct) Gruiformes to be a discrete group with no near relatives, despite superficial resemblances to birds of other orders. Their closest relationships seem to be with the Galliformes (fowl-like birds) on the one hand and the Charadriiformes (shore birds, gulls, and auks) on the other; hence they are placed between these two orders. The order's distribution is world-wide except for the polar regions.

As their fossil history goes back to earliest Tertiary time, the cranes and their allies are of ancient lineage. This is also borne out by the order's large number of distinctive small families of restricted yet widely separated distributions. The order is not only ancient, but seems to be rapidly declining. It has a higher percentage of recently extinct forms and of living forms on the verge of extinction than any other major order of birds.

It is difficult to define the group without recourse to polysyllabic anatomical terms, but its members are more or less aquatic birds, most of them marsh inhabitants. A few dwell on dry plains and even in deserts. They have varied, though always hard, bills, short tails, rounded wings, comparatively long necks, and moderate to long legs. Their toes vary from medium to long. The hind toe when present is sometimes elevated, but in most species is about level with the front ones. The front toes are unwebbed, but in the coots and the finfoots each toe is "lobed" individually with broad membranous flaps. Colours are extremely variable, but are seldom bright. The sexes are usually alike, or nearly so, except in the bustards, where the females always have a more concealing pattern than the males.

Gruiformes are either of large size and strong flight, or of small to medium size and relatively weak flight. A large number are flightless. All members of the order fly with the neck extended straight out in front and usually with the feet trailing conspicuously behind. The young hatch covered with down and leave the nest shortly after hatching. In most families both sexes share the nesting duties. Only in the bustards do the females do all the incubating and rearing of the young. In some of the more primitive families the males assume most of these responsibilities.

MESITAE

GRUIFORMES   MESITORNITHIDAE

This is another of those families that seem to exist just to plague bird classifiers. Its three rail-like members live on the ground in the forests and brushlands of Madagascar, that home of many animal oddities. The native Malagasy call them "roatelos" (of uncertain significance—it means two-three), but ornithologists usually refer to them by their original generic name, *Mesites*, which is a Greek term for a mediator. Unfortunately this seems to have no more significance than the native name for the bird.

The three mesitae are sombre grey-brown to ruddy and olivish birds 10 to 11 inches in length. They run well but fly very little if at all. Reflecting their comparative flightlessness is the reduction of their clavicles to mere stubs. A puzzling anatomical feature is their possession of five pairs of powder-down patches, more than any other bird, and a characteristic which other Gruiformes lack.

One species, *Monias benschi*, sometimes called Bensch's Rail, is believed both flightless and polyandrous—the female mates with several males. In this species the sexes differ in colour, and the male builds the nest and does the incubating. In the other two species, both of the genus *Mesoenas*, the sexes are alike, and the female is believed to do most of the incubating.

Mesitae build frail platform nests of sticks and leaves a few feet above the ground in a low tree or bush. They reach their nests by climbing, not flying. They usually lay a single white or buffy-grey egg, though as many as three have been reported. At hatching the chicks are covered with black down as in the rails. The food of all three species consists of insects, seeds, and small fruit, with an increase in insects during the breeding season.

BROWN MESITES
Mesoenas unicolor
Eastern Madagascar   10 in.

HEMIPODES

GRUIFORMES   TURNICIDAE

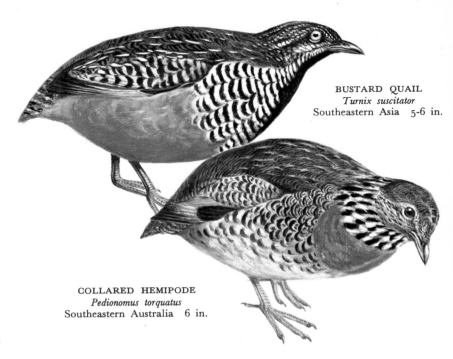

BUSTARD QUAIL
Turnix suscitator
Southeastern Asia   5-6 in.

COLLARED HEMIPODE
Pedionomus torquatus
Southeastern Australia   6 in.

The 16 species in this group are small, dull-coloured, running birds, and comparatively weak fliers. Superficially they resemble the Old World quails. In fact the first ones I encountered in the field in Korea looked so like a quail I did not realize what they were until I had one in my hand. Then its different colour, its lack of a hind toe, and its slender, weaker bill showed it to be the northeasternmost of the hemipodes, the little Chinese Button-quail, which is also the only migratory member of the family.

The family is largely restricted to the southern parts of the Eastern Hemisphere. Its members range from southern Spain throughout Africa and Madagascar, and from India and China southeastward through the Philippines and Malaya to New Guinea, Australia, New Caledonia, and the Solomon Islands. A more fitting name for them is "bustard quail," for they are anatomically nearer the bustards and they inhabit the same sort of open grasslands and brush country.

Hemipodes are tiny birds from 5 to 8 inches in length, and all have similar concealing colours. All run through the grass-lands like small rodents and seldom take flight unless pressed. They fly weakly and for only short distances. Also unlike the quails, the hemipodes are never found in flocks, but usually singly or in pairs. Though the sexes are similar, the female in usually slightly larger and more brightly coloured. This is reflected by their polyandrous nesting habits. The female does the courting, and in some species may take several mates during a season. After she makes a crude nest on the ground, usually concealed under the grass, and lays her 3 to 5 (usually 4) eggs, her mate takes over and does all the incubating and the rearing of the young. The chicks are highly precocial and are able to run almost the moment they leave the shell. The incubation period of only 13 days in the South African species appears to be the shortest known for any precocial bird. The males brood and help the chicks find food for about 10 days.

Fourteen of the bustard quails are united in the single genus *Turnix* and are remarkably similar in size, colour, and habits throughout their extensive range. One aberrant species is the little 5-inch Quail Plover, or Lark Quail (*Ortyxelos*), that lives in the dry, sandy scrub country of north central Africa just south of the Sahara Desert. This bird looks more like a lark than like a quail or hemipode, especially when on the wing. It has white shoulder patches and white tips to its otherwise black wings which contrast markedly in flight. Unlike the other hemipodes it lays only two eggs, but otherwise its habits are reported to be similar.

The most aberrant species is the Collared Hemipode, or "plains wanderer," of the central deserts of Australia. Its behaviour and habits are typical of the hemipodes, but it has a number of structural anomalies which have led some systematists to place it in a family of its own. Among these are its retention of a well-developed hind toe, paired instead of single carotid arteries, and strongly pointed rather than oval eggs. Like the hemipodes it is a shy, retiring bird that runs when disturbed, seldom takes flight, but crouches and hides in the grass. Observed in captivity, the Collared Hemipode seems to be somewhat nocturnal in its activities. It has a peculiar habit of raising itself high on the tips of its toes to survey the country around it.

CRANES

GRUIFORMES   GRUIDAE

No more spectacular group of birds exists than the world's 14 species of cranes, and possibly no group is more in need of protection. Their numbers have been sadly depleted in the last century, and the very existence of several species is now seriously threatened.

All the cranes are large, stately inhabitants of open marsh-lands, wet plains and prairies, and, occasionally, sandy flats and seashores. They are found throughout the world except in South America, the Malayan Archipelago, the Pacific Islands, and New Zealand. As a group they are all long-legged, long-necked birds, usually with the head in the adult partly bare of feathers, with a short, wide tail, and long, wide wings. Their short hind toe is considerably elevated above the others and this normally bears none of the birds' weight when they walk. Cranes always fly with the neck extended straight out in front.

A distinctive anatomical feature is their trachea, or windpipe, which is shaped differently in each species but is always strongly convoluted like the coils of a trumpet. In some species it pierces through the breastbone and the flying muscles.

WHOOPING CRANE
Grus americana
North-central North America 50 in.

CROWNED CRANE
Balearica pavonina
Africa from Nile valley southward 38 in.

SANDHILL CRANE
Grus canadensis
hwestern and southeastern
North America 44 in.

DEMOISELLE CRANE
Anthropoides virgo
South-central Eurasia 38 in.

SARUS CRANE
Grus antigone
India, Burma, Thailand 60 in.

WHITE-NAPED CRANE
Grus vipio
Eastern Siberia 50 in.

This organ gives the cranes their resonant and far-carrying cries, which can be heard several miles away. Most cranes have a loud, clarion-like trumpet note which they utter not only in flight to keep the flock together, but on the ground as well. And on the ground, they add many other notes, some of them quite musical, attractive, and pleasant to hear. They also clack their bills audibly the way storks do.

Most of the cranes are strongly gregarious. They migrate and winter in large flocks. Migrating cranes travelling high in the air in a strong V or a long, extended echelon are a beautiful sight. When travelling any distance, as in their long migrations, they frequently fly at considerable altitudes, reportedly as high as 2 miles. Their wingbeats are regular and steady, usually a slow downstroke followed by a more rapid upstroke. Cranes seldom glide except when they are preparing to land.

Cranes find sustenance in a great variety of foods, both vegetable and animal, and forage in all types of open country, dry upland fields as well as wet marshes. Vegetable matter usually predominates in their diet, and they are fond of all sorts of grains, berries, small fruits, and tender roots. They also eat insects and insect larvae, worms, snails, amphibians and reptiles, small birds and mammals, but very few fish. A common method of feeding is by probing and digging into soft ground with their strong bills for succulent roots and grubs. When foraging in dry stubble fields and open hillsides, which they often do, the flocks fly regularly once or twice a day to the nearest water. They drink by dipping their bill below the surface almost to the nostrils, then raising the head quickly to swallow.

One of the most spectacular habits of the cranes, characteristic of the entire family, is their dancing ceremonies. In these the birds walk stiffly around each other with quick steps, wings half spread. Alternately, they leap high in the air, with wings half spread and legs held gracefully below them. These antics are frequently interspersed with deep bowings and stretchings. The birds pick up sticks or pieces of grass in their beaks, throw them up in the air, and stab at them with their beaks as they come down. Both sexes take part in these antics, and immature birds dance almost as often and as actively as the adults do.

While the dancing is, at times, an integral part of courtship, the birds indulge in it throughout the year and some observers believe it is more an expression of exuberance and general liveliness than an inherent sexual display. Sandhill Cranes have been observed leaping 15 to 20 feet in the air in these dances. Occasionally whole flocks on the wintering grounds, or on the resting grounds while migrating, will go through these antics together. Some observers call them ungainly; others call them very graceful. They may be an outlet of emotion, or perhaps just a playful release of energy. Whatever the reason, it is a fascinating performance greatly enhanced by the immense size of the actors.

All the cranes are ground nesters, and build fairly bulky nests of vegetation in marshy areas, frequently surrounded by water. The normal clutch is 2 eggs; occasionally only one is laid, rarely 3. The eggs are a dull-white to brown and spotted with darker shades of brown, except those of the Crowned Crane which are a clear, pale blue. The eggs are usually laid at 2-day intervals and, as the incubation usually begins with the first egg, the young frequently hatch two days apart. The incubation period in the various species varies from about 28 to 35 days. Both parents share the duties of nest building, incubating, and caring for the young. The young hatch covered with mottled red-brown to greyish down and can run actively as soon as they hatch. Though they grow rapidly, it takes them about 10 weeks to reach the flying stage.

Cranes are traditionally long-lived birds and among the Japanese are one of the symbols of longevity. In Japanese folklore the crane is supposed to live a thousand years, the turtle ten thousand. Both these animals are frequently used as symbols for a long and happy life in birth and wedding ceremonies, the crane frequently perched on the turtle's back. The maximum life span of any crane is probably much less than a hundred years. The oldest crane for which there is a reliable record is one that recently passed its 55th birthday in the Washington Zoo. A long breeding life is to be expected in a bird that has such a slow rate of reproduction, for cranes have small clutches and breed but once a year. This adds to the difficulty these large birds have maintaining themselves in the face of adversity. Such factors as shooting with modern weapons, the encroachment of civilization on their breeding and wintering grounds, disease, storms during migration, excessively cold winters, and bad weather during the breeding season all make survival difficult.

Most typical of the cranes are the 10 species of the genus *Grus*, which has its greatest development across Eurasia, where seven species are found. Best known of these is the Common Crane that breeds widely across northern Eurasia and winters south to Africa. Other palaearctic species include the little-known Black-necked Crane of central Siberia, the White-headed Crane of eastern Asia, the Japanese Crane of Manchuria and northern Japan, and the White and the White-naped cranes of eastern Asia. The stately Sarus Crane breeds across southeastern Asia from India to the Philippines. A close ally is the Brolga, or Native Companion, a tall silvery grey bird with dark-brown wings, and naked red skin at the sides of the face and back of the neck, found in Australia and southern New Guinea. In this genus are the only New World members of the family, the Whooping and Sandhill cranes of North America.

The smallest of the cranes are the two dainty demoiselles, scarcely 3 feet in length. They are soft grey in colour with contrasting black neck plumes and flight feathers and long white plumes curving from behind the eye down to the back of the neck. The true Demoiselle, which is commonly seen in zoos, breeds from southeastern Europe east across central Asia and winters southward to northern Africa, Saudi Arabia, and India. A close relative is the Paradise, or Stanley, Crane of the South African veldt country.

Africa is the home of the other two rather distinct members of the family. One is the majestic Crowned Crane with its conspicuous topknot of stiff feathers that looks like a shaving brush. It has been commonly domesticated, and is reported to be a useful bird around gardens because of its fondness for insects and reptiles. The Crowned Crane has a curious habit of feeding by stamping its feet to scare the insects into flight as it advances through the grasslands.

The Wattled Crane of South Africa gets its name from the two white-feathered wattles that hang from its chin. The front half of its face has conspicuous red warts. The rest of the head, neck, and upper breast are white; the underparts are black. The back and wing coverts are grey.

Biologically everything about the cranes points to their being a very old group, barely able to maintain themselves, and probably on their way out. They are nowhere common today except in some Buddhist countries, where they are protected by religious beliefs and by superstition. The sad history of the magnificent Whooping Crane in North America is well known. Conservationists sparked by the Audubon Society have been fighting hard to save the last remnants of its former extensive population which was down to a low of 23 birds in 1941. In 1960 the Whooping Crane census reported 42 living birds, the highest count in years, 36 in the wild, 6 in captivity. Three of the captive birds were hatched and reared in the New Orleans Zoo. The Whooper's small relative, the less showy Sandhill Crane, has been slightly more fortunate and protection may have come in time to save it from imminent extinction.

Sentiment has also always been on the side of the cranes in Korea and Japan, where the birds have been rigorously protected for half a century and small stocks maintained in several sanctuaries on their wintering grounds. Unrestricted poaching by occupation personnel after World War II drove the cranes from several of these sanctuaries or reduced their numbers. Then in the Korean War armies fought on the age-old wintering grounds of several of the finest Asiatic cranes. The fighting left but a sad remnant of the flocks that formerly graced the rice paddies in winter.

Cranes tame fairly easily and most of them breed well in captivity. Perhaps their only future in a world with an expanding human population is as exotic zoo captives. They are so magnificent in the wild, this seems criminal.

LIMPKINS

GRUIFORMES   ARAMIDAE

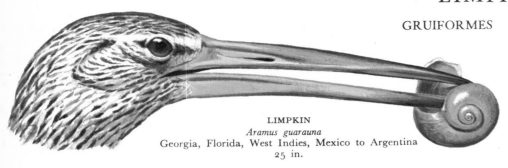

LIMPKIN
Aramus guarauna
Georgia, Florida, West Indies, Mexico to Argentina
25 in.

The Limpkin is a large greyish-brown marsh bird that ranges from the swamps of South Carolina and Florida south through the West Indies, Central and South America to Paraguay, Uruguay, and Argentina. The family contains but a single species divided into five subspecies.

Limpkins are of interest as a connecting link between the cranes and the rails. Their skeletal structure and their manner of feathering are crane-like, but their external characteristics, behaviour, and nesting are like those of the rails, as is their digestive system. Like the rails, they have a long hind toe at the same level with the three front ones, their heads are completely feathered, and their wings are relatively small and rounded. Their antiquity is vouchsafed by the remains of the living species in Pleistocene deposits and by three more species of different genera dating back some 60 million years to Eocene time.

The name Limpkin is of Florida origin and comes from the bird's halting, limping gait. A common vernacular name in the southeastern United States is "crying bird," a fitting title earned by the bird's loud, strident, three-syllable wailing note, heard most often in the early evening and at night.

Limpkins are non-migratory. They live in reedy swamps or marshes, sometimes in damp forests. Though primarily marsh birds, they perch readily in trees and run among the branches. They usually roost in trees at night. Limpkins swim well when they have to and float high on the water as do the coots and gallinules. They do not fly often, and when they do they make a short take-off run and fly weakly, with their wings held high over the back. Their toes are long for walking over mud and swamp vegetation. Their claws are long and sharp.

Limpkins' main food is molluscs, both univalve and bivalve, which they extract cleverly from the shell with their powerful bill. Limpkins also eat small reptiles, insects, crayfish, amphibians, and worms, but they are seldom found far from a supply of the shellfish that are their principal food.

The Limpkin builds a bulky nest of reeds, weeds, and other vegetation, often in tall marsh grass, sometimes in low bushes or trees. Nests have been found as high as 15 feet off the ground. The clutch varies from 4 to 8 eggs, usually 6, which are buff-brown, spattered and spotted about the larger end with darker browns. The incubation period is unknown, but both sexes incubate and both parents care for the young after hatching. The downy young are not black like young rails, but solid dark-brown. Parents usually remain with their young in a family group through the autumn and winter.

Limpkins were once abundant in the swamps of Florida and Georgia. They were such good eating and so tame and trusting, however, that they were almost wiped out by hunters before complete protection was given to them. Now, thanks to wildlife sanctuaries established at Okefenokee Swamp in Georgia and Lake Okeechobee and the Everglades National Park in Florida, Limpkins are once again becoming common enough so that the visitor can be fairly sure of finding them if he looks hard enough.

WHITE-WINGED TRUMPETER
Psophia leucoptera
Amazon forests of Brazil   18 in.

TRUMPETERS

GRUIFORMES   PSOPHIIDAE

In the lowland jungles of northeastern South America lives another small family, which is intermediate in structure and habits between the cranes and rails. The three trumpeters, so called from the males' loud, strident voices, have long legs and necks, but short, rather fowl-like bills. Their plumage is dark and soft, that of the head and neck almost velvety.

Trumpeters are sociable, unwary birds that travel about the forest floor in flocks of a hundred or more. Weak-winged, they can fly only a few hundred yards at a time, and depend more on running to escape danger. They also swim well when they want to cross rivers. Their life history and habits are imperfectly known, but their courtship involves crane-like dancing with exuberant leaps and noisy strutting. Ground nesters, they lay 6 to 10 pure white or green eggs.

Trumpeters are so unwary, so easily caught, and so tasty that they are seldom found near settlements. They tame easily, and Indians often keep them with their poultry as watchdogs. They have never bred in captivity.

RAILS, GALLINULES, AND COOTS

GRUIFORMES RALLIDAE

The rail family is by far the largest and most diverse of the order Gruiformes. All of its 132 species are small- to medium-sized running, wading, or swimming birds. Most are rather soberly coloured, though a few boast brilliant hues. Typically they are marsh inhabitants; some live on open ponds and lakes, a few in woodlands and even on dry plains. Many are very like farmyard hens and are widely known as "water hens" or "moor hens."

The family is an ancient one, with many fossil members dating back 70 million years to earliest Tertiary time. Today the rails are one of the most widespread of all avian families, found practically throughout the world except in the polar regions. Though relatively weak fliers, many species perform long migrations over water as well as land. Rail populations have established themselves on almost all the major oceanic islands and on an astonishing number of the minor ones. Many of these insular populations have been isolated for so long that they have developed into monotypic genera, many of them flightless.

All members of the family are omnivorous and able to sustain themselves on a wide range of both vegetable and animal food. This partly explains their wide distribution and their success in maintaining themselves in so many corners of the globe.

The family includes three fairly distinct types of birds, but these are too closely allied to be separated into subfamilies or even tribes. The gallinules and the coots are merely rails specialized for existence in a particular habitat, and the three types, though distinctive enough by themselves, merge into each other so closely that sharp lines cannot be drawn between them.

Rails are distinguished by the narrowness of their bodies, which are strongly compressed as an adaptation to running through thick marsh grass, weeds, and underbrush. Indeed the common expression "thin as a rail" originally referred to the avian rail and not to the wooden or the steel type. All the rails are rather soberly yet attractively decked out in cryptic colours that blend well with their marsh background. Most are brownish to reddish; a few on the greyish side are attractively striped with darker browns and blacks, occasionally with white. Their legs are stout, of medium length, and their toes are long to facilitate walking over soft marsh mud and grasses. All of them are heard far more often than seen, and their rather strident voices—they are most voluble at twilight and at night—are among the mysterious marsh sounds usually attributed to the "fly-by-night," the bird that we hear but never see.

The rails are of two main types, the long-billed ones of the genus *Rallus*, of which the Virginia, King, Clapper, and Water Rails are examples, and those with short, more conical bills, which are known in Europe as crakes. The Spotted and Corn Crakes and the Sora, the Yellow, and the Black Rails are typical of them.

All the rails and crakes build bulky nests of vegetation well hidden in the grasses on or near the ground, and most of them lay large clutches of from 6 to 16 eggs. The eggs are white or buffy, spotted with red or brown dots. Both parents share incubation duties and care of the young. The young hatch covered with dark, unpatterned down, and leave the nest almost immediately after hatching.

At the other end of the family are the coots of the genus *Fulica*. Their outstanding structural feature is the develop-

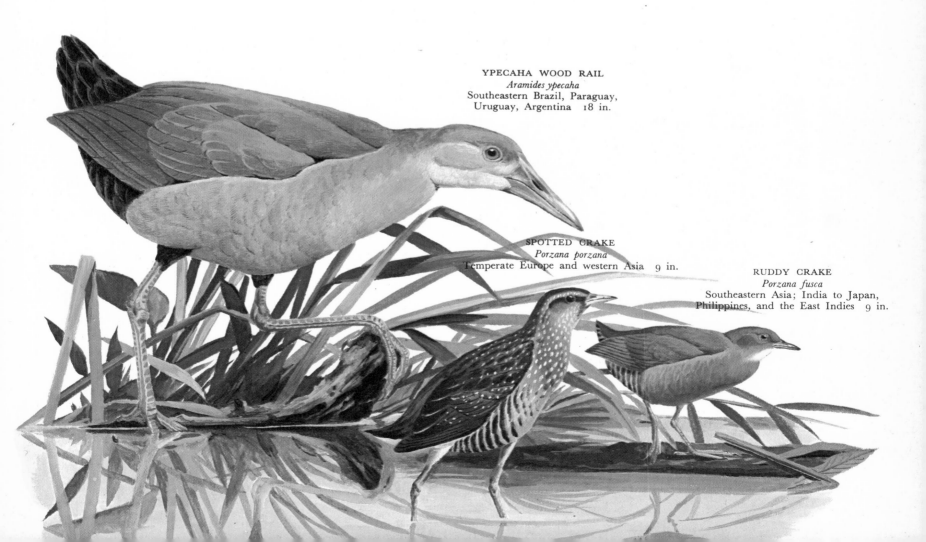

YPECAHA WOOD RAIL
Aramides ypecaha
Southeastern Brazil, Paraguay,
Uruguay, Argentina 18 in.

SPOTTED CRAKE
Porzana porzana
Temperate Europe and western Asia 9 in.

RUDDY CRAKE
Porzana fusca
Southeastern Asia; India to Japan,
Philippines, and the East Indies 9 in.

ment of the marginal membranes of the toes into flaps called lobate webs, similar to those on the feet of the totally unrelated grebes and finfoots. The coots, all good swimmers and divers, spend much of their time like ducks on open water, nodding their heads as they swim. They prefer shallow, muddy lakes bordered by reeds in which they can take refuge and where they nest on a floating platform of vegetation. Except when breeding, coots are quite gregarious and often gather in flocks of several thousands on their southern wintering grounds in both fresh and in brackish coastal waters. Like the rails they are quite noisy. When disturbed they take flight by pattering along the water into the wind until airborne. They appear to run on the surface of the water and kick up quite a splash when they do so. Their pattering in this fashion may be the origin in North America of their common vernacular name, "blue peter."

The common Coot of North America is a 15-inch, solidly grey bird with a conspicuous white bill and a white frontal shield on the forehead between the eyes. It is found from southern Canada to northern South America. A closely allied and very similar coot breeds completely across Eurasia from the British Isles to Japan, and a third coot, with red horny excrescences at the top of its frontal shield, inhabits most of Africa and breeds in southern Europe and southern Spain. The coot group has its greatest development in South America, where seven more species are found. Most of them are birds of open ponds and marshes with the typical swimming habits of the genus. One, the Horned Coot of the Andes, with a large horn-like projection on the frontal shield, occurs

PURPLE GALLINULE
Porphyrula martinica
Southern United States and
West Indies south to Uruguay
and northern Argentina 13 in.

only on a few lonely barren mountain lakes above the 13,000-foot level.

The gallinules have anatomical structures between those of the coots and the rails. Most have the frontal shield even more developed than in the coots, and their bills and shields are frequently coloured in brilliant reds or yellows. Their webless toes are greatly elongated to support them in the marsh and water vegetation which is their home. Like the rails, the gallinules are widespread over most of the temperate and tropical portions of the world and have established themselves on many oceanic islands. The American Common Gallinule and the conspecific Eurasian Moorhen are drab birds with brownish backs and dark-grey bellies. Many of the others, like the gaudy Purple Gallinule, are strikingly coloured in blues and blue greens with contrasting yellow legs. Like the coots, the gallinules sometimes nest on floating vegetation, or else they make rail-like nests in the marshes. Their nesting habits are otherwise similar to those of coots. The young hatch covered with black down (a family characteristic) and are highly precocial.

All the rail family are regarded as game birds and their flesh is quite savoury, though duck hunters are prone to look down their noses at the lowly coot. Rails are usually hunted at high water, when they are unable to escape by running through the grass and are forced to fly weakly away from the hunter.

The family is notable for the number of species that have lost the power to fly. Most of these are of restricted, insular distribution. Living in such limited areas with no terrestrial enemies to bother them, they had no need to fly. When man reached their hideaways and brought with him rats, cats, and dogs, these ultra-specialized populations of rails could no longer survive. The most recent count shows at least 15 distinctive rails and gallinules that have vanished forever during the past century. Many of them are known to science by only one or two specimens. These include rails from the Auckland and Chatham islands off New Zealand, from Tahiti, Fiji, Wake, New Caledonia, Laysan, Hawaii, Kusaie, Iwo Jima, and Samoa in the Pacific, from Jamaica in the West Indies, and from lonely Tristan da Cunha in the mid-South Atlantic. The United States government made valiant efforts to protect and preserve the little flightless rail of Laysan Island. Its restricted population was seemingly doing quite well until World War II, when rats from a naval vessel inadvertently got ashore on Laysan and destroyed them. The monotypic little Wake Island Rail was another casualty of World War II. The last birds were probably eaten by the starving Japanese garrison.

These insular flightless rails led a precarious existence long before modern man arrived to disturb them further. A shell collector delving into caves opened by quarrying operations in Bermuda recently stumbled upon a splendid deposit of Pleistocene bird bones that contained no less than four, perhaps five, different species of rails. These were studied at the University of Florida by Dr. Pierce Brodkorb, who tells me these ice-age Bermuda rails ranged in size from that of a living Black Rail to that of a King Rail, say from 6 to 16 inches.

LIMPKIN
Aramus guarauna
Georgia, Florida, West Indies, Mexico to Argentina 25 in.

MOORHEN (COMMON GALLINULE)
Gallinula chloropus
Temperate and tropical wetlands
of the world, except for
Australia, New Zealand,
and Papuan regions 14 in.

SORA RAIL
Porzana carolina
Temperate North America 9 in.

VIRGINIA RAIL
Rallus limicola
Western Hemisphere, southern Canada
to Strait of Magellan 10 in.

Their bones differ from those of all living species, particularly in the markedly reduced keels and wing bones that show beyond question they were flightless. Their ancestors must have reached Bermuda by flying the Atlantic from the mainland, and most likely the flightlessness these rails developed after their arrival in Bermuda contributed in some unknown way to their failure to survive.

Despite the gloomy outlook for rails and many other kinds of wildlife that seem doomed to dwindle and evidently to disappear, ornithologists always have a faint hope that some of these vanished forms, known only from a skin or two, or perhaps from a few scattered bones, may eventually reappear alive in some isolated spot. Such a fantastic dream came true not long ago in New Zealand.

Among that isolated island's vanishing and vanished forms was a large gallinule called *Notornis*, known to the Maoris as the Takahe. It was the size of a small turkey, but a brilliant green-blue in colour with a startling red frontal shield. Only four specimens of this handsome bird were known, the last taken in 1898, though its bones were found plentifully mixed with those of the giant moas in Pleistocene deposits. In 1948, just fifty years after the last live bird was taken, a small population of Takahes was found still living in a little valley 2,000 feet above sea level in the Murchison range of South Island, a good week's trek from the nearest habitation. The birds have since been found to number about 100 individuals, limited to one or two narrow valleys. How these flightless birds have managed to survive in spite of the introduced weasels and stoats and other predators is a mystery. The New Zealand government is doing the best it can to protect the survivors and to save them for posterity. These birds lay but four eggs each, many of which are infertile. In addition to their low reproduction rate, they have all the other characteristics of a senile and declining species as well as a very ancient one.

The New Zealand Wood Rail, the Weka, a brownish bird about the size of a chicken, is one of the few flightless rails in the world that has not retreated before man's satellite predators. The Weka is a pretty fair predator in its own right, and has added the introduced mice and rats as new items to its diet.

AMERICAN COOT
Fulica americana
Central Canada south to Colombia
and Ecuador; Hawaii 16 in.

WEKA
Gallirallus australis
New Zealand   20 in.

FINFOOTS

GRUIFORMES   HELIORNITHIDAE

The three finfoots, or sun grebes as they are sometimes called, are shy, retiring marsh birds closely related to the rails but quite distinctive in themselves and of a peculiar relict distribution. One is found in Central and South America, the second in tropical Africa, the third in tropical Southeast Asia and Sumatra. They are nowhere plentiful, even in large museum collections, and they are so shy and retiring in life that their nesting, feeding, and other habits are only imperfectly known.

The bodies of finfoots are elongated, their necks and bills quite long, their tails long, stiff, and rounded. Their feet are short and their toes bear scalloped, lobate webs like those of grebes and coots. Finfoots are not related at all to the grebes and only distantly to the coots, which may be their nearest kin. Their long, stiff tails, and their habits of perching on branches over the water and of swimming partly submerged, are suggestive of the anhingas. Their plumage, however, is dense and firm like that of a duck, except for the plumage on the head and neck which is short and soft like that of the rails. Their food is primarily fish and other small aquatic animal life. They are also known to eat some vegetation, especially seeds.

The smallest of the three finfoots is the American Sun Grebe, a 12-inch bird ranging from southern Mexico south to Paraguay and northern Argentina, usually found singly or in pairs along stagnant streams and heavily wooded rivers. It is largely plain olive-brown above, whitish below, and has a white streak extending backward along the side of the head, behind the eye.

The African Finfoot is similar but twice as large. An inhabitant of the denser wooded streams, it may be seen swimming low in the water. It spatters along the water in coot fashion when disturbed, but takes cover ashore in the forest undergrowth along the banks. The Asiatic species is slightly smaller. Found in jungle streams in Malaya and Sumatra, it is shy, rather rare, and has been little studied.

KAGU

GRUIFORMES   RHYNOCHETIDAE

The Kagu is another aberrant relative of the cranes and rails with no close affinities. It is limited to the forested highlands of the island of New Caledonia in the South Pacific, where the native Melanesians knew it long before Europeans arrived. This long-legged, greyish bird, with a startling reddish-orange bill and feet and a pronounced crest on its large head, is barely able to fly. It runs rapidly through the forest underbrush. Generally noisy at night, it has a loud, piercing, yelping cry, almost a scream, that can be heard a mile or more.

Its breeding habits in the wild have never been studied, but it is known to display with its wings half spread much the way a sunbittern does. The Kagu goes through a crazy, grotesque running and skipping dance when courting. In captivity it builds a nest of twigs and leaves on the ground and lays a single egg which is a smooth, pale brown dotted and streaked with reddish brown; both parents incubate the egg, which hatches in 36 days.

Formerly quite plentiful, the Kagu is now in danger of extinction. Much of its forest habitat has been cut off, and Europeans have introduced cats, dogs, pigs, and rats to this island, which formerly had no predatory mammals. If the development of New Caledonia continues, the Kagu will probably survive the century only in captivity.

AFRICAN FINFOOT
Podica senegalensis
Africa south of the Sahara 24 in.

CRESTED SERIEMA
Cariama cristata
Tablelands of Brazil, Paraguay,
and northern Argentina 36 in.

KAGU
Rhynochetos jubatus
New Caledonia 22 in.

SUNBITTERN
Eurypyga helias
Southern Mexico to Peru, Bolivia,
and Brazil 18 in.

SERIEMAS

GRUIFORMES   CARIAMIDAE

This family is composed of two generically distinct species, the Crested Seriema (*Cariama*) and Burmeister's Seriema (*Chunga*). Both are greyish brown, long-legged, running ground birds with a peculiarly erect posture, distinctive erectile crests, short, broad, down-curved bills, longish necks, short wings, and long tails. Their range is from central Brazil to Paraguay and northern Argentina. The Crested Seriema is a bird of the open grassland pampas; Burmeister's Seriema lives only in sparse brushy forests.

Both Seriemas stalk about in a stately manner, usually in pairs or small flocks, and when disturbed run rapidly, holding their heads down. Both species roost in trees at night. They fly weakly, and only at utmost provocation. They feed pri-

marily on insects, especially large ants. They eat some snakes and lizards, also berries, fruit and other vegetable food. The Crested Seriema nests on the ground, Burmeister's Seriema in low bushes and trees. The males display to the females in bustard-like fashion. When courting in spring, their loud, far-carrying cries sound like crazy laughter or the sharp yelping of puppies. The clutch is two eggs incubated by both sexes. Both species tame easily, are good zoo subjects, and have been raised in captivity.

The Seriemas are the only living descendants of a group of large, carnivorous ground birds that lived in South America from early Oligocene to Pliocene time. *Mesembriornis* and *Brontornis* attained heights of up to eight feet or more, and must have been awesome predators. Closely allied to these ancient Gruiformes was the ferocious *Diatryma*, whose remains have been found in Eocene deposits in North America and in Central Europe. In bulk of body the *Diatryma* probably equalled all but the largest of the Moas. It stood nearly 7 feet high and had a heavy bulky body, a short and massive neck, and a large head with a tremendous, compressed, hatchet-like beak. In its day it must have been one of the most fearsome animals alive.

SUNBITTERN

GRUIFORMES   EURYPYGIDAE

This elegant wading bird of Central and South America is another of the aberrant Gruiformes placed in a family by itself. It is a shy, timid species, found only along the wooded margins of streams and ponds in tropical rainforest country, usually solitarily or in pairs, never in flocks. It is non-migratory and tends to be resident throughout its range. Three geographical subspecies are recognized, one from southern Mexico to Ecuador, one in south central Peru, the third from Venezuela to central Brazil.

Graceful in its movements, the Sunbittern walks along stream banks with slow, deliberate steps, hunting minnows, insects, and small riparian life. It stalks its food carefully, with neck drawn in until close enough to lash out with a lightning stroke to spear its victim. When disturbed it flies up lightly into the shelter of the trees. Its call note is a soft, plaintive, long-drawn whistle.

Like the Kagu of New Caledonia, to which it seems most nearly allied, the Sunbittern executes a fantastic dance when excited. It displays with its delicately patterned brown, grey, and black wings and tail spread out in a threatening posture which it may hold as long as a minute or more. For a nest, both sexes work together to build a rather bulky mass of mulch and dry leaves low in a small tree with a semicircular entrance on one side. The two eggs in the clutch are a delicate grey spotted with red. Though the precocial young hatch covered with spotted and striped down, they may remain in the nest several weeks. Both parents feed them. They grow rapidly and at 2 months are indistinguishable from the adults.

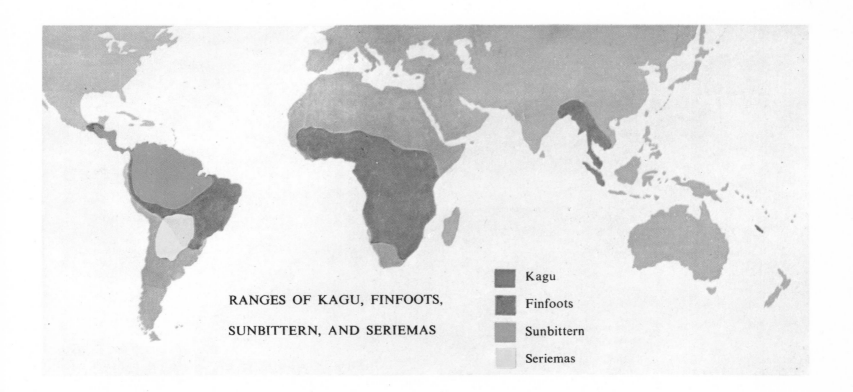

RANGES OF KAGU, FINFOOTS,
SUNBITTERN, AND SERIEMAS

Kagu
Finfoots
Sunbittern
Seriemas

BUSTARDS

OTIDAE

The bustards are a well-marked family of large cursorial upland ground birds that live on open grassy plains and brushy savannahs of the Old World. They have their greatest development in Africa, where 16 species are found. Six more occur in central and southern Eurasia, and one in Australia. Their antiquity is attested by fossil forms more than 50 million years old from the Eocene of Europe. Bustards show their closest affinities to the seriemas of South America.

All the bustards are shy, wary, keen-sighted birds of open, treeless country. They can fly strongly, but usually depend on running to escape their enemies. They normally walk with a stately, deliberate gait. While several African species are the size of a hen, standing only a foot high and weighing less than 3 pounds, most of them are considerably larger. The Kori or Giant Bustard of the South African veldt is perhaps the heaviest of all flying birds; males weigh up to 50 pounds and are strong fliers.

Their usual colours are brown to grey, attractively barred and spotted with darker shades above and either white, pale buff, or solid black below. Several species are crested; others have long bristly feathers on the sides of the head and neck. All have fairly long, strong legs, a rather long neck, a short tail, and broad wings. The soles of their feet are broad, and their claws are peculiarly flattened. In common with many other running birds, they have completely lost their hind toe.

The bustards are great wanderers, and some of the northern species perform extensive migrations. They fly in typical crane fashion with the head and neck straight out in front. Their wings beat strongly and steadily. Bustards can be told at a distance from geese, which they strongly resemble in flight,

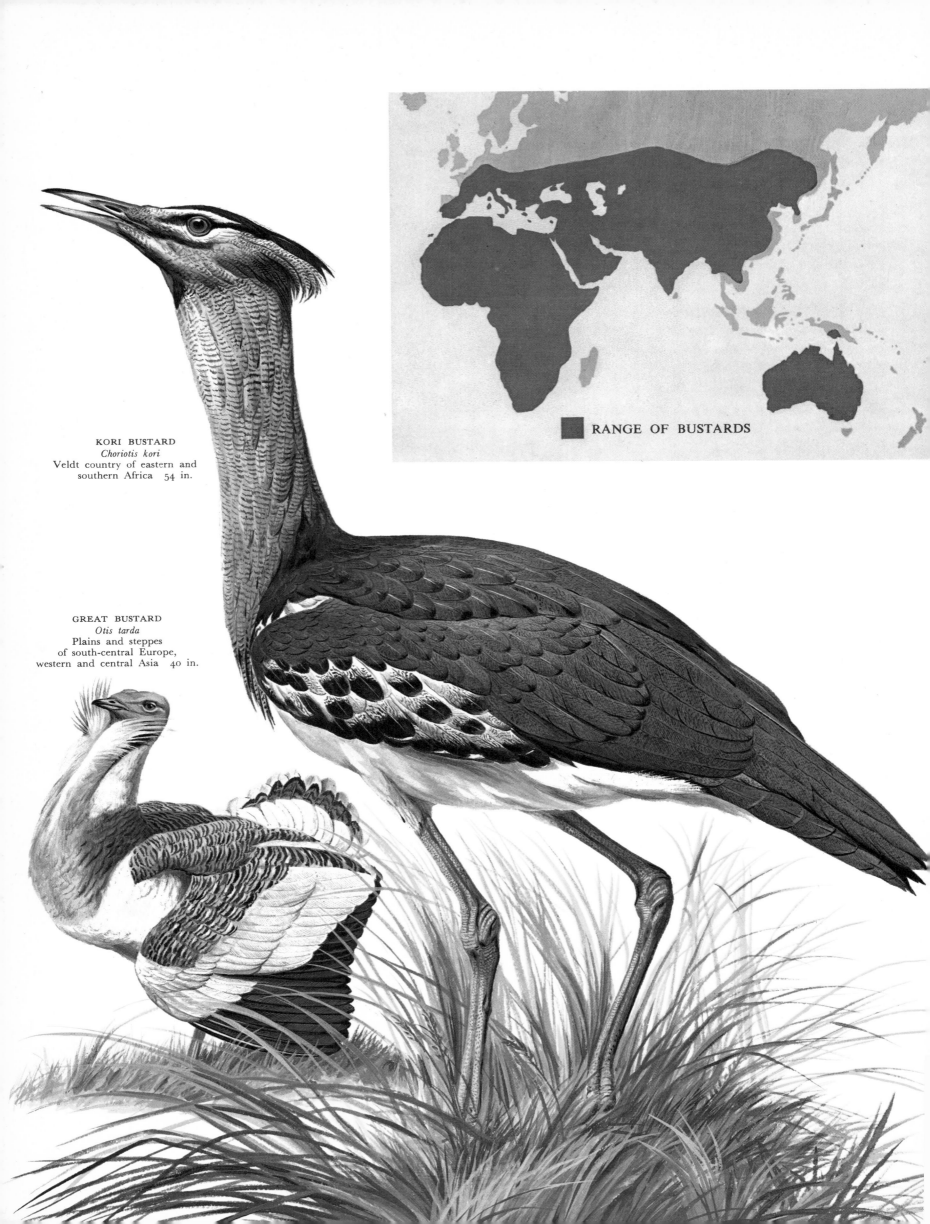

KORI BUSTARD
Choriotis kori
Veldt country of eastern and
southern Africa 54 in.

GREAT BUSTARD
Otis tarda
Plains and steppes
of south-central Europe,
western and central Asia 40 in.

RANGE OF BUSTARDS

by the long legs trailing behind the tail and by their curious aerial posture with the rear of the body sagging low. Unlike cranes and geese, they are not high fliers, and even on long migrations bustards seldom rise more than 200 or 300 feet above the ground.

As a rule bustards travel in small flocks of a dozen or so birds. Highly popular as game birds, they run so rapidly they are difficult for a hunter to approach on foot. However, they often crouch and hide, depending on camouflage to protect them. Unfortunately, they show so little fear of a man on horseback or camelback or in a car that they have little chance against modern weapons. Like all large birds of savoury flesh, they have now become quite rare near centres of human population. They survive in parts of their former range only because of strict protection.

The hundreds of Great Bustards that roamed the Russian and Siberian steppes less than a century ago are now a thing of the past. Small numbers can still be found in the more remote sections of their range, which once extended completely across Eurasia. In winter occasional individuals still wander to the British Isles, where the last resident bustards were extirpated about 1833. On the other side of the continent, wintering bustards still straggle southward from Manchuria into Korea, and once in a while to western Japan.

Bustards are primarily vegetarians and are fond of grains, but are actually omnivorous. They are great insect hunters and kill so many locusts that in much of Africa they are regarded as beneficial to agriculture. They also eat small animals and nestling birds when they can catch them. They are comparatively silent birds, and their voices are not outstanding but most species have chuckling, crowing, grunting, and sometimes booming calls.

Many species of bustards have concealed patches of white on the wings and on the body which show strongly when they fly. These are particularly noticeable in the marvellous display of the male Great Bustard, who seems to turn himself inside out when he struts and postures for the female, changing himself in a twinkling from a drab brownish bird to a fluffy white one. Some species are thought to be polygamous.

Bustards lay their eggs on the ground and make little or no nest. Their eggs are red-brown to olive green, generally blotched with dark markings. The Black-billed Bustard of Africa lays a single dull greenish egg. The Australian Bustard, which rivals the Great Bustard in size and is locally called "wild turkey," also lays one egg, occasionally two. Other species may lay as many as five, but as they nest only once a year, their reproductive rate is slow. Incubation is by the female alone and takes from 20 days in the smaller species to 30 days in the larger ones. The highly precocial young are covered with mottled brown or black down. They leave the nest at hatching and are usually able to fly in 5 to 6 weeks, long before they reach their full growth.

WADERS, GULLS, AND AUKS

CHARADRIIFORMES

The 16 families in this diverse, cosmopolitan order fall roughly into three groups, each of which is sometimes given subordinal rank. The first includes the 12 families of shorebirds known as waders; the second combines the skuas, the gulls and terns, and the skimmers; the third contains the auks, murres, and puffins. Despite their superficial diversity, the 306 species in these 16 families form a natural group, for they share a number of structural peculiarities and growth and behaviour characteristics.

Their anatomical similarities involve their type of palate bones and voice box, and the manner of insertion of the tendons that connect the leg muscles to the toes. They also show affinities in the arrangement of their secondary flight feathers. Most species have 11 primaries, a few only 10. All have a tufted oil gland and a small aftershaft on their body feathers.

Members of the order range in size from 5 to 32 inches. Their plumage is usually dense and frequently waterproof. Bright colours are rare among them; black, white, and various shades of greys and browns predominate. The sexes are usually alike; sexual dimorphism is pronounced only in the painted snipes, the phalaropes, and the Ruff. The shape and size of their bill and feet are extremely variable. With one exception, the seedsnipe, they live primarily on animal food.

The reproductive rate throughout the order is comparatively low. Most species breed but once a year, are single-brooded, and lay from 1 to 4 eggs. Incubation sometimes begins before the clutch is complete, and lasts from 2½ to 4 weeks or longer. The precocial young hatch covered with down. Some leave the nest immediately, while others remain in or near it to be fed by the parents until almost fledged. Typically, the adults share the duties of natal care, but in the snipes the female does most of the incubating and rearing of the young. In the phalaropes and in a few other waders the male assumes these responsibilities.

Found practically everywhere in the world, including the polar regions, most Charadriiformes are inhabitants of coastal waters, beaches, marshes, and meadows. A few are pelagic, and some stay well inland and never come near salt water. Their fossil record goes back some 75 million years to the Palaeocene, and they seem most nearly related to the Gruiformes, to which the jaçanas, the seedsnipe and the thick-knees in particular show decided affinities.

JAÇANAS

CHARADRIIFORMES   JACANIDAE

Jaçanas are at home in tropical and subtropical pools and lakes overgrown with lilies and other low-water vegetation. Here they walk daintily in search of insects, small molluscs, and an occasional unwary minnow. They also eat the seeds of water plants. The correct pronunciation of their name is zhá-sa-ná, with accents on the first and last syllables and the *c* soft. It came into English from the Portuguese, who adopted it from the Tupi Indians of the Amazon basin. Jaçanas are also called "lily-trotters" or "lotus-birds."

The eight species of this family have a number of unique characteristics, the most outstanding of which are their exceedingly long toes and claws which allow them to walk with ease over floating vegetation. Other distinctive features are a frontal shield much like that of the coots and gallinules, and sharp, horny spurs on the bend of their wings which are formidable fighting weapons. These wing spurs occur elsewhere among birds only in the screamers, sheathbills, certain plovers, and in two waterfowl.

As the jaçanas stalk over water hyacinths and water lilies they look something like long-legged gallinules, and they fly much the same way, with their necks extended and their long legs trailing behind. Though seldom noisy, they have a variety of grunting calls and whistles. When bickering together and threatening each other with uplifted wings, they chatter with scolding, chuckling notes.

Jaçanas have such complete confidence and security in their remarkable ability to walk on floating vegetation that they are not at all shy and can often be approached quite closely. When alarmed, however, they will frequently "freeze" and, despite their bright colouring, can be hard to see. They can swim well when they have to, and can even dive to escape enemies in emergencies.

Though the sexes are similar in colour, the female is often larger, and the male does most of the incubating and caring for the young. The nest is a mass of loose, floating vegetation that often drifts on the surface with the wind. The usual clutch is four glossy, dark-brown eggs heavily spattered and marked with black. The incubation period is reported at 22 to 24 days. After the breeding season, jaçanas congregate in small flocks and fly lightly in unison over lakes and marshes the way so many other waders do. When they alight they have a curious habit of stretching their wings upward until they almost meet over the back.

The American Jaçana is an attractive cinnamon-red bird about 10 inches in length. The gaudy yellow-green patches in its wings flash conspicuously in flight. Over its range from Mexico south to Argentina, nine distinct, strongly marked geographical populations have developed. Most of these have the typical cinnamon-red body with a black head and bright yellow frontal shield. One population is entirely black, and several other colour phases occur.

One of the most striking of all the jaçanas is the Pheasant-tailed Jaçana, found from India across southeastern Asia to the Philippines. It is a bronzy, brown-backed bird with black underparts, white face and neck, and contrasting yellow nape and conspicuous white wing patches. Though its body is only a little larger than those of the other jaçanas, its long tail makes the Pheasant-tailed Jaçana the largest species, 20 inches in length. In Africa there are two species of jaçanas. The smaller one of these is the smallest species in the family.

AFRICAN JAÇANA
Actophilornis africana
Africa south
of the Sahara
12 in.

AMERICAN JAÇANA
Jacana spinosa
Mexico and West Indies south to
western Panama   10 in.

PHEASANT-TAILED JAÇANA
Hydrophasianus chirurgus
India to Java, Malaya,
and the Philippines   20 in.

PAINTED SNIPE
Rostratula benghalensis
Africa south of the Sahara, Egypt and
Asia Minor across Asia to China, Japan,
the Philippines, and Australia 9½ in.

PAINTED SNIPES

CHARADRIIFORMES   ROSTRATULIDAE

The two species in this small family are similar in appearance and habits but widely separated geographically. One ranges from Japan southward to Australia and westward to central Africa; the other is limited to southern South America.

The better-known Old World species is a greenish-brown bird, whitish below and cryptically marked above with stripes and crossbars of black, brown, and white. While quite snipe-like in appearance, it is rail-like in many of its actions. A bird of reedy marshes, it is usually seen singly or in small wisps of 10 to 12 birds. It skulks during the day, but is more active at night, and is always difficult to flush. It flies weakly, with its legs trailing behind in rail fashion, and can swim short distances when it has to.

The painted snipes reverse the usual pattern of nuptial behaviour. The slightly larger and more brightly coloured females initiate the courting and are believed to be polyandrous. In courtship both birds bow low to each other and display by moving their tails up and down. The female does most of the displaying to the male who, as soon as the eggs are laid, takes over and does the incubating and the rearing of the young. The usual clutch is 4 eggs, though 2 to 6 have been recorded. The incubation period is 19 days. The nest is a compact, flat mass of reeds and other vegetation built on the ground or half floating in wet paddies and marshes, frequently in lotus beds.

The painted snipes eat worms, molluscs, other small swamp invertebrates, and some vegetable food. While they are not migratory in the true sense of the word, there seems to be considerable local movement, especially of northern populations moving somewhat southward in the wintertime.

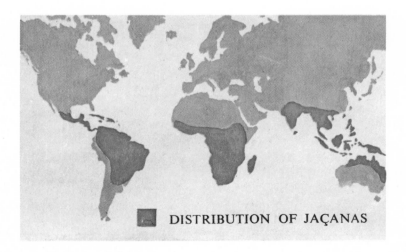

DISTRIBUTION OF JAÇANAS

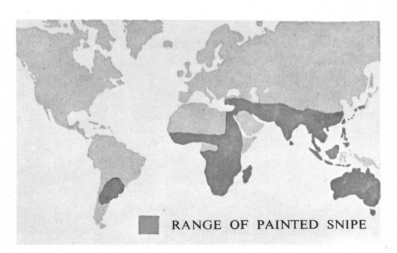

RANGE OF PAINTED SNIPE

OYSTERCATCHERS

CHARADRIIFORMES HAEMATOPODIDAE

The oystercatchers are large, conspicuous, noisy plover-like birds seen on open beaches and rocky coasts throughout the world except in the polar regions and on oceanic islands. Their outstanding feature is their long, blunt, vertically flattened bill, much like a double-edged oysterman's knife, and used for the same purpose. With this powerful tool the birds chisel limpets off the rocks and open oysters, mussels, and clams with great facility. They also use their bill to kill small crabs and to probe deeply into mud for worms. Nowhere are oystercatchers abundant.

Most of the six generally recognized species have fairly wide ranges, and several of them divide into a number of geographical races. All are very similar and exhibit one of two major colour patterns: either solid sooty black or, more commonly, boldly pied brown or black above and white below, with broad white wing patches that show conspicuously in flight. In both colour types the legs and bill are a contrasting red, the feet usually duller or paler than the bill.

The oystercatcher's call note is a loud, shrill, far-carrying, repeated whistle. Their flight is strong and direct. They nest on open shingles, laying 2 to 4 eggs in a shallow depression sometimes lined with debris. Both sexes incubate and care for the young. Incubation is 24 to 27 days. The young remain with the parents about 5 weeks.

PLOVERS AND LAPWINGS

CHARADRIIFORMES CHARADRIIDAE

This large but fairly distinctive family of 63 species consists mainly of chunky, strongly patterned, small- to medium-sized birds of extremely wide distribution. They are found in ice-free lands practically throughout the world. All are plumpish birds, distinguished most easily from other waders by their pigeon-like bills, which are always shorter than the head and slightly swollen near the tip. While few are brightly coloured, many have bold patterns of black or brown and white that show strongly when they fly. Most are gregarious, and on migration flocks of thousands are sometimes encountered. The family is divided into two subfamilies, mainly on the basis of minor skull differences; 38 species are true plovers and 25 are lapwings, many of which are commonly called plovers.

Plover is supposedly a corruption of the Latin *pluvius*, meaning rain, with which ancient folklore somehow associated these birds. Their name in German, *regenpfeifer*, means "rain sandpiper." Nobody has ever explained this association satisfactorily. The birds are neither more active nor more vocal before or during rains than at other times. It has been suggested that the dappled back patterns of many species, particularly of the Golden and the Black-bellied plovers, suggest rain drops, but this seems far-fetched.

Typical of the true plovers (Charadriinae) are the 21 species of the genus *Charadrius*, which are common inhabitants of ocean beaches, sand and mud flats, and open grassy or cultivated fields the world around. All have brownish backs, white underparts, and one or more distinctive bands of black or dark grey across the upper breast. This gives them the general name of "ringed plovers."

The smaller ringed plovers, of which there are several closely allied species and many geographical races, are widespread along the coasts and waterways of the Northern Hemisphere. They breed as far north as the arctic tundras and migrate across the equator to southern beaches in winter. Marked by a single neck ring, these fairly tame little birds can be approached closely as they run along the beaches at the water's edge, often in flocks of hundreds. In common with other plovers, they wade very little but run up the beach as the surf pounds in and follow a receding wave back to pick up the small invertebrates left in its seething wake. Their melodious, double-noted whistle is heard frequently during migration.

A close relative of the small ringed plovers is the familiar slightly larger Killdeer of North America, with its double black collar. This inland and upland species is fond of open prairies, grasslands, and cultivated fields, where its loud, oft-repeated "kitledee, kitledee, kitledee" tells the farmer that the ploughing season is at hand.

The little Piping and Snowy plovers of temperate and southern beaches are also members of this ring-necked group, similarly patterned but so light in colour they are almost invisible on the white sandy beaches that are their home. Their plaintive notes are usually heard before one sees the birds that utter them. The dotterels of the Old World are true plovers also, prettily coloured, with attractive splashes of ruddy brown on the belly and a broad, grey breast band margined with white. The Dotterel, a tundra-nesting bird, breeds in the mountains of northern Europe eastward to Mongolia, and migrates to southern Asia and northern Africa in winter. It is seldom found near the coast, but usually on open, sunny deserts and barren plateaus.

Among the larger species are the Golden and the Black-bellied plovers, each about 11 inches in length. In breeding plumage these birds have coal-black throat, breast, and underparts margined with white which contrast strongly with the adjacent dappled brownish or greyish back. In spring the Golden Plover's back is dappled with golden-yellow spots; the Black-breasted Plover's back is barred in light grey and black. In immature and nonbreeding plumages, these birds are rather nondescript. Circumpolar in distribution, these plovers breed in the high north and migrate southward to tropical shores in winter. They frequent coastal uplands as often as beaches, and are commonly seen during migration running about golf fairways and the grassy strips of airfields. The Black-bellied

Plover has a rudimentary hind toe, which all other members of the family lack.

The lapwings (Vanellinae) are slightly larger than the true plovers (10 to 16 inches in length). Almost all are inland and upland species. An ancient and cosmopolitan group, lapwings are found today in all temperate and tropical countries except North America, where they died out in Pleistocene time.

The prototype of the group is the Lapwing of Eurasia, which breeds from the British Isles and France eastward through Siberia to Mongolia. A conspicuous, noisy bird, its ancient name refers not to a lapping or crossing of its wings, but to a peculiar, irregular lag in its wingbeats in flight. The Lapwing has been so exploited in Europe for its flesh and for its eggs that its survival seems little short of miraculous. Lapwing eggs are the "plovers eggs" of European epicures. These were formerly marketed by countless thousands. The species is now protected in much of northern Europe, but it is still "egged" in Belgium and the Netherlands. There, government regulation prohibits taking eggs after a certain date in May. Studies have shown that birds whose nests are robbed before this date will lay another clutch.

Several lapwings, particularly the so-called "blacksmith" group of Africa, have sharp-pointed spurs on the bend of the wing which they use in fighting. The loud, echoing cries of these lapwings have the metallic ring of iron being pounded on an anvil. Another heavily spurred lapwing is the large Masked Plover of Australia and Malaya, a pugnacious, 15-inch species well able to protect itself against most small predators. Other lapwings in Africa, southern Asia, and Malaya have prominent red or yellow wattles at the base of the bill. Lapwings are alert, nervous birds and quite noisy, especially during the breeding season. They take wing with loud cries of alarm the moment anything strange appears and alert all the game within earshot, to the disgust of hunters.

Plovers and lapwings nest on the open ground, and depend upon their concealing colouration for protection. The shallow hollow they scoop in the ground for their eggs is sometimes lined with pebbles, shells, or plant material. The usual clutch throughout the family is 4 eggs, though occasionally 3 and rarely 5 are reported. The one exception is the peculiar little (6-inch) Wrybill Plover of New Zealand, which maintains itself with a clutch of only two eggs. The Wrybill, which looks and acts like a little ring-necked plover, nests on the inland river beds of South Island and migrates to the North Island, where it winters sometimes in flocks of up to 1500 birds. It is the only bird whose bill is bent laterally, always to the right. Just why has yet to be explained. The bent bill was supposed to be useful in chasing small insects and other invertebrates around pebbles, but recent careful studies of the bird in life show no satisfactory explanation for this peculiar anomaly.

Throughout the family both sexes share the incubation duties, which take about 20 days in the smaller species and from 28 to 30 days in the larger ones. Both sexes take care of the highly precocial young, which leave the nest almost immediately after hatching. Their barred and patterned grey and brown down blends into the background. When threatened by enemies the parent plovers lead intruders away with bold "distraction" displays. Calling attention to itself with loud cries, the adult pretends to have a broken wing and flutters as though helpless in front of the intruder to lead him away from either the nest or the young. The young mature rapidly and are usually able to fly by the third to the fifth week.

SANDPIPERS AND ALLIES

CHARADRIIFORMES   SCOLOPACIDAE

The 82 species of wading birds grouped in this family can be told readily from the plovers by their thin, straight, or down-curved bills, which are always as long as the head and sometimes much longer. Their general lack of bold markings in the colour pattern, and their possession of a hind toe in all except one species, the Sanderling, also sets them off.

The family is essentially one of the Northern Hemisphere. Though a few snipe breed in widely separated parts of the Southern Hemisphere, in South America, Africa, and New Zealand, all the other species breed in the Northern Hemisphere, most of them at high latitudes. They perform prodigious migrations between their breeding grounds and their winter homes at the opposite end of the globe.

The family breaks naturally into four subfamilies: first, the Tringinae (tattlers, curlews, godwits, willets and their allies); second, the Scolopacinae (snipe and woodcock); third, the Eroliinae (sandpipers and their relatives); and, fourth, the Arenariinae (turnstones and surfbirds).

The tattlers and their allies breed widely in the Northern Hemisphere, mainly in northern sections. They winter southward, some considerably below the equator. As their name implies, tattlers are noisy birds whose loud whistles are far-carrying, piercing, yet pleasant. Typical of the tattlers is the Greater Yellowlegs of North America, with a slender, straight bill and long brilliant-yellow legs. The Yellowlegs breeds in marshy ground across northern Canada and winters southward through the United States to the coastal salt marshes and mud flats along the Gulf of Mexico. Its close relative, the Lesser Yellowlegs, is only 10 inches in length but otherwise is almost indistinguishable from the Greater except by its call note. Close Old World relatives of similar habits and appearance are the Redshank and the Greenshank.

Three smaller tattlers, the Solitary Sandpiper of North America and the Wood and Green sandpipers of the Old World, are among the few members of the entire order that do not nest on the ground. These three similar species nest in trees, usually in the abandoned nests of other birds. The nesting habits of the Solitary Sandpiper were unknown until about 1903, when the first authentic set of eggs was found in an American Robin's nest. It uses the abandoned nests of several passerine species, usually in evergreens near swamps. The Wood and the Green sandpipers similarly appropriate the nests of Eurasian passerine birds. Eggs of the Green Sandpiper have been found in old squirrel nests.

Smallest of the tattler group are the Spotted Sandpiper of North American inland waterways and its close relative, the Common Sandpiper of Eurasia. These little brown-backed, white-bellied birds breed along river and lake shores, laying their four eggs on the ground in a shallow depression often lined with grass or dead leaves. They are frequently called "peet-weets" from their oft-repeated call and alarm note. Common American names are "tip-ups" or "teeter-tails," from their habit of continually wagging their rump and tail up and down as they walk along the water's edge.

Largest and most distinctive of the tattler subfamily are the eight curlews of the genus *Numenius*, typified by the circumpolar Whimbrel, known in America as the Hudsonian Curlew. Most curlews breed in the northern tundra and all migrate southward in winter, frequently across the equator. All are brown birds, backs streaked with black, with long legs and a long down-curved bill. The largest of the group is the Longbilled Curlew of North America, 25 inches long. Only slightly smaller is the Madagascar Curlew of eastern Siberia, which

winters southward to Malaya and Australia but which has never been found in Madagascar. (It was named in error for Macassar Straits near the Celebes, whence the first specimens reached Europe in the 18th century.) A Eurasian Curlew now holds the longevity record for a ringed wild bird. One ringed as a chick in Finland in 1926 was shot in Norfolk in 1958—in its 32nd year!

On migration, curlews often frequent dry uplands, feeding on berries, seeds, and insects. Their more usual haunts are coastal marshes and mud flats where they probe deeply with their long bills for worms and other invertebrates. The curlew population has declined markedly during the last century through overshooting for sport and for market. With the legal protection now available some curlews are once again becoming more common. Protection came too late to save the 12-inch Eskimo Curlew, which, after the breeding season, moved eastward to Labrador and Newfoundland, then south off the Atlantic coast to South America. Along the Atlantic coast the birds were slaughtered by the barrel for market.

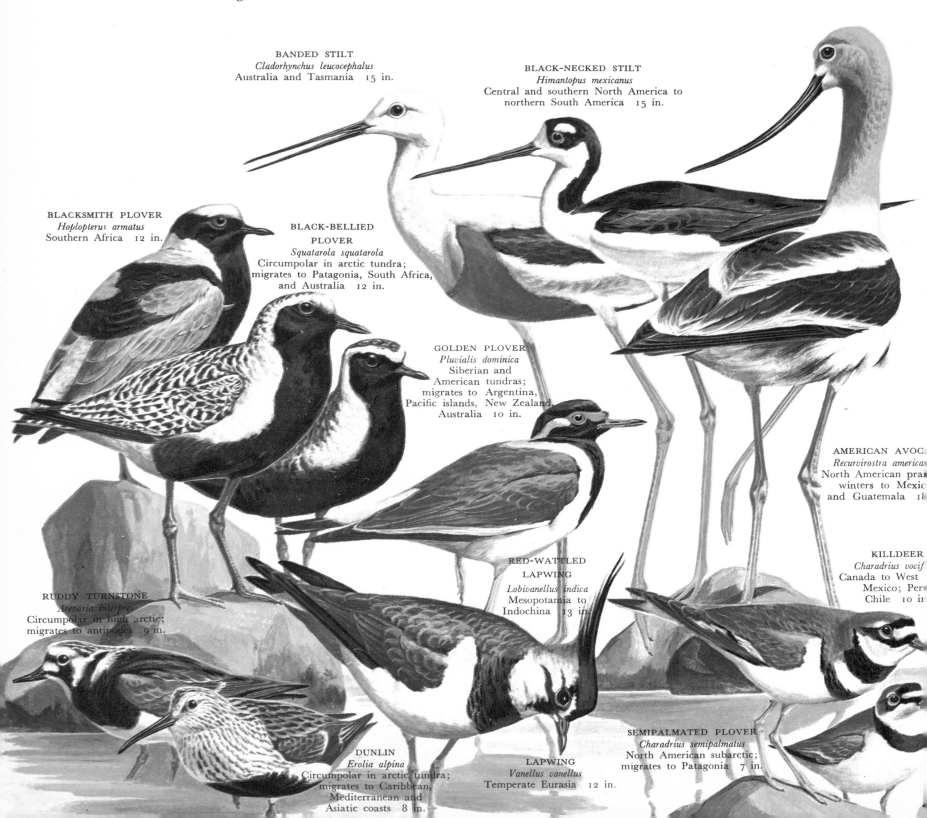

BANDED STILT
Cladorhynchus leucocephalus
Australia and Tasmania 15 in.

BLACK-NECKED STILT
Himantopus mexicanus
Central and southern North America to
northern South America 15 in.

BLACKSMITH PLOVER
Hoplopterus armatus
Southern Africa 12 in.

BLACK-BELLIED
PLOVER
Squatarola squatarola
Circumpolar in arctic tundra;
migrates to Patagonia, South Africa,
and Australia 12 in.

GOLDEN PLOVER
Pluvialis dominica
Siberian and
American tundras;
migrates to Argentina,
Pacific islands, New Zealand,
Australia 10 in.

AMERICAN AVOC
Recurvirostra america
North American pra
winters to Mexic
and Guatemala 18

RUDDY TURNSTONE
Arenaria interpres
Circumpolar in high arctic;
migrates to antipodes 9 in.

RED-WATTLED
LAPWING
Lobivanellus indica
Mesopotamia to
Indochina 13 in.

KILLDEER
Charadrius vocif
Canada to West
Mexico; Per
Chile 10 in

DUNLIN
Erolia alpina
Circumpolar in arctic tundra;
migrates to Caribbean,
Mediterranean and
Asiatic coasts 8 in.

LAPWING
Vanellus vanellus
Temperate Eurasia 12 in.

SEMIPALMATED PLOVER
Charadrius semipalmatus
North American subarctic;
migrates to Patagonia 7 in.

Another curlew that makes a long overwater flight is the Bristle-thighed Curlew, whose thigh feathers have no vanes on their shafts. This species winters on mid-Pacific islands, where it has the disturbing habit of feeding on the eggs of nesting sea birds. Its nesting grounds remained a mystery for a long time but were finally discovered in 1948 high in the mountain tundras of inland Alaska. These curlews make a non-stop 5,000-mile flight over water from their Alaskan breeding grounds to their wintering grounds in the mid-Pacific. Closely related to the curlews are the four godwits, large, handsome, brownish or greyish shore birds with long, straight bills. Formerly abundant, the godwits have continued to decline in numbers despite protection, and are now among the rarer of the large shore birds.

Another large member of the tattler group is the Willet, a large, grey bird that breeds in two areas along the Atlantic coast, in Nova Scotia and from Virginia southward to the Gulf States. Willets were very rare 30 years ago, but have responded to protection and are now quite common. They show a strong white patch in the wing when they fly, and are the only seashore tattlers that like to perch on telephone poles and wires. This habit of perching on posts is also characteristic of the one exclusively inland member of the tattler group, the 12-inch Bartramian Sandpiper, or Upland Plover. This bird breeds on the western plains and in open cultivated fields in the northern United States and well into Canada. It migrates south to the Argentine pampas.

The snipe subfamily contains 25 species of small- to medium-sized birds, 10 to 16 inches long with comparatively short legs and very long bills which they use for probing in

BAR-TAILED GODWIT
Limosa lapponica
Subarctic Eurasia and Alaska;
winters to Africa, Australia, New Zealand   16 in.

LONG-BILLED CURLEW
Numenius americanus
North American prairies; winters to
Gulf Coast and Guatemala   23 in.

AMERICAN OYSTERCATCHER
Haematopus palliatus
Coastal California to Chile and
New Jersey to Argentina   18 in.

SHORT-BILLED DOWITCHER
Limnodromus griseus
Alaska to n. Quebec; winters to
n. South America   12 in.

GREATER YELLOWLEGS
Totanus melanoleucus
Alaska to Newfoundland;
winters to Patagonia   14 in.

SPOTTED SANDPIPER
Actitis macularia
Temperate North America;
winters to Brazil, n. Chile   8 in.

GREAT KNOT
Calidris tenuirostris
Eastern Siberia; winters
to Australia   11 in.

LEAST SANDPIPER
Erolia minutilla
Boreal North America; migrates to
n. South America   6 in.

RUFF ♂
Philomachus pugnax
Northern Eurasia, migrates through
Eurasia and Africa 12 in.

COMMON SNIPE
Capella gallinago
Circumpolar in
Northern Hemisphere;
winters below equator 11 in.

EURASIAN WOODCOCK
Scolopax rusticola
Temperate Eurasia;
winters irregularly southward 14 in.

the mud. Snipes of the genus *Capella*, of which a dozen species are recognized, breed on all the continents except Australia. The bird known in Australia as the "Australian snipe" is more properly called the Japanese Snipe, for this large relative of the American Wilson Snipe and the European Common Snipe nests only in the northern islands of Japan. It flies all the way to Australia to winter.

All snipes have a fascinating courtship flight, during which the male circles high in the air and zooms downward over the female with a loud buzzing sound made by air rushing through its narrow wing and tail feathers. The snipes and the closely related woodcocks are largely inland birds that nest in fresh-water marshes or in damp forests. The Woodcock lives in open wet forests with swampy hollows, where it probes the soft ground for worms. The Woodcock's eyes are placed almost on the top of its head, and it can also open just the end of its bill—a help in grabbing food with its bill hilt-deep in the mud. The Woodcock sings its spectacular courtship flight song late in the afternoon or early evening, particularly on foggy, damp nights. It whistles a beautiful series of trills in circling flight high above the coy female sitting on the ground below before fluttering down, still whistling, beside her.

One group of the snipe subfamily, the North American dowitchers, breeds in the muskeg region from Alaska across to Hudson Bay and winters southward along coastal mud flats and beaches, usually in large flocks. In spring these handsome birds have brilliant red breasts which give them the common name of red-breasted or robin snipe. Dowitchers are the only snipe found regularly on open beaches.

The sandpiper subfamily contains 23 species of small, running beach birds, so similar that they are the despair of amateur bird watchers. Most of these birds are highly gregarious, and are often found in immense flocks during migration. Largest of the sandpipers is the 10- to 11-inch Knot, which breeds circumpolarly in the high northern tundra and migrates southward to New Zealand, Australia, South Africa, and southern South America. Knots sometimes gather in flocks of several hundred along North American coasts during migration.

The smallest of the sandpipers and typical of the group are the 5-inch Least Sandpiper of North America and the closely related stints of Eurasia. There are some 16 more of these so-called "peeps," all of which breed in the tundra regions of the Northern Hemisphere and migrate southward along the coasts of all the continents, though a few follow some of the inland waterways southward.

All these small sandpipers are brown or greyish above and lighter below. In spring plumage they frequently assume a more colourful dress, such as that worn by the circumpolar Dunlin or Red-back Sandpiper, recognizable from others by its slightly down-curved bill. This 8-inch bird is solid grey in autumn and winter, but in spring has a broad black patch on its belly and a lovely rufous colour on its back. Tremendous flocks winter along the shores of North America, Europe, and temperate Asia. Two other little sandpipers, the Semipalmated Sandpiper and the Western Sandpiper, which can be told apart only with difficulty, have the front toes connected with very short webs.

The most aberrant and the largest of the sandpiper group is the 11-to 12-inch Ruff. In winter plumage the Ruff and its female, the Reeve, are similar, plain birds that look like large Knots. In springtime, the male develops an extraordinary collar or ruff of long feathers around the neck which he expands when displaying to the female. This collar is of varied combinations of brown, white, black, and buff, and no two males are exactly alike. In courting, males go through a weird little dance in which they posture with their collars expanded, point their bills to the ground, and quiver all over. They have particular dancing grounds, usually on open hillsides, which the females visit for mating. Incubation and care of the young in the Ruff is entirely by the female, and the males are polygamous. Ruffs breed across northern Europe from France and Scandinavia to central Siberia and migrate southward to southern Asia and northern Africa.

In this sandpiper group also belongs the almost cosmopolitan Sanderling, the only three-toed member of the family, and the lightest coloured of the sandpipers. The Sanderling is a circumpolar, high-northern breeder that migrates southward all the way to the Antipodes.

Sandpipers travel in large, loose flocks and fly with rapid steady wingbeats. When playing along beaches or over marshes, the huge flocks turn and wheel in unison as though on signal, although there is no apparent leader and no regular formation to the flocks. How the sandpipers perform these marvellous evolutions has yet to be explained satisfactorily.

Least typical of the family, though perhaps nearest the ancestral stock from which it sprang, are the turnstones, which have long given systematists trouble. Three species make up the subfamily: the Turnstone, the Black Turnstone, and the Surfbird. As they show certain characteristics of both plovers and snipes, they have, at times, been placed in a family by themselves. Externally they resemble the plovers more than they do the snipes. The bill is short, thin, flattened, slightly upturned at the tip, but not swollen as in typical plovers, and their plumage is broadly patterned with contrasting light and dark patches. They are plump short-necked birds with a well-developed hind toe, and the bone structure of their skulls shows them to be snipes.

In breeding plumage the Turnstone is one of the prettiest of all shore birds. Its bright chestnut upperparts, its white underparts set off by a broad black chest band, and its whitish head are broadly patterned with black and white into a tortoise-shell appearance. Its legs are orange, its bill black.

The Turnstone is one of the highest northern breeders. It nests in the arctic tundra completely around the North Pole. It migrates southward down both coasts of both oceans to Cape Horn, the Cape of Good Hope, Australia, and New Zealand. In migration, it is mostly seen in loose flocks of up to 50 or 100 birds on open coastal beaches feeding along the wet sands, pebbles, or rocks in the wake of the receding tide. It is aptly named for its peculiar habit of flipping over pebbles and bits of shell and seaweed with its bill to expose the small marine life hidden beneath. On the nesting grounds its food is primarily insects. Turnstones nest on the ground; they lay four eggs, and both parents incubate and tend the young. The Black Turnstone is a darker but otherwise similar species in appearance and habits, and is limited in its breeding to the west and south coasts of Alaska. It migrates along the Pacific coasts as far as Cape Horn.

The Surfbird has a migration and winter distribution similar to that of the Black Turnstone. A bird of the surf line, dull greyish in colour, it has light wing patches that show in flight. As its name implies, it prefers kelp- and weed-covered rocks to sandy beaches. Its nesting ground was not discovered until the late 1920's. Instead of nesting in the coastal tundras, as the Turnstones do, the Surfbirds turn inland when they reach Alaska on their northward trek in spring. They fly to the alpine tundra of the mountains, well above timber line, and nest at altitudes of 4,000 feet or more. There, typical of the order, they lay their four eggs in a shallow cup on the ground, but the male Surfbird does most of the incubating and takes care of the young until they are able to fly.

STILTS AND AVOCETS

CHARADRIIFORMES   RECURVIROSTRIDAE

The seven species in this family are characterized by their extremely long legs. Those of the stilts are the longest in proportion to body size of any bird except perhaps the flamingo. All have slender necks, small heads, and very long, thin bills. The stilts have straight bills. The avocets' are gently up-curved, and the Ibisbill's is down-curved. The shapes are correlated with the birds' feeding habits. The stilts probe deeply into the mud for their food; the Ibisbill is also a prober. Avocets wade in the shallows, sweeping their bill back and forth either at the surface or near the bottom in a wide arc with the mandibles partly open.

The Black-necked, or Pied, Stilt, the most widespread member of the family, occurs in temperate and tropical regions practically throughout the world. Six geographical populations are currently recognized, each varying slightly in size and colour. All are black-backed and white-bellied. In New Zealand a small population of all-black stilts occurs with the others. Whether these are simply a melanistic colour phase or a separate species has not as yet been determined. The Banded Stilt of Australia is a slightly larger bird with a white back, head, and neck. It has a broad chestnut band across the breast, a dark-brown abdomen, and bright pink legs.

Avocets are similar widespread, but their distribution is more disrupted. The Avocet of Eurasia and Africa is boldly black and white; the North American Avocet and the Australian Avocet have the head and neck washed with brown. The fourth avocet is limited to the saline lakes in the high Andes of Chile and Bolivia.

The aberrant Ibisbill of mountain lakes and streams in the high Himalayas lives 10,000 feet or more above sea level. It is a slightly heavier-bodied bird than the other species, uniform grey in colour with a bright-red bill.

Stilts and avocets are wetland birds fond of shallow, muddy pools, where they wade slowly and sedately, lifting their legs deliberately one after the other. They swim readily when they

have to and fly strongly. Their call notes are loud, harsh, and far-carrying. They also have a musical twittering, flute-like song, so soft it can be heard only when the birds are close at hand.

Avocets take very little vegetable food, and live mainly on aquatic invertebrates, a variety of crustaceans, molluscs and insects, also some fish and small amphibians. They are gregarious and often breed in small, loose colonies, laying their 3 to 5 (usually 4) eggs in a rough scrape on the ground, occasionally lined with grass or pebbles. Stilts usually build bulky nests of vegetation partly floating in the shallow edges of marshy ponds. Young of both leave the nest shortly after hatching and are tended by both parents.

PHALAROPES

CHARADRIIFORMES   PHALAROPODIDAE

The three dainty little phalaropes are the most aquatic members of the wader complex, and can swim as well as they can wade or walk. An adaptation to their aquatic life is the individual lobate webs on each toe, similar to those developed by the unrelated grebes, coots, and finfoots.

One species, Wilson's Phalarope, breeds around sloughs and potholes in the central plains of northern North America and winters southward to the Argentine pampas. The other two species, the Northern and the Grey phalaropes (the latter is called the Red Phalarope in America after its summer plumage), nest in the arctic and subarctic tundra regions of both hemispheres, usually on the banks of small freshwater pools. They winter southward off both coasts of both oceans to the warm temperate latitudes of the Northern Hemisphere. Each species occupies a somewhat restricted wintering range at sea, usually many miles off the coast. These birds are seldom seen near shore in winter unless driven in by storms.

In the phalaropes the roles of the sexes are strongly re-

versed. The females are larger and much more brightly coloured than the males, and they take the initiative in courtship. The males not only build the nest, but do all the incubating and rearing of the young. The nest is a neat cup in the open tundra, always near water. After the female lays her 4 (rarely 3 or 5) heavily speckled olive-buff eggs, she deserts the nesting grounds. Phalaropes often breed in small loose colonies. While the males tend to do all the domestic chores, the females gather offshore in small flocks.

In the water, phalaropes float very buoyantly and swim rather jerkily, bobbing their heads back and forth. They are quite tame and unafraid, and will let a small boat approach closely before flushing. They then fly in typical sandpiper fashion—the flock wheels erratically over the water, the birds turning and twisting in perfect unison. Phalaropes swim about rapidly in small circles when feeding, sometimes spinning like a top to disturb small floating organisms which they pick daintily off the surface with their thin pointed bills.

WILSON'S PHALAROPE ♀
Steganopus tricolor
North American prairies;
winters to Argentine pampas   10 in.

RED PHALAROPE ♀
Phalaropus fulicarius
Circumpolar in high north;
winters at sea to Southern Hemisphere   9 in.
(summer plumage)

NORTHERN PHALAROPE ♀
Phalaropus lobatus
Circumpolar in arctic tundra;
winters at sea in temperate latitudes   8 in.

CRAB PLOVER
Dromas ardeola
Coasts of East Africa, southwest Asia 15 in.

STONE CURLEW
Burhinus oedicnemus
Europe, northern Africa,
southwestern Asia 16 in.

PRATINCOLE (SWALLOW PLOVER)
Glareola pratincola
Southern Eurasia, Africa 9 in.

CRAB PLOVER

CHARADRIIFORMES   DROMADIDAE

This curious, conspicuous wader is so distinct that it is placed in a family by itself. An oustanding feature is its long, strong, pointed, tern-like bill. Its internal anatomy is plover-like, its long legs with partly webbed front toes resemble those of the avocets, but it has a much larger hind toe. Its nesting habits are most anomalous, for it is one of the few burrow-nesting Charadriiformes, and the only one whose eggs are pure white, a common characteristic of other hole-nesting species.

Crab Plovers lay but a single egg, which is large for the size of the bird. They breed in small colonies and dig their nesting holes 4 to 5 feet back in a sand bank. The precocial young hatch covered with grey down and, though able to run soon after hatching, remain in the burrow for some time while both parents feed them. Crab Plovers inhabit the coasts of east Africa and southwest Asia on the Indian Ocean.

Crab Plovers are sociable birds, easily approached and not at all shy. They are usually found in flocks of 6 to 8 up to several hundred, feeding on coastal mud flats, sand beaches, and coral reefs. As their name implies, they feed on crabs and other crustaceans and on molluscs which they pound to pieces easily with their heavy bills. They are noisy birds, and utter their loud, chattering, hoarse, crow-like cries both when flying and when running about on the shore. They have a peculiar upright stance, with the head and neck pulled down onto the shoulders like a thick-knee, but in flight the neck sticks straight out in front and the feet trail out behind.

THICK-KNEES OR STONE CURLEWS

CHARADRIIFORMES   BURHINIDAE

The nine species of thick-knees, so called because of their perceptibly swollen heels or "knee" joints, are usually known as stone curlews because of their fondness for rough, dry pebbly areas. Their closest anatomical affinities are to the shore birds, but in external appearance and habits they strongly resemble the bustards. All are dull, grey-brown birds streaked and barred with darker browns and blacks. Standing one to almost two feet tall, they have short, plover-like bills, large, broad heads, and the very large eyes of essentially nocturnal species. Their legs are fairly long. The front toes show traces of webs between them and, like so many other running birds, they have no hind toe.

Thick-knees are found in the temperate and tropical parts of most of the world except North America, New Zealand, and the Pacific islands. Typical of the group is the 16-inch Stone Curlew that breeds from southern Britain and western Europe eastward across southern Eurasia to India and in northern Africa. The northern populations migrate southward in winter. Those of more tropical climes wander during the non-breeding season but are not truly migratory. Only one species, the Water Thick-knee of South Africa, lives near water. An inhabitant of sandy or stony borders of rivers and lakes, it is rather tame and unafraid and is often found in the company of crocodiles. Other species are found in South Africa and Southeast Asia, and two species live in Central and South America, one breeding from southern Mexico southward to northern Brazil; the other occupying the Pacific coast of South America from Ecuador to Peru. The Beach Stone Curlew of Australia and Malaya, largest of the thick-knees, is a more coastal species than any of the others.

Most thick-knees are birds of dry uplands and semideserts—strange surroundings indeed for wading birds. They often fly long distances to find water to drink. During the day they crouch quietly on the ground with their long legs doubled under them. In this position they are hard to see, especially as they remain still until almost stepped on. Thick-knees are active in the evening and at night.

When abroad at night, thick-knees are noisy birds and have a vocabulary of wailing, croaking cries. Their food is largely animal. They lay their 2, rarely 3, eggs directly on the ground or in a shallow scrape usually in the open. Incubation is largely by the female, assisted occasionally by the male, who always stands by to warn of approaching danger. Incubation takes 26 to 27 days. The downy young are highly precocial.

COURSERS AND PRATINCOLES

CHARADRIIFORMES GLAREOLIDAE

This Old World family of 16 small aberrant waders contains two subfamilies. These are closely related structurally, but are greatly different in appearance and habits. All are gregarious birds that wander erratically when not nesting, and all are insect eaters, though the two groups feed in radically different ways. Both have their greatest diversity in Africa and southern Asia. Some also occur in temperate Eurasia and in Australia.

The first subfamily, the 9 coursers (Cursoriinae), are long-legged, short-winged, plain-coloured running birds of dry, sandy desert regions, with long, pointed, down-curved bills. They have a peculiar habit of stretching upward on tiptoe with necks outstretched to peer around the horizon. When danger threatens they crouch and depend on their camouflage to hide them. They fly only when pressed, but then swiftly, and they can run faster than a man can walk. Like many other running birds, they have lost the hind toe. One species, the Egyptian Plover, is a beautiful grey and white, with strong markings of black and metallic green. It lives along the sandy river banks of central and northeastern Africa. Tame, friendly, unafraid of humans, it is said to run into crocodiles' open mouths to pick food from between their teeth, but it is probably taking leeches from the reptile's tongue.

Swallow-plover is a more fitting name for the second subfamily, the Glareolinae, than pratincole, which is a Latin concoction meaning "meadow dweller." The seven species are dainty birds, brown or olive above and lighter below, with short legs, long, pointed wings, and long forked tails. Their bills are short, but they can open their mouths very wide when hawking insects on the wing, their preferred method

CREAM-COLOURED
COURSER
Cursorius cursor
Southwestern Asia
and Africa 9 in.

INDIAN COURSER
Cursorius coromandelicus
Northwestern India to Ceylon 9 in.

of feeding. They also run insects down on the ground, and are such efficient locust killers that in South Africa they are called "locust birds." They have the coursers' habit of stretching on tiptoe to look around.

Both groups are ground nesters, and lay from 2 to 3 eggs, with incubation mostly by the female. The Egyptian Plover incubates only at night and buries its eggs in the sand during the daytime so that the sun will keep them warm.

SEEDSNIPES

CHARADRIIFORMES THINOCORIDAE

PATAGONIAN SEEDSNIPE
Thinocorus rumicivorus
Ecuador and Bolivia to
Tierra del Fuego 7 in.

The seedsnipes are small, strange relatives of the waders that have adapted themselves to a vegetarian diet. Though they eat some insects, their food is largely seeds, buds, and other plant growth. The four known species range from the sea-level tundras of the Falkland Islands and Patagonia northward through the Argentine pampas and along the barren Andean highlands from Chile to Ecuador. The highly migratory southern populations fly northward in winter.

Plump little birds with short legs and long, tapering pointed wings, the seedsnipes have stout, conical, sharp-pointed bills much like a sparrow's. A curious anatomical feature, found in no other wader, is the thin opercular flap that covers their slit-like nostrils. Its function is not certain, but it may serve as a protection against the sand and dust carried by the high winds in the dry, barren areas the birds frequent.

Seedsnipes are usually encountered in small flocks. They run rapidly over the ground with the head forward, plover fashion, and are hard to flush. When danger threatens they squat and conceal themselves on the ground with the head and neck extended out flat. When they do take wing they fly rapidly and erratically like a snipe.

They nest on the ground in a scantily lined scrape and lay 3 to 4 clay-coloured eggs which, like those of most waders, are heavily marked and spotted. The Patagonian Seedsnipe covers its eggs with dry earth when it leaves the nest. The precocial young hatch covered with down and leave the nest almost immediately. Little more is known about their nesting habits.

SHEATHBILLS

CHARADRIIFORMES CHIONIDIDAE

Sheathbills are found only on antarctic and subantarctic coasts and islands. They range from the southern tip of South America to the Falkland Islands and the Palmer Peninsula and eastward to Kerguelen and Heard Island south of the western edge of the Indian Ocean. The name sheathbill refers to the peculiar, horny, saddle-like sheath that extends over the base of the upper bill, partly shielding the round nostrils.

Contrary to their peaceful dove-like appearance, sheathbills are bold scavengers. They hang about the fringes of sea-bird colonies to filch what eggs and chicks they can, and flock around calving sea elephants to gorge themselves on the afterbirths and droppings. At other times, they comb the shoreline for seaweeds and whatever molluscs, crustaceans, and other sea life they can find. Sheathbills are quick to locate rubbish dumps when human visitors come to their cold, inhospitable homeland. They are tame, curious, and unafraid.

Structurally the sheathbills are a connecting link between the waders and the gulls, and are perhaps fairly direct descendants of the ancient common ancestor from which both

groups diverged. They have a short, stout bill, short neck, compact body, and fairly long pointed wings. Their legs are short and stout and their feet have rudimentary webs between the three front toes, plus a well-developed hind toe. Sheathbills have wattles about the bill and face and a rudimentary spur at the joint of the wing like those of some plovers. Though they swim well when they have to, these birds avoid the water if they can. They are largely terrestrial, but fly strongly and can make long overwater flights.

The two known species are similar, differing mainly in facial markings and wattles. They usually occur in small flocks of a dozen or so—or a score or more where the pickings are good. No ornithologist has as yet had the opportunity to live near them long enough to give their habits the thorough study they deserve. Sheathbills nest on the ground and lay 2 to 3 white eggs, heavily marked with brown and black blotches. Both sexes incubate and care for the precocial young. Further researches on the behaviour of these relict birds would be interesting and profitable.

SKUAS AND JAEGERS

CHARADRIIFORMES   STERCORARIIDAE

Skua is the old Norwegian name which we use for all four species of these bold, rapacious sea birds, but Americans call three of the species jaegers (pronounced yá-ger), a name taken from the German and Dutch word for hunter. All four are strong-flying, wide-ranging, largely pelagic, piratical birds of high latitudes that strongly resemble their close relatives, the gulls. They differ from gulls structurally in having a fleshy cere across the base of the upper bill, through which the nostrils open. They probably branched off from gull-like ancestors in the Northern Hemisphere.

The Great Skua (Skua to the Americans) is the largest, darkest, and most widely distributed member of the family. It has the distinction of being the only bird species that breeds in both the Arctic and the Antarctic. One population is restricted to the North Atlantic. It breeds on open coastal tundras and moors in Iceland and the Faroes, Orkney, and Shetland islands, and winters at sea south to the Grand and Georges banks off New England and to the latitude of Gibraltar in Europe. Leif Ericson and other northern sailors doubtless knew these birds well, and probably called them skuas in imitation of their cries in flight when chasing their prey.

At least four populations of Great Skuas nest circumpolarly

in the Antarctic, around the fringe of that continent, on the subantarctic islands, and on the coasts of southern Chile and New Zealand. These southern birds winter northward in the warmer waters of all the southern oceans, and cross the equator into the North Pacific. There is no evidence that the birds of the Atlantic population cross the equator, or that the northern and southern Atlantic birds meet on the wintering grounds. The Great Skuas from opposite poles are so similar, however, that only comparison of museum specimens shows the slight differences in colour and size between them.

They are far more plentiful in the Antarctic than they are in the north, and are among the commoner birds of the southernmost coasts and waters. The explorers and whalers who have invaded their ice-fringed home always speak of them as "skuagulls." In appearance and in flight they resemble large, heavy gulls, uniformly dark brown in colour, relieved by a small patch of white on the wings at the base of the flight feathers, which identifies them at a distance.

At sea Great Skuas obtain much of their food by harassing other sea birds and forcing them to disgorge their catch. They also fish for themselves and scavenge along shores and beaches for any sort of dead animal matter. They will settle on the water to pick food from the surface as gulls do. While they do

SHEATHBILL
Chionis alba
Subantarctic coasts and islands 16 in.

ARCTIC SKUA
(PARASITIC JAEGER)
Stercorarius parasiticus
Circumpolar on arctic coasts
and islands 18 in.

LONG-TAILED SKUA
(LONG-TAILED JAEGER)
Stercorarius longicaudus
Circumpolar on arctic coasts
and islands 22 in.

not habitually follow ships, they gather about fishing boats dressing a catch and hang around the whale factory-ships in the Antarctic to feast on the waste and offal thrown overboard.

On their breeding grounds they feed themselves and their nestlings largely on the eggs and young of colonial seabirds. In Antarctica they nest on the fringes of penguin colonies, and their numbers maintain a nice balance with those of the nesting penguins—usually about 1 to 100. Thus a colony of 2,000 pairs of Adélie Penguins will have about 20 pairs of Great Skuas nesting on its flanks, ready to pounce on any egg or chick that is left unattended by its parents. This predator-prey balance has evidently endured for geological ages, and is a control on the numbers of both penguins and skuagulls. They also prey on colonies of petrels and shearwaters.

Great Skuas lay two heavily spotted brown eggs in an open scrape on the ground, but seldom do they raise more than one young. In cold climates the parents must start incubating when the first egg is laid; the second egg is laid and hatches several days later than the first, for each egg requires 28 to 30 days of incubation. When the first nestling starts to wander away from the nest, it is often killed and eaten by its parents or is fed to its sibling, suggesting that the birds' sense of territory is stronger than their recognition of their own young. Ringing in the Antarctic has shown that once individual Great Skuas establish a nesting site, they return to it year after year.

The Pomatorhine, Arctic, and Long-tailed Skuas (known to Americans as the Pomarine, Parasitic and Long-tailed Jaegers), are all northern species that nest circumpolarly in the arctic tundra and winter southward in both the Atlantic and the Pacific, frequently well south of the equator. All are smaller than the Great Skua, and have two colour phases, all brown or, more commonly, brown with white underparts. They are easily identified by their elongated central tail feathers, which project well beyond the rest of the tail. These are square in the Pomatorhine, and longer and pointed in the Arctic and Long-tailed Skuas.

Like the Great Skua, they are predators and strong, fast fliers. In winter they wander over the seas, usually near flocks of other sea birds, particularly Terns and Kittiwakes. While they catch some fish, they subsist mainly by chasing and attacking smaller sea birds, forcing them to disgorge or drop fish they have just caught. On the nesting grounds they feed their young on lemmings and other small rodents, also the eggs and nestlings of other arctic birds. Both sexes incubate the two eggs in a ground nest for 23 to 28 days and tend the offspring for another 6 to 7 weeks until the young are able to fly.

These strong-winged birds fly long distances over the polar ice. The Arctic Skua has been observed within a few miles of the North Pole, and has visited explorers' camps on the barren, foodless Greenland ice cap, well inland and 6,000 feet and more above sea level. Antarctic explorers have reported Skuas hundreds of miles inland on the frozen Antarctic continent (Scott saw one about 150 miles from the South Pole) where they wander apparently following the explorers' trails.

GREAT SKUA
Catharacta skua
Iceland, Faroes, Shetlands;
circumpolar in coastal Antarctica and
subantarctic islands   23 in.

POMATORHINE SKUA
(POMARINE JAEGER)
Stercorarius pomarinus
Circumpolar on arctic coasts
and islands   20 in.

GULLS AND TERNS

CHARADRIIFORMES   LARIDAE

This family of long-winged, web-footed water birds is divided into two well-marked subfamilies, both of which lack the cere on the bill that distinguishes the Skua family. Typically birds of the seashores and coastal waters, many species find their way far inland wherever there are large rivers, lakes, or marshes. Members of the family are found throughout the world except on the driest deserts and the permanently frozen parts of the polar regions. The 43 species of gulls (Larinae) are generally large heavy-bodied birds, 11 to 32 inches in length, with fairly long, stout bills curved downward at the tip into a sharp hook. The 39 species of terns (Sterninae) are smaller, more streamlined birds, 8 to 23 inches in length, with narrower, more pointed wings and thin, sharp-pointed bills.

Gulls are probably the most familiar of all sea birds, for they are common and conspicuous around harbours and beaches where people live. Though often spoken of as "sea gulls," they are seldom found far at sea. The gulls that follow every ocean-bound ship out of harbour hoping to salvage some titbit thrown overboard usually turn back before the vessel leaves soundings. Only one species, the dainty little Kittiwake of northern waters, is found regularly out of sight of land.

The Kittiwake breeds on seaward-facing cliffs along the North Atlantic and in the North Pacific as far north as such cliffs exist. Kittiwakes range far at sea after the breeding

COMMON TERN
Sterna hirundo
Temperate Northern Hemisphere 15 in.

FAIRY TERN
Gygis alba
Islands in tropical Pacific,
Indian, and South Atlantic oceans 12 in.

CALIFORNIA GULL
Larus californicus
Western North America 22 in.

ROYAL TERN
Thalasseus maximus
Coasts of southern U.S.,
West Indies, and West Africa 21 in.

BLACK SKIMMER
Rynchops nigra
Western Hemisphere coasts from Massachusetts
and northwestern Mexico to Strait of Magellan 20 in.

BROWN NODDY
Anoüs stolidus
Tropical Atlantic, Pacific,
and Indian oceans 15 in.

HEERMANN'S GULL
Larus heermanni
Lower California and Mexico 20 in.

HERRING GULL
Larus argentatus
Circumpolar in Northern Hemisphere 24 in.

LAUGHING GULL
Larus atricilla
...tic and Gulf coasts of
...rth America 17 in.

GREAT BLACK-BACKED GULL
Larus marinus
North Atlantic coasts 29 in.

BLACK-HEADED GULL
Larus ridibundus
Temperate Eurasia 15 in.

season, usually following the fishing fleets. As proof of their oceanic wanderings, a score or more Kittiwakes ringed in Great Britain have been recovered in Labrador and New-foundland. Other gulls occasionally wander far across the sea from their normal habitats. Several Black-headed Gulls, a sedentary European species that performs only local migra-tions, have been picked up on the American side of the Atlan-tic. The dainty 11-inch Little Gull of Eurasia, one of the smallest, is another occasional vagrant to American shores. Such wanderers are usually birds only a year or two old. Ring-ing studies have shown that gulls travel farthest during their early years. Young Herring Gulls winter much farther south-ward than do breeding adults 3 or more years old.

Though they prefer animal food and fish when they can

get it, gulls will eat almost anything. With few exceptions they are not good fishermen and seldom catch live food unless it is crippled. But they are good scavengers, not at all finicky in their choice of food, and perform a useful service around harbours and beaches cleaning up fish stranded by the tide and any edible garbage they can find. Every sewage outlet and rubbish dump in coastal cities usually has its attendant gulls, especially in winter when pickings are lean elsewhere. Shell-fish are relished, and the hardest shell is no protection to the animal within. The gull simply flies up in the air with the clam and drops it on a hard surface to break it open, following it down as fast as possible to prevent some marauding neighbour from snatching it first. On sandy coasts they learn quickly that clams break more easily on the hard surface of a nearby bridge or road or even on the flat roof of a cottage or a car.

Gulls are such opportunists that few sources of food go unnoticed. Inland and where agriculture is practised near the coast, gulls follow the plough for grubs and worms. When large insects swarm, as locusts do, gulls gather from miles around to feast on them, as did the California Gulls that nest on Great Salt Lake in Utah when a hatch of "crickets" threatened the first crops of the Mormon settlers. At any rate the gulls are credited with cleaning up enough insects so that the Mormons harvested a crop and were able to survive the winter. This phase of the Mormon saga is commemorated in the lovely statue to the gulls in Salt Lake City.

The California Gull that saved the Mormons' crops is one of a number of gulls that breed on inland lakes. Another American species is the smaller, dark-headed Franklin's Gull that nests around small lakes and potholes in the western prairies of northern United States and Canada. Old World counterparts are Saunders Gull of northern China and Mongolia, the Brown-headed Gull of the Himalayan foothills, and Buller's Gull of New Zealand. All these inland-breeding gulls repair to coastal salt waters in the winter. Franklin's Gull is one of the few that crosses the equator. Migrating southward across the interior of North America, a few winter in the Gulf of Mexico, but most push on to the coasts of Peru and Ecuador.

Where young and old are gathered together in flocks of wintering gulls, the uninitiate may think several species are present, so different are they in colour. Usually the differences between the brown birds and the white ones, and all the intermediates between them, are of age. The Herring Gull, a widespread Northern Hemisphere species, is perhaps the commonest gull on the Atlantic coasts of North America and Europe. For the first winter after leaving the nest, Herring Gulls are a uniform brown with a black bill. In their first spring moult (gulls moult twice a year in spring and autumn), their new feathers are lighter, and their bill becomes flesh-coloured. It takes them three years to assume the full adult plumage. They come nearer and nearer to it with each successive moult, and the sequence is so regular the age of an immature specimen can be told accurately.

Other species show variations on this general pattern. One of the largest gulls, the 32-inch Glaucous, or "Burgomaster," Gull of northern waters, is almost pure white, as is the smaller Iceland Gull, a rare winter visitor to the New England coasts. Several gulls, like the Great Black-backed Gull, aptly dubbed the "minister gull" in New England, have the back and wings black which, with their white heads and bodies, gives them

their clerical aspect. Another group of gulls have the entire head dark-coloured in the breeding plumage, but lose the dark feathers in the autumn moult and are white-headed in winter. These include the Brown-headed Gull and Franklin's Gull, already mentioned, the Black-headed Gull of Europe, and the very similar Laughing Gull of North America's Atlantic coastal waters, whose cackling cry vaguely resembles human laughter.

Some of the smaller gulls acquire their adult plumage more rapidly; several in two years and a few of the smallest in the first year. The state of their plumage reflects their sexual development, for moult is triggered by a sex hormone. Gulls are unable to breed until they are fully adult.

Ringing studies show that gulls are long-lived. Mortality is high on the nesting grounds and remains high during the first year while they are learning to take care of themselves, to find food and to avoid enemies. Once past the crucial first year, their mortality is low, about 33 per cent, and their life expectancy fairly high. The oldest ringed Herring Gull on record was ringed as a chick in Denmark in 1925 and recovered in 1953, 28 years later.

In all their activities gulls are sociable birds, migrating, hunting, resting, scavenging, and quarrelling together. Nowhere are they more social than on their breeding grounds, for most of them prefer to nest together, sometimes in large colonies. Such a colony may be entirely of one species, often of several species of gulls together, and even with other species of sea birds, whose eggs and young the gulls snatch when given the opportunity. The Herring Gull commonly nests in close association with terns, as do the Black-backed and Laughing gulls. The Glaucous Gull and the Kittiwake frequently nest on ledges with auks and murres. The California Gulls at Great Salt Lake nest in association with White Pelicans, Double-crested Cormorants, and Herring Gulls.

Most gulls nest on the ground (a few in low trees) and build a bulky structure of seaweed and whatever other vegetation is handy. They lay 2 or 3 brownish eggs heavily spotted with darker brown or black. Both sexes share the incubation duties, which may last from 20 days in the smaller species to 30 in the larger ones; both feed and protect the chicks. The precocial young hatch covered with greyish down dotted with black. They are able to stand and walk soon after hatching, but they tend to stay in or near the nest until they are fairly well grown. Young birds that wander too far from their own nest are likely to be pounced upon and eaten by a neighbour. They fly at 4 to 6 weeks.

Most gull colonies are on small coastal islands, safe from foxes, weasels, skunks, and the like, but within easy reach of a man with a boat. Egging was a common practice along the Atlantic coast of the United States in the 19th century, and gull eggs were brought to market by the thousands, as they still are elsewhere in the world. Egging and plume hunting almost wiped gulls off American coasts before both practices were stopped by law 50 years ago.

Under protection the gulls have gradually recovered, and now breed in New England and the Middle Atlantic states where they were absent for decades. The most recent threat to their security is the development of shore properties for summer vacationers. Fortunately many of the gull islands are small sand spits too insecure for the building of cottages.

Some of the best-known breeding islands have been purchased and protected by the Audubon societies.

Gulls and terns seem to go through cycles on these protected islands, alternating with each other for periods that may last for 15 to 30 years. Herring Gulls come into a tern colony and gradually take it over until they occupy it solidly for a period of years. Then they leave it and the terns come back. In recent years the Herring Gull has increased greatly along the New England coast to the detriment of the terns.

Gulls are usually noisy, and their raucous cries are familiar sounds in populated harbours and particularly in fishing villages where refuse is plentiful. They seem to lose their fear of man when food is plentiful and they are not harmed. Among their favourite sources of food are fishing boats dressing their catch. As the refuse is thrown overboard the gulls gather close around the vessel and quarrel among themselves for each titbit. The two common gulls of New Zealand, the red-billed Silver Gull and the black-billed Buller's Gull, inhabit the parks of the coastal cities like so many pigeons.

The common wintering gull of southern U.S. coasts is the Ring-billed Gull, which breeds in the Great Lakes region and winters southward to salt water. Slightly smaller than the Herring Gull, it is similarly patterned in grey and white, and identified by the black band around the end of its yellow bill. Like the Herring Gull, it is a beach scavenger. With protection it has become abundant and tame. It feeds among the bathers along the Florida beaches.

Gulls are fine soarers, able to ride updrafts from the waves, from the sterns of vessels, and from dunes, cliffs, or buildings. At sea they circle until they spot some floating object that might be food. They sometimes pick it off the water in flight but usually land next to it to pick at it. Gulls swim well, but they cannot swim underwater, or dive under the surface from the air as do the terns. The best they can do is reach down a foot or so, the length of their neck and bill.

The terns are generally smaller, more slender, more graceful birds than the gulls, and are more selective in their feeding habits. The terns seldom soar, but fly on steady wingbeats, often with the head and bill pointed down instead of forward. Although terns are not above picking small floating titbits from the surface, most of their food is live small fish or shrimps which they capture by plunging under the surface from the air. Inland terns also feed on insects they hawk on the wing.

Although they are web-footed and float buoyantly on the surface, terns are poor swimmers, as their feet are too small and weak to propel them efficiently. When feeding, most terns dive in with a splash and immediately fly out of the water with their catch. The Sooty Tern, one of the most pelagic of all terns, practically never enters the water, but snatches its food daintily from the surface in flight. Another pelagic species, the Brown Noddy, often settles on water where fish are schooling and feeds like a gull.

Most terns resemble gulls in general colour pattern, being white-bodied with a grey back and wings, but they usually have a black crown, and several sport a nuchal crest as well.

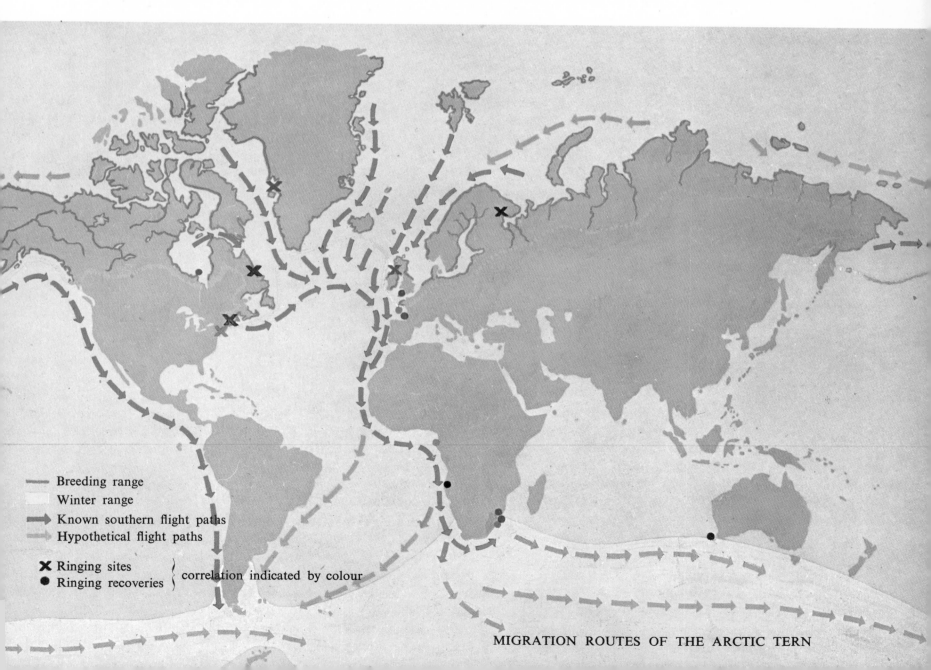

Breeding range
Winter range
Known southern flight paths
Hypothetical flight paths

X Ringing sites ⎱ correlation indicated by colour
● Ringing recoveries ⎰

MIGRATION ROUTES OF THE ARCTIC TERN

Like the gulls, terns moult in spring and autumn, and have a 2- to 3-year adolescent period before they breed, but their immature plumages are not distinctive, and closely resemble those of the adults in winter dress. The tails of first-year birds are usually squarish instead of deeply forked as in most adults. The arctic Sabine's and the Galapagos Forktailed Gulls have forked tails, but the latter never occurs in temperate latitudes. Some of the larger terns, such as the Caspian and Royal of American waters and the Crested Tern of the Western Pacific and Indian oceans, are larger than medium-sized gulls. Their different bills and tails and manner of flight readily identify them as terns.

The bills and feet of terns vary from coal black to bright red or yellow, and bill colour is often the most obvious distinguishing mark between species. Some terns are so alike—the Common, Arctic, and Forster's Terns, for instance—that they are very difficult to tell apart in the field, and even experts sometimes have to rely on their voices as clues. All terns have similar sharp, rasping cries, but with distinctive differences between the various species that are easily recognized.

Though white and grey with a black crown is the commonest tern colour pattern, there are many exceptions. The Brown Noddy reverses the pattern and is solid brown with a pale-grey crown. The Black Tern, a small North American and Eurasian species that nests inland in marshes and reed-bordered lakes, is almost entirely black in adult plumage, but first-year birds have white bellies and dark-grey backs. The lovely Fairy Tern of the Central Pacific is pure white with a black bill. This dainty little bird has the curious habit, for a tern, of nesting in low bushes, usually mangroves. It perches its single egg precariously on a bare branch scarcely larger than the egg, and there it sits and incubates. After hatching, the young bird stays in the tree for several days, until it falls or jumps to the ground. Another unusually coloured species is the Inca Tern, which breeds in company with the

Guanays and Brown Pelicans on the guano islands off the west coast of South America from Peru to Chile. The Inca Tern is the only member of the family that nests under cover. It lays its eggs in rock crevices or in holes in the guano.

Best known and most adequately studied of the terns is the Common Tern, which breeds around the world in north temperate latitudes on coasts and offshore islets and on inland lakes and marshes. It migrates southward across the equator in both hemispheres. More Common Terns have been ringed than any other single species of bird. On the famous colonies on Cape Cod, almost 500,000 terns have been ringed during the past 30 years, most of them as young birds. About 50,000 of these have been recaptured as adults.

The terns appear on Cape Cod from their southern wintering grounds in May and tend to return to the same place where they bred the year before. When they arrive the birds are already paired, but they continue their courtship as they select their breeding sites and build their nests. The male tern courts the female with a small fish which he brings in his beak and offers her as a token of his regard. Each pair selects its breeding site, usually as close as possible to where it bred the year before, and drives all other terns from this limited stretch of ground which may be only a few feet in diameter. Fighting and bickering over territory causes most of the noise and squabbling typical of all tern colonies.

Each pair of terns scoops out a shallow depression in the sand. Resting on its breast, the bird pushes the sand backwards with its feet, turning round and round to make the nest circular. The scrape may be lined with a few pebbles, bits of shell, or seaweed, but often is bare. In this depression the female lays 2 or 3 eggs, on rare occasions 4. The average of thousands of clutches counted is 2.3 eggs per pair. Both sexes share the incubation duties alternately, and some courtship with mutual feeding continues through incubation. Incubation lasts from 21 to 28 days, depending on just how attentively the parent birds keep the eggs warm. Terns incubate most avidly

ARCTIC TERN
Sterna paradisaea
Circumpolar in
Northern Hemisphere 15 in.

ROSEATE TERN
Sterna dougalli
Coasts and islands of North Atlantic,
Indian, and western Pacific oceans 16 in.

INCA TERN
Larosterna inca
Coasts of Peru and Chile 16 in.

SOOTY TERN
Sterna fuscata
Tropic and subtropic Atlantic, Pacific,
and Indian oceans 16 in.

on hot, bright days when temperatures on the sand may rise to over 120°, covering the eggs to keep them cool.

The chicks at hatching are fluffy balls of greyish or brownish down with black markings. They remain in the nest only for the first day or two, where the parents brood them from the hot sun and from occasional chilly rain. Both parents feed the young and frequently poke fish that are longer than the chick itself down their gullets. The young bird stands with the tail end of its dinner waving from its beak waiting for the lower half to digest to make room for the rest. Within a few days the chicks start to run about. When they wander on to the territories of nearby birds, they are driven off with sharp pecks that are frequently fatal.

Other vicissitudes face the growing young tern. Food is perhaps the most critical factor, for their rate of growth depends largely on how fast the parents are able to find fish to cram down waiting gullets. When, as occasionally happens, small fish disappear from the vicinity of the ternery, the young soon starve to death. Occasionally storm-driven tides inundate an entire colony and sweep away both eggs and young. Long periods of stormy weather may be equally disastrous. Diseases, caused by epizootics of which we know little, sometimes wipe out the young before they are 2 or 3 days old. Predators also take their toll. Owls prey upon both adults and young during the night. When rats are able to reach a ternery, they can be a terrible scourge and have wiped out colonies of ten thousand pairs of birds in a few days.

Studies of the mortality of ringed adult birds have shown that 23 per cent of the adult Common Tern population dies each year. The mortality in the young is so high that the terns have difficulty in maintaining their numbers, and over the past several decades the Cape Cod populations have been slowly dwindling. Some years no young mature at all. This is balanced by the occasional good years in which half or more of the young may reach the flying stage.

It takes young terns from 3 to 5 weeks to develop their flight feathers. For the first several weeks after they leave the ternery, the young remain with their parents, who continue to feed them on nearby shorelines until they develop sufficient skill to catch fish for themselves. Some young terns never learn to fish well enough for themselves, and many die of starvation during the first year. Their southward route can be traced by the young birds picked up dead along the beaches. The Cape Cod terns fly southward along the Atlantic coast about as far as Hatteras, where they take off over the blue water and next appear either at the Bahamas or at the eastern end of Cuba. From there they fly through the West Indies to their wintering grounds from Trinidad southward along the east coast of South America, from the Amazon delta south to Rio de Janeiro.

The young terns remain on their southern wintering grounds through the next summer and frequently through their second summer. Occasional young individuals accompany the adults back to the northern breeding grounds, but none breeds in its yearling summer, and very few in the second summer. Most breed for the first time when 3 or 4 years old. For the next 15 years the mortality rate of the adults, shown by thousands of ringed birds recaptured on their nests, remains fairly constant at 23 per cent. Thus the greater part of the population on the breeding grounds is made up of birds anywhere from 4 to 15 years of age. By the time the birds are 18 or 19 years old, the steady decline at 23 per cent a

year leaves only one or two out of each thousand. The oldest tern so far on record on Cape Cod was 25 years old.

Ringing has shown that the young terns return to nest to the area where they were hatched. Once having bred, they return to the identical spot year after year, or as close to it as suitable nesting conditions are available. This trait is called "site tenacity" — the faithfulness of a bird to territory. Since its discovery in the terns, this trait has been demonstrated in many other species. Site faithfulness is always greatest to the breeding grounds, and to a lesser extent to the migration routes and to the wintering grounds.

Comparison of recoveries of various Common Tern populations shows that each group has separate wintering areas. Recoveries from the thousands of young Common Terns ringed in the Great Lakes terneries show that the birds winter mostly in the Gulf of Mexico and on the west coast of South America. When these birds leave their Great Lakes terneries, they fly eastward through gaps in the Appalachian Mountains to the Atlantic seaboard, from Long Island to Chesapeake Bay, not down the Mississippi as once thought. This is probably the ancient route by which ancestral terns reached the Great Lakes when the Pleistocene ice first receded and the Great Lakes drained to the sea through the Hudson and not the St Lawrence. Instead of flying south to Cuba and the Bahamas as the New England terns do, the Great Lakes birds continue southwestward along the Atlantic coast past Florida and then across the Gulf of Mexico. Apparently they retrace the same route in the spring.

A few Arctic Terns nest with the Common Terns on Cape Cod. This is the southernmost breeding place of Arctic Terns in North America. Their breeding habits are similar to those of the Common Tern, but when the nesting season ends the two species part company. The Arctic Terns head northeast toward Newfoundland, where they meet others of their kind from the northern breeding colonies along the Nova Scotia and Labrador coast, and continue eastward and southeastward across the Atlantic following a great circle route toward the west coast of Europe and the Canary Islands. From there they follow the west coast of Africa to the Cape of Good Hope, which they may round, almost as far as Madagascar. They winter in the waters off South Africa southward toward the Antarctic circle.

This amazing migration route was revealed by recoveries of young Arctic Terns I ringed in Labrador almost 35 years ago. One of these was picked up on the coast of France scarcely 6 weeks after it had left its Labrador birthplace. Another was reported from the coast of Natal in southeast Africa, 90 days and 9,000 miles away. For many years this particular bird held the individual record for long-distance travel by a ringed bird. Only a few years ago the Danes started ringing Arctic Terns in Greenland. One ringed near Disco Bay, half way up the west coast of Greenland, was recovered still farther around the southeast coast of Africa and now holds the long-distance record of more than 10,000 miles. One young Arctic Tern ringed in northern Russia was recovered in Australia. An Arctic Tern also holds the longevity record among terns. One ringed in Norway as a chick died on the same ternery 27 years later.

The Arctic Terns breed circumpolarly at high latitudes completely around the Northern Hemisphere from as far north as northern Greenland south to Cape Cod on the Atlantic coast, and in Europe to the northern British Isles and Norway. Most of the birds seem to funnel to the Atlantic and travel down its eastern shores. Those nesting in northeastern Siberia and Alaska fly southward down the eastern Pacific. As many Arctic Terns both nest and winter where the sun seldom sets, they probably see more continuous daylight each year than any other living animal.

Two widespread terns of tropical waters frequently found together in breeding colonies are the Sooty Tern and the Brown Noddy. Populations of each of these birds are found the world around, breeding on isolated islands in the Atlantic, the Pacific, and the Indian oceans.

The Sooty Tern nests in colonies of almost countless thousands on tropical oceanic islands. One of the most famous colonies is the "Wideawake Fair" on Ascension Island in the eastern Atlantic, just south of the equator. This population has freed itself from the yoke of the sun and has abandoned the annual breeding cycle followed by most other birds. It nests at 10-month instead of yearly intervals, which is one way of slightly increasing the number of young birds to replace the yearly mortality of adults. It has not yet been determined whether other populations of the Sooty Tern follow a similar shortened breeding cycle.

The Sooties that breed on the Dry Tortugas just off the Florida Keys, where the seasons are more pronounced, breed on an annual schedule, coming ashore to nest in late May or early June every year. Like most tropical terns, the Sooty lays but a single egg, which, at least in the Dry Tortugas population, seems sufficient to keep its population up to the mark. It lays its egg in a bare scrape on the ground, and often the nests, only a foot or two apart, occupy every bit of suitable territory.

The Dry Tortugas colony of Sooty Terns was almost wiped out during the 19th century by egging. How many thousands of eggs were taken from the island during its heyday is hard to estimate because they were sold not by the dozen or the hundred, but by the gallon, to wholesale bakers. Fortunately the Dry Tortugas are now a National Monument under the protection of the United States National Park Service, and the "Wideawakes," as the Sooty Terns are generally called, and the Noddy now breed there undisturbed by vandalism.

It was on the Dry Tortugas colony that Dr. J. B. Watson made his classic experiments more than 40 years ago proving that individual terns can find their way back over trackless seas to their nesting colonies. This was before the days when birds were ringed systematically. Watson marked his birds with oil paint. The first ones, released 70 miles away at Key West, returned within the day. Later he sent Sooty Terns and Noddies to Havana and Cape Hatteras. The Havana birds came back in 2 to 3 days. It took the Hatteras birds 10 to 12 days to travel the some 1,200 miles they probably flew around the Florida peninsula to their nesting ground.

The Noddies on the Tortugas build a firm platform of sticks and seaweed from 1 to 5 feet off the ground in a low bush. They are so tame and trusting that an incubating bird can often be lifted off her nest by hand. The Noddy sometimes builds its nest on the ground, and occasionally on cliff edges.

It lays but a single egg, and the chicks usually remain in or close to the nest until almost ready to fly.

Apparently the single-egged birds have an advantage over the multi-egged terns of similar size and similar habits in suffering a lower mortality to the eggs and young. The Sooty Tern and Noddy are the most pelagic of the terns and are seldom seen near land except in breeding season. While other terns frequently rest along the shore, these seldom do, and of the thousands and thousands of Sooties ringed at the Dry Tortugas very few are picked up dead along the beaches the way ringed Common, Arctic, Forster's, and Roseate terns are. While figures are not sufficient as yet, the Sooties apparently have a lower adult mortality rate. The oldest Sooty Tern recorded to date was 25 years old and still breeding.

Another widespread species is the Roseate Tern, which is almost cosmopolitan in distribution. A 16-inch bird similar in size to the Common Tern, it has a longer, more deeply forked tail and to the practiced eye it is more graceful in flight. The Roseate often shares nesting colonies with the Common Tern, but instead of nesting in the open on the sand, it usually hides its nest under beach grass and other vegetation. Like all the terns, it defends its nest vigorously when the colony is invaded. Terns not only shriek at the invader but they hover over him and swoop down, striking out at him with their sharp bills. Many times infuriated Common and Arctic terns have pecked my scalp open. Sooties and Noddies are not so ferocious.

One of the most attractive terns is the dainty Least Tern, the smallest of the family, only 8½ inches long. A white bird with a light-grey back, a black cap on its head, and a white forehead, it is identifiable immediately by its bright yellow bill which it carries pointed down in flight. It is now such a common bird, nesting on the open sandy beaches all the way from Cape Cod south to Florida, that it is hard to realize that a scant 50 years ago it was almost extinct.

The Least Tern was one of the birds most sought by plume hunters, for there was a steady millinery market for its skins. Today its shrill little cries are again one of the pleasant sounds along the beaches. Least Terns breed in smaller groups than the other species. Seldom do more than 200 or 300 pairs nest together, and usually there are less than a dozen in a favourable spot on some lonesome beach. It has never been possible to ring Least Terns in as large quantities as the more colonial nesting species. Hence we know much less about their survival rates. Evidently they are as long-lived as the other terns. One Least Tern that I ringed as a nestling on Cap Cod 30 years ago was found dead 23 years later within a hundred yards of where I had ringed it. This seems to indicate that size has little to do with longevity in terns.

The latest threat to tern survival has been the mass spreading of insecticides, mainly DDT, on the coastal marshes to eliminate mosquitoes. Very seldom in the past were adult terns found dead on New England beaches. In recent summers large numbers have been found, among them a score or so of our Cape Cod tern population, aged anywhere from 5 to 12 years. Autopsies showed these birds had been killed by DDT which they had undoubtedly acquired from fishes, which had in turn acquired it from the spraying of the coastal marshes.

SKIMMERS

CHARADRIIFORMES   RYNCHOPIDAE

Skimmers, the only birds whose lower bill is longer than the upper, have a peculiar method of fishing all their own. They skim close to the water with the long lower mandible just cutting the surface. When this strikes a small fish or a shrimp, the upper bill clamps down tightly. The bird flips its prey out of the water, swallows it without missing a wingbeat, and lowers its bill into the water again for more.

Other structural peculiarities connected with this extraordinary fishing technique set the three skimmers apart from their nearest relatives, the gulls and terns. The outer halves of both bills are knife-like, but broader toward the mouth. The outer portion of the lower bill has a single sharp cutting edge, which fits tightly into a groove in the upper bill to hold slippery prey. To withstand the shock of impact with its prey, the neck muscles are strengthened and extra bony processes attach the skull firmly to the neck.

As skimmers' bodies must stay close to the water as they cruise along on steady beats of their long, pointed wings, the wing strokes are kept above the birds' horizontal plane. Skimmers forage singly or in small flocks, weaving back and forth over the smooth, quiet surface of coastal inlets and backwaters. When a feeding skimmer comes close enough on a quiet evening, you can actually hear the bill zip through the water.

Skimmers feed mostly in the early evening and at night when the water is calm and fish and shrimps come to the surface. By day they roost in flocks on open beaches. To protect their sensitive eyes, necessary for nocturnal fishing, against the sun's glare off the water and the white sand, they have vertical pupils that can be narrowed to a slit. Skimmers' yapping calls sound at a distance like the baying of hounds.

The Black Skimmer of North America (p. 130) is the largest of the three. It ranges on the Atlantic coast from Long Island southward and down both sides of South America to Argentina and Chile. The other two species are similar but slightly smaller birds, and have the upper parts blackish brown instead of black. The African Skimmer, found throughout the coasts, rivers and lakes of Africa, has a bright yellow bill. The Indian Skimmer has a bill black at the base and yellow at the tip. It is seldom seen along seacoasts, but ranges along the large rivers from India through Burma to Indochina.

Skimmers nest colonially on sandy beaches, hollowing out a bare spot in the sand by rotating their breasts. Here they lay from 2 to 5 eggs. Incubation is almost entirely by the female. The precocial young are covered with light grey down and can be very difficult to see as they crouch flat on the open sand. Both bills are of equal length at hatching, and the lower one does not start to grow longer than the upper until the birds are almost full-grown.

AUKS AND ALLIES

CHARADRIIFORMES   ALCIDAE

The members of this family are known by so many well-established common names—auk, auklet, murre, murrelet, guillemot, dovekie, puffin—that ornithologists usually refer to them collectively by the convenient term "alcid," derived from their scientific family name. The 23 Recent species of alcids are the northern counterparts of the penguins of the Antarctic. In fact the name penguin was originally applied to the now extinct Great Auk of the North Atlantic, and was somehow transferred to the southern birds more than a century ago. Except for size (the largest auks being only slightly bigger than the smallest penguins), the two groups are remarkably similar in both appearance and habits. Like the penguins, the alcids are heavy-bodied swimming birds with legs placed far back on the body, rather clumsy, awkward, and even comical on land. They are fine swimmers and divers, and obtain their food by chasing it beneath the surface, actually "flying" underwater with their wings.

Here the resemblances end, for all the living alcids are fairly strong fliers, and even the flightless Great Auk had well-developed flight feathers on its wings which the penguins lack. The alcids are as far removed from the penguins evolutionally as they are geographically. Their anatomy shows them closely related to the waders and the gulls, from which, as their fossil record shows us, their ancestors had separated by earliest Tertiary time, 70 million years ago. They offer an example of parallel evolution—of distinct groups developing similar traits as the result of variation and selection by similar environments.

The alcids are holarctic in distribution, breeding circumpolarly around the fringes of the Arctic Ocean. The family stronghold is the Bering Sea and adjacent shores of the Arctic Ocean, where 19 of the living species occur. Three of these, the Black Guillemot and the Common and Brünnich's guill-

GREAT AUK (extinct)
Pinguinus impennis
Islands in North Atlantic   30 in.

emots, live also in the North Atlantic and its arctic extensions, to which three additional species are limited—the Common Puffin, the Little Auk and the Razorbill.

Also limited to the North Atlantic was the Razorbills' large relative, the flightless Great Auk, of which fewer than 100 specimens remain today in museums. Large numbers once nested on small islands from Newfoundland past Greenland and Iceland to the northern British Isles and Scandinavia. So helpless were the Great Auks on land that the early navigators who chanced on their breeding islands were able to fill their boats by herding them over a gangplank or a sail stretched from the shore. The last living pair was slaughtered and their eggs destroyed on a rocky islet off Iceland in June, 1844.

No scientist ever studied the birds in life. What little we know of them has been gleaned from museum specimens and from bones found in prehistoric kitchen middens. Some details are given in the casual writings of early navigators and explorers.

The Great Auk was about 30 inches long and stood well over 2 feet tall. The birds came out of the sea to breed in May and laid a single egg on the rocky ground. It was about 5 inches long, strongly pear-shaped like those of a Razorbill or a guillemot, white in ground colour, and heavily spotted with brown and black. The incubation period was probably about 6 weeks, and if the development pattern followed that of the closely related Razorbill, the young probably took to the sea within 2 or 3 weeks after hatching. Remains found in Indian kitchen middens suggest that the Great Auk migrated far southward along the coasts and travelled amazing distances for a non-flying bird. The numbers of Great Auk bones found in prehistoric deposits as far south as Gibraltar and Florida indicate that the birds once occurred that far south regularly.

The largest of the living alcids are the circumpolar Common and Brünnich's guillemots (Common and Thick-billed murres in American parlance) and the Razorbill. Guillemots and Razorbills breed on narrow ledges on seaward-facing cliffs. They make no nest, but lay their single egg on the bare rock. Their eggs, heavily spotted, vary considerably in colour from white to brown or greenish blue. They are strongly pear-shaped so that if dislodged they will rotate in a small circle around the pointed end instead of rolling off the ledge.

Ringing has shown that the auks and guillemots have strong faithfulness to their breeding sites. Individuals return to lay in the same spot on the same ledge on the same cliff year after year. Both sexes incubate and feed the young, which hatch covered with grey down and mature very rapidly. About 2 weeks after hatching, when still about half the size of adults, their waterproof body feathers have matured, and though their flight feathers have not yet appeared, the young birds flutter down to the water where one or both parents accompany them swimming seaward. This early desertion of the nesting ledge avoids excessive predation by the gulls that constantly harry the open cliffs for unguarded fledglings. The pattern is quite different in the burrow-digging puffins and in the Black Guillemot and the Little Auk which

BRÜNNICH'S GUILLEMOT
Uria lomvia
Northern Atlantic, Pacific,
and Arctic coasts 17 in.

RAZORBILL
Alca torda
Coasts of northern North Atlantic 16 in.

BLACK GUILLEMOT
Cepphus grylle
North Atlantic, North Pacific,
and Arctic Ocean coasts 14 in.

LITTLE AUK
Plautus alle
Greenland to Novaya Zemlya 8 in.

nest in rock crannies where eggs and young are hidden from sight. In these species the young remain in the nest for the 6 to 8 weeks it takes their flight feathers to develop, and usually fly to sea on their own, unattended by their parents.

The puffins with their gaudy parrot-like bills are the clowns of the alcid family. The two Pacific species, the Horned Puffin and Tufted Puffin, have additional head decorations—long crests of feathers in the Tufted, and fleshy excrescences over the eye in the Horned. Puffins' beaks are brilliant only during the breeding season. During the postnuptial moult they shed the outer covering of the bill and spend the winter with a much less gay and noticeable proboscis. They are the best walkers among the alcids. Instead of shuffling along on the foot and tarsus, as all other alcids do, puffins stand upright on their toes and waddle with a comical, stiff, rolling gait.

Puffins nest in burrows; they dig 3 to 4 feet into the turf of grassy slopes near the sea, chiselling the dirt loose with their beaks and shovelling it out with their webbed feet. The single egg each female lays is rounder than those of the guillemots and auks, but there is no danger of its rolling to destruction. As in many hole-nesting birds, puffin eggs are almost white, though some retain faint markings that suggest they once needed camouflaging. The female puffin does most of the incubating, but the male takes short turns on the egg. He also helps feed the young, which is usually stuffed with fish twice daily, in the morning and evening. They feed the young for about 6 weeks, and then suddenly desert it. The chick remains in the burrow another week, living on accumulated fat while the last of the down wears off its body and the flight feathers finish growing. Then at night, when there is less danger from predators, it comes out and flutters to the sea by itself.

Smallest of the Atlantic alcids is the Little Auk, 8 to 9 inches in length, that nests in the crevices of rocky cliffs in far-northern Greenland, Jan Mayen Island, Spitsbergen, and Franz Josef Land, often at some distance from the sea. It migrates southward in winter in large flocks along both coasts of the Atlantic, commonly to the British Isles and New England, occasionally as far as the Mediterranean and Florida. It is occasionally driven ashore, and sometimes far inland, by storms. These fat little birds, commonly called "pineknots" in New England, are a favourite food of the Eskimos, who catch them in dip nets as the flocks wheel by their nesting cliffs. Their usual American name is Dovekie.

Among the more spectacular of the North Pacific alcids is the solid-grey Crested Auklet, whose forward-curving topknot resembles that of the California Quail, and is doubtless responsible for its local name of "sea quail." Smallest of the family is the 6-inch Least Auklet, a plain little black and white bird sometimes encountered on the rough waters of the northern Pacific in flocks of thousands. The Least Auklet and the other small auklets and murrelets from 7 to 10 inches in length are frequently called "sea sparrows." One of the rarest and least known of the alcids is the Japanese Murrelet, which breeds only on a few small islets in the Izu archipelago south of Tokyo. The southernmost are Xantus' and Craveri's Murrelets, which nest in Lower California and range northward to colder waters after breeding, instead of southward as do their northern relatives. Other distinctive species include the Rhinoceros, the Whiskered, and the Parakeet Auklets, all of which have distinctive plumes or beaks during the nesting season. The nest and eggs of one species, the Marbled Murrelet, which is thought to nest on islands off the Alaskan or British Columbia coasts, have yet to be discovered. The nesting of its close relative, Kittlitz's Murrelet, was long a mystery. This little sea bird nests in Alaskan mountains well above the tree line on bare patches of ground amid the melting snow.

COMMON GUILLEMOT
Uria aalge
Coasts of North Atlantic
and North Pacific   17 in.

COMMON PUFFIN
Fratercula arctica
North Atlantic coasts   12 in.

TUFTED PUFFIN
Lunda cirrhata
Bering Sea and North Pacific coasts   15 in.

CRESTED AUKLET
Aethia cristatella
Bering Sea and North Pacific coasts   9½ in.

ANCIENT
MURRELET
*Synthliboramphus
antiquum*
North
Pacific coasts   9 in.

PIGEONS, SANDGROUSE, DODOS

COLUMBIFORMES

Though their fossil record goes back only some 40 million years to Oligocene time, the pigeons and their allies are doubtless of much earlier origin. They are a distinctive group of rather primitive, though fairly specialized, birds that show no close ties to any other order. They agree anatomically with the charadriids in palate and wing structure, but differ in their types of vertebrae, sternum, feet, and other essential features. The order's distribution is world-wide except for the north and south polar regions. One extinct and two living families make up the order.

The Columbiformes are all land birds with thick, heavy plumage, whose feathers are loosely attached in the skin. All live on vegetable foods—fruits, grains, herbage—and all feed their young by regurgitation from a large crop. They lay small clutches of eggs, usually 2, rarely 3, but often only 1. A most distinctive characteristic is their unique method of drinking. No one knows how the dodos drank, but the sandgrouse and pigeons are the only birds able to suck up water. They immerse their beaks and drink their fill without raising their heads as practically all other birds have to do.

SANDGROUSE

COLUMBIFORMES   PTEROCLIDAE

Sandgrouse live in sandy, open, treeless country and are highly regarded as game birds. They vaguely resemble squat, short-legged grouse—hence their name—but have pigeon-like heads and necks. Structurally sandgrouse are very close to the pigeons, though their short pointed bills lack the pigeons' fleshy cere, and their skin is thicker and tougher. Their wings and tails are long and pointed, and their extremely short legs are feathered down to the toes, which also are feathered in two Asiatic species.

Rather plump, medium-sized, streamlined birds, 9 to 16 inches long, all the sandgrouse are protectively coloured. Their greys and browns, cryptically dappled with orange, chestnut, black, and white, melt into their semidesert and steppe surroundings. The 16 species inhabit the drier parts of Africa and Madagascar, southern Europe, central and southern Asia. Their feathered legs and their thick skins doubtless help them resist the extremes of daily temperatures they encounter in these habitats. They never perch, but walk about quietly on the ground with short, mincing steps, foraging on berries, seeds, and buds and on an occasional small insect.

Sandgrouse have all the attributes of a good sporting bird. They are markedly gregarious, their flesh is succulent and tasty, and they are swift of flight, shy, wary, and difficult to approach within gun range. When disturbed they rise with a laboured pigeony clattering of wings, quickly get up speed,

and fly away straight and fast with short, quick wingstrokes that produce a faint whistling sound. On long flights they continually twitter to one another. Their vocabularies include whistles and clucking and croaking noises.

Though they live in dry regions, they must have water daily, and will travel far every morning or evening or both to get it, a habit which is to the hunter's advantage. So wary are they that when the flock reaches the water-hole, the birds first pitch down several hundred yards away and watch quietly for 5 or 10 minutes to make sure the coast is clear and no danger threatens. Then they fly to the water's edge, wade in up to their bellies, and sometimes even paddle a few strokes. (A few species swim readily.) Lowering their beaks, they suck up their fill, pigeon fashion, without raising their heads until they are full. Flocks return again and again to the same water-hole.

Sandgrouse differ from pigeons in nesting habits, for their precocial young hatch out covered with down and soon desert the nest. Their eggs are longer than pigeons' eggs, though similarly rounded at each end, and are protectively coloured buff to greenish, variously marked with brown or violet. The usual clutch is 2, sometimes 3, eggs, laid in the open in an unlined scrape. Both sexes incubate, and the period is rather long, 23 to 28 days. Several species are known to raise two or three broods a season. Sandgrouse reverse the pigeon routine; the female sandgrouse incubates by day, the male by night, and during the day the male brings food and water to his mate in the nest. Both parents feed the young by regurgitation, and lure predators away with a distraction display strongly reminiscent of the plover's broken-wing act.

Some sandgrouse are migratory, and a number of them tend to wander sporadically, often far from their usual haunts. Pallas' Sandgrouse of central Asia, for instance, appears irregularly in western Europe, usually during or after hard winters in their normal range. On at least three occasions, in 1863, 1888, and 1908, the species irrupted into the British Isles by the thousands, extending as far west as Ireland and north to the Outer Hebrides.

PIN-TAILED SANDGROUSE
Pterocles alchata
Spain, North Africa, Asia Minor   12 in.

DODOS AND SOLITAIRES

COLUMBIFORMES   RAPHIDAE

The Dodo is one of the most widely known symbols of extinction, of something lost and gone forever. All that remain of it are two heads and two feet in European museums, and a fair number of skeletons. The bird's probable appearance in life is familiar to most people through Sir John Tenniel's illustrations for "Alice in Wonderland," which Tenniel based on drawings Dutch artists made of Dodos that reached Europe alive in the 16th and 17th centuries.

Though they vanished only a few centuries ago, very little reliable information survives about these gigantic, aberrant flightless pigeons that developed from some flying ancestor that reached the tiny, isolated Mascarene Islands in the Indian Ocean many geological ages ago. By sifting the surviving evidence in old ships' logs and travellers' accounts, scholars have determined that three species of these birds roamed the forests of these faraway islets until man discovered their peaceful sanctuary early in the 16th century. The Dodo itself lived on Mauritius Island; one of the two similar and closely related solitaires (also called dodos) lived on Reunion, the other on nearby Rodriguez.

All were large birds, the size of a turkey or larger, and weighed up to 50 pounds. They had tremendous heads, bulbous hooked beaks, heavy fat bodies, stout strong legs, ridiculous short wings, and a tail of loose, curly feathers. In colour they were greyish brown to white; the males were larger, the females more brightly coloured. They ate fruit, seeds, berries, and leaves, and laid a single egg on the ground, which both sexes incubated.

The sailors of the ships that visited these islands killed quantities of them for food, but the birds were exterminated by the pigs and monkeys that the Portuguese introduced in the islands in the 16th century and which ate the birds' eggs and young. The Dodo disappeared from Mauritius around 1680; the Reunion Solitaire survived until about 1750; the Rodriguez Solitaire until almost 1800.

Recent studies of skeletal remains found on Mauritius and Rodriguez have led European systematists to believe that the Dodos were possibly allied to the rails, and to suggest placing them in a separate order lineally between the rails and the pigeons.

DODO (extinct)
Raphus cucullatus
Mauritius Island   About 3½-4 ft.

PIGEONS AND DOVES

COLUMBIFORMES   COLUMBIDAE

The pigeon family is found throughout the world in temperate and tropical regions. It has its greatest development in the oriental and Australasian regions where almost two-thirds of the family's 289 species occur. Despite their great variety in size, colour, and habits, all members of the pigeon family are so distinctly pigeons that they are easily recognized as such. All are stout-bodied birds with rather short necks and uniformly small heads. All have short, slender, rounded bills, usually thickening toward the tip and thinner in the middle. These always have a fleshy cere at the base through which the nostrils emerge. Most pigeons are sleek, strong-flying birds with a thick, heavy coat of strong-shafted feathers that are so loosely attached to their thin skins that they drop out very easily, perhaps as a protective mechanism against certain predators. Their voices are a soft plaintive cooing or booming which can get to be monotonously repetitive. A few species have whistling or hissing notes.

The terms "pigeon" and "dove" have no technical significance and are used interchangeably throughout the family.

Pigeon is the term generally applied to the larger, plumper species with square or rounded tails, and dove to the smaller, more graceful species with pointed tails. But there is no hard and fast rule. Whether a species is called a pigeon or a dove in its vernacular name depends largely on custom and usage.

Most pigeons subsist almost entirely on vegetable food; seeds, grains, and fruits are favourite items of their diet. Acorns, some leaves, and other vegetable matter occasionally are eaten. A few species take insects, worms, and grubs, and many pigeons show a strong need and liking for salt. Their unique ability to drink by sucking has already been mentioned in the introduction to the order.

The pigeon family is likewise remarkably uniform in its nesting habits. They nest in many situations, mostly in trees, many on the ground, some on cliff ledges or buildings, a few in holes in trees or burrows. Yet practically all pigeons construct a flimsy platform of sticks on which to lay their 1 to 3, usually 2, eggs. The eggs are slightly elongated, rounded uniformly at each end, and most are pure glossy white (a few tropical species lay yellow to buffy eggs). Both sexes incubate, the female usually by night, the male by day, with the period lasting from 12 days in the smallest species to almost 4 weeks in the giant crowned pigeons. The young hatch practically naked and with their eyes closed, and are brooded and fed by both parents until they are able to fly.

Both parents feed the young on what is known as "pigeon's milk." During the incubation period the lining of the pigeon's crop thickens and, when the young are ready to be fed, the lining sloughs off into a cheesy curd which the adults regurgitate into the young. This substance has much the same food value as mammals' milk. To obtain their food, the young birds poke their beaks inside the throats of the old birds. In later states of growth the young are fed with half-digested grain from the crop. The young mature rapidly and leave the nest anywhere from 2 to 3 weeks after hatching. Most species of pigeons compensate for their small clutches by rearing two or more broods each year.

Most familiar and largest of the several groups (some natural, some frankly artificial) into which the members of this unwieldy family are divided are the true pigeons, sometimes called wood pigeons, of the subfamily Columbinae, found in temperate and tropical areas throughout the world. Typical of this group is the common Rock Dove, or Rock Pigeon, of temperate Europe and western Asia, which is the wild progenitor of the common feral street pigeons, and of all the many varieties of domestic pigeons.

These pigeons were probably among the first wild birds man domesticated, for they have played a prominent role in the folklore and religions of almost all early peoples. They are mentioned in several ancient scrolls and appear in early legends. The story of Noah shows how long ago man recognized pigeons' phenomenal ability to find their way home over strange terrain. Pigeons have been used to carry messages for several thousand years. The ancient Romans used them to relay back to Rome the news of Caesar's conquests of Gaul. Word of Napoleon's downfall at Waterloo reached England by pigeon four days before the fastest couriers could carry the news by horse and ship. As recently as World War I, carrier pigeons earned their keep by carrying messages where all other means failed. "Cher Ami," the famous pigeon that brought help to Wittlesy's Lost Battalion in the Argonne Forest, is only one of a number of the birds that made military history. Today electronics has largely displaced the pigeon's usefulness as a message carrier, but carrier pigeons are still raised, trained, and raced by thousands of fanciers.

Pigeons have long been used as laboratory animals by biologists because they are so easy to raise and maintain. Recently they have been used experimentally to try to determine just how birds find their way over strange terrain. These experiments show that pigeons do some navigating by the sun and must have some sort of a built-in mechanism for judging time of day and the angles and directions of heavenly bodies. Just what these mechanisms are and how they operate is still unknown. Evidence does show, however, that pigeons near their roosts are guided by landmarks, and "pilot" their course rather than navigate it.

Large numbers of pigeons are also raised for food, squab being one of the great delicacies. The birds are bred for their beauty, and hundreds of varieties, far removed from their parent stock in colour, shape, and feathering, have been named.

A second large group consists of the fruit pigeons of the Old World, so called because they feed largely on fruits and berries. The fruit pigeons, many of them brightly coloured, are forest birds. One natural group (Treroninae), the 20 species of green pigeons of southeastern Asia, Malaya, and Africa, all are similarly coloured in pale yellowish green, variously hued with yellows, blacks, and greys. Like all the fruit pigeons, they have the tarsus partially feathered, rather broad feet, and a very wide gape for swallowing large fruit whole. They are almost completely arboreal, feeding primarily in trees and seldom coming to the ground. None of them migrates, but they shift their feeding grounds throughout the year following the fruiting of various trees, and may move considerable distances.

Another well-marked group of fruit pigeons consists of the 37 species of imperial pigeons (Duculinae), also called "nutmeg" pigeons because many of them live on nutmegs and other hard nuts and fruits that are often larger than their heads. Their jaws have elastic sockets, like a boa constrictor's, that stretch to accommodate large objects. These pigeons range through Malaya, the Philippines, and northern Australia eastward through most of the larger islands of the South Pacific to the Marquesas and Tuamotu archipelagos. Most of these large pigeons, from 12 to 20 inches in length, are coloured in rather sombre greys. One species, the Green Nutmeg Pigeon, is a metallic iridescent green above and pale lavender below. Another, the Pied Nutmeg Pigeon, is largely creamy white except for black wings and tail. The imperial pigeons usually travel in flocks, sometimes of several hundred birds, and often make long overwater flights from island to island in search of food. They stay largely in the crowns of the tallest trees of the jungle and mangrove forest, 200 and more feet above the ground, well out of shotgun range.

Brightest coloured of the fruit pigeons are the highly variegated fruit doves, or "painted pigeons," of the subfamily Ptilinopinae, whose 39 species are found mostly in the South Pacific islands, a few in extreme southeast Asia. Most of these are smallish birds from 9 to 12 inches long. They are very gaily coloured in greens and yellows and greys with bold contrasting markings of reds and blues and blacks. Though many of them are astoundingly gaudy at close range, these colours are extremely concealing in their natural environment, the leafy canopy of jungle trees where contrasting splashes of sunlight filter through. While collecting in the Solomon Islands I am sure I passed them often without seeing them. Often when I finally managed to spot one in a tree and shot it, a whole previously unnoticed flock flew out.

The aberrant Tooth-billed Pigeon of Samoa is placed in a subfamily by itself (Didunculinae). A greenish-black and chocolate-brown bird about 13 inches long with a bright red bill and feet, it lives largely on the fig-like fruits of the banyan tree. The large bill is high, sharply down-curved, and has two serrations near the tip giving the bird a vague resemblance to the dodo. It has managed to survive in its restricted forest habitat only because it is very shy. When cats were introduced to the island by whaling ships, the Tooth-billed Pigeon was adaptable enough to abandon its ground-nesting habits and take to nesting in trees out of reach of the new predators.

MAGNIFICENT
FRUIT PIGEON
Megaloprepia magnifica
New Guinea,
northern Australia   14 in.

LARGE GREEN PIGEON
Treron capellei
Malay Peninsula, Sumatra,
Java, Borneo   14 in.

IMPERIAL FRUIT PIGEON
Ducula concinna
East Indies   22 in.

JAVA TURTLE DOVE
Streptopelia bitorquata
East Indies and Philippines   12 in.

YELLOW-BELLIED FRUIT PIGEON
Leucotreron cincta
East Indies   12-13 in.

ORANGE DOVE
Chrysoena victor
Fiji Islands   8 in.

BLUE-CROWNED PIGEON
Goura cristata
New Guinea   33 in.

BLEEDING
HEART PIGEON
*Gallicolumba
luzonica*
Philippine Islands   12 in.

Another small and equally distinctive subfamily is the Gourinae, or crowned pigeons, of New Guinea. Its three species are the giants of the pigeon family, ranging from 26 to 33 inches in length. They differ from other pigeons in having 16 instead of 12 tail feathers, in the scaling of their legs, in lacking an oil gland and a gall bladder, and in possessing a large, fan-shaped crest of erect lacy feathers. They feed on the ground but take refuge in the trees when disturbed. Crowned pigeons are rather stupid birds, and after being flushed from the ground sit on an open limb, where they are an easy mark for any hunter. As their flesh, like that of all pigeons, is good eating, these fine, large birds, though now protected by law, have largely disappeared near human habitations, but are reported to be still fairly common in the wilder jungles of New Guinea.

To return to the large and poorly defined subfamily Columbinae, one of its most famous—and most tragic—North American members was the Passenger Pigeon, which a century or so ago was perhaps the most abundant bird in the world. Flocks literally darkened the skies of Colonial America. Contemporary accounts of their abundance, though hard to credit today, cannot be doubted. One of the first reputable American ornithologists, Alexander Wilson, estimated a flock that passed over him about 1810 to contain over two thousand million birds! The great colonial nestings of the Passenger Pigeons were fabulous. The birds occupied vast stretches of oak and beech forests 20 miles or more in extent. Every tree contained at least one nest and sometimes hundreds. Birds perched in such numbers that their weight broke the branches.

The last great nesting in Wisconsin, in 1878, covered about 850 square miles and contained conservatively 136 million birds. This nesting was the Passenger Pigeon's swan song. For several decades the birds were netted, shot, and trapped mercilessly as they bred and their carcasses were shipped to market by the freight-carload. The species never recovered. The last bona fide wild pigeon nest was found near Minneapolis in 1895. The last definite record of a wild specimen was made in 1899, and the last living Passenger Pigeon in the world died in captivity in a Cincinnati zoo in 1914.

Certainly the species' passing is to be mourned, and one cannot but lament the greed and cruelty of the men who con-

ROCK DOVE
Columba livia
Southern Eurasia, North Africa   13 in.

MOURNING DOVE
Zenaidura macroura
Temperate North America
West Indies to Panama   12

GROUND DOVE
Columbigallina passerina
Southern U.S. and
West Indies to Brazil and Ecuador   7 in.

INCA DOVE
Scardafella inca
Southwestern U.S.
to Costa Rica   8 in.

WHITE-WINGED DOV
Zenaida asiatica
West Indies;
southwestern U.S.
to Panama; Ecuador
to north Chile   12 in

tributed to its extinction by exploiting this seemingly inexhaustible natural resource. Yet the biologist realizes that the eventual demise of the Passenger Pigeon was preordained. It was an ultraspecialized species that showed all the signs of old age, such as its tremendous numbers, which many extinct forms have reached just before their demise—the dinosaurs, for example. The Passenger Pigeon's greatest specialization apparently was in its nesting habits. To be successful the birds had to breed in large colonies. After the last great nesting was broken up, many birds survived, but they were unable to reproduce in small numbers successfully.

Had the Passenger Pigeon been able to nest alone or in small colonies, it might have survived into the age of intelligent game management which was just dawning at the

144

beginning of the 20th century. Its disappearance, however, gave dramatic force and impetus to the conservation movement, and encouraged intelligent management of our rapidly vanishing wildlife resources. Hence, though it was doubtless on its way out, it went out in a good cause, and much as all regret its passing, it has not been in vain.

Best known of the wild pigeons in North America today is the Mourning Dove, which has the distinction of being the only North American bird to nest in every state in the Union except Hawaii. It is a favourite sporting bird throughout the southern states, but is protected as a songbird in the North. Because of its economic importance as a game species, it has been the subject of intensive studies and, largely through ringing, much has been learned of its life history, particularly in the last decade or so.

Mourning Doves are not long-lived in the wild. Though individuals have lived in captivity to 16 years, the oldest wild bird to date was 10 years old. Data from the thousands of birds ringed show the mortality in the first year to be more than 80 per cent, which drops, as the birds mature, to 66 per cent. With such an annual death rate, few doves live in the wild more than 4 or 5 years, and the population must renew itself almost completely every 3 to 4 years. Federal protection under the Migratory Bird Treaty Act was first denied the Mourning Dove, on the grounds that the species occurs the year round in the southern states, and hence was non-migratory and not subject to federal regulation.

Recoveries of ringed birds showing the seasonal movements of the Mourning Doves have demonstrated that all of the populations migrate southward in winter, those nesting farthest north moving farthest south. This type of information has proved invaluable in helping authorities to regulate hunting, keeping the annual kill of birds within the limits that the species can withstand. Hence the fine sport of dove hunting is in no immediate danger of being curtailed further; nor is the Mourning Dove likely to follow its predecessor, the Passenger Pigeon, into limbo.

Mention should also be made of the turtle doves of the genus *Streptopelia*, some 15 species of which are widespread throughout Eurasia and Africa. The Turtle Dove of Europe is well-known in poetry and folklore, and remains today fairly plentiful even though it is hunted throughout many parts of its range. Some of the closely related ring doves of China and other parts of the Old World have been introduced widely in other countries, notably in Hawaii and Australia. One species, the Collared Turtle Dove of the eastern Mediterranean region, has recently expanded its range into northern and western Europe by nesting in city parks, where it cannot be shot.

Some of the tropical columbine tree pigeons are exceedingly beautiful. The Bleeding Heart Pigeon, found in the islands of the Philippines, a gentle little grey and white bird with a bright red spot on its breast, forages on the forest floor and flies up into trees when disturbed. Though rather shy in the wild, it tames easily and is a favourite cage bird often seen in aviaries and in zoos throughout the world.

Australia is the home of a group of handsome 12- to 13-inch pigeons with attractive metallic colours known as the bronzewings. These birds feed on the seeds of a poisonous plant which does not affect their flesh, and the birds are hunted and eaten by Australian sportsmen. The poison lodges in the en-

PASSENGER PIGEON (extinct) ♂
Ectopistes migratorius
Temperate central and
eastern North America 17 in.

trails and bones, and is strong enough to kill any domestic dog or cat that eats these parts.

The pigeon family has many more members worthy of mention, such as the attractive little 7-inch friendly Ground Dove of southern North American coasts, and the equally attractive scaled Inca Dove and the larger White-winged Dove of the southwestern states that is one of their fine game birds. Indeed, pigeons of all sorts are hunted wherever men hunt, for without exception they are all fine eating.

The Passenger Pigeon is the only one that has been exterminated by hunting so far, though it is not the only pigeon known to have become extinct within historic time. Several small island populations, notably the Blue Pigeon of Mauritius which was last taken in 1826, and one race of a pigeon of Norfolk Island off New Zealand, are gone. Two rare pigeons have survived solely because one of their favourite foods, the fruit of a New Zealand yew, makes their flesh distasteful. The Puerto Rico Blue Pigeon has not been recorded since 1926, and there are others. Still other doves and pigeons of limited distribution, such as the Wood Pigeon of Japan and the Ryukyu Islands, and the Madagascar turtle doves, are in danger of being wiped out, as much by the destruction of their habitat as by hunting.

One mysterious pigeon that has disappeared for reasons unknown was a little crested pigeon (*Microgoura*) of the Solomon Islands known only from the island of Choiseul, where an Australian collected the six known specimens in 1904. It has not been seen since. It was an attractive little brown ground pigeon about 12 inches in length, with a startling crest on the back of its head. It may have been a small relict population that the head-hunting cannibals who occupy Choiseul Island exterminated. Perhaps like the Notornis of New Zealand, it may have retired into some unexplored part of this small island, and may yet be rediscovered. Though this seems improbable, such is the hope of all who, myself included, have searched for them in vain.

YELLOW-HEADED
AMAZON
Amazona ochrocephala
Mexico to Ecuador
and Brazil 15 in.

AFRICAN GREY PARROT
Psittacus erithacus
Forests of
central Africa 13 in.

BLACK-CAPPED LORY
Domicella domicella
Ceram and
Amboina islands
11 in.

SLATEY-HEADED
PARAKEET
Psittacula himalayana
Northwest India
to Thailand, Laos,
Annam 15 in.

MASKED
LOVEBIRD
Agapornis personata
Tanganyika, Africa
5 in.

RAINBOW
LORIKEET
*Trichoglossus
haematodus*
East Indies and
Australia
east to
New Hebrides 10-11 in.

GOLDEN CONURE
Aratinga guarouba
Eastern Brazil 12 in.

PARROTS AND
THEIR ALLIES

PSITTACIFORMES   PSITTACIDAE

The 315 parrots, parakeets, cockatoos, cockateels, lories, lorikeets, macaws, lovebirds, and budgerigars are a diverse group; yet they are so uniform in their diagnostic features that all are recognizable at a glance as members of the parrot order and family. They range in size from the little 3½-inch pygmy parrots of the Papuan region to the gaudy, long-tailed, 40-inch macaws of the Amazon jungles. They vary in shape from plump African lovebirds and South American amazons to the slender lories and wildly crested cockatoos of the Australo-Malayan region. Their colouring defies summing up in a sentence, but their bodies are usually a solid green, yellow, red, white, or black, with contrasting patches of red, yellow, or blue on the head, wings, or tail.

Identifying characteristics are the large head and short neck, and particularly the strongly down-curved, hooked bill. An equally important structural feature is the parrot's strong, grasping feet with two toes in front and two behind. Parrots also have a broad cere at the base of the bill through which the nostrils open and which is feathered in many species. Their smallish eyes are often bordered by patches of bare skin, particularly in the larger species. Their rather sparse plumage has powder-downs (p. 50) scattered all through it.

The parrots are a distinctive ancient group well warranting their ordinal rank. They show some affinities in anatomy and in habits to both the pigeons and to the cuckoos. Being essentially arboreal birds, their fossil record is poor. The earliest so far unearthed are of Miocene age, less than 15 million years old. These show parrots were formerly more widespread in temperate latitudes than they are today, spreading north almost to Canada in North America and to France in Europe.

The parrots' present distribution is pan-tropical. They occur on all lands in the Southern Hemisphere except the southern tip of Africa and the more remote Pacific islands. In the Northern Hemisphere they now reach northern Mexico (central United States, until recently) in the New World and southeastern Asia in the Old. Parrots fall into six major groups, which are sometimes given family rank, but the structural differences between them are so slight that most students today accord them subfamily rank at best.

While they have never been domesticated in the sense that chickens, ducks, and pigeons have, probably more species of parrots have been tamed and raised in captivity than any other group of birds. Primitive tribes have kept them as pets since time immemorial. The talking ability of the African Grey Parrot is mentioned in ancient Greek and Roman writings. The parrots' appeal is partly aesthetic, partly anthropomorphic. Coupled with their attractive hues and the ease with which they are tamed and maintained in captivity are their intensely human traits of imitating the human voice, of showing affection to each other, of reacting to flattery, and of using their feet almost as hands. No other bird holds food in one foot and bites pieces off, much as one eats a sandwich. Parrots are extremely long-lived. How long the birds live in the wild, where natural enemies take their toll, is unknown, but individuals have lived upwards of 50 years in captivity, and one is reported to have reached 80.

Parrots develop their ability as mimics only in captivity. In the wild they are raucous-voiced birds that shriek or squawk or twitter, depending on their size, and have a poor range of vocal expression. Yet in captivity they learn to imitate all

146

sorts of sounds, some species better than others. The African Grey Parrot is considered one of the best mimics, closely followed by the green amazons of Central and South America. The larger and the smaller species do not do so well. Cockatoos and macaws can learn a phrase or two, and the little budgerigars and parakeets can be taught to whistle a tune if one has patience enough.

Though parrot-lovers will cite examples to prove the contrary, talking parrots haven't the slightest idea of what they are saying. Often it takes a bit of imagination to put the proper words to the syllables they utter. Parrots learn best when young and repeat the simpler sounds they hear most often with little choice or selectivity. A friend kept a young Yellow-headed Amazon on her porch while a house was being built on the next site. Intrigued by the zipping sound of hand saws, the bird made this the favourite item of its vocabulary. My friend soon tired of hearing carpenters sawing all day every day and gave the bird to the zoo.

Parrot fanciers had a severe blow in the 1930's when it was discovered that parrots suffer from a virus disease, originally called psittacosis, which they can transmit to humans, sometimes in a virulent form. To combat this disease, the importation of wild parrots was prohibited, and the traffic in caged parrots suffered a severe setback. Later researches revealed that "parrot fever" occurs in almost all birds, including domestic fowl and pigeons, and the disease is now more appropriately called ornithosis. Antitoxins and antibiotics have been developed that greatly reduce the severity of the virulent strains, and fear of the disease has now been largely overcome. Parrots are again gaining favour as cage birds, particularly the little budgerigars, which are now bred in whites and yellows, far removed from the blues and greens of their wild Australian progenitors.

The kings of the parrot family are the 15 gaudy macaws that live in the tropical rainforests from Mexico south through Central and South America. One of the largest and handsomest is the Red-and-green Macaw found from Panama to Bolivia. When fully developed its tail alone is more than two feet long. The slightly smaller Hyacinth Macaw, highly prized by parrot fanciers for its lovely colouring, lives only in the jungle vastnesses of interior Brazil. The commonest macaws seen in zoos are the Scarlet Macaw and the Gold-and-blue Macaw. Another species widespread from Mexico southward is the Military Macaw, the all-green one with a red forehead. Macaws usually travel in pairs. As these magnificent birds fly screeching on strong rapid wings over the high panoply of their native jungles, they are a far more stirring sight than their tamed counterparts on a zoo perch, and one never forgotten. Other members of the group are smaller; all have long graduated tails.

Perhaps best known of the New World parrots are the 25 or so species of amazons, often kept as cage birds. These are the stout-bodied green parrots with short square or rounded tails, most of them marked with yellow, red, or blue. One of the largest, the Yellow-headed Amazon, is among the best talkers of the American parrots. Other commonly caged amazons are the Yellow-faced and the Red-fronted, one with a yellow and the other with a reddish forehead. One of the smallest is the 10-inch White-fronted Amazon, with a white forehead, bright red lores, and a red wing patch in the male.

Among the less familiar groups of New World parrots are the conures, which are smaller and more slender-bodied than the amazons and have longer, pointed tails. Most striking of this group is the Golden Conure of Brazil. Also classified here is the only parrot native to the United States, the recently extinct Carolina Parakeet, a pretty little parrot about 12 inches long with a yellowish green body, a long pointed tail, and an orange-yellow head.

In the early 19th century Carolina Parakeets ranged from North Dakota and central New York south to eastern Texas and Florida, and were abundant in the heavily forested bottom lands of the Mississippi Valley and the Atlantic seaboard. Slaughtered for sport and to control their depredations to fruit and grain crops, flocking parakeets had an unfortunate habit of hovering in curiosity or concern over a fallen bird, so that the hunter could often kill them all. They had become exceedingly rare by 1900. The last ones were seen in the Florida Everglades in the early 1920's. Though kept commonly as cage birds in the 19th century, they were never raised successfully in captivity and the species vanished before any determined effort could be made to save it.

Similar in size and form to the amazons is the African Grey Parrot, which commands the highest price of all parrots among bird dealers because of its excellence as a mimic. This grey, red-tailed bird is at home in the rainforests of the Congo from the Gold Coast to Kenya and Tanganyika. Like so many of the smaller parrots in the wild, it is generally seen in screaming, chattering flocks flying bullet-like over the tops of the trees. In western Africa it does considerable damage to grain.

The lovebirds are a group of small, heavy-bodied, pointed-tailed Old World parrots best developed in Africa and Madagascar. They are highly prized as cage birds, partly for their attractive colours, partly for their human trait of liking each other's company. Caged pairs sit huddled together by the hour, giving every evidence of fondness for each other. In the wild, lovebirds usually travel in large flocks and often damage crops. In most the sexes are alike, but in the gaudy Eclectus, of the South Pacific islands, the sexes are so different in colour (the male bright green, the female soft maroon) that they were once believed to be different species.

The true parakeets are a widespread Old World group centred in the Indo-Malayan region. Most of these small parrots have long pointed tails. Many live in cultivated areas and eat grain as well as fruit. They travel in large chattering flocks and often feed on the ground. Best known of the group is the Budgerigar of Australia, now popular as a cage bird. A weird group is the hanging parakeets, tiny green birds found from India to the Philippines that sleep at night hanging upside down from their perches like bats.

Another distinctive group of Australo-Malayan parrots consists of the 16 noisy

BUDGERIGAR
Melopsittacus undulatus
Australia 7 in.
(Domestic colour variety)

LEADBEATER'S COCKATOO
Cacatua leadbeateri
Australia 15 in.

GREAT BLACK (PALM) COCKATOO
Probosciger aterrimus
New Guinea, northern Australia 32 in.

SULPHUR-CRESTED COCKATOO
Cacatua galerita
Australia and New Guinea 18 in.

cockatoos, which differ from other parrots in having a crest of long, pointed feathers they can raise and lower at will. Most are fair-sized white birds, frequently washed or tinged with pinks or yellows, and in some the crest colour varies. Wild cockatoos are noisy, gregarious birds that travel in small loose flocks through the treetops and perch on exposed limbs, where they stand out conspicuously against the dark foliage. The Solomon Islands White Cockatoo was a familiar bird to Americans there during World War II, and men got live ones from the natives as pets. A Seabee outfit taught one bird to repeat monotonously "Bledsoe said so," to the delight of the troops and the annoyance of their imperious executive officer, Mr. Bledsoe. Among the commoner white cockatoos seen in zoos are the Sulphur-crested Cockatoo with its bright yellow crown, and the pink-shaded Leadbeater's Cockatoo.

The largest is the 31-inch Black Cockatoo of New Guinea, whose tremendous curved bill ends in a long, sharp point. With it the Black Cockatoo cracks and digs the meat out of hard-shelled nuts that a man has trouble breaking with a rock. Unlike the white cockatoos, the Black Cockatoo is a solitary bird, usually seen alone or in small groups of two or three in the tops of tall jungle trees. Also unlike other cockatoos, the Black Cockatoo has a bare face, and its cheeks change from pink to red with the bird's emotions.

The lories and lorikeets of the Australasian region, 6 to 15 inches long, brilliantly coloured in greens, blues, reds, and yellows, have their tongues edged with a brushy fringe for lapping up nectar and fruit juices. Unlike other nectar-eating birds that siphon flower nectar with thin, tube-like bills, the lorikeets crush flowers with their beaks and lap up the extruded juices with their tongues. A common bird in the

coconut plantations throughout the South Sea islands is the Painted, or Rainbow, Lorikeet, a slender, long-tailed bird that breaks into many geographical races, each island population varying slightly in colour and size. Large flocks of these birds dash twittering and chattering through the treetops and alight in the palm fronds like so many bright flowers. Just as suddenly they take flight again with a great rushing of wings, still chattering.

Smallest of the family are the tiny pygmy parrots, only 3 to 5 inches in length, whose six species range from New Guinea eastward through New Britain and the Solomons. These midgets act more like small woodpeckers than parrots. They creep about the trunks and large limbs of forest trees prying insects out of bark crevices. They have stiff woodpecker-like tails with spiny tips, and long claws for clinging to bark. They are not so common or gregarious as most other parrots, and are quiet and hard to find in their jungle haunts. They have never been kept successfully in captivity.

Strangest and most aberrant of all the parrots is the Kakapo, or Owl Parrot, of New Zealand. This very rare bird is threatened with extinction by New Zealand's introduced predators, for it has lost the power of flight. A large parrot about 20 inches long, its soft feathers are cryptically streaked with greens, yellows, browns, and blacks. Largely nocturnal, it hides during the day in holes in rocks and under tree roots, and comes forth at evening to feed. It runs rapidly on the ground and when in a hurry often spreads its wings. It climbs trees for fruit and nectar and then glides down to the ground. Its longest glide recorded is about 90 yards. In the forest habitat it frequents it keeps paths and trails open by snipping off roots or vegetation in its way as it walks along. The Kakapo is believed extinct on North Island but a few have recently been reported still surviving in the extensive beech forests of South Island.

Equally distinct and abnormal are the two other New Zealand parrots, the Kea and the Kaka, both fairly large birds about the size of a crow, brownish-green in colour, variously marked with reds and yellows. The Kea is a highland form living above the tree line in the alpine regions of South Island, where it nests in crannies and fissures under rocks. In summer it lives on a normal parrot diet of fruit and buds, supplemented with insects, grubs, and worms. In winter it descends to lower levels where it becomes a scavenger, and it has acquired the obnoxious habit of pecking into the backs of living sheep for their kidney fat. To curb their sheep killing, a bounty was put on Keas, and paid on almost 30,000 during an 8-year period. This had little effect on their numbers, which apparently increased because of the plentiful food supply. Removing all sheep refuse after butchering was found a more effective way of controlling them.

The Kea's close relative, the Kaka, lives in low-level forests on both islands. It is a noisy bird usually seen in flocks. It lives on fruits and nectar, and on grubs it digs out of rotten wood with its powerful beak.

Parrots are remarkably uniform in their nesting habits. Parrot eggs are quite round, always white, and fairly glossy. The number per clutch varies from 1 in some of the larger species to 9 or 10 in some smaller ones, and averages 3 to 5. Most parrots are cavity nesters and they usually lay in an unlined hole in a tree. Some nest in burrows on the ground, some in rock crevices. The pygmy parrots and several other small Australasian species dig their nests in termite houses. Incubation is normally by both sexes; in a few species by the female alone. The young usually hatch naked but soon sprout a down coat which makes them look remarkably like fledgling owls. Little is known of their incubation periods, but in the smaller parakeets they run from about 17 to 20 days. Both sexes feed the young by regurgitation, much as pigeons do.

The Grey-breasted Parakeet of Argentina nests colonially in huge structures built of twigs high in trees in which each pair of birds has its own private compartment. The birds use these huge nests as sleeping quarters the year round and add to them from year to year until the wagonload or more of twigs breaks down the supporting branches. Other birds, such as tree ducks, sometimes occupy vacant nests in these colonies with the parakeets, and once in a while opossums move in and apparently live at peace with them.

SCARLET MACAW
Ara macao
Mexico to Bolivia   36 in.

GOLD AND BLUE MACAW
Ara ararauna
Panama to Argentina   31 in.

MILITARY MACAW
Ara militaris
Mexico and western
S. America   30 in.

HYACINTH MACAW
Anodorhynchus hyacinthus
Brazilian forests south of
the Amazon   34 in.

KEA
Nestor notabilis
ith Island, New Zealand
18-19 in.

CUCKOOS AND ALLIES

CUCULIFORMES

The cuckoos and their allies are most closely related anatomically to the parrots. Members of both orders have two toes in front and two behind, but the cuckoos' feet are not so prehensile, and are differently muscled and tendoned. Their upper bill is not movable as in the parrots, is never strongly hooked, and has no cere at the nostrils. The slim-bodied cuckoos have long tails of 8 to 10 feathers instead of 12 to 14 as in the parrots.

Fossil cuckoos go back to Oligocene time. Two rather distinctive families comprise the order, the bright-coloured, fruit-eating touracos of Africa, and the less imposing, largely insectivorous cuckoos found in temperate and tropical regions almost throughout the world. Both families are essentially arboreal, the touracos strictly so, and the sexes are generally alike. Their flight varies from fairly strong to very weak. Their voices are typically loud and monotonous.

TOURACOS

CUCULIFORMES   MUSOPHAGIDAE

The 19 species of soft-feathered birds that constitute this African family are also called "plantain-eaters," for they subsist largely on plantains and other fruits, plus a few insects and grubs. Several South African brushland species, grey and brown with white markings, are called "go-away birds." Their loud, nasal "go-way, go-way" alerts all the game within earshot when a hunter appears.

Most touracos live in the deep forest. They have striking green or blue bodies with red markings on the wings. Most bright colours in birds are produced physically by refraction from microscopic feather structures, but the greens and reds of the touracos are true pigments. Their singular rich red pigment, called turacin, is soluble in water. A red touraco feather stirred in a glass pales out and dyes the water pink, but the heavy jungle rains are shed without fading the colour. In museum specimens the red deepens with age, for the copper in turacin darkens as it slowly oxidizes.

Touracos are fairly large (15 to 25 inches), and have long tails, usually a pronounced crest, and stubby, often bright-coloured bills. They can direct their outer toe either backward or forward as the owls and Ospreys do. Touracos climb vines and run along tree limbs like squirrels; some run fast on the ground. They fly short distances with a weak, dipping flight.

Touracos live in pairs or small family parties. Though noisy and active, they usually keep well hidden in the foliage, where they are inconspicuous despite their bright colours. They nest sporadically throughout the year, building a bulky but fragile platform nest of twigs. Most nest high in forest trees. Their 2 to 3 eggs are usually white, sometimes greenish, and unmarked. Both sexes incubate and feed the young pulpy fruit by regurgitation. The young hatch covered with sooty grey down, and remain in the nest only about 10 days. Long before they can fly, they start crawling out on nearby branches, where their parents continue to feed them until they mature.

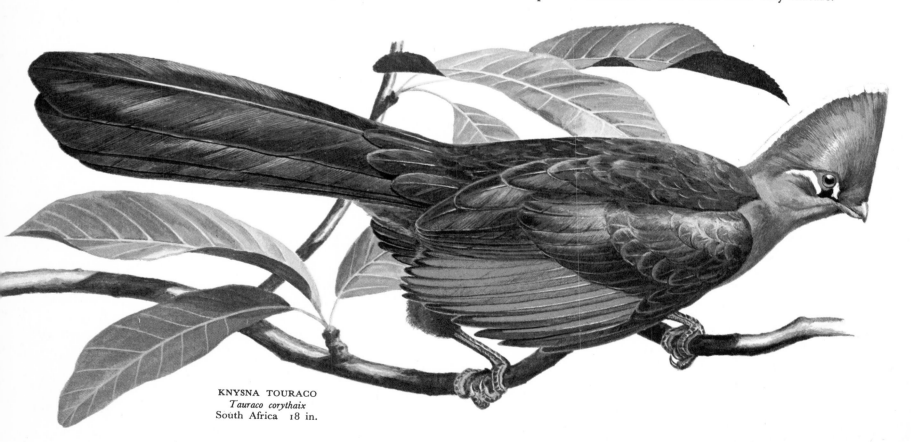

KNYSNA TOURACO
Tauraco corythaix
South Africa   18 in.

CUCKOOS, ANIS,
ROADRUNNERS AND COUCALS
CUCULIFORMES   CUCULIDAE

Despite their diverse and unconventional breeding habits, the cuckoos and their immediate relatives are a fairly close-knit group, well distributed through the tropical and temperate regions of the world. The 127 species are all rather slender-bodied, long-tailed birds with medium to stout down-curved bills, pointed wings, and rather short legs (long in only the terrestrial species). Most of them are forest birds; quite a few inhabit brushy savannahs. A few cuckoos live on mice and other small vertebrates; some eat fruits and other vegetable matter, but insects are the mainstay of most species. Insect larvae are highly relished, and cuckoos are among the few birds that regularly eat fuzzy, hairy caterpillars.

First of the five subfamilies into which the family is split is the "typical" cuckoos of the Old World, the nominate Cuculinae, all 42 of which are parasitic in their breeding. Best known is the Common Cuckoo, the only one that distinctly says its name. This it repeats so clearly, so loudly, and so insistently that it long ago became the bird's name in all languages across its temperate Eurasian breeding ground. The French spell it *coucou*, the Dutch *koekoek*, the Germans *kuckuk*, the Russians *kukushka*, the Japanese *kak-ko,* but no matter how it is spelled, it is the same name for the same bird whose voice announces spring from the Cotswold Hills to the slopes of Fujiyama. Only the males "lhude sing cuccu." It is their springtime mating song, and it sounds in life exactly as the cuckoo clock imitates it. The female has a sort of bubbling chuckle, and both sexes have other harsher but less obtrusive notes at other seasons.

The ancients were familiar with the Common Cuckoo's habit of laying its eggs in the nests of other birds, and from it the earthy Anglo-Saxons bequeathed us our word "cuckold." Social parasitism of this sort, duping another species into assuming the chores of incubation and of feeding the young, is by no means limited to the cuckoos. It is highly developed in the honeyguides and in several weaverfinches of Africa. Its practice in various stages short of perfection by the New World cowbirds shows how this form of parasitism probably evolved (p. 289). Nowhere is this parasitism more widely practised or carried to such degrees of diversity and refinement as in the Cuculinae proper. None of them, so far as it is known, builds a nest or rears its own young.

Though the cuckoos' wantonness (to human morals, that is) has become apocryphal, the cuckoos adhere strictly to their set patterns of reproduction, which their success in surviving proves biologically sound, regardless of how human moralists or other birds may view them. This breeding behaviour has been studied intensively within the last few decades, and some of its complexities and ramifications prove to be almost as incredible as some avian folklore.

The eggs of each individual female Common Cuckoo are uniform in appearance, but those of different birds may differ greatly in colour, though not in size or shape. Each female normally lays 4 or 5 eggs at 48-hour intervals, each in a different nest, and only in nests of one particular species, usually one whose eggs most nearly resemble hers. In areas where conditions for selection are at their best, a cuckoo that lays bluish eggs will lay them in nests of hedge sparrows that lay blue eggs. One whose eggs are brown will put them among the brownish eggs in a pipit's nest. Whether or not egg colour and the accompanying host specificity are hereditary has yet to be determined. One cuckoo that was watched closely laid 25 eggs in 25 different Meadow Pipits' nests in 50 days.

The gravid cuckoo selects her intended dupes carefully, watches them as they build their nests, and usually lays each egg in the afternoon of the same day the prospective foster parent lays one. Taking one egg out of the nest in her bill, she sits on the nest, lays her own egg, then flies off with the stolen egg, which she may swallow or drop. Because cuckoo eggs are often found in domed nests with small entrances like those of willow warblers, which obviously the cuckoo cannot enter, it was believed for years that the cuckoo laid her egg on the ground and put it in the nest with her bill. Careful observations have shown that this never happens. When a cuckoo wants to parasitize such a nest, she props herself with outspread wings and tail against its entrance and ejects her egg directly into it. This awkward manoeuvre is not always successful, and if the egg lands on the edge of the nest without going in or falls to the ground, the cuckoo makes no further attempt to put it where she meant to lay it.

As the incubation period of the cuckoo's egg is 12½ days, it may hatch before, and often simultaneously with, the remaining eggs in the nest. Soon after hatching, the naked fledgling cuckoo starts to work ejecting from the nest any other nestlings or eggs therein. It scrunches down until it gets anything in the nest on its back, and then rises until the egg or the nestling tumbles over the edge. Occasionally two cuckoo eggs are laid in the same nest, usually by different females, and if one hatches before the other, the second egg is soon tumbled to destruction. Sometimes both hatch simultaneously, and both young cuckoos struggle inconclusively, neither able to throw the other out. After the third or fourth day, the instinct to eject all companions from the nest dies, and the two cuckoos settle down peacefully together.

Ridding itself of sibling competition is of vital importance to the young cuckoo, for it soon grows much larger than its foster parent, and it needs all the food that the step-parents would normally bring to their own brood of four or five. It is a ridiculous sight to see a tiny little warbler or titmouse feeding an immense young cuckoo several times its size. Yet the instinct to rear the youngster it has hatched is so strong as to overpower any possible perception or realization on the parents' part that this incubus is not of their own making.

COMMON CUCKOO
Cuculus canorus
Eurasia, Africa   13 in.

COMMON CUCKOO
fledgling, with
LESSER WHITETHROAT
Sylvia curruca
Temperate Eurasia   5 in.

EMERALD CUCKOO
Chrysococcyx cupreus
South Africa   7-8 in.

RED-WINGED
INDIAN CUCKOO
Clamator coromandus
India to Indochina,
Java, Borneo   18 in.

BLACK COUCAL
Centropus grilli
Central Africa   13 in.

YELLOW-BILLED CUCKOO
Coccyzus americanus
Southern Canada to Mexico   12 in.

They faithfully feed and care for the monster for the full 20 to 23 days it takes the cuckoo to fly off and fend for itself.

The cuckoos' reputation as deceivers is based on more than their success in foisting their eggs on other species. Many of them bear striking though superficial resemblances to other birds. The Common Cuckoo in flight looks so much like a Kestrel or a Sparrow Hawk it has been suggested this may have some aggressive value in frightening small birds away from their nests. Other cuckoos resemble shrikes, and several dark Asiatic species so resemble the drongos or king crows they parasitize that they are called drongo-cuckoos. It is doubtful, however, that these resemblances are more than fortuitous, and whether they are of behavioural or other significance remains to be proved.

Each of the cuckoos has its particular pattern of parasitism, and much remains to be learned about these. The Great Spotted Cuckoo, for instance, almost always lays its eggs in the nests of crows and jays. Its Indian relative, the Red-winged Cuckoo, confines its attentions largely to babblers and laughing thrushes. The lovely Emerald Cuckoo of Africa parasitizes many small African species, mostly those that nest high in trees, such as bulbuls and weaverfinches. The Shining Cuckoo of Australia and New Zealand, a brilliant bronzy green above, barred black and white below, regularly violates the domed nests of wrens and fantails. Forcing its way into the nest's small opening, it

ROADRUNNER
Geococcyx californianus
Southwestern U.S. and Mexico   23 in.

pokes its head through the far wall, lays its egg, and then pushes on through and out. The dupe, who soon returns, repairs the ruptured wall, and continues its interrupted incubation.

Most temperate-zone cuckoos are migratory to some extent, and many make long flights. The Common Cuckoo migrates from Europe to central Africa and from Asia to the East Indies. The Shining Cuckoo makes one of the most marvellous flights of all—from New Zealand northward over 2,000 miles of the trackless South Pacific to the Solomon Islands. These long migrations are all the more remarkable because the young birds make them with no guidance from their real parents. Adult cuckoos often leave the breeding grounds weeks ahead of the young birds, who follow along later on their own and find their way unerringly to their species' regular wintering ground. Thus they inherit both the urge to winter in a certain given region, and the ability to find their way to it.

On their wintering grounds the cuckoos are quiet and hard to see in the leafy treetops. As spring approaches they become extremely noisy, particularly the males, and each species has a characteristic loud call, for which it is often named, and which, like the Common Cuckoo's double-barrelled plaint, it often repeats to the point of annoyance.

The second subfamily of cuckoos (Phoenicophaeinae) contains 32 species of medium-sized birds found in the Americas, in Africa, and in the Oriental region. The chief difference between the first subfamily and this group is the fact that none of the members of the latter is parasitic. All build a rather flimsy nest of twigs, in which they incubate their eggs and rear their own young; both sexes take part in these duties. The American members of this group are mostly brown-backed, white-bellied birds with clucking, chuckling call notes. Typical of them are the familiar Yellow-billed and Black-billed cuckoos that breed in the deciduous woodlands, suburbs, and parks of North America where they perform a valued service in destroying tent caterpillars. Both species winter southward into Central

and South America. Old World members of the group are the handsome malcohas, which have a metallic sheen in their plumage and bright green, red, or yellow bills. Malcohas live in vine-tangled tropical forests, are weak fliers, and are largely non-migratory.

The third cuckoo subfamily (Crotophaginae) contains the aberrant Guira Cuckoo, a crested, slender-billed resident of the Argentine pampas, and the three queer anis of the American tropics, found from the West Indies and Mexico southward to Argentina. Anis are shiny black cuckoos with long tails and peculiarly high-crowned, laterally compressed bills. They are the most gregarious of all the cuckoos, and are usually seen in small flocks foraging through open brushlands and isolated clumps of trees.

Anis carry their sociability into their nesting, and often nest colonially. Their nesting habits are most irregular, for they seem to have no particular breeding season, but nest at random any time of the year. Sometimes pairs nest by themselves, building a loose platform of twigs and leaves fairly high in a tree. Here the female lays her normal clutch of 4 or 5 chalky white eggs. More often a group of anis builds one cooperative nest, in which all the females in the company lay. As many as 25 eggs have been found in a single nest, but the number is more often 10 to 15.

The Roadrunner of the American southwestern deserts, sometimes called the "chaparral cock," is the best known of the ground-cuckoo subfamily (Neomorphinae), whose 13 species have longer, stouter legs than the other cuckoos. Roadrunners feed largely on small snakes and lizards, which they kill by pounding with their heavy bills, before they swallow their prey head first. Their running speed has been timed at up to 23 miles per hour, but they are weak fliers and non-migratory.

Ten more of these terrestrial cuckoos are New World birds, found from Arizona and New Mexico southward to Paraguay and Brazil. The other two live in Malaya and Indochina. The Malayan Ground Cuckoo, largest and most striking of the group, is 2 feet in length, has a black head, brown upper parts marked with metallic violet green, and barred black and white underparts.

Three of the tropical American ground cuckoos are parasitic. These are the Striped Cuckoo (*Tapera*), and the Pheasant and Peacock cuckoos (*Dromococcyx*) found from southern Mexico to Argentina. All the others build their own nests and rear their own young.

The last subfamily, the Coucals (Centropodinae), contains 38 species of medium-sized to large, slow flying, mostly terrestrial cuckoos that range from Africa through Australia as far eastward as the Solomons. Ten of these species, the

little-known Couas of Madagascar, are sometimes regarded as a separate subfamily.

The Coucals are mostly dark-coloured birds from 12 to 30 inches in length, with rather long, heavy legs, short, rounded wings, long, rounded tails, and stout, down-curved bills. They are further characterized by the stiff, sparse feathering of their heads, necks, and breasts and by the long, sharp, straight claw on the hind toe, as long as or longer than the toe itself.

None of the Coucals is parasitic. All of them build bulky domed nests on or near the ground with a small entrance on one side. They line the nest with green leaves and grasses and invariably renew them as they dry and shrivel. Coucals lay 3 to 5 rather roundish white eggs, which both sexes incubate for about 14 days.

OWLS

STRIGIFORMES

The world's 133 species of owls form one of the more distinctive of bird groups. Their most obvious definitive characteristics are their forward-facing eyes set in a pronounced facial disc, their large heads set on seemingly short necks, and their soft fluffy plumage which renders their flight so silent. Owls live on animal food which they catch alive by using their hooked beaks and strong grasping feet. They were at one time classified with the hawks and eagles, which feed the same way, but the owls' superficial resemblance to the diurnal birds of prey is a case of parallel development. Structurally the owls

are most closely allied to the goatsuckers, while the hawks' closest relatives are thought to be the herons.

Owls occur throughout the world except in Antarctica and a few isolated oceanic islands. They have adapted themselves to almost every available ecological niche from barren deserts and the arctic tundra wastes to the most lush of the tropical rainforests. Owls are divided into two families, the barn owls and the typical owls. The differences between these are so slight that many ornithologists, particularly the Europeans, place them all in a single family.

BARN OWLS

STRIGIFORMES   TYTONIDAE

Of all the owls the widespread Barn Owl is the most closely associated with man. Its natural nesting sites are hollow trees, cliffs, or old hawks' nests. Now it nests most often in buildings, particularly in abandoned or little used ones, such as church steeples or barn lofts. Ruins are favourite sites, and the unsuspected presence of a pair of Barn Owls has given many an old building its reputation for being haunted, so unbird-like are their cries. Their typical note is a shrill, long-drawn, eerie scream. Barn Owls also have an assortment of chuckling notes, and one like a snore.

Barn owls differ from the typical owls in their heart-shaped facial disc, which is so simian in aspect that the birds are often called "monkey-faced owls." Among their other distinguishing characteristics are their long legs, which are longer than the tail and completely feathered down to their feet, and their short thigh feathers. Another peculiar feature is a serrated comb on the claw of the middle toe, found elsewhere only in herons and some goatsuckers.

Living barn owls are from 13 to 18 inches long, and females are usually larger than males. Numerous remains of a tremendous barn owl, twice the size of any living today, have been found in Pleistocene cave deposits in the Bahamas

and West Indies. When great quantities of sea water were locked in the continental ice sheets during the Ice Age, these islands were much larger than they are today, and many were connected. With the remains of these huge owls are the bones of large rodents on which they probably fed, and which also disappeared when their habitat shrank to its present size.

Barn owls are not migratory and tend to be resident wherever they occur. They show a great faithfulness to breeding sites and use the same one year after year. Presumably they stay mated as long as they live. The common Barn Owl breaks into many distinct geographical populations throughout its almost world-wide range. Golden brown above and lighter below, it is prettily spangled and barred with white, black, and grey. The other nine species in the family are of Old World distribution only, found in Africa, Madagascar, southern Asia, the East Indies, and Australia. (The family is strangely absent from New Zealand and has not reached the oceanic islands.) Most of these Old World barn owls inhabit open grassy plains, and are commonly called "grass owls." All are ground nesters. One species, the Bay Owl of Africa and southeast Asia, lives in deep forests and is so shy and nocturnal that almost nothing is known of its habits.

The common Barn Owl is highly nocturnal and is seldom seen abroad during daylight, though occasionally one is surprised hawking over the fields at dawn. It prefers broken, open country with low brush and grassy fields and, as its diet consists almost completely of rats and mice, it is one of the farmer's best friends. The Barn Owl hunts by sound perhaps more than by sight, and can locate its prey by ear in total darkness. In recent experiments captive Barn Owls placed in a blacked-out room were watched with infra-red equipment. Mice released in the room were safe as long as they kept still. The moment they rustled the leaf litter on the floor, the owls pounced on them with unerring accuracy.

Barn Owls are fairly long-lived, the oldest known to date in the wild being a bird ringed in Heligoland and recovered almost 15 years later.

TYPICAL OWLS

STRIGIFORMES   STRIGIDAE

Owls are probably the most poorly known and most misunderstood of all our familiar birds. For ages these creatures of the night have been regarded with a mixture of fear, suspicion, and superstition. They occur and reoccur in legends and folk tales. To some primitive peoples, they are birds of sorcery and ill omen, in league with evil spirits, the consorts of witches and demons. Even today superstitious country folk believe the hooting of an owl presages death or misfortune. The happiest of the legends concerning the owl is its reputation for wisdom, which, as we all know, the bird gets by looking wise and saying nothing.

Not the least of the owls' outstanding characteristics, and largely responsible for their unsavoury reputation, are their distinctive calls, which vary from the soft, musical, pleasing, plaintive trilling of the misnamed Screech Owl to the strange, eerie, gobbling, hooting, wailing, and crying of many of the larger species. In some owls the males and females have different notes, with the calls of one sex of a different pitch or a different combination of syllables than those of the other. Pairs call back and forth to one another in a sort of duet in the night. Practically all owls express anger and irritation by clacking their bills.

The owls have their senses of sight and hearing particularly well developed. Their eyes are tremendous, actually far larger than they appear from the outside, where only the iris and pupil show. The eyeball of a 2-foot Snowy Owl is almost as large as a man's. Small wonder they can see so well in the dark! Contrary to popular fancy, they are not blind in the daytime and many species are daytime hunters. Their nictitating membrane, or third eyelid, is especially developed to shield the highly sensitive retina from bright daylight.

Owls' hearing is highly acute, and many species hunt by sound rather than by sight. The characteristic facial disc is believed to have an acoustical function in gathering and concentrating sound waves much like the parabolic reflectors sound technicians use. Owls' ears, though completely hidden under their feathers, are also large, and partly covered by flaps of skin. In many species the right and left openings differ in size

MILKY EAGLE OWL
Bubo lacteus
South Africa   26 in.

BURROWING OWL
Speotyto cunicularia
Western Hemisphere plainslands
from prairie states and
Florida to Tierra del Fuego   9 in.

SNOWY OWL
Nyctea scandiaca
Circumpolar in arctic tundra 25 in.

GREAT HORNED OWL
Bubo virginianus
Western Hemisphere from tree line
to Patagonia, except West Indies 25 in.

SPECTACLED OWL
Pulsatrix perspicillata
Mexico to
northern Argentina 17 in.

ELF OWL
Micrathene whitneyi
Southwestern U.S.
and Mexico 5½ in.

BARN OWL
Tyto alba
N. & S. America,
Europe, Africa, A
southeast Asia, Au
Tasmania 15

and shape, doubtless to increase their binaural efficiency in locating prey by sound.

The noiseless flight of owls, which supposedly helps them pounce on unsuspecting prey, is more likely a refinement to increase their hearing powers. The sound-deadening filaments at the tips of the flight and contour feathers are not so well developed and are sometimes absent in the owls that hunt primarily by day, such as the northern circumpolar Hawk-owl and the little Burrowing Owl.

Their long, loose feathers make owls appear short-necked. Actually their necks are rather long and very pliant. This partly compensates for the tunnel vision attendant on the forward-facing placement of their eyes. Owls' eyes are also less mobile in their sockets than those of most other birds, whose eyes on either side of the head give them a far wider field of vision. Hence owls turn their heads to see things on either side or behind. They can twist their heads around a full 180 degrees. This is the basis for the old story that if you walk around an owl sitting in a treetop, it will keep turning its head to watch you until it twists its neck off.

Owls usually swallow their prey whole, and when the strong stomach juices have removed all the nutrients, the indigestible bones, fur, and feathers are formed into neat pellets and coughed up. Owls usually bring their prey back to a favourite perch to eat. There they sit quietly while they digest their food and regurgitate the remains. Sometimes hundreds of pellets are available on the ground for the curious naturalist to gather, dissect, and analyze. As owls usually hunt within a few miles of these perches, the pellets indicate the relative abundance of the various small mammals in the vicinity, and occasionally lead to welcome discoveries. The presence of the northern Red-backed Pine Mouse (*Pitymys*) was unsuspected in central Connecticut until a number of skulls were found in pellets of Barn Owls roosting and nesting in a college belfry in Middletown. Intensive search of possible habitats

OILBIRD
Steatornis caripensis
Northern South America and Trinidad 13 in.

SCREECH OWL
Otus asio
Temperate North America
and Mexico 10 in.

TAWNY FROGMOUTH
Podargus strigoides
Australia and Tasmania 19 in.

BARRED OWL
Strix varia
Central and eastern North America
and Mexico 20 in.

FERRUGINOUS
PYGMY OWL
Glaucidium brasilianum
Southwestern U.S.
to Patagonia 7 in.

PELL'S FISHING OWL
Scotopelia peli
Africa south of the Sahara   22-24 in.

the surrounding country. Incubation is by the female alone, and the male brings her food while she sits.

As daylight is continuous above the Arctic Circle in summer, the Snowy Owl is then perforce a daylight hunter. It also hunts to some extent by day during the winter. Fast enough fliers to catch and kill ducks on the wing, Snowy Owls eat any animal they can kill, but their mainstay is lemmings and arctic hares. When these are plentiful at their periodic peaks, the Snowy Owls lay 7 to 10 eggs. When the lemming and rabbit cycle wanes and hunting is poor, they lay only 2 or 3 eggs per clutch, and in really bad food years they may make no attempt to nest at all. During the cyclic lows that occur once every 5 to 7 years, Snowy Owls are forced far southward in winter in search of food. They then appear in numbers as far south as the British Isles, northern Germany, central Russia, southern Siberia, northern Japan, and central and eastern United States.

Most striking and imposing of the larger owls are the Horned Owls of the genus *Bubo*, whose 11 species range almost throughout the world. These are all large owls, 2 feet and more in length, with conspicuous ear tufts and a ferocious mien enhanced by their large, yellow eyes. Northern Hemisphere representatives include the familiar Great Horned Owl of North America and the very similar Eagle Owl of Eurasia. Brownish to greyish owls, attractively dappled and barred with black, most are forest inhabitants. Geographical populations vary greatly in colour. Eagle Owls that live in open desert lands in northern Africa and Asia Minor are much lighter-hued than their forest-inhabiting relatives.

Horned Owls do most of their hunting at night along the edges of clearings or in the open, wherever food is plentiful. They are often seen abroad during the day. Because of their forays on ducks, grouse, and other game, these big owls have a bad reputation with sportsmen. Actually they do a great deal more good than harm, for they are one of the few predators able to kill skunks, rats, and other mammals that take a far higher toll of game than do the owls themselves. One of the largest and handsomest of the horned owl group is Verreaux's (or Milky) Eagle Owl, a dark blackish-grey owl of the deepest African forests. Its loud mournful cries have given rise to many legends and superstitions among the African tribes. The Spotted Eagle Owl of South Africa, another greyish horned owl, prefers rocky country. It lives and hunts for small animals in steep, bush-clad ravines.

The smaller owls of the genus *Otus*, called Scops or Screech Owls, are one of the most widespread in America. The 36 species in this genus are all very similar. Typical of them is the friendly and misnamed Screech Owl that nests in hollow trees close to dwellings.

The Tawny Owl is found throughout Europe and western Asia. In Great Britain it occurs everywhere except the outer islands of Scotland, and has been introduced into Ireland. Although typically a woodland species it uses small clumps of trees, or scattered trees in parkland. It hunts by night, and rests by day sitting bolt upright in a hollow or on a branch pressed against the trunk. It is the owl most often seen or heard in Britain. Also known as the brown owl, it has two colour phases, grey and brown.

soon revealed a small colony of these interesting but shy little rodents in an isolated clump of pines in a nearby marsh.

With few exceptions owls are cavity nesters. Most nest in hollow trees, some on cliff ledges or in ground burrows. A few appropriate abandoned hawk or crow nests. None uses much if any nest material. All owls lay pure-white, almost spherical eggs. Clutches vary from 1 to 7 or more. Usually both sexes incubate, and in all both parents feed the young.

One of the most striking and distinctive of the 123 species in this extensive family, and one of the most unusual in its nesting habits, is the great Snowy Owl that breeds circumpolarly in the barren northern tundras. One of the few owls that nest in the open, the Snowy Owl usually nests on top of a slight rise of ground that gives it a vantage point to watch

The pygmy owls of the genus *Glaucidium* are stocky, round-headed birds from 6 to 8 inches in length. Twelve species range widely throughout North and South America, Africa, and southern Eurasia. These little birds may be seen abroad during the day, but usually hunt in the evening twilight. Inhabitants of brush regions and sparse woodlands, they feed on insects and small birds and to a large extent on small reptiles. They are bold and active and are known to catch small birds in flight.

One of the smallest owls is the little Elf Owl, only 5½ inches in length, of Mexico and the American Southwest. Though largely desert residents, Elf Owls are also found in pine forests and oak woodlands. They live almost entirely on insects, which they catch on the wing and on the ground. Their voices are astonishingly loud for such small birds, and pairs often sing duets on bright moonlight nights during the breeding season. Their distinctive calls are barks, whines, and yaps much like those of a young puppy. A favourite nesting site is abandoned woodpecker holes in the big saguaro cacti.

Two widely separated groups of owls are known as hawk-owls. The name is most fittingly applied to the northern Hawk-owl, a circumpolar species that breeds across northern North America and northern Eurasia at the tree line. Like the Snowy Owl it is occasionally forced southward in winters when food is scarce. This grey, medium-sized owl, 15 to 17 inches in length, is strikingly hawk-like in appearance and actions. Its tail is longer and its wings more pointed than those of most other owls. It is markedly diurnal in its hunting. It hunts by sight rather than by hearing. Its feathers are more compact and harder than those of other owls, and its facial discs are neither as pronounced nor as complete.

The 18 species of small owls of the genus *Ninox* of eastern Asia, the East Indies, Australia, and New Zealand are also called hawk-owls. The Oriental Hawk-owl of eastern Asia is probably the best known of this group. It is a woodland owl, quite diurnal, which lives largely on insects. The northern populations are migratory and travel mostly by day.

The 11 species of wood-owls of the genus *Strix* are essentially birds of the Northern Hemisphere, though several species are found in South America and in the East Indies. A member of this genus is the 2½-foot Great Grey Owl of northern North America and western Eurasia, one of the largest of all owls. Typical of the group are the familiar Barred Owl of eastern North America and its western counterpart, the Spotted Owl. Wood-owl pellets show their tremendous range of food—insects, occasional lizards and other reptiles, amphibians, and birds—even including smaller owls. But squirrels and wood rats form the bulk of their diet.

Worth mentioning, in passing, are the three spectacled owls of the genus *Pulsatrix*. These New World jungle owls, found from southern Mexico southward through Brazil, have a most striking facial pattern. Then there are the strange fish-eating owls, three species of one genus in Africa and four of another in southeastern Asia. Their legs are unfeathered and the feet have rough scutellations on their underside like those of the Osprey to help them hold on to their slippery prey.

The widespread Short-eared Owl is circumpolar in the Northern Hemisphere and also occurs in South America and on a number of oceanic islands. The northern populations are highly migratory and the migrating flocks often roost on the ground. Short-eared Owls are ground nesters and usually inhabit open lands around both fresh- and salt-water marshes. They feed largely on insects and on small rodents and are frequently seen coursing over the meadows at dusk.

One of the most comical owls is the Burrowing Owl, a 9-inch bird found in southern Florida, the West Indies, and from the Western states southward through Central and South America to Tierra del Fuego. These long-legged little owls live in open prairie lands and nest in burrows which they dig themselves, often in small colonies. By day one of the pair usually stands solemnly at the mouth of the burrow and bobs up and down politely as one approaches before ducking out of sight into its hole or flying away, low to the ground. They feed mainly at dusk and in the early evening. While they take some small mammals and an occasional bird, their main food is insects, especially locusts, crickets, and grasshoppers. Their calls are a low chuckling.

GOATSUCKERS AND ALLIES

CAPRIMULGIFORMES

This is an order of five families of nocturnal or crepuscular birds. All have long, pointed wings, small, insignificant feet, equally insignificant bills, and tremendous gaping mouths. All but one, the Oilbird, feed exclusively on insects which—again with one exception, the frogmouths—they catch on the wing. Most goatsuckers have evolved as highly efficient flying insect traps.

As befits birds that are active mainly at night and hide by day, all are sombrely decked in browns and greys, cryptically mottled, barred, or streaked with black, darker greys, and browns. Their soft, loose, fluffy plumage resembles that of their nearest relatives, the owls.

Their unlovely ordinal name stems from an ancient fallacy, based on their huge mouths. These birds were reputed to milk goats at night. The common names of many species, however, are imitative of the birds' loud, distinctive cries, which have earned them such epithets as Nightjar, Whip-poor-will, Chuck-will's-widow, Poor-me-one, Potoo, and Pauraque. The voices of some tropical species are so weird that local folk have a superstitious dread of the birds.

OILBIRD OR GUACHARO

CAPRIMULGIFORMES   STEATORNITHIDAE

Strangest of the many weird goatsuckers is the almost un-believable Oilbird (p. 157) of northern South America and Trinidad, so named because for centuries the Indians of Venezuela obtained their cooking oil from its incredibly fat young. The Spaniards call it *Guacharo*, the one that wails or cries, from its piercing shrieks and plaints that grate harshly on the human ear.

The Guacharos spend their days deep in seaside or mountain caves and come out to feed only at night. The lean-bodied adults measure only 13 inches in length, but their long, pointed wings span 2½ feet. Oilbirds' feathers are rich cinnamon-brown lightly spangled with small white dots. Their flight is light, swift, strong, and undulating. Their small feet are almost useless, and they never perch. When not squatting on their nests or on ledges in their cave hideaways, they cling to rock walls like swifts.

So singular it merits a family all to itself, the Guacharo is the only vegetarian among the goatsuckers. It lives exclusively on fruits, mainly on the oily fruits of palm trees which it plucks with its stout hooked bill while hovering next to them like a helicopter. Venturing forth just as the early tropical night falls, flocks of Guacharos may travel 50 miles or more to find palm fruits in just the right stage of ripeness. Before dawn breaks they streak back unerringly to their cave entrance, and by daylight are safely hidden in darkness, deep in the bowels of the earth.

Guacharos roost and nest colonially on ledges, sometimes a half mile back from the cave entrance, where they share the Stygian blackness with bats, secure from all enemies except adventurous speleologists. Their nests are truncated cones of their own droppings, mixed with palm seeds which often germinate but wither and die from lack of light. In a shallow cavity on top of the cone they lay 2 to 4 white eggs, which both sexes incubate. The young hatch naked, but soon acquire a sparse down. Stuffed with the same rich, oily fruit, they become helpless masses of fat, which they do not shed until their flight feathers mature. At their maximum they weigh almost twice as much as their tough, stringy parents, and it is at this stage that the Indians harvest them for their oil.

Most marvellous of the Guacharo's attributes is its ability to fly with unfailing accuracy in absolute darkness through the narrow, twisting passages of its underground retreat. This it does, recent studies have shown, by a sonar device located in its ears, similar to a bat's, which measures the distance and direction of obstacles by reflected sound waves. Unlike the bat's sonar, which operates on supersonic waves beyond the range of human hearing, the Guacharo's echo-ranger works on an audible frequency of 7,000 cycles per second. Its pulsations can be heard plainly whenever the birds are in flight as a continuous metallic clicking underneath the birds' wails, screams, and guttural croaks.

The Venezuelan government has recently set aside as a National Park the site of a large Guacharo cave near Caripe and plans to develop it as a tourist attraction complete with guides and electric lights. It should be worth the trip to hear the Guacharos clicking their way through the darkness.

FROGMOUTHS

CAPRIMULGIFORMES   PODARGIDAE

The frogmouths are a small family of 12 peculiar goatsuckers found from Australia north to Malaya and the Philippines and eastward to the Solomons. They differ from other members of the order in their large, flat, horny, triangular, sharply hooked bills, and in their method of feeding. Instead of catching insects on the wing, frogmouths prey on creeping, crawling things such as beetles, centipedes, scorpions, and caterpillars. The big Tawny Frogmouth of Australia even catches mice on occasion. This ground feeder watches quietly from a convenient stump or branch until it spies its quarry and then flutters down on it. Other species are reported to scour the larger branches of jungle trees for their food, though they seem poorly adapted structurally for this type of hunting. Their legs are very short and their feet small and weak. They are somewhat lethargic in their movements, and are the weakest fliers in the order. Their rounded wings are only of moderate length.

Frogmouths range in length from 9 to 21 inches. Their soft silky plumage is patterned with cryptic streaks, barrings, and vermiculations. The sexes are alike or nearly so. Dichromatism occurs frequently in the family, and most species have ruddy brown and greyish colour phases.

Frogmouths always nest in trees, usually in the forks of a horizontal branch. Some build a frail platform of sticks, others a pad of their own feathers, which they camouflage with lichens, mosses, and spider webs. They lay 1 or 2 white eggs, which both sexes incubate, usually the female by night, the male by day. The young are covered with down at hatching and remain in the nest until able to fly.

During the day frogmouths sleep perched lengthwise on a branch with their heads up and their eyes closed. Their colour so matches the branch that they look like part of it and are almost impossible to see. Their nocturnal habits and their relative scarcity make them so difficult to study that comparatively little is known of their biology and behaviour. Their calls are typically a low, hoarse booming. The Tawny Frogmouth repeats through the night a grunting "oom-oom" which has a distinct nasal quality.

POTOOS

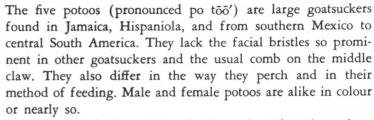

CAPRIMULGIFORMES   NYCTIBIIDAE

The five potoos (pronounced po tōō′) are large goatsuckers found in Jamaica, Hispaniola, and from southern Mexico to central South America. They lack the facial bristles so prominent in other goatsuckers and the usual comb on the middle claw. They also differ in the way they perch and in their method of feeding. Male and female potoos are alike in colour or nearly so.

Potoos perch bolt upright on broken stubs or branches, where they look like a continuation of the tree. At night their large orange-yellow eyes reflect the glare of headlights as they sit on top of a roadside fencepost. Like the nightjars, the potoos live on flying insects, but instead of hawking them in continuous flight, the potoos hunt in flycatcher fashion. They watch quietly from a perch and dash out to grab their prey as large tropical night insects flit by, returning to the perch between each mouthful.

Potoos' calls are loud and distinctive. The Mexican Potoo has a loud "baw-woo," strong enough to be the yowl of a big cat. The call of the 19-inch Giant Potoo of Surinam is a drawn-out "ooroo." The sentimental Trinidadians call the resident Common Potoo the "Poor-me-one," from its sad, self-pitying cry, which it varies with series of 7 or 8 clear whistled notes.

Potoos lay their single spotted egg on top of a broken stump where both sexes incubate it in turn, sitting bolt upright. The chick hatches covered with white down and as it sits motionless on its exposed perch might be mistaken for a piece of bracket fungus. Nevertheless the old birds brood it closely to hide it until its camouflaging contour feathers appear and it assumes the peculiar vertical posture that makes it look like part of the tree.

COMMON POTOO
Nyctibius griseus
Mexico to Argentina 14 in.

GREY OWLET FROGMOUTH
Aegotheles albertisi
New Guinea 6 in.

OWLET FROGMOUTHS

CAPRIMULGIFORMES   AEGOTHELIDAE

Dumpy little birds, the largest a bare 12 inches long, the eight owlet frogmouths of Australia and New Guinea resemble tiny, long-tailed owls. Australians call them "moth owls," for they hawk night-flying insects in flight. They also feed like frogmouths on ground insects, ants, and millepedes. They have large, rounded heads and tiny feet.

Owlet frogmouths are shy, solitary forest dwellers. Strictly nocturnal, they hide by day in hollow trees. They fly less erratically than most goatsuckers, perch crossways on branches instead of lengthways, and sit more erect than any but the potoos. They lack their relatives' loud cries; some have flute-like whistles, while others utter faint churrings in flight.

Owlet frogmouths nest in hollow trees and lay 3 to 4 roundish eggs, slightly pointed at one end, usually clear white, sometimes spotted. Some species line the nest cavity with green leaves; others leave it bare. The young hatch covered with down and are reared in the nest. In southern Australia they nest in spring and often rear two broods.

NIGHTJARS

CAPRIMULGIFORMES   CAPRIMULGIDAE

The largest and most widely distributed family of the goat-suckers is the nominate group known as nightjars. Some 67 species are scattered throughout the world in tropical and temperate regions. The family is absent only from New Zealand and the oceanic islands. Nightjars are famed for their loud, persistent, monotonous calls, which actually do jar the night, and their calls are often more familiar to people than the birds themselves. Most members of the family spend the day sleeping or resting and take to wing at dusk. A few are active by day as well as by night. One of the most diurnal is the common Nighthawk, which, of course, is no more a hawk than it is completely nocturnal.

All the nightjars feed on insects that they catch in flight. Occasionally they scoop up a late-flying small bird or two. Warblers have been found in Chuck-will's-widows' stomachs, but such items in their diet are fortuitous exceptions. Their flight seems light and bouncy as they wheel and turn in an erratic zigzag pursuit of food, yet it is markedly strong and deliberate. Their wingbeats are slow and leisurely, in fact almost lazy, interspersed with short bits of soaring.

Nocturnal birds are never brightly coloured, and all the nightjars are sombrely dressed in browns and greys, pencilled and stippled with browns, black, and white in concealing patterns to hide them during the day. The sexes are similar in appearance, but the white patches on the wings or tails that show in the flight of some males are often brown in their mates. Nightjars are so protectively coloured that they spend

their days in the open, sitting lengthwise along a bare branch where they pass unnoticed as a loose bit of bark. Those that rest among dead leaves on the ground are so confident of their invisibility that they do not move until almost stepped on, when they suddenly take flight from under your very feet. When resting during the day they usually keep their large lustrous eyes closed, whether in sleep or to avoid revealing their presence is not known.

Nightjars' legs and feet are so small they are of little use to their owners on the ground. The birds can shuffle a few steps, but they seldom do. They alight from the air and then fly, rather than walk, to a new spot, even if is only a few feet away. A peculiar feature is the comb of serrated notches on the underside of their middle claw, similar to that found in herons and a few other unrelated species. Its function is unknown, but is thought to be for dressing the feathers in some way. Nightjars might find it useful for removing insect scales from the long facial bristles that increase the effective diameter of their gaping flytrap mouths.

Their insect diet restricts the nightjars to climates where insects are plentiful. Most tropical species tend to be sedentary. Those that venture north or south into temperate latitudes to breed in summer perform long migrations to more insect-ridden climes in winter. The Common Nighthawk, which breeds widely throughout North America north to southern Alaska and Newfoundland, migrates south to Argentina. The European Nightjar winters in central Africa. The Pen-

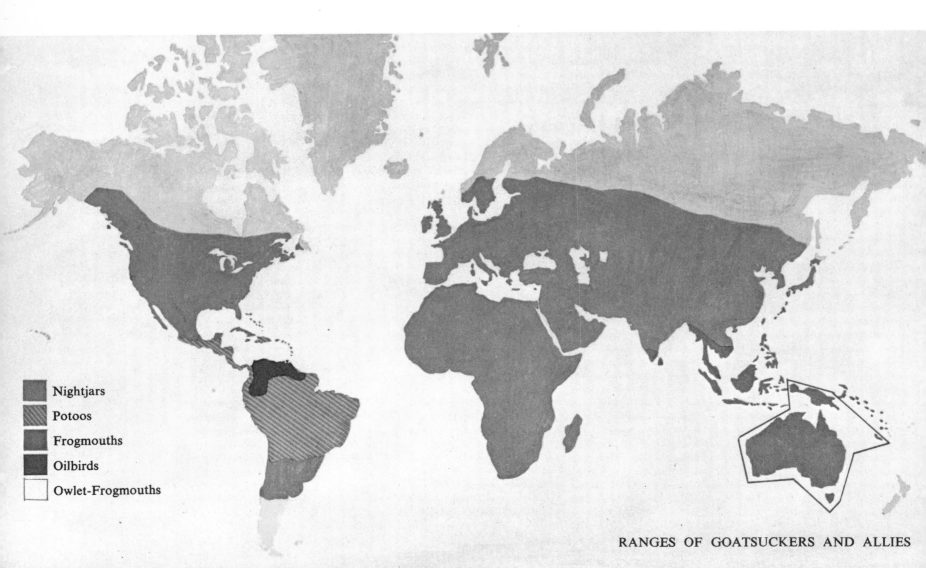

Nightjars
Potoos
Frogmouths
Oilbirds
Owlet-Frogmouths

RANGES OF GOATSUCKERS AND ALLIES

nant-winged Nightjar of South Africa starts northward when summer begins to wane in March, and spends its nonbreeding season in the central Congo.

The Pennant-wing (p. 164) measures only 11 inches from bill tip to tail tip, but as the males don their spring plumage the innermost pair of primaries grow into fluttering pennants 2 feet or more in length. Displayed during the sailing, soaring courtship flight, these pennants apparently take the place of the calls other nightjars use when courting, for the Pennant-wing seems to be voiceless. As valuable as these streamers may be for winning a mate, they must hamper flight to some extent. The moment their usefulness in courtship is over, in February or March, they are broken off—some think by the birds themselves, for the stubs are not shed until the annual moult starts in June. In another showy African species, the Standard-winged Nightjar, the male has the inner pair of primaries similarly elongated during the breeding season. But in this case the feathers' vanes are left like tiny flags only on the outer 6 inches of the 2-foot shafts. The displaying male flies slowly around the female with its arched wings vibrating rapidly to blow the two flags into the air directly above it.

Only within the past decade has it been proved that one nightjar, the Poor-will of western North America, avoids the rigours of an insect-free winter the way many insects, amphibians, and some reptiles do—by hibernating! Prior to this amazing discovery ornithologists scoffed at the idea that any bird could lower its high metabolism enough to pass the winter successfully in a torpid state.

Not that the possibilty of bird hibernation hadn't been thought of before. The untravelled medieval naturalists believed that the swallows which disappeared every autumn and reappeared so regularly every spring hibernated in the marshes where the large flocks were seen to roost at night just before they disappeared. This we know was just another ancient fable, like the one about the northern geese hatching from barnacles, conceived in ignorance to explain a mysterious phenomenon. So when Arizona Indians a century and more ago told of birds that slept away the winter in crevices in rocky cliffs, this was duly recorded by cultural anthropologists, but dismissed by ornithologists as a charming Indian folk tale. It wasn't until 1946 that the sceptical white man learned that this tall Indian tale is quite true.

Whether or not all Poor-wills hibernate instead of migrating is not known, but at the onset of cold weather some of them creep into crevices or niches in the canyon walls. Their body temperatures drop from a normal 102° to about 65° F. Their breathing slows to almost nothing, and their digestive processes cease. They sleep through the cold months until the returning warmth of spring awakens them and their insect food again. Ringed hibernating Poor-wills have been found sleeping in the same niches in successive winters.

Though nightjars often alight and roost in trees (customarily lengthwise with the branch), they always nest on the ground. They make no pretence at a nest, but lay their eggs on the bare earth or in the leaf litter, where the heavy spotting on a white or cream shell makes the eggs as inconspicuous as the birds themselves. Most tropical nightjars lay a single egg, but they may nest twice each season. The temperate zone species usually raise a single brood of two young.

The rather long incubation period, 16 to 20 days, is shared by both sexes in some species, accomplished by the female alone in others, but with her mate in close attendance. The young hatch covered with a concealing coat of mottled down and stay quietly hidden in the ground litter. Both parents feed the chicks with insects from their bills for the 16 to 25 or more days it takes them to mature their flight feathers and take wing to feed themselves.

Nightjars are among the few birds that will move their eggs or young when disturbed or alarmed by the threat of discovery. This has been questioned ever since Audubon described a Chuck-will's-widow moving its eggs in its capacious mouth a century ago. But the phenomenon has been observed in this species often enough since to validate it. Chuck-wills have also been reported to carry their young to a safer place between their thighs the way a Woodcock will. Nighthawks have been known to move their eggs unintentionally as much as 50 feet during their 19-day incubation period. Every time the bird drops on them from the air, it moves them an inch or two by the impact of its body as it lands. As it usually comes in from the same direction each time, the eggs move continually in the opposite direction. Strangely, however, if the eggs are moved during the incubating bird's absence as little as 5 feet from where she left them, though still in plain sight, she is often unable to find them. Memory of the exact spot where they should be is dominant, and she fails to recognize them if they are too far out of place.

The Nighthawk has a number of unusual facets to its character. It is one of the few members of the family that calls in flight. The Poor-wills and all their loud-voiced kin cry out their plaints while perched on the ground or on a branch. The Nighthawk is usually silent when perching, but calls incessantly on the wing, typically a nasal, buzzing "peent" reminiscent of the snipes' plaint. This is evidently a recognition call designed to advertise the individual's position and to keep the loose parties together. It plays little if any part in courtship. The courting Nighthawk dives down out of the sky at its mate on the ground, brakes, and turns upward with a loud zoom produced by the wind vibrating through his primaries—again reminiscent of the snipes' courtship.

Essentially a bird of open country, the Nighthawk is fond of coursing over marshes, wet pastures, and clearings. It has taken comfortably to urban life since the development of flat, gravel-surfaced roofs. It has learned these rooftops make fine nesting sites, and the plaintive buzzing calls of Nighthawks are now commonly heard above the traffic noises of many American cities as the birds course high over the rooftops in their buoyant, dancing search for flying insects.

Much has been written about the monotonous persistence with which the loud-voiced nightjars repeat their courting calls. For several springs a male Whip-poor-will made my doorstep his favourite calling perch. Many a night I retired to his shrill refrain and put myself to sleep counting its phrases. My record count was 402 "whip-poor-wills", repeated a second apart, before the bird stopped or I went to sleep. A Southern friend boasts of counting 834 successive Chuck-will's-widow calls, and I don't doubt him one bit. The all-time high seems to be John Burrough's record of hearing a bird "lay upon the back of poor Will" 1,088 blows in succession.

COMMON NIGHTHAWK
Chordeiles minor
Temperate North America 9 in.

SWIFTS AND HUMMINGBIRDS

APODIFORMES

The unquestioned kings of flight, each in its own fashion, are the swifts and the hummingbirds. In achieving their superb aerial skill, their wings developed at the expense of their feet which, though tiny, are not missing as their ordinal name, "the footless ones," implies. The two groups are so different in appearance and action, each is sometimes given ordinal rank, but the many structural characteristics they share show them more closely related to each other than to any other bird group. They doubtless shared a common ancestor very long ago.

Characteristic of the order are the relative proportions of the swifts' and hummers' wing bones. Their upper arm bone, the humerus, is short and stout, and their wings are formed mainly by the elongated elements beyond the "elbow." This gives their wings greater strength at their junction with the body, and their large flying muscles better leverage. They also show distinctive reproductive similarities. All lay long pure-white eggs, equally rounded at each end. They lay small clutches, often 1 egg in tropical species, usually 2; though some swifts lay 6. The young hatch naked and blind, remain in the nest for relatively long periods, and are capable of extended flight when they leave.

The fossil record of these fragile birds is poor. Fragmentary remains of swifts from Oligocene rocks in France show the family well differentiated at least 40 million years ago. The Apodiformes seem distantly related to the goatsuckers.

PENNANT-WINGED NICHTJAR
Semeiophorus vexillarius
South Africa 12 in.

WHIP-POOR-WILL
Caprimulgus vociferus
Eastern North America 10 in.

CHIMNEY SWIFT
Chaetura pelagica
Temperate central and
eastern North America 5 in.

BROWN-THROATED
SPINETAIL SWIFT
Chaetura gigantea
India to Indochina,
Philippines, East Indies 7 in.

WHITE-RUMPED SWIFT
Apus caffer
Africa south of
the Sahara 6 in.

INDIAN CRESTED SWIFT
Hemiprocne longipennis
India to Indochina
and Celebes 8-9 in.

SCISSOR-TAILED
SWIFT
Panyptila sancti-hieronymi
Honduras and
Guatemala 8 in.

SWIFTS

APODIFORMES   APODIDAE

The aptly named swifts are exceptionally fast fliers. Though not all are speed kings, some are able to fly above 100 miles per hour. The speediest things in feathers are the large spinetailed swifts of eastern Asia, whose flight speeds have been estimated between 150 and 200 miles per hour.

Swifts live entirely on insects they catch in flight, usually high in the air where they have plenty of flying room and their speed can be used to best advantage. They are not related to the swallows, which resemble them and feed somewhat similarly. Swifts' flight is usually straighter, faster, and less erratic than the swallows'. Their streamlined bodies are stouter, their tails shorter and stiffer. Their thin, pointed wings curve back in a graceful crescent. Their beaks are tiny and their mouths open back behind the eye, but the swifts lack the stiff facial bristles that augment the wide gape in most other flying flytraps. Their compact body plumage is usually plainly coloured in solid greys or browns; many have lighter patches on the rump and underparts. The sexes are alike.

Typical swift flight is a series of rapid, shallow wingbeats interspersed with short glides. Their wingstrokes are so fast they are hard to follow with the eye, and often as swifts rocket and turn, their wings seem to beat alternately. Highspeed photographs show that some swifts can and do move one wing faster than the other. Their short tails are inefficient rudders, so they steer partly with their wings, beating them slightly out of phase, though not actually alternating.

The swifts' short legs and small, weak feet will not support them in normal fashion. They never perch on tree branches, and few can raise themselves high enough off flat ground to give their wings play to take flight. They roost upright to vertical surfaces with their sharp toenails, propped against cliff walls, tree trunks, or chimneys by their short tails. In several genera all four toes project forward for firmer gripping, and in one, the spinetails, the tail-feather shafts project beyond the vanes as sharp needles.

Their flight is so effortless that swifts apparently need little rest. They probably spend more of their waking hours in the air than do any other land birds. An ancient belief had it that swifts roosted in the Heavens. In recent years two lines of research have been used to show that some swifts do spend the night on the wing. One was to fix an automatic device to the entrance to the nests to register whether the birds entered or left them during the hours of darkness. The other was to go up in an aeroplane and actually see the birds in the air at night.

The swift family contains some 67 species scattered throughout the world, principally in tropical and subtropical lands where insects are plentiful. Absent from New Zealand and from southern South America, the half-dozen species that nest in the temperate Northern Hemisphere migrate to the tropics in winter. They travel by day in loose-knit flocks, feed as they go, and roost at night in cliffs, caves, large hollow trees or chimneys, often in tremendous numbers.

Swifts fall into eight main genera, each distinctive in its choices of nesting sites and materials. All have one peculiarity in common: they glue their nests into place with their sticky saliva, and the salivary glands of both sexes are greatly enlarged during the nesting season. Both parents build the nest and share incubating and feeding duties. The clutches of elongated white eggs are small, usually 1 or 2, rarely 3, and in a few groups 4 to 6. Incubation periods range from about 16 to 20 days, and the fledging periods are very long, from 4 to 6 weeks. Young swifts do not leave the nest until they are capable of sure, sustained flight, for should one flutter to the ground it might never again take off. They are so able to care for themselves when they leave the nest that the northern migratory species start southward almost immediately afterwards. Ringing statistics show that young swifts escape the high first-year mortality suffered by most other birds.

Most widespread are the 18 spinetailed swifts (*Chaetura*) found on all continents. All nest and roost in hollow trees which they dive into from above. Several species find chimneys a serviceable and more plentiful substitute. For nesting and roosting, the Chimney Swift of North America now uses chimneys almost exclusively. Flocks of migrating Chimney Swifts commonly roost in large disused school or factory chimneys, where they have been ringed

AFRICAN PALM SWIFT
Cypsiurus parvus
Africa, southeastern Asia,
Philippines. East Indies 4 in.

in wholesale quantities. Ringed birds return to the same chimneys to roost and to nest year after year. Preparing to roost at dusk, Chimney Swifts circle, often in thousands, in a twittering, funnel-shaped cloud over their chosen chimney. As darkness deepens they drop, still twittering, from the base of the funnel shape they have formed, into the chimney.

Chimney Swifts scatter out to nest, but large chimneys may hold several pairs. They build their nests of twigs, which they break off with their feet in flight and glue together into a hammock-shaped bracket against the inside of the chimney. All the spinetails build similarly, so far as known, except the Brown-throated Spinetail, one of the largest as well as the fastest of the swifts. It lays its eggs in the bottom of a tree hollow, perhaps because of the difficulty of gluing a nest strong enough to hold its weight.

The 10 Old World swifts of the genus *Apus* are cliff breeders. Their usual nest is a shallow cup of straw, feathers, or other light material snatched up in flight and loosely glued together on the floor of a crevice. Like the spinetails, they have found man-made structures convenient, and the Common Swift of Europe and several others now regularly nest on buildings, often using abandoned nests of swallows or martins as foundations for their own.

Equally distinctive in their nesting are the nine dark swifts of the genus *Cypseloides* in the American tropics. One, the Black Swift, nests northward along the Pacific coast to southern Alaska. These cliff nesters prefer rocky escarpments close to water, usually in inland canyons, sometimes by the sea. They glue a stout, cone-shaped structure of mosses and twigs to the rocks, sometimes using mud as well as saliva, and line the nest with bits of fern. Several South American black swifts nest behind waterfalls and fly through the cascade. The wall of water is an effective barrier against potential enemies.

A vastly different type of nest is built by the two scissor-tailed swifts (*Panyptila*) of Central America and northern South America. Among the more striking patterned swifts (p. 165), the scissor-tails build a tubular stocking from 7 inches to 2 feet in length of dry plant down matted with feathers and plant fibres, but with thinner walls and usually the round entrance at the bottom and lay their eggs on a flat shelf built within the widened top. They usually hang the nest under an overhanging rock shelf or from a large high branch, but have found house eaves good substitutes. The two American palm swifts (*Tachornis*) of the West Indies and northern South America build similar felted tubes of feathers and plant fibres, but with thinner walls and usually set within the hollow spathe of a palm flower or under a drooping palm frond.

One of the weirdest nests is that built by the little African Palm Swift (*Cypsiurus*), which glues a small, flat, rimless pad of feathers to the inner side of a broad drooping palm, banana, or dracina leaf. To the top of this tiny platform, much too small for the bird to crouch on, the Palm Swift glues her one or two eggs upright with saliva. This holds them firmly in place, even though the wind may turn the swaying leaf upside down. The adults incubate clinging to the platform with their toes and sitting bolt upright. The young hatch naked like other swifts, but soon develop a protective coat of down. They cling tightly to the nest, squatting with their heads up, backs out, and breasts against the leaf, and there they stay until they develop their flight feathers fully.

Last of the better-known swifts are the plethora of small cave swiftlets of the Indo-Australian region and the Western Pacific islands. Their saliva nests are used in the Orient for soup—and a delicious, nourishing consommé it is, too. The cave swiftlets are a bewildering group of little birds, from 3½ to 6½ inches in length, all assigned to the genus *Collocalia*. Most of them are dull greys and browns with lighter rumps and underparts, some tinged with metallic blues and greens. They are so varied and yet so similar that they are a systematist's nightmare. Scores have been described, but the differences between them are so slight and their distributions so complex that no one is positive how many species they represent—probably about 15 or 20.

The cave swiftlets are neither fast nor high fliers. They feed like swallows in forest clearings, often close to the ground, and flit about lightly in a most erratic manner. Their nesting habits provide one of the best clues to their relationships. All glue a cup-shaped bracket to a vertical surface, some on tree trunks, some on cliffs. Most nest in mountain or sea-coast caves, sometimes in tremendous colonies. One group uses bits of bark, another favours lichens or vegetable fibres, a third mixes feathers with other nest material—but all use more saliva in their nests than other swifts. The Grey and the Grey-rumped swiftlets of Malaya and Indochina make their nests entirely of saliva. These are the top-grade nests of commerce.

This centuries-old Oriental gastronomic treat is still a thriving business, and nests worth forty thousand pounds or more are harvested each year. The best nests come from the large seaward-facing limestone caverns in coastal Indochina, where the tiny birds breed in tremendous numbers. Native gatherers use bamboo ladders and long poles to knock the nests down from the cave walls and ceilings as the birds finish them. The birds have enough saliva to build a second nest of pure hardened fluid, but their third one is apt to be mixed with impurities and is of lower commercial value. The clean first nests are marketed as they are, and command the highest prices. The others are processed to remove the impurities, and the protein-rich gelatin is rehardened into chips which Chinese merchants sell as "dragon's teeth."

EDIBLE-NEST SWIFTLET
Collocalia inexpectata
India to Indochina,
Philippines, East Indies 4-4½ in.

CRESTED SWIFTS

APODIFORMES   HEMIPROCNIDAE

Restricted to southeast Asia and adjacent islands are three distinctive swifts with crests and long forked tails. They roost and nest on tree branches. Other points of difference are their softer plumage, brighter colours in the males, and a distinctive juvenile dress. Their blue-grey to brownish feathers show bronzy iridescence on the back, and two species have bold streaks of long white plumes above and below the eye.

Crested swifts frequent open woodlands where there are high, bare branches. They feed, like the other swifts, entirely on insects caught on the wing, but their fast, erratic flight is not as sustained. Between sporadic feeding forays the small flocks perch huddled together on a lofty bare limb. Usually found near water, they are fond of swooping down from a height, barely touching the surface, and soaring up again in a long graceful arc. They spend much of the day perched and are most active at dawn and dusk. Their twittering voices are louder than those of most other swifts, and they are particularly noisy during their evening flight before going to roost for the night.

Crested swifts build the tiniest of nests, a thin platform of bark flakes and feathers, seldom more than a quarter inch thick and no bigger than a half-crown, glued on top of a lofty tree limb. This flimsy structure is barely large enough to hold the single elongated bluish-grey egg the bird glues to its centre. The limb beneath, rather than the nest, supports the weight of the incubating adults.

HUMMINGBIRDS

APODIFORMES   TROCHILIDAE

The Western Hemisphere's richest gift to the avian world is the fantastic family of hummingbirds, whose 319 species combine brilliant colour with diminutive size. Their dazzling iridescent colours surpass those of the birds of paradise, and are matched in brilliance, though not in variety, only in the Old World sunbirds.

So brilliant and gem-like are these tiny birds that at one time they were used for jewellery, and the trade in them was tremendous. During the 19th century ·millions of hummingbird skins were shipped from northern South America and the West Indies to European markets, where they were fashioned into pins, brooches, and other accessories for feminine adornment. One London dealer imported more than 400,000 skins from the West Indies in one year alone. The centre of this trade, which has now fortunately subsided, was Bogotá, Colombia, in the centre of the family's abundance and diversity. "Bogotá trade skins" form the nucleus of many scientific collections of hummingbirds still in existence, and many species were first described by European "cabinet ornithologists" from these commercial skins, which lacked data and were of uncertain source. Some distinctive species are still known only from one or two such native-collected specimens, and have yet to be found in the field by ornithologists.

We have no fossil clues to the ancestry of these small, dainty creatures, but their anatomy and their present distribution suggest they arose from some primitive swift-like progenitor in the American tropics—just how long ago is anybody's guess. The great diversity within the family's anatomical framework points to a long period of radiative development, probably since earliest Tertiary time. From their ancestral home in northern South America, hummingbirds have spread southward to Tierra del Fuego and northward to Alaska, Quebec, and Nova Scotia. They have never crossed the ocean barriers to the Old World, where no other birds have succeeded in paralleling their way of life exactly, and where the peculiar ecological niche they occupy in the New World remains essentially unfilled.

Hummingbirds have capitalized on their small size and exceptional flying abilities to invade a biological stratum not conquered by any other birds and shared with only a few insects—the world of flowers. They get their tremendous energy from the quick sugars in flower nectar, and their proteins for growth from small insects captured in the same flowers. While other birds in both hemispheres have adopted nectar-feeding as their livelihood—the honeyeaters, honeycreepers, sunbirds, flowerpeckers, certain parrots, warblers, and tanagers, for instance—few live as exclusively on nectar, and none gathers it entirely in flight as do the hummers.

The wide availability of flowers from ground level to treetop has encouraged among hummingbirds an amazing diversification in form, structure, and colour. The smallest members of the family are the tiny Bee Hummingbirds of the West Indies. The Cuban Bee Hummer is the smallest bird known, 2¼ inches from the tip of its bill to the tip of its tail. Its body is the size of a large bumblebee and it weighs less than

2 grams. The largest of the group is the 8½-inch Giant Hummingbird of the high Andes, which weighs about 20 grams and is one of the few that flaps its wings slowly enough for them to be seen in flight.

The family's greatest diversity, other than in the shimmering splendour of the males, is in their beaks and tongues. All hummingbird bills are slender, thin, and pointed, and most are straight or nearly so. A few have the bill curved gently downward, and one, the Sicklebill found from Costa Rica south to Ecuador, has it curved almost into a half-moon. The bills of the flashy Andean rainbows curve slightly upward at the tip. That of the Swordbill of northern South America is longer than its owner's head, body, and tail together, and capable of probing the depths of the deepest tubular flowers.

Another adaptation for nectar feeding is the hummingbirds' ability to project their tongues some distance beyond the bill. The tongues are tubular at the tip in many species for sucking; others have brushy tips which are effective in gathering both nectar and insects. With this varied kit of tools, the hummers are able to feed from almost any type of flower.

In addition to their vivid colour, many male hummingbirds also sport a bewildering array of crests, fans, chinwhiskers, and other gay ornaments for use in courtship, and their tails also vary greatly from short and square or rounded to long and deeply forked. The rare and little-known Loddiges' Racquet-tail has only 4 instead of the normal 10 tail feathers; the two central ones are long spikes, and the outer pair cross one another to trail the purple flags at their tips behind the bird in flight. Exactly how these are used in courtship has not been determined, for their owner is one of the rarest of hummingbirds. Described from a single trade skin without data in the 1840's, the type remained unique for almost 40 years until professional collectors discovered it in one little valley 9,000 feet up in the Peruvian Andes. It is still known from a mere handful of specimens, all from this same valley, and its habits in life have never been studied.

Hummingbirds' wings beat so fast in flight they produce the humming sound responsible for their name. Their moving wings are practically invisible, just a blur to human eyes. They never soar, but in all other departments of powered flight they yield the palm to no other birds save in straight speed. Though pacing with cars has indicated speeds up to 60 miles per hour for the Ruby-throated Hummingbirds, the common (and only) species of eastern North America, wind-tunnel tests have recently proved half that to be this species' maximum air speed. On its prodigious annual migrations between North America and its ancestral tropical home, the Ruby-throat flies non-stop 500 miles or more across the Gulf of Mexico. A physiologist once proved by metabolic tests in his laboratory that the Ruby-throat cannot possibly store enough fuel within its tiny frame for such a lengthy flight, but the birds, never having read this report, continue to do so twice each year.

In quick, darting flight, in sudden stops and starts, and in complete mastery of movement in the air, hummingbirds are supreme. They can hover motionless like a helicopter, move straight up or down or sideways and even backwards. Though time and again people watched hummingbirds dart bullet-like up to a flower, stop in mid-air to sip for a moment, back away, and move nimbly on to the next flower, they were assured that the backward flight was an optical illusion. It took studies with the ultra-rapid stroboscopic camera to prove that their backward flight is no illusion. Analysis of these camera studies, coupled with researches on the birds' anatomy, has now given us a fair idea of how they fly.

A hummingbird's wing loading, the ratio between the area of wing surface and the weight of the bird it supports, is roughly comparable to that of most other birds that use flapping flight. (Soarers have more wing surface per unit of body weight.) However, their flying muscles are tremendous, larger in proportion to their size and weight than in any other bird, and attached to a proportionately deeper and sturdier keel on the breastbone. This power, coupled with their small size, allows them to beat their wings faster than any other bird. Stroboscopic studies of the western Broad-tailed Hummingbird show that in hovering flight its wings beat 55 times per second. At this rate there is no humming sound. When the bird moves off in level flight the rate rises to 75 beats per second, and a distinct hum is audible. The humming is loudest during the male's spectacular courtship display, when he zooms up and down before the female in U-shaped arcs, and the air zips with a loud buzz between the narrow tips of his primaries, which are then vibrating at 200 beats per second.

As in the swifts, the hummingbirds' wing structure is designed to give the muscles that power the wings maximum leverage. Their tremendous wing muscles average 25 to 30 per cent of their body weight. The upper arm is comparatively short and the expanse of the wing is supported mainly by the elongated wrist and hand bones. The attachment of the wing bones to the shoulder girdle is uniquely swivelled, which allows the bird to adjust the angle of attack of the wing surface to the air to produce motive thrust on the upstroke as well as on the downstroke, and to fly in practically any direction. These mechanical features, coupled with small size, are the secret of hummingbird flight.

The camera also revealed that the Broad-tailed Hummingbird actually takes flight before it leaves its perch. The take-off takes only 7/100 of a second, and instead of pushing with its feet, it pulls the perch up with it momentarily before it lets go. Hummers use their tiny feet only for perching, never for walking or climbing. If a hummer wants to move only an inch or two along a branch, it flies those few inches.

The hummers' body metabolism is extremely high, and their dashing, powerful flight burns up a great deal of fuel, which for long non-stop migratory flights they stow, as do all migrants, in a thick layer of fat under the skin. The Ruby-throated Hummer takes on a subcutaneous fuel load that adds almost 50 per cent to its body weight before take-off. Non-migratory species build up no such fat reserve, and the migratory species do so only at flight time in response to an endocrine stimulus triggered by length of daylight. Hummingbirds with no fat reserve must take on carbohydrate fuel from nectar at frequent intervals to keep going.

It has recently been learned that hummingbirds conserve their energies in other ways. Most diurnal birds' body temperatures drop from 5 to 10 degrees at night, from about 105°-110° F. to about 100° F. Tests on Anna's and Allen's hummingbirds in California reveal that their temperatures may drop at night as low as 65°, almost to that of the surrounding air. The birds thus go into a sort of nocturnal hibernation that slows their rapid metabolism and conserves their energies. Mountain species in the Andes have similarly been seen to go into a state of torpidity during cold spells, and to revive and become active again the moment the sun comes out and the weather warms up.

While hummingbirds get their quick sugar principally from nectar and show a preference for tubular flowers such as trumpet vine, columbine, and honeysuckle, they will also sip tree sap oozing from a wound, and occasionally indulge in fruit juices. They are easily attracted to feeding stations with tubes of water sweetened with sugar or syrup. They are most satisfactory guests, not only for their beauty but for their fearless unconcern of man, which amounts almost to indifference. They are readily encouraged to sip from a phial held in the hand. After they have fed from flowers, pollen is often visible on hummingbirds' heads, and they perform the same cross-pollinating service that so many insects do.

Hummingbirds also eat small insects, most of which they find in flowers in conjunction with the nectar. They are occasionally seen hunting insects on the wing in the open air, or foraging for them among tree leaves and branches. Some hunt them flycatcher-fashion, dashing out and back as insects come within range of an exposed perch, often a telephone wire. Some species make a practice of raiding spiders' webs.

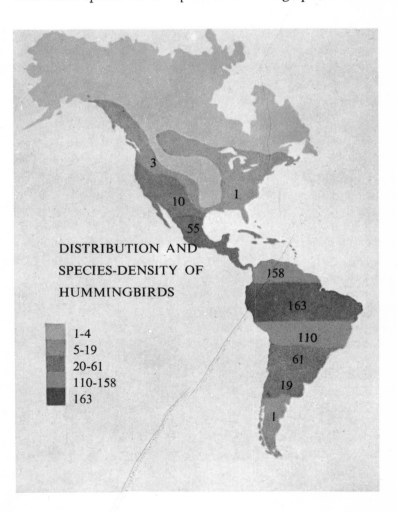

DISTRIBUTION AND
SPECIES-DENSITY OF
HUMMINGBIRDS

1-4
5-19
20-61
110-158
163

VIOLET SABREWING ♂
Campylopterus hemileucurus
Mexico to Panama   5 in.

WHITE-NECKED JACOBIN ♂
Florisuga mellivora
Southern Mexico to
Peru and Brazil   4½ in.

LODDIGES' RACQUET-TAIL ♂
Loddigesia mirabilis
Highlands of northern Peru   6½ in.

CRIMSON TOPAZ ♂
Topaza pella
Guianas to Ecuador   7½ in.

ADORABLE COQUETTE ♂
Paphosia adorabilis
Costa Rica   3 in.

Hummingbird voices are not noteworthy. Most of them have thin squeaky warblings and twitterings that are not audible at any distance. They make their loudest noises with their wings, and these particularly at courting time.

As might be suspected from the brilliance of their courting plumage, male hummingbirds are not model spouses. A number of species are known to be polygamous, and only in one group has the male been observed to incubate and to help with the rearing of young. These are the fairly widely distributed Violet-eared Hummingbirds of northern South America in which, unlike most other hummingbirds, the sexes are almost identical. The usual pattern is for each male to establish a territory which he defends bravely and ferociously against all other males of his kind. Here he attracts and courts his mate or mates by a dashing aerial dance, swooping up and around in wide arcs, buzzing his wings and flashing his colours. Mating is often consummated in flight, after which the male loses interest in his partner.

The female builds the tiny, deep, cup-shaped nest of plant down and spider webs, often on top of a branch, sometimes in the fork between two branches. In some tropical species the nest is placed underneath the top of a palm leaf; in others it is attached to the sides of cliffs or of overhanging rocks,

POPELAIRE'S
THORNBILL ♂
Popelairia popelairii
Colombia, Ecuador,
Peru   4½ in.

GOLDTHROAT ♂
Polytmus guainumbi
Venezuela and Trinidad to
Paraguay and Bolivia   4½ in.

GEOFFROY'S WEDGEBILL ♂
Schistes geoffroyi
Colombia to Peru and Bolivia   3½ in

COLLARED INCA ♂
Coeligena torquata
Colombia to Peru   5½ in.

GOULD'S VIOLET-EAR ♂
Colibri coruscans
Colombia to northern Argentina   5½ in.

FRILLED COQUETTE ♂
Lophornis magnifica
Central and southern Brazil   2¾ in.

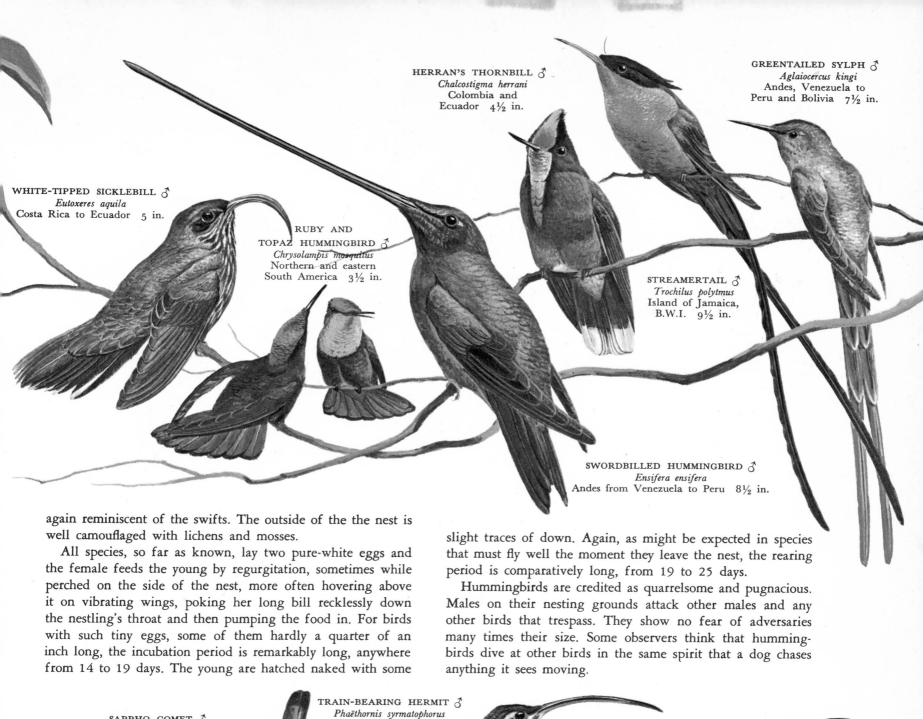

WHITE-TIPPED SICKLEBILL ♂
Eutoxeres aquila
Costa Rica to Ecuador 5 in.

RUBY AND
TOPAZ HUMMINGBIRD ♂
Chrysolampis mosquitus
Northern and eastern
South America 3½ in.

HERRAN'S THORNBILL ♂
Chalcostigma herrani
Colombia and
Ecuador 4½ in.

GREENTAILED SYLPH ♂
Aglaiocercus kingi
Andes, Venezuela to
Peru and Bolivia 7½ in.

STREAMERTAIL ♂
Trochilus polytmus
Island of Jamaica,
B.W.I. 9½ in.

SWORDBILLED HUMMINGBIRD ♂
Ensifera ensifera
Andes from Venezuela to Peru 8½ in.

again reminiscent of the swifts. The outside of the the nest is well camouflaged with lichens and mosses.

All species, so far as known, lay two pure-white eggs and the female feeds the young by regurgitation, sometimes while perched on the side of the nest, more often hovering above it on vibrating wings, poking her long bill recklessly down the nestling's throat and then pumping the food in. For birds with such tiny eggs, some of them hardly a quarter of an inch long, the incubation period is remarkably long, anywhere from 14 to 19 days. The young are hatched naked with some

slight traces of down. Again, as might be expected in species that must fly well the moment they leave the nest, the rearing period is comparatively long, from 19 to 25 days.

Hummingbirds are credited as quarrelsome and pugnacious. Males on their nesting grounds attack other males and any other birds that trespass. They show no fear of adversaries many times their size. Some observers think that hummingbirds dive at other birds in the same spirit that a dog chases anything it sees moving.

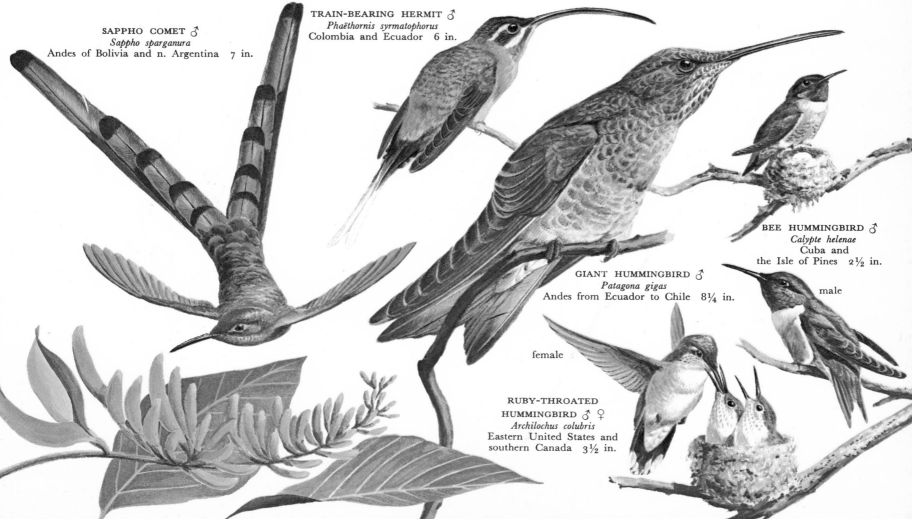

SAPPHO COMET ♂
Sappho sparganura
Andes of Bolivia and n. Argentina 7 in.

TRAIN-BEARING HERMIT ♂
Phaëthornis syrmatophorus
Colombia and Ecuador 6 in.

BEE HUMMINGBIRD ♂
Calypte helenae
Cuba and
the Isle of Pines 2½ in.

GIANT HUMMINGBIRD ♂
Patagona gigas
Andes from Ecuador to Chile 8¼ in.

male

female

RUBY-THROATED
HUMMINGBIRD ♂ ♀
Archilochus colubris
Eastern United States and
southern Canada 3½ in.

QUETZAL ♂♀
Pharomachrus mocinno
S. Mexico to Costa Rica 14 in.
(add 2 ft. for tail plumes)

male

female

BAR-TAILED TROGON ♂
Trogon collaris
Mexico to Bolivia 10 in.

TROGONS

TROGONIFORMES TROGONIDAE

Typical of everyone's idea of what tropical birds should look like are the 34 bright-coloured trogons, a distinctive and uniform family—and order—of quiet, sedate, solitary inhabitants of tropical forests the world around. Trogons are most plentiful and most richly developed in the New World, where 20 species occur from southern Arizona, Texas, and the West Indies south through the equatorial belt to northern Argentina. Another 11 species live in the oriental region from India eastward to the Philippine Islands and southward to Sumatra and Java; three inhabit the African jungles south of the Sahara.

Trogons are non-migratory and move but little locally. Their sedentary nature makes it difficult to account for the family's widely disrupted pan-tropical distribution, which is paralleled by few other animal or plant groups. Their uniformity of structure and behaviour allows no possibility of parallel development from different stocks. The three widely separated populations are unquestionably of common ancestry, but in what part of the world they arose or from just what parent stock, we cannot even venture a guess. The fossil remains of a primitive trogon (*Archaeotrogon*) dug out of Oligocene deposits in France suggest the living trogons are relict survivors of some long-vanished type of bird that must have had a much wider and more continuous distribution in past geological areas when milder climates permitted tropical forests to extend far beyond their present limits.

The trogons have a number of anatomical peculiarities, chief among which is their foot formation. Their legs are

ORANGE-BREASTED
TROGON ♂
Harpactes oreskios
Thailand, Indochina, Malaya,
Java, Sumatra 11 in.

WHITE-TAILED TROGON ♂
Trogon viridis
Costa Rica to Brazil 9½ in.

small and weak, their tarsi are feathered, and they have two toes in front and two behind, a condition known as "yoke-toed." This arrangement is found elsewhere in such arboreal groups as the parrots, cuckoos, toucans, and woodpeckers. But in all other yoke-toed birds the outer, or fourth, toe has moved backward to give the foot firmer grasping power. In the trogons alone it is the inner, or second, toe that has shifted to the rear. Also their two front toes are joined together at the base.

One of the trogons' most peculiar and outstanding characteristics is their exceptionally thin, tender skins. Their soft, fluffy feathers are very loosely attached to the flimsiest imaginable excuse for an epidermis, which has the consistency and strength of wet tissue paper. They are notorious among ornithologists as the most difficult of all birds to prepare as museum specimens, for their skins are so tender they tear almost at a glance, and are virtually impossible to remove intact from the body. Even well-prepared specimens have to be treated gently, for the feathers continue to drop out with the least handling.

Trogons are medium-sized birds between 10 and 14 inches long with short, rounded wings and long, squared tails. All are brightly coloured, the males especially so. Their upperparts are a shiny metallic green or brown, and their heads, breasts, and bellies are variously painted in bold contrasting reds, greens, blues, or yellows. The sexes are unlike in most species. Despite their gay and showy colours, their broken patterns give them excellent concealment among the broken lights and shadows of their leafy jungle habitat. They are not overly active, but sit still for minutes at a time on an open branch in the middle storey of the forest, perched very upright and dignified, moving only their heads as they keep sharp watch with their large eyes for some passing insect. You hear their soft, rather melancholy cooing calls far more often than you see the birds, for their voices are ventriloquial as well as far-carrying, and can be difficult to trace to their source amid the leafy branches overhead.

Trogons have short but very broad, flat bills with prominent bristles at the base. They feed extensively on insects—the oriental species exclusively so—which they capture in flight. They forage flycatcher fashion, watching quietly from their perch until they spot their prey flying by or crawling on a leaf. Then they dart out, grab it, and return to the perch to swallow it. The Narina Trogon of Africa eats a few berries on occasion, but all the American trogons take small fruits as a large part of their diet. They harvest fruit in the same way as they catch insects, snatching it from its stem in flight and then perching to swallow it. Possibly in response to their fruit-eating habits, the edges of the bills of American species are more notched and serrated than those of the Old World trogons. All trogons have a fast, peculiarly twisting flight when in pursuit of prey, but they are not strong-winged and seldom fly any great distance.

Trogons are hole nesters and many of them lay their eggs in natural cavities in trees and stumps. Most of the New World species prefer to excavate a nest for themselves, but as their beaks are ill suited to digging or chiselling, they have to work in rotten wood or other similarly soft material. Ter-

mite nests are favoured by many species as a good workable medium. The Gartered Trogon of Central America and northern South America habitually digs its nesting cavity out of the large paper nests built high in trees by certain tropical wasps. Before going to work on a nest the pair first gobble up all the wasps, to whose stings they appear to be immune or indifferent. They then feast on the larvae within the nest as they dig.

Trogons add no lining to their nesting cavity, but deposit their eggs directly on the bottom of the hole. They lay 2 to 4 rather round eggs which are usually white, sometimes pale buff or greenish blue, and always unmarked. Both sexes share all the nesting chores. Incubation in the few species studied lasts about 19 days. The young are naked at hatching and are reared in the nest until ready to fly, which takes from 15 or 16 days in the smaller species to 23 or more in the largest ones.

One of the largest and most ornate of the trogons, in fact a leading contender for the title of most beautiful bird in the world and certainly one of the showiest, is the Quetzal (p. 172). Resident in the heavy rainforests from the highlands of southern Mexico south to Costa Rica at altitudes up to 9,000 feet, the Quetzal, a brilliant bronzy green with bright red and white underparts, measures 14 inches from bill to tail tip. In breeding males four of the upper tail coverts grow into long, shimmering green plumes, the two central ones trailing gracefully 2 feet behind the tail.

The almost breath-taking splendour of the Quetzal intrigued the ancient Aztecs and the Mayas, who worshipped it as the god of the air and treasured the male's long plumes for ceremonial use. They never killed the birds to obtain the feathers, but plucked them from the living Quetzal, which they then released to grow more. The Mayas incorporated the Quetzal into their stylistic art and formalized it in their pictorial representation of Quetzalcoatl, the principal god of the Toltec pantheon, commonly referred to as the "plumed serpent." Today the Quetzal is the national bird of Guatemala. Patriotic Guatemalans regard it as symbolic of the spirit of freedom, and stoutly maintain that when deprived of its liberty the Quetzal soon dies of a broken heart. This may or may not be so, but Quetzals have seldom survived long in captivity. The Quetzal also appears on the Guatemalan state seal, postage stamps, and coins. It has given its name to Guatemala's second largest city and to the country's standard monetary unit, which is not a peso or a dollar, but a quetzal.

As in all trogons, the Quetzal is a hole nester and the male does his share of the incubating. Guatemalans have always claimed that the Quetzal selects a nesting hole with two entrances, so the male will not injure his gorgeous plumes when on duty. Recent studies have shown this to be pure legend. The Quetzal nest cavity has but one entrance. When the male takes his turn on the eggs he goes in and turns around, thus facing outward and leaving his plumes doubled forward over his back with their tips outside the hole waving gently in the breeze like fern fronds. By the end of the nesting season his plumes, much the worse for wear, are often ragged, frayed, and broken from the rough treatment they have thus had.

COLIES OR MOUSEBIRDS

COLIIFORMES   COLIIDAE

The colies are strange African birds that are almost as much trouble to the bird classifier as they are to the farmers whose crops they despoil. There are only six species in the group, all so similar they are united into the single genus *Colius*, yet all are so different from other birds they are placed in an order by themselves.

Colies are slender-bodied birds about a foot long with prominent crests and long, thin tails more than twice the length of their bodies. All are a sombre grey or brown in colour, with red feet and legs and often with patches of red or blue skin about the eyes. The sexes are alike. They are called "mousebirds" from their habit of scurrying rodent-like among the foliage, creeping along on their short tarsi and long toes, their bodies hugging the branches. They are quite acrobatic, and, like parakeets, use their bills to help them in climbing. They often hang upside down, and they feed from almost any position.

Structurally the colies show no close affinities to any other group of birds. Their chief peculiarity is their outer toes, which are reversible and can be used either forward or backward. Their long claws are sharp, and curved for clinging and climbing. Their wings are short and rounded. Their rather hair-like contour feathers grow continuously over the body instead of in tracts. Their bills are short, stout, down-curved, somewhat finch-like, and fleshy about the nostrils. Some students consider colies possibly distant relatives of the parrots, which they vaguely resemble in feeding and climbing habits. Others point out that their nesting behaviour parallels that of the touracos.

All colies are highly gregarious and usually travel in chattering flocks of 20 or 30 birds, moving from tree to tree and bush to bush along the forest edges with rapid wingbeats interspersed with long glides. They have a peculiar habit of flying directly into a tree before braking and alighting. When foraging they fly from the top of one tree to the bottom of the next, work their way up, and repeat the process. They often run on the ground, occasionally bask on bare earth during the heat of the day, and are fond of dust bathing. When perched together colies preen each other. They roost huddled together in clusters, clinging to a vertical surface or a branch with their tails pointing straight down and their heads up. Several species sleep hanging upside down. They have no true song, but a variety of harsh calls, and short twittering notes. Some utter a clear trilling whistle in flight.

Colies live largely on buds, tender leaves, berries, and fruits; they also eat quantities of insects, and are especially fond of aphids. They are such voracious feeders that farmers and fruit growers detest them, and in farming areas where they are plentiful, control measures have to be taken to prevent their depredations. They strip off green shoots and eat flower buds, berries, and small fruits. They eat the pulp of large fruits through a hole pecked in the side, leaving only the empty skin. As they also prey on nestlings, they are often mobbed by other small birds.

At breeding time the flocks of colies disperse to nest. Each pair builds a bulky nest well hidden in thick foliage. On a small platform of twigs they fashion a neat cup of grasses, bark, and rootlets; they line their nests with green leaves and grasses which they renew constantly as they wither. Colies lay 2 to 4, rarely 7, rough-textured white eggs, streaked with brown in some species. Both sexes share the nesting duties. Incubation takes 12 to 14 days. The young hatch naked, but soon grow a sparse coat of down. They are fed partly digested food by regurgitation. When a few days old, they leave the nest and creep about the nearby branches, crawling with their wings and beak as well as feet, but return to be brooded at night. The parents tend them constantly until they can fly, which usually requires 17 to 21 days.

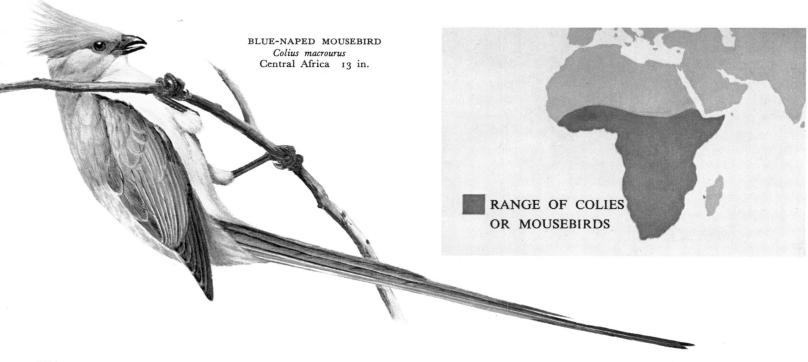

BLUE-NAPED MOUSEBIRD
Colius macrourus
Central Africa   13 in.

RANGE OF COLIES
OR MOUSEBIRDS

KINGFISHERS
AND ALLIES

CORACIIFORMES

The seven well-defined families united in this order are a varied assemblage of essentially tropical and subtropical land birds characterized by having their three front toes joined for part of their length, a condition known as "syndactyly." Other less prominent structural similarities involve the form of their palate bones and leg muscles, the way the tendons of their leg muscles are attached, and the distribution and arrangement of feathers in their feather tracts.

Most Coraciiformes are brightly coloured birds with large, distinctive bills. They vary in size from the 3½-inch todies to 5-foot hornbills. They tend to be noisy and many are somewhat social in their habits. Most are carnivorous and live on fish, reptiles, amphibians, small mammals, and insects. A few eat some fruit and berries. All are cavity nesters, digging holes in banks, rotten trees, or insect nests. Most lay from 3 to 6 eggs (a few kingfishers lay as many as 10), which are white or slightly tinted and are rarely marked. Their young are born blind and naked (except in the hoopoes which are down-covered), and are reared in the nest.

The order's distribution is cosmopolitan in tropical and temperate regions, and is predominantly Eastern Hemisphere. Only the kingfishers occur in both the Old and New Worlds. The motmots and the todies, the only exclusively American families, occupy much the same biological niche that the rollers and bee-eaters do in the Old World. The few temperate zone species are migratory; the rest are sedentary. Their relationships to other orders are obscure, but they show distant affinities to the trogons, to the Piciformes, and to the swifts. Except for an Eocene hornbill, their fossil record is limited to the late Tertiary.

KINGFISHERS

CORACIIFORMES   ALCEDINIDAE

A charming old legend tells us that the perky little Common Kingfisher of Eurasia was originally a nondescript grey bird that acquired its bright colours when it left Noah's Ark. It flew straight westward into the setting sun, which scorched its breast a rusty red, and its back reflects the greenish blue of the evening sky. The ancient Greeks, believing that kingfishers nested on the open sea, called them *halkyons*, from *hals* (sea) and *kyon* (conceiving). The gods so favoured the halkyons (*halcyon* in Latin) that they calmed the waters for them at their nesting time, the fortnight preceding the winter solstice, and periods of calm and peace have been "halcyon days" ever since. In Greek mythology Alcyone (Alcedo in Latin), one of the Pleiades, married Ceyx, son of Hesperus. When he perished in a shipwreck she threw herself into the sea in grief, and the pitying gods changed them both into kingfishers. Their memory is perpetuated in the kingfishers' scientific names.

Technically the kingfishers are a well-marked family of cosmopolitan distribution, absent only from the polar regions and some oceanic islands. They are of ancient lineage, though their fossil record goes back only to the Ice Age. The 84 living species have their greatest development and abundance in the Old World, particularly in southeastern Asia and the East Indies. Six species occur in the New World, and only one of these, the Belted Kingfisher, north of Mexico. Europe also has but a single species, the widespread Common Kingfisher found throughout Eurasia, northern Africa, and eastward to the Solomon Islands. In Africa some 15 species are represented; the remaining 60-odd kingfishers range from cen-

tral and eastern Asia southward to Australia and eastward in the Pacific islands to Samoa.

Kingfishers are thick-set birds with short necks, short tails, and large heads, accentuated in many species, particularly the American ones, by an erectile crest. Their bills are long, strong, and usually pointed; their legs are short, their feet small and weak. Diagnostic of the family is the joining of the front toes for more than a third of their length. Most kingfishers are brightly coloured, mainly in greens and blues with contrasting patches of dull red and white; some are barred and spotted, and many have a conspicuous red or yellow bill. The sexes are usually alike or closely similar, the females somewhat duller coloured in a few species. The female Belted Kingfisher has a broad band of chestnut across the chest which the male lacks.

The kingfishers are divided into two subfamilies. The Alcedininae include the familiar fishing kingfishers found around the world. The Daceloninae, or forest kingfishers, are a more primitive, much larger, and more diversified, though less familiar, Old World group whose members often, though not always, live far from water. The fishing kingfishers have strong but narrow, sharp-pointed bills; the bills of the forest kingfishers are broader, more flattened, and in some species are slightly hooked at the tip.

Best known and most widespread of the fishing kingfishers are the already mentioned Common Kingfisher of the Old World and the Belted Kingfisher of North America. Both species dwell mainly along the shores of fresh-water streams and lakes, but visit salt and brackish waters in autumn and winter. Their principal food is small minnows, though when these are scarce they will take small crustaceans, reptiles, amphibians, and aquatic insects of many sorts. Their preferred method of fishing is to watch motionless from an exposed perch overhanging the water, where they sit in a characteristic upright stance. When they spot their prey, they plunge on it directly, grab it in their strong, sharp-edged beak, and carry it back to their perch to kill and eat, juggling it to get it headed right before swallowing. Both species also hunt by hovering 20 or 30 feet in the air over the water on rapidly beating wings, their bodies almost upright, bills pointed downward, until their quarry comes close enough to the surface for a quick spearing dive.

Similar in feeding habits are all the other fishing kingfishers, such as the Amazon Kingfisher of South American jungle streams, and the black and white Pied Kingfisher of eastern Asia and Japan. The Pied Kingfisher is fond of crayfish, which it pounds to pieces with its bill before swallowing. The gems of the subfamily are the little 5-inch kingfishers of the genus *Ceyx*, which have only two toes in front and one behind. Ten species of these bright-billed, jewel-like birds live along forested streams of the Oriental tropics from India to the Philippines and the Solomons and southward to Australia. They eat small fish, crustaceans, newts, frogs, and quantities of insects and other invertebrates.

The fishing kingfishers dig nesting burrows into vertical banks, usually along watercourses, chiselling with their beaks and scraping the loose dirt out with their feet. Though their legs seem small and weak for such work, their joined front toes make fairly efficient scoops. The tunnels extend horizontally, sometimes slightly upward, from 3 to 10 feet back into the bank, and end in a round chamber where the 5 to 8, usually 6 or 7, white eggs are laid on the bare earth. No nest lining is used, but the burrows soon become littered with food scraps, and the young are often raised on a pad of fish bones and scales and crayfish carapaces.

Both parents incubate and feed the young. The incubation period varies from 18 to 24 days, and the young remain in the nest 3 to 4 weeks after hatching. They hatch naked and blind, but within a week start sprouting their feathers, which retain their waxy sheaths until just before the young leave the nest, giving them a strange bristly appearance. The parents

GREY-HOODED KINGFISHER
Halcyon leucocephala
Africa south of the Sahara 7 in.

LAUGHING KOOKABURRA
Dacelo gigas
Eastern and southern Australia 17 in.

BELTED KINGFISHER ♀
Megaceryle alcyon
Temperate North America 13 in.

WHITE-THROATED KINGFISHER
Halcyon smyrnensis
Asia Minor to Formosa 11 in.

COMMON KINGFISHER
Alcedo atthis
Eurasia and Africa eastward to Solomons 6½ in.

AMAZON KINGFISHER
Chloroceryle amazona
Mexico to n. Argentina 11 in.

remain with their young for several days after they leave the nest, feeding them until they acquire enough skill to fish for themselves. Most temperate species are double-brooded, and the tropical ones may nest twice each year too.

The flight of kingfishers is swift, strong, and direct, usually a succession of rapid wingstrokes followed by a short glide on half-closed wings, then another flurry of wingstrokes. It is seldom long-sustained, except in the migratory northern species. When moving between fishing spots the birds fly along the water courses close to the surface. Their voices are loud but not musical, and their calls, often given in flight, are typically successions of harsh rattles, much like the whirring of a football fan's rattle. Many of the smaller species have sharp, shrill, whistling notes.

The forest kingfishers (Daceloninae) are a large and varied group, some of which never go near the water but hunt in forests and dry savannahs for large insects, reptiles, amphibians, and even small mammals and birds. Others live along streams and feed on fish, and some are coastal birds partial to brackish mangrove swamps. They take their name from one of the biggest and most outstanding members of the family, the Kookaburra, or Laughing Jackass, of Australia, whose generic title *Dacelo* is just an anagram of *Alcedo*, the old Latin name for kingfisher and for the nominate genus of the fishing kingfishers.

The Kookaburra's weird laughing cries are strangely human in aspect, very loud and disturbing, and even alarming to the uninitiate. The birds raise a wild chorus of crazy laughter as they go to roost in the tree-tops at dusk, and again wake everyone within hearing just as dawn breaks, so regularly that in the hinterlands of Australia they are known as the "bushman's clock." Australians value the Kookaburra, not only as an intriguing member of their strange fauna, but for its habit of feeding on snakes and lizards. The Kookaburra seizes snakes behind the head and kills them by dropping them from a height, or else carries them to a perch and batters them senseless with its big bill before swallowing them. Less welcome is the Kookaburra's fondness for the young of other birds, and its occasional raids on farmyards for ducklings and baby chicks.

The largest group of the forest kingfishers consists of the 38 species assigned to the genus *Halcyon*, which range widely over Africa, much of Asia, the East Indies, Australia, and the islands of the Southwest Pacific. One of the most widespread is the noisy, 8-inch White-collared Kingfisher, a striking light greenish blue above and white below, that frequents coastal areas and mangroves all the way from the Red Sea to Samoa, and breaks into almost 50 named local races recognizable from minor variations in size and colour. Often confused with the White-collared is the very similar but smaller Sacred Kingfisher ("sacred" from its scientific name, *H. sancta*, perhaps of mythological but of no sanctimonious significance) that nests inland

in Australia and migrates northward to spend the antipodean winter fishing along coral beaches and mangrove-lined inlets from Malaya to the Solomons.

Inland-dwelling halcyons include the brilliant White-throated Kingfisher with its bright-red beak, common in dry uplands in India and southeastern Asia, and the closely related Grey-headed Kingfisher of Africa. A most colourful representative is the Ruddy Kingfisher of eastern Asia. The Japanese claim that its reflection in the water so astounds the bird that it cannot drink. Hence it is always thirsty, and on bright days calls continually in its forest home for rain.

These inland kingfishers live on large insects and small vertebrates and, like their littoral kin, prefer to watch for their quarry from a commanding perch. Occasionally they dart out to snatch a flying locust. wasp, or butterfly from the air. More often they pounce down to grab a crawling beetle or unwary lizard from the ground. Invariably they carry their catch back to their perch to pound and macerate it before swallowing. To move about on the ground kingfishers do not walk, but hop stiffly.

Again in true kingfisher fashion, all the Daceloninae nest in holes, often dug in banks like those of their fishing relatives. But some nest in hollow trees—the Kookaburra and the Ruddy Kingfisher among them—and many of the tropical species excavate their burrows out of termite nests. None so far as is known uses any additional nesting material, and all pay little or no attention to nest sanitation. Their nests are always fouled with excrement and littered with food remnants.

TODIES

CORACIIFORMES   TODIDAE

Tiny relatives of kingfishers and motmots, the five todies, grouped in the single genus *Todus*, constitute the only avian family restricted entirely to the West Indies. Three of them live, respectively, in Cuba, Puerto Rico, and Jamaica, and two on Hispaniola, one in the mountains, the other throughout much of the lowlands.

The todies' peculiarly flattened bills have fine serrations along the edges. All have prominent facial bristles, beady grey eyes, bright green backs, and pale underparts. Their blazing red bibs are absent in the immatures.

Todies chatter harshly and sit with their flat bills pointed upward at a 45° angle. They watch for insects from an exposed branch, usually fairly near the ground. When one comes within range, they dart out with a curious whirring rattle of wings, and bring the prize back to their perch to eat.

Tame and unsuspicious, todies can sometimes be approached closely enough to be caught in a butterfly net. Jamaicans call them "robins," Cubans "cartacuba" (their colours are those of the Cuban flag) and in a more vulgar vein "pedorrera" (flatulence), from their buzzing flight. In Puerto Rico and the Dominican Republic they are "barrancoli," the bank dwellers.

Todies usually live in pairs, each pair keeping to its own territory, which the male defends pugnaciously, chasing away intruders with a great rattling and clattering of his bill. Displaying males droop their wings and fluff out their loose body feathers so that they look twice their normal size.

Like kingfishers and motmots, todies nest in ground burrows. Though their front toes are similarly joined, they dig mostly with their bills. Their narrow tunnels are usually about a foot deep and turn sharply near the entrance. In a fist-sized chamber at the end, they lay their 3 or 4 roundish, translucent, white eggs. Both sexes incubate and feed the young. The todies' chief enemy in Haiti are native children, who like to dig out the tiny eggs to eat.

MOTMOTS

CORACIIFORMES   MOMOTIDAE

Forming a discrete New World family are the eight motmots, long-tailed, jay-sized forest inhabitants found from Mexico to northern Argentina. Motmot is a crude English simulation of their low-pitched calls, which the Indian "hu-tu" copies more closely. Their placid, stolid demeanour leads the Spanish to dub them "bobo," or fool.

Motmots are soft-feathered birds coloured in subdued brownish greens, prettily marked about the head and breast with bright blues and browns. The long tails of the six larger species have the two central feathers greatly elongated and racquet-tipped. These feathers grow with vanes along the entire shaft, but those along the subterminal section are weak and brittle, and gradually break away as the bird preens them, leaving the characteristic small fans at the tip. Their broad and gently down-curved bills have small saw-tooth serrations along the cutting edges.

Motmots are usually found singly or in pairs, perched quietly on a branch in the forest, and one can walk close to them before they fly away. They sit calmly for long periods, twitching their tails mechanically from side to side. At times they hold the tail skewed to one side so that they look off balance. They live mainly on large flying insects they sometimes catch in flight, but also eat snails, lizards, and some fruit. They have the kingfishers' habit of carrying their prey to a perch to pound and swallow.

The motmots' nesting habits closely parallel those of the kingfishers. A few nest in rock crevices, but most dig 4- to 6-foot tunnels in a bank with a terminal chamber for the 3 to 4 white eggs. Both sexes incubate and rear the young. Incubation takes about 21 days and fledging from 4 to 5 weeks.

Despite the long rearing period, the young often leave the nest before their wing and tail feathers grow fully and the bill develops its serrations. Motmots never clean their nests, which soon become filthy with their droppings and the remains of discarded food.

**RANGE OF TODIES
AND MOTMOTS**

■ Motmots

▨ Todies

BEE-EATERS

CORACIIFORMES   MEROPIDAE

Among the most attractive Old World birds are these graceful, colourful, sociable relatives of the kingfishers. The 24 bee-eaters range throughout most of the tropical and temperate lands of the Eastern Hemisphere, both in forests and in open country. They have sleek, streamlined bodies, small, weak legs, and feet with the front toes partly joined in true coraciid fashion. Their long, sharply pointed, and somewhat down-curved bills are frequently ridged on the top. Also diagnostic are their tails, which are forked in one African species and square in one small African genus (see the Red-throated Bee-eater, p. 180), but in all the others have the two central tail feathers noticeably elongated beyond the rest. Most bee-eaters are predominantly green in colour, with a black line through the eye and bold patches of yellows, reds, or blues about the head and rump. Country folk commonly call the brighter ones "rainbow birds."

Bee-eaters eat many kinds of insects, but their name is not unfitting, for more than half the insects they choose are members of the bee and wasp family. This makes them unpopular with apiarists, but otherwise they are regarded as highly beneficial birds. In Africa, where more than half of the bee-eater species occur, they often do yeoman service during locust plagues.

Bee-eaters catch their insects on the wing, either dashing out from an exposed perch in short, swift sallies like flycatchers, or hawking them in flight like swallows. Their easy graceful flight becomes quite erratic as they zigzag among their swarming prey. Some African species are fond of sailing about on moonlight nights, chirping and chattering to one another as they flutter and swoop about high in the air. Most bee-eaters are quite sociable, and they like to perch and rest together on exposed branches, telegraph wires, and rooftops, twittering interminably to one another. Though highly vocal, their voices are not overly melodious; short trills, whistles, and chirps are interspersed with hoarse chuckles and croaks.

As with most insectivorous birds, the temperate zone bee-eaters are migratory. In winter the Australian and South African forms travel northward to where food is more plentiful, and the northern Eurasian species return southward to the tropical regions which were doubtless the home of their ancestors. The Madagascar Bee-eater crosses the Mozambique Channel to winter throughout the African mainland. The tropical species move locally in response to the available food supply. The larger species travel about in large flocks, sometimes of 300 birds or more.

Though strictly arboreal at all other times, bee-eaters nest in ground burrows. Most dig into vertical banks, often in colonies like so many Sand Martins. The Rainbow Bee-eater, which the Australians call the "golden spinetail" or "golden swallow", digs downward at an angle in flat ground a foot or two before levelling off. The pure-white eggs, which may vary from 2 to 8 per clutch, are laid in a chamber at the end of the shaft. As with kingfishers, no nest lining is provided and the birds don't clean their nests; so eggs and young are soon surrounded by droppings and indigestible parts of insects.

Both sexes share nesting chores from digging the burrow to feeding the young. Often both parents spend the night in the burrow, which they enter by diving precipitously head first from the air, though the entrance is scarcely larger than the bird itself. Incubation takes about 22 days, and the rearing period is even longer, some 4 weeks. The young bee-eaters, again like kingfishers, retain the sheaths on their growing body feathers until just before they leave the nest, which gives them a hedgehoggy look. In their first juvenile plumage the young are usually duller coloured than their parents. So far as known, all bee-eaters are single-brooded.

ROLLERS

CORACIIFORMES   CORACIIDAE

Centred in the Old World tropics are the 17 species of conspicuous pigeon-sized rollers, noted and named for their spectacular aerial acrobatics. The five ground-rollers (Brachypteraciinae) and the single cuckoo-roller (Leptosomatinae) are aberrant species limited to Madagascar. Of the 11 "true" rollers (Coraciinae), 7 live in Africa south of the Sahara, 4 range widely across warm temperate Eurasia, southward to northern Australia and eastward to the Solomons. Rollers differ from other Coraciiformes in foot structure; their two inner front toes are connected for much of their length, but the outer toe moves freely.

The prevailing colour of the true rollers is blue, often with blended brown markings on the body and light patches in the wings or tails. English-speaking residents of India and Africa call them "blue jays" incorrectly, though not unfittingly, for they look something like jays. The sexes are alike, the bill is stout and strong, the head large, and the neck short. The wings and tail are long, the legs short, and the feet weak. Rollers do not walk, but hop clumsily on the ground. In trees they seldom climb about, but fly from perch to perch.

Rather solitary birds, rollers are usually seen singly or in pairs, sitting quietly on an exposed perch from which they sally out to seize a passing locust or butterfly, or swoop on some luckless lizard or grasshopper on the ground. Numbers gather from miles around to feast when locusts swarm or hatches of flying ants fill the air. They are among the first birds to appear when brush or grass fires drive the small animal life into the open.

TURQUOISE-BROWED MOTMOT
Eumomota superciliosa
Mexico to Costa Rica 13 in.

One of the commoner African species, the Lilac-breasted Roller, has a deeply forked tail. The Abyssinian Roller and the Racquet-tailed Roller of South Africa also have forked tails, the long outer pair in the latter expanding into miniature flags at the tip. The common European Roller, the Indian Roller, and the Broad-billed Roller of the Orient all have square tails.

The Broad-billed Roller is a rich greenish-blue with bright-red bill and feet. It is better known throughout its wide range as the Dollar Bird, from the light circular patches on its wings about the size of a silver dollar that look almost transparent in flight. The Dollar Bird is one of the few species that have maintained resident populations in their tropical centres of origin while other populations have spread both north and south into temperate regions, each migrating back to the tropics in winter. Dollar Birds arrive in northern Australia to breed in October and leave for their New Guinea wintering grounds in March. The northernmost Dollar Birds reach Korea and Japan in May and leave in October to winter from the Malay Peninsula southward to Sumatra. Ten more geographical races are resident from southern India through the East Indies to the Solomons.

On Guadalcanal, where I first made the species' acquaintance, the resident Dollar Birds inhabit open second-growth jungle. They sit stupidly like stolid lumps on dead branches above the brush through most of the hot day, stirring only when some tempting insect flies within range. Toward evening they become more active, and spend the last daylight hours hawking insects back and forth over the tree-tops. They fly strongly and buoyantly with slow, steady wingbeats, uttering

JAMAICAN TODY
Todus todus
Island of Jamaica,
B.W.I. 4½ in.

LILAC-BREASTED ROL
Coracias caudata
South Africa 16 in

EUROPEAN BEE-EATER
Merops apiaster
Southern Europe, southwestern Asia, Africa 11 in.

CARMINE BEE-EATER
Merops nubicus
Central Africa 13 in.

RED-THROATED BEE-EATER
Melittophagus bulocki
Central East Africa 9 in.

GREAT HORNBILL
Buceros bicornis
India to Indochina and Sumatra 60 in.

harsh, croaking cries. I was never fortunate enough to see their amazing courtship flight until I met them again some years later in Japan. There they live in the giant cryptomerias around old temples and shrines. Climbing high above the trees, the wooing birds dive steeply and swoop upwards in barrel rolls and an occasional somersault, calling loudly. The Japanese Dollar Birds have recently taken to courting around tall factory chimneys, always those of yellow or brown brick, which they are apparently substituting for dead tree stumps.

Rollers usually nest in hollow trees, either in natural cavities or in old nesting holes left by woodpeckers or barbets. Some of the tropical species dig into tree termite nests. In Korea and northern China the Dollar Birds often use the huge magpie nests, and in Japan they occupy bird boxes erected for them on the tall yellow chimneys they favour for their nuptial displays. Like most Coraciiformes they use little or no nesting material, and lay roundish white eggs, the clutch varying from 2 to 4. Incubation, believed to be by both sexes, takes 18 to 23 days. The young remain in the nest another 3 to 4 weeks, and are often fed by both parents for some days after they depart.

The five ground rollers of Madagascar are more protectively coloured than the true rollers, most of them clothed in yellows and greens with heavy mottlings. Much more terrestrial in their habits, they have longer legs, shorter wings, and longer, pointed tails. Four live in heavy forest, one in sandy brushlands. They have the roller habits of sitting quietly on high perches, and of a tumbling flight when excited. More nocturnal, they continue their evening feeding into the night.

The Madagascar Cuckoo-roller is so aberrant that some students give it family rank by itself, which may well be justified. It is the only coraciid with well-marked powder-downs. Cuckoo-rollers differ from the other two roller sub-families in that the sexes are unlike, the male a glossy green above and white below, the slightly larger brownish female barred above and spotted below with black. Both sexes have short crests. Cuckoo-rollers feed largely in tree-tops, and small flocks fly evolutions together above the forest. Otherwise their habits, so far as known, are those of the other rollers.

HOOPOE
Upupa epops
Eurasia, Africa,
Madagascar 11 in.

HOOPOES AND WOODHOOPOES

CORACIIFORMES   UPUPIDAE

The seven members of this small Old World family are distinctive among the Coraciiformes for their long, thin, pointed bills and the fusing of only their inner two front toes at the bases. The sexes are similar, the female slightly smaller and duller than the males. The monotypic Upupinae contains only the strikingly crested Hoopoe, with nine subspecies ranging over southern Europe and Asia and southward into Africa and Madagascar.

The eye-catching Hoopoe commands notice wherever it occurs. Its delicate fawn colour, its high black-tipped crown extending from bill to nape, and the strong black and white bands which show conspicuously in flight across its wings and tail make it unmistakable, even at a glance. Both its scientific and common names are onomatopoeic for its low, soft, mellow "hoop-hoops," several times repeated, with considerable carrying power.

Hoopoes are pictured on the walls of ancient tombs and temples in Egypt and Crete. Medieval writers mention them in connection with magic and the supernatural. Soothsayers recommended using various Hoopoe organs in concoctions to stimulate vision or aid the memory. The species appears in the Old Testament list of foods proscribed by the sanitary laws, incorrectly translated from the Hebrew in the Authorised Version as "lapwing."

Hoopoes frequent open and cultivated lands with some trees, often alone, seldom more than two or three together. Common around the outskirts of towns, they dust-bathe in the parks of Tel Aviv and other Near Eastern cities. Though they occasionally hawk insects on the wing, Hoopoes feed mainly on the ground, and can run fairly rapidly. They probe in the earth and in dung and garbage heaps with their long thin bill for worms, grubs, ants, and other small animal life. They seem to have little need of water, for apparently they never drink. Their erratic, undulating flight is much swifter than it seems. At night Hoopoes roost in trees, on roofs, ridge poles, or in wall crevices.

A favourite nesting site is a tree cavity, but crevices in walls and buildings also serve. Some Hoopoes line the hole with bits of straw or feathers, but usually they use no nesting material. The clutch is 4 to 6 pale blue eggs that are soon stained brown by the bird's excreta. The female incubates closely alone for about 18 days, and the male feeds her on the nest. The young hatch covered with sparse down. In the early stages of the 3- to 4-week fledging period the female broods its young closely and relays to them the food the male brings. When they begin to feather out she ventures forth and helps her mate forage for them.

Hoopoes are notorious for their foul, smelly nests, from which they never remove droppings or food debris. In addition the female has a strongly repulsive musty smell that emanates from her preen gland, and is believed to have a protective function like attar of skunk. Their filthy nesting habits were doubtless responsible for their place on the ancient Hebrews' proscribed list, yet other peoples eat them readily, and some even consider them a delicacy.

The six woodhoopoes (Phoeniculinae) are often accorded full family rank. Sometimes called "scimitar-bills," they are found only in forested Africa south of the Sahara. Uncrested, and with long, pointed tails, all six are coloured in metallic blues, greens, and purples. They feed occasionally on the ground, but glean most of their food from tree trunks and branches, searching the bark like creepers, often upside down. More gregarious than the Hoopoe, they fly gracefully from tree to tree in small noisy family parties. They share the Hoopoes' unattractive nesting habits, and have the same musty body odour during the breeding season.

HORNBILLS

CORACIIFORMES   BUCEROTIDAE

Enormous down-curved bills, usually surmounted by a grotesque horny casque, are the hallmark of the hornbills. Forty-five species are widely spread through the Old World tropical and subtropical forests—in Africa, southeastern Asia, and the East Indies east to the Philippines and the Solomons. They are the largest birds of the order; only a few are less than 2 feet long, and some exceed 5 feet. By no stretch of the imagination can these birds be considered beautiful, yet hornbills are attractive and intriguing, fascinating, and even amusing in many of their unique habits.

Hornbills are dressed in blacks and dark browns, relieved by bold patches of white or cream on the body, wings, and tail. Their huge bills and casques are usually horn-coloured, but some are black, and others are bright red or yellow. They are often deeply sculptured and chiselled, and have serrated edges. The bill and casque are usually hollow or filled with a comb of cells, but those of the Helmeted Hornbill of Malaya are of solid hard ivory, which Borneo natives carve into ornaments and fetishes. Some hornbills have coloured patches of bare skin about the eyes and throat, and a peculiar feature is their well-developed eyelashes, which few other birds (the Ostrich, Hoatzin, a few cuckoos and hawks) possess. Hornbills' feathers are coarse and loose-webbed. Their wings are strong, their tails long and usually rounded. Their legs are typically short, but their coraciiform feet, with the three front toes partly joined, are broad-soled and stout.

Most hornbills live in heavy forests, and go about in pairs or small flocks of a dozen or less. They are fairly quiet through the heat of the day, and most active and vocal in the cool of the morning and in the late afternoon and evening. Their voices are extremely variable, but loud and far-carrying. The Casqued Hornbill of Africa brays like a donkey; others have honking, tooting, bugle-like notes. Some squeal harshly or whistle shrilly, while others have an amazing variety of roars, grunts, bellowings, and cacklings.

Hornbills fly strongly, usually alternating a series of slow, heavy wingbeats with short sailing glides. All except the smallest species fly with noisy wingbeats audible for some distance. Their underwing coverts do not cover the bases of their flight quills, and with each wingstroke the wind rushing between the gaps makes a loud "whoosh" that sounds in the distance exactly like the chuffing of an old steam locomotive.

As a family hornbills are practically omnivorous, but their specific food choices vary considerably. Most eat fruits, berries, various insects, and small animals. Those that live mostly on fruits usually live in the tops of tall trees where they hop from branch to branch, usually with the wings closed, and reach out awkwardly to pluck the fruit, which they often toss playfully into the air before catching and swallowing. They do the same thing with grasshoppers, locusts, small reptiles, and amphibians which, like other birds of the order, they beat with their bills to kill before eating. Hornbills swallow most of their food whole, and regurgitate the indigestible fruit pips, insect carapaces, and animal bones. Some species feed extensively on the eggs and young of small birds, and in parts of agricultural Africa others damage fruit crops. Smaller species catch insects in flight, and most will travel far to reach a grass fire in order to feast on the small animal life fleeing incautiously before it. Several African hornbills habitually follow army ant columns for the same purpose. When feeding on the ground, hornbills hop about in rather ungainly fashion. Tropical villagers often keep them as pets. They tame easily, and are amusing, playful, and fond of tossing sticks and bits of food into the air.

Most peculiar of all the hornbills' idiosyncracies are their nesting habits. Hornbills are believed to pair for life. A few species nest in caves or in rock crevices, but most use natural tree cavities, or enlarge abandoned woodpecker holes for the purpose. The nesting hole may be near the ground, or a hundred feet or more up in a forest tree. When the female is ready to lay, she goes into the hole and is sealed in "for the duration," as it were.

In some species the male seals the female in, but usually both work together at the task, the female from within, the male from without. With a combination of mud, dirt, their own ordure, and sometimes with matter regurgitated from the crop or stomach, they plaster up the hole, leaving a narrow slit in the centre just wide enough for the female to poke her bill through. The wall soon hardens to a brick-like consistency that even the strong-billed birds have difficulty chipping away when the time comes. As a defensive measure against the raids of monkeys and tree snakes this device is uniquely effective. Few predators would care to face the sword-like bill guarding the narrow aperture.

Hornbill clutches vary from 1 to 6 white, somewhat roundish eggs; the usual clutch is 2 to 4. Incubation periods vary from 28 to about 40 days, and it takes another 4 to 8 weeks for the young to mature. Throughout the entire incubation period and usually until the young are at least half grown, the fe-

male remains sealed in her prison, a minimum of 6 weeks, and in some species nearly 3 months. She fits into her cramped quarters by turning her tail forward over the back, and takes advantage of this period of inactivity to go through her moult. She often sheds her tail entirely soon after she starts to incubate, but the flight and body feathers are usually replaced in rotation.

Throughout this entire period her faithful mate keeps her well fed through the slit passing food at the tip of his bill. Males of the fruit-eating species bring in a cropful of food, regurgitate it piece by piece to the end of the bill, and pass it in, sometimes 15 or 20 figs at a time. In some species the male is reported to pass in a conglomerate of partly digested fruit and insects in a regurgitated sac formed of the lining of the gizzard or the crop, a phenomenon which needs further investigation and verification.

To pass food into the entrance hole, the male clutches the vertical trunk of the tree just below the hole and props himself in position with his tail, which at the end of the nesting period is frayed and worn. The burden on the male to keep his mate and offspring fed increases as the young grow, and usually when the nestlings are half grown either the male or the female chips enough of the hard entrance block away for her to get out and assist him with the chores. The young frequently plaster the hole up again from the inside, leaving just enough room for food to be passed in to them.

Unlike their relatives the hoopoes, the hornbills are fairly clean nesters. The female drops fruit pips and other indigestible food remains outside the nest, and she as well as the growing young void accurately through the opening. As their tails grow, the young birds hold them over the back in the same way as the female keeps hers. When the female comes out of her prison, she is so fat and flabby and stiff from her confinement that she can hardly fly. The young likewise leave the nest before their flying powers are fully developed, and may spend several days hopping around the trees and strengthening their wings before taking off on their own.

Because of the hornbills' unique nesting habits, primitive bush peoples regard these birds with a superstitious awe and use them or representations of them in tribal rites as symbols of purity and marital fidelity. In Central Africa they are not only regarded as tribal fetishes, but are left unmolested because they are good scavengers, particularly the two large species of ground hornbills. These big 4½-foot birds have longer, stronger legs than the other species, and feed largely on the ground. Small flocks forage in more or less open country, consume quantities of locusts, grasshoppers, and other injurious insects, and kill snakes and lizards as well. The casque of the ground hornbills is open in the front, giving it a rather peculiar appearance. The ground hornbills nest on or near the ground in tree stumps or in clefts among rocks, and the female is not imprisoned in the nest.

The Great Hornbill illustrated on page 181 is a common species of southeastern Asia, ranging from western India through Indochina and south through Malaya to Sumatra. A bird of heavy rainforests from sea level up to about 5,000 feet, it is primarily a fruit eater. It is an enormous bird, one of the largest of the hornbills, and its long, white tail with a black band near its tip frequently reaches 3 feet in length.

In life this bird's feathers are frequently stained a bright yellow by the oil from its preen gland which the bird spreads liberally over itself. The colour disappears after death and is not apparent in museum specimens. Its loud barking calls resound in the evening as it flies over the forest with alternate sailing and flapping wings, each downward beat producing the chuffing locomotive sound.

As would be expected in so distinctive a family, the hornbills are an ancient group which developed from some primitive coraciid stock in pre-Tertiary time, probably the same stock from which the hoopoes descended. Fossil remains of a primitive hornbill, *Geisiloceros,* found in Eocene deposits in Europe attest the family's antiquity and show it then lived far beyond its present range.

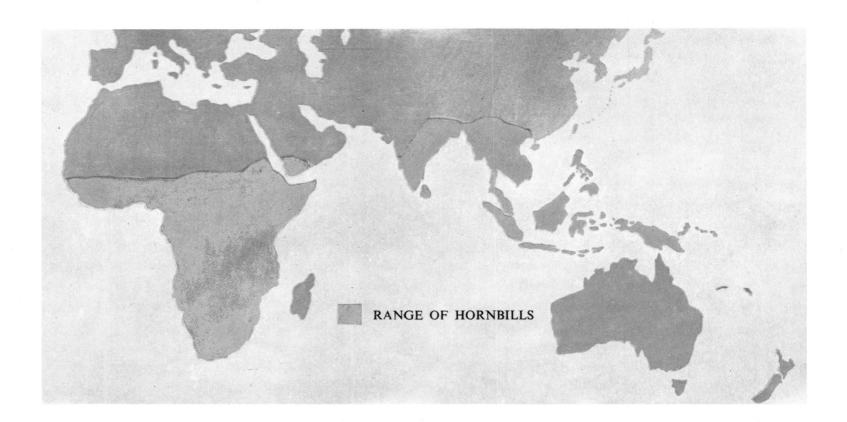

RANGE OF HORNBILLS

WOODPECKERS AND ALLIES

PICIFORMES

The woodpeckers and their picarian allies are distinguished by their zygodactylus (yoke-toed) feet, a feature they share with the trogons, parrots, and cuckoos. In most Piciformes the outermost of the front toes is reversed to parallel the hind toe, giving the birds two toes in front and two behind. In a few woodpeckers the outer front toe has disappeared, and these birds have two toes in front and one behind. Accompanying this shift of toes, and found in no other order of birds, is a distinctive arrangement of the thigh muscles and the tendons that move the feet.

The six families of the order are all arboreal, and most tend to be solitary. Usually encountered alone or in pairs, seldom do more than a few flock together. Their colours vary considerably, from brilliant hues in bold patterns to dull and nondescript. They range in size from 3 to 24 inches. Most live entirely on insects; a few eat fruit as well. Their flight may be weak or strong, but is seldom sustained and is typically undulating. All except a few temperate zone woodpeckers are non-migratory.

All members of the order are cavity nesters, and dig nest holes in the ground, in trees, or in termitaries. One family, the honeyguides, is parasitic in its breeding behaviour, but usually parasitizes hole-nesting species. The nests of the other families are not elaborate, and usually have little if any lining. All lay pure-white, somewhat roundish eggs, and both sexes share the nesting chores. The young hatch blind and usually naked (jacamar hatchlings have long white down), and are reared in the nest.

The Piciformes inhabit forests and brushlands of the tropic and temperate zones. They are absent from the Australia-New Zealand region, from Madagascar, and from the oceanic islands. Their distribution gives no clue to the order's affinities or place of origin. The woodpeckers and the barbets occur in both Eastern and Western Hemispheres; the honeyguides are essentially Ethiopian; the jacamars, puffbirds, and toucans are limited to the New World tropics. Fossil woodpeckers are known from the Eocene of North America and Europe.

BARBETS

PICIFORMES   CAPITONIDAE

The gaudy little barbets are plump birds with short necks, big heads, and large, heavy bills. Their beaks have conspicuous bristles or, in one group, tufts of feathers over the nostrils which early cabinet ornithologists thought gave them a bearded look—hence their name. A few barbets are plain-coloured, but most are splashed with gay greens, reds, yellows, and blues. As their wings are short and rounded, the barbets' flight is weak, and seldom long-sustained. They are not migratory and tend to be resident wherever they occur.

Barbets are at home in the lush growth of tropical forests. The family has its greatest development in tropical Africa, where more than half the 72 recognized species occur. Some 23 species live in the oriental region from India to the Philippines and southward to Sumatra and Borneo. Another 12 range the American tropics from Costa Rica south to Paraguay and Brazil. This broken pan-tropical distribution closely parallels that of the trogons and must have come about in much the same way. The barbets' anatomy shows they probably descended from the same primitive stock that produced the honeyguides, puffbirds, and toucans. This ancestor must at one time have been more continuously distributed in the tropical forests that covered much of the land surface when the world was younger.

Barbets are seldom seen on the ground. Most of them investigate the outer tree branches for fruit, buds, flowers, and insects; some climb around trunks in woodpecker fashion. Some live almost exclusively on vegetable matter—but feed their young on insects. Others live entirely on insects, and tree ants and termites are favourite foods.

The larger barbets, often noisy, conspicuous, and quarrelsome, drive other birds away when they are feeding. All like to sit for hours in one spot, calling monotonously, jerking their heads or flicking their tails each time they call. Pairs commonly answer one another antiphonally. Their voices are usually loud and strident, though some have pleasing low whistles. The calls of many Old World species have a ringing metallic quality that has earned the birds such sobriquets as coppersmith, blacksmith, and tinkerbird. They repeat these monosyllabic clangings so interminably that they become annoying and exasperating in hot weather. Barbets are among the several such persistent singers called "brain-fever birds" by those who have to endure their noise in the heat.

The Crimson-breasted Barbet of India is the "coppersmith" of Kipling's "Rikki-Tikki-Tavi," whose metallic "took" spread the welcome news when Rikki killed the cobras Nag and Nagaina. This coppersmith's note is like the tap of a small hammer on metal. It never varies, and the hotter the day, the more the birds sing. The Crimson-breasted Barbet is a fruit eater and partial to wild figs. It feeds gluttonously, picking at the fruit on the trees, spoiling and knocking off more than it eats.

Barbets dig their nesting holes with their beaks, and since these are less efficient as chisels than those of the woodpeckers, the barbets are forced to use a softer medium. One African species digs in earth banks, and East Indian barbets chip into termite houses, but most hew their nest holes in the trunks or branches of dead trees that have started to soften and rot, usually high above the ground. Both sexes work together at the task. The entrance hole is small, just large enough to admit the bird, and often placed under a branch or below an overhang that shelters it from the rain. The birds dig in several inches before turning to make the nest cavity. Some species use the same hole year after year, digging it farther each season, and sometimes adding a second entrance.

The usual clutch is 2 to 4 white eggs, and the incubation period is 13 to 15 days. The nestling period is believed to be considerably longer, but nesting habits of only a few species have been thoroughly studied, owing to the inaccessibility of most nests. Barbets keep their nests quite clean and remove all the young's excreta, carrying it away and dropping it at a distance. Both parents sleep in the nest at night, and often use it for roosting throughout the year. Though the barbet is usually a solitary bird, in some species they roost together.

TOUCAN BARBET
Semnornis ramphastinus
Andes of Colombia and Ecuador   8½ in.

GOLDEN-THROATED
BARBET
Megalaima franklini
Southeastern Asia   9 in.

GREATER HONEYGUIDE
Indicator indicator
Central and South Africa   7½ in.

BLACK-COLLARED BARBET
Lybius torquatus
Africa south of the Sahara   7½ in.

HONEYGUIDES

The honeyguides are a small family of dull-coloured little picarian birds closely allied structurally to the barbets, but differing from them greatly in appearance and habits. Both their vernacular and scientific family names are based on the unique and extraordinary habit developed by several African species of the genus *Indicator* of leading man and other animals through the forest to bees' nests. Another singular characteristic is their brood parasitism. No honeyguide, so far as is known, builds a nest of its own or rears its own young. All lay their eggs in the nests of other species, for foster parents to hatch and rear. This reproductive pattern is found elsewhere only in the Old World and a few New World cuckoos, in some of the New World cowbirds, in a small group of African weaverfinches, and in one South American duck.

Predominantly an African family, 9 of the 11 honeyguides are found in forests and brushlands south of the Sahara. One species lives in the foothills of the western Himalayas. The eleventh is a rare and little-known jungle inhabitant of Malaya, Sumatra, and Borneo. All are essentially solitary birds, usually encountered singly or in pairs. Though their typically undulating flight is strong and swift, no honeyguide is known to be migratory. Some of the African species, however, show evidence of local seasonal movements, evidently in response to the availability of food.

The honeyguides are nondescript birds of sparrow to thrush size (4½ to 8 inches), grey to brownish above, lighter below, and variously mottled and streaked. Some have a few yellow markings; all have white patches on the tail that are conspicuous in flight. Their short bills are typically stout and blunt, but are slender and thin in one genus. Their tails are graduated (lyre-shaped in one species) and their wings are long and pointed. The family is unique among the nonpasserines in having only nine primaries.

The honeyguides' basic food is insects, and they consume a great variety. High in the list of their choices are bees and wasps. Some honeyguides live on these almost exclusively, eating the flying adults and raiding hives for larvae. Honeyguides have tough, thick skins, which are thought to be impervious to the insects' stings, and some are reported to have a strong musty body odour (though this has been questioned) that might act as an insect repellent. At any rate, honeyguides are seldom found where bees and wasps are absent.

So avid are several species of honeyguides for bees' nests that they have established a unique mutual-assistance relationship with animals that can facilitate their access to them, notably the ratel, or African honey badger, and primitive African man. The best-known and most inveterate "guider" is the Black-throated, or Greater, Honeyguide, found over most of equatorial and southern Africa. The Greater Honeyguide calls the ratel's or man's attention by persistent loud chattering. Once attention is gained, it calls more loudly and flies a short distance. When followed it repeats the manoeuvre until it has led its ally close to a bees' nest, usually less than a quarter of a mile away. It sits by quietly waiting for the badger or the man to dig the nest out and take most of the honey.

Then the bird moves in for its share of the bees' honeycomb.

African tribesmen have all sorts of superstitions about this bird. Natives who find a honey tree are very careful to leave some honey for the birds who have guided them to it, believing if they fail to do so the bird will not lead them again, but will come and chatter around them the next time they are hunting and drive the game away. It is even riskier not to open a hive if a bird has led you to one, for the next time he will lead you to a dangerous snake or a lion.

It has only recently been proved that the honeyguides' interest in bees' nests is not for the honey, or for the eggs or larvae, but for the wax in the comb! What role this normally indigestible material of low nutritional value plays in the honeyguides' internal economy has not been learned. But stomachs of most species, including those that do not guide, frequently contain pieces of honeycomb. Their digestive tracts show no special modifications for wax-eating, but it has recently been demonstrated that these birds have a peculiar intestinal flora of bacteria that help them digest it.

Of even more interest than the mechanics and physiology of the wax-eating habit (known technically as cerophagy) is how such a distinctive pattern of soliciting other animals' assistance in obtaining the wax could develop to the point where it is instinctive—as it definitely is in the Greater Honeyguide. The problems of the origin and inheritance of wax-eating and guiding traits are intensified by the honeyguides' parasitic nesting habits. As the young are reared by foster parents, they are never fed wax as nestlings. They have no parental guidance to encourage them to eat wax, or to teach them to lead ratels or men to beehives. These behaviour patterns must be inherited.

The honeyguides have developed specialized techniques in their brood parasitism unknown to other practitioners of the art. One group of rather primitive African honeyguides lays its eggs in the open nests of white-eyes, warblers, and flycatchers. The Greater Honeyguide and its nearer relatives parasitize only hole-nesting species, and mostly their own close relatives that lay similar white eggs. Barbets and woodpeckers are their principal hosts, with bee-eaters, kingfishers, woodhoopoes, and starlings next in the list of some 35 or 40 species they commonly impose upon.

Honeyguides sometimes destroy the eggs of the nest's rightful owner when depositing their own, but depend on a far more insidious and certain device to insure the exclusive care of foster parents. The honeyguide hatchlings have at the tip of their bill a sharp hook with which they bite any nestmates fatally. The hook is a calcareous growth comparable to the egg tooth, and usually drops off when the young honeyguide is about a week old and has no further use for it. Whether or not they are able to pierce unhatched eggs with the hook is debatable, as is the claim that the young honeyguides eject eggs and other nestlings from the nest in cuckoo fashion. The one certainty is that week-old honeyguides usually have the nest to themselves and their foster parents' exclusive care and attention from then on.

JACAMARS

PICIFORMES   GALBULIDAE

The 14 species of jacamars form a distinctive American family of slender, graceful, iridescent forest inhabitants found from southern Mexico southward through Central America and the Amazon region to southern Brazil. They can be told at a glance by their lean tapered bodies, their long, thin, sharp-pointed bills, long, gracefully graduated tails, and their shining colours, in which green, blues, and bronzes predominate. Jacamars are as brilliant as the hummingbirds that share their habitat, and even more showy because of their larger size. The sexes are unlike, the females usually having brown instead of white throats.

Jacamars are seldom found in deep jungle, but are commoner along the forest edges near roads and clearings, or along streams and in ragged second-growth timber. Solitary birds, they sit so quietly on a commanding branch they almost seem to be asleep, their bodies erect, their rapier bills slanted upward at a saucy tilt. They move only their heads back and forth as they watch sharply for food to come within range. Then out they dash in a sudden swift sally of whirring wings to pick an insect from the air with an audible snap of the bill, and return with it to their perch.

Jacamars live exclusively on insects and catch most of their prey in flight. Their needle-like bills seem ill adapted for this type of feeding, for the narrow biting surfaces demand considerable accuracy when small flying insects are the target. This is probably why jacamars specialize in the large showy butterflies and dragonflies. It is quite a sight to watch a jaca-mar catch and eat one of the big blue *Morpho* butterflies. The bird beats the gorgeous insect mercilessly against its perch, knocks off the beautiful cobalt wings, and swallows the soft body.

Vocally the jacamars are inferior, for their call notes are unimpressive little squeaks. Some species have a pleasant, melodious trilling song, but it is so unobtrusive you have to listen hard to hear it. Yet their bright iridescence and their dashing sorties when feeding make them sufficiently conspicuous. Their vernacular name was given them by the Amazon Indians.

Jacamars nest in burrows in the ground, usually in a steep hillside or a convenient bank. Both sexes co-operate in digging, loosening the soil with their bills and kicking it out with their feet. The finished burrow has a round entrance hole too small for a man's arm, and extends back only a foot or two before expanding into the chamber, where the female lays 3 to 4 pure-white eggs. Both sexes incubate, the female usually at night, for the 19 to 21 days it takes the eggs to hatch. Both parents feed the young, which remain in the burrow for another 3 weeks. Jacamars make little attempt to clean their quarters, which are soon littered with the regurgitated indigestible chitinous parts of insects. The sheaths stay on the growing feathers for a long time, giving the nestlings a bristly look. When they leave the nest in their first juvenile plumage, the young strongly resemble their parents, but are slightly duller in colour.

PUFFBIRDS

PICIFORMES   BUCCONIDAE

Closely related to the jacamars and paralleling them in distribution is another distinctive group of New World picarians, the puffbirds. The 30 puffbirds are, like the jacamars, small-to medium-sized forest birds, but they are more heavily built and lack the jacamars' bright plumage. Most are dull browns and dark greys, but a few are strikingly patterned in black and white, often with a broad contrasting breast band.

Puffbirds have noticeably large heads and short necks, and their heavy bills are usually broadly flattened, usually hooked at the tip, and surrounded by conspicuous bristles. Their wings are short and rounded, their tails of medium length with square or rounded tips. Their centre of distribution is the Amazon basin, and they have spread from there in diminishing numbers (both of species and individuals) northward to southern Mexico and southward to Paraguay.

As a family, the puffbirds tend to be silent, rather inactive birds with unimpressive voices, thin weak whistles or wheezy peeps. They like to sit on an exposed perch with their thick, fluffy body and neck feathers puffed out—hence their name. Notably unsuspicious and unafraid, they allow a close approach. Because of their quiet demeanour and sombre dress they are called "nunbirds," "nunlets," or "monklets." Less reverent Brazilians call them *João bobo*, or "stupid John."

Puffbirds feed much as jacamars do, flying out from their perch for passing insects, and with their broader bills they are more skilled at snatching small insects from the air. They also poke about among the leaves, and not infrequently pounce on creeping things on the ground.

Again like the jacamars, most puffbirds nest in a burrow, often in some convenient bank, sometimes slanted downward in level ground; a few dig into tree termites' nests. Both sexes dig the burrow, which may extend 3 or 4 feet into the earth. Some species pile sticks and leaves around the entrance, evidently to hide it, and they usually line the nest chamber with a few grasses or leaves. Their method of carrying the earth away (little is found outside the burrow) has not been observed, but they probably do so in their beaks. Pairs wait around the site a week or so after finishing the nest before laying. The normal clutch is 2 to 3 roundish white eggs, which both parents incubate. Their nesting habits have not been well studied, and nothing is known of their incubation periods or care of the nestlings.

TOUCANS

PICIFORMES   RAMPHASTIDAE

Their tremendous bills, sometimes almost as big as their bodies, make the 37 toucans one of the most unmistakable of all bird families. Vaguely resembling those of the Old World hornbills, toucan bills are even larger, more canoe-shaped, and brighter coloured. Smooth and never incised, they lack the hornbill's ornate casque. Toucans are found wild only in American tropical forests.

Toucans in captivity will eat and thrive on many kinds of food, but in the wild they live essentially on fruit, with occasional side dishes of large insects and fledgling birds. They handle all sorts of food with ease and facility, but there is no denying that their bill seems unnecessarily large, and not well designed for fruit eating. The toucan's bill may even be as much a hindrance as a help in feeding, though the birds certainly do well enough with it.

The toucan's cumbersome beak may be a persisting anachronism, originally developed to eat some peculiar large soft fruit or insect that has long since vanished. But this seems unlikely. Its length is a help in reaching fruits and berries

hanging far out, but reach is no problem to fruit eaters with much shorter beaks. As a defensive weapon, the bill is awesome enough perhaps to have a greater frightening value than capacity to inflict damage. It is apparently little protection against the few predators that bother toucans, mainly weasels and large hawks.

The toucan's bill may have developed in response to needs other than feeding, aggression, or defence. The distinctive bills of the various species may serve as recognition marks be-

CUVIER'S TOUCAN
Ramphastos cuvieri
Colombia to Bolivia and Brazil   24 in.

PARADISE JACAMAR
Galbula dea
Venezuela to Bolivia   12 in.

GREAT JACAMAR
Jacamerops aurea
Costa Rica to the Guianas
and Ecuador   11½ in.

WHITE-NECKED PUFFBIRD
Notharchus macrorynchos
Mexico to Argentina   9½ in.

LAMINATED HILL TOUCAN
Andigena laminirostris
Colombia and Ecuador   17 in.

COLLARED PUFFBIRD
Bucco capensis
Colombia to Peru and Brazil   7 i

TOCO TOUCAN
Ramphastos toco
The Guianas and Brazil 25 in.

tween species of similar body colours. Also, they may play some part in courtship display, though none has been observed. Perhaps the toucan's bill has no particular adaptive function, but developed more or less fortuitously, and its owners have been able to use it well enough to survive and prosper.

Though toucans seem to be all bill and out of balance, the bill is an efficient fruit-picking tool and a wonderful piece of structural engineering. It is amazingly light in weight, for inside its outer horny sheath it is trussed with a honeycomb of stiff cellular fibres that impart strength with lightness. The tongue, which extends almost to its tip, is very thin and narrow, rather stiff and hard, and fringed on both sides with bristles. The function of these bristles is uncertain, and perhaps as ambiguous as the bill itself.

To eat fruit, toucans tear a chunk free with the bill's sharp, serrated cutting edges, juggle it around a bit at the bill tip,

SULPHUR-BREASTED TOUCAN
Ramphastos sulfuratus
Mexico to Venezuela 23 in.

EMERALD TOUCANET
Aulacorhynchus prasinus
Mexico to Peru 14 in.

GREEN ARAÇARI
Pteroglossus viridis
Colombia through Brazil 13 in.

DOUBLE-COLLARED ARAÇARI
Pteroglossus bitorquatus
Central Brazil 15 in.

RANGE OF TOUCANS

Toucanet of Central America is a highland species; it is seldom found below 3,000 feet and prefers the virgin cloud forests that grow at 9,000 feet and higher.

That the toucan's colouring has significant concealing value is open to question, for the birds seldom seem to take advantage of it. They are one of the noisiest of the jungle dwellers. The larger ones croak loudly throughout the torrid day and their harsh cries carry a half mile or more in the still jungle. They travel about actively in small noisy flocks of half a dozen or so birds, and when feeding in the tree-tops chatter to one another with coarse, grating chucklings, interspersed with the hollow clacking of their bills. Toucans often fence with one another with their bills and toss berries into the air at one another or pass them along from bill to bill. Whether this apparent playing has some courtship significance or is just joyful high spirits is not known.

Toucans fly gracefully but weakly, and seldom for long distances. A series of 8 or 10 rapid wingbeats ends in a slight upthrust, followed by a short glide on stiff wings. In flight over the jungle their silhouette is unmistakable, for the tremendous bill, carried out in front and pointed slightly downward, gives them a nose-heavy look. Some have a curious habit of jerking their tails upward as they fly. The peculiar muscular and bony attachment of their tails permits more vertical than lateral movement, and helps them fit into the cramped tree cavities where they roost and nest. A toucan preparing to sleep folds itself together, first resting the bill down the centre of the back, then covering it with the tail, which hinges forward so that its tips are up around the shoulders and the bird looks like a ball of feathers.

Toucans nest in tree cavities, either natural ones in some rotted stump or old woodpecker holes, which they may enlarge slightly. Height above the ground makes little difference; nests have been found near ground level and high in tall trees. Some large toucans line the bottom of the nest cavity with a few green leaves, but most species leave it bare, cleaning out any debris or loose wood before laying their 2 to 4 glossy white eggs in the bottom. The toucanets keep their nests fairly clean, but the larger species do not. Both adults and young regurgitate indigestible fruit pips, which soon make a cobbly bed in the bottom of the nest.

Both sexes incubate and tend the young. Incubation takes only about 16 days, but the nestling stage is markedly long, 6 to 7 weeks in the Keel-billed Toucan. The young hatch naked, and at first do not look like toucans at all. Their beaks are broad and flat, the lower bill projects beyond the tip of the upper, and the soft tongue completely fills the bill cavity. As they grow, the bill gradually assumes its bulky adult proportions, but does not achieve its full growth and colouring for several months.

Another distinctive feature of nestling toucans is the prominent pads on their "heels" at the upper end of the tarsus. These bear most of the birds' weight while in the nest. Similar pads occur on other hole-nesting species whose young are reared on hard, unpadded surfaces, such as the jacamars and hornbills, but in no other group are they as prominent and well developed as in the toucans. The heel pads remain until the young fledge, and then start to slough off. They disappear by the time of the first post-juvenal moult, and adults show no trace of them.

and then throw their heads back so the morsel falls into their throats. They drink the same way, dipping the end of the bill into the water and then raising it up so the water flows down into their gullets.

Toucans range from southern Mexico southward to Paraguay and northern Argentina. Their centre of abundance is the Amazon region, where they probably developed from some unknown generalized picarian ancestor. The larger, crow-sized species with the biggest bills, such as the Toco and Keel-billed toucans of the genus *Ramphastos*, live mainly in the heavy lowland rainforest. The native Tupi Indians still call them "toco," which European explorers corrupted to "toucan" centuries ago. These large toucans have black bodies, contrasting throat patches, and upper and under tail coverts of red, yellow, or white.

Some smaller toucans occur in the lowlands, but more inhabit mountain forests higher up. Most brilliantly plumaged and widest ranging of the family are the silky-bodied araçaris (the Tupis call all smaller toucans "arassaris") of the genus *Pteroglossus*. Found from Mexico to Argentina at various altitudinal ranges, the 11 araçaris are among the most gregarious of the toucans (which are the most gregarious of the piciform families). They move about the jungle in small flocks, and roost together at night in hollow trees. Another gaudy group consists of the hill toucans (*Andigena*), which move seasonally up and down the Andean mountainsides as various fruits and berries ripen.

As with other bright-coloured forest birds, the toucans' broken patterns harmonize with their surroundings, and the birds can be hard to see, especially when they sit quietly in the tree-tops for a midday siesta. The eye that notices their vivid splashes of colour disregards them as a flower or fruit among the foliage. Most concealingly coloured are the green jay-sized toucanets. These are the smallest toucans and have the smallest bills in proportion to body size. The Emerald

WOODPECKERS

PICIFORMES   PICIDAE

Their adaptations to a life centred about the trunks of trees make the woodpecker family one of the most distinctive and easily recognizable of all land birds. Though largely limited to forested regions, woodpeckers have spread through almost the entire world, failing only to reach Australia, the oceanic islands, and Madagascar. Fossil woodpeckers from Eocene deposits in both hemispheres show them to be an ancient group. The family is a large and compact one of 210 species, divided into three subfamilies, 179 true woodpeckers (Picinae) and two smaller, less specialized, more primitive groups, the wrynecks (Jynginae) and the piculets (Picumninae).

The most primitive members of the family are the two wrynecks, so called from the snake-like way they twist their heads when feeding. The Eurasian Wryneck breeds across northern Eurasia from Great Britain to Japan and migrates southward in winter. The other species, a resident of Africa, is slightly larger and has a red-brown upper breast and chin. Both are insect eaters, particularly fond of ants, and partial to open brushlands. Wrynecks feed on the ground and in trees, and make short dashes into the air for flying insects.

Wrynecks' tails are soft instead of stiff-shafted as in the true woodpeckers. When wrynecks alight in trees, they usually perch across a branch in normal perching-bird fashion, not along it or upright on the trunk as do the woodpeckers. Nor do they peck or bore for their food, but pick it up from the surface with rapid flickings of their long tongues. As their bills are not efficient chisels, they depend on natural cavities or deserted woodpecker holes for nesting sites. In northern Japan they use nesting boxes in the parks. They lay large clutches of 6 to 9 pure-white eggs, which hatch in 12 to 14 days. Both parents feed the nestlings, largely on ants and beetle larvae, for the 21 to 24 days it takes them to fledge.

The tiny piculets also perch crossways and have soft tails of no use as props. Unlike the wrynecks, piculets seldom feed on the ground, but forage through tangled vines and low bushes along forest edges. These rather solitary birds are continually on the move, climbing about nervously in search of small insects. They fly weakly with the undulatory up-and-down movement of all woodpeckers.

Piculets are wren-sized; the largest of the 29 species is only 5 inches long. All are mottled in olive-green, greys, and browns, often with pepper-and-salt patches about the head. Best developed in the American tropics, 25 species range from the West Indies and Honduras south to northern Argentina. Three more species occur in the forests of southeastern Asia, and a single isolated piculet has survived in tropical West Africa. This disjointed distribution attests their antiquity.

True woodpeckers have invaded the realm of tree trunks and large branches more successfully than any other birds. Most of them live an upright life on vertical surfaces, and are structurally modified for this purpose. Their legs are short; their toes, only two of which face forward, are long, strong, and tipped with sharp curved nails for clinging to bark. They prop themselves erect resting against their tails, whose feathers are always pointed and have stiff, strong shafts.

The typical woodpecker bill is straight, hard, and pointed, an ideal chisel for digging into bark and wood. This chisel beak, backed by a large head with a strong, thick-walled skull to absorb the shocks of pounding, is driven by powerful muscles in the slim but wiry neck.

Woodpeckers have a long extensile tongue, which most species can stick out to astonishing lengths beyond the bill. The tongue has backward-pointing barbs at its tip, and the salivary glands of many species secrete a gluey substance that coats it so that insects adhere to it. When a woodpecker opens the tunnel of a borer, the long tongue snakes into it to spear the grub and hook it out.

Woodpeckers start feeding near the base of a tree and work their way spirally upward around it, probing into each likely cranny as they go. They explore the promising larger limbs as well, often clinging to the underside of a horizontal branch to get at a borer there. When they reach the top they swoop down to the base of the next tree and repeat the manoeuvre as long as they are feeding.

Woodpeckers fly strongly, but not swiftly and seldom for long distances. They are easily recognized by their undulating flight—a succession of four or five rapid wingstrokes carries them upward; they swoop downward with wings closed a few seconds; another flurry of wings, another swoop, and they continue climbing and swooping on their wavy course. Very few woodpeckers are migratory, though some of the northern species move irregularly southward in winter. Their food supply is not seriously affected by cold weather, for they can support themselves on pupae and larvae that hibernate under the bark or in rotted wood out of reach of most other birds. Migration is most pronounced in those woodpeckers that probe for their food the least, the flickers of North America and the green woodpeckers of Eurasia, both fond of lapping up ants from the ground. Others that wander seasonally in search of food are the few that, in addition to insects, eat some fruit and nuts, and one small North American group that drills for sap—the well-named sapsuckers.

Most woodpeckers have loud, harsh voices, and many repeat their sharp, ringing call notes in successive peals. Woodpeckers have no true song, but during courtship they call more vigorously and repeatedly. They also advertise their presence, desires, and intentions by drumming a loud rolling tattoo on a dead limb—or on a tin roof or a metal stovepipe.

Woodpeckers work hard for their living, and their feeding habits do not encourage gregariousness. They are seldom seen in flocks. The smaller species are often tame and unsuspicious, but the larger ones tend to keep their distance. They usually keep a tree trunk between themselves and an intruder.

Most familiar are the small- to medium-sized woodpeckers of the genus *Dendrocopos*, collectively known as the "pied woodpeckers." These are a Northern Hemisphere group of some 30 species scattered widely across North America and Eurasia. Several closely allied species occur in central Africa and in South America southward to Argentina. The pied woodpeckers are black or greyish-brown birds conspicuously barred or mottled with white. The males usually have patches of red on the head, lacking in the females. In parts of their range, two similar species of this genus, almost identical in colour but different in size, live side by side. The Downy and Hairy woodpeckers of North America are examples. The Downy is 6 inches long; the 10-inch Hairy is twice or more its bulk. Living similarly together through European woodlands are the almost identically coloured 6-inch Lesser and 10-inch Great spotted woodpeckers. These "sympatric pairs" of species do not compete with each other. The smaller birds scour the smaller twigs and outer branches while the larger birds work the main trunks.

Very similar to the pied woodpeckers in habits and appearance are the three-toed woodpeckers, which are similarly black and white but have yellow in the crown. These have lost one of their two hind toes—a distinguishing characteristic useful only with the bird in the hand. Only two species are known, one with a solid-black back, the other with the back barred white. The 9-inch "ladder-backed," or Northern, Three-toed Woodpecker is circumpolar in the spruce-larch belts across northern North America and the Eurasian taiga. It breaks into a dozen or so geographic races, with populations

IVORY-BILLED
WOODPECKER ♂
(probably extinct)
Campephilus principalis
Southeastern
United States 20 in.

YELLOW-BELLIED SAPSUCKER ♂
Sphyrapicus varius
Temperate North America 8½ in.

JAMAICAN WOODPECKER
Centurus radiolatus
Island of Jamaica, B.W.I. 11 in.

YELLOW-SHAFTED FLICKER ♂
Colaptes auratus
Temperate North America 13 in.

RED-HEADED
WOODPECKER
Melanerpes erythrocephalus
Central and eastern
North America 10 in.

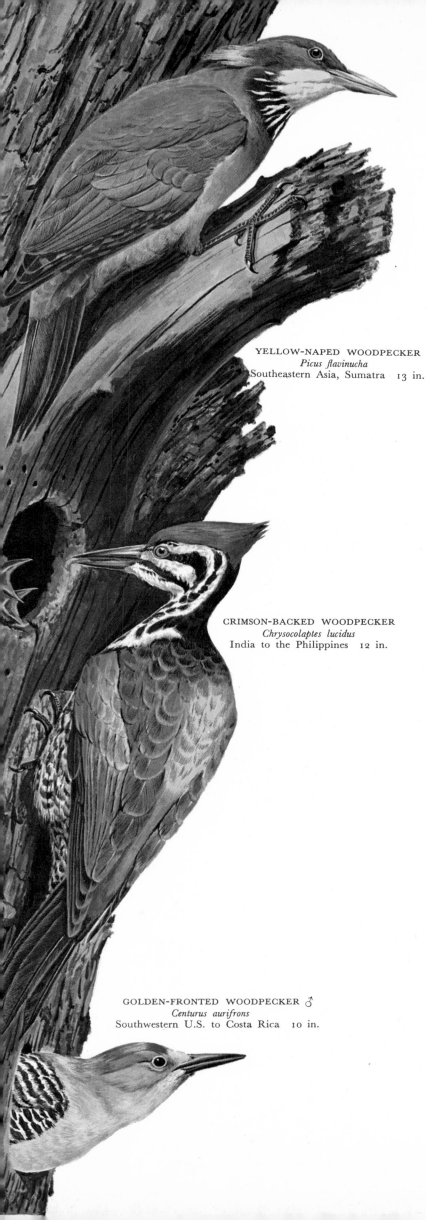

YELLOW-NAPED WOODPECKER
Picus flavinucha
Southeastern Asia, Sumatra   13 in.

CRIMSON-BACKED WOODPECKER
Chrysocolaptes lucidus
India to the Philippines   12 in.

GOLDEN-FRONTED WOODPECKER ♂
Centurus aurifrons
Southwestern U.S. to Costa Rica   10 in.

isolated in mountain regions south of its normal range—in the Alps and the Carpathians of Europe, in the Altai Mountains of Asia, in the Rocky Mountains of North America southward to Arizona and New Mexico, and in the White Mountains of New England.

The 10-inch Black-backed, or American, Three-toed Woodpecker is commoner in North America than its circumpolar relative. It follows the spruce-larch belt from Alaska across to Labrador and south to Nevada, Wyoming, northern New York, and Maine. Both species are active, restless birds that live almost entirely on wood-boring insects and move into burned lands to feed on beetle larvae they find under the bark of the dying or dead trees, wedging off whole sections of the bark to expose the borers in the wood beneath.

Another widespread New World genus is the *Melanerpes* group, typified by the familiar and widespread Red-headed Woodpecker. This common inhabitant of open woodlands throughout temperate North America east of the Rockies, unmistakable with its startling red head and neck, is less orthodox in its feeding habits than many other species. While it digs for borers in the bark, it frequently flies out to catch insects on the wing. It is also fond of berries and fruit, and will come to feeding stations for bread crumbs. It often digs its nesting holes in telegraph poles along roadsides in the Southern states. Its Western relative, the Acorn Woodpecker, is a provident species that stores food for future use. It drills holes just the right size in the bark and sticks acorns in them to eat when times are leaner. Tree trunks are often riddled with its empty storage holes. The *Melanerpes* group has some 18 species ranging from southern Canada through the West Indies, Central America, to Argentina and Paraguay. Closely related are the *Centurus* woodpeckers, which include the Red-bellied Woodpecker of the Southern states, replaced by the pretty Golden-fronted Woodpecker from Oklahoma and Texas south through Central America to Costa Rica. The Jamaican Woodpecker is also a member of this group.

The two sapsuckers, the Yellow-bellied and Williamson's, form a peculiar North American genus of woodpeckers. As their name implies, sapsuckers drink the sap that oozes from the holes they drill in the tender bark of deciduous trees. They also eat the insects that come to feed on the sap, and the tender cambium layer underneath the bark. Sapsuckers are often accused of damaging fruit trees, but while their work disfigures the bark, it seldom causes permanent damage. Studies of their food habits show the beneficial effects of the sapsuckers' consumption of boring insects far outweigh the harmful effects of the small holes they make in the bark. In healthy trees the wounds heal over quickly, and the birds are never numerous enough to be much of a problem.

Another American group is the flickers (*Colaptes*). The Yellow-shafted Flicker of eastern North America is the distinguished owner of the 132 different vernacular names which one assiduous compiler dug out of the North American literature—highholder, yellow-hammer, golden-wing, wakeup, and hairy wicket are but a small sample. It is replaced in the West by the Red-shafted Flicker, very similar in colour, appearance, and habits, but with the shafts of the wings and tail feathers red instead of yellow. Intermediate forms are common where the ranges overlap, and many students now

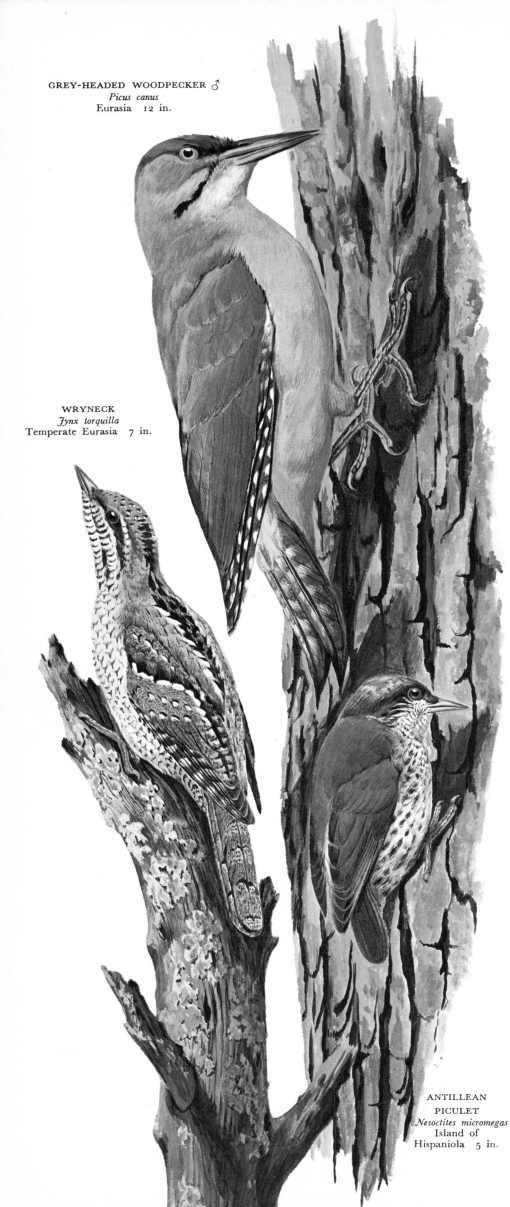

GREY-HEADED WOODPECKER ♂
Picus canus
Eurasia 12 in.

WRYNECK
Jynx torquilla
Temperate Eurasia 7 in.

ANTILLEAN
PICULET
Nesoctites micromegas
Island of
Hispaniola 5 in.

regard them as conspecific. Other members of the genus are found southward into South America.

Flickers feed on the ground more than most other woodpeckers and are particularly fond of ants. Driving their bills into ant burrows, they extend their long, sticky tongue, and withdraw it loaded. The sticky substance from the salivary glands which coats their tongue is strongly alkaline, perhaps to counteract the ant's formic acid. Flickers normally chisel their nests out of upright dead trees, but may use telephone poles or the eaves of country houses. In spring they pound a rolling tattoo on dead limbs, stovepipes or even tin roofs.

The Old World green woodpeckers of the genus *Picus* number some 15 species ranging across Europe and Asia and southward to Borneo and Java. The green woodpeckers occupy the same ecological niche in Eurasia that the flickers occupy in the New World. They dig their nests out of tree trunks and also feed largely on ants. The striking Crimson-backed Woodpecker is one of three similar species of open forests from India through Malaya to the Philippines. Most terrestrial of the family is the Ground Woodpecker of South Africa, which digs in the ground, and excavates its nest like a kingfisher.

The true Woodpeckers, except for a few terrestrial species that nest in dirt banks, dig their nests in tree trunks, usually hewing a hole inward a few inches and then downward, sometimes a foot or more, slightly expanded at the bottom. They use no nest lining except a few wood chips, and lay roundish, glossy white eggs. Their incubation period is short, from 11 to 14 days in the smaller species and to only 18 in the largest ones. The fledging period is much longer, from 2 ½ to 3 weeks in the smaller species and as long as 5 weeks in the largest ones. Both sexes share the work of digging the nest hole and incubating and feeding the young. Many species dig several holes, nest in one, and roost in the others at night.

The group of crested ivory-bills, most of which are rapidly nearing extinction if not already extinct, are the largest and most imposing of the woodpeckers. The Ivory-billed Woodpecker, formerly found widely in the mature forests of North America and in Cuba, has not been reported reliably during the last decade and is feared to have gone to join the Dodo and Passenger Pigeon. The status of the related Imperial Woodpecker of the Mexican highlands and the Magellanic Ivory-bill of southern South America is equally tentative. The disappearance of these birds is largely attributed to the cutting of big trees where they lived. We still hope that a few Ivory-bills may survive in forests of the Gulf Coast, and perhaps a few in the mountains of Cuba.

Very similar to the Ivory-bill and often mistaken for it is the Pileated Woodpecker, still fairly common in the southeastern United States. The Pileated is slightly smaller than the Ivory-bill and has a dark instead of a yellow-white bill. Both sexes have red crests and at rest show little white on the wings. The Pileated Woodpecker is a member of the circumpolar genus *Dryocopus*. The Pileated and the Great Black woodpeckers of northern Eurasia both have black bellies. A similar but white-bellied form is found in eastern Asia and southward to the Philippines, Java, and Borneo. A few of these still persist in Korea, but the small population that once inhabited the island of Tsushima between Japan and Korea has not been reported for several decades.

PERCHING BIRDS

PASSERIFORMES

The Passeriformes, commonly known as the passerine or perching birds, are by far the largest, most complex, and most highly developed order of birds. The order contains about 5,100 species, roughly three-fifths of the known living birds. All are land birds of small to medium size. The largest passerines are the Raven and the two Australian lyrebirds.

The passerines' outstanding characteristic is their perching feet, with four unwebbed toes joined at the same level, three in front and one behind. The hind toe is usually the strongest and best developed and is never reversible. Among the passerines' other features are the peculiar structure of their palate bones, a reduction of their cervical vertebrae (usually 14, 15 in the broadbills alone), and a distinctive type of spermatozoa. All have altricial young which hatch naked (or nearly so) and helpless and are reared in the nest.

Members of the Passeriformes are found on all major land areas except Antarctica, and on most oceanic islands capable of supporting bird life. Their ancestry and kinship to other orders of land birds are an enigma. They probably arose very early in Tertiary time, or earlier, from several parent stocks. The few early Tertiary remains are too fragmentary to be identified with certainty, and offer no clues to the perplexing questions of the order's antecedents and relationships. Only within the last few decades have palaeo-ornithologists begun to sift fossil deposits for tiny bird bones. These are now yielding some clues to the pre-Ice Age distribution and relationships of a few passerine families.

During and since Tertiary time, the passerines have evolved more rapidly and successfully than any other avian order. So rapid and so recent has been their development that the lines of demarcation between many groups are not well defined. The differences between some passerine families are not so great as those between many non-passerine genera. This, and the persistence of primitive forms that do not manifestly link more highly developed stocks, makes subdividing the order into "manageable" families most difficult.

Ornithologists are by no means agreed on the exact delineation of passerine families or on their lineal sequence, particularly in the oscines, or "true song birds." Recent classifications have lumped them into as few as 50 families, and divided them into as many as 70. The adoption of 57 families in this book is perhaps on the low side.

More than a century ago, the German anatomist Müller pointed out basic differences in the number and attachment of the muscles of the voice box, or syrinx, which permit the recognition of four suborders. The first three, with 4 or fewer pairs of syrinx muscles, are the more primitive passerines, the so-called "suboscines." These are the suborder Eurylaimi with the single Old World family of broadbills; the suborder Tyranni, a group of 13 essentially New World families that includes the ovenbirds, tyrant flycatchers, pittas, and their allies; and the Menurae, containing only the two lyrebirds and two scrub-birds of Australia.

The fourth suborder, the Passeres, or "true oscines," have 5 to 8 pairs of syrinx muscles. This large aggregation of true singing birds contains slightly more than 4,000 species, almost half of the world's birds. Students now divide it into from 36 to 55 or more families. Efforts to unite these families into larger natural groups have met with little success, and the sequence in which they are listed is still a matter of contention, depending largely on the characteristics considered most important by the individual systematist.

Most Europeans put the crows at the apex of the family tree because of their supposed higher intelligence, and the related bowerbirds and birds of paradise for their complex development of behaviour patterns and plumages. The American school of thought places the seedeaters and related nine-primaried oscines in the top position. These are today the dominant and most successful of all bird groups. They show the greatest and most recent adaptive radiation and development. Many ornithologists, myself among them, feel they represent the main stream of songbird evolution.

BROADBILLS

PASSERIFORMES   EURYLAIMIDAE

The 14 species of broadbills are a distinctive family of bright-coloured perching birds distributed erratically in the Old World tropics. Their simple syrinx controlled by a single pair of muscles, the partial joining of their front toes, and their 15 (instead of 14) neck vertebrae set them so apart from all other passerines they are placed in a separate suborder. Their primitiveness and disjointed distribution suggest the living broadbills are the remnants of an ancient group that was once of wider distribution and now past its peak of development. Their relationships are uncertain, but they seem closest to the New World cotingas and puffbirds.

Plump birds from 5 to 11 inches in length, the broadbills have disproportionately large heads set on short necks and, as their name implies, heavy, wide, flattened bills hooked at the tip. Their short legs add to their squat appearance, but their feet are strong and their toes are tipped with long curved claws. Their soft, silky plumage is brightly coloured green and blue in most Asiatic species; the African forms are more sombre but relieved with gay patches of red, yellow, and lavender. Their bills and large eyes are often a vivid hue. Females are usually duller than the males.

The family is divided into two subfamilies, the typical

broadbills (Eurylaiminae) and the green broadbills (Calyptomeninae). The typical broadbills are uncrested and have 11 primaries, and graduated or rounded tails. Seven species of five genera range across southeastern Asia from the Himalayas to the Philippines and southward to Sumatra and Borneo. Four species are limited to the forests of central and southern Africa. The single genus of green broadbills is found only in the oriental region. Its three species have 10 primaries, short, square tails, and their smaller bills are partly hidden by a frontal crest of thick feathers.

All the broadbills are birds of wet jungles and cloud forests. Some live continually near the ground; others inhabit the tree-tops. Most are sedentary, and some are extremely restricted in their movements. Two of the green broadbills, the rare Magnificent and the Black-throated, are found only in the mountain forests of northern Borneo. Rarest of all is Grauer's Broadbill, of which fewer than a dozen specimens are known, all taken in a small tract of bamboo forest in the mountains near Lake Tanganyika. It is a tiny greenish bird, scarcely 5 inches long, with a blue throat and breast. It apparently lives in the tree-tops and catches insects in flight.

Commoner and better known is the Long-tailed Broadbill, widespread from the Himalayan foothills through southeast Asia to Sumatra and Borneo. These plump birds work through the jungles in small flocks, climbing through the lianas in parrot fashion in search of insects, chattering continually to one another. They are remarkably tame and unsuspicious, even failing to take alarm when some of the flock are shot.

The typical broadbills are insectivorous, and also take occasional small frogs and lizards. They find much of their food on foliage and catch flying insects on the wing. The green broadbills, of which the Lesser Green Broadbill of Malaya is the most widespread and best known, live largely on fruit and berries. They are rather solitary, silent birds.

Broadbills have superlative skill at nest building. They weave a long, hanging, purse-like structure of grasses, rootlets, and other fibres, tapered gracefully at top and bottom. This they suspend by a slender string, woven of the same materials, from a branch or vine in the forest, often over a stream or pool. The nest proper in the centre is entered through a hole in the side which may have a sheltering portico and doorstep perch.

Within this intricate nest the broadbills lay from 2 to 8 (usually 3 to 5) white or buffy eggs, sometimes spotted around

LESSER GREEN BROADBILL
Calyptomena viridis
Malaya, Sumatra, Borneo 6 in.

LONG-TAILED BROADBILL
Psarisomus dalhousiae
Himalayas to Indochina, Sumatra, Borneo 10 in.

the larger end. Beyond these few facts little is known of their breeding habits. Both sexes have been observed building the nest, and for the Dusky Broadbill of Thailand there is evidence that as many as 10 birds may work on the same nest. Both sexes have been seen bringing food to the young, but whether they share incubation duties is unknown, as is the length of the incubation period.

Several broadbills have specialized courtship displays involving the sudden flashing of bright patches of feathers on the back, usually concealed under the wings. The Red-sided Broadbill of Africa, which the Congo natives call the "cock of the forest" because it is the first bird to greet the breaking day, makes sudden short display flights in which the bird flits in a small circle a foot or two in diameter above its perch with a trilling frog-like croak made by the vibrating stiff wing feathers.

WOODCREEPERS

PASSERIFORMES   DENDROCOLAPTIDAE

Strongly resembling the Brown Creeper of America's northern woodlands in appearance and actions, though usually somewhat larger and darker, are 48 species of slender, brownish birds found in American tropical and subtropical forests from Mexico to northern Argentina. These are the woodcreepers, a well-marked family of very similar birds in no way related to the true oscine creepers, but belonging to the more primitive suborder Tyranni, whose members have much simpler vocal organs. The woodcreepers' closest relatives are the ovenbirds, with which they share such structural characteristics as two pairs of syrinx muscles and partially joined front toes. Some students classify the woodcreepers and the ovenbirds as subfamilies of the same family.

The woodcreepers' superficial resemblance to the oscine creepers is a fine example of parallel evolution in widely separate stocks which have similar needs in comparable ecological niches in their respective parts of the world. Both live chiefly on the trunks of forest trees, clinging to the bark with their sharply curved claws and propping themselves upright, woodpecker fashion, with their stiff, spiny tails.

The woodcreepers are not shy birds, but are so protectively coloured they are hard to observe. All are dull brown with ruddy brown wing and tail feathers. A few, such as the Olivaceous and Ruddy woodcreepers of Central America, are plain immaculate browns. Most species, however, have the head, back, and underparts variously streaked, mottled, or barred with black, buff, grey, or white. Though their patterns are distinctive enough, they are hard to discern at a distance, especially against the birds' usual background of brown bark. Easier field marks are the relative sizes of the different species, and the length and shape of their bills.

Woodcreepers vary in length from 5½ to 14 inches. Their laterally compressed bills range from short and straight to long and sharply down-curved—adaptations for searching bark crannies, probing into mosses, ferns, and epiphytes, or for picking grubs out of their burrows. Their beaks are not the strong chisels of the woodpeckers and are used essentially as probes. Most woodcreepers work methodically when feeding. Starting near the base of a tree, they move spirally upward, searching each crack and fissure. A few species feed occasionally on the ground, working over fallen logs.

Woodcreepers usually travel about singly or in pairs. Often one or two are found among the mixed flocks of antbirds, flycatchers, and tanagers that move irregularly through the rainforests. None is migratory, but individuals wander considerably. They fly strongly, but only from tree to tree.

Woodcreepers are quite vocal and their simple repetitive calls are commonly heard in the tropical American forests. Their range of expression is limited by the primitive structure of their sound-producing organs. The calls may be flutey trills or loud, harsh nasal notes. Some woodcreepers rap with their bills on hollow trunks in woodpecker fashion as part of their courtship, but their tapping does not have regular cadences.

Woodcreepers are cavity nesters, but as their beaks are not strong enough to chisel into wood, they use natural hollows in rotten stumps or take over those abandoned by woodpeckers. They tend to pick sites with very small entrances, barely large enough for passage. Some remove chips or debris from the hole and use it bare. Others make a crude pad of bark flakes or dead leaves, which they renew constantly through the nesting period, a habit shared by the related ovenbirds.

The normal clutch is 2 to 3 white eggs, sometimes with a greenish tinge, always unspotted and rounded at both ends. Both sexes incubate, and they relieve each other frequently through the day. The incubation period averages about 15 days. The young hatch naked except for a slight fuzz on the back and remain in the nest about 3 weeks. Their parents continue to feed them several weeks after they leave the nest.

RED-BILLED SCYTHEBILL
Campyloramphus trochilirostris
Panama to Argentina   9 in.

OLIVACEOUS WOODCREEPER
Sittasomus griseicapillus
Mexico to Argentina   6½ in.

BARRED WOODCREEPER
Dendrocolaptes certhia
Mexico to Brazil   11 in.

OVENBIRDS

PASSERIFORMES   FURNARIIDAE

The ovenbirds are a large family of primitive passerines noted for their extremely varied nesting habits and named for the intricate clay nests, shaped like an old-fashioned Dutch oven, a few build. Found from southern Mexico to Patagonia, the family has its greatest development and diversity in southern South America. The North American Ovenbird is not a member of this family, but a wood warbler (p. 285).

The 215 species in the ovenbird family are small to medium in size, to 11 inches long. Most are plain, brownish above and lighter below, often with contrasting white throats. Some are spotted or streaked with black, white, or rufous, and only a few have distinctive colour patterns. The sexes are alike or nearly so. Ovenbirds differ from the closely allied woodcreepers in having elongated instead of round nostrils. Their front toes are not joined together as far, and their outer toes are not distinctly larger than the inner.

Though predominantly forest birds, the ovenbirds have a wide range of habitats. A few occupy coastal sand dunes, many live on the open pampas and adjoining brushlands, and others dwell at considerable altitudes above the tree line in the Andes. All are insect eaters, but a few eat some seeds and vegetable matter. One group, the treerunners, climb tree trunks and brace themselves with their tails like the woodcreepers. Another, the foliage-gleaners, forage among the

WHITE-CHEEKED SPINETAIL
Schoeniophylax phryganophila
Brazil, Paraguay, Argentina   7½ in.

RUFOUS OVENBIRD
Furnarius rufus
Southern Brazil and Argentina   8 in.

PLAIN XENOPS
Xenops minutus
Mexico to Brazil and Paraguay 5 in.

PALE-BREASTED SPINETAIL
Synallaxis albescens
Costa Rica to Argentina   5½ in.

leaves and branches. The leaf-scrapers turn over the litter on the jungle floor. One small group, the spinetails, is made up of marsh inhabitants that look and behave like large marsh wrens. The shaketails live along watercourses and wag their tails continually the way dippers, wagtails, and many other stream-loving birds do. But most ovenbirds feed on the ground and behave more like larks or thrushes.

So far as known both sexes share the nesting duties. Ovenbirds lay from 2 to 6 eggs, usually white (pale bluish in one group) and unmarked. Incubation varies from 2 to 3 weeks, and the young usually remain in the nest from 12 to 18 days. They show great variety in their choice of nesting sites and type of nest. About the only type of nest they do not seem to build is the simple open cup.

Many terrestrial ovenbirds dig nest tunnels in the earth. One group, the miners, excavates burrows 5 to 10 feet into a bank, ending in a round chamber which the birds line with soft grasses. Other tunnel nesters include the foliage-gleaners of the genera *Automolus* and *Philydor*, and the little whiskered *Xenops*, one of the smallest members of the family, with a strangely up-curved bill. The terrestrial shaketails and the earthcreepers shelter their nests in rock crannies, and some build in natural cavities in trees and stumps.

The widespread spinetails build complex covered structures of twigs and grasses, sometimes on or near the ground, sometimes high in trees. The castle-builders and firewood-gatherers build bulky nests of sticks that seem too big for these 6- to 8-inch birds to carry. The Red-fronted Thornbill builds a huge columnar, communal nest, usually around a bare branch high above the ground. Four or five pairs build the castle together, and each occupies a separate compartment within it. Other spinetails make rounded twig nests with pipe-like entrances at one side; some have complex entrances leading downward from the top. Still another group, the marsh inhabitants, builds domed nests of reeds plastered with mud.

Best known, and largely responsible for the family name, is the Rufous Ovenbird of southern Brazil, Paraguay, and Argentina, which Spanish Americans call *el hornero*, the baker. The baker is a drab 8-inch bird, rather thrush-like in aspect, that prefers open country. It is plentiful around houses and along roadsides. It walks about conspicuously in the open, but takes shelter in trees when disturbed.

The baker nests during the rainy season, from December to February, when mud is plentiful. Its domed, oven-like nests, usually about 12 inches long, 8 inches wide, and 10 inches high, are built of mud reinforced with grass and straw. The entrance hole near the bottom is separated from the nest chamber by an inner spiral threshold. The birds build these nests in the open on fence posts, bare limbs, and often on the eaves of houses. Strong and durable, the nests last for several years, and are often appropriated by swallows and other cavity nesters. The bakers build new nests each year.

ANTBIRDS

PASSERIFORMES   FORMICARIIDAE

Another tremendous family of primitive passerine birds limited in range to continental Central and South America is the bewildering array of antbirds. The family numbers 221 species divided among some 50 genera that range through the forests and scrublands from southern Mexico to Paraguay and northern Argentina. Their centre of abundance is in the rainforest jungles of the vast Amazon basin.

Like the ovenbirds, to which they seem most nearly related, the antbirds are small- to medium-sized birds ranging from 4 to 14 inches in length. They are rather dull-coloured and patterned inconspicuously, for the most part in drab browns, russets, greys, and blacks. Their front toes are slightly joined at the base, and their plumage is rather loose-webbed. Antbirds differ from the ovenbirds structurally in the manner of the scaling of their legs, and in having their beaks always hooked at the tip, strongly so in some genera. Also, male and female antbirds are usually unlike in colour, often markedly so, and

their nest construction is simpler and more uniform. A few antbirds build covered nests on the ground, a few line tree cavities, but most make open cup nests, occasionally on the ground, more often between the forks of a low branch.

Antbirds are largely forest dwellers, and most of them haunt the dark lower strata on or near the jungle floor, where, as their name implies, most are fairly intimately associated with ants. Some species, notably the antcatchers, live largely on ants and termites, but most antbirds follow the wandering columns of ants to feed on the insects and other small life the ants disturb. As the files of voracious army ants move inexorably through the jungle, everything able to move gets out of their way in a mad scramble for safety, throwing caution to the winds as though fleeing a forest fire. This makes very good hunting indeed for all avian insectivores, and the antbirds make a special practice of taking advantage of it. Individual antbirds of several species can usually be found harrowing the flanks of an active phalanx of army ants.

These loose bands that follow an ant column seldom contain more than one or two antbirds of any one species, for the antbirds are not as a rule gregarious. I have seen as many as six White-faced Antcatchers hunting together in the Guiana forests, but these birds may have been a family group which had not yet separated. This startlingly crested species, however, is reported to move about in small, tight flocks. Antbirds are weak fliers and none is migratory.

STRIATED EARTH-CREEPER
Upucerthia serrana
Peruvian Andes 8 in.

WHITE-FLANKED ANTWREN ♂
Myrmotherula axillaris
Honduras to Brazil   4 in.

WHITE-FACED ANTCATCHER
Pithys albifrons
Venezuela, the Guianas, Brazil   4½ in.

BLACK-SPOTTED BARE-EYE
Phlegopsis nigro-maculata
Central Brazil   7 in.

BARRED ANTSHRIKE ♂
Thamnophilus doliatus
Mexico to Argentina   6 in.

GREAT ANTSHRIKE ♂
Taraba major
Mexico to Argentina   8 in.

CHESTNUT-BACKED ANTBIRD
Myrmeciza exsul
Nicaragua to Ecuador   5½ in.

SCALED ANTPITTA
Grallaria guatimalensis
Mexico to Peru and Brazil   7½ in.

SPOTTED ANTBIRD
Hylophylax naevioides
Nicaragua to Ecuador   4½ in.

STREAK-CHESTED ANTPITTA
Grallaria perspicillata
Nicaragua to Ecuador   5½ in.

Few of the antbirds are conspicuous or distinctive enough to have earned well-established common names and, except for the commonest and best-known species, the names that have been manufactured for them have yet to be confirmed by usage. The more distinctive groups of antbirds are generally distinguished by the names of the types of birds they seem to resemble. The smallest of the antbirds, for instance, are commonly called antwrens, though to me they are wren-like only in size. The antwrens do scurry through the underbrush and are hard to see, but otherwise they are not wren-like in either appearance or actions.

A more aptly named group is the antvireos, slightly larger birds, 5 to 7 inches long, that work the lower branches of trees in vireo fashion and build vireo-like nests suspended between forked branches. A group of still larger species that feed both on the ground and in the brushy undergrowth are called antthrushes. Other fairly well-marked groups are the antcreepers, antshrikes, and antpittas. Those that fit into none of these handy categories retain the collective family name of antbird. One small genus of Brazilian antbirds with unfeathered facial patches is justly called the bare-eyes, and another with bright irises is known as the fire-eyes.

The antpittas are so distinctive they are sometimes given subfamily rank. These are stocky birds often the size of a quail or larger, with comparatively long legs, noticeably large heads, and short stubby tails. Like the Old World pittas, which they strongly resemble in everything but colour, the antpittas are shy, retiring birds of the forest floor and hard to observe. They have loud voices, and pairs are given to the common antbird habit of calling back and forth antiphonally to one another.

For birds with such primitive vocal organs—some have only a single pair of syrinx muscles—the antbirds are surprisingly vocal. Their calls are so distinctive that they are often more easily recognized than the birds themselves, which constantly stay hidden in the thick forest cover.

Perhaps the best known and most familiar of the family are the antshrikes, all of which have the bill strongly hooked and with a small tooth. All are somewhat shrike-like in their actions. One of the most widespread is the Barred Antshrike, found from Yucatan, where I first met it, southward to Bolivia. The male is strikingly barred in black and white, the female a plain dull brown. It is a noisy, active species that frequents roadside thickets and brushy tangles, and announces itself with a series of rapidly descending trilling calls. It also has quite a vocabulary of whines and chattering notes that it utters when disturbed.

The nesting habits of the Barred Antshrike have been well studied, and are apparently typical of most of the family. These birds build a simple cup nest in the branches fairly near the ground. Both sexes share all the duties of reproduction from nest building to caring for the young till they are on their own. Male and female alternate incubating at 1- to 2-hour intervals throughout the day, but the female takes the night shift alone. The normal clutch is 2 to 3 eggs, which are buffy white and lightly spotted. The incubation period is 15 to 16 days. The young hatch naked, but mature very rapidly and are usually able to leave the nest in from 8 to 11 days.

ANTPIPITS

PASSERIFORMES   CONOPOPHAGIDAE

The antpipits, also called gnateaters (the translation of their family name), are a poorly known group of 10 species in 2 genera found in the Amazon rainforests and adjoining Andes foothills. All are tiny birds, the largest only 5½ inches long, dressed in sombre browns and olive greens relieved in most species by a conspicuous white line over the eye.

Antpipits are smooth, sleek, stocky birds that, except for their small size and dull colours, resemble Old World pittas more than they do pipits. Like the pittas, they live on or close to the forest floor, and have comparatively large heads, long legs, and stout feet. Their feathers are soft and loose-webbed, those of the rump being very long and lax. Yet antpipits present a singularly well-groomed appearance, with never a feather ruffled or out of place. Short and rounded wings mark them as weak fliers. They are non-migratory.

Antpipits differ from antbirds in the shape of the bill which, though similarly hooked, is much broader and flattened, like that of a flycatcher. Structurally the antpipits are most closely allied to the tapaculos, with which they share the distinction of being the only passerine birds having the posterior end of the sternum with 4 instead of 2 notches.

While antpipits are neither overly timid nor shy, they are nowhere plentiful. They live in thick, impenetrable cover where they are hard to find and even harder to observe. Their voices consist of simple, unimpressive, rather sibilant call notes. One of the best-known species, the Black-cheeked Antpipit, makes a sucking noise. The Brazilians inelegantly call it "chupadenta," the toothsucker, or "cuspidor," the spitter.

Little is known of antpipits' breeding habits. The few nests that have been reported were simple cups of sticks and moss built on or close to the ground, containing buffy eggs with dark markings. Antpipit courtship, nest building, incubation, and care of the young have never been described.

BLACK-CHEEKED
GNATEATER
Conopophaga melanops
Eastern Brazil   4 in.

BLACK-BREASTED GNATEATER
Conopophaga melanogaster
Central Brazil and Bolivia   5½ in.

TAPACULOS

PASSERIFORMES RHINOCRYPTIDAE

When Charles Darwin encountered one of these birds in Chile during the *Beagle's* voyage in 1834 he wrote: "It is called *Tapacolo,* or 'cover your posterior'; and well does the shameless little bird deserve its name; for it carries its tail more than erect, that is, inclined backward toward its head." The perky little birds have earned other appropriate vernacular names. Argentinians call them "gallitos," the little cocks; one Chilean species is known as "el Turco," the Turk. Onomatopoeic names based on their distinctive calls include "huet-huet," "chucao," and "tococo" for the one Darwin wrote about.

The 26 species of tapaculos are terrestrial, non-migratory birds of dry grassy plains and scrublands or of the thick undergrowth of montane forests. They are most numerous in the temperate southern third of South America, where they inhabit dry and barren hillsides from Tierra del Fuego northward to southern Brazil. A few species have extended the family's range at higher elevations into southern Central America. The northernmost form, the Silver-fronted Tapaculo, lives in cloud forests and wet ravines 6,000 to 10,000 feet above sea level in western Panama and Costa Rica.

Stout-bodied little birds from 4½ to 10 inches long, tapaculos have large, strong legs and feet as befits ground-living species. Their rounded wings are short and weak, and as a group they are perhaps the poorest fliers of all the passerines, with the possible exception of the New Zealand wrens. They seldom flutter more than a few yards, and escape danger by running or hopping. The flying muscles of their breasts are rather flabby and underdeveloped compared to the strong, firm thigh muscles that power their legs.

The tapaculo's plumage is soft and loose.

The sexes are coloured alike in sombre browns and greys, often attractively barred and scalloped with reddish browns or black. Their closest relatives are the antpipits, with which they share a unique four-notched sternum, but they differ in the scaling of the tarsus, which more nearly resembles that of the antbirds. Tapaculos' nostrils are covered with a movable flap, or operculum, which may keep out dust during windstorms.

Tapaculos eat insects and some vegetable matter such as buds and seeds. Many of them scratch in the dirt or in the litter of the forest floor like chickens. They are active and inquisitive, and are experts at keeping out of sight. The brushland species, like the gallitos of Argentina, keep to shrubby cover and dart across open spaces with amazingly long strides. When surprised in the open they scurry into hiding like so many mice. The little 7-inch Brown Gallito is a fabulous runner, and takes 6-inch strides as it scurries in erratic zigzags out of the way of the intruder. Though most tapaculos run, the Chilean Turko hops. Darwin described it in the following manner: "With its tail erect, and stilt-like legs, it may be seen every now and then popping from one bush to another with uncommon quickness."

OCELLATED TAPACULO
Acropternis orthonyx
Andes, Venezuela
to Ecuador 8 in.

GREY GALLITO
Rhinocrypta lanceolata
Argentina, Paraguay 8 in.

The forest tapaculos are usually solitary, but those that live in open country often travel about in small flocks when they are not nesting. They are notably loud-voiced, with a repertoire of weird, harsh clucks, cackles, and gobbles.

The tapaculos' nesting habits are varied. Some forest species nest in rock crevices or in hollow tree trunks close to the ground. The Grey Gallito builds a bulky domed nest of grasses and bark with a side entrance, usually 2 or 3 feet up in a thick thornbush. The Brown Gallito, which the Argentinians call the "barrancolina," or little bank-dweller, digs a narrow 3-inch tunnel a foot or so into a bank, ending in a rounded chamber which the birds cushion with grass for their two white eggs. The Chilean Turko is also a tunnel nester.

Tapaculos' courtship and incubation have never been described, and little is known of the fledgling stages except that the hatchlings have a sparse down and are reared in the nest by both parents. Birds in their first juvenile plumage show conspicuous rusty bands.

COTINGAS

PASSERIFORMES   COTINGIDAE

This is a large and diverse family of New World primitive passerines. Among 90 species of some 30 genera are some of the gaudiest and most striking of all neotropical birds, as well as many that are drab and nondescript. Cotingas range in size from 3½ to 18 inches. Some are crested; some have brilliant patches of bare skin on the head; some have fleshy wattles or excrescences about the bill; and one group has a weird feathered lappet hanging from the throat. Despite their great variation in colour, size, and form, all cotingas are united by a combination of anatomical characteristics involving the peculiar structure of their vocal organs and of their legs and feet. They are most closely related to the manakins and to the tyrant flycatchers, which several of the smaller cotingas resemble in appearance and habits.

Cotingas are essentially solitary forest dwellers, usually encountered singly or in pairs, occasionally in small family groups with young. They occupy all types of woodland from the heaviest rainforests to the pine and oak cover of the highlands. Most live in the tree-tops or in the middle storeys of the jungle, a few in the brushy forest edges; one small group, the cocks-of-the-rock, is terrestrial.

Cotingas are most common in tropical forests along the Amazon and in southern Central America. From this centre representatives of the family have spread southward to Paraguay, Bolivia, and northern Argentina, and northward to the southern border of the United States. A single species, the Jamaican Becard, has secured a foothold in the highlands of Jamaica and is the only member of the family found in the West Indies.

"Cotinga" comes from the Amazon Indians' name for one of the more bizarre members of the family, the White Bellbird, and means literally "washed white." This bird of the deep forest, the Snowy Cotinga, and several other close relatives are among the very few white or mostly white tropical forest birds. White occurs sparingly in land birds, except in those of the snowy arctic regions, and its natural advantage, if any, to these birds of the dark tropical jungles has never been satisfactorily explained.

Many of the cotingas are almost as conspicuous in other bright, gay colours as the few white species. They exhibit lovely and unusual shades of reds, purples, and blues. These colours occur mainly in the males, the females' being drabber browns and greys. Unfortunately we know little of how the males use them in display, for most cotingas carry out their courtship in the privacy of the high leafy tree-tops.

The cotingas' unusual colours, particularly the violet shades, are not produced by a prismatic feather structure that refracts light, as are most such colours in birds, but by a true pigment within the feathers. This pigment has been isolated and is known as cotingin. An example of it is the lovely red lavender of the Pompadour Cotinga, which was named not for any peculiarity of its own but for the noted French courtesan who made the upswept hairdo famous. Madame de Pompadour set a fashion of elaborate coiffures adorned with ribbons, flowers, feathers, and even whole birds.

The first specimen of this unusual bird to reach Europe was in a shipment of bright-coloured bird skins sent to Madame de Pompadour for this purpose from French Guiana. The French ship carrying it from Cayenne was captured by the British, and George Edwards, the eccentric British naturalist and artist who first described and portrayed the bird, gallantly named it in honour of its intended recipient.

Edwards, and other 18th-century European naturalists who knew nothing of cotingas' habits and behaviour, called them "chatterers" from their fancied resemblance to waxwings. No name could be more unfitting. No cotinga can possibly be said to chatter and many are notably quiet. Some have faintly musical lisping subsongs; some make grunting, rumbling, un-bird-like sounds; a few utter shrill whistles. The notes of the bellbirds are loud, explosive metallic peals that carry half a mile or more through the jungle.

The four bellbirds are odd-looking, jay-sized fruit eaters. The White Bellbird has a peculiar erectile black spike sparsely covered with small white feathers growing from the base of its upper bill. The male Naked-throated Bellbird of southeastern Brazil is also pure white, but instead of the wattle has a verdigris throat and face, bare of feathers but covered with scattered bristles. The male Black-winged Bellbird of Trinidad, Venezuela, and the Guianas has thin fleshy wattles hanging from its throat. This bird's body is white, with the wings black and the head brown. The females of both these species are soft-olive-green birds with blended yellow markings. The Three-wattled Bellbird of Middle America has, as shown in the illustration on page 204, three pronounced wattles, and it displays with its mouth wide open.

Several cotingas show peculiar aberrant development of the wing feathers. One such is the curled coverts of the Pompadour Cotinga. Others have one or two of the outer primaries twisted or sharply narrowed. Whether these abnormalities are used for courtship display is uncertain.

Most singular of these anomalies in the cotingas are those of the crow-like umbrellabirds, so named for their crests of retractile feathers which they expand like a parasol when displaying. Each of these birds also has an inflatable lappet hanging from its throat. In the 16-inch Ornate Umbrellabird shown on page 205, the lappet is feathered and sometimes reaches 13 inches in length. In other forms, which are considered only subspecifically distinct, the lappet is shorter, and in one it is unfeathered and bright red. Little is known about how the umbrellabirds use these excrescences, for they are birds of the tree-tops and have been little studied. Like the bellbirds, they are fruit eaters.

Another group of tree-top-inhabiting, fruit-eating cotingas is the fruit-crows. The Crimson Fruit-crow, an 18-inch strawberry-coloured bird found in eastern Brazil and the Guianas, is the largest member of the family. The smaller 11-inch Purple-throated Fruit-crow ranges from Costa Rica southward through the Amazon region. Black with a patch of stiff, glossy maroon feathers on its throat, at a distance it resembles a stout, heavy-bodied jay.

Among the handsomest of the family are the two cocks-of-the-rock, the males of which are a bright orange in one species, a soft red in the other, while the females are a warm brown. Their outstanding feature is the large, flattened, disc-like crest extending from the top of the head to the tip of the bill. Terrestrial birds of the undergrowth and forest floor, the cocks-of-the-rock have stronger, heavier feet than other cotingas, and have a communal courtship dance reminiscent of the Sage Grouse's. Groups of up to a score of males and females gather in a forest clearing, and one male at a time goes through a series of hopping antics to show off before the females. Cock-of-the-rock nests are shallow mud cups reinforced with sticks and decorated with leaves. The few that have been found were on ledges near the mouths of sheltered caves near jungle streams.

A better-known group of cotingas is made up of the three tityras, the commonest being the Masked Tityra which occurs from Mexico to Brazil, not only in the rainforests but in drier areas with scattered trees. Though birds of the tree-tops, the tityras are frequently found in the open where they are easily observed. Small flocks or family parties rove through the woodlands in search of the fruits and berries that compose the greater part of their diet. They also eat quantities of insects, which they occasionally catch in flight but more often snatch from the foliage. Tityras are vaguely shrike-like in appearance, with sharply hooked bills, but they are chunkier, heavier-bodied, and have shorter necks and larger heads. In the bright tropical sunlight the light grey of the male tityras looks almost white, contrasting with the black marks on the wings and tail. The brown-backed female Masked Tityra lacks the male's black forehead, and her bare facial patches are not so red. Their voices are strange frog-like croakings.

Tityras invariably nest in high tree cavities, which they usually appropriate from other species. They drive away the owners, usually woodpeckers or toucans, by filling the hole with twigs and leaves in their absence. This they keep up until the rightful proprietors tire of cleaning away the mess and abandon the site. The only tityra nest ever examined (they are hard to reach, high up in precarious dead trunks) contained two buffy brown eggs heavily marbled with darker brown, almost buried in the leaf litter lining the cavity. Incubation is by the female alone. The male stands by to guard the hole during her frequent absences on feeding trips, and helps feed the young. The incubation period has never been determined, but the young remain in the nest 3 weeks or more. Tityras are multibrooded, and often lay a second clutch of eggs a few weeks after the first young leave the nest.

The 15 species of becards are found through most of the family's range. Becards are small dull-coloured birds 5 to 8 inches long with large heads and thick, slightly hooked beaks (hence their name). Blacks, greys, and brown predominate in their colouring, with the females always less imposing than their mates. The northernmost species, the Rose-throated Becard, nests from the Arizona and Texas border southward to Costa Rica.

Like most cotingas, the becards live mostly in the tree-tops, but occasionally forage at lower levels. They eat some berries and small fruits, but their diet is chiefly insects, which they capture both in flight and from the foliage. A favourite method of feeding is by hovering close to the leaves of outer branches and plucking caterpillars without alighting.

Becards build large, bulky nests of twigs and leaves, domed over the top, with the entrance at the side or through the bottom. They make no attempt to conceal these imposing structures, but usually build them in full view near the end of a branch at some height above the ground. They often build near nests of stinging wasps, a habit adopted by many tropical species, apparently for protection.

The female becard does most, if not all, the nest building. In some species the male brings nesting material. The clutch varies from 3 to 6 eggs, which are usually buff-coloured, variously marked with brown. Incubation, so far as we know, is entirely by the female, and takes 18 to 19 days in one of the smaller species, the 5½-inch White-winged Becard of Panama, one of the very few cotingas whose incubation period is known. The young are fed by both parents, almost entirely on insects, and remain in the nest 3 weeks or longer.

THREE-WATTLED BELLBIRD ♂
Procnias tricarunculata
Nicaragua to Panama 11½ in.

LOVELY COTINGA ♂
Cotinga amabilis
Mexico to Costa Rica 7½ in.

MASKED TITYRA ♂
Tityra semifasciata
Mexico to Brazil and Bolivia 8 in.

BLACK-NECKED RED COTINGA
Phoenicircus nigricollis
Northern Brazil 9 in.

MANAKINS

PASSERIFORMES   PIPRIDAE

The pert, bright-eyed, active, chubby manakins are among the most conspicuous small birds of American tropical and subtropical forests. The bright colours of the males, their constant activity, comparative tameness, and unusual songs make them more noticeable than many species just as common and several times their size. Residents of woodlands from southern Mexico to Paraguay and northern Argentina, their centre of abundance is Venezuela, the Guianas, and Brazil.

Unlike their nearest relatives, the cotingas, the 59 species of manakins form a fairly homogeneous group. All are tiny birds, most less than 5 inches long. The few that exceed 6 inches are no larger in body size, but have longer tails that add a few inches to their length. Typically their tails and wings are short, their legs and feet are slender, and their middle front toe is joined at the base to one or the other of

ORNATE UMBRELLABIRD ♂
Cephalopterus ornatus
Costa Rica to Brazil 16 in.

PERUVIAN COCK-OF-THE-ROCK ♂
Rupicola peruviana
Northern Andes, Colombia to Peru 12 in.

COCK-OF-THE-ROCK ♂
Rupicola rupicola
Guianas and
northern Brazil 12 in.

POMPADOUR COTINGA ♂
Xipholena punicea
Guianas and
northeastern Brazil 8 in.

CIRRHATE MANAKIN ♂
Teleonema filicauda
Venezuela and Colombia to Peru 5½ in.

PEARL-HEADED MANAKIN
Pipra iris
Northern Brazil 3½ in.

YELLOW-THIGHED MANAKIN
Pipra mentalis
Mexico to Ecuador 4½

its neighbours. The manakins' stubby beaks are broad at the base and pointed at the tip. The upper mandible overhangs the lower slightly, and has a small notch near the end.

In most manakins the sexes differ. The males have brilliant patches of red, yellow, or blue on the head, back, or thighs that contrast vividly with their brownish-green to velvety-black bodies. The females are all little olive-green birds that are likely to escape notice as they flit quietly through the forest. In one small relatively unstudied group, which may be misplaced in this family, the sexes are alike. This group includes the Thrush-like Manakin (*Schiffornis*), a rather shy and secretive reddish-brown bird that lives in forest undergrowth from Mexico to Brazil.

Manakins wander through the forest singly or in small bands. They feed on small berries and insects, and a few can usually be found in the mixed flocks of antbirds, tanagers, and other insect eaters that follow army-ant trains for the small animal life they panic out of hiding. Manakins seldom pick insects from the ground, but snatch those that climb into the foliage to escape the ants. They swallow small insects at once; larger ones they pound to pieces with their bills. Manakins show little fear of man, and go about their business near him as unconcerned as titmice.

The noises the manakins make include strange unbird-like sounds—sharp crackings like the snapping of a dry stick or a flag whipping in the wind, and odd mechanical raspings as though a nail were drawn across a comb. The call notes their primitive vocal organs produce are simple unobtrusive chirps and thin, high-pitched whistles. A few sing melodious, bell-like little songs of low intensity and short duration. Their spectacular noises are made mechanically with their wings. The flight feathers of most male manakins show peculiar modifications, apparently for this purpose. In the Yellow-thighed Manakin, the secondary wing feathers are enlarged, stiffened, and curved. In some species the outer primaries are narrowed at the tip; in a few they are twisted. The long-tailed species usually have the bases of the primaries curiously thickened. Just how the rattlings and buzzings are produced has yet to be demonstrated conclusively—whether by the wings striking each other, by the shafts vibrating together, or by air rushing between the feathers. When producing these sounds, the birds flutter their wings too rapidly for the eye to follow.

In several manakins whose breeding habits have been well studied the males are highly polygamous, and this pattern is apparently the rule in all the sexually dimorphic species. At the start of the breeding season (in January or February north of the equator), the males repair to a suitable part of the forest and establish individual display territories where they go through a highly intricate series of antics, calling attention to themselves by dancing about, flashing their bright colours, and making their loud noises. These dancing grounds may be isolated, but in some species a score or more males may have territories within the space of a few acres.

Gould's and Black-and-white manakins each establish display territories between two small saplings a few feet apart. Each bird cleans the jungle floor between them bare of all leaves and litter. At intervals the males flit back and forth between their two saplings, springing from one to the other and back again, buzzing and snapping with their wings at each flit. Male Yellow-thighed Manakins set up dancing territories higher in trees. Each picks a bare branch in an open spot in the foliage from which to execute its bouncing, snapping displays.

When a female approaches, the males increase their activity; each makes short buzzing flights to show his charms. When the female makes her choice there is no poaching, and no nearby males leave their territories. After copulating the female flies away as quietly as she came. The males remain on their territories throughout the breeding season, and each presumably serves as many females as he attracts.

Each female builds her nest, incubates her eggs, and rears her young by herself. She may build near the male's territory, or some distance from it. She weaves a frail little basket of grass and fibres between the forks of a horizontal branch from 5 to 75 feet above the ground, depending on the species. She lays two spotted eggs which she incubates for 19 to 21 days. She feeds the young by regurgitating insects and occasional berries carried to the nest in her throat. The young fledge in about 2 weeks. In juvenile plumage, young males resemble adult females. They retain this plumage most of their first year, and some come into breeding condition while still in it. This may account for reports of females taking an active part in the courtship dances.

206

TYRANT FLYCATCHERS

PASSERIFORMES   TYRANNIDAE

This large New World family of insect-eaters is the most aggressive and the most successful, biologically speaking, of the primitive passerine groups. Its 365 species are widely spread over the Americas from the tree limit across northern Canada southward to Patagonia. The Tyrannidae are most plentiful in tropical lowlands, where they probably originated, but they have spread into the temperate zones to occupy successfully almost every available ecological niche where insects are to be found. Almost all tyrant flycatchers are arboreal, except for a few terrestrial species in southern South America that hunt insects on the ground somewhat like pipits. These aberrant flycatchers have longer, stronger legs than the rest of the family, and are more gregarious.

Like all primitive passerines, tyrant flycatchers have a comparatively simple voice box. The partial joining of two of their front toes at the base and other similarities show their relationship to the cotingas and the manakins, with which they doubtless shared a common ancestor millions of years ago—in earliest Tertiary time if not earlier. Their superficial resemblances to many species of the large family of Old World flycatchers (p. 259) in appearance and habits are the result of convergent evolution. The Old World family consists of oscines that apparently arose at a later date from an unrelated parent stock on the other side of the world.

Most of the tyrants are plain-coloured birds, mainly olive-green, brown, and grey. The sexes are usually alike; only in a few bright-coloured species do the females differ markedly from the males. Despite their sombre garbs, the tyrants are conspicuous, for they are active, audacious, and often quite noisy. They like to forage in the open, where they are easy to see. Some of the smaller species are so alike that it is next to impossible to tell them apart in the field, but most are easy to recognize as members of the tyrant flycatcher family. Their peculiar upright perching stance is unmistakable.

Tyrant flycatchers range in size from 3½ to 16 inches, but typically they are medium to small birds less than 10 inches in length, with large heads and flattish beaks, which are strongly hooked in all the northern species, less so in some tropical forms. Most have prominent bristles at the base of the bills. Their wings are usually pointed, their tails rounded to shallowly forked—deeply forked in a few long-tailed species. Their legs and feet are small and weak.

In most of the family the crown feathers are more or less erectile. Many species have a distinct crest, often with a streak of bright red, yellow, or white feathers in the centre that may or may not be partly concealed. The birds use the crest both for display and intimidation, rais-

GREAT KISKADEE (DERBY FLYCATCHER)
Pitangus sulphuratus
South Texas to Argentina 9 in.

ACADIAN FLYCATCHER
Empidonax virescens
Eastern United States 6 in.

EASTERN WOOD PEWEE
Contopus virens
Eastern North America 6½ in.

NORTHERN ROYAL FLYCATCHER ♂
Onychorhynchus mexicanus
Mexico to Venezuela 6½ in.

VERMILION FLYCATCHER ♂
Pyrocephalus rubinus
Southwestern U.S. to Argentina   5½ in.

SCISSOR-TAILED FLYCATCHER
Muscivora forficata
South-central United States   15 in.

EASTERN KINGBIRD
Tyrannus tyrannus
Central and eastern North America   9 in.

GREAT CRESTED
FLYCATCHER
Myiarchus crinitus
Eastern North America   9 in.

EASTERN PHOEBE
Sayornis phoebe
Eastern North America   7

ing and expanding it to show the colour mostly in moments of stress. The crest reaches its greatest development in the little Royal Flycatcher, a resident of rainforests from Mexico to Brazil. Despite its flaming crown, the Royal Flycatcher is not conspicuous in the half-light of the lower and middle storeys of its tropical forest home. It keeps its crest lowered and its colours hidden except when excited.

Most flycatchers feed in a distinctive manner by capturing insects on the wing in short sallies from a prominent perch, where they sit quietly upright and alert until their quarry ventures within range. Then they dash out suddenly, snap their prey out of the air with an audible click of the bill, and return with it to their perch to eat at leisure. They often beat large insects loudly against their perch into bite-size pieces for swallowing. Insects are their mainstay, and they consume practically any and all kinds. Some of the smaller species hunt through trees like vireos or warblers, scouring the foliage for their prey. A number of tropical flycatchers supplement their diet with small berries. These genera usually have the rictal bristles poorly developed. The larger species, like the strong-beaked Boat-billed Flycatcher, pick up small reptiles and amphibians when they can, and the Derby Flycatcher has learned to catch fish.

Among the more conspicuous of the North American members of the family are the kingbirds of the nominate genus *Tyrannus*. Kingbirds are aptly named, for they are indeed monarchs who brook no intrusion into their nesting territories by birds many times their size. Typical of the group is the Eastern Kingbird, a bird common on roadsides east of the Mississippi which the Indians, who knew it well before the white man came, called "Little Chief." This 9-inch bundle of feathered ferocity is unmistakable with its dark back, white breast, and white-tipped tail. Concealed within its crest is a crown of orange which it flashes when courting or when angry. From its commanding perch on a fence, bush or telephone wire, the Kingbird dashes out fearlessly to harass every passing crow, hawk, or other large bird that dares trespass on its domain. Invariably the trespasser flees ignominiously, but the Kingbird keeps attacking until the interloper is well on his way. The Kingbird's fearlessness and audacity have made it a favourite with all who know birds— all except apiarists, who resentfully call it the "bee martin." Bee stings hold no terrors for the Kingbirds, and their inroads on hives of honeybees can be considerable.

Other North American flycatchers are less showy than the Kingbird in appearance as well as actions, and many lack conspicuous field marks. A number so closely resemble one another, particularly the little olive-green members of the genus *Empidonax,* that they are the despair of bird watchers. Three of these "empidonaces," the Least, the Acadian, and the Alder (or Traill's) flycatchers, can be told apart only with difficulty even from specimens in the hand. They are most easily recognized in the field by their distinctive calls, but this is little help when they are migrating in the autumn, for the birds are then quite silent. Skilled field observers often have to list migrants they see as *Empidonax,* sp?," meaning they are certain of the genus only, not the species.

Many of the flycatchers are exceedingly vocal, and their voices are so distinctive that a number have named themselves. The dull-coloured Wood Pewee of North American forests utters his plaintive "pee-a-wee" all day long until it actually gets tiresome. Another flycatcher that announces itself is the Phoebe, the pert olive-grey bird that plasters its mud and moss nest under bridges over country streams. The Pewee and the Phoebe usually call incessantly from a perch; the Kingbird utters its harsh grating chatter in flight.

In common with most insect-eaters that nest in temperate latitudes, all the North American flycatchers migrate southward when winter cuts down the food on which they depend. Phoebes winter in the Southern states and never go south of Mexico, but other northern flycatchers travel on to Central America and northern South America. Most are night migrants, but the Kingbirds travel by day in loose, widely scattered waves. A few of the flycatchers that breed in the high mountains of Central and South America migrate vertically, moving up and down the slopes with the seasons.

One of the few tyrants that migrates in flocks is the lovely Scissor-tailed Flycatcher, whose long, trailing, deeply forked tail makes it the longest (16 inches) of the family, though shorter species surpass it in body size. The Scissor-tail breeds in the open lands of the south-central United States and is a conspicuous inhabitant of the Texas plains, where it sits quietly on telephone wires and trees along the roadsides, a trim symphony in pastel pink and grey, with its long tail closed and hanging straight down. Its flight in pursuit of prey or when chasing an intruder from its guarded preserve is dashing and swift with rapidly fluttering wings, tail streaming straight behind. The Scissor-tail is also fond of performing acrobatics high in the air, flying in erratic zigzags with abrupt

sharp turns facilitated by pivoting on its widely spread tail. It winters from Mexico to Panama, travelling by daylight and often in sizeable flocks.

The most brightly coloured member of the family is the fiery male Vermilion Flycatcher, resident from southwestern United States southward through Central and South America to Argentina. Strangely, this brilliant little bird has never got to the West Indies, but is well established on most of the Galapagos Islands 500 miles out in the Pacific west of Ecuador. It is one of the few flycatchers that show strong sexual dimorphism, the female being a dull brownish grey.

Among the many distinctive tropical species, one of the most familiar is the large, stout-bodied, brown and yellow Derby Flycatcher, widely known as the Kiskadee from its rasping cry, paraphrased as "kiss-me-dear" by the romantic, as *bem-te-vi* (I see thee well) by the Brazilian Portuguese, and as *bien-te-veo* by Spanish-speaking peoples. The Kiskadee is a noisy, conspicuous busybody found from southern Texas to Argentina in semi-open lands, and is common almost wherever there are trees. Though essentially insectivorous, the Kiskadee also frequents mangroves and other riverside vegetation in the tidelands, where it has acquired an un-flycatcher-like habit—it fishes like a kingfisher, splashing boldly into the water for small fish.

The nesting habits of flycatchers are considerably varied. Typically they weave open, cup-shaped nests of grasses and twigs in trees. The Phoebe builds a mud base for its nest of moss under a streamside ledge or under bridge rafters. Many tropical species make large purse-shaped or domed nests with an entrance at the side or in the bottom. Some of the Brazilian and Argentinian species appropriate the mud-and-stick nests built by ovenbirds. Not a few species are cavity nesters, like the Great Crested Flycatcher of eastern North America which stuffs its untidy nest into old woodpecker holes, bird boxes, open-ended mail boxes, or even into the metal receptacles put up for the daily paper along rural roads.

The Crested Flycatcher's fondness for decorating its nest with cast-off snakeskins has provoked much speculation. The oft-proposed theory that the birds use pieces of snakeskin consciously as a protective measure to frighten predators is hardly tenable. Its use is probably fortuitous, as a convenient material of desirable consistency. Pieces of cellophane and waxed paper occur just as frequently in the nests. Unquestionably protective, however, is the common flycatcher habit of building their nests near those of wasps.

The eggs of different species of flycatchers also show considerable variation. Some are pure white; others are spotted or streaked. Clutches vary from 2 to 6 and are usually smaller in tropical species, many of which maintain their numbers by nesting several times instead of once per year as do most temperate zone species, though these also are sometimes multi-brooded.

While both sexes co-operate in nest building, the usual pattern in flycatchers is for the female alone to incubate. Rarely does the male assist in this duty, though he always helps feed the nestlings. The incubation period varies from 12 days in the smallest species to 21 days in some of the larger ones, and the young remain in the nest for a roughly equal length of time before taking flight.

PLANTCUTTERS

PASSERIFORMES   PHYTOTOMIDAE

In temperate South America, from western Peru southward to Patagonia, live three species of plump, finch-like birds that look so much like grosbeaks they were for many years thought to be sparrows. Their syrinx muscles and their foot structure, however, show them to be related to the cotingas, from which they differ mainly in the arrangement of their thigh muscles and in their finch-like conical bills, which are short, strong, and finely sawtoothed.

Each of the three plantcutters is about 7 inches in length. The sexes differ in colour. Best known and most widespread is the Reddish Plantcutter of Argentina, Uruguay, and Bolivia. The female is brownish and sparrow-like. The Peruvian Plantcutter, isolated along the dry northwest coast of Peru, has less red in its plumage; the Chilean species is grey.

Plantcutters live in open woodlands, dry brushy country, and in cultivated regions. They earn their name by their gross manner of feeding; they clip off leaves, buds, fruits, and shoots, and sever small plants at the base, wasting far more than they eat. In farming country, particularly in Chile, they are reported occasionally so destructive to crops and gardens that control measures are necessary. Plantcutters are often tame and fearless, and permit a close approach as they perch quiet and upright on top of a bush. When disturbed they seldom fly far, but take cover in nearby foliage. Their flight is weak and undulating and seldom prolonged. They flutter their short, pointed wings rapidly enough in flight to produce an audible whirring.

Plantcutters often gather in small, loose flocks that move erratically about the countryside when the breeding season is over, and show some seasonal movement in shifting their feeding grounds. Their harsh and unmusical calls have been likened to the squeaking of tree limbs rubbing together, to the croaking of frogs, and to the bleatings of lambs.

Plantcutters build open round nests of twigs lined with finer vegetable fibres. The Chilean Plantcutter nests fairly high in trees; the Reddish Plantcutter usually nests closer to the ground, often in the sanctuary of a thorn bush. The clutch is 2 to 4 bluish-green eggs spotted with dark brown. Incubation is by the female alone; care of the young is by both sexes.

SHARPBILLS

PASSERIFORMES   OXYRUNCIDAE

Little is known about the sharpbills beyond what the few scattered museum specimens reveal. They have been collected in six countries: Costa Rica, Panama, Venezuela, British Guiana, southeastern Brazil, and Paraguay. Nowhere are they plentiful, and each known population seems to be extremely localized.

The Brazilian and Paraguayan groups live in lowland rain-forests 3,000 feet or so above sea level. Specimens from the six widely scattered localities differ slightly in size (6½ to 7 inches) and in the yellow to white shading of their underparts. All are regarded as geographical representatives of a single species which was probably more widespread and of continuous distribution in the distant past.

The sharpbills have no close relatives and their systematic position is uncertain. Anatomically they seem closest to the tyrant flycatchers, for they have the same type of syrinx muscles and foot structure. The partly concealed bright-red median crest (usually paler in females) is strongly reminiscent of that of many of the tyrants, but sharpbills' legs and toes are stouter and stronger. They differ markedly from the tyrants in their straight, sharp-pointed, unhooked bills, which are uniquely rimmed at the base with short, fine, bristly feathers instead of with rictal bristles. Their nostrils are covered by an opercular flap, and are elongated instead of round. Pending further research that may show their affinities more clearly, most students place them in a family by themselves.

No one has observed sharpbills enough in life to describe their habits and behaviour. They are apparently solitary birds; at least, flocks have never been reported. They are known to eat fruit. Their actions in the field reminded one collector of those of the Old World wrynecks; others who have seen them report that they act like cotingas or tanagers. Their breeding habits are unknown and their nests and eggs have never been described.

CRESTED SHARPBILL
Oxyruncus cristatus
Costa Rica to Paraguay 7 in.

REDDISH PLANTCUTTER ♂
Phytotoma rutila
Bolivia, Paraguay,
Uruguay, Argentina 7 in.

STEERE'S PITTA
Pitta steerii
Philippines 8 in.

GARNET PITTA
Pitta granatina
Malaya, Sumatra, Borneo 6½ in.

PITTAS

PASSERIFORMES   PITTIDAE

Plump-bodied small birds from 6 to 11 inches in length, pittas have stout, slightly down-curved bills, large heads, short necks, short rounded wings, and rather long, strong legs and feet. Their most distinctive feature, other than the variegated gay colouring of their loose-webbed plumage, is their abnormally short, stumpy tails. These have degenerated in some species to mere tufts of short, stiff feathers. A few species have a crest or ear tufts. In each species the sexes are similarly coloured in a gaudy assortment of contrasting patches that includes almost the entire spectrum from greens to purples, reds, and yellows. The females are usually duller than the males.

Technically the pittas are a distinctive and closely knit group, so close that all 23 recognized species are placed in the single genus *Pitta*. Their centre of distribution is southeastern Asia and adjacent Malaysia. A single species, the Blue-winged, or Fairy, Pitta, ranges from northern India across China to southern Japan. Others are found eastward to the Philippines and to the Solomons and southward to Australia, where three species occur. Two species are isolated in eastern and central Africa. Many of the tropical pittas are of extremely limited distribution. One of the most beautiful, Steere's Pitta, lives only in the mossy undergrowth of the wet mountain forests of three of the Philippine Islands.

The pittas have no close relatives, and their affinities to other existing families are uncertain. Their primitive syrinx structure is responsible for their placement in the suborder Tyranni, to whose New World members they show no other close ties. Their homogeneity as a group and their disrupted distribution suggest the living pittas are the surviving representatives of a primitive stock of forest-inhabiting birds formerly more widely distributed over the Old World tropics.

The pittas' bright hues are seldom seen to best advantage in the dim light of their usual habitat, the floor and lower stories of wet, tropical forests. These solitary birds stay in the thickest cover, where they are hard to see. When ap-

proached they scurry away through the underbrush like some rodent. When pittas do fly, they fly straight and fast with rapid wingbeats. Many are migratory. Those that nest in temperate China, Japan, and Australia winter in the tropics, and several of the tropical forms are believed to move to fresh feeding grounds in the nonbreeding season.

Pittas feed entirely on insects and other small animal life. Some species live largely on termites, others on millepedes. The Noisy Pitta, whose showy colours have earned it the name of "dragoon bird" in Australia, is fond of slugs and land snails, and usually has a particular stump or stone within its territory that it uses for cracking open their shells.

Though the pittas feed and spend most of their days on the ground, they roost in trees at night, and usually hop up into the branches when calling. Their call notes are loud double- or triple-noted whistles of considerable carrying power, but so ventriloquial they are difficult to trace to their source. Some pittas call to one another across the jungle on moonlight nights; others make peculiar grunting noises. The African species make whirring and rattling sounds, apparently with their wings, in short courtship flights.

Pittas build large globular nests, loosely put together of twigs and vegetable fibres, with an entrance on the side. The nest is usually on or near the ground, often in a thorny bush, but may be as high as 30 feet up a tree.

Pitta eggs are almost round, highly glossed, white to buffy in colour, and covered with flecks of dark brown. The normal clutch is 4 to 6, though as few as 2 and as many as 7 eggs have been reported. Both parents incubate and care for the altricial young, but the length of the incubation period has not been determined accurately. The northern species breed from May to August; those south of the equator in Africa and Australia breed in the southern summer, from November to February. The oriental tropical species tend to nest during the rainy season from February to April, probably because their insect food is then most plentiful.

NEW ZEALAND WRENS

PASSERIFORMES   ACANTHISITTIDAE

BUSH WREN
Xenicus longipes
New Zealand   3½ in.

Four species of tiny, insect-eating New Zealand birds constitute this family. Three are 4-inch brownish, wren-like birds (*Xenicus*) that scurry with their tails cocked up through the underbrush or on rocky ground. The fourth (*Acanthisitta*) is the 3-inch, yellowish-green Rifleman, New Zealand's smallest bird, a creeper-like inhabitant of deep forests.

The Rifleman is still fairly common, though limited to the beech forests. The Bush Wren and Rock Wren are now rare, having suffered from such introduced predators as stoats, rats, and cats. The Stephen Island Wren is extinct. It had probably the most limited range of any known bird—a wooded islet scarcely a mile in area in Cook Strait.

The extant species are weak fliers. The most capable of the three, the Rock Wren, is able to flutter only a hundred feet or so. Their primitive vocal organs produce simple nasal chirps, calls, and alarm notes, but no true song. All three build covered nests with side entrances, the Rifleman in tree cavities, the two wrens in hollow logs or stumps, rock crevices, or holes in the ground. Their clutches range from 2 to

5 pure-white eggs, and both sexes share the nesting chores.

The affinities of these distinctive tiny birds are uncertain, but they show similarities in structure and behaviour to the pittas. They probably evolved from some remote pitta-like ancestor that became isolated in New Zealand long ago.

ASITIES AND FALSE SUNBIRDS

PASSERIFORMES   PHILEPITTIDAE

In the forests of Madagascar live four little-known small birds that are evidently the sole survivors of some primitive passerine stock that has long since vanished elsewhere in the world. Though quite different in build and habits, the two asities (*Philepitta*) and two false sunbirds (*Neodrepanis*) share anatomical characteristics that suggest they evolved from the same ancestor.

WATTLED
FALSE SUNBIRD
Neodrepanis coruscans
Eastern Madagascar   3½ in.

VELVET ASITY
Philepitta castanea
Eastern Madagascar   6½ in.

The asities are plump, stout-legged, completely arboreal birds that vaguely resemble pittas. The commoner Velvet Asity inhabits the humid forests on the eastern slopes from sea level to 5,000 feet. It is reported as a quiet, stolid bird, that allows a close approach. It works rather sluggishly through the middle storeys and brushy ground cover of the forest in search of fruits and berries, usually alone, sometimes in small parties of two or three. Its voice is seldom heard, but it has a soft, thrush-like song. The only member of the family whose nesting is known, the Velvet Asity weaves a hanging, pear-shaped nest of mosses and palm fibres, lined with dead leaves. The side entrance is sheltered by a small portico. The one clutch reported contained three white eggs. On the western side of Madagascar lives Schlegel's Asity, a smaller and more brightly coloured bird.

Sharing the wet forests of the eastern slopes with the Velvet Asity is the Wattled False Sunbird, a much smaller and very different species, with small, weak legs and a long curved bill. So closely does it resemble the true sunbirds (p. 278) that for years it was classified as one until anatomical studies showed its true affinities. It lives and feeds exactly as do the sunbirds, dipping into flowers to sip nectar and pick up small insects. Like the asities, it is a solitary bird, and, though reportedly not uncommon, seldom are more than two or three seen together. Its call is a soft hissing note. The second false sunbird, the Small-billed Neodrepanis, is known from seven specimens taken in the forests of northeastern Madagascar. It is a small, inconspicuous bird, apparently easily overlooked and, like all the unique Madagascar fauna, in danger of extinction as its forest habitat disappears.

LYREBIRDS

PASSERIFORMES   MENURIDAE

Not the least of the marvels of Australia, that continent of many zoological and botanical anomalies, are the wonderful lyrebirds, so named from the tail of the male Superb Lyrebird. Two species constitute the family, the Superb and the slightly smaller Albert's Lyrebird, named for Prince Albert, Queen Victoria's consort. Brown-backed, ashy-bellied birds the size of a rooster with elongated pointed bills, longish necks, large, strong legs and feet, and fantastic long tails, the first lyrebirds to reach Europe at the close of the 18th century were thought to be pheasants by the naturalists who studied them.

Much later, when their anatomy was studied, the lyrebirds were found to have an oscine type of syrinx, but with only 3 pairs of muscles instead of the oscine's 5 to 7. Other anatomical peculiarities include their long, narrow breastbone, which resembles that of most water birds rather than the short, squarish passerine type, a tail of 16 feathers instead of the usual 12, and 6 feathers on the thumb joint, or alula, instead of the usual 3 or 4. To show their anomalous systematic position, the lyrebirds are placed with the order Passeriformes, but in a suborder of their own, the Menurae, together with the distantly related Australian scrub-birds.

The Superb Lyrebird is widely familiar through its symbolic use on Australian seals and stamps. The traditional posture of the bird as pictured on postage stamps and in books, with the tail erect and partly spread into a perfect lyre, has caused Australian ornithologists some embarrassment because it is not typical, though it occurs momentarily during the courtship display.

The frame of the lyre is formed by the outer pair of the male Superb's tail feathers, which are almost 2 feet long and gracefully curved and banded. The next six pairs of quills form the strings; these are brown above and almost white below and, lacking barbules to hold the vanes together, are lacy in texture. The central pair of feathers are long and narrow and lack the outside web; they cross one another just behind their insertion and sweep out gracefully to opposite tips of the lyre. The male Albert's Lyrebird is a redder brown and its fanciful tail lacks the lyre frame. Its central tail feathers are like the Superb's but all the other seven pairs are lacy quills. The females of both species are coloured similarly to the males, but have ordinary tails. Young males resemble the females, and do not develop their distinctive tail plumes until they are about 3 years old.

Both species are residents of the forests and scrublands of eastern Australia, Albert's being the more northerly of the two. They are shy, solitary birds that reportedly keep to thick cover. Largely terrestrial, they seldom fly, but run and leap with great speed through the underbrush. When they do fly they usually glide for considerable distances. At night they roost in the branches of tall trees. Their food is reported as almost entirely animal—insects, worms, land crustaceans, and molluscs which they obtain by scratching like fowl among the leaf litter and by tearing rotten logs apart.

Most famous of the lyrebirds' attributes is their extraordinary skill as mimics. They are credited as being the most ac-

SUPERB LYREBIRD ♂
Menura novaehollandiae
Southeastern Australia   38 in.

complished of all birds in this respect, and connoisseurs regard Albert's as the better imitator. While they have distinctive notes of their own, such as the Superb's resounding "choo! choo! choo!" usually heard at dawn, they can reproduce practically all other sounds they hear with fantastic accuracy, especially the calls and songs of other birds. Lyrebirds also copy the cries of animals and mechanical noises—the neighing of a horse, the bleating of sheep, the barking of dogs, the whine of a saw, the sounds of vehicle horns and motors—in fact anything they hear that strikes their fancy.

Male lyrebirds are thought to be polygynous, for they take no part in nest-building, incubation, or rearing of the young. Each male establishes a large territory for himself, sometimes half a mile or so in extent, within which he tolerates no other males. Within this area he establishes a series of perhaps a dozen display grounds, which he visits in turn throughout the day to perform his magnificent courtship antics. The Superb Lyrebird rakes damp soil into mounds about 3 feet across on which he dances; Albert's Lyrebird scrapes out shallow craters about 2½ feet in diameter.

Climbing his mound or entering his scrape, the displaying male starts his performance vocally, and he chortles and bubbles and sings from his extensive repertoire throughout the action. After a few moments of singing he unlimbers his tail, slowly expands it, and raises it up and forward over his back until its shimmering silvery cascade covers him completely, the lacy feather tips touching the ground in front of his lowered head. This is the climax of the display. He ends it suddenly with a few high-pitched notes, folds his tail to its normal position, and stalks away.

The female spends about a month building her nest. On or near the ground, often between two trees, in a hollow stump, or within the crown fronds of a leaning tree fern, she builds a bulky domed structure with a side entrance. Its exterior of sticks, dry fern fronds, moss, and bark has an inner wall woven of rootlets and bark fibres. She lines her nest with long downy feathers she plucks from her back and thighs. A week or so after the nest is finished, she lays her single egg, and she may wait another week before she starts incubating.

The lyrebird egg is dark grey with inky markings, and is the largest laid by any passerine bird. Also the incubation period is the longest reported for any passerine. A lyrebird egg was hatched under a domestic hen in 28 days, but in the wild, lyrebirds are reported to incubate 35 to 40 days. The chick hatches almost naked, but soon grows a covering of long black down. It is raised in the nest in typical passerine fashion, and grows so large before leaving that toward the end of the rearing period it sometimes pokes its head through the domed roof to be fed.

SCRUB-BIRDS

PASSERIFORMES ATRICHORNITHIDAE

Allied to the lyrebirds and apparently stemming from some common ancestral stock are the two Australian scrub-birds. Little is known of these shy, skulking, brownish birds, somewhat wren-like in appearance and actions. The larger of the two, the 8½-inch Noisy Scrub-bird of the brushlands of Southwestern Australia was thought to be extinct. Only about 20 museum specimens existed, the last having been taken in 1889. In 1960 it was found to be still extant. The slightly smaller Rufous Scrub-bird still persists in small numbers in the subtropical coastal scrublands of eastern Australia. Observers claim it is almost flightless; it flutters feebly for short distances, but can scuttle speedily on ground through the tangled vines and underbrush.

Scrub-birds show affinities to the lyrebirds in having the same oscine type of syrinx, but powered by only two pairs of muscles. Also they have large, strong legs and feet, and scratch the ground for snails, worms, insects, and occasional seeds. Their chief anatomical distinction, probably connected with their weak flight, is their greatly reduced clavicles. They are the only passerine birds in which these two bones are not fused to form a wishbone. The sexes are unlike, the females being duller and smaller.

Scrub-birds further resemble the lyrebirds in vocal powers. They are said to be accomplished mimics, and are famed for their loud and penetrating calls. Those of the male Noisy Scrub-bird are so shrill, one listener reported, "as to produce a ringing sensation in the ears, precisely the effect produced when a shrill whistle is blown in a small room."

The Rufous Scrub-bird builds a miniature version of the lyrebird's domed nest on or close to the ground. Loosely woven of dried grasses and dead leaves, it is lined uniquely with a peculiar tough substance resembling rough cardboard. The birds gather soft decayed wood and plaster it when wet around the inside of the nest. The usual clutch is two pinkish-white eggs speckled with brownish-red. Little is known of their breeding behaviour other than that the female alone incubates and rears the young in the nest.

Reduction of habitat and introduced predators are largely responsible for the scrub-birds' rarity. Much of the present range of the Rufous Scrub-bird lies within the boundaries of Lamington National Park, where the bird's chances of survival should be good.

RUFOUS SCRUB-BIRD
Atrichornis rufescens
Eastern Australia 7 in.

LARKS

PASSERIFORMES   ALAUDIDAE

Small, dull-coloured terrestrial birds famous for their inspired song flights, the larks are essentially an Old World group. The family is well represented across Eurasia from the tundra southward, but is best developed in Africa where almost two-thirds of the world's 75 species occur. Two species have pushed southeastward to northern Australia, and a single species, the Horned Lark, has invaded the New World. Readily recognized by its black ear tufts, the Horned Lark breeds circumpolarly in the arctic tundra, southward in the Old World to North Africa, and throughout most of North America to southern Mexico. One isolated population of Horned Larks has established itself in the savannahs of the Colombian highlands in South America.

Larks form one of the most distinctive and well-defined of all the passerine families. They differ from all other perching birds in that the back of the tarsus is rounded and scaled instead of sharp and unsegmented. This suggests early differentiation of the family from other passerine stock and, added to certain primitive features of their five-muscled syrinx, places them at or near the base of the oscine family tree—as primitive true singing passerines. The larks' long, pointed wings have 10 primary feathers, but the outermost one is very short, almost obsolete in some genera. The long straight claw on the hind toe, a feature shared with the pipits and wagtails, is another identifying characteristic.

Despite their diversity—the 75 species are divided among 15 genera—the larks are quite uniform in general appearance, in habitat, and in habits. Small birds, from 5 to 9 inches in length, most of them are sombrely clad in streaked browns and greys, darker above than below. All have pointed, slightly down-curved bills and most have crested or tufted heads. Except in the Black Lark of northern Eurasia and the finch-larks (*Eremopterix*) of Africa and India, the two sexes are quite similar; the females are sometimes duller and slightly smaller than the males. Some widely distributed larks show minor colour or size differences between geographically separated populations. In the widespread Horned Lark, for instance, 15 such subspecies, as these recognizable populations within a species are called, are known in the Old World, 26 in the New.

Most larks live in open country, on grassy plains, treeless moors, cultivated fields, deserts, or beaches. Save for a few species, such as the bush larks that habitually alight on low bushes or posts, they usually dwell on the ground, where they walk or run instead of hopping. They are so well camouflaged that they are not always easy to see until they fly, and usually allow a close approach before they flush. Their diet is almost equally animal and vegetable and encompasses insects and their pupae and larvae, seeds, and other plant material. Larks are generally gregarious, and gather in flocks when not breeding. Most of them are migratory to a degree. Some perform lengthy flights between breeding and wintering grounds.

Larks are renowned as songsters the world over. The spectacular song flight of the courting male Skylark is one of the most beautiful of natural sounds. The Skylark is small, drab, and unpretentious, but his music belies his looks. This is the bird that has inspired so many poets—Shelley, Wordsworth, and Tennyson among them. To know why, you should meet your first one as I did one spring morning in a lonely wheat field. Suddenly a small brown bird whisks from the ground at your feet and spirals swiftly high into the air, showering the countryside with his rippling, bubbling melody.

The "blithe spirit" of Shelley's verse nests across Eurasia from the British Isles to Kamchatka and from northern Siberia southward to India and North Africa. Europeans so love the Skylark they have carried it with them to many other parts of the world. It has been introduced successfully to New Zealand and the Hawaiian Islands. A colony established on Long Island, New York, in the 1880's persisted for a time but gradually died out and has not been reported since 1913. Skylarks introduced to Vancouver Island off British Columbia have fared better and are still thriving.

Despite high sentimental regard for them as songsters, larks were at one time a great table delicacy. It takes many of the tiny birds to make a meal, but they are still shot and netted for food in some countries. Such occasional persecution has not seemed to affect their numbers. The forest clearing and field cultivation that accompany human expansion encourage their increase, and larks are quick to expand into new territory where the habitat becomes suitable for them.

Most larks build open, cup-shaped nests on the ground and lay from 2 to 6 speckled white eggs. Exceptions are the bush larks of the genus *Mirafra*, which build domed nests. Incubation is predominantly, if not exclusively, by the female. She builds the nest alone, too, but the male stands by and encourages her with his courtship song flights. He brings her food during the 11 to 12 days she incubates, and helps feed the young for the 10 to 12 days it takes them to fledge. Larks typically rear two or more broods each year.

HORNED (SHORE) LARK
Eremophila alpestris
Eurasia, North Africa,
North America, Mexico,
Colombia   6½-7 in.

SKYLARK
Alauda arvensis
Temperate Eurasia,
n. Africa   7 in.

SWALLOW
(BARN SWALLOW)
Hirundo rustica
Holarctic; Eurasia, North America 7½ in.

TREE SWALLOW
Iridoprocne bicolor
Temperate North America 5½ in.

CLIFF SWALLOW
Petrochelidon pyrrhonota
Canada to central Mexico 6 in.

ROUGH-WINGED SWALLOW
Stelgidopteryx ruficollis
Southern Canada to Argentina 5½ in.

SWALLOWS AND MARTINS

PASSERIFORMES   HIRUNDINIDAE

No group of birds is more loved by people throughout the world than the swallows and martins. Nearly cosmopolitan in distribution, the family is absent only from the polar regions and a few oceanic islands. "Swallow" goes back to the Old Norse "svalva," and Anglo-Saxon "swalewe." "Martin" is of more recent medieval etymology, but was well established in heraldry. The terms swallow and martin are used somewhat interchangeably today. Americans restrict martin to some of the larger species, but Europeans apply it to a number of the smaller birds which Americans call swallows. The usage seems largely fortuitous, but swallow is more widely used for the family.

Swallows are often confused with the swifts, but are not related to them. Though the two groups resemble each other superficially, they differ widely in anatomy and their similarities are "analogous rather than affinitive," the result of convergent evolution in two discrete stocks that have become adapted to the same ways of living. Though not as thoroughly aerial as swifts, swallows probably spend more of their waking hours on the wing than any other passerine birds.

In the hand swallows can be told at once by their 12-feathered tail (swifts have only 10 rectrices), and by the presence of facial bristles which swifts lack. Swallows have a less speedy and (usually) more erratic flight. Their longer tails are often forked, their bodies less cigar-shaped, and the leading edge of their wings is less smoothly curved.

Otherwise there is no mistaking a swallow or martin. Small birds 4 to 9 inches long, their bodies are slender and sleek, their wings long and pointed. Their plumage is compact, often

with some metallic sheen, usually darker above than below. Their legs are short, their feet small and weak. Their tiny triangular bills belie their wide gape, made more effective by bristles which act as an aerial fly scoop.

Though the swallows have their primary feathers reduced from 10 to 9, an indication of high specialization, they are placed low in the passerine family tree because of certain primitive structural features, notably the incomplete development of their bronchial rings. Swallows are indeed highly specialized and peculiarly adapted to an aerial life. They show no close ties with any other avian group. Apparently the family branched off long ago, probably from some primitive perching, insect-eating stock, but just what stock and in what part of the Eocene world is anyone's guess. The 79 living species, in some 20 genera, are scattered so widely and so evenly throughout the world that their distribution affords no clue to their probable place of origin.

Swallows spend much of their time on the wing hawking back and forth for insects. They are exceedingly graceful and among the most accomplished of all fliers, but they are no match for the swifts in speed, and generally do not fly as high. Also unlike the swifts, which alight seldom during the day and then only on vertical surfaces, the swallows perch readily on twigs, branches, wires, and roofs. The only time they are normally seen on the ground is when gathering nesting material. They walk short distances with difficulty and have an awkward shuffling gait.

Swallows are widely beloved because of their value as insect eaters and because they are common, friendly, and attractive birds. While they are not accomplished songsters, they twitter cheerfully and chatter to one another both in flight and at rest. They show little fear of man and nest on and about his dwellings. Not least of the reasons for their popularity in temperate climes both north and south is their age-old reputation as harbingers of spring.

Few signs of spring are more certain than the appearance of flocks of swallows. As swallows migrate by day and must feed as they travel, their northward advance requires the presence of insects in the air, which in turn depends on warm weather. The swallows' northward migrations coincide nicely with the northward movement of the isotherms that, plotted fortnightly, tell the weatherman spring is on the way. The Swallow usually follows close on the heels of the 48° F. isotherm. One or two hardy individuals often arrive ahead of the main flocks before spring has really settled in and suffer from late freezes, proving the old adage that "one swallow doth not a summer make."

As the swallows' northward movement is governed largely by the weather, it is equally uncertain, and careful records show their arrival dates vary from spring to spring by as much as 2 weeks, which is the normal spread of the isotherm advance. There is a legend that the swallows return to the Mission San Juan de Capistrano in California infallibly on the same day each spring which is a charming folk tale, but like many such tales isn't quite true. The Cliff Swallows do come to Capistrano faithfully enough each spring to nest, but their actual arrival dates are as variable as those elsewhere.

One of the most familiar and widespread members of the family is the bird known in Britain just as the Swallow. The French and Germans refer to it as the Chimney Swallow, and the Americans, Dutch and Norwegians call it the Barn Swallow. It breeds throughout the North Temperate Zone, in both North America and Eurasia. North American Barn Swallows are slightly smaller than the European subspecies; their underparts are usually washed with brown, and the dark band across the chest has a break in its centre. North American Barn Swallows winter in South America; the European subspecies travel to Africa, and the Asiatic populations mi-

grate to Malaya and the Philippines. Close relatives of the Barn Swallow are resident in the Old World tropics; some nest in the South Temperate Zone and winter northward, among them the Welcome Swallow of Australia.

Throughout their extensive range the Barn Swallows and their kin (the genus *Hirundo*) nest in close association with man, and have done so since the dawn of history. Written records of them go back to early Greek civilization. In North America, they favour barns and sheds, as their name implies, and plaster their open cup of mud to the top or sides of rough-hewn rafters. European birds pick similar sites in outbuildings. In Korea and Japan a swallow nesting on one's house is a sign of good luck, and the rice farmers encourage the birds by nailing small shelves for them under the eaves of their thatched roofs. The spread of man has doubtless increased the population of these swallows by providing nesting sites where none existed previously. Before man built houses and barns, the Swallows apparently nested on cliff ledges or on sheltered tree branches, where very few still nest today.

Swallows show strong faithfulness to their nesting territory and return year after year to the same site, often to the same nest. Occasionally they renovate the old nest; more often they build a completely new one near it. Both sexes work together, bringing little pellets of mud in their bills which they plaster in place and strengthen with grass and straw. The usual clutch is 4 or 5 white eggs, rarely 3 or 6. Incubation is entirely by the female, and the male usually sleeps beside the nest at night. He occasionally sits on the eggs during the female's absence by day, but he is unable to keep them at the proper temperature, for he lacks the brood patch—the bare space on the breast amply supplied with blood vessels—that incubating birds use to warm the eggs. Incubation takes 14 to 16 days, depending on the attentiveness of the female to her task. As in all weak-legged species that must be able to fly well on leaving the nest, the fledging period is comparatively long, from 20 to 24 days. The young usually return to roost at the nest for the first few nights after leaving.

Swallows frequently rear a second brood and occasionally a third. The later clutches are usually smaller than the first—

GREY-BREASTED MARTIN
Progne chalybea
Texas to Argentina 8 in.

male

female

PURPLE MARTIN
Progne subis
Temperate North America 8 in.

BROWN-CHESTED MARTIN
Progne tapera
Colombia and Venezuela to Argentina 8 in.

2 to 4 instead of 4 to 5 eggs. The young of the first brood usually stay in the vicinity, and often help the parents feed the later young. Adults not otherwise engaged or those that have lost their own broods frequently help feed the young in nearby nests. Ringing studies have shown that young returning to breed for the first time nest a week or two later than older birds, and that third clutches are laid only by the oldest pairs. Swallows are surprisingly long-lived—16 years is the record set by a Swallow ringed in Britain.

Another mud-nest builder is the common House Martin of Eurasia, a small green-backed, white-bellied swallow. This species plasters its mud cups under house eaves, leaving a narrow entrance at one edge. Originally House Martins were cliff nesters. Large colonies of them still nest on rocky cliffs in the Japanese Alps, just as their ancestors have done for ages, and often in unbelievable numbers. The Japanese value them as a tourist attraction, and establish colonies at large resort hotels by taking young birds from their nests and rearing them by hand where they want the birds to settle. These young birds migrate southward with their kind in late summer, and return in spring to the place where they were reared, not where they were hatched.

Other mud-nest builders among the swallows are the Cliff Swallow of Capistrano fame and the similar Red-rumped, or Mosque, Swallow of south temperate Eurasia. These birds build retort-shaped nests like a bottle lying on its side, with a small round entrance through the neck. They plaster them under the eaves of buildings, including temples and mosques in the Orient.

Many swallows are cavity nesters. Typical of this group is the Tree Swallow, common throughout most of temperate North America and much like the House Martin. The Tree Swallow's normal nesting site is a hole in a tree, either a natural cavity or one made and abandoned by woodpeckers, which the birds line first with grasses and then with feathers. Such sites are not too plentiful, and the Tree Swallow's numbers have always been limited by available nesting places rather than by food supply. Populations of Tree Swallows can readily be built up by supplying them suitable housing. The erection of bird boxes has encouraged their steady increase, and they have become one of the commonest bird-box occupants in North America.

One of the most popular bird-box users is the Purple Martin, largest of the American swallows, and one of the few members of the family in which the sexes differ markedly. The Purple Martin will nest in colonies and use houses divided into compartments. Long before the arrival of the white man, the southeastern Indians hung gourds on poles for them, a practice still widely continued in the South today. A South American relative, the Brown-chested Tree Martin, commonly uses the abandoned nests of ovenbirds (p. 198) and has been known to appropriate occupied ones.

Despite the site fidelity shown by all swallows to their nesting places and their strong territorial sense, many cases have been recorded of swallows nesting on moving vehicles—boats, trains, cars, tractors. I remember the pair of Grey-breasted Martins that occupied a bird box tacked to the taffrail of a little river steamer in British Guiana long ago. These birds stayed faithfully with the boat and successfully reared brood after brood as it went its weekly rounds up and down the Essequibo River, a round trip of 180 miles.

The simplest of swallow nests are those of the burrowing species, typified by the widespread Sand Martin, which breeds circumpolarly around the Northern Hemisphere. Americans call it the Bank Swallow. Sand Martins nest in colonies in vertical clay or sand banks, frequently along rivers. They dig horizontal tunnels 2 to 3 feet deep near the top of the bank, chipping the dirt free with their bills and scraping it out with their feet. They line the nesting chamber at its end with grass stalks, rootlets, and small sticks, and make a padded bed of feathers for their 4 to 5 white eggs.

The Rough-winged Swallow, so called because of the serrated web of its outer primaries, is another tunnel nester, but unlike the Sand Martin, the Rough-winged does not nest in colonies, though several pairs may nest fairly near one another where conditions are favourable. A group of African swallows of the genus *Psalidoprocne* are also called Roughwings. These birds live along forest edges and in open jungle clearings, and tunnel their nests into the banks of streams and into the walls of pitfalls the natives dig for big game. Most of these tropical species lay only two eggs.

The temperate zone Swallows are among the earliest of autumn migrants. As soon as nesting duties are over in summer, the birds start gathering in large flocks, often in thousands, and take their departure southward late in summer or very early in the autumn, moving by day and feeding as they go. Large mixed flocks of several species together can often be seen swooping over waterways, marshes, or fields where insects are plentiful, or resting on telegraph wires. Reedy marshes are favourite night roosts for the migrating flocks.

This was doubtless responsible for the medieval European belief that swallows were one of the "seven sleepers." People with no knowledge of far-off Africa, where the European swallows winter, thought the birds hibernated like frogs or turtles in the marsh ooze. This belief persisted well into the 19th century. Naturalists investigating reports of swallows found hibernating in the marshes invariably found dead ones, killed by starvation or cold. Though some birds do hibernate (see goatsuckers, p. 163), and others become torpid during a cold wet spell and recover (hummingbirds, p. 169), this phenomenon has never been demonstrated conclusively in any of the swallows.

Occasionally swallows delay their mass autumn departure until early cold snaps clear the air of flying insects. The Tree Swallows are often caught off their guard in this manner on Cape Cod, Massachusetts, in October and November. The birds then may be seen hovering over the bayberry bushes along the coastal moors, stoking up on the waxy fruit.

Africa is the home of an aberrant swallow, the African River Martin, sometimes put in a family of its own because of its complete bronchial rings. This large black swallow has a red beak and red eyes. It nests on the sandy shoals exposed when the Congo River is low during the dry season, often in colonies of several hundred pairs, and lays its three eggs at the end of a burrow dug slanting down from the surface. When the rains come and the river rises the birds move southwestward and spend the wet season in coastal marshes.

CUCKOO-SHRIKES AND MINIVETS

PASSERIFORMES   CAMPEPHAGIDAE

Cuckoo-shrike is an unfortunate name for this group of Old World birds. While some of them resemble shrikes and show vague similarities to cuckoos, they are not related to either family. More fitting is their family title, Campephagidae, which means "caterpillar eaters." Actually the cuckoo-shrikes

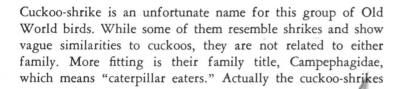

I ROSY MINIVET
Pericrocotus roseus
Afghanistan to S. China 8 in.

2 RED-SHOULDERED
CUCKOO-SHRIKE
Campephaga phoenicea
Africa south of the Sahara 8 in.

3 BARRED CUCKOO-SHRIKE
Coracina lineata
Australia and New Guinea
east to the Solomons 9½ in.

4 WHITE-WINGED TRILLER
Lalage sueurii
Java, Celebes, New Guinea,
Australia 7 in.

5 FLAMED MINIVET
Pericrocotus flammeus
India to the Philippines
and Borneo 9 in.

are rather primitive insect-eaters of uncertain antecedents and relationships, perhaps distantly allied to the Old World fly-catchers. Their distribution is Africa and the warmer parts of Asia from India northward to Manchuria and Japan, southward to Australia, and eastward to Samoa.

The 70 members of the family are small- to medium-sized arboreal birds, 5 to 14 inches long. Family characteristics are a stoutish down-curved bill, notched and hooked at the tip; nostrils partly hidden by short bristles; pointed wings with 10 primaries, the outermost shortened; tail long, graduated or rounded; legs usually short; feet rather weak. Their plumage is soft and fluffy, and an outstanding feature is the dense patch of thick, often light-coloured feathers on the lower back. These have large, stiff shafts and are so loosely attached they probably function as a defence mechanism, as do the loose feathers in certain pigeons and the easily shed tail of many lizards.

Most cuckoo-shrikes are a rather plain grey, black, or white, with barred underparts. The minivets are generally more brightly coloured in reds, yellows, and oranges. The sexes are similar in a few species, but are usually unlike, the females usually being duller, brown birds. All feed on insects, other small animals and occasionally berries. Some species, particularly the northern minivets, are migratory; the tropical and subtropical forms are essentially sedentary. Fairly conspicuous birds, they are often gregarious. When not nesting, small noisy flocks wander through the tree-tops, sometimes in company with other species of similar habits, such as flycatchers and orioles.

Breeding patterns, so far as known, are much alike throughout the family. Campephagid nests are typically shallow open cups on a horizontal branch or fork, built of twigs and grasses, often camouflaged with lichens and spiders' webs, and small for the size of the bird. The 2 to 5 eggs are white, green, or blue and usually blotched or speckled. Both sexes usually build the nest, incubate, and rear the young. In some species only the female incubates, but the male stands by and feeds her on the nest. The incubation period is 13 to 14 days in the smaller species. The nestlings of many cuckoo-shrikes are covered with a snowy white down, which is replaced before fledging by a juvenile plumage closely resembling that of the female.

Representative of the family are the 41 cuckoo-shrikes of the genus *Coracina*; these range widely from Africa through Malaya and Australia to the Solomons. About 8 to 13 inches in length, the Coracinas are often called "grey birds" from their predominant colour, or "caterpillar shrikes" from their favourite food. Some are quite shrike-like in appearance, a few species even having the black mask across the eyes. In their undulating flight, alternating flurries of rapid wingbeats with short glides, they suggest cuckoos. They inhabit heavy forest, most often living in the tree-tops. Their voice range is limited to harsh churrs and whistles; they often call in flight, but their notes are seldom loud or far-carrying.

The several species of the nominate genus *Campephaga* are African. In this group the males are glossy black, some with patches of red or yellow on the shoulders, the females brownish. Several closely related African species (*Lobotos*) have fleshy lobes of yellow or orange at the corner of the mouth. The Wattled Cuckoo-shrike, also called the Oriole Cuckoo-shrike from its resemblance to a forest oriole in size and colouring, is an example.

Another well-marked group consists of the smaller (6- to 8-inch) cuckoo-shrikes known as trillers (*Lalage*) from the loud, clear whistling notes of the males when courting. Trillers range from southern Asia to Australia, the Philippines, and the western Pacific islands. The males are mostly black and white, the females brownish. The White-winged Triller of Australia is the only member of the family to moult twice a year. The male goes into an eclipse moult after the breeding season and assumes a brownish dress like that of the female which he discards for his marked black and white nuptial garb the following spring. In southern Australia the White-winged Triller is migratory.

Australia is also the home of the largest member of the family, and one of the most aberrant, the 14-inch Ground

BLACK DRONGO or KING CROW
Dicrurus macrocercus
India to Formosa, Indochina, and Java   13 in.

Cuckoo-shrike. While this species spends much of its time foraging on the ground, it nests like the rest of the family in trees, 30 feet or so up, and builds the usual small, shallow nest for its 2 to 3 brown-spotted green eggs. After fledging in November or December, the young remain with their parents and wander about the countryside in small flocks until September, when they scatter to breed.

The 10 minivets (*Pericrocotus*) are neat, slender birds with sharply pointed tails, and so different from the other campephagids that some ornithologists give them subfamily rank. Minivets are birds of the tree-tops, ranging throughout southern and eastern Asia from Afghanistan to Japan and southward to Malaysia and the Philippines. While they forage among the leaves and branches like the rest of the family, minivets frequently catch insects on the wing in flycatcher fashion. One of the larger and brighter species, the 8-inch Flamed Minivet, common from India to the Philippines, is quite gregarious. Noisy bands of 20 or more birds rove through the tree-tops in the high green jungle. They are conspicuous both for their gay, striking colours and their endless melodious chattering.

The northernmost species, the Ashy Minivet, is patterned more sombrely, like the cuckoo-shrikes, in greys, black, and white. In Japan and Korea it vies with the swallows as a herald of spring, arriving from the south in April. A slender, grey bird with long wings and graduated tail, it flies high in the sky and proclaims the season with a pleasant, far-carrying note cool as the peal of a bell. It nests in the deciduous woodlands of the foothills, building a small, delicate, thin-walled nest of lichens, mosses, pine needles, and small twigs cleverly fastened together with spider webs. Its normal clutch is 4 to 5 bluish-grey eggs spotted heavily with purplish brown at the large end. Incubation is by the female alone. She raises but a single brood each summer.

DRONGOS

PASSERIFORMES   DICRURIDAE

The 20 species of drongos are Old World arboreal birds found throughout Africa south of the Sahara and in Asia from India and China southward to northern Australia and eastward to the Solomon Islands. They live in deep forests, in wooded savannahs, and in cultivated lands and gardens, and may be found from sea level up to perhaps 10,000 feet. A few species are migratory.

Drongos range from the size of a starling to that of a large jay. Their stout arched bills are slightly hooked and notched, and prominent bristles shield the nostrils. Their legs are short, their feet strong. Except for the highly variable Grey Drongo of southeastern Asia, drongos are black with bright metallic sheens of green to purple. A few species have white patches on the head or underparts. Many have a crest, or ornamental plumes on the head or neck, and most have a rather long, deeply forked tail. In some, the outer tail feathers are greatly elongated, curved, and variously ornamented. The Great Racquet-tailed Drongo of the Indian and Malayan forests has wire-like outer tail feathers tipped with miniature flags which extend a foot beyond the rest of the tail and almost double the length of the bird.

Drongos are conspicuous birds fond of sitting in the open on exposed dead branches and electric wires, where they watch for passing insects. They pounce on the insects ferociously and carry them back to the perch to eat. Large prey, such as locusts or grasshoppers, they hold down with one foot and tear to pieces with their beak before swallowing. Some species like to hang around cattle, feeding on the insects disturbed by their passage; others accompany troops of monkeys through the tree-tops for the same purpose. Most drongos are fairly noisy; their calls are varied and harsh. Some have melodious, attractive songs as well, and a few mimic other species of birds with considerable skill.

The relationships and systematic position of the drongos are uncertain. Kinship to the shrikes, the orioles, the jays, and the birds of paradise has been proposed, and to all of these the drongos show some resemblances. In behaviour they seem closest to the Old World flycatchers. The most recent revision of the group unites 19 species, all with 10-feathered tails, in the single genus *Dicrurus*. The 20th species, the diminutive Mountain Drongo (*Chaetorhynchus*) of New Guinea, has 12 tail feathers and strongly resembles a flycatcher. This jungle dweller is considered the most primitive of the drongos.

Throughout their wide Old World range the drongos are famed for their pugnacity and for their aggressive protection of their nesting territory. Like the American Kingbirds, they promptly attack any and every large bird that trespasses on their domain, and no predator cares to arouse their fury. Hawks, eagles, and crows flee before their aerial onslaught, though in fair combat any of these large predators should be more than a match for the much smaller drongos. Congo tribes call the Velvet-mantled Drongo "Nkandongoe," which roughly translated means "angry leopard." The name drongo, by which all members of the family are known, is the native Malagasy name for the Crested Drongo of northern Madagascar.

The commonest and most conspicuous drongo of India and southeastern Asia is a 12-inch shiny black bird with a forked tail. It is called the King Crow, not because of its black colouring, but because it is the master of these traditional nest robbers and drives them and other predators larger than itself away fearlessly. Drongos seem to limit their attacks to potentially dangerous animals and birds, a trait of which less aggressive species of equal and smaller size take advantage. A tree with a King Crow's nest may also shelter nests of orioles, doves, and other gentle species enjoying safety from marauders because of the drongos' presence.

Comparatively little is known of the breeding behaviour of the drongos. Most of them build a small, fragile, saucer-like nest, usually in a forked branch fairly high up. They lay anywhere from 2 to 5 (usually 3 to 4) eggs, which may be pure white or speckled with browns and grey. Incubation is believed largely by the female, though the male may assist at times. Both sexes co-operate in rearing the young. Drongos are frequently parasitized by cuckoos, and one Asiatic cuckoo, called the Drongo-cuckoo (*Surniculus*), looks so much like a drongo it is often mistaken for one, which is thought may facilitate its parasitizing of drongo nests.

OLD WORLD ORIOLES

PASSERIFORMES   ORIOLIDAE

The English word "oriole" stems from the Latin *aureolus*, meaning golden or yellow, and was originally applied most appropriately to the brilliant Golden Oriole that breeds widely throughout Europe and western Asia, wintering southward into Africa. This bird is the only European representative of a family of some 28 species of brightly coloured Old World birds, essentially tropical and subtropical in distribution. They range widely throughout Africa, southern Asia, and the East Indies to New Guinea and eastern Australia. These "true" orioles are 10-primaried birds allied anatomically to the crow and jay group, and are not related to the birds that are called orioles in the New World. Though the American orioles resemble the true orioles superficially, they have only nine primaries. They are of Western Hemisphere origin and closely allied to the tanagers.

The Old World orioles are all forest dwellers that live, feed, and breed in the tree-tops. Starling-sized birds from 8 to 12 inches in length, all have 12 tail feathers and short, fine bristles concealing the nostrils. Throughout the genus *Oriolus*, which embraces all but three members of the family, the sexes differ in colour. The males are predominantly yellow and black, and most of them have reddish bills. The females are much duller, usually greenish, and the young in their first juvenile plumage are even drabber, though frequently streaked and speckled with brown.

Orioles are strong, fast fliers, and have a characteristic undulating flight reminiscent of that of the woodpeckers. Despite their brilliant colours, the males are far more often heard than seen in their leafy tree-top habitat. Their call notes are loud, flutey whistles, and most species have a pleasant, melodious song as well. Some of the tropical forms, notably the Black-headed Oriole of Africa, are excellent mimics and include startlingly accurate imitations of the songs of other species in their courtship repertoires.

The 30-odd species of the genus *Oriolus* are essentially a tropical and subtropical group, with their greatest development in diversity of species in the jungles of central Africa, southern Asia, and Indonesia. From this centre of distribution several forms have spread into more temperate regions to breed during the clement summer months, migrating back to warmer climes during the colder parts of the year. Typical of such species are the Golden Oriole of Europe and its eastern Asiatic counterpart, the Black-naped Oriole, which breeds northward to Korea and Manchuria and winters southward to Malaya and Indonesia. These birds are highly regarded as songsters in their northern breeding grounds, and their appear-

BLACK-NAPED ORIOLE
Oriolus chinensis
India and Manchuria to the Philippines
and Celebes 9 in.

MAROON ORIOLE
Oriolus traillii
Himalayas to Formosa 9 in.

YELLOW FIGBIRD
Sphecotheres flaviventris
Northern Australia 10 in.

ance in late spring, with bright colours suggestive of exotic warmer lands, is welcomed as the surest sign that summer has really arrived.

Orioles are not gregarious and are usually encountered singly or in pairs, foraging through the tree-tops. They eat many kinds of insects, particularly during the breeding season, and are among the few birds that consume quantities of woolly caterpillars, which they first pound against a branch to remove the fuzz. Later they augment this diet with fruits, showing a fondness for cherries, mulberries, currents, figs, and loquats, which does not endear them to fruit farmers.

These orioles weave intricate cup-shaped nests of grasses and strips of bark, usually between the forks of a high horizontal branch, slinging the structure like a hammock attached firmly to branches on each side. They lay 2 to 5 eggs (usually 3 to 4), which are commonly white, more or less heavily speckled with brown or black. In the northern species both sexes build the nest and share the incubation and rearing duties. In the few tropical species that have been adequately studied, incubation is largely by the female. The male feeds her on the nest. In most orioles the incubation period is 14 to 15 days, and the young remain in the nest another two weeks before they take flight.

Somewhat aberrant members of the oriole family are the two figbirds (*Sphecotheres*) of eastern and northern Australia and New Guinea. The figbirds differ from the *Oriolus* group in having the bill slightly down-curved and the lores and the eye region bare of feathers. These handsome birds also differ somewhat from the nominate group in habits, mainly in being far more gregarious. They tend to travel in small, noisy flocks and, as their name implies, feed largely on fruits and berries. Their nesting habits are similar to those of other orioles, except that they usually lay but three eggs, which are predominantly greenish and brown in colour, heavily spotted with reddish or brownish markings. Also classified tentatively with the orioles is the little-known Kinkimavo (*Tylas*) of the Madagascar forests. Recent studies suggest the Fairy Bluebirds (p. 245), now classified with the leafbirds, may be aberrant orioles.

CROWS AND JAYS

PASSERIFORMES   CORVIDAE

Among the 102 species assigned to the Corvidae are some of the world's most familiar birds. Possessors of conspicuous personalities, bold, active, noisy, and aggressive, the crows, ravens, rooks, jackdaws, jays, and their kindred have always claimed man's interest and attention. The distinctive vernacular names he has given them are household words in many tongues. No other group of birds has earned for itself a more prominent place in legend, folklore, literature, and common everyday speech.

Though best developed in the Northern Hemisphere, the crow family is almost world-wide in distribution, absent only from Antarctica, New Zealand, certain oceanic islands, and southern South America. Ornithologists generally divide the crow family into two subfamilies, the larger, more sombre crows (Corvinae) and the smaller, more colourful jays (Garrulinae). The crows have relatively long, pointed wings and short tails, the jays shorter, rounded wings and longer tails. The structural differences between the two are not always well marked. Several genera are difficult to assign positively to either subfamily.

As a family the corvids are a generalized, relatively unspecialized group of considerable age, evolutionarily speaking, and probably closest to the ancestral stock from which over the ages they and their more specialized relatives, the orioles, birds of paradise, bowerbirds, and others, have developed. Technically they are diagnosed as medium- to large-sized, 10-primaried oscine birds with strong, unnotched bills, the nostrils usually covered with forward-directed bristles, the legs and feet large and strong, the tarsus scaled in front, smooth behind, and terminating in a ridge. Typically inhabitants of forests, brushlands, and grasslands, crows and jays are seldom finicky in their choice of food. Many will eat almost anything they can swallow, animal or vegetable, and so are able to survive changing conditions in a variety of habitats. At the same time some groups have strangely limited distributions, apparently restricted by some particular environmental factor. Several species have widely disrupted ranges.

From its present distribution the family is thought to have arisen in what are now the northern temperate and subtropical portions of the Old World and to have spread from there into the rest of its present range. (Corvids left their fossil remains in Miocene deposits in Europe 25 million years ago.) The great development of the jay subfamily in Central and South America suggests an ancestor's early invasion of the New World, possibly in mid-Tertiary time. The absence of jays from Africa south of the Sahara suggests a later Old World conquest by jays from the Western Hemisphere.

The crow subfamily seems to have reached the New World considerably later than the jays, for its members have pushed southward only as far as Honduras, and are absent from South America. Yet the crows are more aggressive and more adaptable than the jays, and are stronger fliers. They have established themselves in many more island regions—the West Indies, Australia, the Philippines, and other smaller Pacific islands in which jays are unknown. Crows have been in the West Indies long enough to develop four distinct though similar species, one each on Cuba, Hispaniola, Puerto Rico, and Jamaica. Pleistocene deposits in the West Indies have yielded bones of still two more crow species, either or both of which may have been ancestral to the present forms.

Possibly no bird or group of birds is better known to more people than the crows of the nominate genus *Corvus*. The Common Crow, which is widespread in North America, the very similar Carrion Crow of temperate Eurasia, the House Crow of India, the Jungle Crow of eastern and southeastern Asia, the Pied Crow of South Africa, and some 26 other members of the genus are large, black, black and grey, or black and white birds with raucous voices. All are called "crows" wherever English is spoken, and they all say "crow," "craw," "caw," or "krahe."

The crows are the largest-bodied of the passerine birds, and the largest of them is the Raven, which measures 26 inches from tip of bill to tip of tail. (The Raven is exceeded in length by the Ribbon-tailed Bird of Paradise, by the lyrebirds of Australia, and by the handsome, slender 28-inch Magpie Jay of Central America, all of which have smaller bodies.) The Raven is the most widespread as well as the largest species in the family, for it occurs, or did until the last century or so, in practically all the arctic and temperate Northern Hemisphere. The Raven is difficult to distinguish in the field from other black corvines other than by its more guttural croaking calls. Its slightly larger size, heavier bill, and more pointed, shaggier throat feathers are hard to discern at a distance. The Raven has not fared so well in competition with mankind as some of its smaller relatives. It is now found only in the wilder, uninhabited parts of its range, and is most common today north of the tree line.

CHOUGH
Pyrrhocorax pyrrhocorax
Europe, south-central Asia   15 in.

A singular attribute of most crows is their ability to co-exist with man. Their adaptability and their boldness and sagacity, coupled with their extensive dietary range—they are practically omnivorous—have enabled them to live and thrive in country radically altered by man's activities. In agricultural regions crows are a mixed blessing, for their inroads on sprouting grain are partly offset by their consumption of enormous numbers of injurious insects and larvae.

Crows are widely credited with being the most "intelligent" of all birds. Though much of the evidence supporting this is blatantly anthropomorphic, there is no question that crows do have mental qualities of a high order. Experiments with captive crows show they have considerable learning ability, that they can count up to three or four and learn to associate various noises and symbols with food. That crows have a language of their own and that their calls have recognizable meanings (as indeed do those of all birds) has long been known. Before the days of modern behaviour studies and scientific analyses of bird noises with hi-fi equipment and sound spectrographs, most country boys knew the difference between the various crow calls: the loud, clear

RAVEN
Corvus corax
Northern Hemisphere 26 in.

COMMON CROW
Corvus brachyrhynchos
Temperate North America 21 in.

HOODED CROW
Corvus cornix
Europe, western Asia 18 in.

assembly "caaw," the rapid "ca-ca-ca-ca" of alarm, and the excited scolding when mobbing an owl. Crows have some imitative skill, and with patience captive ones can be taught to say a few words, but they are not as good at it as mynahs and parrots.

The best proof of crows' intelligence is their adaptability to change and their success in withstanding constant persecution. Almost everywhere man is against them, and in North America they have never been protected. Their well-known penchant for the eggs and young of other species turns sentimental bird-lovers against them, and their forays on nesting waterfowl and game birds make every sportsman their enemy. Still they manage to survive and prosper—despite wholesale dynamiting of their winter roosts that slaughters thousands at a time in America.

Nor is the crows' rate of reproduction abnormally high. They are typically single-brooded, and the clutch varies from 3 to 5 (occasionally 6) greenish eggs heavily spotted with brown. Most of the family are tree-nesters; the raven and a few others often nest on cliffs. All build substantial open nests of twigs and sticks. Incubation is entirely by the female, who sits closely and is fed on the nest by the male. Incubation in the Carrion Crow takes 18 to 19 days, and the fledging period is about 3 weeks.

A distinctive Eurasian member of the genus *Corvus* is the slightly smaller Rook, whose habit of nesting in large colonies gives us the term rookery for any such assemblage regardless of species (even breeding colonies of seals are called rookeries). Another still smaller species is the Jackdaw which is black with a grey head. Other genera in the crow subfamily include two other fairly well-known northern birds, the choughs and the nutcrackers.

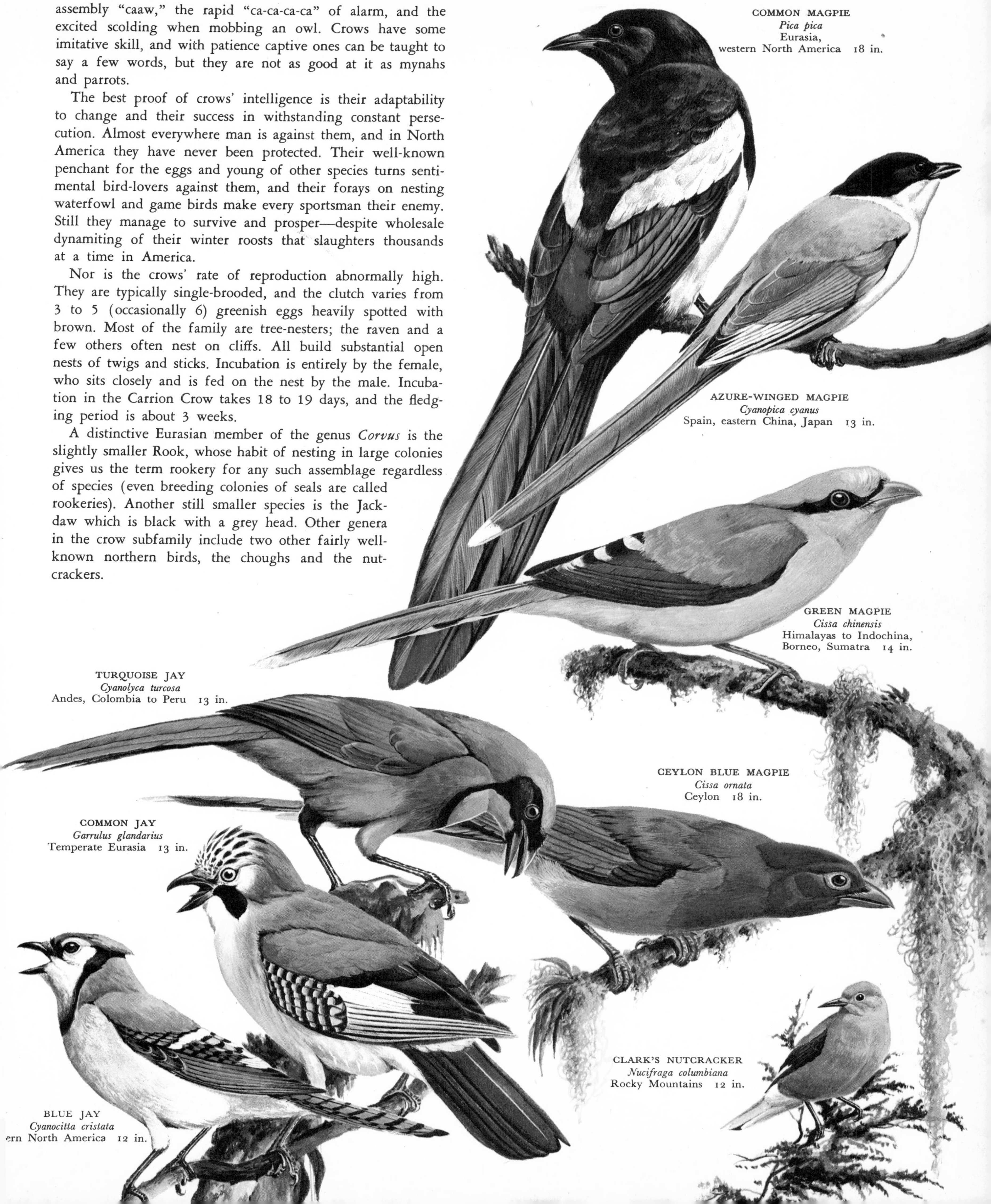

COMMON MAGPIE
Pica pica
Eurasia,
western North America 18 in.

AZURE-WINGED MAGPIE
Cyanopica cyanus
Spain, eastern China, Japan 13 in.

GREEN MAGPIE
Cissa chinensis
Himalayas to Indochina,
Borneo, Sumatra 14 in.

CEYLON BLUE MAGPIE
Cissa ornata
Ceylon 18 in.

TURQUOISE JAY
Cyanolyca turcosa
Andes, Colombia to Peru 13 in.

COMMON JAY
Garrulus glandarius
Temperate Eurasia 13 in.

CLARK'S NUTCRACKER
Nucifraga columbiana
Rocky Mountains 12 in.

BLUE JAY
Cyanocitta cristata
ern North America 12 in.

The choughs inhabit rocky heights in Europe and south-western Asia. These rather small corvids are glossy black like most of the group, but are distinctive in their thinner, pointed, and strongly down-curved bills, which are bright red in the Common Chough and yellow in the Alpine Chough, the only two species in the genus *Pyrrhocorax*. The Common Chough nests on ledges along inaccessible sea cliffs. The Alpine Chough prefers ledges in the mountains. Both are noted for their aerial acrobatics. Individually and in flocks they perform all sorts of flight evolutions around their cliffs, wheeling and dashing back and forth, climbing high and diving like a plummet with closed wings, even turning somersaults — all seemingly for the fun of it.

Nutcrackers are jay-sized inhabitants of mountain forests in northern Eurasia and western North America. The Nutcracker of Eurasia is a brownish bird handsomely spangled with white (the Japanese call him the star crow); Clark's Nutcracker (discovered by the Lewis and Clark expedition in 1805) is a pale-grey bird whose black wings and tail have white patches that show conspicuously in flight. Nutcrackers prefer evergreen forests, but are often found above the timber line in the mountains. Omnivorous like most crows and jays, they eat all sorts of insects, grubs, and the eggs and young of other birds, but their principal food is nuts and seeds. They are adept at hacking pine cones open, holding a cone with one foot and hewing it apart with pickaxe strokes of their strong bills. The nutcrackers are notorious food-storers. They make caches of pine cones and hazel nuts in summer and autumn, and show a phenomenal ability to return to the exact spot to dig out their supply even when it is covered with snow. They are not infallible, however, and nuts and cones nutcrackers bury and fail to retrieve help reforest barren mountain regions.

The jays are a more varied group than the crows, and much more colourful in appearance. The subfamily is exceptionally well diversified in Central and South America where no less than 28 of the 32 New World species occur, and in south-eastern Asia where more than half of the Old World forms live, including some of the most brilliantly coloured members of the family, such as the Green, the Ceylon Blue, and the Red-billed Blue magpies.

The somewhat more specialized feeding habits and nesting behaviour of a number of jays and their strangely restricted and disrupted distribution patterns suggest that the group may be an earlier, more ancient one than the crows. Small colonies of the Azure-winged Magpie, for instance, are woodland residents of extreme eastern Asia and Japan. The species suddenly reappears on the other side of Eurasia in the highlands of Spain. The North American Scrub Jay shows a similar relict distribution. This species breaks into a number of races on the west coast from Washington to southern Mexico, and is absent from the rest of the continent except for a population resident in the scrublands of central Florida.

Widest ranging and most familiar of the Old World species is the Common Jay, found in temperate Eurasian woodlands from the British Isles to Japan. Although the Common Jay is fairly omnivorous and fond of all sorts of animal food, its diet is almost three-fourths vegetable matter. Acorns are its mainstay, and its distribution closely coincides with that of the oak trees that produce them. In much of its range it is regarded as a game bird and shot for sport and food. In England and parts of Europe gamekeepers kill it whenever they can because of its fondness for the eggs and young of game birds. That the Common Jay still manages to remain fairly plentiful throughout its extensive range speaks highly for its adaptability and reproductive powers. It is single-brooded, but lays from 5 to 7 eggs. It nests in trees and builds a well-constructed and fairly bulky open cup of twigs usually lined with grass. As in most jays, but not in crows, the male shares the incubation duties. The incubation period is 16 to 17 days. Fledging takes another 19 to 20 days.

The Common Jay's New World counterpart is the cocky Blue Jay of temperate North America east of the Rockies. Essentially a woodland species fond of open forest, the Blue Jay has become a common resident of the parks and suburbs of most North American cities.

Most corvids tend to be residents and few have well-marked migrations. They do wander considerably after the breeding season, often in small flocks. Ringing has shown that the Blue Jay seldom travels more than a few hundred miles. Blue Jays also are fairly long-lived; a number of ringed individuals have lived 10 to 12 years, the oldest to date, 15 years. Though length of life is roughly a corollary of size, with larger animals living longer, the oldest wild crow on the ringing records was 13 years old when killed. However, crows have lived in captivity beyond 20 years.

Northernmost of the jays are those of the circumpolar genus *Perisoreus*, resident in the boreal birch and conifer forests. The American species, widely known as the Canada Jay, is a mischievous bird familiar to all north woods travellers. The Siberian Jay is similar in appearance and habits, but browner in colour.

The only jay species common to both hemispheres is the Common Magpie, which ranges across Eurasia and into western North America. Its only close relative, the Yellow-billed Magpie, is limited to the valleys and foothills of California west of the High Sierras. Conspicuous black and white birds with very long tails, these magpies are more like the crows in certain aspects, particularly their nesting behaviour, and some students consider them intermediate between the two subfamilies.

Birds of semi-open countryside, the Common Magpies are thoroughly at home in Old World farmlands. They usually go about in twos or threes, are as noisy and mischievous as any member of the family, and are one of the most notorious thieves, prone to pick up all sorts of bright objects and carry them away. Their fondness for the eggs of other species led to their persecution by gamekeepers, but their diet is as varied as that of most corvines. They hang about cattle and other large ungulates more than other corvids do, and may even be seen perched upon an animal's back.

Magpies make a large bulky stick nest from 1 to 3 feet in diameter, usually in the trunk fork of a deciduous tree. Nest-building is part of the magpies' courtship, the male bringing the material, the female arranging it. The tremendous nests are often used and added to year after year. Incubation by the female alone is one of their crow-like idiosyncracies. This takes 17 to 18 days, and fledging of the young, which the male helps feed, lasts another 22 to 27 days.

WATTLEBIRDS

PASSERIFORMES   CALLAEIDAE

Three distinctive New Zealand forest birds, each placed in a separate genus, form this small family—the extinct Huia, and the still extant but rare Saddleback and Wattled Crow. All three have rather weak wings, large, strong legs and feet, and large fleshy wattles at the corner of the jaws, bluish grey in the Wattled Crow, yellow to orange in the others. They are believed offshoots of the primitive crow-like stock that produced the bowerbirds, birds of paradise, mudnest builders, and bellmagpies.

Most interesting of the three species was the Huia. The whitish bills of the male and female were so different that the first specimens to reach Europe were considered distinct species. The male's beak was stout, straight, and chisel-like; the female's was longer, thinner, and gracefully down-curved. Pairs of these large, glossy-black birds hunted together on or near the ground in deep forests for wood-boring grubs, the male chiselling away the hard wood to get at the grubs, the female probing soft, rotten branches to extract the grubs. The Maoris valued the Huias' white-tipped tail feathers, which they used in chiefs' ceremonial headdresses. Living Huias have not been reported reliably since 1907. Over zealous hunting by the Maoris and by European collectors of museum specimens has been blamed for the Huia's extinction, but destruction of its primaeval forest habitat was a far more important factor. The Maoris hunted it for years before Europeans arrived without seriously affecting its numbers. A recent survey showed only 67 specimens traceable in museums of the world today, and

it is doubtful whether Europeans ever collected more than two or three times that number.

The Saddleback, or Tieke as the Maoris call it, is also glossy black, but has a conspicuous chestnut back. The sexes are alike and both have black, straight, pointed bills. Saddlebacks are smaller than the Huia, about 10 inches long. They are poor fliers but flit from branch to branch through the forest undergrowth and hop on the ground. Their food is mainly insects, also some fruits and flower nectar. They build a cup-shaped nest deep in a tree-fern stem or in rock crevices, and lay 2 to 3 brownish-grey eggs heavily spotted with brown which are incubated 20 to 21 days. Saddlebacks are now limited to a few of the smaller offshore islands where they are protected and reported still to be thriving. They are rarely reported on the main islands.

The Wattled Crow, or Kokako, a large blue-grey, jay-like bird with a short, heavy, down-curved beak, was plentiful a century ago but is now restricted to the few stands of highland forest remaining on the main islands. It flies weakly, but moves through the trees and over the ground in long hops, aided partly by its wings. It lives more on fruit and berries than the other two species, and its song is considered the most beautiful of all New Zealand bird music. The Kokako builds an untidy open nest of twigs lined with bark and moss, usually 20 to 30 feet up in a tree. The clutch is 2 to 3 spotted greyish eggs. The incubation period is unknown, but the young remain in the nest 4 weeks.

MUDNEST BUILDERS

PASSERIFORMES   GRALLINIDAE

The four members of this odd little antipodean family all build similar nests—deep open bowls of mud strengthened with hair, feathers, and grass, usually on a high horizontal branch. All are somewhat gregarious, fly rather weakly, and have peculiar jumping gaits both on the ground and in trees. They live in open woodlands, along lake shores and stream banks, and in marshes and cultivated areas; they are usually found near water.

The mudlarks (*Grallina*) are the smallest members of the family. The 11-inch Australian Mudlark, also called Magpie-lark or Pee-wit, is a graceful, boldly black and white, rather tame inhabitant of open stream banks, lake shores, and

marshes. The slightly smaller but similarly coloured Papuan Mudlark is the least gregarious member of the family, and lives solitarily or in pairs along rushing streams in the forested mountains of western New Guinea. The Australian species gathers in flocks of up to 500 birds in winter, but the pairs establish individual nesting territories in spring. Magpie-larks are believed to pair for life, and each pair maintains the same nesting ground, which may be as large as 15 or 20 acres, year after year. Both sexes defend it, and sing antiphonally while courting. When one bird sings the first two syllables of the song, a shrill whistled "te-be," its mate immediately finishes the remaining "pee-o-wit" in perfect synchronization.

Mudlarks lay four heavily spotted white eggs and are multibrooded. Their peculiar mud nests are often washed away by heavy rains. They are thought to build a new one for each brood. They feed on insects and small aquatic life, and as they consume quantities of molluscs that are the alternate hosts of sheep-infecting flukes, they are regarded as highly beneficial birds.

The Apostle Bird, or Grey Jumper (*Struthidea*), of eastern Australia has earned its two unusual common names. First, it travels about the open forests and farmlands in small flocks of about a dozen birds; second, it jumps in long leaps over the ground and from branch to branch. Dark-grey birds the size of a large jay, Apostle Birds feed largely on the ground on insects and seeds. They are reported to nest communally.

The fourth and largest member of the family is the glossy black White-winged Chough (*Corcorax*), also a resident of eastern Australia. Like the Apostle Bird, the White-winged Chough goes about in small flocks and feeds mostly on the ground on insects, but also eats fruits and berries. It flies with slow wingbeats, and its white wing patches are conspicuous in flight. When disturbed it hops off through the trees in a series of long jumps from branch to branch It also is reported to be multi-brooded and a communal nester, three birds usually combining to build the typical mud nest, in which several females may lay. How many eggs each lays is unknown, but as many as eight have been found in a nest. Like those of the other members of the family, the eggs are whitish and spotted with brown.

AUSTRALIAN BUTCHERBIRDS
AND BELLMAGPIES

PASSERIFORMES   CRACTICIDAE

This small group of 10 Australian and Papuan birds shows strong affinities to the crows and jays and probably developed from magpie-like ancestors that became isolated in the antipodes fairly early in Tertiary time.

The Grey Butcherbird, common and widespread throughout temperate Australia, is remarkably like the northern shrikes, and has the same habit of impaling insects, lizards, small birds, or rodents on thorns or hanging them on twigs to be eaten later. It uses the thorn or a convenient tree fork to hold its prey firm while it tears it into small pieces.

Australians rate the butcherbirds, with their clear, mellow calls, among their finest songsters. The butcherbirds sing practically all the year round, are noted for their duetting or antiphonal singing, and are also accomplished mimics.

Pairs of butcherbirds apparently stay mated and defend their territories throughout the year. The females take as active a part in this and in the singing courtship as do the males. They build untidy, crow-like nests of twigs lined with softer material in a tree fork, and lay 3 to 5 varicoloured, heavily spotted eggs. Their incubation period is rather long

MAGPIE-LARK
Grallina cyanoleuca
Australia 11 in.

WHITE-WINGED CHOUGH
Corcorax melanorhamphus
Southeastern Australia 18 in.

for a passerine bird—23 days, followed by a fledging period of 25 to 26 days.

Bellmagpies, 14 to 20 inches in length, resemble magpies in their black and white colouring but have much shorter tails. All are fine singers and have ringing, gong-like calls that resound through the bush. The Grey Bellmagpie, the largest of the family, is disliked by fruit farmers for its fruit-eating and by bird lovers for its fondness for the eggs and young of other birds. It also eats insects in quantity.

The Western Bellmagpie has territorial relationships unknown in any other bird, for it lives in clans of from 6 to 20 individuals of varying sex ratios that establish clan territories up to 100 acres in extent. Members of the clan remain within its boundaries throughout the year and defend the frontiers against incursions from neighbouring clans. Individuals seem to be promiscuous, and the clan relationships are apparently somewhat communistic.

At mating time all the clan participates in a carolling song-festival, which dies down during the incubation period. Nest-building and incubating are entirely by the females, but the males assist in feeding the young and in protecting them. Aggressive in defence of their nests, they attack all other species that approach, including humans. The nest is large and bowl-shaped, and usually placed high in a tree fork. Made of sticks and lined with finer grasses and leaves, a peculiar feature in its construction is the frequent use of heavy wire. One Western Bellmagpie's nest is reported to have weighed 13¾ pounds. It contained 286 pieces of miscellaneous wire, some of it barbed wire from stock fences, varying in length from 4 inches to 4 feet and totalling 338 feet.

GREY BUTCHERBIRD
Cracticus torquatus
Australia and Tasmania 11 in.

BOWERBIRDS

PASSERIFORMES   PTILONORHYNCHIDAE

The most remarkable characteristic of the 17 species of bowerbirds is the extraordinary display grounds the males of most species build as part of their courtship. While a number of other birds establish special plots for courting and clear or modify them to suit their fancy (manakins, lyrebirds, and certain grouse are examples), none builds such elaborate structures as the bowerbirds. Some bowerbirds erect such large edifices it is hard to believe they are the work of one small bird. In fact the first ones seen by early explorers were thought to be playhouses built by native children.

Bowerbirds are so closely related to the birds of paradise that some students consider them subfamilies of the same family. The two groups have almost identical ranges—they are known only from New Guinea and northern Australia—and the structural differences separating them are not particularly well marked. They show minor divergences in palate structure and in the arrangement of the feather tracts, and differ in the relative length of the hind toe, which is always shorter than the middle front toe in the bowerbirds, but as long or longer in the birds of paradise. While the sexes are unlike in most bowerbirds, they are similar in the more primitive species. Some male bowerbirds are brilliantly coloured, and a few have crests and elongated head feathers, but none has the distinctive gaudy plumes of the male birds of paradise. The outstanding difference between the two groups is their courtship behaviour. Whereas male birds of paradise attract their mates by displaying their outrageously showy plumes, the male bowerbirds' forte is making their surroundings attractive. They have developed skills as architects and decorators found nowhere else below man in the animal kingdom. In their respective methods of display, the bowerbirds and the birds of paradise are unquestionably the most highly specialized wooers among all birds.

A noteworthy and curious aspect of bowerbirds' activities is that the male's skill as a builder is not used for nest construction. Each male builds his bower or stage by himself and performs there alone. The bower's sole function seems to be to attract a female and to stimulate her to mate, and mating takes place within it. After mating, the male takes no further part in the reproductive duties. The female goes off by herself and alone builds her shallow cup-shaped nest of twigs, lays and incubates her two eggs, and rears the young. While suspected, polygamy has not been proved in the bowerbirds.

Bowerbirds are classed for convenience into four groups according to their type of bower: those that build no bower, the stage makers, the maypole builders, and the avenue build-

SATIN BOWERBIRD ♂
Ptilonorhynchus violaceus
Eastern Australia 13 in.

REGENT BOWERBIRD ♂
Sericulus chrysocephalus
Eastern Australia 11 in.

ORANGE-CRESTED
GARDENER ♂
Amblyornis subalaris
Southeastern New Guinea 9

MOCHA-BREASTED BOWERBIRD
Cnemophilus macgregorii
Central New Guinea 9½ in.

ers. The first group, considered the most primitive of the family, contains two species, the Green Catbird of eastern and northern Australia and the Aru Islands, and the congeneric White-throated Catbird of western New Guinea (both unrelated to American catbirds). These two species have feline mewing call notes and hissing, spitting alarm cries. In both species the sexes are alike. Catbirds have shorter, heavier, and stouter bills than the more highly developed bowerbirds, are more arboreal, and are seldom seen on the ground. Their food is fruit, berries, seeds, and some insects, mainly beetles. Beyond the fact that the males build no bower, little has been published about their breeding behaviour. Whether or not the males assume more of the nesting and rearing duties than in the other species is unknown. The catbird nest is like that of the other bowerbirds, a cup-like structure of twigs, usually fairly high in a forest tree. The normal clutch is two cream-coloured eggs.

The simplest bowers are those built by the three so-called stage makers, best known of which is the Toothed-billed Bowerbird of the scrubby highland forests of northeastern Australia. The sexes are similarly plain and protectively col-

oured in this species—olive-brown above and streaked brown and white below. Both have deep saw-like notches near the tip of both upper and lower mandibles, with which the male cuts the leaves it uses to decorate its playground. This stage maker clears a space 3 to 5 feet in diameter on the ground in the forest. It covers this stage with fresh leaves, often of one particular kind. As the leaves wither, the bird replaces them with fresh ones. Well-used playgrounds are surrounded by a circle of the discarded debris. The male spends much of his time calling and singing from special perches above the plot, and is renowned as a ventriloquist and mimic.

Sanford's Golden-crested Bowerbird builds a similar but fancier circus ring on the floor of the mossy palm forests of New Guinea, some 8,000 feet above sea level. It mats its dancing ground with fern fronds and decorates the edges with piles of beetle wings, snail shells, and pieces of resin. Then it hangs a curtain of bamboo strands and wilted ferns from vines around its arena, among which it scatters pieces of bark, berries, and an occasional snail shell. The male maintains this stage throughout the breeding season, and daily redecorates it and poses and sings in and around it.

CRESTLESS GARDENER
Amblyornis inornatus
Western New Guinea 9 in.

SPOTTED BOWERBIRD
Chlamydera maculata

BLACK-FACED
GOLDEN BOWERBIRD ♂
Sericulus aureus
New Guinea and
northern Australia   10 in.

SPOTTED BOWERBIRD ♂
Chlamydera maculata
Eastern Australia   11-12 in.

GREEN CATBIRD ♂
Ailuroedus crassirostris
Northern Australia   14-15 in.

The maypole builders number five species. The Golden Bowerbird of northern Australia, only 9 inches long and one of the smallest of the family, builds one of the largest bowers, a roofed gazebo that in extreme cases may tower 9 feet in height. The other four maypole builders live in the New Guinea jungles at considerable altitudes. These birds plant mosses in their dancing grounds and are hence often referred to as the "gardeners." These four congeneric New Guinea species are the Crested, the Orange-crested, the Crestless, and the Golden-fronted gardeners. The Golden-fronted is one of the great ornithological rarities. The three known specimens reached Europe in 19th-century shipments of bird-of-paradise plumes. Though every expedition to New Guinea has sought it, the bird has yet to be found in the wild.

The maypole builder starts his bower by piling sticks and twigs horizontally around the base of a small tree until they reach the desired height, usually 4 to 6 feet. He then builds a similar but smaller pyramid around the base of another sapling or shrub a few feet away and arches over the inter-vening space with vines and sticks so that it resembles a thatched roof. These structures are often used season after season, repaired and added to each year, and the largest ones may represent years of work. The birds decorate the walls and the ground under and around the bower with mosses, ferns, orchids and other flowers, and little orderly piles of bright berries and snail shells. As the flowers fade, the owner re-moves them and replaces them with fresh ones.

The nine species of avenue builders are considered the most highly specialized of the family. Though their bowers are not as massive as those of the maypole builders and are only partly roofed, if at all, their construction is more intricate. At least two species, the Satin and Regent bowerbirds of

Australia, use tools—paint daubers—when decorating them. The male avenue builder starts his bower by flooring a cleared space about 4 feet in diameter with a mat of well-trodden sticks and twigs several inches thick. In the centre of this he erects two parallel walls of upright sticks firmly implanted and entwined together and sometimes arched over at the top. Dimensions vary somewhat between species. The Spotted Bowerbird of Australia makes a mat 6 to 8 inches thick with avenue walls 2 to 3 feet long and 16 inches high. The Regent Bowerbird builds walls only 8 inches long and 6 inches high. The walls are just far enough apart for the bird to walk through without brushing the sides with its wings. The birds decorate this playground with all sorts of strange objects such as pebbles, bleached bones, shells, leaves, and flowers.

The Regent and the Satin bowerbirds daub the inside walls of the bower with a bluish or greenish paint made of charcoal and other pigments mixed with saliva. The Regent takes a wad of green leaves in its beak and daubs the paint around with it; the Satin Bowerbird uses a wad of bark. The only other use of a "tool" by a bird that I can think of is that of the probing thorn of one of the Galapagos finches (p. 297).

In five of the avenue builders, the Satin and Regent of Australia and the Black-faced Golden, the Yellow-throated Golden, and Baker's bowerbirds of New Guinea, the males are brightly coloured, the females relatively drab and dull-coloured. In the other four, all of the genus *Chlamydera*, both sexes are dull and nearly alike, their main colouring being a patch of elongated pink feathers on the nape, on the male alone in some, in both sexes in others. The *Chlamydera* group in both Australia and New Guinea live in open scrublands and often near grasslands. The largest member of the family, the 15-inch Great Grey Bowerbird of Australia, belongs to this genus.

The avenue builders are somewhat more gregarious than other bowerbirds, and outside the breeding season often travel about in small flocks of 4 to 6 birds. Their diet is prin-cipally fruits and berries, supplemented by insects of various sorts. The range of the Spotted Bowerbird in western Aus-tralia is apparently limited by the distribution of its principal food, a wild fig. Orchardists complain of their depredations, particularly of those of the Satin Bowerbird, which loves soft fruits. The call notes of this group are not particularly at-tractive, being guttural cries or saw-like wheezes, but like most bowerbirds they are good mimics and include the songs of other species in their repertoire when displaying.

LITTLE KING BIRD OF PARADISE ♂
Cicinnurus regius
New Guinea 7 in.

SUPERB BIRD OF PARADISE ♂
Lophorina superba
New Guinea 9½ in.

WILSON'S BIRD OF PARADISE ♂
Diphyllodes respublica
New Guinea 6½ in.

BIRDS OF PARADISE

PASSERIFORMES   PARADISAEIDAE

In this family is the most ornate and colourful assemblage of birds in the world. In the male birds of paradise the development of special feathers for the attraction of the opposite sex reaches its peak, not only in varied bright colours but in weird and fanciful shapes. Yet the family is of lowly origin, for these 40 gorgeous birds evolved from some drab generalized, crow-like ancestors that became isolated in the Papuan region, probably fairly early in Tertiary time. Their closest living relatives are the bowerbirds, from which they differ in a few minor anatomical points such as relative length of toes, but primarily in their courtship behaviour and in the ornamental plumages that are an integral part of their sex life.

The home of these splendid creatures is the forests of New Guinea and neighbouring small islands. Four species occur in the mountain forests of northeastern Australia. Much of their habitat has only recently become accessible and is still relatively unexplored. Some forms are still known only by a specimen or two collected without data by native hunters. Only a score of trained ornithologists have had the good fortune to study these birds in their native haunts, and few have been able to spend more than several months in the field with them. Hence our knowledge of their behaviour and life histories is rather sketchy. Much of what we know about their display has been learned by watching captive birds in zoos.

Yet modern knowledge of birds of paradise dates back 450 years. Primitive New Guinea tribes have used the plumes as ornaments from time immemorial, and Chinese voyagers and traders brought them to the Orient long before the 16th century. The first known in Europe were two native-made skins sent to the king of Spain by the ruler of Batjan, one of the Molucca Islands, and carried home aboard Magellan's circumnavigating *Victoria* in 1522. So unbelievably beautiful were these two birds that the Spaniards believed them visitors from paradise instead of from the Papuan jungles, and

birds of paradise they have been ever since. The 16th- and 17th-century Portuguese traders knew them as "manucodiata," a corruption of the Malay phrase "manuq dewata," meaning "birds of the gods." This name survives in the five manucodes of New Guinea and the closely related Trumpeter Manucode of New Guinea and northeastern Australia, a shiny blackish bird that displays by erecting its long, shiny neck feathers in a wide ruff and produces its loud, deep notes in the long windpipe coiled about under the skin of its chest.

Most of the bird of paradise specimens that filtered back to Europe in the early days were native-made trade skins from which the savage taxidermists had removed the legs and feet. This gave rise to all sorts of fanciful tales—the birds were supposed never to alight, but to live on the wing and to fly continually toward the sun, and the female was supposed to lay her eggs in a hole in the male's back. The level-headed European naturalists of the 18th century must have known that these were just travellers' tales, and doubtless the great Linnaeus had his tongue in his cheek when, in the 1758 edition of his great "Systema Natura," he named the best-known one *Paradisaea apoda*, "the footless paradise bird." Linnaeus gave the locality for this species as "India" and that of the Little King Bird of Paradise, which he called *Paradisaea regia*, as the "East Indies." Both we now know came from the Aru Islands, the little group of satellite islands lying just southwest of the New Guinea mainland.

The actual source of the trade skins that were delighting European naturalists was not discovered until 1824, when the French explorer-naturalist René Lesson collected specimens of the Trumpeter and Black

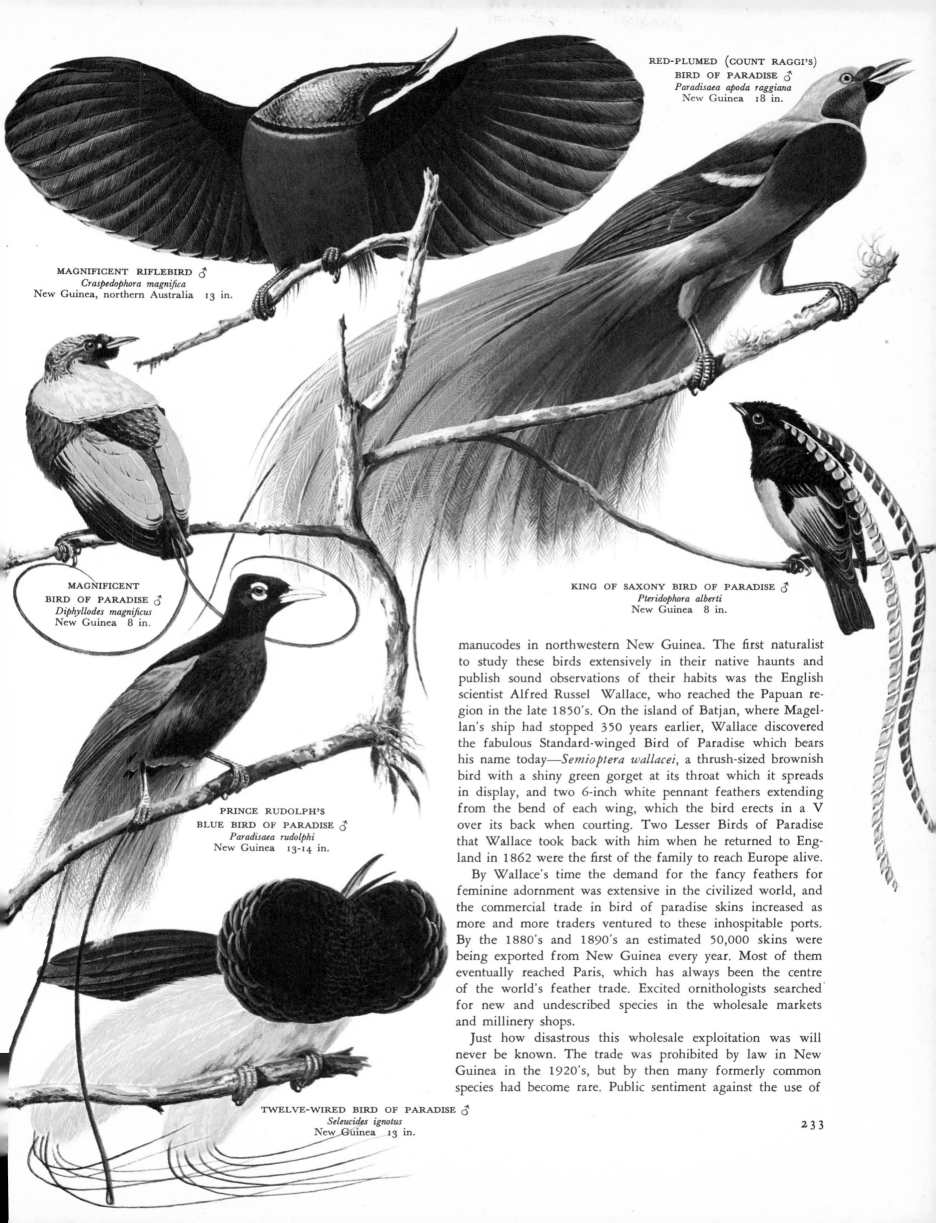

RED-PLUMED (COUNT RAGGI'S)
BIRD OF PARADISE ♂
Paradisaea apoda raggiana
New Guinea 18 in.

MAGNIFICENT RIFLEBIRD ♂
Craspedophora magnifica
New Guinea, northern Australia 13 in.

MAGNIFICENT
BIRD OF PARADISE ♂
Diphyllodes magnificus
New Guinea 8 in.

KING OF SAXONY BIRD OF PARADISE ♂
Pteridophora alberti
New Guinea 8 in.

PRINCE RUDOLPH'S
BLUE BIRD OF PARADISE ♂
Paradisaea rudolphi
New Guinea 13-14 in.

TWELVE-WIRED BIRD OF PARADISE ♂
Seleucides ignotus
New Guinea 13 in.

manucodes in northwestern New Guinea. The first naturalist to study these birds extensively in their native haunts and publish sound observations of their habits was the English scientist Alfred Russel Wallace, who reached the Papuan region in the late 1850's. On the island of Batjan, where Magellan's ship had stopped 350 years earlier, Wallace discovered the fabulous Standard-winged Bird of Paradise which bears his name today—*Semioptera wallacei*, a thrush-sized brownish bird with a shiny green gorget at its throat which it spreads in display, and two 6-inch white pennant feathers extending from the bend of each wing, which the bird erects in a V over its back when courting. Two Lesser Birds of Paradise that Wallace took back with him when he returned to England in 1862 were the first of the family to reach Europe alive.

By Wallace's time the demand for the fancy feathers for feminine adornment was extensive in the civilized world, and the commercial trade in bird of paradise skins increased as more and more traders ventured to these inhospitable ports. By the 1880's and 1890's an estimated 50,000 skins were being exported from New Guinea every year. Most of them eventually reached Paris, which has always been the centre of the world's feather trade. Excited ornithologists searched for new and undescribed species in the wholesale markets and millinery shops.

Just how disastrous this wholesale exploitation was will never be known. The trade was prohibited by law in New Guinea in the 1920's, but by then many formerly common species had become rare. Public sentiment against the use of

233

plumes has increased ever since, and it is now illegal to import wild-caught skins into the United States and most European countries. Some species have been reported to have made a good comeback in the last several decades. However, the eventual deforestation of New Guinea for agriculture could certainly be disastrous to the survival of these magnificent birds, whose fascinating courtship habits we are just beginning to understand.

The birds most people picture as typical birds of paradise are the six jay-sized species of Linnaeus's genus *Paradisaea*. These inhabitants of the wet lowland coastal jungles were common species of commerce. Their long, filmy flank plumes extend well beyond the tail when the bird is at rest and are raised over the back in a fountain-like spray in display. The shafts of the central tail feathers of the male are elongated thin wires or flattened narrow or twisted plumes. Their bodies are predominantly mauve, and they usually have patches of bright yellow on the back and head, and a brilliant greenish gorget at the throat. In the typical race of the Greater Bird of Paradise (Linnaeus's *apoda*), the trailing flank plumes are a bright yellow shading to mauve. These vary through orange to red in the Red Bird of Paradise, found only on the island of Waigeu off the northwest coast of New Guinea. Most of these birds display by crouching on a branch and waving their plumes above them. The Emperor of Germany Bird of Paradise starts his display right side up, and gradually tilts forward from the branch until he is hanging upside down with his plumes cascading around him. The rare and lovely Blue Bird of Paradise of the mountain forests of eastern New Guinea hangs upside down to start his display and then waves his gorgeous blue plumes in a lacy mist of blue spray around him.

Another species common among trade skins is the Twelve-wired Bird of Paradise found in the mangroves and sago swamp forests of coastal central and western New Guinea. Its six brilliant yellow plumes growing from each flank have long wiry tips bending sharply forward. When displaying to the drab brownish-barred female, the male Twelve-wire expands its bib of iridescent black-and-green throat feathers up around the bill and opens its bill to show its bright greenish-yellow mouth lining.

The 6-inch King Bird of Paradise is the smallest member of the family and one of the most brilliant; it is bright scarlet above and white below, and has bright blue legs and green plumes. Two of its tail feathers are elongated wires that end in curly metallic-green rackets. Conspicuous birds of the tree-tops, the male Kings apparently establish territories around the tall jungle trees where they display. This is the only species in the family known to nest in a hole in a tree.

Closely related to the King Bird of Paradise are two slightly larger species, the Magnificent and Wilson's. The Magnificent, found over much of the drier lowlands of New Guinea and up to about 5,000 feet in the mountains, makes a display ground for itself on the floor of the forest, stripping all vegetation from a stage some 15 feet in diameter and plucking the bark and the leaves from the saplings growing within it. The male dances up and down on these saplings, expanding his brilliant yellow crest in a fan like a cape and puffing out his glossy green chest feathers to reflect the light.

Because of the double cross of small, black velvety feathers

on the bare blue skin of its crown, Wilson's Bird of Paradise is often called the "cross of Christ." Named *Paradisaea wilsoni* in 1850 by John Cassin, the Philadelphia naturalist, in honour of his friend Alexander Wilson, the same specimen had been named six months earlier by Charles Lucien Bonaparte, a nephew of Napoleon who spent some time in the United States and wrote extensively on American birds. Bonaparte called it *P. respublica* (the scientific name Wilson's Bird of Paradise holds today by right of priority) partly in honour of the French republic, partly to express his disapproval of some "republicans," for he commented, "Even though a paradisaean Republic does not exist, at least there is now a *Paradisaea respublica*."

Many birds of paradise have been named after royalty. One of the earliest was Queen Victoria's Riflebird (*Ptiloris victoriae*) of Australia, named after his monarch by John Gould, the English artist-naturalist, in 1850. The Germans, who were active in New Guinea in the 1880's, named two outstanding species after their then emperor and empress (*P. guilielmi* and *P. augustaevictoria*). The Austrian Otto Finsch named the Blue Bird of Paradise *P. rudolphi,* in honour of Archduke Rudolph of Hapsburg, who died so tragically a short while later at Mayerling, and Princess Stephanie's Bird of Paradise (*Astrapia stephaniae*), one of the ribbon-tailed group, after Rudolph's Belgian consort.

Princess Stephanie's Bird of Paradise is another of the very few species that have bred in captivity, and is representative of a group of long-tailed birds of paradise sometimes called paradise magpies. All are inhabitants of the high mountain forests of New Guinea, where very few of them were caught for the feather trade. All have a shining metallic-black body, and many are endowed with brilliant, reflective neck ruffs and long, ornate tails. The male Ribbon-tailed Bird of Paradise has two white central tail feathers which stream 3 feet behind him in flight. This bird, discovered in 1939, has a total length of 42 inches and is the longest of all the passerine birds.

The largest-bodied birds of paradise are the crow-sized Sickle-bills of the New Guinea highlands, seldom found below 5,000 feet. In display the Sickle-bill raises epaulettes of long metal-tipped feathers growing along his flanks up over his head until they meet over his back; he opens and closes his long central tail feathers, and opens his bill to show the bright yellow lining.

Best known of the so-called flag birds is the Six-plumed Bird of Paradise, which has three wire-like plumes growing out of each side of the head, each tipped with a black racket. Another is the King of Saxony, or Enamelled, Bird of Paradise, a little 7-inch mite known only from the mountains of central New Guinea. Males have two long 18-inch plumes trailing backward from the head, each of which bears a series of 30 to 40 miniature flags along one side of the vane, a brilliantly enamelled blue outside, brown inside. This bird, described in 1894 from a specimen found in a Paris market, is so unbelievable that conservative ornithologists of the time refused to believe that it was real, and suspected that it was an artifact.

While their habits in the wild are still imperfectly known, a number of these fantastically plumed birds are polygamous, and as usual in such circumstances, all the nesting duties from building of the nest to feeding and rearing of the young are done by the duller, browner females. This, however, is not true throughout the family. The more primitive species, the manucodes and the wattled birds of paradise of the genera *Macgregoria* and *Paradigalla,* are often brilliantly coloured, but have few or no plumes, and the male and female are similar in colour. In the Black Manucode of New Guinea the males are monogamous, and while the female alone incubates through the 15- to 18-day incubation period, the male brings nest material for the female to work with, helps bring food to the young, and occasionally broods them.

The Magnificent Riflebird is found in both New Guinea and northeastern Australia. Its flank display plumes are soft and hairy and much shorter than those in many of the other groups. The bird has a brilliant throat of glossy purplish blue and poses with wings spread wide and its head thrown back to catch the rays of the sunlight on the throat. Riflebirds get their peculiar name from their call, a loud two-syllabled whistling note reminiscent of the whine of a bullet.

Related to the flag birds is the Lesser Superb Bird of Paradise, a small starling-sized species with two sets of plumes,

a cap of more than 100 velvety black feathers behind the crown which can be elevated into a huge fan over the head, and a breast plate of metallic-green feathers which expands almost to meet the crown plumes. These plumes are so firmly muscled that the displaying birds can fly with them erect. From the centre of this feathery shield the bird opens its mouth to show the brilliant lining.

The soundest biological explanation so far proposed for the development of these fancy plumes and elaborate display patterns is the need for pronounced recognition marks between species to prevent hybridization between these promiscuous, polygamous birds. A score or more wild hybrids are known, more of them between than within genera. All of them occur between the most highly developed types, none among the more primitive forms. As most such hybrids are sterile and of no value in species survival, species recognition is highly important in these highly specialized forms that do not form permanent mating pairs. Some of the most gaudy patterns and weirdest displays have possibly evolved through the need to avoid such disadvantageous hybridizing.

TITMICE

PASSERIFORMES   PARIDAE

No more friendly group of birds exist than the 65-odd species of active tits, titmice, and chickadees. Bright-eyed, pert, curious, and unafraid, they go about searching twigs and small branches for minute insects with little concern for humans. These wild birds can be tamed to take food from one's hand. Their lisping, reedy calls and their simple whistled songs are among the best known and best loved of bird sounds. Many species nest in bird boxes. The vernacular names "tit" and "titmouse" generally used for the group are of Anglo-Saxon origin, "tit" meaning a very small object, and "mouse" a corruption of "mase," an Anglo-Saxon name for several small birds.

The titmouse family is fairly well defined. Most of its members are very small birds less than 6 inches in length, the smallest measuring only 3 inches from tip of bill to tip of tail, the largest a bare 8 inches. All have soft, thick plumage, and the sexes are usually alike in colour, mostly greys and browns, often boldly marked with black and white or blues and yellows, but never very bright, and never barred, streaked, or mottled. All have short, stout, pointed bills, the nostrils partly concealed by bristles, and small but strong legs and feet. Their rounded wings are of medium length and have 10 primary feathers, the outermost one only half the length of the second. Their tails vary from quite short to very long in a few species.

The relationships of titmice to other families are obscure, but the titmice show affinities in distribution, structure, and behaviour to the crow-jay complex. Their present distribution strongly parallels that of the crow subfamily and suggests a similar Old World origin. Titmice have their greatest development in the Northern Hemisphere, are well represented in Africa south to the Cape of Good Hope, but are absent from the Australian region and from the oceanic islands. They

have pushed southward in the New World only to the Guatemalan highlands.

Titmice are among the most adaptable and teachable of the very small birds—another similarity to the corvids. Laboratory tests have proved the titmice's ability to solve simple problems connected with obtaining food, a skill long known to cage-bird fanciers. The tricks tame titmice can be taught are amazing. The Varied Titmouse is the little bird that tells fortunes at shrine festivals and street fairs in Japan. At the command of its master it hops to its perch, takes a coin from your fingers, drops it into a cash box, opens the door of a miniature shrine, takes out your paper fortune, and tears off the wrapping so that you receive it ready to read.

After the breeding season titmice roam through the woodlands in small family groups, and later gather in flocks of considerable size. These loose bands may include several

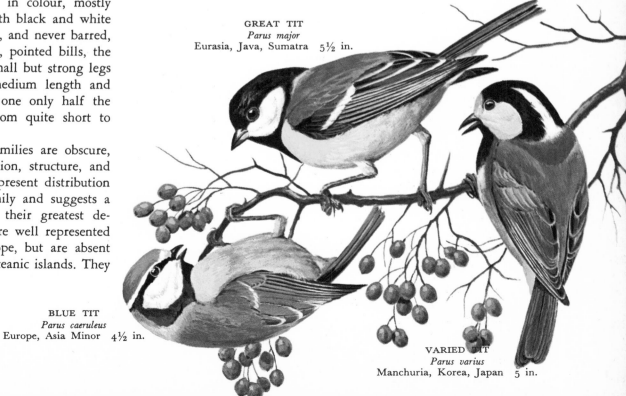

GREAT TIT
Parus major
Eurasia, Java, Sumatra   5½ in.

BLUE TIT
Parus caeruleus
Europe, Asia Minor   4½ in.

VARIED TIT
Parus varius
Manchuria, Korea, Japan   5 in.

species of titmice and sometimes nuthatches, creepers, kinglets, and woodpeckers, all moving steadily, working a limb here, a branch there, and then flitting on to the next tree.

While insects are their mainstay, titmice eat seeds, small fruits, and berries, especially in winter when insects are scarce. They come readily to bird-tables in suburban areas and are particularly fond of suet and sunflower seeds, which they hold between their feet and pound with their bills jay-fashion to open. The Crested Tit of northern Eurasia has the usual titlike habit of storing food, caching spruce and pine seeds and insect pupae in bark crevices for later use.

Though titmice wander widely when not breeding and northern species may retreat hundreds of miles southward in severe winters, they are not strongly migratory. Their seasonal movements, as revealed by ringing, are sporadic and irregular and seem conditioned by local availability of food.

Some 45 species, almost three-quarters of the family, are grouped in the single genus *Parus* of the subfamily Parinae. Typical of them is the familiar Willow Tit, which gave Gilbert and Sullivan one of their happier inspirations—though "tit willow" is not part of the birds' vocabulary by any stretch of the imagination. In North America lives the very similar Blackcapped Chickadee, whose clearly whistled "spring soon" or "sweet weather" cheers the New England countryside as the bleak days lengthen in late winter. The genus is represented by 11 species in North America and Mexico, and by 18 more in temperate Eurasia. The 5½-inch Great Tit, while the largest and commonest of Europe, is not the largest member of the family. This distinction goes to the 8-inch Sultan Tit, a resident of the hill forests from the eastern Himalayas through Burma, Siam, and Malaya to Sumatra. The Sultan Tit is a stocky black bird with golden-yellow underparts and a long yellow crest.

A number of titmice of the genus *Parus* have distinctive head crests which stand up all the time. The Crested Tit of northern Eurasia is one example, the Tufted Titmouse of the southeastern United States another. The 6½-inch Tufted Titmouse, a mouse-coloured bird with rusty flanks and all the friendly characteristics of its chickadee relatives, is the largest member of the family in North America.

Practically all the parine titmice are cavity nesters. A few chip their own holes out of half-rotten stubs or fenceposts; others use available natural cavities in trees or those deserted by woodpeckers. Still others nest in nooks and crannies in rocky cliffs. Nesting behaviour is similar throughout the subfamily. The female usually builds the nest, and the male sometimes assists by bringing material to her. In the Willow Tit both sexes work at hewing out the nesting cavity and lining it with grasses, feathers, and hair; in the Crested Tit the female does all the nest building. Incubation is always by the female alone, but the male feeds her while she is incubating. Both sexes feed the young.

The parine titmice are normally single-brooded, but they lay large clutches, rarely as few as 5 to 6 eggs, more frequently 7 to 11, and as many as 15 have been recorded. In a few species the eggs are pure white; in most they are speckled with reddish brown. Large families are needed to offset the high natural mortality in the titmice, which averages 70 per cent in the adults and is even higher in the young during their first year. With almost three-fourths of the population dying each year, less than one per cent of the wild birds live more

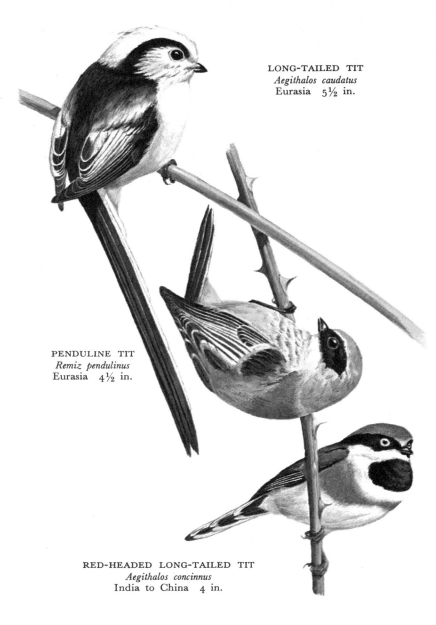

LONG-TAILED TIT
Aegithalos caudatus
Eurasia 5½ in.

PENDULINE TIT
Remiz pendulinus
Eurasia 4½ in.

RED-HEADED LONG-TAILED TIT
Aegithalos concinnus
India to China 4 in.

than 4 years. The longevity record for wild titmice is 8 years, attained by a Black-capped Chickadee ringed on Cape Cod.

The subfamily Aegithalinae contains a dozen tiny titmice with long tails. Typical of this group is the Long-tailed Tit of Eurasia, a tame and confiding little mite that can be approached within a few feet. One of the smallest is the Pygmy Tit of Java, barely 3 inches long, and most of it tail. Close relatives are the sociable little Bush Tits of the western U.S.A. and the Mexican highlands, dull grey and brown little birds with the roving habits typical of the family.

The Long-Tailed Tits make beautiful bag nests with a side entrance, woven of mosses, lichens, and spider webs and lined with feathers. Pairs spend 2 to 3 weeks together building it in a bush or tree. As in the chickadee group, the male feeds the female on the nest. So small is the nest's cramped interior that the sitting bird has to curl her tail to fit in. The Long-tailed Tit lays from 7 to 12 eggs, white with small red spots. Incubation takes 12 to 13 days.

A third subfamily, Remizinae, consists of the eight species commonly known as the Penduline Tits because of the long hanging bag nests most of them make. The side entrances of their nests are usually protected by short tunnels, which some African species are reported to bite shut behind them. The

Penduline Tit of Eurasia, with its distinctive black facial mask, is one of the better-known species. The only American member of this subfamily is the Verdin, a tiny olive-grey bird that lives in western chaparral country. The Verdin builds a large globular nest of thorny twigs that is so impregnable the bird makes no attempt to conceal it, but places it conspicuously near the end of a branch of a shrub or low tree.

The Penduline Tits lay smaller clutches than the other titmice, usually 4 to 5 eggs, but most of them are double-brooded. The males seem to do most of the nest building, and the females all the incubating and rearing of the young. The males often make several nests, and the female chooses one to lay in. The others are used for roosting at night. Roosting within their nesting cavities is a common habit among all titmice.

CREEPERS

PASSERIFORMES   CERTHIIDAE

There is no mistaking these slender, little brown birds that creep unobtrusively up and around tree trunks. Streaked and spotted above and whitish below, they are almost invisible against the bark. They have thin, pointed, down-curved bills for probing into bark crevices, and long, stiff tail feathers pointed at the end. Creepers use their tails as props for climbing, as do woodpeckers, and they moult their tail feathers in the same way, from the outermost pair inward in succession. They are the only passerines in which the central pair of tail feathers remain in place until all the others are replaced.

These "true" creepers number five species, all placed in the single genus *Certhia*, which is restricted to the Northern Hemisphere. The principal species is called the Tree Creeper in Europe, the Brown Creeper in North America. This wide-ranging little bird, found throughout the forested portions of North America and Eurasia, breaks into about a dozen geographical races on each continent. The four other species are all very similar birds found along the southern periphery of the family's range in the Old World. In the New World the Brown Creeper has reached southward to the mountains of Nicaragua, but its ecological niche is filled from Central America southward by the strikingly similar woodcreepers (p. 196).

Creepers are generally solitary birds that stay by themselves and go their own way. They live almost entirely on bark insects, and their eggs and larvae. Unlike the nuthatches, which search trees up, down, and sideways, head down as well as head up, the Tree Creeper usually works steadily up the tree trunk in a spiral, working systematically to the top and then fluttering down to the base of the next tree to repeat the manoeuvre. To rework a rewarding section of bark, it drops down backwards a few feet, tail first, with a fluttering of wings, and climbs back up again. It explores the bottoms and sides of horizontal branches as well as their tops, and has no trouble clinging to the underside of a limb like a fly on the ceiling.

The call notes of the Tree Creeper are high-pitched, sibilant squeaks, weak and hard to hear, though the bird utters them frequently while feeding and occasionally in flight. The species also has an attractive little musical song in the spring. Clear, sweet, polysyllabic, and pitched very high in the upper registers of human hearing, its low intensity is in keeping with the singer's small size and unprepossessing manner.

The Tree Creeper builds a hammock-shaped, elongated cup nest, usually wedged against the trunk of a dead tree behind a piece of loose bark. Cunningly woven of thin strips of bark, mosses, and fine grass on a base of slender twigs, it is lined with soft bark, spider webs, and feathers. Both sexes work at nest building. In the American races, only the females incubate, though the male is believed to assist in some of the European forms. The eggs number 6 to 7, occasionally as many as 9, and are white with a fine peppering of small reddish-brown dots. The incubation period is from 13 to 15 days, and the young spend another two weeks in the nest, where both parents feed them until they are able to climb out and creep over the surface of the bark to find food for themselves.

NUTHATCHES AND ALLIES

PASSERIFORMES   SITTIDAE

The acrobatic nuthatches are the only tree-trunk foragers that habitually hunt downward. Perhaps from their head-down viewpoint they find titbits the competing creepers and small woodpeckers overlook. Nuthatches live largely on the small insects and spiders they ferret out of crannies in the bark, but also eat some seeds and nuts. Several Old World species hew acorns and hazelnuts open by wedging them in crevices and hacking them with the bill, swinging their tiny bodies to drive home each blow. The name comes from this habit, rarely observed in the New World nuthatches, and is a corruption of "nuthack." It has nothing to do with incubating.

The name nuthatch is most properly applied to the 15 species of the genus *Sitta* and the subfamily Sittinae found throughout the forested regions of the Northern Hemisphere. These are stocky, short-necked little birds dressed in plain solid colours, usually grey to blue above and white below. Many have the underparts tinged with reddish brown, and the top of the head is often black or brown. Their bills are thin, straight, and sharp-pointed, and their legs short but stout. Their long, strong toes are tipped with sharp claws that give them sure footing on vertical bark surfaces. Unlike the woodpeckers and the true creepers, nuthatches do not use their tail in climbing but rely entirely on their feet to hold them in place. Instead of being stiff and spiny, their tails are soft, short, and squared or rounded.

Like their nearest relatives, the titmice, the nuthatches are best developed in the Old World, where they doubtless had their origin. Only four species occur in the New World, and the family is unknown south of central Mexico. Largest of the North American species is the White-breasted Nuthatch, common in the deciduous woodlands of the United States and a frequent visitor to city parks and suburbs. The Red-breasted Nuthatch prefers coniferous forests and breeds from the Canadian spruce zones southward through the Appalachians and the Rockies to northern Mexico. The Pygmy Nuthatch is a western species; the Brown-headed is a resident of the southeastern U. S. lowlands.

Widest ranging of the Old World species is the common Eurasian Nuthatch, which strongly resembles the Red-breasted. It breeds across the continent, usually in deciduous woodlands, from Great Britain and Spain to Kamchatka, Japan, and China. One of the most striking is the blue-backed Velvet-fronted Nuthatch, found in southeastern Asian forests from India to the Philippines. Similar to the Velvet-fronted, but with the head and abdomen velvety black, is the southernmost of the *Sittas,* the Azure Nuthatch of the mountain forests of Malaya, Java, and Sumatra.

Two *Sittas* have left the woodlands to live among the bare rocks of highland cliffs, canyons, and gorges. These are the rock nuthatches of southeastern Europe and the Himalayas. Light-grey birds with brown washings on their white underparts, they hop and climb around the rock faces with the same agility and mannerisms that their tree-trunk-loving relatives display.

Nuthatches are droll, earnest little birds, quite tame and fearless and always busily searching for food. Rather solitary and usually met singly or in pairs, they come to feeding places readily and can be induced, with patience, to take food from the fingers. Though they roam widely when not breeding, nuthatches are not strongly migratory, and most are resident where they occur. Northern forms move slightly southward in search of food during the winter, and mountain species seek lower levels during cold weather. One or two can often be found with the loose flocks of titmice, kinglets, and small woodpeckers that rove the temperate woodlands in winter.

Most nuthatches have distinctive metallic and penetrating call notes, easy to recognize. The American White- and Red-breasted nuthatches utter unmistakable nasal "yank-yanks" as they clamber about. Many of them also have unprepossessing spring songs, varied, bubbling, and quite musical, but hard to hear; these are delivered quietly as if the bird were singing under its breath.

All the *Sittas* are cavity nesters, and all but the rock nuthatches use natural holes in trees. Both sexes work at lining the cavity with grasses, mosses, and very often with animal hair. The Old World species have the peculiar habit of reducing the size of the entrance to their nest cavity by

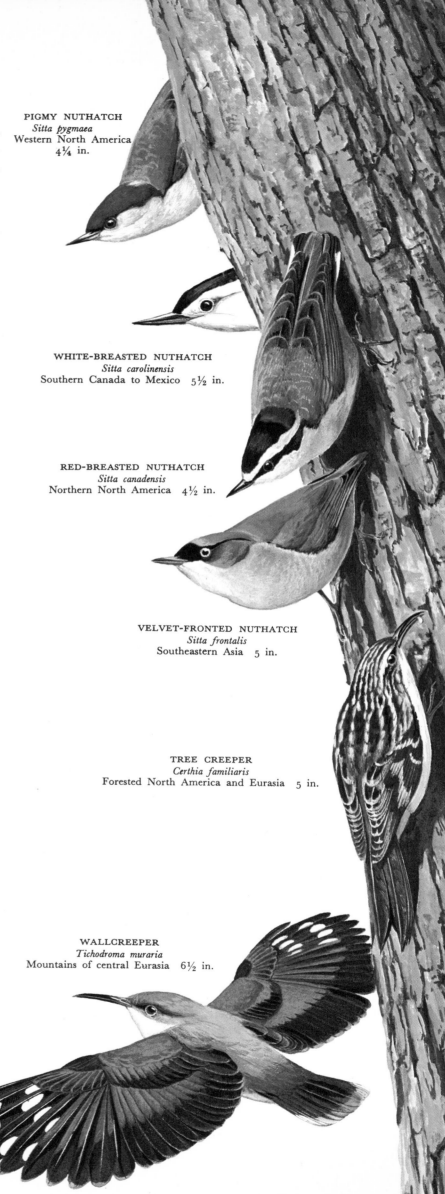

PIGMY NUTHATCH
Sitta pygmaea
Western North America
4¼ in.

WHITE-BREASTED NUTHATCH
Sitta carolinensis
Southern Canada to Mexico 5½ in.

RED-BREASTED NUTHATCH
Sitta canadensis
Northern North America 4½ in.

VELVET-FRONTED NUTHATCH
Sitta frontalis
Southeastern Asia 5 in.

TREE CREEPER
Certhia familiaris
Forested North America and Eurasia 5 in.

WALLCREEPER
Tichodroma muraria
Mountains of central Eurasia 6½ in.

plastering it with mud, presumably for added safety. This technique is most pronounced in the rock nuthatches, which build cone-shaped nests entirely of mud in cavities between the rocks, or projecting 6 or 8 inches from a rock face. Strangely, none of the New World nuthatches does this, though the Red-breasted Nuthatch smears the edges of its nesting hole with pine pitch.

The sittine nuthatches lay white eggs speckled with red-brown. The clutch may vary from 4 to 10, and incubation is apparently by the female alone. The male feeds her on the nest throughout the 12- to 14-day incubation period, and he always helps feed the young until they fledge. Nuthatches are generally multi-brooded.

Classified with the nuthatches are 15 Old World birds of uncertain systematic position, some formerly placed with the creepers. Most have slender, down-curved bills, and are commonly called "creepers," but as they lack the creepers' stiff, springy tails, they are now included tentatively as subfamilies of the nuthatches. Some perhaps deserve separate family rank, such as the Coral-billed Nuthatch (*Hypositta*) of Madagascar, a little greenish-blue bird with a short, slightly hooked, reddish bill that suggests possible affinities to the vanga-shrikes. It is reported as fairly common in the wet forests of eastern Madagascar. It forages for the most part on tree trunks and the larger branches, and it apparently never perches head downward. Instead it works spirally upward as the creepers do.

Largest of the nuthatches and placed in a subfamily by itself is the singular Wallcreeper with its startling red wing coverts. Wallcreepers inhabit rocky cliffs in the mountains of southern Europe and eastward through the Himalayas. Wallcreepers climb over the sheer rock walls hunting insects. They assist their progress up the vertical rock faces with short wing flicks that flash their red and white markings, darting out occasionally to snatch a passing insect on the wing. Their flight is peculiarly halting and butterfly-like; in fact, mountaineers call them "butterfly birds."

The Wallcreeper builds a nest of grasses and moss lined with hair and a stray feather or two, deep in an inaccessible crevice. The male may bring nest material and he helps feed the young, but the female builds the nest and does all the incubating. In winter Wallcreepers retreat to lower altitudes, where they sometimes have trouble finding the precipitous surroundings they prefer, and are seen scaling the walls of tall buildings.

Placed in another subfamily are the two Spotted Creepers (*Salpornis*) of Africa and India, and the three small Sitellas or tree runners (*Neositta*) of Australia and New Guinea. These birds act and look like true creepers, except for their soft tails, but they build open cup nests in forked branches. One of the rarest and least-known members of the family is the Red-fronted Creeper (*Daphoenositta*) of New Guinea. In Australia are five species of streaked brownish birds 5 to 6 inches long called treecreepers (*Climacteris*) that feed on the ground as well as on tree trunks, and are hole nesters like most nuthatches. Possibly allied to them are two aberrant Philippine creepers (*Rhabdornis*), the Striped-headed and the Plain-headed, both also hole nesters. These birds not only take insects from bark crevices, but have brush-tipped tongues and feed among flowers.

CORAL-BILLED NUTHATCH
Hypositta corallirostris
Madagascar 5½ in.

SPOTTED CREEPER
Salpornis spilonotus
Tropical Africa 5 in.

STRIPE-HEADED CREEPER
Rhabdornis mystacalis
Philippines 6 in.

RED-BROWED TREECREEPER
Climacteris erythrops
Eastern Australia 5½ in.

RED-CAPPED BABBLER
Timalia pileata
Himalayas to Indochina and Java 7 in.

STRIPED JUNGLE BABBLER
Pellorneum ruficeps
India to Indochina 6½ in.

PEKIN ROBIN
Leiothrix lutea
Himalayas and
southern China 6 in.

SILVER-EARED MESIA
Leiothrix argentauris
Himalayas to Indochina 7 in.

GREY-CROWNED SCIMITAR-BABBLER
Pomatostomus temporalis
Eastern Australia 10 in.

CINNAMON QUAIL-THRUSH
Cinclosoma cinnamomeum
Interior of Australia 9 in.

WHITE-CRESTED LAUGHING THRUSH
Garrulax leucolophus
Himalayas to Indochina 12 in.

RED-WINGED (BLACK-CROWNED) SHRIKE-BABBLER
Pteruthius erythropterus
Himalayas to Indochina 6½ in.

BABBLERS AND ALLIES
PASSERIFORMES   TIMALIIDAE

This large assemblage of some 280 Old World forest birds is one of the most diverse of all passerine families. Its members range from tiny birds such as Bearded Tits or wrens to some the size of small crows. Some look and act like tits, others like woodland rails or pittas, still others like thrashers, thrushes, or crows. Many are dull-coloured and undistinctive; others are brightly hued and strongly patterned. Some build open cup-shaped nests, others build domed structures with side entrances, but all nest on or fairly near the ground. Most of them are noisy birds (hence the name babblers) of woodlands or brushlands that travel through the undergrowth in small flocks and keep up a more or less continual chatter of chirps and churrs. All are insect eaters; a few add small fruits and seeds to their normal diet of small animal life.

Anatomically the family is poorly defined and loosely delimited, but all its members have soft, fluffy plumage and comparatively large, strong legs and feet. All are rather weak fliers with short rounded wings that curve to fit closely to the body. All have wings with 10 primary feathers, the first 3 unequal in length and shorter than the longest one. Normally the 12-feathered tail is fairly broad and square or rounded, though it is long and pointed in a few species. The bills vary from short and stout to slender and down-curved, but are always shorter than the tarsus. The culmen is more or less ridged and curved at the tip, and sometimes ends in a shrike-like hook. The upper mandible usually has a slight notch near its tip.

The babbler family's distribution is essentially the wooded portions of Old World central and southern land masses. The greatest number of them are found in the oriental region, and the family is well represented in Australia and in Africa. Its northernmost members are the little crowtits that range from southwestern Europe eastward across temperate Asia to Korea. Another, the Wrentit of United States west coast scrublands, is the only member of the family in the New World. A number of genera have disjointed ranges in Africa and Asia.

If the family as now constituted is a natural assemblage (which is open to question), its diversity and the patchy, scattered distribution of many of its components suggest it is of ancient lineage. Its members show similarities to so many other passerine families that the affinities of the group as a whole cannot be determined. They probably represent early offshoots from some primitive Old World insect-eating ancestor or ancestors that also gave rise to the Old World bulbuls, warblers, thrushes, and flycatchers. Only within the last few decades has some order been made out of the welter of different species assigned to the family Timaliidae. They are now sorted into seven fairly distinctive subfamilies, some of which are so divergent in appearance, habits, and distribution that many students accord them full family rank.

The ground-babbler subfamily (Cinclosomatinae) contains a scant score of terrestrial species restricted to the Australo-Papuan region, though one species, the Malay Rail-babbler, extends northward into Malaya. The ground–babblers are varicoloured birds with very soft, fluffy plumage, long legs, rather small feet, and thin necks. They live on the forest floor, often near fallen timber, and scurry through the underbrush much like rails or pittas.

Typical of the group is the Cinnamon Quail-thrush of Australia. These birds go about in pairs or small parties and, though fairly noisy, keep well hidden in the undergrowth. They fly with an audible whirring of wings, but only when closely pressed, and then for a very short distance. They drop quickly into cover, run off through the underbrush, and are difficult to flush a second time. The quail-thrushes build open cup-shaped nests on the ground, in which they lay 2 to 3 heavily spotted eggs.

Other interesting Australian members of this group are the logrunners, or spinetails (*Orthonyx*), which are similarly retiring birds of the underbrush, but have more pleasant voices.

BALD CROW
(BARE-HEADED ROCK FOWL)
Picathartes gymnocephalus
Tropical West Africa 14 in.

VINOUS-THROATED CROWTIT
Paradoxornis webbiana
Manchuria and Ussuria to Burma 4½ in.

They scratch in the ground debris for their food, mainly insects, slugs, and snails, and reportedly use their tails as well as their feet for the purpose, raking the ground sideways, with the spiny tips of their short tail feathers, a most unusual habit known in no other bird. The spinetails build a domed nest of sticks and moss with a side entrance on or near the ground. They lay two pure-white eggs which take about 3 weeks to hatch.

The jungle-babbler subfamily (Pellorneinae) contains some 30 species of small, secretive, brownish birds from 6 to 8 inches in length found from the Philippines through the oriental region, where they are most plentiful, and in Africa. Jungle-babblers have rather slender bills, often strongly hooked at the tip, and look much like some of the Old World warblers (p. 255). They inhabit low forest thickets where their sombre plumage and skulking habits make them extremely hard to observe. Representative of the group is the Striped Jungle-babbler, which ranges from India to Indochina in the low brushwoods and bamboo jungles from sea level up to perhaps 4,000 feet. Fairly common throughout its range, the Striped Jungle-babbler is more often heard than seen. Its loud mellow calls and whistled chatterings are familiar sounds in the Burmese jungles. Jungle-babblers travel about in small flocks and feed largely on insects and small molluscs. They build large globular nests of leaves and moss on or close to the ground, often in the shelter of a low shrub, and lay 2 to 4 heavily spotted eggs.

The third subfamily, the Pomatorhininae, is commonly known as the scimitar-babblers and wren-babblers. The group's 33-odd species range throughout the Orient from India to eastern China and south through the East Indies into Australia. All are sombrely streaked and mottled in browns. The scimitar-babblers are thrush-sized birds 7 to 11 inches long, with long tails and long down-curved bills, that superficially resemble the thrashers of the New World. Wren-babblers are smaller birds 3½ to 6 inches long, wren-like in appearance as their name implies. The two extremes are connected by many intermediate forms.

Shy, retiring denizens of the forest undergrowth, the scimitar-babblers and wren-babblers feed on or near the ground and are known for their habit of digging into the earth with their bills. Many of them have pleasant songs. All build domed nests of rather loose, fragile construction. Their eggs vary greatly, some being pure white, others heavily spotted with dark browns. The Grey-crowned Scimitar-babbler of eastern Australia has the typical babbler trait of traipsing through the forest undergrowth in small noisy bands. Its gregariousness and its distinctive calls have earned it such local names as apostle bird, happy family, chatterer, cackler, and yahoo.

The 37 species classified as tit-babblers (Timaliinae) include some of the more brightly coloured members of the family. Their fluffy plumage often exhibits contrasting patterns of white and black, browns, greys, and yellows. They have short titmouse-like bills and large, strong legs and feet. They range from the Philippines westward through the oriental region to India, and four species of one genus, *Neomixis*, are marooned in Madagascar. While they have the general flocking habits of the family, the tit-babblers are not noisy, few have a real song, and all tend to be less terrestrial. Some live entirely in trees, a few live in evergreen forests in the highlands, and a number are addicted to open scrub country and grasslands. Most of them make bell-like domed nests, but a few build deep cups. The striking Red-capped Babbler, which ranges from India to the Philippines and southward to Java, is fairly typical of the subfamily. This species is partial to canebrakes and grassy plains.

The largest, most widespread, and perhaps most typical group of babblers consists of the 140-odd laughing thrushes of the subfamily Turdoidinae. The laughing thrushes are found in Africa, throughout India and the oriental region, and south into the East Indies. They are a highly variable group ranging from about 4 to 12 inches in length. Some are dull-coloured; others show the gayest hues of any member of the family, with bright yellows, reds, and greens showing in bold patterns. The laughing-thrush complex is best developed in the hill forests from India through southern China and Malaya where some of the brightest and most colourful species occur. Here live the Red-winged Shrike-babbler and the Red-billed Leiothrix, which, though a bird of the Himalayan foothills, is commonly known as the Pekin Robin. Its bright colours and attractive song have made it a popular cage bird in India and elsewhere.

Laughing thrushes are noisy birds with wide vocal ranges, given to chattering choruses that have the quality of distant human laughter. Essentially arboreal forest dwellers, many of them feed on the ground, and some are common garden residents in India and the Orient. Primarily insectivorous, many of them eat seeds and small fruit as well. Most build cup nests in trees or bushes; a few have domed nests on or near the ground.

The sixth subfamily of this widely varying family, the Paradoxornithinae, contains the northern outliers of the group, the dozen or so species of crowtits or parrotbills of central and eastern Asia. Once classified as titmice, crowtits have short, heavy bills, laterally compressed like a parrot's—hence the name parrotbill often used for the group. Crowtits are active little birds that wander through grasslands, brushlands, hedgerows, and thickets in flocks of 50 or more, hunting seeds, berries, and small insects. They work over reed stems and thicket twigs at gravity-defying angles while keeping up a twittering chattering to one another. They act so much like the non-tippable "daruma" dolls set on a round base that the Japanese name "daruma tit" for the Vinous-throated Crowtit of China and Korea is most apt.

Another member of this subfamily formerly classified with the titmice is the Bearded Tit, so called for the male's black moustache stripes. A resident of reedy marshes from southern Europe to Manchuria, the Bearded Tit behaves much like the parrotbills, and is similarly gregarious, acrobatic, and garrulous. All these tit-like babblers build deep cup nests of grasses and reeds lined with plant fibres, hair, and a feather or two. In the Bearded Tit both sexes build the nest and the male adds the lining. Their clutches are large for timaliids, 5 to 7 white eggs, heavily blotched with brown. Both sexes incubate for a period of 12 to 13 days; the fledging period is 9 to 12 days, and the species is multi-brooded.

Now thought a possible offshoot from the crowtits is the

unique Wrentit, isolated in the scrublands west of the Rocky Mountains from Oregon south to Baja California. If it is a crowtit, it is the only member of the family to have reached the New World. This fluffy little grey-brown bird shows no close affinities to any of the American passerines, and the American Check-list places it in a family by itself—the Chamaeidae. Wrentits are weak fliers and move through the thickets by hopping from twig to twig. Though the immature birds wander widely in the autumn and winter, adults are very sedentary. Wrentits appear to mate for life, and each pair to remain all year within its acre or two of territory. Ringing has shown these little 6-inch mites may live 10 years, a long life span indeed for so small a bird.

Recently placed with the babblers as a seventh subfamily, the Picathartinae, are two strange birds of West Africa known as Bare-headed Rock Fowl. The two species differ largely in the colour of their heads, the bare skin being blue and red in the Cameroon species, bright yellow in the bird of Sierra Leone. Both species live on the ground in wet highlands where tall forest trees shelter large moss-covered boulders. Few Europeans have ever had the opportunity to study the Rock Fowl in their native haunts, and the African natives attribute magical powers to them. They are reported to be somewhat gregarious, to fly little, to move gracefully on the ground, and to be curious enough to investigate anything unusual in the vicinity. Rather quiet birds, Rock Fowl have low croaking calls, and feed on insects, small frogs, crustaceans, and snails. Rock Fowl build mud nests lined with vegetable fibres and a few feathers; the nests are plastered to cliff faces 5 to 15 feet above the ground, often sheltered from rain by a rocky overhang. They lay two creamy-white eggs heavily mottled with brown.

BULBULS

PASSERIFORMES   PYCNONOTIDAE

Bulbuls are among the better known and more familiar of the local songbirds throughout the family's extensive range in southern Asia and Africa. Many have adapted themselves to cultivated lands and have become common residents around villages, in suburban gardens and orchards, and even in city parks. Of moderate size and rather plainly garbed, most bulbuls are not striking in appearance, but they generally make themselves conspicuous by their actions. They are gregarious, industrious and inquisitive, and fairly bold and noisy. Their most winning attributes are their cheerful friendliness and their constant musical chattering. Many have pleasant songs.

The bulbul family is large, with 119 species, and fairly well defined. An outstanding characteristic, though sometimes partly concealed, is a patch of hair-like, vaneless feathers on the nape. Bulbuls range in length from 6 to 11 inches. Their necks and wings are short, their tails medium to long and sometimes slightly forked. Bills are somewhat slender, slightly down-curved, and hooked and notched in some species. Most bulbuls are sombrely clad in greys, browns, dull greens, or black, often relieved by patches of yellow or red and white about the head and undertail coverts. A number of species are crested. The sexes are similarly coloured but males are sometimes slightly larger.

The bulbuls are a rather primitive group of Old World oscines, believed most closely allied to the babblers, from which they differ mainly in having shorter legs and feet and well-developed rictal bristles. Their dull colours and their soft, fluffy plumage, especially their thick patch of long rump feathers, suggest possible affinities to the cuckoo-shrikes. Like both the babblers and cuckoo-shrikes, the bulbuls are essentially forest inhabitants, though a number live in scrub country and in open grasslands if shrubby cover is available. They have adapted well to man-made changes in their natural environment. Their altitudinal range extends from sea level up to 10,000 feet in the Himalayas.

The bulbul family is best developed in Africa and Madagascar, where all but one of its 14 genera occur. Nine of the African genera are either monotypic or have only two or three species. Four of the larger genera have representatives ranging widely from Africa across southern Asia to Japan, the Philippines, and the Moluccas. The largest and most familiar group consists of the 47 species in the nominate genus *Pycnonotus*, of which the Red-whiskered Bulbul is typical.

The Red-whiskered Bulbul, a common Asiatic species, is found from India to China and south through Malaysia. Always lively and on the go, this bird prefers human settlements to the heavy jungles. Its short, bright call notes vie with the chatterings of sparrows and starlings around rural oriental villages. A cheerful and conspicuous resident of orchards and

RED-WHISKERED BULBUL
Pycnonotus jocosus
India to China, Indochina, Java, Sumatra   8 in.

243

YELLOW-STREAKED GREENBUL
Phyllastrephus flavostriatus
Tropical Africa 8 in.

gardens, it scurries through the trees looking for ripening fruit or over the grass in search of insects, its tail cocked at a jaunty angle, and bathes in puddles left by a passing shower. It tames easily and is a popular oriental cage bird. Introduced to New South Wales some years ago, the Red-whiskered Bulbul has become well established in suburban Sydney and Melbourne. It is something of a nuisance to fruit growers, often damaging crops enough to become a problem.

While bulbuls eat some insects and other animal food, their mainstay is berries and fruit. They are gross and intemperate feeders, and occasionally get tipsy on overripe fermenting fruit, a frailty they share with a number of other fruit-eating birds.

Most bulbuls are gregarious and when not nesting go about in small flocks searching for food and taking an alert interest in everything that goes on. They are not strongly territorial and do not establish property rights, but they are keen to potential danger and spread the alarm when they spot a prowling cat or snake. If an owl appears all bulbuls in the vicinity gather to mob and harass it until it moves on. They will also attack nest-robbing crows and magpies.

The short-winged bulbuls are not strong fliers and tend to be resident wherever they occur. Highland species move to lower levels in winter, and some of the lowland tropical species shift their feeding grounds seasonally, following the ripening fruit. The only truly migratory members of the family are the northern populations of the Brown-eared Bulbul of eastern Asia and Japan.

The Brown-eared Bulbul is representative of some 20 species of the genus *Hypsipetes*, found widely from eastern Asia and the Philippines westward to India and southward on islands in the Indian Ocean to Madagascar. Their habits are those of the rest of the family, but their voices are more raucous. The Japanese Brown-eared Bulbuls all move southward in winter, travelling by day, and are often seen in large flocks flying across the straits from one island to another. The bulbul population of Hokkaido, the northernmost of the Japanese islands, crosses the Japan Sea and winters in Korea and eastern China.

So far as known all bulbuls build open cup nests woven of grasses and fibres in the branches of a shrub or tree. The nesting habits of the Brown-eared Bulbul are typical of the family. It makes a deep cup of leaves, grasses, moss, and bark, often lined with pine needles, rootlets, and the slender leaves of bamboo, from 5 to 15 feet up in a tree or thicket. The nest is always cleverly concealed and hard to find. In it the female lays a single clutch of 3 to 5 (usually 4) eggs, pinkish grey marked with red, black, and purplish spots. Incubation is mainly, if not entirely, by the female. The male feeds her on the nest and helps brood and feed the nestlings. The young are fed at first on insects, later on small berries. The tropical bulbuls usually have smaller clutches, 2 to 3 eggs, and pairs are multi-brooded.

African representatives of the genus *Pycnonotus* include the Black-capped, White-eared, and White-vented Bulbuls. Like the Red-whiskered Bulbul, all are tame, cheery, conspicuous inhabitants of forest edges, gardens, and villages. More strictly forest dwellers are the shyer and less well known leaf-loves and bristle-bills. The best known of these African forest bulbuls are the 22 members of the genus *Phyllastrephus*, commonly called greenbuls or brownbuls. These birds all have greenish to brownish backs and yellowish underparts, and many are so alike they are hard to tell apart in the field. The females in this genus are noticeably smaller than the males and have shorter bills. The greenbuls eat more insects than they do fruit, and many are fine singers. They share the common bulbul traits of being active, curious, and rather tame, but have a characteristic habit of flicking their tail and wings—often one wing at a time.

How the odd-sounding name bulbul became attached to these birds is uncertain. Bulbul is an ancient Arabic name for a small bird, and was probably imitative in origin. It occurs frequently in the 12th-century poetry of Omar Khayyam, and English versions of the *Rubaiyat* usually translate the name as nightingale, perhaps incorrectly. The true Nightingale is a small European thrush (p. 252), which occurs in Iran as a migrant, but neither breeds nor sings there. The bird the medieval mathematician, astronomer, and poet Omar mentioned so often in his quatrains probably was the White-cheeked Bulbul, a cheerful and familiar resident of the palm groves, gardens, and hedgerows of the Tigris-Euphrates Valley and western India.

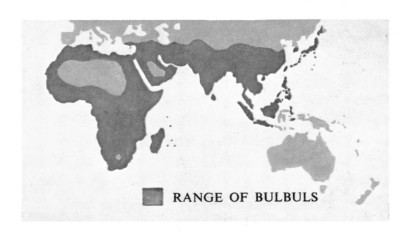

■ RANGE OF BULBULS

LEAFBIRDS AND ALLIES

PASSERIFORMES   CHLOROPSEIDAE

Closely related to the bulbuls and sometimes classified with them are 14 species of more brilliantly coloured forest birds of southeastern Asia. Divided among three distinct genera, they are known respectively as leafbirds, ioras, and fairy blue-birds. They share a number of characteristics with the bulbuls, including the long, fluffy rump feathers and the patch of hair-like feathers on the nape. But unlike the bulbuls, the males are always more brightly coloured than the drab females.

Leafbirds are medium-sized (7 to 8 inches) denizens of the forest crown. The eight species are all predominantly bright green, variously marked with blue, orange, yellow, and black. Typical is the Golden-fronted Leafbird, a common species from northern India to Burma and the Sumatra highlands. When not nesting leafbirds travel through the woodland canopy in small noisy bands. Despite their bright colours they are difficult to see in the tree-tops. They eat some seeds and insects, but fruit and nectar are their mainstay, and they often gather with other species to feast in the tops of fruiting or flowering trees. They are especially fond of the nectar and the berries of the oriental mistletoes (*Loranthus*), and are a factor in both pollinating and spreading these common tree parasites.

All leafbirds are fine singers and accomplished mimics that copy the songs and calls of other species. Their rich and varied singing, bright colours, and adaptability to confinement make them popular cage birds that find a ready market in the Orient. They are so aggressive and pugnacious, however, that they are not suitable for mixed aviaries.

Leafbirds build small, shallow cup-shaped nests of fine roots and grasses, unlined but coated on the outside with soft fibres, on a bough or fork 20 feet or so above the ground. When nesting they are exceedingly alert and watchful; but they are so noisy and excitable that when danger threatens they usually betray the location of their nests by their obviously anxious behaviour.

The four ioras are smaller birds, 5 to 6 inches long, with yellow or olive-green and black their predominant colours. Like the rest of the family, ioras are arboreal birds, but they feed almost entirely on insects, are not gregarious, and usually frequent the forest borders and edges of clearings. The Common Iora, a common resident of village gardens, is plentiful from India to all Malaya.

The courtship of the Common Iora includes a striking song flight. Flying up into the air, the male fluffs his feathers, especially those of the rump, until he is as round as a ball. Then he spirals slowly to his perch whistling a thin piping note like that of a cricket or a tree frog. He continues the display on his perch, posturing with feathers still fluffed and wings drooping, spreading and flicking his tail and whistling steadily. Ioras build neat, frail cup nests of grasses bound together with spiders' webs, usually in a fork 5 to 30 feet above the ground. They lay 2 to 4 creamy-white eggs streaked with grey or brown.

The two fairy bluebirds are larger species, about 10 inches long, one ranging from India to Indochina and Malaya, the

1 GOLDEN-FRONTED LEAFBIRD ♂
Chloropsis aurifrons
India to Annam and Sumatra 8 in.

2 FAIRY BLUEBIRD ♂
Irena puella
India to Indochina and East Indies 10 in.

3 COMMON IORA
Aegithina tiphia
India to Indochina 6 in.

other limited to the Philippines. The males are handsome black birds with bright-blue mantles, the females much duller. Recent skeletal studies suggest they are misplaced in this family, and may be more closely related to the forest orioles (p. 221).

Like the leafbirds and orioles, fairy bluebirds live in the forest crown and feed largely on fruit. They are particularly fond of wild figs, and also eat some flower nectar. While not migratory, they wander locally depending on the seasonal abundance of fruit. They usually travel quietly in pairs through the forest, but when a large fig tree is bearing, scores of birds may gather for the banquet together with orioles, leafbirds, hornbills, bulbuls, and other fruit eaters, drawn by the same magnet.

Fairy bluebirds build rather frail saucer nests of twigs and moss, usually in saplings or thin bushes deep in the forest gloom. They normally lay two greenish-white eggs heavily marked with brown splotches.

245

DIPPERS

PASSERIFORMES   CINCLIDAE

The only truly aquatic passerines are the dippers, whose habitat and mode of life are shared by no other bird. Dippers live only on cool, clear, rushing mountain streams. Their element is the spray-drenched rocks where the roar of the water fills one's ears. This environment has become their very own. They go in and out of the water with gay abandon, and walk into it and under the surface with utter unconcern.

The four species of dippers are all similar in size, structure, and habits, and are all placed in the single genus *Cinclus*. The uniform brownish-grey North American Dipper lives in the western mountains from Alaska to Panama. The White-headed Dipper ranges down the Andes from Colombia to northern Argentina. The Common Dipper of Europe, brown with a white throat and breast, lives on mountain streams from Scandinavia to northwest Africa and eastward to the Himalayas. The all-brown Asiatic Dipper is spread across Siberia and China, north to Kamchatka and south to Formosa.

Just where and from what ancestral passerine stock dippers developed is uncertain. One school holds they evolved in central Asia from some thrush-like forebear and invaded the New World by way of the Bering land bridge. In support of this theory is the dippers' thrush-like tarsus and the mottled breasts of the immature birds in the Old World species. It seems more likely, however, that the dippers arose in the western American Cordilleras from a wren-like ancestor and worked their way westward into Eurasia. They show more similarities to the wrens than to the thrushes—in their nesting habits as well as in their short stubby wings and tails, thick brownish plumage, and distinctive musty body odour. The dippers are unquestionably a relatively ancient group.

Chief among dippers' unique adaptations to their unparalleled way of life are their soft, filmy plumage with a very thick undercoat of down and their tremendous preen gland, ten times the size of that of any other passerine bird. The gland provides the oil to keep their feathers waterproof. Other structural modifications are a movable flap over the nostrils (to keep out water) and a highly developed nictitating membrane, or third eyelid which they use for keeping their eyes clear of droplets in the splashing spray of falls and rapids.

Dippers have stout, strong legs and feet, but their toes are not webbed. They do not swim well on the surface, but pitch along with a jerky motion until their feet hit bottom. They swim expertly under water, using their wings for propulsion, and have been known to fly down through 20 feet of water to feed on the bottom. The length of their average dive is about 10 seconds, with a probable maximum of perhaps 30 seconds. Whether or not they actually walk on the bottom is debatable. As their specific gravity is much lower than that of water, they cannot stay on the bottom without exerting some force to keep them from bobbing up to the surface. Their wings doubtless help keep them under, but it is also thought they set the angle of their bodies against the current to plane down, a possible reason why they prefer fast-running streams.

Dippers fly straight and fast with a quail-like buzzing of their stubby wings, usually close to the water. They seldom fly far, and are quite sedentary. Dippers are solitary birds, seen in one another's company only at nesting time. Each individual or pair seems to occupy its own half mile or mile of stream, where they remain the year round unless forced to move by the drying up or freezing over of the waters. Cold does not seem to bother them, for they play merrily along the mountain torrents, even when the surrounding countryside is blanketed deep in snow.

Dippers feed mainly on water insects. They pick adult mayflies, stoneflies, and caddisflies from along the banks, and seek out their larvae among the rocks and gravel of the stream bed. Nor do they disdain other small aquatic life such as newts and minnows. They are so fond of fingerlings and trout fry that they become real nuisances around fish hatcheries.

The dippers' call and alarm note is a sharp piercing "djii" that carries clear and far above the roar of the waters. They also have a lovely, burbling wren-like song that they sing throughout the year except during the postnuptial moulting season in late summer and early autumn. The song is not so loud and piercing as the call note, and difficult to hear except when sung in the quiet reaches of some backwater.

In their nesting habits the dippers are very wren-like. They build large domed nests of moss, sometimes lined with grass and leaves, and always with a side entrance. The nest is usually hidden in rock crevices, or between tree roots, close to the water. Protected ledges and nooks behind waterfalls are favourite sites. The clutch is 3 to 6, usually 4 or 5, pure-white eggs which the female incubates alone for the 16 days it takes them to hatch. Both parents feed the young, though the female seems to do most of the work. The young remain in the nest 15 to 24 days, and the moment they leave are as much at home in the water as their parents, walking into it immediately with the same facility and unconcern. Dippers nest early in the spring and usually rear at least two broods each year.

NORTH AMERICAN DIPPER
Cinclus mexicanus
Alaska to Panama 8 in.

COMMON DIPPER
Cinclus cinclus
Europe to Himalayas 7 in.

WRENS

PASSERIFORMES TROGLODYTIDAE

Few small birds are as unmistakable as the familiar, busy brown wrens—the small birds with the big voices. Few have a firmer niche in men's hearts and folklore and legend than the bird the Americans call the Winter Wren and which we have known simply as The Wren since early Anglo-Saxon days. In English nursery tales the wren is traditionally feminine, and given such endearing titles as Jenny Wren or Kitty Wren. Continental folklore makes the wren masculine, as in the German "Zaunkönig," king of the hedges, and the Dutch "Winterkoning." The French "troglodyte mignon," or little cave dweller, also masculine, is reflected in its scientific name, *Troglodytes*. This derives partly from the large covered nest the wren makes, partly from its habitual skulking and roosting in rock crevices and root tangles.

How the tiny wren won its legendary position as king of the birds is one of the oldest of European folk tales. At a caucus to decide which should be their ruler, the birds agreed that the title should go to the one that flew the highest. The eagle promptly soared above all the others, but when he was about to proclaim his majesty from the heights, a little wren that had stowed away unnoticed on his back flew up a few feet higher and trilled out his triumph to the world below. The wren was used symbolically as king of the birds in medieval feasts and celebrations, some of which persist to this day in rural parts of Europe and the British Isles.

The Wren, the traditional king of the birds, is, oddly enough, the only member of an extensive New World family found outside the Americas. How long ago it invaded Eurasia, probably via Alaska, we have no way of knowing. Its remains have been found in Pleistocene deposits in Europe, and the species has been in Eurasia long enough to differentiate into 26 distinct geographical races. The Wren occurs south to Formosa, northern India, and northwest Africa, and populations are resident on the Hebrides, Shetland, and Faroe islands, and in Iceland. In North America the same species (their Winter Wren) breeds across the Canadian woodlands from Alaska to Newfoundland and south in the mountains to California and Georgia. Here there are 8 geographical races, 5 of them on various islets in the Aleutians. These island populations do not migrate, but the continental Winter Wrens winter southward to the Gulf of Mexico.

The most recent revision of the wren family lists 59 species divided among 14 genera and ranging from Canada southward to the tip of South America and out into the Falkland Islands. Wrens are most abundant and diversified in Central and South America. Strangely, the family is almost absent from the West Indies. The House Wren has extended its range northward from South America through the Lesser Antilles as far as Dominica. The only other wren known from the islands is the Zapata Wren, which undoubtedly has the most restricted range of any American bird. It is known to live only in one swamp, scarcely 5 square miles in area, on the south coast of Cuba, where it was discovered in 1926. The Zapata Wren resembles Bewick's Wren of North America. These little wrens never

SHORT-BILLED MARSH WREN
Cistothorus platensis
Southern Canada to
Tierra del Fuego 4 in.

WREN (WINTER WREN)
Troglodytes troglodytes
Northern Hemisphere 4-5 in.

leave Zapata Swamp, but hide in its dense scrub. When they fly, which is seldom, they only flutter weakly for a few feet.

The 59 wrens form one of the better defined and cohesive of the passerine families. Their distribution shows them unquestionably of Western Hemisphere origin, but their ancestry is obscure. Their closest ties are to the dippers and to the mockingbirds. All three groups probably stemmed originally from some primitive insect-eating oscine of early Tertiary time that was probably akin to the ancestor of the thrushes.

All the wrens are similar in appearance and are easily recognizable as wrens. Most are less than 6 inches long and the largest barely reaches 9 inches. All are soberly dressed in browns or brownish greys, variously striped, streaked, spotted, or mottled with black, grey, white, or contrasting shades of brown. The sexes are alike. All have slender, sharp-pointed bills, which vary from short to fairly long, usually slightly down-curved. All have comparatively large, stout legs and feet and short rounded wings. Wrens fly rather weakly, but have a quick, straight, buzzing flight. They characteristically carry their stubby tails cocked bolt upright.

Most wrens live close to the ground in the tangled underbrush where they search for insects. They are adaptable little mites and have successfully invaded many habitats. The Cactus and the Rock wrens are at home on dry, treeless mountain slopes. The Short-billed and the Long-billed marsh wrens spend their lives in the reeds and cattails of salt- and fresh-water marshes. The White-breasted and Grey-breasted wood wrens live on the floor of tropical forests from southern Mexico to Bolivia. Others, like the House, Bewick's, Winter, and Carolina wrens, live in garden shrubbery and hedgerows, and nest around houses and outbuildings.

Wrens are highly vocal. They may be hard to see as they scamper through undergrowth, scurry mouse-like among tree roots, or hide in tangled swamp sedges, but they invariably betray their presence with their harsh, chattering, scolding calls. Almost all are fine singers that delight the ear with intricate burbling melodies, which seem much too loud and rich to come from such small throats. Both sexes sing, and they sing practically throughout the year, which may be a way pairs keep in contact with one another in impenetrable habitats where vision is limited. Some tropical wrens sing antiphonal duets between pairs, one bird singing the first few notes, its mate finishing the strophe.

Wrens build large bulky nests, which typically are domed with a side entrance, and are mostly the work of the male. Male wrens have such a strong urge to build nests that each usually builds several in his territory, sometimes as many as half a dozen. This is evidently an integral part of nuptial display and courtship. The female selects one of the nests for the brood—one perhaps meant for the purpose, for it is usually better built and better hidden than the others. The female lines

HOUSE WREN
Troglodytes aëdon
Southern Canada to
Tierra del Fuego 4½-5½ in.

ZAPATA WREN
Ferminia cerverai
Cuba 6¼ in.

CACTUS WREN
Campylorhynchus brunneicapillus
Western United States
and Mexico 8 in.

this nest and finishes it for occupancy. The extra "cock nests" are usually flimsy structures and poorly, if at all, concealed. The cock often sleeps in one or another of them. Another purpose these dummy nests may serve is to fool cowbirds into laying in them instead of in the real nest.

Many wrens are cavity nesters, and these will use almost any natural hole they find on or near the ground—tangled roots, clefts in rocks, and abandoned woodpecker holes. The Winter Wren's favourite site is among the upturned roots of a fallen tree. Other cavity-nesting species, Bewick's Wren and the Carolina Wren among them, find sites around dwellings. Most familiar of these is the common House Wren, a widespread species of 30-odd races which ranges from southern Canada south to Cape Horn and the Falkland Islands. The House Wren is one of the most frequent users of bird boxes wherever people put them up. The House Wren isn't particular, and almost any bird box will do, provided the entrance is large enough for it to enter. The minimum diameter, the size of an halfpenny, keeps out House Sparrows, but House Wrens prefer wider holes that let them lug in larger sticks. If several houses are put up near one another the male defending the territory will, in true wren fashion, fill most of them with debris. If houses aren't available, the House Wren will use holes in trees and stumps, empty tin cans, rural mail boxes and old wasps' nests. It may also use the space behind a loose board in an outbuilding or under the dashboard of an unused motor-car, tractor, or piece of farm machinery.

Wrens are generally multi-brooded, and some are polygamous. Incubation is usually by the female alone. The male sometimes feeds her on the nest, and he helps rear the young. The eggs vary from pure white to dark brown, and are often speckled. Clutches range from 2 or 3 in most tropical forms to 8 or 10 in some temperate zone species. The House Wren usually lays 4 to 6 speckled white eggs and incubates 12 to 15 days, averaging 14. The nestling period varies from 12 to 18 days, depending on the size of the brood and how well the young are fed. Usually the smaller the brood, the more food each nestling gets, and the quicker it grows.

Except for a few tropical species that are slightly gregarious when not nesting, wrens are typically solitary and do not form flocks. They like to roost under cover at night, and when away from their nests will creep into crevices and crannies to sleep. They have been found dozing in scarecrows and in pockets of shirts hung on clotheslines.

MOCKINGBIRD
Mimus polyglottos
Southern U.S. and Mexico 10½ in.

BLUE MOCKINGBIRD
Melanotis caerulescens
Mexico 10 in.

BROWN THRASHER
Toxostoma rufum
Eastern U.S. and
southern Canada 12 in.

CATBIRD
Dumetella carolinensis
Southern Canada to
Gulf States 9 in.

MOCKINGBIRDS, CATBIRDS, AND THRASHERS

PASSERIFORMES   MIMIDAE

An even more thoroughly American family than the wrens, and closely allied to them, are the 31 species of mockingbirds and their relatives, the catbirds and thrashers. All these birds are fine singers and most are excellent mimics, the mockingbirds especially so—hence their family name of Mimidae. One occasionally hears them referred to collectively as the "mimine thrushes." They probably developed, as did the wrens, from some thrush-like ancestor.

In many ways the Mimidae are intermediate between the wrens and the thrushes. Their nesting habits are distinctly thrush-like in that they build open cup nests. In other features of behaviour and in colour pattern they resemble the wrens. The thrashers, in particular, look and act like overgrown wrens. Medium-sized birds from 8 to 12 inches in length, the mimids are more slenderly built than thrushes and have longer tails, and slender, more wren-like bills. The sexes are alike. All are active, inquisitive, aggressive birds that live near the ground and eat insects, fruit, and berries.

Most famous of the family is the Mockingbird of the southern United States, which is as symbolic of the Old South as magnolias, hominy, "chitlins," and mint juleps. Selected as "state bird" by five Southern states—Tennessee, Arkansas, Florida, Mississippi, and Texas—the Mockingbird has earned this perhaps empty and unrewarding honour by its vocal powers and its conspicuousness. Mockingbirds draw attention to themselves not only by their wonderful singing, but by their constant activity and their staunch defence of their territories against intruders. They love to chivvy the household cat or dog.

Mockingbirds sing all the year long, and usually pick an exposed place to sing from, a roof eave, telephone wire, or the top of a fencepost. They pour forth their matchless melodies at odd times throughout the day and often sing at night when the moon is full. Then, when other bird voices are stilled and the noises of civilization quieten down, their song is heard at its best. While Mockingbirds have burbling wren-like songs of their own, most of their melodies are imitations of the sounds of other birds they have heard. Typically they repeat each phrase three or four times before changing tune.

Individual mockers have been credited with rendering perfect imitations of the songs of 30 or more different species in succession, and with giving recognizable replicas of such un-bird-like sounds as the postman's whistle and a squeaking cart wheel. They are quick to pick up any new song they hear and add it to their repertoire. When caged Nightingales were brought from Europe and housed in the gardens of the Bok Singing Tower in Florida, the local Mockingbirds were soon singing the same lovely liquid notes. Sound spectrograph records of the Mockingbirds' versions compared with the original Nightingale songs show them to be exact reproductions of each phrase in all its parts, including vibrations beyond the range of the human ear.

The Mockingbird builds a stout, cup-shaped nest of short, stiff twigs lined with grasses and rootlets, usually well hidden in the shrubbery or the lower branches of a tree, seldom less than 3 or more than 20 feet above the ground. Both sexes bring material and work hard enough to finish the nest in 3 or 4 days, sometimes by dint of excess zeal in as little as 2 days. The clutch is 3 to 6 greenish eggs spotted with red-brown. Incubation is mainly by the female, though the male may take a short stint on the eggs during her absence. Incubation takes 12 to 14 days, and both parents feed the young. The fledglings mature rapidly and are often able to leave the nest in another fortnight. Hence the entire breeding cycle is seldom more than a month. Pairs usually raise two or more broods each year.

The common Mockingbird is the northernmost of nine similar species assigned to the genus *Mimus* which range from the central United States southward through the West Indies and Central America to Argentina and Chile. All are slim, slender birds, grey to grey-brown above, lighter below, and usually with white or pale-grey markings in the wings and tail. One species, with a larger bill and legs and narrower nostrils that justify placing it in a genus of its own, *Nesomimus,* is resident in the Galapagos Islands. The two Blue Mockingbirds of Mexico are an exception to the family's dull colours. One is solid blue; the other has a white belly. Like their grey relatives, the Blue Mockingbirds are notable singers and good mimics.

One of the most distinctive members of the family, and the least variable, is the friendly grey Catbird, unmistakable for its black cap and russet undertail coverts, and its feline mewing call. While no vocal match for the Mockingbird, the Catbird has a pleasant song and ventures some imitations, which are not as loud, accurate, or varied as the mocker's, though recognizable for what they are meant to be. Also, the Catbird never repeats its phrases.

Like the Mockingbird, the Catbird likes to live around houses and becomes very tame. It builds a similar cup nest of twigs in the shrubbery and lays 4 to 6 glossy, greenish-blue eggs, which take 12 to 13 days to hatch. While primarily insectivorous, the Catbird consumes quantities of berries and small fruits, and is occasionally accused of raiding grape-vines and blackberry patches. These depredations are seldom serious, and most country and suburban folk regard the Catbird as a pleasant neighbour and are glad to see it return in the spring.

The Catbird breeds across most of North America from southern Canada southward to the northern edge of the Gulf States. It winters from the southern states through the West Indies and Central America to Panama. A small population resident in Bermuda is inseparable from the mainland Catbirds. A close relative is the Black Catbird of Yucatán and British Honduras, exactly like the Catbird in size, shape, and habits, but glossy black in colour.

The thrashers are a more varied group of slightly larger birds with noticeably long tails. Most of them are brownish above and have white breasts and bellies streaked with brown. Ten of the 17 species are grouped in the genus *Toxostoma,* typical and best known of which is the Brown Thrasher, a common resident of most of the eastern and central parts of the United States. The Brown Thrasher is less companionable than the Catbird and Mockingbird. It lives in the wilder copses and forest edges and searches through the undergrowth and ground litter for its food. Its song is louder than that of the Catbird, and it makes no attempt at mimicry. While it occasionally sings from an exposed perch, it sings more often from cover, and its song is easily recognized by the bird's tendency to repeat each phrase twice.

Eight other species of thrashers are found in the western United States and southward into Central America. Largest of the family is the 12-inch California Thrasher, a tawny bird that feeds largely on the ground in chaparral country and in mixed brushlands, avoiding the solid forests. The Sage Thrasher, the Crissal Thrasher, and the Le Conte's Thrasher inhabit the more arid regions of the West, feed largely on the ground, and usually nest in thorny cactus or stiff-twigged desert brush.

Four species of thrashers are limited to the West Indies. Two of them are exceedingly rare and in danger of extinction. The White-breasted Thrasher, brownish above and white below, occurs only on the islands of Martinique and Saint Lucia and is seldom reported nowadays. It is wren-like in its actions and it chatters and cocks its tail as it moves about the underbrush.

Another rare species is the Trembler, a ground forest dweller of the smaller islands, now extirpated from most of its former haunts. This species' peculiar habit of shivering and trembling has never been satisfactorily explained. The decline of both the Trembler and the White-breasted Thrasher has resulted from human persecution, from the cutting of forest cover, and from introduced predators.

The Scaly-breasted Thrasher of the Lesser Antilles and the Pearly-eyed Thrasher, which ranges from the Bahamas south to many islands in the southern Carribbean, are not as rare, possibly because they are tree dwellers, less molested by rats and other introduced predators. These island thrashers have low reproductive rates. They lay only 2 to 3 eggs per clutch, against double that number in the mainland species.

THRUSHES

PASSERIFORMES   TURDIDAE

In this large family are some of the most highly regarded songbirds in the world. The thrushes are such renowned songsters that the name has become a common synonym for a singer. No other family has so many members famed for their music—the Nightingale, Song Thrush, Hermit Thrush, Wood Thrush, to name but a few. Other well-known thrushes, loved for their beauty as well as their song, include the robins and bluebirds. Less familiar groups are the solitaires, chats, wheatears, shortwings, cochoas, and forktails. Still others have no common names.

The thrush family is practically cosmopolitan, absent only from the Antarctic, the frigid parts of the Arctic, some Polynesian islands, and from New Zealand (where the European Blackbird and Song Thrush were successfully introduced in 1862). The family has its greatest development in the temperate and tropical regions of the Old World, where it is believed to have originated. If so, its conquest of the New World must have occurred very early, for a number of thrush groups are thoroughly established and well developed in North and South America and in the West Indies.

The thrush's closest relatives are two other equally large families of predominantly Old World birds, the warblers and the flycatchers. All three are fairly generalized, insect-eating oscines with 10 primary feathers on each wing. While most members of these three families—Turdidae, Sylviidae, and Muscicapidae—can be assigned to their respective families with little trouble, the lines between the three are not sharp. The number of borderline species difficult to assign to one or another confirm their close relationships. The differences between them are so slight they are sometimes considered subfamilies of a single family. As the three groups contain more than a thousand species, almost one-eighth of the world's birds, the tendency today is to give family rank to each.

The thrushes are slightly larger, plumper birds than the Old World warblers and the flycatchers, and typically have the tarsus unscaled or "booted." Though essentially insectivorous, thrushes do not catch insects in flight. They feed on the ground as well as in trees, and eat more vegetable food, particularly fruit, than warblers and flycatchers do. All build open cup nests, usually in trees or bushes, some on the ground, and a few in rock crevices and tree cavities.

Being stronger fliers and perhaps more vigorous and adaptable, the thrushes have been more successful than the warblers and flycatchers in spreading over the world. Thrushes colonized the New World in several invasions, and populations have reached and settled on many oceanic islands—Tristan da Cunha in mid-South Atlantic, the Hawaiian and Bonin islands, and the West Indies. Many of these small island populations became so specialized that when man arrived and changed their environment they disappeared rapidly. Several Hawaiian and West Indian thrushes have vanished within the last half century. The Bonin Island Thrush has not been seen since four specimens were collected in 1828. The species was probably wiped out shortly thereafter by rats that escaped from whaling ships.

The 306 species currently assigned to the thrush family are divided among about 45 genera. The most widespread and best known of these is the nominate genus *Turdus*, to which some 60-odd species are ascribed. These are the largest members of the thrush family, medium-sized birds from 8 to 12 inches in length. As typical as any is the American Robin, one of the most familiar backyard birds of temperate North America. The American Robin is one of the most companionable of their thrushes, and replaces the swallow as the traditional herald of spring in North America. Its "cheerily-cheerily-cheerily," full-throated and sweet, means spring has really arrived in New England.

This Robin breeds across North America from the tree line southward to the southern United States and winters from the Gulf States southward into Central America. Normally a bird of sparse woodlands, forest edges, and open scrublands, it has found the changes brought by civilization much to its liking, and now nests more commonly near dwellings in cultivated lands and city suburbs than it does in uninhabited regions. It builds its well-formed open nest of straw and other fibres reinforced with mud usually in a shrub or tree from 5 to 30 feet up, often in a sheltered recess on a building. Nest building and incubation are almost entirely by the female. The clutch of four clear blue-green eggs takes 12 to 14 days to hatch, and the young fledge in another 2 weeks. The male stands by and helps guard the nest and feed the young. The American Robin is multi-brooded except in the North, where the summers are too short.

TOWNSEND'S SOLITAIRE
Myadestes townsendi
Western North America   9 in

ORANGE-BILLED NIGHTINGALE-THRUSH
Catharus aurantiirostris
Mexico to Venezuela   6½ in.

A typical thrush, the American Robin eats a varied menu of insects, small fruits, and berries. His diet is roughly 60 per cent vegetable, most of this small fruits. Stories of Robins getting tipsy from eating overripe wild cherries are quite true, fortuitous intemperance being a weakness it shares with many fruit-eating birds. Less than a century ago Robins were shot for sport and for food in America, as some of their relatives still are elsewhere. They were sold in eastern U.S. markets for 60 cents a dozen as recently as 1913. Most Americans today would as soon think of eating the family dog.

The American Robin's popularity and adaptability seemed, until recently, to assure its perpetuation as a favourite songbird. Its existence is now threatened seriously by the wholesale broadcasting of new powerful insecticides, whose residual effects, long after they have stopped working on the insects, kill birds. As the rains wash DDT into the soil, it impregnates earthworms. These come to the surface where Robins eat them and die. Municipalities that fog their residential areas regularly with DDT have witnessed marked declines in Robin populations. Some Midwestern cities have succeeded in wiping these birds out entirely.

Though this Robin is the only *Turdus* in North America, the genus has established itself firmly to the southward. More than a score of other turdine species live in the West Indies and from Mexico southward throughout South America to Tierra del Fuego and the Falkland Islands. Gray's Thrush of Central America and northern South America is one example, and the White-chinned Thrush of Jamaica another. The tropical forms are usually resident; those breeding at higher latitudes and altitudes move with the seasons.

The genus *Turdus* is best developed in the Old World. The European Blackbird, a close relative of the American Robin, is a familiar bird on British lawns or singing his melodious spring song from a conspicuous perch. About the same size as the American bird he is all-black with a yellow bill, the female a nondescript brown. Both male and female birds can be very pugnacious.

Other European turdine species are the Ring Ouzel, a black thrush marked with a white chest band and common in higher country; the sweet-singing Song Thrush; the Mistle Thrush, so called because of its fondness for mistletoe berries; the Fieldfare, which has recently established itself in Greenland;

WOOD THRUSH
Hylocichla mustelina
Eastern North America   8 in.

NIGHTINGALE
Luscinia megarhynchos
Europe, southwestern Asia   6½ in.

HERMIT THRUSH
Hylocichla guttata
North America   7 in.

EUROPEAN BLACKBIRD ♂
Turdus merula
Europe, North Africa,
south-central Asia   10 in.

and the Redwing. Almost a score more are found in Asia—the Siberian Red-throated, Black-throated, Eyebrowed, Dusky, and Naumann's thrushes among the better known. All these Eurasian thrushes are similar to the American Robin in the essential features of their habits and behaviour. All are migratory; they travel and winter similarly in loose flocks, sometimes of considerable size, and usually congregate where berries are plentiful. Both Song and Mistle Thrushes use a stone 'anvil' on which they break open the shells of the snails which form part of their diet.

A distinctive group of North American thrushes are the five species of *Hylocichlas,* the Wood, Hermit, Swainson's, and Grey-cheeked thrushes, and the Veery. Slightly smaller than most of the *Turdus* group, these North American thrushes are uniformly brown above and white below, and have spotted breasts. All are forest inhabitants that search the forest floor for grubs, insects, fruits, berries, and leaf buds. Swainson's and the Grey-cheeked thrushes breed in the Canadian zone evergreen forest. The Hermit Thrush breeds across northern North America in mixed woodlands. The Veery summers in deciduous forests, as does the Wood Thrush of the eastern United States, the only one of the group that commonly nests in suburban shrubbery.

These forest thrushes are all fine singers. Their voices are somewhat similar, but each species pipes a distinctive pattern of song that plays an essential part in territorial relationships and courtship. All build well-formed, cup-shaped nests of twigs, grasses, and leaves, often strengthened with mud. The Veery and the Hermit Thrush usually nest on the ground, the other three in shrubs and low trees, seldom more than 10 feet up. All lay 3 to 4 eggs, greenish blue in colour, sometimes spotted with brown, which are incubated entirely by the female, the male standing by to help feed the young. The Wood and Hermit thrushes winter to the Gulf States and Mexico, the other three species travel on to northern South America.

In Central America and northern South America are seven species of the genus *Catharus* known as nightingale-thrushes, whose habits and behaviour are so similar to those of the *Hylocichla* group they might be considered congeneric. The nightingale-thrushes have largely lost the spotting of the breast and are non-migratory, but they are ground-feeding forest dwellers and sing the same sort of bell-like songs.

The three American bluebirds of the genus *Sialia* are typified by the familiar Eastern Bluebird with its blue back and reddish breast. The Western Bluebird and the Mountain

EASTERN BLUEBIRD ♂
Sialia sialis
Eastern North America   7 in.

EUROPEAN REDSTART
Phoenicurus phoenicurus
Europe to central Asia   5½ in.

AMERICAN ROBIN
Turdus migratorius
North America   10 in.

WHITE-RUMPED
SHAMA ♂
Kittacincla malabarica
India to Indochina
and East Indies   11 in.

EUROPEAN ROBIN
Erithacus rubecula
Europe, Asia Minor   5½ in.

BLUE (RED-BELLIED)
ROCK THRUSH
Monticola solitarius
Southern Eurasia,
Spain to Japan   9 in.

Bluebird are similar 6- to 7-inch birds that have replaced the red on the breast with blue or white. Bluebirds are gentle birds whose soft warbling songs are neither as loud nor as impressive as those of other thrushes. Partial to open woodlands, they are cavity nesters. Bluebirds nest in natural tree holes and often occupy bird boxes, in which they build a typical thrush cup nest. Bluebirds raise 2 and sometimes 3 broods in a season. The female does all the incubating; the male helps rear the young. After the young have flown, the parents often pick new mates for the next brood.

The solitaires (*Myadestes*) are a group of largely tropical American thrushes found from Mexico and the West Indies southward through Brazil. Townsend's Solitaire, the only temperate zone member of the group, breeds in the western mountains from Mexico north to Alaska. Solitaires are rather shy, trim, plain-coloured birds, difficult to see in their forest homes. Their colours are mostly olive-brown to grey; the bills are always black, and the tails are usually longer in relation to the body than those of the other American thrushes and are frequently edged with white. As befits members of the thrush family, solitaires are outstanding singers, and their flute-like melodies, unhurried and simple, are among the loveliest of tropical bird songs.

Oddest of the New World thrushes is the tiny Wren-thrush (*Zeledonia*), a shy resident of the high mountain forests above 5,000 feet in Costa Rica and western Panama. It creeps and hops around, wren fashion, on the forest floor. The Wren-thrush is unique among thrushes in having its 10th primary so greatly shortened that some students put the bird in a family by itself. Its voice is reported as a clear, musical whistle repeated 6 or 8 times at equal intervals. In its short tail and short, rounded wings it seems most closely related to the shortwings (*Brachypteryx*), a small group of six Asiatic thrushes ranging from the Himalayas across southern China to the Philippines and southward through the East Indies to Java. The shortwings are also wren-like birds of forest thickets at high altitudes, but unlike the Wren-thrush, the shortwing sexes differ in colour.

Among the more distinctive of the many Old World thrush groups are the eight rock thrushes of the genus *Monticola*. These are medium-sized thrushes 8 to 9 inches in length found widely over Eurasia and Africa. Most of them

are blue with some admixture of browns and reds. As the name implies, they are partial to open rocky country. Most of them, like the Blue Rock Thrush of Eurasia, are mountain dwellers living in rocky gorges, stony cliffs, and boulder-clad hillsides. They are not gregarious, but are usually encountered in pairs or small family groups. Some of these birds are also at home on sea coasts.

The Red-bellied Rock Thrush of eastern Asia is one of the few passerine species that has adapted itself completely to a beach life. It perches on the boulders in the salt spray on the rocky shores of Japan and Korea and feeds among the kelp and seaweed exposed at low tide. It is seldom found inland, but is a common backyard bird in coastal fishing villages. It builds its typical thrush nest of grasses and rootlets in a crevice in the rocks at the edge of the beach and lays 4 to 5 clear pale-blue eggs.

Another outstanding Eastern Hemisphere group is formed by the 20-odd wheatears (*Oenanthe*). Wheatears are thrushes that have left the woodlands and live mostly in open country, bare hillsides, coastal downs and dunelands, and in deserts of Eurasia and Africa. All are dapper ground birds from 5 to 7 inches long, often attractively marked with contrasting black and white. Most species have black facial markings, black on the wings and tail, and a distinctive white rump. The name "Wheatear" has nothing to do with wheat or ear, but is a euphemism for the Anglo-Saxon "white arse." The common Wheatear is widespread across the northern Palaearctic and breeds in the tundras of Greenland, northeastern Canada, and western Alaska. It winters southward to Africa. When wheatears flock to migrate southward, they are usually very fat. For years, they have been a gourmets' favourite. In parts of Europe and Africa they are still netted for market.

The Old World is also the home of a large complex of small thrushes of several genera, most of them less than 7 inches in length, sometimes called collectively the "chat thrushes" from their tendency to chatter and scold. Here are grouped some of the most familiar of European birds, the original Robin and such appropriately named birds as the Whinchat (which lives in whins—wet grassy meadows) and the Stonechat, which lives in neglected gorse country and old pastures and has a call note like two stones clicked together.

STONECHAT
Saxicola torquata
Eurasia, Africa, Madagascar   5 in.

BLUETHROAT
Luscinia svecica
Eurasia   5½ in.

WREN-THRUSH
Zeledonia coronata
Costa Rica and Panama   4½ in.

WHEATEAR
Oenanthe oenanthe
Eurasia, Alaska, Labrador,
Baffin Is., Greenland, Iceland   6 in.

Here are the descriptively named Bluethroat and Rubythroat, and the original Redstart (not to be confused with the unrelated American Redstart, a wood warbler, p. 285). Here also are such notable singers as the White-rumped Shama and the Dyal Thrush of India, and the most famous singer of all, the Nightingale.

The Robin of legend and story is a small, plump, friendly bird, which is common about gardens, hedgerows, and farmyards throughout Europe and the British Isles. The Robin has always been so well-liked in Britain that Britons have carried the name wherever they went and given it to foreign species that reminded them of the familiar native bird. So we find robins, related and unrelated, the world around, in America, Australia, India, Africa—wherever English is spoken.

The Robin's appeal stems from its engaging manners and friendly tameness. While it is a good singer, its voice is not as outstanding as those of the Nightingales and many other thrushes. It chatters and scolds a great deal, and its song, while not loud, is varied and musical, and has a wistful quality.

Most of the chat thrushes are birds of open woodlands and brushy fields and most of them nest on or near the ground. A few, such as the Redstart, are cavity nesters. Their eggs are usually pale-green to blue, and may or may not be spotted. Those of the Robin are white with fine brown speckling.

All lay slightly larger clutches than the bigger thrushes do, usually from 5 to 6 eggs. Their breeding patterns are likewise much the same, with the female assuming most or all of the nest-building and incubating duties, the male encouraging her with his singing, and standing by to help feed the young. Incubation and fledging times last 12 to 15 days. Many of the chat thrushes are multi-brooded, and the male sometimes takes complete charge of the first brood when the female starts incubating her second clutch.

In addition to their chattering, the chat thrushes sing fairly complex melodies, which they deliver with energy and enthusiasm. This is particularly true of the Nightingale, whose vigorous song seems much too loud to come from so small a bird. The Nightingale is unimpressive in appearance, a nondescript plain brown above and white below. It acts much like the Robin and frequents the same surroundings, but is shyer and seldom comes out of the undergrowth to feed in the open. It usually sings from cover and, despite its name and reputation, sings more freely during daylight than at night. It does sing habitually at night, however, and its song is most impressive in the quiet of the moonlight, when other voices and noises are stilled. Its song is exceptionally rich and varied. Pleasing and melodious though the Nightingale's song is, I have always been impressed more by its strength and vigour than by its beauty.

OLD WORLD WARBLERS

PASSERIFORMES   SYLVIIDAE

With a few exceptions the 398 species gathered in this tremendous family are small, dull-coloured, active birds with thin bills and rather weak legs and feet. The sexes are usually alike or similar in colour. Old World warblers differ from thrushes and Old World flycatchers principally in having unspotted young. The tarsus may be either scaled or booted, and rictal bristles may be well developed or absent. These warblers are not to be confused with New World, or wood, warblers (page 284), which are a totally unrelated group of birds having only 9 instead of 10 functional primary feathers and differing in other structural features and in habits.

The family Sylviidae is something of a catch-all. As currently assayed, it consists of four subfamilies, each of which some students regard as worth family rank. These are the Sylviinae, or true warblers, of the Old World; the Polioptilinae, or gnatcatchers, of the New World; the Regulinae, or kinglets, of panboreal distribution in the Northern Hemisphere; and the aberrant Malurinae, or Australian warblers, limited to Australia, New Zealand, and the East Indies.

In addition to their similar structural characteristics, members of each of these subfamilies show fairly close affinities in habits and behaviour. All live primarily, some exclusively, on insects. Most are arboreal, though a few groups live in weedy swamps, grassy meadows, or brushlands. Song is well developed throughout the family and, though none is equal to the best thrushes, many Old World warblers are exceptional vocalists. The species of temperate distribution are mostly migratory, some of them highly so, while those of the tropics and subtropics tend to be sedentary. Old World warblers vary considerably in nesting habits. Most of them build an open cup nest, but many lay their eggs in a domed or covered one. Incubation may be by the female alone or by both sexes, but the pair bond is strong. When the female incubates alone, the male usually feeds her, and helps feed the young.

The true warblers, or Sylviinae, form by far the largest of the four subfamilies. They number about 300, or better than three-fourths of the family's species. The nominate genus *Sylvia* contains many common European birds, including such familiar species as the Garden Warbler, the Black-cap, and the Whitethroat. The Garden Warbler is a nondescript 5-inch bird, brownish above, pale-buffy below, that lives in the tangled forest undergrowth and skulks through hedgerows and shrubbery borders. All the members of the genus are active little birds that hunt for insects in this way, and all migrate southward in winter. All have rather monotonous, short, "tac-tac" call and alarm notes, and all have sweet, pleasant, warbling songs that make them as welcome in the garden as their insect-eating does. Their

LONG-TAILED TAILORBIRD
Orthotomus sutorius
India to southern China, Malaya, Java   5 in.

songs are usually distinctive and, as throughout this family of many closely similar species, the birds can often be told apart more easily by their songs. All the members of the genus *Sylvia* build open nests, usually fairly near the ground, in the shelter of bushes, brambles, or hedgerows. The males often make "cock nests" as do the wrens, either as an outlet for excess building drive, or for a roosting place, or to confuse predators and nest-parasitizing cuckoos. Both sexes incubate the 4 to 5 eggs, which take 11 to 12 days to hatch. The young usually remain in the nest another 9 to 10 days before fledging.

The some 30 species of leaf or willow warblers of the genus *Phylloscopus* that breed across temperate Eurasia and migrate southward in winter to southern Asia and Africa are one of the most exasperating of all bird groups to identify in the field. One species, the Arctic Willow Warbler, has extended its breeding range across Bering Strait into Alaska. The only member of the subfamily to reach the New World, the Alaskan birds retrace their paths each autumn and migrate down the Asiatic coast to Indochina and the Philippines.

All the willow warblers are slim, greenish to greenish-yellow birds 4 to 5 inches in length. They lack distinctive field marks, and are hard to observe because they spend most of their time in the tree-tops hunting among the leaves for small insects. Field experts depend more on their songs and their actions to tell them apart than on their appearance. Their songs, while not impressive, are sweet, pleasing, musical warbles and are distinctive between species. One of the most distinctive songs is that of the

Chiffchaff, one of the commoner European species. The song consists of two syllables, one higher than the other, repeated in irregular order: "chiff-chaff, chaff-chiff, chaff." Other species such as the Willow Warbler, the Greenish Warbler, and the Wood Warbler have characteristic combinations of trills and repeated notes that are easier to recognize than the little dull-coloured bird uttering them from the tree-tops or the depths of a thicket.

Though all the willow warblers tend to feed in the higher foliage, all nest on or near the ground, and most of them build round domed nests with entrances on the side. Nest building and incubation are by the female alone. The eggs are white, lightly speckled with brown in some species, and usually number 6 to 7 in the first clutches. Second broods are generally smaller, from 4 to 5. Incubation is 12 to 13 days, and the young, fed by both parents, fledge in 13 to 15 days.

Nine species of rather plain, brownish warblers of the genus *Locustella* are known as grasshopper warblers because their thin, unimpressive buzzing songs seem more like the notes of an insect than those of a bird. The grasshopper warblers live in open brushlands, grassy meadows, and marshlands, and all are shy and hard to observe. During the breeding season the males perch momentarily on the tops of reed stems to sing their short, thin, little chirping songs, which are more like series of alarm notes. They stay in sight only a few moments while singing, then dive out of sight into the cover below.

Breeding patterns vary somewhat in the grasshopper warblers. All nest on or near the ground in thick cover. Some build a fragile open nest, others a closed one with a side entrance. Nest building and incubation may be by the female alone or by both parents. The eggs number 4 to 7, and are usually white with brown spottings. Incubation is usually 12 to 14 days; fledging takes another 10 to 15 days.

The dozen reed warblers of the genus *Acrocephalus* are another fairly distinct complex of warblers breeding across temperate Eurasia. Here again the species are so similar that their songs are more easily recognized than the birds themselves. Their voices are rather loud, and their songs are a strident but pleasant chattering that once heard can be easily re-identified. The song of the Great Reed Warbler, one of

GREAT REED WARBLER
Acrocephalus arundinaceus
Central Eurasia,
Spain to Japan 7½ in.

PALLAS'S GRASSHOPPER WARBLER
Locustella certhiola
Western Siberia to Japan 5½ in.

BLACK-CAP
Sylvia atricapilla
Europe, western Asia 5½ in.

COMMON
FAN-TAILED WARBLER
Cisticola juncidis
Southern Europe, Africa,
southeastern Asia 4 in.

the larger members of the family, can be heard long distances over the marshes in summer. During the breeding season the reed warblers sing by night as well as by day.

Always found in marshes, as their name implies, the reed warblers hang their deep open nests on reed stems a few feet above the ground or water. Nest building is chiefly by the female, assisted in some species by the male, who usually also shares the incubation duties. The eggs may number 4 to 6 and are usually greenish to bluish, blotched or spotted with dark brown. In the Great Reed Warbler incubation is 14 to 15 days; the young leave the nest in another 12 days, but do not fly well for another 3 or 4 days. Both incubation and fledging times are shorter in the smaller species.

The fantail, or grass, warblers of the genus *Cisticola* are one of the most widespread of all the warbler groups. Some 75 species are recognized in this single genus, most of them in Africa, where they occupy many types of country, but always in or near grass. Other species are found from the Mediterranean region across Asia to Japan and southward to Australia. Some live in wet marshes, others in dry fields. All are little brown birds streaked above and lighter below, with rather broad, often light-tipped tails. All nest on or near the ground, some building an open cup, some a hanging purse, others a domed nest.

The Common Fan-tailed Warbler of Eurasia breeds in grassy plains and river meadows. The male has an interesting song flight. Starting from its perch on a grass stem, it circles 50 to 100 feet in the air with a series of whistles which change to a guttural "dja-dja-dja" in its gradual fluttering descent. This species builds a bulky, bottle-shaped nest in the meadow grass, using slender leaves, rootlets, and the cottony flowers of marsh grasses which it weaves together with spiders' webs. Most *Cisticolas* line their nests with plant down and continue to add to them during incubation.

The most ingenious of all warbler nests are those built by the tailorbirds, nine species of which are found in southeast Asia from India to the Philippines and southward through the East Indies. A common and familiar bird of gardens and scrub country, the Long-tailed Tailorbird, the Darzee of Kipling's jungle tales, is one of the widest ranging, found from India eastward to southern China and southward to Java. Like all the tailorbirds, it is an unprepossessing little 4-inch skulker with a streaked olive-green back and a lighter belly. Thoroughly domesticated and not at all shy, it lives around

human dwellings. Like most warblers it is extremely active and hops about the vines and bushes around the veranda in search of insects. It carries its tail cocked stiffly over its back wren-fashion, and jerks it up and down as it makes its short flights. Its shrill discordant calls are so loud and persistent they can become annoying on a hot day.

The tailorbird builds its nest within a cup made by sewing the edges of one or of two leaves together. It fills this cavity, lined with fine grasses and sometimes animal hairs, mainly with plant down. To sew the leaves together the bird first pierces holes in the leaf with the point of its beak and draws the thread through, knotting it on the outside enough to prevent its slipping back. Each stitch is made separately. For thread the tailorbird uses plant fibres or silk from insect cocoons or spiders' webs. The nests are usually within 6 feet of the ground, but may be considerably higher, the main requisite being the presence of leaves to be sewn together. Tailorbirds lay from 3 to 6 long pointed eggs which vary from buffy to greenish and are boldly spotted and splotched.

The five species of kinglets, three in the Old World, two in the New, all placed in the single genus *Regulus*, form a well-marked subfamily. Kinglets are tiny birds barely 4 inches in length with soft, fluffy olive or greyish-green plumage. All have brilliant, sometimes partly concealed crown patches of yellow to orange, except the American Ruby-crowned Kinglet, whose crown patch is bright red. These feathered mites are residents of the circumpolar conifer belt and nest from the tree limit southward in both hemispheres. The two American species breed side by side across the Canadian zone and southward at favourable altitudes in the western Cordilleras almost to the Mexican border. Both migrate in winter to the Gulf States, Mexico, and Guatemala.

The Goldcrest is so similar to the New World Golden-crowned Kinglet that some students regard the two as conspecific. The Goldcrest nests in the taiga zone of conifers southward to central Europe and Asia. Insular populations are isolated on the Azores and Canaries and on the larger Mediterranean islands. A second common European species, the Firecrest, is lighter green in body colour and has a deeper-orange crown without the Goldcrest's yellow borders. The Firecrest breeds through most of continental Europe south to the Mediterranean islands and Asia Minor in mixed woodlands and deciduous scrubby growth. The little-known Formosan Kinglet, found only in the high mountain forests of Taiwan, closely resembles the Firecrest but has a brighter crown, a yellow rump patch, and black and white wing bars.

The kinglets are all active, unsuspicious birds that search tree needles and leaves for minute insects, eggs, and larvae, and pay little heed to humans close at hand. Outside the breeding season they travel in small scattered bands, often in company with the mixed flocks of titmice, creepers, and woodpeckers that roam through the northern woodlands. When insect food is scarce, they eat small seeds and other vegetable matter. Their call notes are a thin "zee-zee-zee," so high-pitched it takes sharp ears to hear them. Their spring songs are pleasant little warbles, not very loud and, again, so high-pitched that, with one exception, you have to listen hard to hear them. The Ruby-crowned Kinglet is the exception—its

BUSH WARBLER
Cettia diphone
Eastern Asia 6 in.

WILLOW WARBLER
Phylloscopus trochilus
Northern Eurasia 4¼ in.

257

EMU WREN ♂
Stipiturus malachurus
Southern Australia
and Tasmania 7½ in.

VARIEGATED WREN ♂
Malurus lamberti
Southeastern Australia 5 in.

Typified by the Blue-grey Gnatcatcher of the United States and Mexico, the Polioptilinae are dainty, slender little birds, 4 to 5 inches long, with rather long, thin, pointed bills. All are dressed in soft greys, usually with some white on the rather long tail. Some species have black marks on the head. Extremely active, they strongly suggest tiny mockingbirds. Their long tails are continually in motion, bobbing up and down and from side to side as the birds work through the foliage in search of small insects.

Gnatcatchers forage through the outer leaves and twigs of trees, seldom on the trunks or main branches. Like the kinglets, they work the underparts of the leaves carefully, and when an insect takes flight will flutter after it and catch it on the wing. They also have the kinglet habit of hovering to pick the insects that can't be reached from the branch off a clump of leaves. Though the gnatcatcher's simple short "zee" call notes are easily heard, their songs are whispered rather than sung. The little birds have a varied repertoire of high-pitched trills and warblings. They also mimic the songs of other species, though always in a quiet monotone that one has to listen hard to hear. The gnatwrens inhabit the lower levels of the tropical forests and are usually encountered in pairs, hopping about through the vines of the undergrowth with their long tails cocked up. Their song is a soft whistled trill on a single note.

Gnatcatchers build beautiful nests—compact little cups of plant down and flower petals bound together with spiders' webs and camouflaged on the outside with small bits of mosses and lichens. Usually the nest is saddled on a horizontal limb; sometimes it is placed within a forked branch. Gnatcatchers lay 4 to 5 pale bluish eggs finely spotted with brown. Both sexes incubate for the 13 days it takes the eggs to hatch. The young are fed entirely on insects by both parents, and one observer counted 43 feedings within 20 minutes. The young usually leave the nest 10 to 12 days after hatching.

song is surprisingly loud, highly varied and prolonged, sweet, fluent, and pure of tone. This may be compensation for the Ruby-crown's relatively small crown patch, which the female lacks entirely. Other kinglets display their brilliant crests to attract the opposite sex and to warn off rivals. The Ruby-crown seems to use music instead.

Kinglets build marvellous hanging purse nests of mosses, woven together with spiders' webs and thickly lined with bits of fur, feathers, and plant down. Both sexes work at building the nests, the female doing most of the construction. She incubates her large clutch of 7 to 12 tiny spotted eggs alone. The nest's interior is so small that the eggs are often deposited in two layers. The incubation period is long for such small eggs—usually from 14 to 17 days—and though both parents work hard to feed the young, it takes almost 3 weeks to fledge them.

If the 12 species of gnatcatchers and gnatwrens are correctly placed with the Old World warblers, they must be the descendants of sylviid ancestors that invaded the New World long ago, perhaps as early as Miocene time. The eight gnatcatchers of the genus *Polioptila* range from the northern United States southward through Central and South America to Argentina. One species is endemic to Cuba. The four gnatwrens (*Ramphocaenus* and *Microbates*) are found from southern Mexico to Brazil.

FORMOSAN KINGLET ♂
Regulus goodfellowi
Formosa 3½ in.

RUBY-CROWNED KINGLET ♂
Regulus calendula
Northern North America 4 in.

BLUE-GREY
GNATCATCHER
Polioptila caerulea
United States to Guatemala 5 in.

The most aberrant of the sylviids are the 80-odd species of wren-warblers, the Malurinae of the East Indies, Australia, and New Zealand. Unlike the other three subfamilies, many of these little birds are brightly coloured in contrasting shiny blues, reds, blacks, and whites. They carry their long tails perpetually cocked up over the back in wren fashion, and most of them are commonly called wrens in the antipodes. Most are good singers, and a few are clever mimics. Active birds of the scrub and heath lands, the wren-warblers keep to the cover of the underbrush as they search industriously

for small insects and larvae. They are usually encountered in small flocks, even in the breeding season.

Though a few of the wren-warblers build open cups, most of them make domed nests with entrances on the side or near the top for their 2 to 5 eggs. The nests are composed of plant fibres and grasses, often matted together with spiders' webs and other insect fibres and lined inside with plant down and feathers. The Variegated, or Purple-backed, Wren is typical of the group. One of the most curious is the tiny Emu Wren, whose tail is composed of 6 delicate feathers about 4 to 5 inches long, considerably longer than the body of the bird. The Emu Wren holds its tail upright as it works through the underbrush, and lets it stream out behind when it flies from bush to bush.

WILLIE-WAGTAIL
Rhipidura leucophrys
Australia and New Guinea to the Solomons 8½ in.

GOLDEN WHISTLER ♂
Pachycephala pectoralis
Java and Australia to the Fiji Isls. 7 in.

OLD WORLD FLYCATCHERS

PASSERIFORMES   MUSCICAPIDAE

Old World flycatchers live almost entirely on insects and catch them the same way the more primitive New World tyrant flycatchers do. Some have expanded their hunting methods to include gleaning insects from the foliage in warbler or vireo fashion. A few habitually pounce on insects on or near the ground. Unlike the thrushes and the warblers, with which they undoubtedly shared a common ancestor early in Tertiary time, Old World flycatchers have never successfully invaded the Western Hemisphere.

In physical equipment Old World flycatchers feature a comparatively broad, flat bill with a subterminal notch. They have well-developed rictal bristles about the nostrils which are a help in catching insects in flight. They are tree dwellers with little need for stout underpinning, their legs are rather short, and their feet are weak. They resemble the thrushes in that the young are usually spotted, but their tarsi are scaled, not smooth, in front.

Old World flycatchers vary greatly in colour. Some groups

are plain greys and browns, others are boldly patterned in black and white, still others sport brilliant blues, yellows, and reds. Some are crested; a few have bright facial wattles. In the duller-coloured species the sexes tend to be alike; in many of the brighter ones sexual dimorphism is marked. While song is fairly well developed in a few species, the flycatchers are by no means the match musically of either the warblers or the thrushes. Most of them have rather harsh call notes, and their songs tend to be weak, monotonous, and repetitive, with very little individual variation.

Flycatchers' nesting habits are fairly uniform. Most of them build neat cups in the branches of trees or bushes using shredded leaves, mosses, and lichens, often tied together with spiders' webs. Some nest in holes in trees, under banks, or in clefts of rocky cliffs. Both sexes share all the nesting chores, but the female usually does most of the work. The flycatchers' 2 to 7 eggs may be white, greenish, or buffy in ground colour and are often heavily spotted.

The muscicapids range throughout the Old World and have their greatest development in Africa and the Indo-Australian region. Most of the species that breed across Eurasia from the tree line southward are migratory. Members of the family have pushed eastward through the Pacific islands as far as the Marquesas and Hawaii. The some 378 species in the family are divided among four subfamilies, the largest and most widespread of which is the nominate subfamily Muscicapinae.

Among the commoner and less showy of these "typical" flycatchers are the Spotted Flycatcher of Europe and the similar Broad-billed Flycatcher of Asia. Sombre grey birds about 5 inches in length, both are common summer residents in sparse woodlands, farms, suburbs, and parks. Their songs are undistinctive and somewhat unmelodious little warbles. The Spotted Flycatcher frequently nests around buildings. It builds a rather slight structure of moss and plant fibres tied together with cobwebs, sometimes on the deserted nest of another bird, often against a tree trunk. The sexes share the incubation (typical in most of the family), but the greater part of the burden falls on the female, whom the male feeds on the nest. Incubation takes 12 to 14 days, and the fledging period varies from 11 to 15 days.

One of the more brightly coloured members of this subfamily is the Narcissus Flycatcher of eastern Asia, a flashy little black and yellow bird that summers in China, Korea, and Japan and migrates to the Philippines and the East Indies. Common in summer in deciduous forests up to 6,000 feet in the Japanese Alps, the Narcissus Flycatcher is one of the better singers of the family. It builds a nest of leaves, moss, and rootlets, usually on a branch well above the ground. It occasionally uses nesting boxes.

Another fine Asiatic singer is the Japanese Blue Flycatcher, a conspicuous summer bird in Japan that winters southward to Malaya. The male pours out his melodies from an open perch throughout the breeding season. The Japanese Blue Flycatcher builds a nest of mosses lined with rootlets, usually near the ground in crevices in rocky slopes or among exposed tree roots.

Africa, the wintering ground for many of the European and western Asiatic flycatchers, has perhaps a hundred resident species of its own. One of the most interesting is the Black-throated Wattle-eye, so named for the conspicuous red fleshy wattle above its upper eyelid. The wattle-eyes are representative of a group known as the puff-backed flycatchers. The members of this group raise and spread out their long rump feathers when excited. These restless birds flit conspicuously through the middle layers of the forest. They click their bills when catching insects as do their northern relatives, and also flick their wings audibly in flight.

The puff-backs build a typical flycatcher nest, a small cup of fine grasses and other fibres bound together with spider webs and camouflaged with lichens, usually in a forked branch. Like many small African passerines, these flycatchers are parasitized heavily by honeyguides and cuckoos, whose young soon grow to be twice the size of their foster parents. It is absurd, amusing, and pitiful to see a little flycatcher trying to brood and feed such an outsized incubus, whose demands for food must be enormous (p. 152).

In Australia and from New Guinea to the Fiji Islands live a group of small muscicapids that the Australians call robins. The five Australian robins of the genus *Petroica* are tame, friendly grey birds with red or pink markings on the breast and head. The Scarlet Robin and the Red-capped Robin live along roadsides and in gardens and have cheerful trilling songs. Their anatomy, habits, and behaviour, however, are those of the flycatchers, not of the thrushes.

Most striking of the flycatchers are the monarch and paradise flycatchers of the subfamily Monarchinae. Most of them are boldly patterned in blues, red-browns, or black and white. Many are crested, and in the paradise group the tails of the males are greatly lengthened. The sexes are unlike in this subfamily, and the usually unspotted young resemble the female. Their bills are broad, flat, and ridged, their wings rather long, their legs and feet small. These beautiful flycatchers are forest dwellers, and all are active, restless, and industrious. While they occasionally dash out to catch a passing insect on the wing, they hunt typically by scouring the foliage and smaller branches for their prey. They are usually solitary, but when not breeding may be found in small parties or accompanying the mixed flocks of other woodland birds that traipse through the forest in loose, scattered bands hunting insects.

The shorter-tailed monarchs, whose tails are only medium-long, range across southern Asia from India to the Philippines, south through the East Indies to Australia, and eastward in the South Pacific to the Solomons. One of the handsomest of the group is the Black-naped Blue Monarch. This widespread species, found from India to the Philippines and southward through Malaya, breaks into a number of distinct geographical populations over its wide range. Tamer and more friendly than others of the monarch group, its harsh call notes

JAPANESE BLUE FLYCATCHER ♂
Cyanoptila cyanomelana
Manchuria, Korea, Japan 5½ in.

BLACK PARADISE FLYCATCHER ♂
Terpsiphone atrocaudata
Japan, Ryukyus, Formosa   20 in.

PARADISE FLYCATCHER ♂
(white phase and red phase)
Terpsiphone paradisi
India to Manchuria,
Indochina, and East Indies
19 in.

and rather pleasant trilling song are heard frequently from the trees in the native villages. It builds a deep cup nest of fine grasses coated with cobwebs, mosses, and lichens, usually in a forked branch at no great height. It lays from 2 to 4 pinkish-white eggs freckled with fine brown spots.

The exquisite long-tailed paradise flycatchers of the genus *Terpsiphone* range from Africa and Madagascar through India and Malaya, the Philippines, and northward to China and Japan. The tropical forms are sedentary, the northern ones migratory. The development of the male's long central tail feathers strangely parallels that of the American Scissor-tailed and Fork-tailed flycatchers (p. 208). In the New World species, however, the outer instead of the inner pair of feathers are elongated, and the birds acquire them in their first post-juvenile moult. The male paradise flycatcher's longer central tail plumes, which reach three times the length of his body, do not attain their full 18- to 20-inch growth until the bird moults into his third winter plumage.

The Japanese Black Paradise Flycatchers reach Honshu in early May and establish their breeding territories in the mixed woodlands of the foothills. They are one of the most charming of the bird inhabitants of the extensive forests around the base of Mt. Fuji. Their striking cobalt-blue bill and wattled eyelids are as conspicuous in the field as the male's long tail, which streams behind him as he flies through the forest and does not seem to interfere in the least with his foraging. Nor does it prevent him from

SPOTTED FLYCATCHER
Muscicapa striata
Eurasia   5½ in.

BLACK-NAPED BLUE MONARCH ♂
Hypothymis azurea
India to the Philippines and East Indies   6 in.

NARCISSUS FLYCATCHER
Ficedula narcissina
Eastern Asia   5 in.

taking his regular turn at incubating. The paradise flycatchers build small but well-formed cup nests of thin grasses, moss, and bark tightly bound with spiders' webs and lined with thin rootlets. They lay 3 to 5 creamy eggs spotted with brown, and their 12- to 14-day incubation period is normal for the family.

A third and well-marked subfamily of Old World flycatchers is made up of the fantails (Rhipidurinae), found from southeastern Asia southward to Australia and New Zealand and eastward on most of the South Pacific islands. The fantails all have long, rounded tails, which they keep moving constantly from side to side and up and down, spreading them in a fan and closing them again. They also droop their wings as they hop about. Restless, active birds of the forest undergrowth, the fantails are fond of brushy forest edges and clearings, and many are habitually found near water, along sea beaches and the banks of fresh lakes and streams. Tame and inquisitive, they make themselves at home around settlements. The sexes are similarly coloured, usually in rather nondescript browns and greys, but the best-known members of the group are the conspicuously black and white birds typified by the Willie-wagtail of Australia.

The Willie-wagtail is a bird of the clearings. It followed the axe and the plough as Australia was settled to become one of the most familiar birds around farmsteads and suburbs. The constant companion of farm stock, the Willie-wagtail uses the backs and horns of cattle as a convenient perch from which to sally after the insects the grazing animals disturb. Strongly territorial, it defends its domain vigorously, and in kingbird fashion drives off species much larger than itself. Like all fan-

tails, the Willie-wagtail builds a small, neat cup nest, usually low in a bush or on a horizontal branch, and bound together so tightly with spiders' webs that it is extremely durable and hard to tear apart. Fantails' nests often have a tail of loose material.

The Pachycephalinae, or thick-heads (the fourth subfamily), are commonly known as the whistlers from their melodious flutey calls. Stocky-bodied birds with large rounded heads, the whistlers have rather heavy bills with a shrike-like hook at the tip. Most strongly developed in Australia and New Guinea, they range northward through Malaya and the Philippines and eastward through most of the South Pacific islands. Most of them are brownish to greenish grey above, lighter, often yellow, below. The throat is usually white, and the head and neck are variously patterned with black or yellow. Typical of the group is the Golden Whistler, found from the Malay Peninsula, Java, and Australia eastward to the Fiji Islands. This species breaks into some 80 or more subspecies over its wide range. In most populations the males are markedly brighter than the females; in some the sexes are alike. Their unspotted young resemble the female.

Whistlers are inhabitants of scrublands and the forest undergrowth, where they search industriously for insects among the twigs and foliage. During the breeding season they are strongly territorial, and pairs call back and forth to one another antiphonally. When not breeding they may be found with loose flocks of other species wandering through the woodlands. They are active and curious, and can be whistled up by imitating their call. Whistlers build a fairly large and substantial cup nest near the ground which is the work of the female alone. The clutch is 2 to 3 eggs.

HEDGE SPARROW
Prunella modularis
Europe, Asia Minor 6 in.

ALPINE ACCENTOR
Prunella collaris
Mountains of Eurasia,
Spain to Japan 7 in.

ACCENTORS

PASSERIFORMES   PRUNELLIDAE

Across Eurasia occur 12 species of small, inconspicuous, sparrow-like birds that are something of a puzzle to classify. Accentors look and act much like buntings, but they have thin, sharp-pointed, thrush-like bills, and rounded wings with 10 primaries. Rather robust little ground birds, quietly streaked and spotted in soft browns and greys, all but one of them, the Dunnock, are hardy inhabitants of high plateaus and mountaintops or tundra country above the tree line.

The 12 accentors are so similar to one another they are placed in the single genus *Prunella.* Their affinities are uncertain, but they seem most closely related to thrushes. The young are spotted, and they have moderately strong legs and feet, but their rather short tarsus is scaled, not booted as in thrushes. While they have melodious little warbling songs, their voices are neither as loud nor as outstanding as their common name suggests. In summer they eat quantities of insects, but in winter they subsist largely on berries and seeds. Like most seed eaters, they have a crop and a muscular gizzard, and they swallow grit to help their digestion.

Representative of the family is the widespread Alpine Accentor, resident in the Atlas Mountains of northwest Africa and from the Pyrenees and Alps of Europe eastward through the Himalayas to the highlands of Manchuria and Japan. While not uncommon, Alpine Accentors are extremely localized in their distribution, and eight geographical races are currently recognized. In summer they live well above the tree line. In winter they move to lower levels, usually in small, loose flocks. They are not shy, and will gather closely around mountain climbers to feed on crumbs from their lunches. They move over the ground with quick little hops or short darting runs. Their gait has a peculiar shuffling quality and they flick their wings and tails frequently as they run about.

Courting Alpine Accentors sing a warbling song from the top of a rock or a low bush, and the males make short, lark-like song flights. They build a neat cup of leaves, grasses, rootlets, and a few feathers in crevices in rocky screes, and lay 3 to 5 pale greenish-blue eggs, which both sexes incubate about 15 days. They feed their young at first on soft insects, later on seeds from their crop. The young sometimes leave the nest before they can fly, and may be attended by the parents for some time. Usually Alpine Accentors raise two broods each summer.

The Dunnock, which is widely called the Hedge Sparrow, lives at lower levels in scrub country and open moorlands, usually where there is some bush growth or shrubbery. It is also found along the European coasts and on rocky coastal islands where the winds and salt spray prevent forest growth. Though not particularly shy or uncommon, the Dunnock is rather quiet and unobtrusive, and remains close to the ground, usually in the shelter of hedges and shrubbery. It nests in hedges, in low evergreens, or in brush piles. In this species nest building and incubation are by the female alone. The male does not bring her food, and she leaves the nest regularly to forage. Incubation takes about 12 days, and the young remain in the nest another 12, being fed by both parents. The clutch is four eggs which, as throughout the family, are a clear blue-green, rarely with light spottings. The Dunnock starts nesting fairly early in spring, and customarily rears two broods each year, sometimes three. It migrates southward to the Mediterranean region in winter.

Two stray specimens of the Mountain Accentor collected in autumn on Nunivak and St. Lawrence islands off western Alaska admit it to the American list. Normally this Siberian species breeds from the Urals to the Chukotski Peninsula, in willow thickets along tundra streams. It migrates in winter to central Siberia, northern China, and Korea.

PIPITS AND WAGTAILS

PASSERIFORMES   MOTACILLIDAE

Trim, slender-bodied ground birds that walk and run rapidly but never hop, the pipits and wagtails have thin, pointed bills and live almost entirely on insects, which they capture on or near the ground. Essentially birds of open treeless country, most live on moors and prairies, arctic tundras, seacoasts or along streams and lakes.

The 54 species in the family are divided among 3 genera of pipits and 2 of wagtails. The pipits, so called from their twittering voices, are a streaked and mottled brown. The sexes are alike or closely similar. The wagtails, which continually pump their long tails up and down, are more boldly patterned. The male wagtails are the more forcefully coloured, and the juveniles often have a distinctive plumage. Both groups usually have the outer tail feathers white, or edged with white, which shows conspicuously in flight. They fly strongly with marked undulations, and call constantly on the wing. Most are migratory.

Pipits and wagtails have pointed wings and rather long, slender legs with partly scaled tarsi. An outstanding feature is their possession of 9 instead of the usual 10 primary wing feathers. Their structure and behaviour suggest affinities to Old World warblers and thrushes. Their distribution points to an Eastern Hemisphere origin, and their fossils are found in upper Oligocene deposits 30 million or so years old.

The largest group in the family consists of the 34 very similar pipits of the genus *Anthus*, one of the most widely distributed of all passerine genera. Best developed in Eurasia and Africa, pipits occur practically throughout the world, but are absent from the Pacific islands. One species lives on South Georgia at the edge of the Antarctic. These pipits are all so alike they are very difficult to tell apart in the field. Their superficial resemblance to the larks both in appearance and habits is pronounced. Hence they are often called titlarks or fieldlarks.

Pipits migrate and winter in flocks and roost at night on the ground. They often forage in pastures among cattle for insects. Species that nest and winter along seacoasts hunt along beaches and around tide pools at ebb tide. Several pipits have the same tail-pumping habit as the wagtails, though it is usually less pronounced. One of these, the Tree Pipit of Eurasia, though essentially a ground bird, takes cover in trees and sings from a tree perch.

One of the most widespread species is the Water Pipit, or Rock Pipit, which nests in the arctic tundra the world around and winters southward. Another is Richard's Pipit, found from eastern Europe and Africa eastward to China, Australia, and New Zealand. Both these pipits are represented by many geographical races. Sprague's Pipit, a common American resident of northern prairies, is known for its spectacular courtship flight. Sprague's Pipit was discovered by Audubon, who named it after one of his field companions. Representative Eurasian forms include the Meadow Pipit, the Pechora Pipit, the Red-throated Pipit, and the Tawny Pipit, the subject of a most delightful English film some years ago. Africa has more than a score of pipits, some wintering, others resident.

Pipits build deep cup nests on the ground neatly woven of fine grasses and well hidden. Incubation is entirely by the female, but the male stands by and feeds her and the young. The eggs are usually white to buffy, heavily spotted with browns, and may number from 3 to 7. The incubation period in pipits runs from 12 to 16 days, and it takes the young another fortnight to fledge. Most are multi-brooded.

One aberrant African group of pipits is fittingly called the longclaws. These eight species of the genus *Macronyx* have an exceedingly long hind toe and claw which facilitates their running over the tufted grasses of the veldt country. The hind toe of the common Yellow-throated Longclaw is almost

2 inches long, and the foot spans 3½ inches, almost half the bird's length. The longclaws have their upperparts cryptically coloured for concealment, but most of them have brilliant yellow underparts crossed by a crescentic breast band. This gives them an astounding resemblance to the unrelated meadowlarks of North America.

Most of the 10 wagtails of the genus *Motacilla* live near water, along mountain streams and lake shores, and in swampy meadows or marshes. Wagtails are most plentiful in the temperate parts of Eurasia and Africa. Several species winter in southeastern Asia. The Pied Wagtail straggles occasionally to western Alaska, but only one species has successfully invaded the New World. The Yellow Wagtail breeds from Britain across Eurasia to Point Barrow, northern Alaska, and the northern Yukon. Alaskan wagtails migrate back to the Old World of their ancestors in winter, retracing their steps westward to Siberia, then southward.

Among the most unmistakable of Old World small birds are the several species of the widespread Pied Wagtails. Their contrasting black and white colouring is conspicuous. They are not at all shy, and they move about actively in the open. Pied Wagtails live across Eurasia and in Africa in a variety of habitats, always in open country and seldom far from water. Inland populations are found commonly in cultivated lands and around farms. Coastal Pied Wagtails are familiar in fishing villages, where they flit tamely along the shore and chase flies among the drying nets and lines.

The Yellow Wagtail and the very similar Grey Wagtail, both with grey-to-brown backs and yellow underparts, are a trifle wilder. They are commoner along streams and in swamps and meadows. One species, the Forest Wagtail of Eurasia, is a woodland inhabitant. Instead of constantly pumping its tail up and down as do all other wagtails, the Forest Wagtail swings its tail in a sideways, somewhat circular motion.

When not breeding, wagtails are gregarious. Unlike the ground-roosting pipits, wagtails roost off the ground, in trees and bushes, or among marsh reeds. Migrating and wintering flocks sometimes roost together in thousands.

Wagtails are essentially ground nesters, and typically build a fragile nest of straw and rootlets lined with hair, feathers, and bits of paper. They may use nests of other birds in trees and bushes. Their eggs are coloured like the pipits', and they lay a similar clutch of 4 to 7. In the wagtails, however, the male often assists in incubation. Like the pipits, wagtails are generally multi-brooded. The northern migratory species usually rear two broods. The more sedentary tropical species space their nestings to coincide with the rainy seasons, when food is more plentiful.

YELLOW-THROATED LONGCLAW
Macronyx croceus
Africa south of the Sahara   8 in.

WATER (ROCK) PIPIT
Anthus spinoletta
Northern Hemisphere   6½ in.

GREY WAGTAIL
Motacilla cinerea
Eurasia   7 in.

PIED WAGTAIL
Motacilla alba
Eurasia, Iceland   7 in.

FOREST WAGTAIL
Dendronanthus indicus
Northern China,
Manchuria, Korea   5½ in.

WAXWINGS AND ALLIES

PASSERIFORMES   BOMBYCILLIDAE

This is something of a hotch-potch family containing four small distinctive groups of birds each of which perhaps merits family rank by itself. Their affinities are obscure, but the three waxwings (Bombycillinae), four silky flycatchers (Ptilogonatinae), the Hypocolius (Hypocoliinae), and the Palm Chat (Dulinae) resemble one another more closely than they do the members of any other family. All are fruit-eating arboreal birds 6 to 9 inches long. All have somewhat broad bills, short legs, and 10 primaries. All but the Palm Chat have soft, silky plumage and are dressed in nicely blended drab colours. Their voices are poorly developed and none has an outstanding song. All are restricted to the Northern Hemisphere, and here their major similarities end.

Only the waxwings occur in both the Old and New worlds. The silky flycatchers are limited to Middle America, the Hypocolius to southwestern Asia, and the Palm Chat to the island of Hispaniola in the West Indies. Their patchy and restricted distributions, coupled with their lack of ties to other families, suggest all four to be relict groups that have persisted in their present ranges while their close relatives have vanished. Their kinship to one another is by no means certain, and grouping them in a single family, though convenient, may not express their true affinities. These await further clarification by more intensive study of their comparative anatomies and habits.

The three waxwings are so similar to one another they are placed in the single genus *Bombycilla*. They are sleek, strongly crested birds with smooth, velvety plumage, mostly fawn-brown in colour, accented by a narrow band of bright yellow or red at the end of the tail. The sexes are alike, but immatures are duller coloured than the adults. Their name refers to the small pellets of bright-red waxy material that form on the tips of the adults' secondaries in the two best-known species. If these peculiar droplets serve any particular function it has yet to be discovered.

The 8-inch Bohemian Waxwing is the largest of the three species and the northernmost in distribution. It breeds irregularly in the evergreen and birch forests across northern Eurasia and in North America from Alaska south to Washington and Idaho. The slightly smaller Cedar Waxwing is similarly coloured but lacks the Bohemian's white wing markings and has yellow instead of chestnut undertail coverts. The Cedar Waxwing nests throughout the woodlands of much of temperate North America and winters irregularly southward to northern South America. The Japanese Waxwing is similar to the Cedar, but lacks the wax droplets on the wings and has a red instead of yellow tail band. It breeds in the taiga forests of eastern Siberia and winters southward to Japan and Korea.

Waxwings are highly gregarious. They migrate and winter in close-knit flocks, and they stay together on the breeding grounds as well. Their flight is graceful, strong and fairly fast. Their migrating and wintering movements are nomadic. They show a marked lack of territorial fidelity, and their annual appearance in places where they winter commonly is never certain. At 4- to 7-year intervals large flocks of waxwings erupt

BOHEMIAN WAXWING
Bombycilla garrulus
Eurasia, western North America   8 in.

southward far beyond their normal wintering range in both hemispheres into regions where they are seldom seen otherwise.

Waxwings are almost as irregular in their choice of breeding grounds, which they often shift from year to year. Their nomadism may be governed in part by the availability of their preferred foods. They consume a great variety of berries and small fruits, both wild and cultivated. Cherries are a favourite item, as are the berries of cedars and junipers. Waxwing flocks seem to follow ripening fruit. In the spring and summer they eat flower petals in quantity, and are attracted by flowing sap. They also eat some insects, and feed them exclusively to their nestlings. Waxwings have short alimentary tracts for fruit-eating species and digest their food very rapidly, in from 20 to 40 minutes.

Waxwings are quiet, gentle birds, and usually are rather tame. Their call notes are soft, thin, and lisping, and fairly high in pitch. Their songs in spring are faint, unimpressive warblings. They often nest fairly close to one another, each pair building a bulky cup-shaped nest of twigs and grasses lined with finer fibres, hair, and feathers, usually on an open branch with little attempt at concealment. Both sexes share the nesting duties, but incubation is principally, if not entirely, by the female, who is fed by the male. Waxwing eggs are an ashy grey spotted with brown and black. The clutch numbers 3 to 5; incubation takes 12 to 15 days, and fledging another 14 to 16. They are apparently single-brooded.

Best known of the silky flycatchers is the Phainopepla, a fairly common resident of the arid brush country of southwestern United States and Mexico. Three other species assigned to two different genera range from Mexico to western Panama. These birds resemble waxwings in their soft, silky plumage, in their prominent crests, and in their fruit-eating habits, but they eat more insects than other members of the family and catch them, flycatcher fashion, on the wing. They have shorter wings and longer tails than waxwings, and the sexes are dissimilar.

Silky flycatchers are somewhat gregarious and when not nesting usually travel in small flocks. They often sit on exposed perches with their crest raised. Like the waxwings their wan-

derings seem governed by the presence of berries. Mistletoe berries are a favourite food, and the birds doubtless help spread this semi-parasitic plant. Their songs are short jumbles of short notes, on the weak side but nevertheless musical.

The Phainopepla is the only one of the subfamily whose nesting habits have been well studied. It builds an open cup-shaped nest in trees or bushes, much like that of the wax-wings, but smaller. The male does most, if not all, of the nest building and performs a major share of the incubation. The breeding cycle is somewhat irregular, and the species is believed single-brooded. Clutches are small, usually 2 to 3, rarely 4, greyish-white eggs heavily speckled with brown and black. Incubation takes about 14 to 15 days.

Isolated in the Tigris-Euphrates Valley of Iraq but occasionally wandering to Arabia, Afghanistan, and western India and southward to the Persian Gulf is a strange crested bird the size of a Cedar Waxwing but largely bluish-grey in colour and known only by its scientific name of *Hypocolius*. These birds travel about the scrub country in small flocks and live almost entirely on fruits, principally mulberries, dates, and figs. They fly strongly, and when they reach a tree or a bush, they fly directly into it instead of landing on an outer branch. They hide quietly within the foliage and are reported difficult to flush out. Like the other two subfamilies, they are rather quiet birds with low-pitched call notes and no noticeable song. Pairs nest by themselves, building a nest similar to those of the waxwings and silky flycatchers. They lay 4 or 5 milky-white eggs heavily spotted with brown at the larger end.

The fourth subfamily of this conglomerate family contains only the unique Palm Chat of Hispaniola, where it apparently became isolated long ago. In common with the other three groups in this family, it is a fruit eater and is gregarious. It differs in having harder, harsher plumage, olive-brown above, yellowish-white below, broadly streaked with brown. The sexes are alike, and the immatures are darker and duller in colour. The Palm Chat's bill is somewhat heavier and stronger than those of the other 3 groups. Its wings are of medium length and rounded, and its legs and toes are stout.

The Palm Chat also differs greatly from the other members of the family in its breeding habits. The birds are communal nesters and build huge apartment-like structures the size of a bushel basket, of twigs and stick, usually placed conspicuously at the base of the fronds of a palm tree. Anywhere from 2 or 3 to as many as 20 or 30 pairs may combine to build the apartment. Each pair has its own separate compartment with its own private entrance from the outside. They line the interior with softer bark and grass. The clutch is 2 to 4 white eggs heavily spotted with grey. After the breeding season the birds roost in these communal nests.

Palm Chats are common and conspicuous on Hispaniola, for they are noisy birds and usually utter their harsh chattering notes in chorus. They live mostly on berries and flowers, are entirely arboreal, and never feed on the ground. Very little else is known about their habits. It is difficult to say whether the Palm Chats have developed their distinctive peculiarities in their insular isolation, or whether they maintain there the characteristics of a formerly more widespread ancestor that has left no record of its existence elsewhere.

PHAINOPEPLA ♂
Phainopepla nitens
Southwestern U.S. and Mexico   7 in.

HYPOCOLIUS
Hypocolius ampelinus
Arabia, Iraq,
Tigris-Euphrates Valley   7 in.

PALM CHAT
Dulus dominicus
Island of Hispaniola   8 in.

WHITE-BROWED WOOD-SWALLOW
Artamus superciliosus
Australia 8½ in.

WOOD-SWALLOWS

PASSERIFORMES   ARTAMIDAE

The wood-swallows, small, plain-coloured, aerial birds with plump bodies and long, pointed wings, are most plentiful in Australia, where 6 of the 10 known species occur. The others range northward from India to the Philippines in southeastern Asia and eastward in the Pacific to the Fiji Islands. The name wood-swallow, which is applied to these birds in Australia and has become the accepted vernacular term for the family, is an unfortunate choice. In southeastern Asia, English-speaking people call them swallow-shrikes. While they feed almost entirely on insects caught largely on the wing and look something like stocky swallows in flight, the wood-swallows are in no way related to the swallow family.

The ancestry of wood-swallows can only be guessed at, for they show no close ties to any other living species. They show their nearest affinities, and these only vaguely, to the waxwings and to the vanga-shrikes. Their plumage is soft and fine-textured, and their colours are drab browns, greys, or blacks relieved by a white rump or white underparts in some species. The sexes are alike or nearly so. Their bills are longish, stout, and slightly down-curved, and their gape is wide. Their short legs are stout and their feet are strong. Their necks are short. Their medium-length tails are square or slightly emarginate. The wood-swallows' outstanding peculiarity is their possession of powder-downs, a specialized type of feather that grows continually and frays off at the end into a powder used for dressing the other feathers. Found in the tinamous, herons, parrots, and in the strange mesitae and cuckoo-rollers of Madagascar, powder-downs are known to occur in no other passerine birds.

Some observers consider wood-swallows to be the most skilful and accomplished fliers among the passerines. They are the only perching birds, other than the Raven, able to glide for extended periods on motionless wings and to sail effortlessly into the sky on thermal updrafts. In flight they resemble stout-bodied swallows, but their flight is slower, more direct and less erratic, and marked by long stretches of soaring. Wood-swallows are usually seen in flocks hawking insects over forest clearings, grain fields, or rice paddies, often soaring high into the sky, almost out of sight. They keep up a harsh nasal twittering that can be heard from above when the birds are almost invisible.

Each flock usually centres its activities around some central vantage point, a high lone tree or a clump of tall waving palms or giant bamboos. There they perch quietly close together and sally forth individually to feed as the spirit moves them. Birds dash out fitfully from their perch after a passing insect and then spiral around in soaring circles a few moments before returning. They feed most actively in the early morning and late evening, and usually remain huddled quietly on their exposed roosts during the heat of the day. During plagues of locusts and other insects, wood-swallows flock to feed on the swarming pests and do yeoman service in controlling them. When flying insects are scarce, they will descend to the ground to feed on crawling insects and larvae. Rarely do they eat seeds, fruit, or other vegetable matter.

Throughout most of their range wood-swallows are common and quite conspicuous, for they are rather noisy and highly gregarious. They are often seen perched in long lines on telephone wires. At night they roost huddled together on high branches. During bad weather they take shelter in close-packed swarms under a leaning tree trunk, a projecting branch, or a loose flap of bark. They sometimes jam into narrow spaces one atop the other like a swarm of huge bees, always with their heads up.

Wood-swallows build frail, loosely constructed, saucer-shaped nests, usually on a branch. The 8½-inch White-browed Wood-swallow of Australia, one of the largest species, generally nests rather low down in a tree or bush. The Ashy Swallow-shrike of southeastern Asia usually nests 30 to 40 feet above the ground, and a favourite site is the shelf formed by a projecting stub where palm leaves have broken away below the crown. The smallest member of the family, the 6-inch Little Wood-swallow of Australia, which looks in flight only half the size of its larger relatives, places its flimsy nest in tree cavities or in rock crevices on a cliff. The Little Wood-swallow often nests in colonies, as do some of the other species. So far as known, nesting duties are shared by both sexes in the wood-swallows. The eggs number 2 to 4; they are white to buffy in ground colour, and are usually heavily spotted around the larger end, in which characteristic they strongly resemble the eggs of shrikes.

BLUE VANGA-SHRIKE
Leptopterus madagascarinus
Madagascar 6 in.

NORTHERN
(GREAT GREY) SHRIKE
Lanius excubitor
Northern North America
and Eurasia 9½ in.

BLACK-HEADED GONOLEK
Laniarius barbarus
East Africa 8 in.

RED-BACKED
SHRIKE
Lanius collurio
Temperate Eurasia 7 in.

GORGEOUS (FOUR-COLOURED)
BUSH-SHRIKE
Telophorus quadricolor
South Africa 8 in.

BLACK-HEADED SHRIKE
Lanius schach
Southern Asia, Iran to China,
Malaya, and New Guinea 9 in.

VANGA-SHRIKES

PASSERIFORMES   VANGIDAE

Isolated insular populations evolve so rapidly that nobody knows just when the vanga-shrikes' ancestors reached Madagascar; nor can we be sure just what those progenitors of the family looked like. As the less specialized vangas bear anatomical resemblances to the African helmet shrikes (Prionopinae), it is probable that some primitive laniid crossed the Mozambique Channel to found this isolated family of 12 distinct species assigned to 8 genera.

Most vangas are metallic black above, white below, or marked with chestnut or grey, and 5 to 12 inches long. Two have white heads, and the gayest of them is the Blue Vanga shown above. Sexes are usually alike, females sometimes duller. Typically, vangas have stout, strongly hooked bills, but one species' is thin and down-curved, and another's bears a casque. Their wings are rounded, the tail usually short and square, the legs and feet short and stout.

All vangas are arboreal, occupying different niches in the forests. Most live in the tree-tops and search the foliage for insects, as do the Blue Vanga and the smaller Red-tailed Vanga, sometimes called the tit-shrike because it hangs upside down to poke under leaves and branches for its food.

The Rufous Vanga lives in the middle and lower forest strata, Lafresnaye's Vanga solitarily in arid brushlands. The Helmet Bird, which boasts a casque on its bill, flies rather heavily through the woodlands in small flocks. The Hook-billed Vanga, one of the more primitive species, ranges widely from the tree-tops to the ground, also in second-growth brushlands and mangroves. A solitary bird and deliberate in its movements, it sits motionless on a branch, turning its head slowly to watch for insects, small reptiles, and amphibians. Its call is a monotonous, long-drawn whistle.

Most gregarious of the family is the thin-billed Sicklebill, which roves through the woods and savannahs in flocks of 25 or more. The Sicklebill builds a large nest of twigs in a tall tree, but its nesting habits and behaviour, like those of the rest of the vanga-shrike family, are practically unknown.

SHRIKES

PASSERIFORMES   LANIIDAE

Dashing and bold are the shrikes, the most truly predatory of the perching birds. They occupy somewhat the same position among the passerines that the hawks and owls do among the non-passerines. Though shrikes are essentially insect eaters, many of them prey on small vertebrates—frogs, lizards, rodents, and even on birds almost as big as themselves. Unlike the hawks and owls, whose chief weapons are their strong talons, shrikes kill with their sharply hooked beaks. Their well-known habit of impaling their prey on thorns has earned them the common name "butcherbird."

Shrikes are small- to medium-sized birds, most of them 7 to 10 inches long, with large, broad heads and stout bills, strongly hooked and notched at the tip. Their shortish rounded wings have 10 primaries, and their tails are usually long and graduated. Their legs and feet are strong and their claws sharp. The more familiar Northern Hemisphere shrikes are plainly coloured grey or brown above and white below, often with contrasting black or white markings on the head, wing, and tail. The black mask of the Northern and Loggerhead shrikes is duplicated in many Old World species. The sexes are generally alike, but are dissimilar in some species.

The shrike family is predominantly an Old World one, with its centre of development and abundance in tropical Africa. As presently constituted it is divided into three subfamilies, the true shrikes (Laniinae), the bush shrikes (Malaconotinae), and the helmet shrikes (Prionopinae). The 39 bush shrikes and the 9 helmet shrikes are limited to Africa. The 25 true shrikes are widespread throughout Africa and Eurasia, but have never reached Australia or the Pacific islands south or east of the Philippines. Two species occur in the New World, the widespread circumpolar Northern Shrike, and the smaller Loggerhead Shrike. The Loggerhead, whose range extends to southern Mexico, is the family's only wholly nearctic species. Shrikes do not occur in Central America or South America.

The shrikes' relationships to other families need further clarification, but with 72 of the family's 73 species of Eastern Hemisphere distribution, there is no question of their Old World origin. They are probably an offshoot from some primitive ancestor of the Old World flycatchers, the Muscicapidae. Their distinctness as a family points to their antiquity. Fossils of several living species are known from early Ice Age deposits, and of one, the Lesser Grey Shrike, from the Pliocene of Europe. The nominate genus *Lanius* is represented in early Miocene deposits in Hungary.

A well-known true shrike is the Northern or Great Grey Shrike, one of the largest species in the subfamily, which nests in the spruce forests completely across northern North America and Eurasia and winters irregularly southward when food is scarce in the north. In North America it divides into two geographical races, an eastern and a western, which then merge in the Hudson Bay region. Eurasia has a score of races, particularly along the southern edge of the species' range in southern Europe, northern Africa, and eastward to the Himalayas. Many Americans are familiar with the nine races of the Loggerhead Shrike, which nests widely across southern Canada and the United States. The Red-backed Shrike is an equally common Eurasian species found in temperate regions across the continent. It breaks into some eight geographical races, most of which migrate to Africa and southern Asia in winter.

Wherever they occur, shrikes are conspicuous birds, for they sit in a prominent open place with no attempt at concealment. Their actions are bold and aggressive. They fly strongly, usually undulating when travelling any distance, gliding shortly between wing strokes. They fly fairly close to the ground and sweep upward to their perch at the last moment. When hunting they may hover momentarily with fluttering wingbeats before striking, but usually they watch quietly from a commanding perch and pounce suddenly and directly when they spy their prey. If it is small and light, they carry it away in their beak; if it is heavier, in their feet.

The favourite food of most shrikes is large insects, such as grasshoppers, dragonflies, locusts, and crickets. These they hold in their feet and tear apart with their beaks. Their curious habit of impaling their prey on thorns (barbed wire is a frequent substitute in cattle and farming country) may have developed from the difficulty of holding tougher animals in their feet while tearing them apart. Originally the thorn may have served them as a butcher's hook to give them better purchase for dismembering their catch, and they left the remains after eating their fill.

Like many predators, shrikes often kill more than they can eat, and when opportunity presents itself seem to kill for the joy of killing. Bird ringers have to watch their traps carefully when there are shrikes in the vicinity, for a wandering shrike that happens into a trap full of birds will kill every bird fluttering within reach before starting to eat. Shrikes usually have a favourite larder within their territory where they hang their catch. It is possible to come across a thorn tree or barbed-wire fence decorated with a dozen or more grasshoppers, locusts, mice, or small birds.

That the shrikes establish such larders in times of plenty against future need has been questioned. They often fail to return, and the carcasses slowly shrivel or rot. Studies on several species show individual birds do remember where they have cached their food. A Japanese ornithologist counted 68 such caches made by one Bull-headed Shrike within its territory during the autumn. The bird returned and gradually consumed its stores during January and February, when live prey was scarce.

Seldom are predators of any sort gregarious, for each individual needs quite a bit of territory to forage over. Shrikes are no exceptions, and throughout most of the year they are encountered singly at intervals over the countryside. While most of the north temperate zone species are migratory to some extent, mass movements are seldom observed in these solitary birds. The migratory instinct is not highly developed, and varies in intensity and regularity. Some may remain near the breeding grounds all year, while others move irregularly southward in winter. Their wanderings seem determined more by food supply than by season. Every two or three winters an influx of Northern Shrikes invades the northern United States; at other times almost none appear.

The Northern Shrike preys more on small birds and mammals than do most other shrikes, particularly in winter when insects are scarce in the north. Its dashing attacks on titmice, sparrows, and other small birds have not made it popular with tender-hearted bird lovers, who fail to realize that the fierce predator is a useful biological regulator of lesser species and is an essential part of the natural scheme of things. Back in the latter part of the 19th century, shortly after the European House Sparrow was introduced to the United States, Northern Shrikes became so numerous on Boston Common one winter that men were hired to shoot them to protect the sparrows. Little did people then realize that the House Sparrow would soon become far too plentiful for man himself, much less for shrikes, to control.

Shrikes start pairing off in late winter as the springtime breeding season approaches. They build bulky, loose, deep cup nests of twigs in a shrub or tree from 5 to 20 feet above the ground. The Northern Shrike lines its nest heavily with grasses, feathers and hair, for it lays very early in spring and, like most shrikes, rears at least two broods each year. Clutches vary from 3 to 6, and the eggs are typically a dirty white or tinted bluish to pinkish in ground colour, always heavily spotted with greys or browns about the larger end. Incubation among the shrikes is almost exclusively by the female. Though the male may take short turns on the eggs, he usually spends his time bringing food to the incubating female. The incubation period is 14 to 16 days, and the young leave the nest 2 to 3 weeks after hatching.

During the breeding season shrikes are rather quiet and go about their business inconspicuously. When nesting is over and the pairs break up and scatter out on their own, shrikes become fairly vocal and announce themselves with unmelodious cries and rattles. The name shrike derives from the same root as shriek, and refers to their shrill calls. They have a wide range of vocal expression, and some species imitate the calls of other birds skilfully. Shrikes are sensitive to the weather and sing but little when it is overcast and wet. They are noisiest on fine, dry days.

The large subfamily of African bush shrikes is divided among seven genera, which vary considerably in appearance. Most of them are much more brightly coloured than the laniine shrikes, and the sexes are generally unlike. Despite their brilliant colours, they are hard to observe, for they are shy birds of dense thickets and heavy cover. They skulk in the underbrush and hunt on or near the ground. They feed mainly on insects, but many of them are predatory on frogs, lizards, snakes, and mice. Some are notorious nest robbers,

taking both the eggs and nestlings of other species. Representative of the bush shrikes are the Gorgeous Bush Shrike and the Black-headed Gonolek.

Most bush shrikes have loud, melodious voices and reveal their presence by distinctive calls. Many of them sing antiphonally, the male piping one phrase, the female answering immediately with another. Bush shrikes build a loose open cup nest in branches fairly near the ground. Their clutches are smaller than those of the true shrikes, two eggs being the usual number, occasionally three. Both sexes build the nest, but incubation is almost entirely by the female, and takes about 12 days. The young are ready to leave about 15 days after hatching.

The helmet shrikes are such a distinctive group that they are sometimes given full family rank. They are boldly patterned, usually black above and white or buffy below. Their stiff forehead feathers project forward over the nostrils, and their eyes are surrounded by a conspicuous wattle. Residents of wooded and forested Africa south of the Sahara, helmet shrikes are markedly gregarious and, as might be expected, are not as predaceous as other shrikes. They live almost entirely on insects, hunting for them like so many large warblers or titmice. They move through the tree-tops in noisy bands of 5 to 20 birds, chattering continually to one another and snapping their bills audibly. This curious bill snapping is typical of the entire subfamily.

Helmet shrikes even remain together in small groups when breeding, and in the Spectacled Crested Shrike three or more individuals may share in the nest building and the feeding of the young at a single nest. Helmet shrikes build a cup nest of grasses and twigs in a tree fork 15 feet or higher above the ground, and lay 3 to 4 eggs, usually pale-blue spotted with brown. They are reported to be pugnacious in defence of their nests, and to attack large animals and even humans who approach too closely.

STRAIGHT-CRESTED HELMET SHRIKE
Prionops plumata
South-central Africa 8¼ in.

STARLINGS

PASSERIFORMES STURNIDAE

Thanks to man's misguided assistance, the sometimes too-familiar Common Starling has become the most widely distributed member of this family of aggressive Old World birds. During the past century man has helped it across the oceans and other natural barriers that originally confined it to the western palaearctic region. Its range is now almost cosmopolitan. South America is the only major land mass on which it has not as yet gained an impregnable foothold.

The 111 species in the starling family are of Old World origin and distribution, with their centres of greatest development in the Ethiopian and oriental regions. All but three of them are grouped in the nominate subfamily Sturninae, which in turn is apportioned among some 26 genera. They are a fairly well-defined group and, though their ancestry is uncertain, starlings most probably arose from primitive thrush-like stock. One of the earliest passerine fossils known is considered intermediate between the starlings and the thrushes. The fossilized impression of the skeleton of this early perching bird, named *Laurillardia*, was found in France in Eocene deposits about 50 million years old.

As a group, starlings are jaunty, active birds of medium size with straight or slightly down-curved bills. They have strong, stout legs and feet, and while a few hop occasionally, most of them walk cockily with a waddling gait. Their flight is strong and direct, and their pointed wings have 10 primaries, the outermost one greatly shortened. Typically the tail is short and square, though it is rounded in some and long and pointed in a few.

Starlings are generally dark-coloured, most of them black with metallic sheens; some are brown or grey, others brightly marked with white, yellow, or, less often, red. Many are crested, and a number sport prominent wattles or bare patches of skin on the head. The sexes may be alike or unlike. The immatures of most species differ from the adults in having a duller plumage often streaked or scaled, which is probably indicative of the ancestral adult type.

Starlings moult but once a year, immediately after breeding. The seasonal variation in their plumage, which is often notable, is accomplished entirely by feather wear. The name starling, meaning little star (some of the smaller gayer species are now called starlets), comes from the spangled appearance of the Common Starling in its fresh autumn plumage. The buffy star-spots at the tips of the fresh feathers wear away gradually during the winter, leaving the bird a shining glossy black by spring. The bill also changes colour in the Common Starling, its horny brown of autumn and winter becoming a bright ivory-yellow as the gonads enlarge and the birds come into breeding condition in the spring.

While starlings probably originated as forest birds, only a few groups live in deep woodlands. Most of them prefer open, broken country. The most successful species have associated themselves with man and are most abundant in cultivated regions. Their basic diet is insects and fruit, but those that live near man are catholic in their food selection, and take a varied diet including birds' eggs and kitchen waste.

Many starlings are insectivores. The Common Starling consumes great quantities of noxious insects. The Grey Starling, which replaces the Common in eastern Asia, is one of the few birds that feed extensively on the rice stem-borer, and for this reason is protected in Japan. The Rosy Pastor of southeastern Europe and southwestern Asia follows the cyclic swarms of locusts, and nests whenever and wherever these periodic pests become plentiful.

Another famous nomadic locust eater is the Wattled Starling of South Africa, where it is widely protected. The Wattled Starling is unique in that the males, and occasionally the females, shed their head feathers and grow conspicuous wattles during the breeding season. This species also has no regular breeding season or place, but nest periodically and colonially when stimulated by a superabundance of food. When the locusts swarm, flocks of Wattled Starlings gather to the feast from miles around.

Most starlings are gregarious, some of them highly so. The temperate zone species are migratory, and usually travel and winter in flocks, sometimes of tremendous size. They often gather in spectacular numbers to roost at night. Just before going to roost, and again at dawn, the flocks climb high into the air and execute a series of mass evolutions. Wheeling and turning in unison with almost military precision, the birds course back and forth in tremendous twittering swarms before settling down for the night or scattering for the day's foraging.

Starlings are generally noisy and garrulous, and chatter to one another continually in flight and when roosting. The Common Starling has a large vocabulary of creaking, grating, wheezing, rattling notes that it intersperses with clear musical whistles. It sings in autumn as well as in spring, and sometimes sings at night in its winter roosts. Many of its notes are too high in pitch to be heard by the human ear, with frequencies above 8,000 vibrations per second. Starlings often incorporate imitations of other birds in their songs, and several rank high as mimics.

Among the best of all talking cage birds are the Asiatic mynahs of the genus *Gracula* that range from India and Ceylon through the oriental region. The Hill Mynah, commonly called a grackle in India, is a large, glossy black starling with yellow head wattles. Isolated populations vary considerably in size, from 12 to 15 inches. Hill Mynahs travel through the forests in small noisy flocks and live largely on fruits. In the wild their notes vary from low, hoarse chuckles to loud, ringing whistles that carry far. In captivity their imitations of human speech are far superior to those of any parrot. I have heard several tame mynahs with astonishingly extensive vocabularies, and with an enunciation so perfect that there was not the slightest doubt of what they were saying.

The Common Mynah (*Acridotheres*) of southern Asia is a stocky, 10-inch brown and black bird with white wing patches, a short crest, and naked patches of orange skin about the eyes. A noisy, vigorous species that prefers open country and feeds much on the ground, it is not as attractive a cage bird as the Hill Mynah and does not learn to talk as well. It has been introduced successfully in almost as many parts of the world as the Common Starling. Similar in appearance to the Hill Mynahs are three species of Papuan Mynahs (*Mino*), found from New Guinea eastward on many of the Southwest Pacific islands. Commonest of the Pacific island species are the 20-odd glossy starlings (*Aplonis*), most of which are black with metallic sheens, and are regarded as one of the more primitive groups of the family. In appearance and behaviour the glossy starlings I encountered in the South Pacific reminded me strongly of American blackbirds.

The Sturninae are well developed in Africa, where a large complex of 16 dark, shiny species with tails of varying lengths is assigned to the genus *Lamprotornis*. Among the more striking of the African forms is the Golden-breasted Starling, a slender-bodied bird whose sleek grace is accentuated by its long, tapering tail. The Golden-breasted Starling feeds largely on termites, opening their ground tunnels with rapid flicks of its bill, and catching the insects skilfully on the wing when they take flight. The Superb Starling is representative of 10 brightly coloured African species of the genus *Spreo* which live on both insects and fruit. This species feeds on the ground in small flocks, and is rather tame and congenial. It builds a round domed nest of thorny twigs lined with feathers, usually in a bush or low tree.

Nesting habits vary considerably in the starling family, but in most of those that have been studied the pair bond is strong and both sexes share the various nesting duties. Starling eggs are usually a clear blue-green; they are white in a few species. In several genera, *Aplonis, Gracula,* and *Mino* among them, the eggs are spotted with brown. Clutch size varies from 2 to 9, but is usually 3 to 5. Most starlings are cavity nesters and build in holes in trees, either natural ones, or holes abandoned by, or usurped from, woodpeckers. Some nest in cliff or wall niches, others under embankments. Those that have associated themselves with mankind, such as the Common Starling, use sites in buildings, behind shutters, under eaves, or on any projecting ledge. They are expert at finding their way into belfries, towers, and attics.

One of the South Pacific glossy starlings (*A. metallica*) builds a large woven hanging nest in the tree-tops, much like that of a weaverfinch. When a hatch of locusts encourages the African Wattled Starling to breed, the birds nest colonially. They build massive covered nests of sticks and twigs, usually within the protection of thorny trees or shrubs. Often several pairs mass their nests together, 2 or 3 touching one another. Sometimes a dozen or more of these double or triple nests occupy the same thorn tree.

The Rosy Pastor is another colonial and opportunistic breeder. It nests in huge crowded colonies when conditions are right, starting suddenly and finishing its breeding cycle in a hurry. Each pair builds a crude, untidy nest, heaping twigs or grasses together in crevices in rock hillsides, cliffs, walls, or ruins. The Rosy Pastor lays 5 to 6 pale bluish eggs, which are incubated by the female alone. The incubation period is short, usually 11 to 12 days, and the young, fed by both parents, leave the nest in 14 to 19 days after hatching. This irruptive breeding behaviour is doubtless conditioned by and adapted to the transitory nature of the insect swarms that trigger it

into action. The Rosy Pastor rears but a single brood, and as soon as the young are securely on the wing the birds quickly wander away in search of fresher and richer feeding grounds.

The Common Starling sometimes nests in small colonies, but more often singly. Like the Rosy Pastor, it makes a loose, bulky open pad of sticks and straws for a nest in any convenient cavity. The normal clutch is 4 to 5 clear-blue eggs, which both parents incubate for 12 to 14 days. The young remain in the nest almost 3 weeks and fledge fully before leaving. This helps reduce the usual high juvenile mortality rate. The Common Starling is multi-brooded, and pairs use the same nest for 2, sometimes 3, successive broods. The nest soon becomes fouled by the droppings of the young, for nest sanitation, practiced by most passerines, is distinctly not a starling trait.

The Common Starling's success in establishing itself when carried by man to corners of the globe far from its natal habitat bespeaks its adaptability and aggressiveness. It is one of four vertebrates, the others being the House Sparrow, brown rat, and house mouse, all originally inhabitants of Europe, which man has spread widely over the planet, purposely for the two birds, accidentally for the two mammals. Most dramatic and best documented of these cases has been the introduction and subsequent spread of the Common Starling in North America during the past half century. This outstanding example of the dangers latent in foreign introductions was largely responsible for the present federal laws controlling the importation and release of wild birds in the United States.

A dozen or more attempts were made to introduce starlings in various parts of the United States and Canada between 1870 and 1900. All failed except one—the 60 birds released in New York's Central Park in 1890, followed by 40 more in 1891. These started to breed at once, and the first nest was found under the eaves of the American Museum of Natural History adjoining the park in the summer of 1890. From these 100 birds have descended the millions of starlings that now occupy most of settled North America.

For the first few years the Central Park starlings remained in New York. As their numbers increased they began to wander, particularly in autumn and winter. By 1900 they had reached New Haven, Connecticut, and Bayonne, New Jersey. In another 10 years they had appeared in most of New England and in the Middle Atlantic states. Their expansion followed a set pattern. The birds invaded new territory during their winter wanderings. Where they found conditions suitable, a few remained to breed instead of returning to their natal area. These remained static until the local population built up, and shortly their descendants moved on to fresh conquests. By the early 1930's starlings had expanded throughout the Middle West, northward into southern Canada, and southward into northern Florida. The first ones crossed the Rockies into California in the 1940's.

Starlings were introduced with the best motives in the world —in Europe they are cheerful and useful bird neighbours that consume great quantities of harmful insects. But by the time they had gained an impregnable foothold in North America and had begun to appear in large flocks in the suburban countryside, it was realized, too late, that their presence had undesirable elements. Though their extensive insect consumption is on the positive side, their inroads on crops of grains and small fruits are considerable. Starlings compete for wild fruits with native thrushes and waxwings, and for nesting sites with highly valued hole nesters, such as bluebirds and woodpeckers, whose numbers decline wherever starlings take over.

The starlings' worst habit has been their flocking into cities in tremendous hordes to roost in winter. In this respect, they have become a prime nuisance. The situation became acute in Washington, D.C., during the early 1930's. Wintering flocks that fed by day over the surrounding countryside streamed into the heart of the city from every quadrant late in the afternoon. The birds lined the ledges on the government buildings, swarmed into the trees on Pennsylvania Avenue, and perched in noisy windrows in every nook and cranny in the foyers of theatres and department stores. Their droppings soiled the buildings, and the streets and pedestrians below them as well. In residential districts their night-long wheezing and chattering kept people awake. In the past two decades other eastern and mid-western cities have been subjected to similar starling plagues. A famous roost is on the girders supporting the Hudson River Parkway viaduct in New York City. Birds stream in every winter evening from the New Jersey and Long Island marshes.

Control of the starling nuisance in cities is a serious civic problem that has yet to be solved satisfactorily. Trapping, netting, poisoning, and shooting have not reduced the birds' numbers effectively. Efforts to drive them away with flares, firehoses, smudgepots, noisemakers of all sorts including electronic magnifications of their alarm notes, and most recently by painting their roosts with sticky pastes, have afforded only temporary relief. Architects are now designing buildings to eliminate all ledges where the birds might roost.

Fortunately the starling problem now shows signs of abating by itself. The first great population explosion seems ended in the eastern states. In places the huge wintering flocks are gradually diminishing, and the birds are settling down into a more static biological niche. Starlings have now established regular migration patterns in North America, largely in a northeast-southwest direction paralleling the movements of their European forebears.

The Common Starling has been introduced to South Africa, Australia, New Zealand, and Jamaica with roughly similar

AMETHYST STARLING
Cinnyricinclus leucogaster
Tropical Africa 7 in.

GOLDEN-CRESTED MYNAH
Mino coronatus
Burma, Thailand,
Indochina 8 in.

HILL MYNAH
Gracula religiosa
India to Indochina and Malaya 13 in.

consequences. In each case the newcomers remained quiescent until they gained strength in numbers. Then they suddenly expanded explosively, with unfortunate effects on native birds, on crops, and on human peace. The species has also increased and expanded in its European home during the past century. It has followed human cultivation northward into northern Scandinavia and the subarctic islands. Starlings reached Iceland in the 1930's, and have been breeding there regularly since 1941.

The Common Mynah, as mentioned above, has also been introduced widely around the world in the past century. It has gained strong footholds in South Africa, Hawaii, New Zealand, Australia, and on many islands in the Pacific, Indian, and South Atlantic oceans. About 1900 the related Crested Mynah of southeast Asia was introduced to Vancouver, British Columbia. They became well established, but fortunately have not as yet been able to expand as they and starlings have done elsewhere. The British Columbia population is believed to number about 20,000 Mynahs today, and seems to be remaining steady. Just what the ecological conditions are that allow it to prosper in this one area around Vancouver without spreading are unknown. Wildlife management experts still have their fingers crossed against Mynahs crossing the barrier of biological intolerance that apparently keeps them from establishing a population in more favourable territory to the south. Straggling Mynahs have been reported in Oregon and Washington. A Mynah plague could be disastrous in the California fruit country.

Despite the rampant success of these adaptable starlings, the family contains several species that became so specialized in limited environments that they vanished when civilization reached them. One such species was a small starling that lived with the Dodo on Rodriguez and Reunion islands in the Indian Ocean. Some 23 specimens of it are known, the last taken in 1840. A handsome, glossy black starling (*Aplonis*) that once lived in the forests of Kusaie Island in

COMMON STARLING
Sturnus vulgaris
Europe, western Asia 8½ in.

ROSY PASTOR
Sturnus roseus
Southeastern Europe,
southwestern Asia 8½ in.

SUPERB STARLING
Spreo superbus
East Africa 8½ in.

GOLDEN-BREASTED
STARLING
Cosmopsarus regius
East Africa 14 in.

YELLOW-BILLED OXPECKER
Buphagus africanus
Africa south of the Sahara 8½ in.

the eastern Carolines is known only from a few skins in the Leningrad Museum. It is thought to have been exterminated by rats that came ashore on Kusaie from whaling ships in the 19th century. Rats from a ship wrecked on tiny Lord Howe Island in the Tasman Sea between Australia and New Zealand in 1918 quickly wiped out another glossy starling there.

Two aberrant African starlings, the Red-billed and Yellow-billed oxpeckers, form the subfamily Buphaginae. These strange starlings have adopted a life with, and actually upon, large animals. Their food consists mainly of the ticks they pull from the animals' hides, and they also sip the blood that oozes from tick wounds. Oxpeckers have broadly thickened beaks; their legs are short, their claws sharp and curved, their tails stiff and pointed. They climb about on all sorts of large wild animals and domestic cattle as a woodpecker climbs tree trunks. The animals seem to pay little attention to the birds unless they get too close to their eyes or noses.

Africans regard oxpeckers with mixed feelings. Hunters dislike them because they warn their animal hosts of danger by flying up with rattling cries. Game photographers love them because of the interest they lend to pictures of big game. Bushmen and primitive farmers value them for ridding their cattle of ticks. Commercial cattlemen are against them because they claim the birds keep tick wounds open in order to drink the blood. However, oxpeckers waste no time on tick-free animals, and soon disappear from ranges where the cattle are dipped regularly and there is no big game about for them to feed from.

Oxpeckers are cavity nesters. The Yellow-billed nests in holes in tall trees. The Red-billed breeds commonly under the eaves of buildings, in the thatched roofs of native huts, in rock cavities, or along embankments. Each builds an untidy nest of grass or straw lined with animal hair, and lays from 3 to 5 white to pale-blue eggs variously spotted with brown in it.

Placed tentatively with the starlings as a third subfamily, the Pityriasinae, is the rare and little-studied Bristle-head of Southern Borneo forests. Although it had long been classified with the helmet shrikes (p. 270) because of its peculiar head feathering, and sometimes placed in a family by itself, what little is known of the Bristle-head's behaviour and habits has led most students today to regard it as a highly aberrant starling.

HONEYEATERS

PASSERIFORMES   MELIPHAGIDAE

The 160 species of honeyeaters form one of the dominant and most characteristic families of Australia, New Zealand, and the islands of the Southwest Pacific. Most are rather small birds, only a few exceeding thrush or jay size. Many are drably coloured in greenish browns, greys, and yellows; others are boldly patterned with blacks, whites, and reds. They live in the forests and brushlands, and feed, as their name implies, mainly on flower nectar and small insects. All have slender, down-curved, pointed bills, and a long extensible tongue with a brushy tip and sides that curls around to form a tube for sucking nectar from forest flowers. All have 10 primaries and rather long pointed wings. The tail may be short or quite long; the legs are normally shortish and strong.

The family has its greatest development in Australia, where more than half the known species occur, and is well represented from the Moluccas eastward through the Papuan region and the South Pacific islands. One branch of the family reached Hawaii, where 5 or 6 forms were once found on as many of the islands. These were the birds the Hawaiians called the O-o and whose yellow feathers they used for the unique capes of their royalty. The O-os lived in the mountain forests and disappeared rapidly when the native woodlands were destroyed. While it is hoped that the O-o (*Moho braccatus*) may still exit on Kauai, the others are certainly extinct, for none has been recorded since early in the 20th century. Persecution by native Hawaiians for their feathers has commonly been blamed for the disappearance of these birds, but destruction of their forest habitat as the island plantations were developed by Westerners is the more likely cause of their extinction.

The Helmeted Honeyeater is typical of a large complex of Australian honeyeaters, most of which are olive-greenish in colour, with tufts of yellow feathers around the head or neck. These honeyeaters of the nominate genus *Meliphaga* are essentially inhabitants of vast eucalyptus forests, though some species prefer oak growth or acacias. A number are common visitors to gardens and city parks when the trees come into bloom. Quite a few antipodean flowering trees are ornithophilous, i.e., dependent on birds for cross-fertilization. Their flowers are shaped to facilitate pollination by honeyeaters and other nectar-sipping birds.

The Helmeted Honeyeater and its relatives travel through the forests in small bands and feed together among the flowers of a tree in bloom. Active, aggressive birds, they quarrel among themselves while feeding and jockey for positions next to favourite flowers. They stop bickering when a bird of another species appears and join forces to drive it away from their feeding site. All honeyeaters build open cup-shaped nests in trees or bushes composed of small twigs and lined with plant down or animal hair. One species, the White-eared Honeyeater, is so tame during the nesting season it sometimes lights on people's heads to steal hair for nest-lining material. Most lay 2 or 3 eggs, which may be white or tinted with markings of darker shades.

Another large group of honeyeaters is formed by the many *Myzomelas*, bright-coloured little birds 4 to 6 inches in length found widely throughout the Pacific islands. In most of these the sexes differ in colour, the males being brilliant blacks and reds, the females dull greenish. Dichromatism varies greatly within the genus. In some species the males are dull-

275

NOISY FRIARBIRD
Philemon corniculatus
Eastern Australia 12 in.

O-O (extinct)
Moho nobilis
Hawaii 13 in.

TUI
Prosthemadera novaeseelandiae
New Zealand 11 in.

coloured like the females; in a very few the females have a bright plumage similar to that of the male. Except when they settle down to rear their broods, *Myzomelas* are nomadic, wandering about in small flocks in search of flowering trees and shrubs. Their nesting habits are typical of those of most of the family in that they build an open cup-shaped nest and lay 2 to 3 eggs. The female does most of the nest building, but the male may do some of the incubating, and always helps feed and rear the young. Incubation in these little birds is fairly lengthy, reported as about 18 days, and the nestling period is equally long.

The friarbirds and wattlebirds of Australia are honeyeaters that have bare spaces or wattles about the head. These jay-sized birds are among the larger honeyeaters, and most are grey in colour. Many are highly vocal. The Noisy Friarbird, whose unattractive naked head of black skin is responsible for its vernacular name of "leatherhead," has raucous calls. It wanders about cultivated lands and settlements and is reported occasionally to damage orchards. Wattlebirds, so called because of the yellow or red wattles behind the eye, likewise eat fruit as well as nectar and insects. Their nomadism has reached the point of seasonal regularity, so that in southern Australia they are classed as migrants. At one time

they were hunted for their flesh, which is excellent eating, and because they are large enough for shooting, and travel about in flocks. They are now protected throughout most of Australia.

Song is highly developed in most honeyeaters, and one of the best performers is the Tui, which New Zealanders consider among the finest of their forest songsters. The Tui's song is loud, varied, musical, and pleasant, and the bird is a competent mimic as well, imitating the songs of the other birds it hears and such unbird-like sounds as the squealing of a pig, a boy whistling to his dog, and even the dog's barking. The Tui's two white patches of curly feathers at the throat, like the collars worn by 19th-century divines, led New Zealand settlers to call it the "parson bird." Though not as plentiful as it was before the original bush was cut, the Tui is still fairly common in New Zealand, for it has been able to adapt itself to man's occupancy of its habitat far better than have two other New Zealand members of the family, the Bellbird and the Stitchbird.

The New Zealand Bellbird, whose notes in chorus sound like the chiming of little silvery bells, is still to be found in some of the few patches of original forest now remaining, and is reportedly plentiful in some of the forest reserves.

CARDINAL HONEYEATER ♂
Myzomela cardinalis
Micronesia, Samoa, Solomons,
New Hebrides 4½ in.

HELMETED HONEYEATER
Meliphaga cassidix
Southeastern Australia 8 in.

CAPE SUGARBIRD
Promerops cafer
South Africa 17 in.

Bellbirds are about 9 inches in length, the male dark green in colour, the female browner. They are shy and are heard more often than seen. Both sexes sing equally well.

The little 7-inch Stitchbird, whose notes sound like two pebbles struck together, was last reported limited to a very small population on one little barrier island off the coast of North Island. The male Stitchbird is velvety black above with prominent white feather tufts on the sides of the head and bands of yellow across the breast and at the bend of the wing. The female is a dull brown with a few whitish feathers on the sides of the head and a small white mark in the wing. The few Stitchbird nests that have been described were in holes in trees, a most unusual site for a member of this family. The nest is made of small sticks and rootlets, and is lined with feathers and tree fern scales. The clutch is five pure white, glossy eggs.

Stitchbirds feed entirely on nectar, and even feed their young on it exclusively. This may be partly responsible for their failure to withstand the radical changes in their environment brought on by civilization. The native Maoris used the yellow feathers from the breast of the Stitchbird for ornamental cloaks the same way the Hawaiians did those of the O-o. The introduction of rats and other predators has also affected the Stitchbird and the Bellbird adversely. There seems little question, however, that here again change of habitat rather than human persecution has been responsible for the disappearance of the bird.

Placed tentatively with the Meliphagidae in the subfamily Promeropinae are the two odd South African sugarbirds, found only from Southern Rhodesia southward. They may not be correctly placed here, for it is difficult to see how honeyeater stock could have reached South Africa from Australia without leaving representatives in southern Asia, the Indian Ocean islands, or elsewhere in Africa. Sugarbirds resemble the honeyeaters strongly in structure and habits. They have the same type of tongue and live largely on nectar, mainly from the flowers of the genus *Proteus*. They also eat insects. Despite their similarities to the honeyeaters, which are the only group of birds they resemble closely, they could have developed from an entirely different stock by the process of convergent evolution.

The male Cape Sugarbird is the largest of the meliphagids; with its long tail, it measures 16 to 17 inches in length. The female is as large-bodied, but is only 11 inches long. Sugarbirds build open cup nests, lined with plant down, usually in a bush. They lay two buffy, blotched eggs.

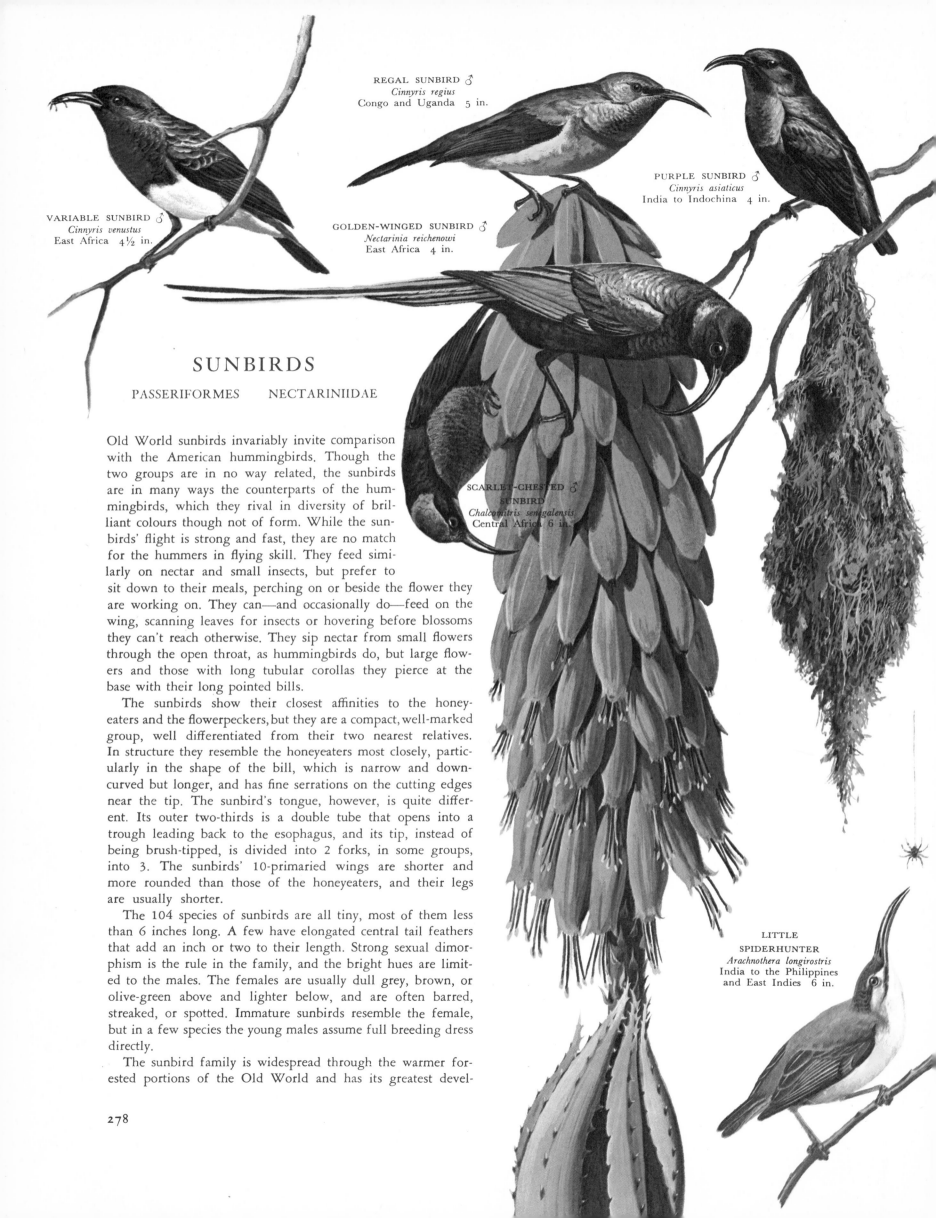

REGAL SUNBIRD ♂
Cinnyris regius
Congo and Uganda 5 in.

PURPLE SUNBIRD ♂
Cinnyris asiaticus
India to Indochina 4 in.

VARIABLE SUNBIRD ♂
Cinnyris venustus
East Africa 4½ in.

GOLDEN-WINGED SUNBIRD ♂
Nectarinia reichenowi
East Africa 4 in.

SCARLET-CHESTED ♂
SUNBIRD
Chalcomitra senegalensis
Central Africa 6 in.

LITTLE
SPIDERHUNTER
Arachnothera longirostris
India to the Philippines
and East Indies 6 in.

SUNBIRDS

PASSERIFORMES   NECTARINIIDAE

Old World sunbirds invariably invite comparison with the American hummingbirds. Though the two groups are in no way related, the sunbirds are in many ways the counterparts of the hummingbirds, which they rival in diversity of brilliant colours though not of form. While the sunbirds' flight is strong and fast, they are no match for the hummers in flying skill. They feed similarly on nectar and small insects, but prefer to sit down to their meals, perching on or beside the flower they are working on. They can—and occasionally do—feed on the wing, scanning leaves for insects or hovering before blossoms they can't reach otherwise. They sip nectar from small flowers through the open throat, as hummingbirds do, but large flowers and those with long tubular corollas they pierce at the base with their long pointed bills.

The sunbirds show their closest affinities to the honeyeaters and the flowerpeckers, but they are a compact, well-marked group, well differentiated from their two nearest relatives. In structure they resemble the honeyeaters most closely, particularly in the shape of the bill, which is narrow and down-curved but longer, and has fine serrations on the cutting edges near the tip. The sunbird's tongue, however, is quite different. Its outer two-thirds is a double tube that opens into a trough leading back to the esophagus, and its tip, instead of being brush-tipped, is divided into 2 forks, in some groups, into 3. The sunbirds' 10-primaried wings are shorter and more rounded than those of the honeyeaters, and their legs are usually shorter.

The 104 species of sunbirds are all tiny, most of them less than 6 inches long. A few have elongated central tail feathers that add an inch or two to their length. Strong sexual dimorphism is the rule in the family, and the bright hues are limited to the males. The females are usually dull grey, brown, or olive-green above and lighter below, and are often barred, streaked, or spotted. Immature sunbirds resemble the female, but in a few species the young males assume full breeding dress directly.

The sunbird family is widespread through the warmer forested portions of the Old World and has its greatest devel-

278

opment in tropical Africa, where more than half the known species live. Sunbirds also range across southern Asia from Israel eastward, and more than a score of species inhabit Malaya. Only one species reaches northern Australia, but several extend out into the Pacific islands. Sunbirds are usually resident wherever they occur. They may move about during the non-breeding season, shifting their feeding grounds as various trees and plants come into bloom, but they show no clear migration patterns.

Though sunbirds often gather together to feed when some favourite tree or patch of flowers comes into bloom, they are not innately gregarious. Some are pugnacious and defend feeding grounds as well as nesting territories against intruders. Their voices are poorly developed, and their thin, metallic calls do not carry far. Courting males utter a twittering, chattering excuse for a song.

An outstanding sunbird characteristic is the hanging, purse-like nests they build of plant fibres woven and matted together or bound with spiders' webs. The nest is usually hung from a branch fairly near the ground, seldom more than 10 feet up, and little attempt is made to conceal it. A few species make neat, compact bags, but most sunbirds' nests are ragged. The bottom is extended with loose trails of fibres with a leaf or two tangled in, so that they are easily overlooked as bits of accumulated rubbish. The nest is lined with plant down, fur, or feathers, and the entrance is on one side near the top and usually covered by a portico.

Though the pair bond is strong and pairs seem to remain together throughout the year, the nesting chores devolve largely on the female sunbird, in some species entirely so. The division of labour is by no means constant within the family and needs further study, but incubation is apparently done by the female alone. In some species, as in the White-breasted Sunbird, the male occasionally helps with nest building and brings food for the young. Sunbird eggs are generally white or buffy and heavily blotched. The usual clutch is 2, rarely 3, and in those species that nest several times yearly, only one. Incubation is reported as 13 to 14 days, and the fledging period another 17 days.

Centred in the oriental region are the nine species of spiderhunters, all of the genus *Arachnothera*, which are such a distinct and uniform group they are sometimes given subfamily rank. The spiderhunters lack the bright metallic hues of the rest of the family, and the sexes are usually dressed alike in grey-browns, dull yellows, or olive-greens. From 6 to 8½ inches in length, they have longer, stronger bills and feed to a greater extent on insects. The Little Spiderhunter of Indochina feeds extensively on the nectar of banana blossoms and probes deep into the flower tubes as it clings to the purple bracts, often upside down.

Most spiderhunters build a unique cup-shaped nest attached to the bottom side of a broad leaf. They sew the rim of the cup to the leaf with cobwebs or vegetable fibres, knotting the strands on the upper side. The leaf forms the roof of the nest, and the entrance is a semicircular hole in the side of the felted cup. Both sexes share the duties of nest building, incubating, and rearing of the young. The eggs are normally 2, though occasionally 3 are reported.

FLOWERPECKERS

PASSERIFORMES   DICAEIDAE

The smallest birds one sees commonly in the oriental and Australian regions are the flowerpeckers. Most of these active, plump little bundles of feathers are barely 3 inches long, and only a few exceed 6 inches from the tip of their bills to the end of their short, stubby tails. The 54 species in the family are divided among 6 genera. The largest, commonest, and most typical group is formed by the 33 species of the genus *Dicaeum*. These are to be found throughout the range of the family, from India to Formosa and the Philippines, southward to Australia, and eastward in the Pacific to the Solomons.

The family is most diversified in the Papuan region, where it is believed to have arisen. The flowerpeckers probably share a common ancestor with the sunbirds, which seem to be their nearest relatives. They have a similar long tubular tongue and fine serrations on the edges of the terminal third of their bills. Flowerpeckers' bills vary somewhat in shape, but are never as long and thin as in the sunbirds. Typically they are shorter, thicker, and slightly down-curved. An important family characteristic is the reduction in length of the outermost primary. This is strongly manifest in the primitive forms, and in the more advanced and typical genera such as *Dicaeum*, the 10th primary is vestigial. Flowerpeckers lack the bare spots or wattles on the head that characterize many honeyeaters and sunbirds, and only one species shows a crest.

Colour patterns vary throughout the flowerpeckers, but generally the birds are dressed in solid hues, and only a few are streaked below. Usually the sexes are strongly unlike, though they are similar in a few species. The males have dark backs, often with a glossy sheen, though this is seldom metallic. Most are lighter, and sometimes white below. Many sport bright patches of red or yellow on the head, back, rump, or breast. The females are usually a duller, plain dark olive-brown above and lighter below. Where the sexes are similar, the colours are usually not bright. In one Philippine group the females are closely similar to the bright males.

True to their names, flowerpeckers spend some of their time pecking around flowers for small insects, and some groups feed extensively on nectar, but the mainstay of most species, especially the dicaeids, is small fruits and berries. A favourite food is

SCARLET-BACKED FLOWERPECKER ♂
Dicaeum cruentatum
India to southern China and East Indies   3½ in.

MISTLETOE BIRD ♂
Dicaeum hirundinaceum
Australia 3¾ in.

YELLOW-TAILED DIAMONDBIRD ♂
Pardalotus punctatus
Southeastern Australia 3¼ in.

the small sticky berries of the tropical mistletoes (*Loranthus*), so much so that one of the common Australian species is called the Mistletoe Bird. Flowerpeckers are roundly blamed for spreading these parasites, which are often a scourge on mango trees.

Flowerpeckers spend much of their time in tree-tops, but frequently descend closer to the ground when low-growing shrubs come into flower or, later, into fruit. Though they are occasionally found in mixed groups with other species attracted to the same food, flowerpeckers are generally not gregarious. In the Solomons I found the Midget Flower-

pecker, singly or in pairs, flitting through shrubs at the edges of forest clearings and around the native villages, never in the heavy forests. Their call notes are short, somewhat metallic chirps, often repeated at some length. Some species are reported to have a simple warbling song as well, but the family is by no means noted for its vocal abilities.

Most flowerpeckers build nests like those of the sunbirds, small, deep purses hung from a branch and woven of plant down and other fibres strengthened with cobwebs into a felt-like consistency. The nest of the Mistletoe Bird is pear-shaped with a slit-like opening near the top. Some species reinforce the entrance by weaving tougher grasses around its edges, and others protect it with a small hood woven of the same materials. Nest building and incubation in the typical flowerpeckers are entirely by the female, though the male often accompanies his mate for nest material. He also helps feed the young.

So different from the typical flowerpeckers as perhaps to deserve subfamily rank of its own is the group of seven chubby little diamondbirds found in Australia and Tasmania. They are sometimes called pardalotes, from their generic name *Pardalotus*, which means leopard-like and refers to their bright spotting. Diamondbirds are similar in size and proportions to the flowerpeckers, but have shorter, deeper bills which are notched behind the tip and are not serrated. They live almost entirely on small insects and insect larvae. They forage for these like titmice, scouring the bark, leaves, and twigs. They are usually encountered in pairs working the outer branches of large forest trees, usually fairly high up.

Diamondbirds differ greatly from flowerpeckers in their breeding habits. While they build a similarly domed nest, they make it largely of strips of bark and grasses, and place it in a cavity. Most of them dig a tunnel 1½ to 2 feet into the earth and build at the end of it. The Yellow-tailed Diamondbird digs down into level or slightly sloping ground; the Spotted Diamondbird burrows into a bank or into the soil around an uprooted tree. The Red-tipped Diamondbird uses the natural holes in trees, and occasionally nests in crevices in buildings, as do several other pardalotes. Both sexes co-operate in digging the tunnels and in building the bulky nest; and the male takes his turn regularly at incubating. The eggs vary from 3 to 5 according to species, and are pure white without markings.

WHITE-EYES

PASSERIFORMES   ZOSTEROPIDAE

The most uniform of the larger passerine families are the small yellowish-green birds called white-eyes from the narrow ring of white feathers around their eyes. With the preceding three families, the white-eyes complete the complex of Old World nectar-eaters. They show their closest affinities to the honeyeaters, for their tongues are brush-tipped instead of tubular as in the sunbirds and flowerpeckers. They are considered the most advanced of the four families because their 10th primary is at best vestigial and usually absent.

White-eyes are very much alike. They are from 4 to 5½

inches long, and their colours range from olive-green to greyish-brown above and from yellow to grey or white below. Their only conspicuous feature is the eye ring, which varies somewhat in width, is partly complete in a few forms, but is rarely absent. The Yellow-spectacled Zosterops of the Lesser Sunda Islands is the only species in which the eye ring is not white. White-eyes' bills vary slightly in length and thickness, but are typically rather slender, pointed, and slightly down-curved. Their wings are generally rounded, their square tails of medium length, and their legs short but strong.

Such slight differences separate the many distinct populations of white-eyes that the group is both the delight and the despair of avian systematists. Very similar forms often occupy different habitats side by side, and apparently never intermingle. The latest revision recognizes 85 species divided among 12 genera. As the differences between these genera are less marked than those between species in other families, some conservative workers lump almost all white-eyes into the nominate genus *Zosterops*.

White-eyes range throughout Africa south of the Sahara, across southern Asia from Arabia to the Pacific, north to China and Japan, and south to Australia and New Zealand. They have pushed eastward in the Pacific to the Carolines, Fiji, and Samoa. Carried by man to Hawaii within the past century, they have spread from island to island. White-eyes seem to be expanding their ranges. The Common White-eye of Australia appeared suddenly in New Zealand in the early 1850's and now occupies most of the outlying islets too. One hardy group settled that antarctic outpost, Macquarie Island.

The family's success in reaching and colonizing oceanic islands is remarkable. White-eyes are not particularly strong fliers and, except for a few populations of high altitudes or latitudes that retreat to warmer climes in cold weather, they are not migratory. Their marked success at island hopping apparently stems from their gregariousness. Except when breeding, white-eyes move in flocks, sometimes of hundred of birds of both sexes. Hence the chances of enough pairs reaching distant islands to colonize successfully when carried there by the vagaries of wind and weather are far better than in less gregarious species.

ORIENTAL WHITE-EYE
Zosterops palpebrosa
India to the Philippines 4 in.

Arboreal birds that eat insects and some fruits and berries, most white-eyes also feed on nectar, a few of them almost exclusively so. They obtain nectar both by poking down into the centre of the flower and by pecking holes through the base of large blossoms. White-eyes also work over leaves and outer branches for small insects. During the breeding season the males have a tinkling, warbling song.

As so often where the sexes are alike, the nesting chores in the white-eyes are divided, with the male assuming his fair share. Breeding patterns show little variation in the widely separated species that have been studied in Africa, India, Australia, and Japan. Each pair selects its territory and builds a dainty open cup nest of vegetable fibres bound with spiders' webs and lined with hair or rootlets. The nest is usually fastened between the tines of a horizontal fork in a low tree or bush. The clutch varies from 2 to 4 eggs, which range from unmarked dark blue to blue-white. The incubation period is 11 to 12 days; the nestling stage usually takes another 9 to 13 days.

VIREOS

PASSERIFORMES   VIREONIDAE

In our lineal sequence the vireos are the first of six families that represent the peak of evolutionary development among New World oscines. These six families contain slightly more than 800 species, almost a tenth of the world's birds. All are distinguished by having only nine functional primaries. Whether they stem from a single or, more likely, from several parent stocks is uncertain, as are their affinities to other passerine families. Members of only two families, the Hawaiian honeycreepers and the New World seedeaters, have expanded beyond the American continental limits. All are unquestionably of Western Hemisphere origin.

Each of these six families forms a fairly discrete unit, but the dividing lines among them are not always clear. Opinions differ on other systematic relationships, and the placement of a few intermediate genera is still somewhat arbitrary. Several shifts in family groupings and realignments of the lineal sequence have been proposed. Researches now being conducted in their comparative anatomies, in their breeding behaviour, and in related fields are certain to result in further refinements in the classification of these birds. Full family rank may prove warranted for several groups treated here as subfamilies.

Vireos are the most sharply differentiated of the six families, and are considered the most primitive because many of them retain a vestigial 10th primary feather. In this respect they parallel the Old World flowerpeckers, but their Eastern Hemisphere counterparts are the white-eyes. Like the white-eyes, the vireos are rather undistinguished small birds, 4 to 6

RED-EYED VIREO
Vireo olivaceus
Southern Canada
to Argentina 6 in.

YELLOW-THROATED VIREO
Vireo flavifrons
Eastern North America 5½ in.

RUFOUS-BROWED PEPPERSHRIKE
Cyclarhis gujanensis
Mexico to Argentina 6½ in.

CHESTNUT-SIDED SHRIKE-VIREO
Vireolanius melitophrys
Mexico and Guatemala 7 in.

GREY-HEADED GREENLET
Hylophilus decurtatus
Mexico to Panama 4 in.

The vireos are among the few well-known birds whose scientific name has become widely accepted as their common name. The only other English name ever used for these birds was the term greenlet, often applied to vireos in the 19th century, but now commonly restricted to members of the tropical genus *Hylophilus*.

Vireos inhabit the outer foliage of trees and shrubs and hop about very deliberately among the branches, searching for small insects. In autumn and winter they supplement their insect diet with seeds and berries. They are partial to the fruits of the elderberry, huckleberry, pokeberry, and magnolia among others. Highly valued as insect destroyers, vireos are notable as the most persistent avian singers. One of the most indefatigable is the Red-eyed Vireo, whose prattling, rather colourless monologues led early New Englanders to dub it "the preacher."

Through the spring and summer the Red-eyed Vireo almost never stops singing from dawn to dusk. It sings a series of short but pleasantly musical phrases of 2 to 5 notes. Each individual bird varies its phrases, and may use a score or more modulations of the theme. Phrases often end on an upward inflection, as though the bird were asking a question, which it answers in the next with a downward strophe, then punctuates momentarily as it grabs an insect before asking the next one. A persevering Canadian ornithologist spent a day counting the songs uttered by a single bird. The grand total was 22,197. Even in Ontario, where the June days are 20 hours long, this is more than 1,000 songs per hour!

The Red-eyed Vireo is one of the 20 species of the genus *Vireo*, and the most widely distributed member of the family. Representative forms of it range from Canada to southern Brazil and Argentina; some 12 geographical races, which differ very little from one another, are recognized. The northern and the southern populations spend their respective winters in the Amazon jungles, which are occupied by resident sub-species that do not migrate.

Eleven other *Vireo* species nest in North America. All are similar to the Red-eyed in general appearance and behaviour, but are individually recognizable by slight differences in colour and pattern when you can glimpse the singer hidden among the leaves. Some have conspicuous wingbars, eye rings, eye stripes, or other features that are responsible for their names —the White-eyed, Black-capped, Yellow-throated, Yellow-green, and Blue-headed vireos. Vireos are more easily recognized in the field by their characteristic songs, which vary so between species that the good field observer soon learns to differentiate among them.

One of the easiest songs to recognize is that of the White-eyed Vireo. It consists of loud, short-phrased warbles interspersed with clear whistles and cat-like mews, each phrase typically beginning or ending with a short "chick." Found throughout the central and eastern United States southward through the West Indies (where several subspecies are resident) and through Mexico to Nicaragua, the White-eyed Vireo is smaller than the Red-eyed and has whitish wingbars in addition to its conspicuously white eye. It is a bird of thickets and shrubbery, partial to brushlands, and a frequent summer resident in suburban gardens. Active, inquisitive, and almost as noisy as the Red-eyed, it is easy to lure into sight by squeaking.

inches long, the sexes dressed alike in plain olive-greens and grey-browns. Their habits are somewhat similar, and they build the same type of nest. These resemblances are the result of convergent evolution, and the two groups are not related. Anatomically and distributively, the vireos' closest living relatives seem to be the wood warblers, from which they differ mainly in their thicker, heavier bills, slightly hooked and with a small notch or tooth near the tip.

The 42 species that form the family are divided into three subfamilies. The vireos and greenlets (Vireoninae) contain 37 species spread widely throughout the forested parts of the Americas from central Canada south to Argentina. The 3 shrike-vireos (Vireolaniinae) and 2 peppershrikes (Cyclarhinae) range from southern Mexico to central South America. The family's distribution is thus centred in the tropics from Central America to northern South America. As practically all the temperate zone breeders in this family, both north and south, migrate to the American tropics to spend their winters, this was doubtless their ancestral home.

The 15 species of greenlets of the genus *Hylophilus* are tropical vireos found from Mexico to Brazil. They are all similar greyish-green birds that differ from the *Vireo* group mainly in having a somewhat longer, more slender bill. They are a maddeningly nondescript genus, and lack the prominent wingbars and head markings that make vireos fairly easy to tell apart in the field. Their habits are essentially those of the nominate group. They live in scrub and tree growth and forage through the foliage for insects with the same deliberate movements. All are persistent singers of the same sort of loud, short-phrased songs.

An outstanding vireonine characteristic is their type of nest, a neat open cup of grasses and insect fibres invariably slung between the horizontal arms of a forked branch. Most vireos build near the ground, from 2 to 10 feet up in a leafy tree or shrub, though some tree inhabitants, such as the Red-eyed, Yellow-throated, and Philadelphia vireos, occasionally build much higher. Nest building in the vireos is almost entirely by the female, but as in most groups where the sexes are alike, with few exceptions the males assist with the incubation. The males' periods of incubating and brooding average shorter than the females', but they take a more active part in feeding the young.

Vireo eggs are white lightly speckled with brown. The clutch varies from 3 to 5, and the eggs are laid a day apart, usually early in the morning. Vireos start incubating when the first egg is laid, and the young hatch a day apart, 13 to 15 days later. It takes them another 10 to 14 days to fledge.

The northern vireos have but one brood a season, but those in warmer regions may raise two. Vireos are exceptionally tame at the nest. Many allow a close approach before flushing, and then stay near the intruder, scolding and trying to drive him off. So strong is the habit of singing that in most vireos the males invariably, and the females often, continue to sing while incubating.

Peppershrikes and shrike-vireos are each frequently given separate family rank, but both are so close to the vireos in behaviour and anatomy this hardly seems warranted. Slightly larger than the typical vireos, the two peppershrikes have much heavier and more strongly hooked bills. They inhabit bush-lands and the forest edges around tropical clearings, and are usually found fairly near the ground, moving through the foliage in deliberate vireo fashion. They eat large insects, which they hold down with their feet and tear apart with their beaks, and also some fruit and berries. Their flight is rather weak, but their voices are loud. They have harsh scolding notes and a musical warbling song that is given as persistently as in the vireos. Peppershrikes build a rather fragile nest hung in a forked branch and lay 2 to 3 pinkish-white eggs blotched and speckled with brown.

The three shrike-vireos have not been well studied and their nesting habits have not been described. The Chestnut-sided Shrike-vireo of southern Mexico and Guatemala is a bird of the tree-tops and lives largely on fruits, supplemented with some insects. It is the most strikingly marked of the family, and has the same type of loud, persistent song.

HAWAIIAN HONEYCREEPERS

PASSERIFORMES   DREPANIDIDAE

Palaeobotanists tell us that the first forests capable of supporting arboreal birds probably developed in Hawaii in mid-Pliocene time about 5 million years ago. The ancestors of the Hawaiian honeycreepers probably arrived soon thereafter. They prospered and diversified so rapidly that it hardly seems possible for such variations to have developed from a single ancestral type in so short a time. Hawaiian honeycreepers provide a dramatic example of adaptive divergence, and are a living (and disappearing) proof that evolution works fastest in small, isolated populations, where random heritable changes have the best chance of surviving.

The 22 highly varied species in this purely Hawaiian family are indeed an oddly assorted group. They are from 4½ to 9 inches long, and their colours range from plain greens and greys to bright yellows, reds, and black, but are never metallic or glossy. Most remarkable is the great variation in the size and shape of their bills, doubtless in response to the availability of particular types of foods. Some drepanidid bills became long, thin, and down-curved for probing flowers for nectar and insects. Others became the short, heavy seed-crushers of a grosbeak or a parrot. One species that probes into bark for insects has a straight bill like that of a woodpecker. The Akepa, now rare, has tips of the mandibles crossed uniquely sidewise, perhaps to help it open leafbuds.

HAWAIIAN HONEYCREEPER ♂
Vestiaria coccinea
Hawaii 6 in.

Recent anatomical studies have shown that despite these divergencies, the Hawaiian honeycreepers are probably descended from a single ancestral stock. Their progenitor was most likely a nectar-sipping insect eater with a relatively unspecialized bill and tongue. As the group shows its closest affinities to the New World nine-primaried oscines, it is now thought that some long-vanished members of this great complex (perhaps tanagers) managed to cross 2,000 miles of ocean from the American mainland to found the dynasty.

The Drepanididae are divided into two subfamilies, representing two main lines of development. The more primitive Drepanidinae, the thick-skinned honeycreepers, are mainly red and black; the sexes are similar, with the male somewhat larger. Their head feathers are stiff and pointed, and their sharp-edged primaries produce a whirring sound in flight. They wander through the forest in small, loose flocks, visiting various flowers as they come into bloom, extracting the nectar by piercing a hole in the base. Some also eat soft-bodied insects. A member of this group was the Mamo, a species the Hawaiians used for their feather cloaks. The Mamo has not been taken since 1892, and was last reported alive in 1898. Four other species the Hawaiians used for cloaks still exist, and two of them, the red Iiwi and the Apapane are fairly common.

The second subfamily, the Psittirostrinae, has mostly greenish plumage. The sexes differ in this group, the males often showing bright yellow or orange. The head feathers are soft and fluffy. The green honeycreepers are insect, seed, and fruit eaters, and probably represent a later evolutionary expansion. They are more sedentary than the Drepanidinae, and strongly territorial. The males have a courtship song, which is lacking

in the thick-skinned group. The commonest of the surviving honeycreepers, the Amakihi, is one of this group. It occurs on all the larger islands.

Drepanidids breed from January to July, making rather simple open cup nests in trees or shrubs, some in the grass. The eggs are white, usually spotted, and number 2 to 4. Incubation is by the female, but both parents tend the young.

Hawaiian honeycreepers demonstrate dramatically that rapid evolution and ultra-specialization usually mean a short species life. Of the 22 species of drepanidids known, 9 are extinct. Another 8 or 10 survive precariously in small, local populations. Several species formerly widespread over all the islands now occur on only one or two. Of 39 known forms, 24 (more than 60 per cent) are now extinct or nearly so. The three commonest species are the least specialized.

The seed and fruit eaters were apparently the most specialized forms and the first to disappear. Two seed eaters of the genus *Psittirostra* have not been reported since the 1890's. Rarest in collections is a pretty little grey and red bird which the Hawaiians called the Ula-ai-hawane (*Ciridops anna*). It is known from only five specimens, all from the island of Hawaii, the last taken in 1892.

The fiction still persists that the Hawaiian honeycreepers were exterminated by Hawaiians who killed the birds to use the feathers for chieftains' cloaks. Their decline actually dates from the arrival of Americans, and its basic cause was the inability of ultra-specialized forms to adapt themselves to the environmental changes initiated by the newcomers. Destruction of the original forests, introduced predators, and little-known bird diseases also played a large part in wiping out so many of the Hawaiian honeycreepers.

WOOD WARBLERS AND BANANAQUITS

PASSERIFORMES   PARULIDAE

Perhaps no group of birds gives the growing coterie of American birds watchers more all-around enjoyment than the wood warblers. No one the least bit interested in birds can fail to be thrilled by a morning afield in spring when a real warbler flight is going through. This always occurs at that delightful time when the trees are just budding. The woods that were barren of birds yesterday are suddenly alive with scores of bright-coloured little warblers of a dozen or more easily identified species in full breeding dress. Yet one of the greatest challenges offered the amateur is to identify these same birds in the autumn when they have moulted into maddeningly similar drab plumages with few distinguishing marks, and those hard to discern.

Americans refer to this family simply as the warblers, a term too ingrained to be changed, yet an unfortunate choice. First, very few of the family can be said to warble in the true sense of the word, which Webster defines as "singing in a trilling manner, softly and quaveringly with rapid modulations in pitch." Second, the term implies a non-existent relationship to the Old World warblers (Sylviidae, p. 255). To prevent confusion the New World family is more accurately called the wood warblers.

The Parulidae are a fairly compact group of New World nine-primaried oscines. Their relationships to the other groups

in this complex are uncertain, but anatomically they seem closest to certain tanagers and emberizine finches. The family now has about 119 species, but may have less if a few birds are reduced to subspecific rank. It is divided into two subfamilies — the 109 insect-eating warblers (Parulinae), widely spread throughout the Americas, and the 10 nectar-eating bananaquits and conebills (Coerebinae) of the West Indies, Central America, and South America. Until recently the latter were classified in a separate family (the honeycreepers, Coerebidae) with 30 other nectar eaters now placed with the tanagers (p. 291).

Wood warblers are small, dainty birds with slender, pointed bills and rounded tails. All have rictal bristles, often inconspicuous, and best developed in the redstarts and other species that capture insects on the wing. Most warblers glean small insects among the leaves and twigs—each species in its preferred niche: some in the tree-tops, others in low shrubbery, a few on the ground. Many species also eat small berries and seeds in the autumn and winter.

Wood warblers range from sombre greys and olive-browns to bright yellows, blues, and reds, but yellow is the commonest bright colour in the family. In most of the 59 migrant species that nest in North America and winter southward, the males are more brightly patterned than the females, espe-

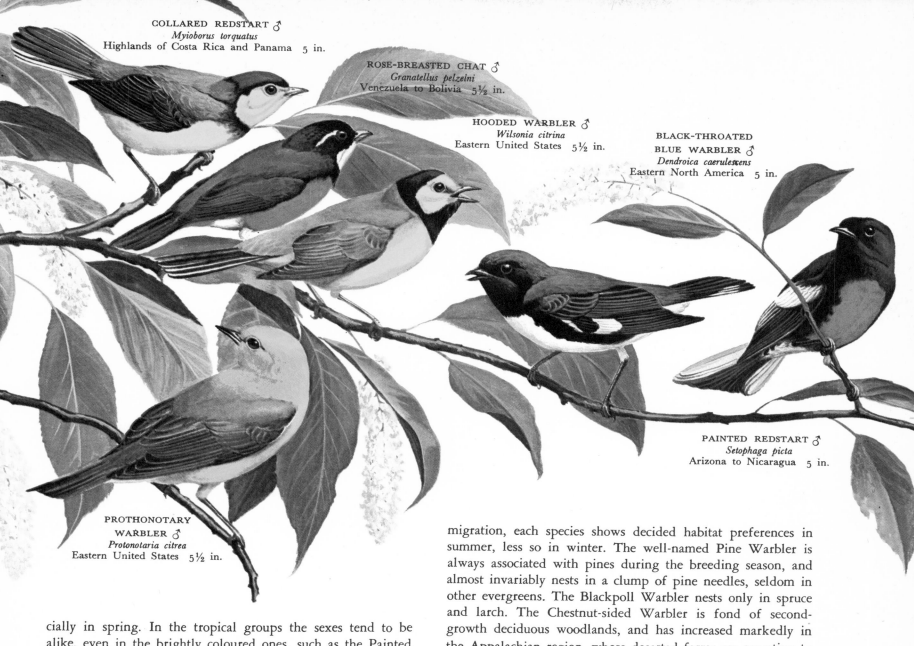

COLLARED REDSTART ♂
Myioborus torquatus
Highlands of Costa Rica and Panama 5 in.

ROSE-BREASTED CHAT ♂
Granatellus pelzelni
Venezuela to Bolivia 5½ in.

HOODED WARBLER ♂
Wilsonia citrina
Eastern United States 5½ in.

BLACK-THROATED
BLUE WARBLER ♂
Dendroica caerulescens
Eastern North America 5 in.

PROTHONOTARY
WARBLER ♂
Protonotaria citrea
Eastern United States 5½ in.

PAINTED REDSTART ♂
Setophaga picta
Arizona to Nicaragua 5 in.

cially in spring. In the tropical groups the sexes tend to be alike, even in the brightly coloured ones, such as the Painted Redstart and the Red Warbler of Mexico.

A peculiar trait of the warblers is their tendency to produce occasional hybrids between species. Crosses between the Blue-winged and Golden-winged warblers, both members of the genus *Vermivora*, produce the fairly well known Brewster's Warbler and the less familiar, recessive Lawrence's Warbler. Further study of these hybrids is needed, but apparently they are fertile and their genetics follow Mendelian lines. More rarely intergeneric hybrids are reported, a recent one being Sutton's Warbler, thought to be a cross between the Parula and Yellow-throated warblers.

With a few exceptions, such as the 7½-inch Yellow-breasted Chat, the largest member of the family, which is strong-voiced and an excellent mimic, the warblers are not outstanding singers. Their voices are weak, high, and insect-like, often with hissing, buzzing, or lisping qualities. Yet the warblers are persistent singers in spring, and each species has a distinctive song of its own. The expert tells warblers apart by their songs as readily as by their appearance, but the notes of some species are so similar that it takes a sharp ear to differentiate between them. Among the more distinctive and easily recognized are the ringing "teacher, teacher, teacher" of the Ovenbird, the thin "witchitee-witchitee-witchitee-widgit" of the Yellow-throat, and the lisping "zee-zee-zee-zee-zee-zewo" of the Painted Redstart.

Though many species of warblers throng together during migration, each species shows decided habitat preferences in summer, less so in winter. The well-named Pine Warbler is always associated with pines during the breeding season, and almost invariably nests in a clump of pine needles, seldom in other evergreens. The Blackpoll Warbler nests only in spruce and larch. The Chestnut-sided Warbler is fond of second-growth deciduous woodlands, and has increased markedly in the Appalachian region, where deserted farms are reverting to hardwood forest.

The wide-ranging Myrtle Warbler, with its bright-yellow rump patch, shows less partiality, but usually nests in conifer forests. It migrates and winters in more open country, and is common in the coastal belt of myrtle, whose waxy berries are its winter mainstay—bayberry in the north, wax myrtle farther south. The Magnolia Warbler is another inhabitant of northern spruce, hemlock, and balsam forests at nesting time. Its discoverer, the pioneering Alexander Wilson, collected the type specimen in a magnolia tree in Mississippi and gave it its inappropriate name.

A number of other warblers were given most unfitting names by their describers, who often christened them for the place where they discovered the bird in transit, far from its customary haunts. The Connecticut, Kentucky, Cape May, Tennessee, and Nashville warblers are victims of such misnaming. The Prairie Warbler inhabits scrublands and seldom visits open prairies. The Palm Warbler breeds across palmless southern Canada and winters from Florida southward, not in palms, but in open fields and scrublands. Efforts to change these and other ill-fitting common names always meet stern resistance.

One of the rarest warblers and most restricted in its breeding range is Kirtland's Warbler, which nests only in a portion of the Michigan jackpine country less than 80 miles in diameter and migrates to the Bahama Islands. A careful census made in 1951 showed the total Kirtland's Warbler population to be less than a thousand individuals, and the species seems to be barely holding its own. A major limiting factor is parasitism by the Brown-headed Cowbird (p. 289). All wood warblers are among the victims the cowbird makes use of but more than half the breeding Kirtland's Warblers rear young cowbirds instead of their own offspring.

Most temperate zone warblers build an open cup nest in the branches of shrubs or trees at moderate heights. Some tree-top species, the Blackburnian, Cerulean, and Pine warblers for instance, may build 50 or more feet up, but most nest less than 10 feet above the ground. Most tropical species nest on the ground. One northern ground-nesting species, the Oven-bird, is so called because of its oven-shaped domed nest with a side entrance. Among the very few cavity nesters in the family is the Prothonotary Warbler, one of America's brightest golden-yellow birds. An inhabitant of the swamp lands of the southern states, the Prothonotary nests in holes in rotten trunks, sometimes in old woodpecker holes or bird boxes. The Catholic Louisiana Creoles christened it the Prothonotary in honour of the papal secretary, who traditionally wears a brilliant orange-yellow robe.

The breeding behaviour of wood warblers follows fairly standard patterns. Nest building is almost entirely by the female, with occasional help from the male in a few species. Warbler eggs are generally white, lightly speckled with brown, often in a ring around the larger end. The northern migratory species lay 4 to 5 eggs and are usually single-brooded. Incubation is always by the female alone, and sometimes, though not regularly, the male feeds her on the nest. Incubation takes 11 to 14 days, and the nestling period another 8 to 14 days.

Warblers migrate at night and frequently come to grief during their long journeys, usually from adverse weather conditions that catch the flocks in transit. Though the migrants take off under clear skies with favourable winds, they have no weather service to warn them of what lies ahead. Occasionally hurricanes carry them far off course and drop them exhausted into the sea. More often the migrants encounter weather fronts of low-lying clouds that force them close to the ground where they collide in the dark with TV masts, buildings, bridges, and other tall obstructions.

Bright lights attract and confuse night migrants forced below their normal flight altitude. Lighthouses on well-travelled flight paths have long been known to lure migrants to their death on foggy nights. The powerful searchlights used at airports to measure the height of cloud ceilings constitute a new and most destructive hazard. On drizzly nights swarms of migrating warblers, vireos, tanagers, and other species fly into the intense vertical beam. Unable to escape from the beam, they

BANANAQUIT
Coereba flaveola
West Indies; Mexico to Argentina   4½ in.

mill around within it in a cloud, crash into one another, and flutter helplessly to the ground in a rain of dying birds.

As yet we have no accurate measure of the mortality imposed by hazards of migration. At times this must be tremendous, and of serious import to species survival. Truckloads of tiny dead birds have been shovelled away under a ceilometer beam after a disastrous night. Countless thousands of additional migrants must perish during storms and other perils of nature. One such debacle during a mass flight could easily wipe out Kirtland's Warbler.

The Parulinae are well represented in tropical Central and South America south as far as Argentina, and in the West Indies, where they are more plentiful in the wooded highlands than in wet lowlands. The two commonest tropical genera are *Myioborus* with some 8 species, and *Basileuterus* with about 22. While some of these are fairly brightly coloured, most tend to be dull browns and yellows. The sexes are alike, and they show no marked seasonal plumage change as do the migratory species. Many build domed nests on or near the ground. Though the males do not incubate, they take an active part in nest building and other breeding chores. These sedentary species are not subject to the hazards of migration, and their reproductive rate is both lower and slower than in the northern breeders. The usual clutch is 2 to 3 eggs, incubation lasts 13 to 16 days, and the rearing period takes 12 to 14 days.

Another tropical group is the Coerebinae, which live mostly in lowland forests, and whose tongues are cleft and fringed for nectar feeding. Typical is the widespread Bananaquit, found from the Bahamas, throughout the West Indies (it is strangely absent from Cuba), and from southeastern Mexico southward to Paraguay and Argentina. These bright little birds are resident throughout their wide range and are often quite abundant. Local populations vary considerably in colour, and some 35 subspecies are now recognized.

Except that they feed extensively on nectar by piercing the base of large flowers with their pointed curved bills, Bananaquits act much like warblers. They flit actively through the foliage in search of food, singly or in pairs, never in flocks. They also consume insects in quantity. Despite their name they are not overly fond of bananas, though they eat some other fruits such as sapodillas. Their voices are thin and warbler-like.

Bananaquits lay 2 to 6 eggs in a bulky domed nest with a side entrance near the bottom, usually in a thicket and fairly near the ground. While only the female incubates, the male is most active at nest building. He not only builds most of the nest, which the female lines and finishes for the eggs, but often builds a series of roosting nests nearby in which he spends the night.

MAGNOLIA WARBLER ♂
Dendroica magnolia
Canada   5 in.

ICTERIDS

PASSERIFORMES   ICTERIDAE

The 94 species of icterids include such common and familiar North American birds as blackbirds, grackles, orioles, meadowlarks, cowbirds, and the Bobolink. Less familiar tropical forms are the troupials, oropendolas, and caciques (ka-seeks'). None of these distinctive groups is truly representative of the entire family, and the names oriole, blackbird, and grackle are confused with Old World species. The term troupials has been used as a family name (this South American oriole was the first to be described), but has never become popular. Ornithologists always refer to these birds as the icterids, and that term is now widely used among amateurs as a convenient label for this all-American family. "Icter" being Latin for yellow, the name best fits the bright-yellow or orange orioles, but yellows occur throughout the family.

The icterids are small- to (typically) medium-sized birds, 6 to 21 inches in length. An integral part of the complex of New World nine-primaried oscines, they are so closely allied to the tanagers and to the cardinal finches that it is difficult to demark all three groups. The icterids lack obvious rictal bristles; most have rounded tails. Their wings are long and pointed, their legs and feet strong, their bills hard, conical and pointed. In the orioles and grackles the bill is moderately slender and down-curved. The oropendolas and caciques have heavier bills topped by a prominent swelling. Meadowlarks' bills are straight and sharp, as are most blackbirds'; those of the cowbirds and the Bobolink are short and finch-like.

The family ranges over all the Western Hemisphere except the extreme north, but is chiefly tropical. Most of its temperate zone members are migratory. Northernmost of the family is the Rusty Blackbird, which nests across the continent from the tree line to the northern United States, often in hemlock and larch swamps, and winters south to the Gulf Coast. The southernmost icterids are the red-breasted, or military, blackbirds of Patagonia. One of these inhabits the Falkland Islands, and another population thrives on Easter Island, where it was introduced.

Icterids have adapted themselves to almost all upland habitats. Most are arboreal, and various species can be found in almost every type of forest, from the Hudsonian conifers to tropical jungle. The meadowlarks and the Bobolink prefer open fields and prairies. The wide-ranging Red-winged Blackbirds and their close relatives, the Yellow-headed and Yellow-shouldered blackbirds, are essentially marsh dwellers. Scott's Oriole is at home in western semi-deserts among the agaves and yuccas.

Icterid food preferences are just as varied. All of them eat insects, and most eat seeds and grains. The tropical orioles and oropendolas are fruit eaters, as are the caciques, which also eat nectar. The grackles are practically omnivorous. Inveterate nest robbers, they also like small reptiles and amphibians, and some have learned to catch small fish.

Icterids that feed on the ground walk about vigorously and seldom hop. All are strong fliers. Their voices are usually loud, somewhat harsh, and vary from guttural burblings, to clear, flutey whistles. Song is highly developed in the orioles. Most of the family are gregarious, many species highly so. The migrant temperate zone species travel and winter in flocks and sometimes roost in tremendous swarms. The oropendolas, caciques, and many blackbirds and grackles are colonial in their nesting.

The family exhibits great divergence in breeding habits, but the nesting duties fall largely on the female, entirely so in many groups. As often happens in markedly dichromatic groups where the males take little part in nesting, many species are promiscuous or polygamous. One group, the cowbirds, has developed brood parasitism to a high degree. Most icterids build conventional open cup nests, either in trees, on the ground, or in marsh vegetation, but the long, hanging nests of the orioles and their immediate kin are marvels of avian architecture. Icterid eggs are usually white, sometimes tinted blue, green, or buff, and typically marked with heavy, irregular black scrawls. In the tropical species the normal clutch is 2 eggs; the temperate forms lay 3 to 7.

Gaudiest of the icterids, as well as among the best singers and nest architects, are the orioles. Some 30 species are grouped in the nominate genus *Icterus*, most of them tropical. The several that come north to nest in spring bring splashes of tropical splendour to the temperate woodlands, and the males' songs are rich, varied, and full-throated. In the tropical orioles the females are often as brightly coloured as the males. The temperate zone females lack the males' gay hues. After breeding the males shed their finery and assume a similar drab dress before migrating.

The male Baltimore Oriole arrives in the eastern woodlands of the United States in spring, flaunting the strong orange and black of Maryland's founding family, the Calverts. His mate is quietly dressed in variable yellowish olives and browns. The Baltimore Oriole is replaced in the west by the similar, but specifically distinct, Bullock's Oriole. Where the two species overlap in Oklahoma and Nebraska they frequently hybridize. A less showy northern nester is the smaller Orchard Oriole, clad in quieter orange-brown and black. A fine singer in spring, the Orchard Oriole is one of our most useful insectivores.

The pair bond is strong in these orioles, but the males take little part in nesting. They spend their time chasing insects and singing while their mates weave the intricate cradles every farm boy knows, and lay and incubate the 4 to 6 eggs. The nest of the Baltimore Oriole is a neat grey bag of fibres about 6 inches deep with a constricted top; it is usually hung from the outer branches of a tall tree.

Among the world's best nest builders are the orioles' larger tropical relatives, the oropendolas and caciques. They weave marvellous long sleeves of grasses with the entrance at the top, the nest proper resting in a pouch at the bottom 3 to 6 feet below. They usually nest in colonies, which are fascinating and noisy bazaars. A colony of Montezuma's Oropendolas above my camp in British Honduras was never still. Throughout the day the birds kept up a continual bubbling chatter, the main theme of which sounded like "bottle-o-glooo."

For their colony these birds pick a tall isolated tree in a clearing or one towering above the surrounding jungle. Under a canopy of the tree's spreading top the female oropendolas weave from a dozen to a hundred long, swaying stockings that can be seen for miles around. The females outnumber the polygynous males, which sit around the top of the tree and act as guardians and watchmen, for they are faithful to the colony if not to a particular mate.

Polygyny occurs in most icterids that nest colonially and in some that do not. It varies in degree between populations of the same species, depending on the sex ratio. In Brewer's Blackbird of western North America the males are polygynous when outnumbered by the females, but not when the sexes are evenly balanced. The same is true of the Boat-tailed Grackles, and of the American Red-winged Blackbird.

The Red-winged Blackbird, with its scarlet epaulets, breeds throughout southern Canada and the United States and southward through the West Indies and Central America. It is replaced in South America by the Yellow-shouldered Blackbird. In the sloughs of the prairie states nests the equally unmistakable Yellow-headed Blackbird. All these birds are highly gregarious; they migrate and winter in flocks, and usually nest colonially, in fresh-water marshes.

In temperate North America the male Red-winged Blackbirds are among the first migrants to arrive in spring, several weeks in advance of their mates. They have usually established their individual territories by the time the smaller and less conspicuous females appear. The last to arrive are the young of the previous year. It is not as yet certain to what extent they breed in their first spring, if at all.

Usually the sexes are evenly balanced and monogamy is the

CHESTNUT-HEADED
(WAGLER'S) OROPENDOLA ♂
Zarhynchus wagleri
Mexico to Ecuador   14 in.

GREEN OROPENDOLA ♂
Psarocolius viridis
The Guianas to
Ecuador and Peru   17 in.

MONTEZUMA OROPENDOLA ♂
Gymnostinops montezuma
Mexico to Panama   19 in.

TROUPIAL ♂
Icterus icterus
Colombia and Venezuela   9½ in.

SPOT-BREASTED ORIOLE ♂
Icterus pectoralis
Mexico to Costa Rica   8½ in.

rule, but it is not unusual to find two or more females nesting within the territory of a single male. Nest building and incubation are by the female alone, though the male is attentive throughout the process, and helps feed the young. The nest is an open cup, woven of coarse grasses in the marsh vegetation, usually only a few feet above the water or ground. Incubation and fledging each take about 12 days.

The young birds in their first juvenile plumage resemble the female, but the sexes are distinguishable by both size and colour. In the annual postnuptial moult an adult male's distinctive black garb is hidden by brown tips to the feathers. These gradually wear off during the winter to reveal his nuptial dress beneath; there is no second moult in spring.

As the nesting season ends, first the young birds and later the adult Red-winged Blackbirds flock to the uplands to feed in open fields, returning to the shelter of the marsh at night. In migration, flocks coalesce and increase in size. On the wintering grounds in the southern states they join with other flocking American blackbirds. Five or six species often roost together in tremendous aggregations of millions of birds.

The birds leave the roosts at dawn and travel as much as 30 to 50 miles in search of good foraging. By mid-afternoon they start heading toward the roost, and converge on it from all directions. The vanguard arrives several hours before dark, and from then on flock after flock pour in until darkness. Roosts of several hundred thousand birds are common, and some of the larger roosts in Alabama and Arkansas have been estimated to contain 5 million birds. Flocks of this size can and do inflict serious damage to grain crops, and this is only partly compensated for by the large numbers of insects the birds also consume. Wholesale killing is sometimes used as a control measure.

Most notorious of the crop damagers used to be the Bobolink, the champion icterid migrant. Bobolinks breed across southern Canada and the northern United States and winter in Argentina, migrating both north and south across the Gulf of Mexico and the Caribbean. In the days of horses, when hay was a standard crop, Bobolinks were common summer residents in New England farmlands. Now that hayfields are few, the species has almost disappeared from the Northeast, but has expanded its range westward. The western Bobolinks retrace their steps eastward in migration before heading southward across the Gulf.

The Bobolinks' breeding pattern is similar to the Red-winged Blackbirds'. Males arrive on the breeding grounds before the females and establish territories. Females build cup nests well concealed on the ground in upland grassy fields. The species is occasionally polygynous, and rears but a single brood of 5 to 7 young.

When rice was a major commercial crop in the Carolinas in the 19th and early 20th centuries, migrating Bobolinks were a serious pest to the sprouting seeds in spring and to the maturing grain in autumn. They were killed in thousands to protect the crops, and marketed as "reed birds" or "rice birds." Autumn migrants are very fat, and they were brought to market skewered a dozen to a stick. In Jamaica, where they stop on their cross-water flight, they are still called "butter birds." Now the Bobolink is protected as a song bird, and "rice birds" are no longer available for the gourmet. Rice growing has

shifted to Louisiana and Texas, where other flocking icterids, notably the Red-winged Blackbird, are occasionally equally harmful to the crops.

Among the North American icterids perhaps the most highly regarded as insect destroyers and as sweet singers are the meadowlarks. They pipe their clear whistles all year, though most ardently at breeding time, and have none of the annoying habits of their more gregarious relatives. They never gather in such large flocks, and they do not attack standing grain. Their vegetable food in autumn and winter is confined to weed seeds and waste grain left in the fields after harvesting. They are not strongly migratory, and will winter as far north as they can find snow-free fields.

The two species, the Eastern and Western meadowlarks, are so similar in appearance they are almost impossible to tell apart by size and colour alone. The Western Meadowlark is only slightly smaller than the Eastern, its yellow breast is slightly paler, and the yellow of its throat extends slightly further into the cheek. These differences are almost useless as field marks, and where both species occur observers depend on their voices to tell one from the other. The Western Meadowlarks' call note is of a different timbre and a full kilocycle lower than the Eastern's, and differences in phrasing and syllabification in the two species' clear, plaintive songs are easily recognized.

Recent studies in Wisconsin, where both Meadowlark species often nest at the same time in the same field, show they apparently do not hybridize in the wild. Their breeding habits are identical and resemble those of the Bobolink. They differ almost imperceptibly in their choice of nesting sites, the Eastern Meadowlark choosing moister spots in the meadows; the Western drier ones. Females have the major role in selecting their mates, and invariably choose males of their own species. They apparently base their unerring choice on differences in voice rather than of appearance or behaviour.

Breeding aberrations among the icterids are most pronounced in the cowbirds, which have brought brood parasitism to the same perfection in the New World as the cuckoos, honeyguides, and a few weaverfinches have in the Old World. Cowbirds are well named, for they habitually hang around cattle. Before livestock were taken to America, the cowbirds followed the herds of buffaloes. Except for the Giant Cowbird of Central and South America, which hunts hides for ticks just as do the oxpeckers of Africa, cowbirds seldom alight on cattle, but flock around to feed on the insects disturbed by their feet.

The degrees of parasitism exhibited by different cowbird species are of particular interest because they suggest how the habit probably developed. The first step apparently was the loss of the inclination, and then of the ability, to build a nest. The non-parasitic Baywinged Cowbird of Brazil and Argentina is at present in this stage. While some individuals can and do occasionally build nests of their own, they are reluctant to do so and prefer to use the abandoned nests of other species.

The next stage, that of dispossessing the owner from a freshly built nest, is evidently quite transitory, and no species shows it today. At this point the birds must learn quickly to leave their eggs for the rightful owner to hatch and rear, but they do not immediately lose all the ingrained habits of nesting behaviour. The widespread Shiny Cowbird of South America, which is

1 BOBOLINK ♂
Dolichonyx oryzivorus
Eastern North America 8 in.

2 RED-BREASTED BLACKBIRD ♂
Leistes militaris
Panama to Argentina 7½ in.

3 YELLOW-HEADED BLACKBIRD ♂
Xanthocephalus xanthocephalus
Western North America 11 in.

4 SHINY COWBIRD ♂
Molothrus bonariensis
Colombia and Venezuela to Argentina 7-8 in.

5 WESTERN MEADOWLARK
Sturnella neglecta
Western North America 9 in.

6 BOAT-TAILED GRACKLE ♂
Cassidix mexicanus
Southern U.S. to Venezuela and Peru 17 in.

parasitic on many small birds, occasionally shows nesting instincts during courtship. Birds pick up nesting material, and sometimes start to build a nest, but they never finish one. Nor has the Shiny Cowbird yet learned to put its eggs out efficiently for adoption. Females waste many eggs by laying them on the ground when they are unable to find a nest, and often put more eggs in a single nest than the foster parent can care for. As many as 37 Shiny Cowbird eggs have been found in one ovenbird's nest.

Some cowbirds have developed host-specificity. The Screaming Cowbird of Brazil and Argentina relies entirely on the non-parasitic Baywinged Cowbird to rear its young for it. The Giant Cowbird chooses oropendolas and caciques for its dupes. The Redeyed, or Bronze, Cowbird of the southwestern United States and Mexico is not so particular. While it specializes in victimizing various orioles, its eggs have been found in the nests of a number of non-icterids. Least selective in its choices and most successful as a brood parasite is the Brown-headed Cowbird of temperate North America. Its eggs have been found in nests of more than 200 other species, mostly smaller birds such as vireos, warblers, and various seedeaters.

Though they shirk the nesting chores, like most other icter-ids Brown-headed Cowbirds establish breeding territoires. They are usually monogamous, though polygyny is thought to occur when there is an excess of females. The female cowbird watches prospective hosts building their nests within her territory, and seems to know in advance where she is going to lay. She usually lays 4 to 5 eggs, each on successive mornings, and each in a different nest unless hosts are scarce. Also she lays as the hosts are still laying and before incubation has started. Unlike the cuckoo, she does not remove an egg when depositing her own, but occasionally returns and removes some, though never all, of the host's eggs.

The Brown-headed Cowbird egg hatches in 11 to 12 days, which is seldom longer than the time it takes the eggs of its hosts to hatch. Nor does the young cowbird push other eggs or nestlings out of the nest, as do nestling cuckoos. Being larger than the young of most of its small hosts, it does manage to get most of the food and fledges more rapidly, usually in 9 to 10 days. Thus while cowbird parasitism greatly reduces the reproductive efficiency of its victims, it does not negate it entirely. There are many records of 2 or 3 other young birds reared successfully in the nest with the cowbird, and this seems to be the general pattern.

TANAGERS

PASSERIFORMES   THRAUPIDAE

"Tanager" is another of the distinctive New World bird names, such as jaçana, jacamar, jabiru, anhinga, ani, araçari, toucan, tinamou, hoatzin, macaw, seriema, and cotinga, that have come into our language from that of the Tupi Indians of the Amazon region. The Tupis, who have always been pretty good birdwatchers, call these gaudy arboreal birds tangaras, which 18th-century European systematists Latinized as tanagra. "Tanager," the English version, has been in common use since early in the 19th century.

The tanager family is a large one of some 222 species confined almost entirely to the tropical and subtropical portions of the Americas. All but the four species that have pushed into temperate North America to breed are non-migratory, though some of the Central and South American highland tanagers wander altitudinally with the seasons. Gay colours the year round are a hallmark of the family, and female tanagers are usually as brightly coloured as the males. Strong sex differences occur in the four migrant species and in the few tropical forms that flock together when not nesting, such as the velvet tanagers and the euphonias. The northern tanagers are among the few that show any seasonal plumage change. In a few genera both sexes are dull, soft browns or brownish reds and greens, but most are as colourful as tropical birds are supposed to be.

The tanagers are small- to medium-sized birds, most of them less than 8 inches in length, and compactly built. Their wings, with nine primaries, vary in length and shape, but are usually short and rounded. The presence of obvious rictal bristles sepa-rates the tanagers from the icterids, but not from the cardinal finches, to which they seem more closely allied. Tanagers differ from the buntings (see p. 295) mainly in their adaptations to a fruit or nectar diet.

The 191 "typical" tanagers of the subfamily Thraupinae have a simple tongue and a fairly distinctive bill. It is short to medium in length, somewhat conical, curved downward along the top ridge, and has a small notch or tooth in the cutting edge near the slightly hooked tip. Best known are the four North American species of the genus *Piranga* that winter

RED-CROWNED
ANT TANAGER ♂
Habia rubica
Mexico to Argentina 7 in.

YELLOW-CROWNED
EUPHONIA ♂
Tanagra luteicapilla
Nicaragua to Panama 4 in.

CINNAMON-BELLIED
FLOWER-PIERCER ♂
Diglossa baritula
Mexico to Honduras 4½ in.

SWALLOW TANAGER ♂
Tersina viridis
Panama to Argentina 6¼ in.

PLUSH-CAPPED TANAGER
Catamblyrhynchus diadema
Colombia and Venezuela
to Peru and Bolivia 5 in.

ROSE-BREASTED
THRUSH TANAGER ♂
Rhodinocichla rosea
Mexico to Venezuela 8 in.

dash or hurry. Their songs are pleasant and musical but not distinctive. The northern tanagers build loose cup-shaped nests well concealed on a horizontal branch. They lay 3 to 5 greenish-blue eggs blotched and spotted with brown. Incubation, which is by the female alone, takes 13 to 15 days. The male helps to feed the young, which require another 2 weeks to fledge.

The eight species of velvet tanagers of the genus *Ramphocelus*, found from Mexico to Argentina, are a tropical group in which the sexes differ. The males of this genus (the Scarlet-rumped Tanager is an example) are glossy, velvety black, variously marked with reds or yellows, and have bright silvery-blue bills. The females are nondescript brownish birds.

The Scarlet-rumped Tanager is one of the better singers in this family. Its songs are notable for length and persistence rather than for musical quality. The females do not sing, but start to build their open cup nests soon after the males come into voice at the start of the rainy season. The species shows little territorial sense, and pairs often nest in groups fairly close together in the lower branches of the forest edges. The female builds the nest, though the male occasionally accompanies her on her trips for material, which she often steals from the nests of other birds. The female incubates unassisted, though her mate usually helps rear the young.

The nominate genus *Thraupis* contains eight fairly large and common tanagers, 7 to 8 inches long, known as "blue tanagers." The sexes are alike, and predominantly blue in colour, as in the Blue-grey Tanager. Though they live in the tree-tops, these active tanagers are easily observed in partly cleared and cultivated areas. They eat fruit and berries, and are adept insect catchers.

When not nesting the blue tanagers sometimes gather in small flocks, but they remain mated throughout the year and usually go about in pairs. Their breeding habits are similar to those of the northern migratory tanagers, but they lay a smaller clutch of 2 to 3 eggs and rear at least two broods annually. The incubation period is from 12 to 14 days, but the young take longer to fledge—up to 20 days.

The 48 species assigned to the genus *Tangara*, which have spread throughout Central and South America, are the epitome of typical tropical tanagers. The sexes are alike in these fruit and insect eaters. Their beauty is feather deep, for they have little or no song.

Best studied and one of the commonest of the *Tangaras* is the Golden-masked Tanager, found from southern Mexico southward through the Amazon basin. It lives in the wet rainforests and in open fields from sea level up to 5,000 feet. It is usually encountered in pairs, for the species stays mated the year round. The Golden-masked Tanager builds an open cup nest well hidden in the foliage anywhere from 5 to 50 feet up. Both sexes work on the nest, but only the female incubates the 2-egg clutch. Incubation takes 13 to 15 days, and the male feeds her on the nest. He also helps feed the young and is very active about it. After a fledging period of about 14 to 16 days, the young leave the nest in a plumage similar to but duller than their parents'. This they soon replace in a post-juvenile moult by regular adult dress. These little birds rear 2 or 3 broods each nesting season, which extends in Central America from February to September.

southward to their ancestral home in the tropics. These are the Scarlet Tanager of the East and Midwest, the Western Tanager of the western states, and the Summer and Hepatic tanagers of the southern United States and northern Mexico.

Despite the males' showy colours these tanagers are not conspicuous. They live quietly at moderate heights in the leafy shadows and do not call attention to themselves by action or voice. In the north their food is principally leaf-eating insects with smaller amounts of fruit and berries. They catch flying insects on the wing and forage efficiently, but without

The genus *Tangara* contains several rare species known by only one or two specimens and never seen in life by an ornithologist. Their skins were found in shipments of bright-coloured birds sent to the European markets during the feather-trade days of the 1880's. Gould's Tanager, a distinctive green, blue, yellow, and black bird, known by a single specimen in the British Museum, is thought to have come from southeastern Brazil. Arnault's Tanager is a unique buff, green, blue, and black. The only known specimen, which is in a Paris museum, reached Europe alive as a cage bird. Just where in South America it came from is unknown. Ornithologists have long searched in vain for these and other little-known birds which may still exist as small isolated populations in the vast forests of the American tropics.

A third rarity, the Azure-rumped, or Cabanis's, Tanager, was described in 1866 from a single trade skin that came from western Guatemala and is now in the Berlin Museum. It is a 6-inch bird with back and rump azure green, crown and neck greyish blue, and wings and tail black, edged with blue. Dr. Pierce Brodkorb of the University of Florida had the once-in-a-lifetime thrill of rediscovering Cabanis's long-lost tanager in Chiapas, southern Mexico, in 1937.

Another large complex of tanagers found from Mexico southward are the 24 small euphonias, whose generic name *Tanagra* is confused with *Tangara* by proof-readers—and others. The euphonias are dumpy little birds, most under 5 inches, with short tails and stubby bills. Unlike most tropical tanagers, the males are prettily patterned in shining dark blues and yellows but the females are dull olive-greens. The Yellow-crowned Euphonia is an example.

Euphonias roam along the forest edges in pairs or small bands searching for berries and small fruits. A favourite food is mistletoe berries. They differ from the larger tanagers in building domed nests, which are chiefly the work of the female, though the male sometimes lends a hand. In true tanager fashion the female does all the incubating (13 to 14 days), and the male helps feed the young. The members of this group feed their young by regurgitation. The parents stand at the nest's entrance and pop berry after berry into the mouths of the nestlings. As in all tanagers the inside of the nestlings' mouths is bright red, and this is believed to stimulate the parents' feeding reaction. The fledging period in the tanagers that build covered nests is considerably longer than in the open nesters, and lasts up to 23 or 24 days.

Closely related to the euphonias are the four slightly larger chlorophonias, 5½ to 6 inches long. The males of these stub-billed tanagers are beautifully tinted in greens, blues, and yellows, the females similar but paler and duller. Chlorophonias (their generic name) are highland dwellers, found for the most part in cloud forests above 4,000 feet. Their habits are essentially those of the euphonias. Their clutch is usually three eggs, and they are double-brooded.

A second branch of the tanager family is the 28 honey-creepers and flower-piercers of the subfamily Dacninae. These birds have longer, more slender bills than the typical tanagers, and brush-tipped tongues. They are still classified by some workers, together with the bananaquit (p. 286), in a separate

BLUE-CROWNED CHLOROPHONIA ♂
Cholorophonia occipitalis
Mexico to Panama 5½ in.

MASKED TANAGER
Tangara nigro-cincta
Mexico to Bolivia 5¼ in.

PARADISE TANAGER
Tangara chilensis
Colombia to Brazil and Bolivia 5¾ in.

BLACK-EARED TANAGER
Tangara parzudakii
Colombia to Peru 6 in.

SCARLET-RUMPED TANAGER ♂
Ramphocelus passerinii
Mexico to Panama 7 in.

BLUE-GREY TANAGER
Thraupis virens
Mexico to Brazil

SCARLET TANAGER ♂
Piranga olivacea
Eastern North America 7 in.

family, but their palate structure and musculature show them to be tanagers modified for nectar feeding.

The Blue, or Red-legged, Honeycreeper ranges widely from Cuba and southern Mexico to Ecuador and southern Brazil, and is often encountered in small flocks. A bird of the tree-tops and forest edges, it is commonest in the humid lowlands. The female is a dull olive-green above and yellowish below. In a post-nuptial moult the male takes on a similar dull green dress, which is gradually replaced with bright blue and yellow before the next breeding season.

Honeycreepers use their long, thin pointed bills to pierce the bases of flowers for nectar, always while perched, never while hovering. They also eat some fruit and small insects. Their breeding patterns resemble those of the true tanagers. Nest building and incubation (12 to 13 days) are by the female, and the male usually follows her about as she works, but is not attentive to her during incubation. He does help bring fruit and insects to the young, which take 2 weeks to fledge. Food is brought in the bill and is not regurgitated. In Central America the Blue Honeycreeper builds an open cup nest of fine fibres tied together with spiders' webs, and lays two spotted white eggs.

Most specialized of the nectar-eating tanagers are the dull-brownish diglossas, or flower-piercers, whose bills are peculiarly and uniquely adapted for their particular method of feeding. The upper mandible is bent upward and strongly hooked at the tip. With this the bird holds the tubular corolla firm while it pierces it with the needle-like lower mandible, and then inserts its tongue for the nectar. The operation takes only a moment, and the birds can sip from a number of blossoms in a short time. Aided by their strong rictal bristles, diglossas also catch small insects on the wing.

The 10 species of flower-piercers are highland dwellers found from southern Mexico to Peru and Bolivia and eastward to Venezuela and the Guianas. They forage alone or in pairs, and both sexes sing a thin, weak, trilling song. The female builds a thick-walled cup nest of mosses in low bushes for her two bright-blue eggs, spotted with brown, which she incubates alone.

Three other aberrant species I have placed with the tanagers as a matter of convenience may each warrant family rank. These are the Swallow Tanager (*Tersina*), the Thrush Tanager (*Rhodinocichla*), and the Plush-capped Tanager (*Catamblyrhynchus*). All three are in need of further study.

The Swallow Tanager has been studied more than the other two species. Tanager-like in appearance, the male is a lovely, soft greenish-blue, the female a plainer green. Found from Panama southward through Amazonia, it seems to be partly migratory. Small flocks wander through the lowland tree-tops, and move to higher country to breed. The species' chief peculiarities are its wide, flat bill, sharp-edged and strongly hooked at the tip, and its distensible throat pouch. This bulges out in weird shapes when the bird stuffs it with fruit. Swallow Tanagers have prodigious appetites, and captive birds will eat two-thirds of their weight in fruit daily. They also catch insects on the wing. Their voices are monotonous, unmusical chirps, and they have no song.

The Swallow Tanager differs from most other tanagers in being a cavity nester. Its nest is in a natural hole in a tree.

RED-LEGGED HONEYCREEPER ♂
Cyanerpes cyaneus
Cuba; Mexico to Ecuador and Brazil 4½ in.

In some parts of their range the birds dig tunnels into earthen banks, or use cavities in houses or stone walls. Nest building and incubation of the 3 glossy white eggs are by the female alone. Incubation varies from 13 to 17 days, and starts with the laying of the first egg, so the chicks hatch on successive days. The male helps feed the young, which take up to 24 days to fledge.

The Thrush Tanager is a skulking bird of the forest floor found from Mexico to Colombia and Venezuela. It is difficult to see despite its bright, soft red colours because it stays in the shadowy underbrush. Anatomically it seems closest to the tanagers, but in behaviour it shows strong similarities to the thrashers and the cardinal finches. Thrush Tanagers feed on the ground, flicking away the leaves like Blackbirds. They have a fine loud song which both sexes sing antiphonally during courtship. Recent studies have shown that the male helps with the incubation as well as with other nesting duties.

Least known of the three is the peculiar Plush-capped Tanager, called the Plush-capped Finch by those who, with equally good justification, classify it with the cardinal finches. Found in high Andean forests, it is named for the unique patch of short, stiff, velvety, orange-yellow feathers on the forehead of both sexes, which are similar in colour. The bill is short, stubby, and slightly hooked. Most of the specimens in museum collections are trade skins. Few ornithologists have ever encountered this bird in the field. It is usually seen alone or in pairs. Its feeding and nesting habits are unknown, and its anatomy has never been studied.

NEW WORLD SEEDEATERS

PASSERIFORMES   FRINGILLIDAE

At the top of the avian family tree is the tremendous galaxy of small- to medium-sized birds known collectively as sparrows or finches. The most recent estimate, which shows 690 species, may be in error by a score of species either way, depending on how a few poorly known forms are classified. The main characteristic of sparrows and finches is their short, conical, pointed bills, adapted principally for eating seeds.

From the evolutionary standpoint the seedeaters are a youthful as well as a dominant group. The seed-bearing plants that furnish their principal food came suddenly into prominence during the Miocene epoch, 25 or 30 million years ago. Other birds turned partially to this new type of food—larks among the passerines, and quail, pheasants, and pigeons among the nonpasserines. But none exploited seeds as food so intensively as did the ancestors of the sparrows. Seed-producing plants, principally grasses and sedges, spread rapidly after the Miocene. So did these small birds that relied on them for food. The presence of seeds allowed sparrows to populate almost all the land areas of the world. They are absent only from Antarctica, where no seed-bearing plants grow, and from a few oceanic islands the birds have been unable to reach. The task of sorting the vast complex of seedeaters into natural groups that reflect their ancestry and relationships to one another has long plagued ornithologists. We are now certain that they arose from 2 or 3 parent stocks, perhaps more, simultaneously in different parts of the world. Complicating the problem has been the marked parallelism of anatomical development of the various groups. Another factor is the successful spread of these similar stocks between continents into each other's natal domains.

Seedeaters fall most logically and conveniently into two large families based on place of origin, the New World Fringillidae and the Old World Ploceidae. Sizable segments of each family occur today in both hemispheres, and some subfamilies in each family are often given full family rank.

The 315 or so seedeaters of New World origin are an integral part of the complex of Western Hemisphere oscines with nine primary feathers. Though the fringillids are the most youthful, widespread, and highly developed of this complex, many students consider them close to the ancestral stock from which they and the vireos, warblers, icterids, and tanagers have branched. New World sparrows are so close to the icterids and tanagers that some species are assigned to one family or another almost arbitrarily. The Dickcissel of the midwestern prairies, for instance, is generally regarded as a fringilline finch. It has also been placed, on good grounds, with the icterids and with the cardinal finches, which some anatomists now place with the tanagers. The lines of distinction, both in anatomy and behaviour, between the three families are indeed fine. The fringillids' strong reliance on seeds as their main food (though there are exceptions) is a major one.

In addition to anatomical criteria involving the form and shape of the palate bones and the attachment and insertion of various head and limb muscles, fringillids show basic traits of behaviour that unite them as a group and help to separate them from their Old World counterparts, the ploceids. Fringillids forage mostly on or near the ground. Most have a well-developed and pleasing song, which they usually give from a perch, rarely in flight. With few exceptions they are strong fliers, and most temperate zone species are migratory. Many are gregarious when not nesting. They migrate and winter in flocks.

None of the fringillids nests colonially, and their breeding habits are catholic, fairly uniform, and show few departures from the norm. Almost all build open cup nests, a very few high in trees, more in low bushes, in the grass, or on the ground. A few tropical species build covered nests, and members of one genus, the saffron finches, stuff them into cavities. All fringillids, so far as we know, are essentially monogamous, none is parasitic, and each pair establishes and defends a breeding territory of its own.

The family divides handily into three subfamilies—the cardinal finches (Richmondeninae), the small group of Galapagos, or Darwin's, finches (Geospizinae), and the nominate Fringillinae, which Americans call sparrows but are called buntings in Britain. The collective names sparrow, finch, bunting, and grosbeak have been so widely and miscellaneously applied to various species of both fringillids and ploceids that they have no taxonomic significance.

The 35 species that constitute the cardinal finch subfamily have rather stocky bodies and stout, strong bills. Essentially arboreal woodland inhabitants, they show a number of other close similarities to tanagers. Though the females are sparrowy browns, the males of most species are brightly coloured in reds or blues. They are not markedly gregarious, and many species remain paired throughout the year. With few exceptions the female does all the incubating, though the male helps build the nest, often feeds the incubating female, and always helps rear the young. Most cardinal finches are better singers than tanagers, and they feed more on the ground. Their centre of distribution is tropical America, and they range northward to southern Canada and southward to Argentina.

Most familiar of the northern members of the subfamily is the Cardinal, the well-loved "red bird" of the southern states. Found throughout the warm temperate parts of eastern North America and southward to Mexico and British Honduras, the Cardinal's six geographical races tend to be resident, the birds showing little seasonal movement. The Cardinal seems to be pushing its range slowly northward. It is now a fairly common resident in the New York area, where it was unknown when I was a youthful birdwatcher there not so long ago. Closely related to the Cardinal is the svelte Pyrrhuloxia found from Texas and southern Arizona southward through Mexico. It feeds more on the ground than does the Cardinal, and is seldom found far from cover.

Other members of this subfamily that have pushed north-

BLUE GROSBEAK ♂
Guiraca caerulea
Southern U.S.
to Costa Rica 6½ in.

PYRRHULOXIA
Pyrrhuloxia sinuata
Southwestern U.S., northern Mexico 8 in.

CARDINAL ♂
Richmondena cardinalis
United States to southern Mexico 8 in.

PAINTED BUNTING ♂
Passerina ciris
Southern U.S. and
northern Mexico 5¼ in.

ward from their tropical homes, such as the Rose-breasted and the Blue grosbeaks, are not so hardy, and retire southward to their ancestral tropics when winter comes. The Rose-breasted Grosbeak of deciduous woodlands in eastern North America and the Black-headed Grosbeak of western North America are exceptions to the usual breeding pattern of the group. The male does much of the incubating and often sings while doing so. The Black-headed Grosbeak is also known for its song flight during courtship, and is one of the few members of the entire family that sings on the wing.

The Blue-black Grosbeak is a dark-blue bird that ranges from Mexico to Bolivia. Both sexes sing to one another as they work at nest building. Incubation takes 13 to 14 days. The young are fed by both sexes and fledge in another 11 to 12 days. A South American representative is the Ultramarine Grosbeak, found from Venezuela down to temperate Argentina. Though the temperate zone grosbeaks all lay 4 eggs, the tropical species lay only 2 per clutch, but are multi-brooded and may raise 3 broods each year.

Smallest and most colourful of the richmondenines are the six buntings of the genus *Passerina*. These range from the United States to Panama, and the three northern species, the

Indigo, Lazuli, and Painted buntings, are migratory. The male Painted Bunting is one of the most startlingly bright birds in North America, and aptly justifies its commonly heard name of "nonpareil." The female is dull greenish above and yellowish below. In spite of its unequalled splashy colours, the nonpareil is not conspicuous, for it stays within the foliage of thickets. For a short time during the breeding season, the male sits out on an open perch and trills a musical little song to encourage his incubating mate and warn other nonpareils away from his breeding territory.

BLACK-HEADED SALTATOR
Saltator atriceps
Mexico to Panama   10 in.

the *Beagle* visited the Galapagos Islands in 1835. His study of these birds, all similar enough to one another to show obvious relationship, yet each markedly different, was instrumental in convincing Darwin of the validity of the first great axiom in the formulation of his theory of evolution—that "species are not immutable."

Darwin's finches are a small, compact group of 14 species divided among 4 genera. They occur only on the Galapagos, the little group of islands on the equator 600 miles west of Ecuador, and on Cocos Island between the Galapagos and Panama. They are all believed to have descended from a single ancestor of early fringillid stock that managed to reach these islands from the American mainland, possibly in Pliocene time, say, 5 or 10 million years ago.

This little group of birds is one of the neatest, clearest, and most clear-cut examples of adaptive radiation—the process whereby the descendants of a single parent stock differentiate and radiate out to fill separate ecological niches close to one another. This process is seldom as apparent in the complex faunas of large land masses, where competition from unrelated forms is stiffer. Evolution works fastest in small isolated populations, away from competition. (Another example is the Hawaiian honeycreepers, p. 283.)

Darwin's finches vary in size from 4 to 8 inches. In most species both sexes are coloured alike in greyish browns; in some the males are black. They show their greatest divergences in their bills, which vary from stout and finch-like to long, thin, and warbler-like. Most of the stout-billed species live on seeds. The one with the smallest, thinnest bill lives on insects. One with a decurved bill and a split tongue probes the flowers of the prickly-pear cactus for nectar and eats its soft, pulpy fruit. One with a short, thick slightly decurved bill lives on buds, leaves, and fruits. One with a stout, straight bill, the Woodpecker Finch (illustrated), has developed one of the

Most tanager-like of the cardinal finches in behaviour are the 11 large, plain-coloured sparrows known only by their generic name *Saltator*. The several species I have met in Central and South America are quiet, sedate, and unobtrusive. Largest of the genus is the Black-headed Saltator shown above. Better known is the slightly smaller 8-inch Buff-throated Saltator found from Mexico south to Paraguay.

Residents of the humid tropics, saltators live in open woodlands and at the edges of forest clearings. They are usually greenish brown above, lighter, sometimes streaked below, and have string markings of white, yellow, or black about the head. The sexes are alike or closely similar. Their bills are large and finch-like, but not so stout and strong as those of cardinals and grosbeaks. While saltators eat some seeds, their diet is essentially berries and fruits, and many of them eat flowers. Another tanager characteristic is their voices, which are somewhat weak for such large, stout birds.

Saltators build a bulky open nest among the foliage fairly near the ground. Nest building and incubation are by the female, but the male stands by and attends her. Incubation of the 2-egg clutch takes 13 to 14 days. Both parents feed the young, often for several weeks after they leave the nest following a 14-day fledging period. They are multi-brooded.

The second subfamily, the Geospizinae, are most fittingly known as Darwin's finches, for Darwin discovered them when

WOODPECKER FINCH ♂
Camarhynchus pallidus
Galapagos Isls.   5 in.

LARGE GROUND FINCH ♂
Geospiza magnirostris
Galapagos Isls.   5¾ in.

WHITE-THROATED SPARROW
Zonotrichia albicollis
Northern North America 7 in.

CHESTNUT-COLLARED
LONGSPUR ♂
Calcarius ornatus
Central North America 6½ in.

SNOW BUNTING ♂
Plectrophenax nivalis
Arctic tundra,
circumpolar
6½ in.

OREGON JUNCO
Junco oreganus
Western North America 6 in.

TREE SPARROW
Spizella arborea
Northern
North America 6½ in.

LAPLAND LONGSPUR ♂
Calcarius lapponicus
Arctic tundra, circumpolar
6 in.

most amazing of all bird habits. Although it chisels into bark for insects, it lacks the woodpecker's long tongue to rake out the grubs after it has opened their burrow. So it picks up a small twig or a cactus thorn and probes with it into the burrow until the insect emerges. It then drops the thorn and grabs its meal. The only other known case of a bird using a tool is the bowerbirds' use of grass swabs for painting their bowers (p. 229).

Despite the wide differences in their bills and feeding habits, studies of their internal anatomy have verified the close relationship of the Darwin's finches to each other. This is further indicated by their breeding habits, which are remarkably similar for a group with such diverse feeding habits. All establish nesting territories, which the males defend and advertise to the females with an unimpressive and not too musical song. All build covered nests, large for the size of the builder, usually out in the open near the end of a branch of a cactus or other growth, from 3 to 30 feet up. Though the eggs differ in size among the various species, all are white with pink spots, and the normal clutch is four eggs. Incubation takes 12 days by the female alone, and the young remain in the nest another 2 weeks. The male feeds the female on the nest and helps her feed the young.

The nominate Fringillinae, the third and last subfamily, is the largest and most widespread of all seedeater groups. It contains some 266 species of about 75 genera. They are most plentiful and best developed in the American tropics and subtropics, where the family is believed to have arisen. From this centre the fringillines have dispersed to occupy all of the Americas south to Cape Horn and north to the frozen lands along the polar seas. Two genera, the longspurs (*Calcarius*) and the snow buntings (*Plectrophenax*), are completely circumpolar in the far north. Some 40 species of three strictly Old World genera have descended from an early invasion of the Eastern Hemisphere, perhaps in late Miocene or early Pliocene time. These are widespread over continental Eurasia,

and a few have managed to push southward in Africa to the Cape of Good Hope. No fringillines have reached beyond the main Old World continents.

The fringilline finches are small birds from 4½ to 8 inches long. Most are clothed in inconspicuous browns, streaked or mottled with greys. Bright colours are rare. Their more striking patterns are formed by contrasting black and white, occasionally with spots of yellow. Usually the sexes are alike or closely similar. In a few the males are more gaily coloured, such as the dichromatic black and white Lark Bunting of the North American prairie states with its drab brown mate, and the black, brown, and white Towhee, whose consort has a less conspicuous brown instead of black.

Most fringillines are birds of grasslands, scrublands, or open woodlands. Some inhabit forest undergrowth, but none is strictly arboreal. Though some nest in shrubs or low trees, most are ground nesters. All forage on or near the ground. Seeds of any and all sorts are their mainstay. To these they add small amounts of other vegetable matter—buds, foliage, or an occasional taste of fruit and berries in season—and varying quantities of insects to boost their protein intake. They feed their young almost exclusively on insects.

The 50-odd species that occur regularly in temperate North America include many familiar garden birds. The friendly Song and Chipping sparrows nest in shrubbery close to houses and sing cheerily in spring and summer. Relatives of the Song Sparrow are the Swamp and Lincoln's sparrows. Close congeners of the Chippy are the Field, Clay-coloured, Brewer's, and Tree sparrows. Field inhabitants are the Lark Sparrow and the Vesper Sparrow (that sings by day as well as at twilight), the widespread Savannah Sparrow, and the Grasshopper named for its insect-like buzzing trill.

A striking group is formed by the crowned *Zonotrichias*, the White-crowned, Golden-crowned, White-throated, and Harris sparrows, that breed in the northern woodlands. All are fine singers, and considered by many the prettiest of the sparrows. Less well known are the Seaside Sparrows of United States eastern coastal marshes and the Sharp-tails that nest in fresh or brackish marshes. Then there are the Sage Sparrows of the western deserts, and the Black-chinned Sparrow of chaparral-covered hillsides, among many others.

Practically all these temperate zone breeders are migratory, most of them flocking in winter to the southern states and northern Central America. Many are hardy enough to withstand the northern winters. Such Canadian and Hudsonian zone breeders as the juncos, the Tree Sparrow, and the *Zonotrichias* winter commonly in fields and suburbs of the northern states, sometimes joined by the Snow Buntings and Lapland Longspurs that come down from the Arctic when the snows get deep.

Among the host of tropical American fringillines are the small finches known appropriately as seedeaters. The genus *Sporophila* contains some 30 species, ranging from southern Texas to Argentina. Tiny 4- to 5-inch birds with very short, heavy bills, seedeaters are common in grassy meadows, reedy marshes, and along roadsides and clearings, often in large, busy flocks. The males are black, marked with white or brown; the females dull brownish. The well-known Black Seedeater is also called the Variable Seedeater because the male's markings are not constant.

Seedeaters are sociable birds and often nest fairly close together. They are not truly colonial in their nesting, but establish small territories and do not defend them avidly. The female builds a flimsy open cup nest near the ground, in a bush or low tree, and incubates the 2 to 3 eggs. The male feeds her while she incubates, and if she is absent when he comes bringing gifts he offers the food to the eggs. Seedeaters feed their young by regurgitation, bringing insects, small seeds, and grasses to the nest in their throats.

The Yellow-faced Grassquit is typical of four species of the genus *Tiaris* found from Mexico to Brazil. Similar in feeding and flocking habits to the *Sporophilas*, the grassquits are among the few continental small birds also found widely through the West Indies. Grassquits build covered nests with a thick roof and side entrance. The male helps with nest building, which is part of the courtship. He usually starts the nest and the female finishes it.

Domed nests are the custom of a few other tropical fringillines, notably some of the forest inhabitants of the genera *Arremon* and *Arremonops*, in which the sexes are closely alike, as in the Olive and Green-backed sparrows, and the Orange-billed Sparrow, whose bright beak, white throat and yellow wing markings are conspicuous recognition marks in the dark undergrowth these birds inhabit.

Most distinctive in nesting habits are the 10 ground finches of the genus *Sicalis* found in open brushlands from Mexico to Argentina, but most plentifully in southern South America, where they are called "wild canaries." Representative of these unusually bright fringillines is the Saffron Finch of South America, common in Jamaica where it was introduced. The Saffron Finches are one of the few cavity nesters in the family. They stuff a messy mass of straw and feathers into a hole in a tree, under the eaves of buildings, or in rock crevices. In southern Brazil they often appropriate abandoned domed nests of ovenbirds (p. 198).

Classified as fringillines and not as richmondenines are the handsome Dominican and Crested cardinals. Residents of southern Brazil and Argentina, they are among the larger and gayer members of the subfamily. The Crested Cardinal has long been a popular cage bird, favoured for its bright red crest and cheerful song. It has been introduced to Hawaii. Limited to the West Indies are several fringilline genera, notably the bullfinches of the genus *Loxigilla*, woodland species that build globular nests with side entrances.

The Old World component of the subfamily contains many common and familiar Eurasian birds. Widespread in Europe and eastern Asia is the Chaffinch, first of the family to be given a scientific name (*Fringilla*) by Linnaeus in 1758. By the inflexible rules of nomenclature this entire family of New World origin and essentially New World distribution derives its name from one of its Old World members.

The Chaffinch breeds throughout the European countryside and is a common summer resident in parks, gardens, thickets, hedgerows, and cultivated lands. Like most northern hemisphere members of the subfamily, it is gregarious when not nesting and migrates in flocks, often composed of one sex. It winters in open stubble fields with other seedeaters. The Brambling, a close relative, shares the genus *Fringilla* with it but is a more northern breeder, nesting in birch and conifer woodlands across northern Eurasia and migrating somewhat

YELLOW-FACED
GRASSQUIT ♂
Tiaris olivacea
West Indies;
Mexico to Venezuela 4 in.

VARIABLE
SEEDEATER ♂
Sporophila aurita
Mexico to Peru 4½ in.

SAFFRON FINCH ♂
Sicalis flaveola
Venezuela to Argentina;
Jamaica (intr.) 5½ in.

erratically southward, sometimes in tremendous numbers. One recent Brambling "invasion" that poured from the north into southern Germany and Switzerland was estimated to number in excess of 70 million birds.

The 30-odd species assigned to the species *Emberiza*, and most commonly referred to as "buntings," are the largest single group of the Old World fringillines. Like most North American species, the emberizids are plain-coloured birds with the sexes alike. Usually cryptically patterned in browns with streakings of black, white, and greys, many are attractively marked with yellow, and most have the outer tail feathers partly or wholly white. The genus has its greatest development across the Eurasian land mass, and most of its members are migratory or partly so.

Emberizid stock expanded successfully southward to invade the African home of the ploceids. The Golden-breasted Bunting lives throughout much of South Africa in open country, in sparse woodlands and cultivated areas, and is also a common resident in suburban gardens. Even more widespread is the Cape Bunting, found in many types of open country but partial to dry regions. It is often called the "rock bunting" because of its addiction to rocky hillside slopes. The Cape Bunting breaks into a number of geographical races over its wide range.

A representative emberizid is the Meadow Bunting of eastern Asia and Japan, an inhabitant of open fields, shrubby hillsides, and young second-growth woodland. It likes thickets along the roadsides and the hedgerows between cultivated fields. Meadow Buntings sing throughout the year, but most ardently in spring and summer. The male pipes his pleasant melody from the topmost twig of a bush, or from the electric wires along the country roads. As in the American Song Sparrow, each individual bird has his own particular melody and phraseology which he repeats over and over, sometimes for hours at a time.

Other well-known Eurasian species include the Pine, Cirl, Reed, and Little buntings. The Yellow Bunting, usually called the Yellowhammer, is one of the commonest finches in Great Britain. Nesting in the northern taiga from Sweden to Kamchatka is the Rustic Bunting, the only member of the genus admitted to the American list, as it occasionally straggles into the Aleutians. The Black-headed Bunting shown below is one of the more strikingly coloured members of the group, and one of the few that lacks white in its outer tail feathers. The Corn Bunting, very common in the British Isles, also lacks the usual distinguishing mark of white in the outer tail feathers. This is one of the very few fringillines in which breeding aberrations are reported. Male Corn Buntings sometimes have as many as 4 or 5 mates.

The Ortolan of epicurean fame is one of the commoner European emberizids. Its name is probably a corruption of its scientific name *hortulana*, or gardener, for it is one of the common European garden residents. Ortolans gather in large flocks to migrate in the autumn. Like most migrants, they take on quantities of fat for their long flight southward. For centuries Ortolans have been netted on their autumn flight and served as a gourmet's titbit. They are often kept in captivity and fattened further before they are marketed.

The nesting habits of the emberizine closely parallel those of the North American fringillines. All build open cup nests, sometimes in bushes or trees, seldom at any great height from the ground and often on it. Nest building and incubation are mainly by the female, though the male lends a hand in a few species. Clutches run from 3 to 6 eggs, usually 4 or 5, and most species are multi-brooded. Eggs vary somewhat in colour, but are typically lightly tinted and finely spotted.

BRAMBLING ♂
Fringilla montifringilla
Northern Eurasia 6 in.

ORTOLAN BUNTING
Emberiza hortulana
Europe, western Asia 6½ in.

MEADOW BUNTING
Emberiza cioides
Turkestan to Japan 6 in.

BLACK-HEADED BUNTING
Emberiza melanocephala
Southeastern Europe,
southwestern Asia 6½ in.

BULLFINCH ♂
Pyrrhula pyrrhula
Temperate Eurasia   6 in.

SISKIN ♂
Carduelis spinus
North temperate Eurasia   5 in.

WHITE-WINGED CROSSBILL ♂
Loxia leucoptera
Northern Hemisphere   5¾ in.

EUROPEAN GOLDFINCH ♂
Carduelis carduelis
Europe, western Asia, northwest Africa   5½ in.

OLD WORLD SEEDEATERS

PASSERIFORMES   PLOCEIDAE

The 375 or so seedeaters of Old World origin fall into three well-marked groups: the 112 goldfinches and allies (Carduelinae), the 107 waxbills (Estrildinae), and the 156 weaver finches, of which the nominate Ploceinae forms the largest of four closely allied subfamilies. The species within each of these three groups are closely related and share common ancestry, but that all three branched from the same parent stock is doubtful. While they share enough basic features to suggest some degree of kinship, many scholars now believe they arose from different stocks in different parts of the Eastern Hemisphere, and hence may each deserve family rank.

The Ploceidae show no close ties to any other Old World family, and we are still hoping to find fossil clues to their ancestry. Their closest similarities are to the New World seedeaters, for, as previously pointed out, the evolution of these two great avian complexes has been closely parallel. In addition to their stout, conical, seed-eating bills, the ploceids also show a reduction in the size of the outermost, or 10th, primary feather, though not so strongly as in their western counterparts. Many ploceids, the goldfinch subfamily in particular, retain a discernible 10th primary, which is usually less than half the length of the 9th. The feather has disappeared only in the most highly evolved types.

Other anatomical points of difference between the two families are manifest in the palate bones and jaw muscles. Rictal bristles, usually obvious in the New World seedeaters, are poorly developed and often absent in the ploceids. Two striking characteristics separating the families are the relative

sizes of their legs and bills. In the Old World family the tarsus is relatively short, never longer than the middle toe with its claw. The exposed portion of the upper bill is relatively long, always more than twice the length of the gonys (the central ridge of the lower bill from its tip to the point of forking). The reverse is true for both these characteristics in the New World Fringillidae.

The goldfinches and their relatives in the subfamily Carduelinae are typified by the European Goldfinch, which feeds commonly on thistle seeds. Its generic name, bestowed on the subfamily, derives from the Latin *carduus*, a thistle. The

HOUSE FINCH ♂
Carpodacus mexicanus
Western North America and Mexico   5½ in.

REDPOLL ♂
Acanthis flammea
Northern Northern Hemisphere,
circumpolar 5½ in.

carduelines are best developed in the Northern Hemisphere, and evidently originated in the Eurasian land mass we now call the palaearctic region, where 64 species of 20 genera exist today. From this centre the goldfinches have spread throughout Africa (30 species) and the Americas (32 species). Several species occur on all three continents. Three species have reached the East Indies and the Philippines, but none is known from Australia or the Pacific islands.

With few exceptions the carduelines are tree-dwelling forest birds, much more so than the fringillines. All habitually sing during their peculiarly undulating flight, and their social instincts are highly developed. Few are strongly migratory, but most northern species move irregularly southward in winter. They travel in compactly unified flocks, and a number of species nest in loose colonies. Unlike the other ploceids, they build compactly woven, open cup nests, usually placed in tree branches well off the ground, except in the few species such as the redpolls that nest in treeless areas. Incubation is usually by the female alone, but the male feeds her on the nest and helps rear the young. A noteworthy aspect of their nesting habits which goldfinches share with the waxbills is their lack of nest sanitation. These are among the very few higher passerines that do not remove the nestlings' faecal matter from the nest.

Colour and moult patterns vary throughout the carduelines. Some are streaked and mottled; others are clothed in solid hues. The sexes may be alike or different, and in many the males don a bright breeding dress of yellows or reds which they moult after breeding. In these species the winter males and first-year young resemble the females. In the European Goldfinch the sexes are alike the year round. In the congeneric American Goldfinch the sexes differ, and the male dons his bright-yellow and black breeding plumage in spring and doffs it in the late summer.

The European Goldfinch's neat beauty, its pleasant song, and the ease with which it is kept in captivity make it a popular cage bird, and thousands used to be caught for this purpose. A number of attempts were made to introduce the European Goldfinch to the United States during the 19th century, and releases were made in Oregon, Missouri, Ohio, New Jersey, and Massachusetts, as well as in Bermuda. Though small populations still persist in favoured spots along the south shore of Long Island, the species found conditions to its liking only in Bermuda, where it is now one of the common resident birds. It has also been introduced in Australia and New Zealand.

Close relatives of the goldfinches are the European Twite and Linnet, and the northernmost members of the family, the circumpolar redpolls that breed in the arctic tundra the world around and migrate southward in winter to temperate latitudes. Widest ranging of the subfamily are the 22 very similar yellowish siskins found in coniferous and deciduous woodlands throughout the Northern Hemisphere. Siskins have acclimatized themselves southward in Africa to the Cape of Good Hope, and have followed the American cordilleras to the Straits of Magellan. They are the only carduelines in South America. One siskin has been isolated in the coniferous mountain forests of Hispaniola long enough to become generically distinct. The only other strictly American genus of carduelines is the strong-billed Evening Grosbeak of northern forests, which flocks irregularly in winter and often comes to window-box feeding places in the northern states for sunflower seeds.

Prominent among the reddish-coloured carduelines is the Purple Finch of North America, replaced in Eurasia by the Scarlet Finch and several rose finches, all of the genus *Carpodacus*. Very similar to the Purple Finch is the slightly smaller and brighter Mexican House Finch, a common garden bird from California southward through Mexico. In 1940 cage-bird dealers in southern California shipped numbers of these birds, caught illegally in the wild, to New York dealers for sale as "Hollywood finches." Alert agents of the Fish and Wildlife Service spotted this violation of the International Migratory Bird Treaty Act and quickly put an end to the traffic. To avoid prosecution the New York dealers released their birds. The species was soon noted in the wild on nearby Long Island, and it has slowly been increasing its range ever since. The Mexican House Finch has now pushed northward into Connecticut and southward into New Jersey. It has also been introduced to Hawaii.

One of the largest carduelines is the 9-inch Pine Grosbeak. The male is dull red, the female greyish brown with a yellowish crown and rump. The Pine Grosbeak breeds circumpolarly in the pine-spruce belt across northern North America and Eurasia, wintering irregularly southward. Similarly distributed are the Red and the White-winged crossbills. Both males are ruddy, both females brownish. The crossbills' strong bill with uniquely overlapped tips is an ideal tool for prying seeds out of tough evergreen cones, and the birds are seldom found far from conifers. They do eat other seeds, and they

RED AVADAVAT ♂
Estrilda amandava
India to Indochina
and East Indies 3 in.

BLUE-FACED
PARROT FINCH ♂
Erythrura trichroa
Micronesia to New Ireland
and New Hebrides 4½ in.

CHESTNUT MANNIKIN ♂
Lonchura ferruginosa
India to Philippines and East Indies 4¾ in.

feed their young on insects. Crossbills have pushed southward following the evergreens in both hemispheres. A population of Red Crossbills inhabits the Central American highlands from Guatemala to Nicaragua. A wandering group of White-winged Crossbills that reached Hispaniola still lives with the endemic siskin in the highland conifer forests.

Well-known Eurasian cardulines include the Hawfinch of Europe, a husky-bodied bird named for its fondness for the seeds of the hawthorn. In eastern Asia, the Hawfinch is replaced by the 9-inch Japanese Grosbeak. Found across Eurasia are 10 geographical races of the Bullfinch, which is admitted to the American list on the basis of straggling records in Alaska. The Bullfinch is popular as a cage bird in Europe and the Orient, and is prized for the lovely pink colour of the male's breast and for its sweet piping calls.

The best known of all cage birds, the Canary, is a cardueline finch of the siskin type. Wild Canaries still exist on the Canary Islands, whence they were imported into Europe as cage birds in the 16th century. They live on the Azores and Madeira islands as well. Other relatives of the same genus occur in Africa and Europe, best known of which is the Serin. The wild Canary stock is olivish above streaked with brown and black, and greenish yellow below. Centuries of selective breeding in captivity both for colour and for song and crossing with closely related species have produced the many distinctive varieties now available.

The second subfamily of Old World seedeaters, the Es-

behaviour. Native to the tropical parts of the Old World, Africa, southern Asia, the East Indies, and Australia, the 107 species are divided among 15 genera. All are very small birds, 6 inches in length at most, with short, stout, pointed bills. They are non-migratory and generally resident wherever they occur. They like open grasslands, reedy marshes, or the brushy borders of forest edges and clearings. All are ground feeders that live mainly on the small seeds of grasses and sedges, augmented by a few insects and an occasional small fruit or berry.

The waxbills are highly gregarious and customarily go about in flocks, sometimes of tremendous size, often containing 3 or 4 species. Many of them nest colonially. All build large domed nests, globular, melon-, pear-, or bottle-shaped, but notably flimsy and of loose construction, and with side entrances. A number of them build separate nests for roosting. They lay large clutches of from 4 to 10 pure-white eggs. Both sexes build the nest and care for the young, and the male usually helps to some extent with the incubation, which runs from 11 to 17 days. While waxbills do not remove their nestlings' droppings, these always dry up quickly, crumble away, and do not foul the nest excessively. The nestlings have bright patches of colour inside the mouths, the sight of which is thought to stimulate the parent's feeding reactions. The young mature rapidly and are able to breed in their first year.

The nominate genus *Estrilda* contains 28 species ranging from Africa to Australia. Typical of the genus is the Common Waxbill, found over most of Africa south of the Sahara

GOULDIAN FINCH ♂
Poephila gouldiae
Northern Australia 5¾ in.

RED-CHEEKED CORDON-BLEU ♂
Uraeginthus bengalensis
Africa, Senegal to the Sudan 4½ in.

YELLOW-BELLIED WAXBILL ♂
Estrilda melanotis
South Africa 4 in.

GREEN-BACKED TWINSPOT ♂
Estrilda nitidula
South Africa 3 in.

LOCUST FINCH ♂
Estrilda locustella
Southeast Africa, Tanganyika 3½ in.

GREEN TIGER FINCH ♂
Estrilda formosa
Central India 4 in.

MELBA FINCH ♂
Pytelia melba
Central and southern Africa 5 in.

trildinae, are also great favourites among cage-bird fanciers. The appeal of the waxbills to aviculturists is their bright colour, spritely liveliness, and ready adaptability to confinement. They are poor singers, and though some males have pleasant warbling notes, most of them are limited to simple chirps, hisses, buzzes, and subdued chatterings. Members of this kaleidoscopic group are known to the trade by such fanciful and descriptive names as mannikins, munias, parrotfinches, negrofinches, firefinches, locustfinches, crimsonwings, cut-throats, silver-eyes, bluebills, cordon-bleus, and grenadiers, to mention but a few.

Despite their great diversity of colour, the estrildids are a remarkably uniform group anatomically and in habits and

in reed marshes. The Yellow-bellied Waxbill lives in small flocks along forest edges or in thick tangles of undergrowth bordering streams. The tiny Locust Finches move about wet grasslands in dense swarms, and are almost impossible to see when feeding on the ground. When disturbed they rise and fly straight and fast with rapidly whirring wings and drop quickly again into concealment in the grass.

Other African species are the Green-backed Twinspot, which eats termites as well as grass seeds, and the Orange-cheeked Waxbill, which has become established in Puerto Rico from escaped cage birds. Other favourite cage birds are the several cordon-bleus, common around villages and cultivated lands in East Africa. The cordon-bleus often build their domed nests near those of wasps for protection, and occasionally use the abandoned nests of weaverbirds, re-lining them with feathers and plant down. The three species of red-faced melba finches are inconspicuous inhabitants of thorny thickets and undergrowth, where they search about quietly on the ground for small seeds.

A brilliant little Asiatic estrildid is the Red Avadavat (a corruption of Ahmadabad, the Indian city from which the first were sent to Europe). Avadavats live in dense swarms in reedy marshes and wet grasslands. They nest irregularly throughout the year, but most often in the rainy season, when food is plentiful. Netted in quantity for the live bird trade, they become tame and confiding in captivity.

WHITE-HEADED BUFFALO WEAVER ♂
Dinemellia dinemelli
Sudan to Abyssinia and Kenya 9 in.

RED-BILLED
QUELEA ♂
Quelea quelea
Africa south
of the Sahara 5 in.

HOUSE SPARROW ♂
Passer domesticus
Eurasia, North
Africa 6 in.

BAYA WEAVER ♂
Ploceus philippinus
India to Indochina
and Malaya 6 in.

EURASIAN
TREE SPARROW
Passer montanus
Eurasia 5½ in.

The 30 munias and mannikins of the genus *Lonchura*, found from Africa across southern Asia to the Caroline Islands and southward to Australia, are one of the largest groups of estrildids. Most of them are reddish brown, variously patterned with black and white. They are grassland birds of savannahs and reedy marshes. These prolific little birds lay 4 to 8 eggs and in captivity rear up to 5 broods a year. The young breed before they are a year old.

Mannikins often congregate in swarms in grain fields. The Chestnut Mannikin is one of the main pests of rice growers in the Philippines and Malaya. Flocks of Bronze Mannikins traipse about the open lands of the Congo following the food supply as grasses and grains ripen. Bronze Mannikins roost communally, jammed in on top of one another in old nests and in special nests they build for sleeping. One of the brighter members of this group is the Java Sparrow, common in bird shops where it is sold as a cage bird. This plump grey bird tinged with pink on the belly has two large white ear patches and a light-pink bill. It makes an attractive pet, but its presence in rice fields is not relished by farmers. Its fitting scientific name is *Padda oryzivora*, which means the paddy-field rice-eater.

Limited to the Australian and Oriental region are 23 species of colourful grass-finches or parrot-finches divided among three genera. Typical of the nine species of the genus *Poephila*, known in northern Australia as painted finches or purple-breasted finches, is the gaudy Gouldian Finch (p. 303). Gouldian Finches have the tail pointed instead of square, and live in small flocks in open grassy country, often near watercourses. A close relative and a common Australian bird is the Zebra Finch, often seen in cages, with its zebra-barred black and white tail, chestnut ear patches, and pink bill. These finches build bottle-shaped nests of dried grasses in a bush or low tree, sometimes in tall grass, and occasionally in tree hollows, an unusual departure in this subfamily.

Also with pointed tails are the nine parrot-finches (*Erythrura*), bright green in colour with contrasting reds and blues. Most of them live along forest edges, and they are frequently found in bamboo tangles, where their green colours are very hard to see. A widespread member of this genus is the Blue-faced, or Three-coloured, Parrot-finch, a resident of many Pacific islands from the Solomons, New Hebrides, and Loyalty Islands, northward to the Carolines and westward to the Bismarck Archipelago. Others occur in the Philippines, Malaya, Papua, and northern Australia.

The third assemblage of Old World seedeaters, the weaverbirds, is composed of four subfamilies, the buffalo weavers (Bubalornithinae), the sparrow weavers (Passerinae), the typical weavers (Ploceinae), and the widow weavers (Viduinae). The weavers have by far their greatest development in Africa, where the group arose. From here members of two subfamilies have pushed widely through the palaearctic and the fringes of the oriental region, and one of the sparrow weavers, the ubiquitous House Sparrow, has, with the help of man, become perhaps the most widely distributed and familiar small bird in the world.

Though a few species are solitary, most weavers are highly gregarious, and some have brought social development to its

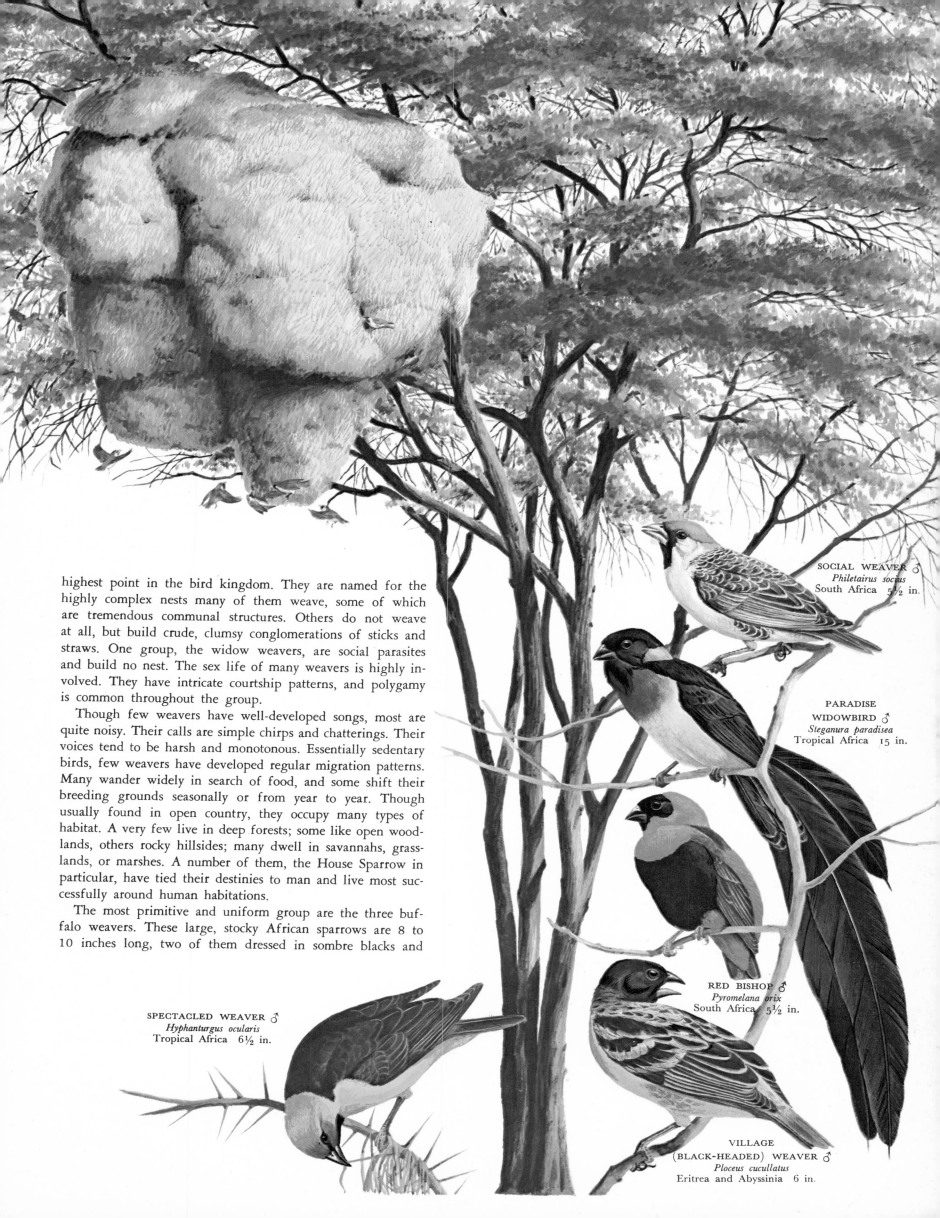

highest point in the bird kingdom. They are named for the highly complex nests many of them weave, some of which are tremendous communal structures. Others do not weave at all, but build crude, clumsy conglomerations of sticks and straws. One group, the widow weavers, are social parasites and build no nest. The sex life of many weavers is highly involved. They have intricate courtship patterns, and polygamy is common throughout the group.

Though few weavers have well-developed songs, most are quite noisy. Their calls are simple chirps and chatterings. Their voices tend to be harsh and monotonous. Essentially sedentary birds, few weavers have developed regular migration patterns. Many wander widely in search of food, and some shift their breeding grounds seasonally or from year to year. Though usually found in open country, they occupy many types of habitat. A very few live in deep forests; some like open woodlands, others rocky hillsides; many dwell in savannahs, grasslands, or marshes. A number of them, the House Sparrow in particular, have tied their destinies to man and live most successfully around human habitations.

The most primitive and uniform group are the three buffalo weavers. These large, stocky African sparrows are 8 to 10 inches long, two of them dressed in sombre blacks and

SOCIAL WEAVER ♂
Philetairus socius
South Africa 5½ in.

PARADISE
WIDOWBIRD ♂
Steganura paradisea
Tropical Africa 15 in.

RED BISHOP ♂
Pyromelana orix
South Africa 5½ in.

SPECTACLED WEAVER ♂
Hyphanturgus ocularis
Tropical Africa 6½ in.

VILLAGE
(BLACK-HEADED) WEAVER ♂
Ploceus cucullatus
Eritrea and Abyssinia 6 in.

browns, the third with a white head and underparts. Buffalo weavers roam the dry savannahs and veldts in small flocks of a dozen or so, feeding on the ground about equally on insects and grass seeds. They build bulky compartmented nests of sticks heaped together on the branches of large trees, and strew thorny twigs along the supporting limbs to discourage climbing marauders. They may build 8 or 10 nests in the same tree, each nest with two or more inner chambers occupied by separate pairs and with separate entrances facing outward in different directions.

Prominent among the 35 sparrow weavers is the House Sparrow, whose generic name *Passer*, Latin for sparrow, is bestowed on the entire order of perching birds. Native to Europe, western Asia, and northern Africa, the House Sparrow is the most successful city and town dweller of all birds, and has followed European civilization all over the world. It was introduced to North America in 1852 (in a Brooklyn, N.Y., cemetery), and its subsequent spread throughout the settled parts of the continent is now practically complete. It has been almost equally successful in South Africa, South America, Australia, New Zealand, and Hawaii. A few introductions have failed. House Sparrows were unable to survive in southern Greenland, which is not surprising. In the Philippines they were unable to compete with their close relative, the Eurasian Tree Sparrow (not to be confused with the nearctic fringilline of the same common name, p. 298), which had already been introduced there from Asia and occupies the same niche around villages.

The Eurasian Tree Sparrow closely resembles the male House Sparrow, and the sexes are alike. Widespread in cultivated regions from central Europe eastward to China, Korea, and Japan, this species is just as ubiquitous around towns as the House Sparrow, and a great nuisance in rice-growing regions. Tremendous flocks descend on the paddies as the rice ripens in the autumn, and all sorts of scarecrows, noisemakers, and smoke bombs are used to discourage them—with little effect. The Japanese net them by the millions—between 5 and 10 million are sold annually. Their plucked bodies hang in the markets, their necks inserted in twists of rice-straw rope in skeins of 10 each. In season they are a common delicacy at Oriental dinners, and in Tokyo little street-side stalls sell them broiled on skewers over charcoal and flavoured with soy sauce. Broiled to a crisp and eaten bones and all, they are quite tasty. A small population of Eurasian Tree Sparrows is resident around St. Louis, Missouri. They were introduced in 1870 but have never spread.

Close to the *Passer* group is the Snow Finch (*Montifringilla*) of the southern Eurasian mountains. The Snow Finch nests above 4,500 feet in the Pyrenees, Alps, Apennines, and the Balkans, and up to 16,000 feet in the Himalayas. Familiar to mountain climbers and common about Alpine hostels, the Snow Finch looks like a female House Sparrow with patches of white in its wings. Another allied group is the rock sparrows (*Petronia*), found on dry rocky slopes and semideserts from South Africa northward to southern Europe and the Himalayas.

These sparrow weavers build untidy bulky nests, always domed with a side entrance when out in the open. More frequently the House Sparrow and its close kin appropriate a crevice among rocks or a hole in a tree or building which they fill with a mass of straw, twigs, feathers, and trash. The House and Tree sparrows frequently nest under house eaves wherever they can jam a cranny with nesting material. The House Sparrow lays 4 to 9 white eggs heavily speckled with grey which the female incubates practically alone. The incubation and fledging periods each average 13 to 14 days, and two or more broods are raised annually.

Most specialized of the sparrow weavers is the Social Weaver of South Africa, whose large communal nests are sometimes mistaken at a distance for native huts. From 100 to 300 pairs of Social Weavers pool their efforts to build their apartment dwelling, which may be 10 feet high and 15 feet in diameter, usually high in the branches of a sturdy tree, preferably one standing by itself in the open. The birds start by building the communal roof, a waterproof canopy of straw thatch. Hanging from its underside, each pair weaves its own retort-shaped nest chamber, entered by a tube woven from the bottom. Sparrow Weavers nest in the South African midsummer, around Christmas time. Each pair lays 2 to 4 dull-white eggs, heavily speckled with dark grey. Each flock remains about its nest tree throughout the year, chattering to one another continually (they have no true song). When not nesting they forage in small flocks for grass seeds and insects, and return at night to roost in the shelter of their dwelling.

The typical weavers of the subfamily Ploceinae number about 109 species, most of them African, a few in southern Asia. In most of this group the sexes are unlike. The dull-brown females resemble female House Sparrows, while the males in breeding dress are usually bright with yellow and black. After the breeding season the males don an "eclipse" dress much like that of the female. The young resemble the female throughout the first year, and do not mature into breeding dress until the end of their second year. A few nest solitarily, but most are highly social and nest in colonies which run from a few pairs to millions. All weave beautiful flask-like or retort-shaped nests, with the entrance either at the side or through a long tube from the bottom.

Representative of the Ploceinae is the Village Weaver, a common resident around native settlements throughout much of Africa. Large isolated trees may contain hundreds of their nests, which are not united into a single structure as with the Social Weaver, but are built separately, each on its own twig or branch. The male bird starts the nest by weaving a frame of palm fibres, obtained by nipping a small slit in the palm frond and tearing off a long strip by flying away with it in his beak. On the framework he weaves an inverted flask, entered through a funnel from the bottom. The female finishes the nest by lining it with softer material. Though in some colonies the sexes are about in balance, there is often an excess of females. When a male has one female safely ensconced on her eggs, he usually starts a new nest at once for another mate.

A similar Asiatic species is the Baya Weaver, an exceedingly common bird in India, Indochina, and Malaya. Its flask nests hang in colonies of 8 or 10, sometimes 50 or 100, from the trees in rural villages. As with the Village Weaver, the male Baya starts the nest, weaving a firm support of grass fibres around a branch, from which he plaits a hanging loop. To the loop he weaves thick walls, and adds a hollow tube for access down one side. This varies in length from a few inches to several feet. When the outside of the nest is complete, the hens begin to appear at the colony, and each makes her choice of the structures built by the males. When she finds one to her liking, the hen finishes off the interior with softer materials while the male completes the outside tube. As soon as she has laid her eggs and started incubating, the male Baya starts a new nest. The polygamous males keep on building nests throughout the season and, except where there is a substantial surplus of females, are often left with unfinished and unoccupied nests.

Several African members of this group have become serious economic pests in agricultural areas. The worst of these is the Red-billed Quelea, a little 5-inch greyish-brown bird with a bright red bill. The male has red markings around the head and a black mask in the breeding season, but at other times it resembles the duller sparrow-like female. Queleas wander about aimlessly in tremendous swarms in the open and semi-wooded savannah country, and when one of these flocks, which may number into the millions, visits crop lands as the grain is ripening, their depredations are so enormous that they have been combated with flame throwers and chemicals spread from aircraft.

The highly prolific Queleas are opportunist nesters and, unlike most other weavers, they are able to breed when they are one year old. Their breeding is triggered by the rainy season and, when conditions are propitious, the birds settle down together to the business of reproduction wherever they happen to be. The great flocks seem to pick fresh breeding grounds every year. These sometimes cover hundreds of acres, every tree of which is festooned with their nests. The males build the nests, which are simple oval structures woven of strips of grass with little or no lining and an entrance at one side near the top. As soon as a nest is finished and the female accepts it, pairing takes place and the eggs are laid within the next day or two. In these mass nestings there seems to be little polygamy, for the male shares some of the incubating duties during the day, the female always incubating at night. The young hatch in 13 days, usually all at once throughout the colony. They leave the nest in another 12 days, and the large flocks are soon on their erratically wandering way again, augmented by the many young.

The most ornamental members of this group are the bishop and whidah weavers. The male Red Bishop is one of the brightest-coloured of all the weavers and has one of the most interesting courtships. He displays in a bouncing flight before his harem of 2 or 3 females, and makes clapping noises with his wings. Bishops nest in reed beds and wet marshes, building an oval shell of a nest slung between upright reeds. Bishops are great termite eaters, but the large flocks often damage crops, and African farmers are not infrequently put to considerable expense keeping them away from their ripening grain.

A closely related group are sometimes called widows, but more properly whidahs (an anglicization of Ouidah, the coastal town on the Gulf of Guinea where the first of them were obtained). These are also small-bodied birds. The males in breeding season are not only bedecked with gay colours but often with long tail feathers. The male Long-tailed Whidah, a shining black bird with scarlet wing patches, is the longest bird in the family, just under 2 feet in length despite its small body. The male Jackson's Widah builds himself a dancing ground. He clears a round arena 4 feet or so in diameter in the grassy veldt, leaving a single column of grass untouched in the centre. Around this he jumps and prances and spreads his tail in a manner which female Jackson's Widahs apparently find irresistible. Whidah weavers are strongly polygynous; each male has a harem of 4 to 12 plain-coloured hens, which nest in groups on the grassy veldt. During the day the male goes from one nest to another encouraging the females with churring notes. At evening he leaves with his long tail streaming behind him to roost in the reeds with other males.

The strangest and most aberrant of all the weavers are nine species of the subfamily Viduinae, the true widowbirds. These birds of open grasslands and savannahs are widespread throughout Africa south of the Sahara. The females are inconspicuous brown birds, but the males in breeding dress with their long fancy tails are among the most striking of all the seedeaters.

All the widowbirds are both polygynous and parasitic, and with these sexual abnormalities have developed intricate courtship displays reminiscent of those of the bowerbirds. Others of these long-tailed weavers make extended courtship flights. Rising 200 to 300 feet into the air, they hover with flapping wings and waving tail. Then they coast down to the female in the grass below, trusting she is entranced into a state of receptiveness by these antics.

In their parasitism the widowbirds are highly selective in their choice of hosts. They lay their eggs chiefly in the nests of certain waxbill finches, each species of widowbird parasitizing only one or a few species of waxbill. Their eggs, instead of being tinted or spotted as in all other weavers, are pure white like those of their estrildine hosts. Even more amazing, the nestling parasites have bright mouth markings similar to those of their hosts. This phenomenon probably stems from the common ancestry of the two groups.

The female widowbird is believed in some cases to remove an egg from her host's nest, but otherwise this parasitism is apparently not unduly harmful to the waxbills. The dupes rear the young widowbirds with their own broods, and the foster fledgling gets along well with its nestmates, which it closely resembles. It would be interesting to know just when and how young widowbirds, conditioned by and "imprinted" to foster parents, suddenly realize they are birds of a different feather and leave to find others of their own kind. We have much to learn about social parasitism, not only in these weavers, but in the cuckoos, honeyguides, and cowbirds that also practise it successfully.

BIBLIOGRAPHY

New information, theories, and discoveries in natural history are seldom announced in books. They usually first appear in technical publications issued serially by museums, universities, or learned societies as their *Proceedings, Novitates, Archives, Bulletins, Annals,* or *Reports*. Most in ornithology now make their debut in journals usually issued quarterly and distributed by subscription only. Files of these magazines are generally available in technical libraries.

Of the several hundred ornithological periodicals now published in various languages throughout the world, the leading ones in England are *Ibis, Bird Study,* and *British Birds*. Their counterparts in North America are: *Auk, Bird-Banding, Condor,* and *Wilson Bulletin*. On the Continent are *L'Oiseau et Revue Française d'Ornithologie, Journal für Ornithologie, Die Vogelwelt, Dansk Ornithologisk Forenings Tidsskrift, Ornis Fennica, Var Fagelwärld,* and others. From South Africa comes *Ostrich*, from Australia *Emu*, from New Zealand *Notornis*, from Japan *Tori* and *Yacho*. And there are scores more that the ornithologist must consult for the latest information on his subject.

Data from such technical journals eventually find their way into books, and these best meet the needs of amateur ornithologists. For the student who wants to delve further into the following selected list of recent major books about birds may be helpful. An exhaustive list of bird books is R. M. Strong's "A Bibliography of Birds" (Field Mus. Nat. Hist. Chicago, 4 parts, 1939-59).

REGIONAL

WORLD

Alexander, W. B. 1954. *Birds of the Ocean*. New York, Putnam. 428 pp.

Gilliard, E. T. 1958. *Living Birds of the World*. New York, Doubleday. 400 pp.

Greenway, J. C., Jr. 1958. *Extinct and vanishing birds of the world*. New York, Am. Comm. Int. Wildlife Prot. 518 pp.

Knowlton, F. H. 1909. *Birds of the World*. New York, Holt. 873 pp.

Sharpe, R. B., and others. 1874-98. *Catalogue of birds in the British Museum*. London, Brit. Mus., 27 vols.

Thomson, Sir A. Landsborough (Ed.), 1964. *A new dictionary of birds*. London, Nelson. 928 pp.

EURASIA

Ali, Salim. 1949. *Indian Hill Birds*. London, Oxford Univ. Press. 188 pp.

Austin, O. L. Jr. 1948. *The birds of Korea*. Cambridge, Bull Mus. Comp. Zool. 301 pp.

Austin, O. L. Jr. and Kuroda, N. 1953. *The birds of Japan*. Cambridge, Bull. Mus. Comp. Zool. 360 pp.

Baker, E. C. S. 1922-30. *Fauna of British India: birds*. London, Taylor & Francis. 8 vols.

Benson, S. Vere. 1937. *The observer's book of British birds*. London, Warne. 223 pp.

Coward, T. A. 1920. *Birds of the British Isles*. London, Warne. 3 vols.

———. 1936. *Birds of the wayside and woodland*. (Ed. Enid Blyton) London, Warne. 352 pp.

Deignan, Herbert G. 1945. *The birds of northern Thailand*. U. S. Nat. Mus, Bull. 186. 616 pp.

Delacour, Jean. 1947. *Birds of Malaysia*. New York, Macmillan. 382 pp.

Dementiev, T. N., and Gladkov, H. A. 1951-54. *Birds of the Soviet Union*. Moscow, State Publ. 6 vols. (in Russian).

Macdonald, J. D. 1949. *Birds of Britain*. London, Bell. 153 pp.

Meinertzhagen, R. 1954. *Birds of Arabia*. Edinburgh, Oliver & Boyd. 624 pp.

Scott, M. K. C. and Henderson J. A. *Birds*. Edinburgh, Nelson. 159 pp.

Smythies, B. E. 1953. *The birds of Burma*. London, Oliver & Boyd. 668 pp.

Voous, K. H. 1960. *Atlas of European Birds*. London, Nelson. 284 pp.

Whistler, Hugh. 1949. *Popular handbook of Indian birds*. 4th ed. London, Gurney & Jackson. 560 pp.

Witherby, H. F., and others. *The handbook of British birds*. London, Witherby. 7 vols.

NORTH AMERICA

Austin, O. L. Jr. 1931. *Birds of Newfoundland Labrador*. Cambridge, Mass., Memoirs Nutt. Orn. Club. 229 pp.

Burleigh, T. D. 1958. *Georgia Birds*. Norman, Okla., Univ. of Okla. Press. 746 pp.

Forbush, E. H. 1925–29. *Birds of Massachusetts and other New England states*. Mass. Bd. of Agr. 3 vols.

Gabrielson, I. N., and Lincoln, F. C. 1959. *Birds of Alaska*. Washington, Wildlife Mgmt. Inst. 922 pp.

Jewett, S. G., and others. 1953. *Birds of Washington State*. Seattle, Univ. of Wash. Press. 767 pp.

Lowery, G. 1955. *Louisiana Birds*. Baton Rouge, L.S.U. Press. 556 pp.

Murphy, R. C., and Amadon, D. 1953. *Land birds of America*. New York, McGraw-Hill. 240 pp.

Palmer, R. S. 1949. *Maine birds*. Cambridge, Bull. Mus. Comp. Zool. 656 pp.

Peters, H. S., and Burleigh, T. D. 1951. *The birds of Newfoundland*. St. John's, Newf., Dept. of Nat. Resources. 431 pp.

Rand, A. L. 1956. *American water and game birds*. New York, E. P. Dutton. 238 pp.

Roberts, T. S. 1936. *The birds of Minnesota*. Minneapolis, Univ. of Minn. Press. 2 vols.

Snyder, L. L. 1950. *Ontario birds*. Toronto, Clarke, Irwin & Co. 248 pp.

——— 1957. *Arctic birds of Canada*. Toronto, Univ. of Toronto Press. 310 pp.

Sprunt, Alexander Jr. 1954. *Florida bird life*. New York, Coward-McCann. 527 pp.

Taverner, P. A. 1938. *Birds of Canada*. Toronto, Musson Book Co. 445 pp.

Todd, W. E. C. 1940. *Birds of western Pennsylvania*. Univ. of Pittsburgh Press. 730 pp.

WEST INDIES AND MIDDLE AMERICA

Blake, Emmet Reid. 1953. *Birds of Mexico*. Univ. of Chicago Press. 644 pp.

Bond, James. 1961. *Birds of the West Indies*. Boston, Houghton Mifflin. 256 pp.

Dickey, D. R. and van Rossem, A. J. 1938. *The birds of El Salvador*. Chicago, Field Mus. Nat. Hist. 609 pp.

Eisenmann, E. 1955. *The species of Middle American birds*. N. Y., Trans. Linn. Soc. 128 pp.

Friedmann, H., and others. 1950-58. *Distributional check-list of the birds of Mexico*. Cooper Orn. Club, Pac. Coast Avif. Pts. 1 & 2.

Griscom, L. 1932. *The distribution of bird life in Guatemala*. N. Y., Bull. Am. Mus. Nat. Hist. 439 pp.

Sturgis, B. B. 1928. *Field book of birds of the Panama Canal Zone*. New York, G. P. Putnam's & Sons. 466 pp.

Sutton, G. M. 1951. *Mexican birds, first impressions*. Norman, Okla., Univ. of Okla. Press. 282 pp.

Wetmore, A., and Swales, B. H. 1931. *The birds of Haiti and the Dominican Republic*. U.S. Nat. Mus. Bull. 155. 483 pp.

SOUTH AMERICA

Chapman, F. M. 1917. *The distribution of bird-life in Colombia*. Bull. Am. Mus. Nat. Hist. 729 pp.

———. 1926. *The distribution of bird-life in Ecuador*. Bull. Am. Mus. Nat. Hist. 784 pp.

Goodall, J. D., Johnson, H. W., and Philippi, R. A. 1946-51. *Las aves de Chile*. Buenos Aires. 2 vols. (in Spanish)

Haverschmidt, F. 1955. *List of the birds of Surinam*. Utrecht, Netherlands. 153 pp.

Hellmayr, C. E. 1932. *The birds of Chile*. Field Mus. Nat. Hist. 472 pp.

Mitchell, M. H. 1957. *Observations on birds of southeastern Brazil*. Univ. of Toronto Press. 258 pp.

Murphy, R. C. 1936. *Oceanic birds of South America*. New York, Am. Mus. Nat. Hist. 2 vols.

Olrog, C. C. 1959. *Las Aves Argentinas, una guia de campo*. Tucuman, Argentina, Inst. "Miguel Lillo", 343 pp. (in Spanish)

Wetmore, A. 1926. *Birds of Argentina, Paraguay, Uruguay, and Chile*. U.S. Nat. Mus. Bull. 448 pp.

AFRICA

Bannerman, David A. 1951-53. *Birds of West and Equatorial Africa*. Edinburgh, Oliver & Boyd. 2 vols.

Cave, F. O., and Macdonald, J. D. 1955. *Birds of the Sudan*. Edinburgh, Oliver & Boyd.

Chapin, James P. 1932-54. *The birds of the Belgian Congo*. New York, Bull. Am. Mus. Nat. Hist. 4 vols.

Mackworth-Praed, C. W., and Grant, C. H. B. 1952-55. *Birds of eastern and northeastern Africa*. London, Longmans, Green & Co. 2 vols.

Roberts, A. 1957. *The birds of South Africa*. (Rev. Ed.) Cape Town, Cape Times Ltd. 504 pp.

Van Someren, V. G. L. 1956. *Days with birds*. Fieldiana: Chicago Nat. Hist. Mus. 520 pp.

ISLAND AREAS

Baker, R. H. 1951. *The avifauna of Micronesia*. Lawrence, Univ. of Kansas Press. 359 pp.

Cayley, N. W. 1931. *What bird is that? A guide to the birds of Australia.* Sydney, Angus & Robertson. 320 pp.

Delacour, Jean, and Mayr, Ernst. 1946. *Birds of the Philippines.* New York, Macmillan. 309 pp.

Falla, R. A., and others. 1953. *Checklist of New Zealand birds.* Wellington, N. Z., Reed Pub. 68 pp.

Iredale, T. 1956. *Birds of New Guinea.* Melbourne, Georgian House. 2 vols.

Mayr, E. 1945. *Birds of the southwest Pacific.* New York, Macmillan. 316 pp.

Oliver, W. R. B. 1955. *New Zealand birds.* Wellington, A. H. & A. W. Reed. 661 pp.

Rand, A. L. 1936. *The distribution and habits of Madagascar birds.* Bull. Am. Mus. Nat. Hist., 72:143-499.

Salomonsen, F. 1950. *The birds of Greenland.* Copenhagen, Munksgaard. 607 pp.

Serventy, D. L., and Whittell, H. M. 1951. *A handbook of the birds of western Australia.* Perth, Paterson Brokensha Pty. Ltd. 384 pp.

Smythies, B. 1960. *The birds of Borneo.* London, Oliver & Boyd. 562 pp.

TAXONOMY AND DISTRIBUTION

Amadon, Dean. 1957. *Remarks on the classification of the perching birds (order Passeriformes).* Proc. Zool. Soc. Calcutta : 259-268.

American Ornithologists' Union Committee. 1957. *Check-list of North American birds.* 5th Ed. 691 pp.

Beecher, William J. 1953. *A phylogeny of the Oscines.* Auk, 70:270-333.

Delacour, Jean, and Vaurie, Charles. 1957. *A classification of the Oscines (Aves).* Los Angeles County Mus. Contr. Sci : 1-16.

Hellmayr, C. E. 1919-49. *Catalogue of birds of the Americas.* Chicago, Field Mus. Nat. Hist. 15 vols.

Mayr, Ernst. 1958. *The sequence of songbird families.* Condor, 60:194-195.

Mayr, Ernst, and Amadon, Dean. 1951. *A classification of recent birds.* Am. Mus. Nov. 1496:1-42.

Peters, J. L. 1931-60. *Check-list of birds of the world.* Cambridge, Mass., Harvard Univ. Press. 8 vols.

Ridgway, R., and Friedman, H. 1901-50. *Birds of North and Middle America.* Washington, U. S. Nat. Mus. Bull. 50. 11 vols.

Storer, Robert W. 1959. *The arrangement of songbird families.* Condor, 61:152-153.

Stresemann, Erwin. 1927-34. *Aves*, in *Kükenthal und Krumbach, Handbuch der Zoologie.* 899 pp. (in German)

———. 1959. *The status of avian systematics and its unsolved problems.* Auk, 76:269-280.

Tordoff, Harrison B. 1954. *A systematic study of the avian family Fringillidae based on the structure of the skull.* Univ. Mich. Mus. Zool. Misc. Publ. No. 81, 42 pp.

Vaurie, Charles, 1959-65. *The birds of the Palearctic fauna, a systematic reference.* London, Witherby. 2 vols.

Wetmore, Alexander. 1960. *A classification for the birds of the world.* Smithsonian Misc. Coll. Vol. 139(11): 1-37.

BIRD BIOLOGY, HABIT, AND BEHAVIOUR

Allen, G. M. 1925. *Birds and their attributes.* Boston, Marshall Jones. 338 pp.

Bent, A. C. 1919-58. *Life Histories of North American Birds.* Bull. U. S. Nat. Mus. 20 vols.

Blaikie, A. H. and Henderson, J. A. *Nests and eggs.* Edinburgh, Nelson. 78 pp.

Goodwin, Derek. 1961. *Bird behaviour.* London, Museum Press. 123 pp.

Hann, H. W. 1953. *The biology of birds.* Ann Arbor, Mich., Edwards Bros. 153 pp.

Heinroth, O. and K. 1958. *The birds.* Ann Arbor, Mich., Univ. of Mich. Press. 181 pp.

Howard, E. 1948. *Territory in bird life.* London, Collins. 224 pp.

Kendeigh, S. C. 1952. *Parental care and its evolution in birds.* Univ. Ill. Biol. Mon., 22, 356 pp.

Lanyon, W. E. 1957. *The comparative biology of the meadowlarks.* Cambridge, Mass., Nutt. Orn. Club. 67 pp.

Lorenz, K. Z. 1952. *King Solomon's Ring.* New York, Crowell. 202 pp.

Macdonald, J. D. 1959. *Bird biology.* London, Museum Press. 128 pp.

Pettingill, O. S. Jr. 1956. *Laboratory and field manual of ornithology.* 3rd ed. Minneapolis, Minn:, Burgess Pub. Co. 379 pp.

Skutch, A. F. 1954. *Life histories of Central American birds.* Cooper Orn. Soc., Pac. Coast Av., 448 pp.

———. 1960. *Life histories of Central American birds.* Part II. Pac. Coast Av. 593 pp.

Sturkie, P. D. 1954. *Avian physiology.* Ithaca, N. Y., Comstock Publ. Assn. 423 pp.

Thomson, J. A. 1923. *The biology of birds.* New York, Macmillan Co. 436 pp.

Tinbergen, N. 1953. *The Herring Gull's world.* London, Collins. 225 pp.

———. 1954. *Bird life.* Oxford Univ. Press. 64 pp.

———. 1958. *Curious naturalists.* London, Country Life Ltd. 282 pp.

Van Tyne, J., and Berger, A. J. 1959. *Fundamentals of ornithology.* New York, John Wiley & Sons. 624 pp.

Wallace, G. J. 1955. *An introduction to ornithology.* New York, Macmillan. 443 pp.

Wing, Leonard W. 1956. *Natural history of birds.* New York, Ronald Press Co. 539 pp.

Wolfson, A. (ed.) 1955. *Recent studies in avian biology.* Urbana, Ill. Univ. of Ill. Press. 479 pp.

MONOGRAPHS ON SPECIES, GROUPS, AND SPECIAL SUBJECTS

Allen, R. P. 1942. *The Roseate Spoonbill.* New York, Nat. Aud. Soc. 142 pp.

———. 1947. *The flame birds.* New York, Dodd, Mead. 333 pp.

———. 1953. *The Whooping Crane.* New York. Nat. Aud. Soc. 246 pp.

———. 1956. *The Flamingos: their life history and survival.* New York, Nat. Aud. Soc. 285 pp.

———. 1957. *On the trail of vanishing birds.* New York, McGraw-Hill Book Co. 251 pp.

Amadon, Dean. 1950. *The Hawaiian Honeycreepers.* Bull. Am. Mus. Nat. Hist. 95(4): 151-262.

Archey, G. 1941. *The Moa.* Aukland, N. Z., Unity Press Ltd. 119 pp.

Armstrong, E. A. 1955. *The Wren.* New York, Macmillan. 312 pp.

———. 1958. *The folklore of birds.* Boston, Houghton Mifflin. 272 pp.

Baldwin, P. H. 1953. *Annual cycle, environment and evolution in the Hawaiian Honeycreepers.* Univ. Calif. Publ. Zool. 52: 285-398.

Banko, W. E. 1960. *The Trumpeter Swan.* Washington, No. Am. Fauna 63. 214 pp.

Bock, Walter J. 1956. *A generic review of the family Ardeidae (Aves).* Am. Mus. Nov. No. 1779:1-49.

———. 1958. *A generic review of the plovers (Charadriinae, Aves).* Bull. Mus. Comp. Zool: 27-97.

Brodkorb, P. 1960. *How many species of birds have existed?* Gainesville, Bull. Fla. State Mus., 5:41-53.

Broun, Maurice. 1949. *Hawks aloft.* New York, Dodd, Mead. 222 pp.

Buxton, John. 1950. *The Redstart.* London, Collins. 180 pp.

Delacour, Jean. 1946. *Les timaliines.* Ois. Rev. Franc. Orn. 16:7-36.

———. 1951. *The Pheasants of the World.* London. Country Life Ltd. 347 pp.

———. 1954-60. *The Waterfowl of the world.* London, Country Life. 3 vols.

Fisher, James. 1952. *The Fulmar.* London, Collins. 492 pp.

Fisher, James, and Lockley, R. M. 1954. *Seabirds.* London, Collins. 320 pp.

Friedmann, Herbert. 1929. *The cowbirds.* Springfield, Ill. 421 pp.

———. 1948. *The parasitic cuckoos of Africa.* Wash. Acad. Sci. 204 pp.

———. 1955. *The honey-guides.* U. S. Nat. Mus. Bull. 208. 292 pp.

———. 1960. *The parasitic weaverbirds.* U. S. Nat. Mus. Bull. 223. 196 pp.

Greenewalt, C. H. 1960. *Hummingbirds.* New York, Doubleday. 250 pp.

Griscom, L., and Sprunt, A. 1957. *The warblers of America.* New York, Devin-Adair. 356 pp.

Jameson, William. 1959. *The Wandering Albatross.* New York, Wm. Morrow & Co. 128 pp.

Knight, J. A. 1947. *Ruffed Grouse.* New York, A. Knopf. 271 pp.

Koford, C. B. 1953. *The California Condor.* New York, Nat. Aud. Soc. 154 pp.

Kortright, F. H. 1942. *Ducks, geese, and swans of North America.* Washington, Am. Wildlife Inst. 476 pp.

Lack, D. 1943. *The life of the Robin.* London, Witherby. 200 pp.

———. 1947. *Darwin's finches.* Cambridge Univ. Press. 208 pp.

———. 1956. *Swifts in a tower.* London, Mittmen. 239 pp.

Lockley, R. M. 1942. *Shearwaters.* London, J. M. Dent & Son. 238 pp.

Lowery, G. H., Jr. 1951. *A quantitative study of the nocturnal migration of birds.* Univ. Kansas Pubs. Mus. Nat. Hist. 3(2): 361-472.

Matthews, G. V. T. 1955. *Bird migration.* Cambridge Univ. Press. 141 pp.

Mayfield, Harold. 1960. *Kirtland's Warbler.* Cranbrook Inst. Sci. 242 pp.

Meyerriecks, A. J. *Comparative breeding behavior of four species of North American herons.* Cambridge, Nutt. Orn. Club. 158 pp.

Nice, M. M. 1937-43. *Studies in the life history of the Song Sparrow.* Trans. Linn. Soc. of N. Y. 2 vols.

Oliver, W. R. B. 1949. *The Moas of New Zealand and Australia.* Wellington, N. Z. 206 pp.

Phillips, J. C. 1922-26. *A natural history of the ducks.* Boston, Houghton Mifflin. 4 vols.

Richdale, L. E. 1951. *Sexual behavior in the penguins.* Lawrence, Univ. of Kansas Press. 316 pp.

———. 1957. *A population study of the penguins.* New York, Ox. Univ. Press. 195 pp.

Schorger, A. W. 1955. *The Passenger Pigeon.* Madison, Univ. of Wisc. Press. 432 pp.

Sladen, W. J. L. 1958. *The Pygoscelid Penguins.* Falkland Ids. Dep. Serv. Sc. Rpts. No. 17. 97 pp.

Smith, S. 1950. *The Yellow Wagtail.* London, Collins. 172 pp.

Stanford, J. K. 1949. *The awl-birds.* New York, Devin-Adair. 90 pp.

Stoddard, Herbert. 1931. *The Bobwhite Quail.* New York, Charles Scribner's Sons. 559 pp.

Tanner, J. T. 1942. *The Ivory-billed Woodpecker.* New York, Nat. Aud. Soc. 111 pp.

Walkinshaw, L. H. 1949. *The Sandhill Cranes.* Bloomfield Hills, Mich., Cranbrook Inst. 202 pp.

Warham, John. 1956. *The technique of photographing birds.* London, Focal Press. 199 pp.

FIELD GUIDES & BIRD WATCHING

Campbell, Bruce. 1952. *Bird watching for beginners.* Harmondsworth, Penguin Books. 240 pp.

Fisher, James. 1941. *Watching birds.* Harmondsworth, Penguin Books. 192 pp.

———. 1948-55. *Bird recognition.* Harmondsworth, Penguin Books. 3 vols.

Hickey, J. J. 1943. *A guide to bird watching.* New York, Oxford Univ. Press. 262 pp.

Hutson, J. P. W., ed. 1956. *The ornithologists' guide.* New York, Philosophical Lib. 275 pp.

Lister, M. 1956. *The bird watcher's reference book.* London, Phoenix House. 256 pp.

McElroy, T. P. Jr. 1950. *Handbook of attracting birds.* New York, A. Knopf. 163 pp.

Peterson, R. T. 1961. *A field guide to western birds.* Boston, Houghton Mifflin. 366 pp.

———. 1947. *A field guide to the birds.* Boston, Houghton Mifflin. 290 pp.

———. 1957. *The bird watcher's anthology.* New York, Harcourt Brace & Co. 401 pp.

———. 1960. *A field guide to the birds of Texas.* Boston, Houghton Mifflin. 304 pp.

Peterson, R. T., and others. 1954. *A field guide to the birds of Britain and western Europe.* London, Collins. 318 pp.

Pough, R. H. 1946–51. *Audubon bird guide: Eastern landbirds; Water birds.* New York, Doubleday. 2 vols.

———. 1957. *Audubon western bird guide.* New York, Doubleday. 316 pp.

Sandars, E. 1927. *A bird book for the pocket.* London, Oxford Univ. Press. 247 pp.

Saunders, A. A. 1951. *A guide to bird song.* New York, Doubleday. 307 pp.

Westell, W. P. *Let's watch birds.* Edinburgh, Nelson. 258 pp.

Zim, H. S., and Gabrielson, I. N. 1956. *Birds.* New York, Golden Press. 160 pp.

INDEX

(Asterisks refer to illustrations; those numbers in italics show text references other than main account, which is either close to the species illustrated or else shown in roman type.)

Acanthis flammea, 302*
Achanthisitta, 212
Acanthisittidae, 212
Accentor, Alpine, 262*; Mountain, 263
Accipiter gentilis, 76*
Accipitridae, 75
Acridotheres, 271
Acrocephalus arundinaceus, 256*
Acropternis orthonyx, 202*
Acryllium vulturinum, 99*
Actitis macularia, 121*
Actophilornis africana, 116*
Aegithalos caudatus, 236*; *concinnus*, 236*
Aegithina tiphia, 245*
Aegotheles albertisi, 161*
Aegothelidae, 161
Aepyornis maximus, 14
Aethia cristatella, 139*
Agamia agami, 54*
Agapornis personata, 146*
Aglaiocercus kingi, 171*
Agriocharis ocellata, 99*
Ailuroedus crassirostris, 231*
Aix galericulata, 70*; *sponsa*, 70*
Ajaia ajaja, 60*
Alauda arvensis, 215*
Alaudidae, 215
Albatrosses, Black-browed, 32, 33; Black-footed, 30*, 32; Buller's, 32; Grey-headed, 33; Laysan, 30*, 32; Light-mantled Sooty, 33; Royal, 33; Short-tailed, 33; Sooty, 33; Steller's, 33; Wandering, 30*, 33*; Waved, 33; Yellow-nosed, 33
Alca torda, 138*
Alcedinidae, 175
Alcedo atthis, 176*
Alcidae, 137
Alectoris rufa, 91*
Alectura lathami, 85*
Alopochen aegyptiaca, 66*
Amazon, Red-fronted, 147; White-fronted, 147; Yellow-fronted, 147; Yellow-headed, 146*, 147
Amazona ochrocephala, 146*

Amblyornis subalaris, 230*
Anas acuta, 68*; *crecca* 68*; *clypeata*, 68*; *cyanoptera*, 68*; *formosa*, 68*; *penelope*, 68*; *platyrhynchos*, 68*; *querquedula*, 68*
Anatidae, 64
Andigena laminirostra, 188*
Anhima cornuta, 63*
Anhimidae, 63
Anhinga anhinga, 41*, 45*
Anhingidae, 45
Anis, 153
Anodorhynchus hyacinthus, 149*
Anoüs stolidus, 130*
Anser albifrons, 64*; *anser*, 66*; *indicus*, 66*
Anseranatinae, 67
Anseriformes, 63
Antbirds, 199; Chestnut-backed, 200*; Spotted, 200*
Antcatcher, White-faced, 199, 200*
Antcreepers, 201
Antpipits, Black-cheeked, 201*
Antpittas, Scaled, 200*; Streak-chested, 200*
Antshrikes, 201; Barred, 200*; Great, 200*
Ant-thrushes, 201
Antvireos, 201
Antwren, White-flanked, 200*
Anthropoides virgo, 103*
Anthropornis, 27
Anthus spinoletta, 264*
Apalopteron, 241
Apapane, 284
Aplonis metallica, 272
Apodidae, 165
Apodiformes, 164
Apostle Bird, 228
Aptenodytes forsteri, 26*, 29; *patagonicus*, 26*, 29
Apterygiformes, 15
Apteryx australis, 15*
Apus caffer, 165*
Aquila chrysaëtos, 78*
Ara ararauna, 149*; *macao*, 149*; *militaris*, 149*
Arachnothera longirostris, 278*

Araçari, Double-collared, 189*; Green, 189*
Aramidae, 106
Aramides ypecaha, 107*
Aramus guarana, 106*, 109*
Aratinga guarouba, 146*
Archaeopteryx, 8*, 12, 63
Archaeotrogon, 172
Archilochus colubris, 171*
Ardea herodias, 50*, 54; *purpurea*, 51*
Ardeidae, 50
Ardeola, 53
Arenaria interpres, 120*
Argusianus argus, 95*
Arremon, 299
Arremonops, 299
Artamidae, 267
Artamus superciliosus, 267*
Asity, Schlegel's, 212; Velvet, 212*
Astrapia stephaniae, 234
Atrichornis rufescens, 214*
Atrichornithidae, 214
Auklet, Crested, 139*; Japanese, 139; Least, 139; Parakeet, 139; Rhinoceros, 139; Whiskered, 139
Auks, 38, 115, 137; Great, 14, 137*; Little, 138*, 139
Aulacorhynchus prasinus, 189*
Automolus, 199
Avadavat, Red, 302*, 304
Avocets, 123; American, 120*; Australian, 124
Aythya marila, 69*; *valisineria*, 69*

Babblers, 240; Ground, 241; Jungle, 242, (Striped, 240*); Malay Rail, 241; Red-capped, 240*; Scimitar, 242, (Grey-crowned, 240*); Shrike-, 242, (Redwinged (Black-crowned), 240* 242); Tit, 242; Wren, 242
Balaeniceps rex, 56*
Balaenicipitidae, 55
Bald Crow, 241*
Balearica pavonina, 103*

Bananaquits, 284, 286*
Barbets, Black-collared, 185*; Crimson-breasted, 185; Golden-throated, 185*; Toucan, 185*
Bare-eye, Black-spotted, 200*
Basileuterus, 286
Becards, Jamaican, 203; Rose-throated, 204; White-winged, 204
Bee-eaters, 179; Carmine, 180*; European, 180*; Madagascar, 179; Rainbow, 179; Red-throated, 180*
Bellbirds, 203, 276; Three-wattled, 203, 204*; Black-winged, 203; Naked-throated, 203; New Zealand, 276; White, 203
Bellmagpies, Grey, 229; Western, 229
Birds of Paradise, *229*, 232; Blue, 233*, 234; Count Raggi's, 233*; Emperor of Germany, 234; Empress of Germany, 234; Enamelled, 234; Greater, 234; King, 234; King of Saxony, 233*, 234; Lesser Superb, 235; Little King, 233*; Magnificent, 233*, 234; Manucodes, 232, 235, (Black, 233, 235, Trumpeter, 232); Prince Rudolph's, 233*; Princess Stephanie's, 234; Red, 234; Red-plumed, 233*; Ribbon-tailed, *233*, 234; Riflebird, Magnificent, 233*; 235, (Queen Victoria's, 234); Sickle-bills, 234; Six-plumed, 234; Standard-winged, 233*; Superb, 232*; Twelve-wired, 233*, 234; Wilson's, 232*, 234
Bishop, Red, 305*, 307
Bitterns, American, 52*; Black Mangrove, 52; Least, 50*, 52; Little, 52*; Tiger, 53
Blackbirds, American, 287; Brewer's, 288; European, 252*; Military, 287; Red-breasted, 287, 290*; Red-winged, 288; Rusty, 287;

Blackbirds (*continued*)
Yellow-headed, 287, 290*;
Yellow-shouldered, 287
Black-cap, 255, 256*
Bluebirds, Eastern, 253*; Fairy,
245*; Mountain, 253; Western, 253
Bluethroat, 254*
Bobolink, 289, 290*
Bombycilla garrulus, 265*
Bombycillidae, 265
Bonasa umbellus, 88*
Boobies, Abbot's, 47; Blue-faced, 47*; Blue-footed, 47*;
Brown, 47*, 48*; Masked,
47; Peruvian, 47; Red-footed,
47*
Botaurus lentiginosus, 52*
Bowerbirds, *195*, 229; Baker's,
231; Gardeners, 231, (Crested, 231; Crestless, 230*,
231; Golden, 231; Golden-fronted, 231; Orange-crested,
230*, 231); Golden, 231,
(Blackfaced, 231*); Great
Grey, 231; Mocha-breasted,
230*; Regent, 230*, 231;
Sanford's Golden-crested,
230; Satin, 230*, 231; Spotted, 231*; Tooth-billed, 230
Brachypteriinae, 179
Brachypteryx, 254
Brain-fever Birds, 185
Brambling, 299, 300*
Branta canadensis, 66*; *leucopsis*, 66*; *ruficollis*, 66*
Bristle-head, Bornean, 275
Broadbills, 195; Black-throated,
196; Dusky, 196; Grauer's,
196; Green, 196, (Lesser,
196*); Long-tailed 196*;
Magnificent, 196; Red-sided,
196
Brolga, 105
Brontornis, 112
Bronze-wings, 145
Brownbuls, 244
Bubalornis albirostris, 304*
Bubo lacteus, 155*; *virginianus*,
156*
Bubulcus ibis, 51*
Bucco capensis, 188*
Bucconidae, 187
Bucephala islandica, 69*
Buceros bicornis, 181*
Bucerotidae, 182
Budgerigar, 147*
Bulbuls, 243; Black-capped,
244; Brown-eared, 244; Red-whiskered, 243*; White-cheeked, 244; White-eared,
244; White-vented, 244
Bullfinch, 301*
Buntings, *295*, 300; Black-headed, 300*; Cape, 300;
Cirl, 300; Corn, 300; Golden-breasted, 300; Indigo, 296;
Lark, 298; Lazuli, 296; Little, 300; Meadow, 300*; Ortolan, 300*; Painted, 296*;
Pine, 300; Reed, 300; Rustic,
300; Snow, 298*; Yellow, 300
Buphagus africanus, 274*
Burhinidae, 125
Burhinus oedicnemus, 125*
Bustards, 113; Australian, 115;
Black-bellied, 115; Great, 113,
114*, 115; Kori, 114*
Butcherbirds, 228, *269*; Australian, 228; Grey, 229*

Buteo jamaicensis, 77*
Butorides virescens, 50*, 53
Buzzards, 73, 75, 79; English,
79; Honey-, 77

Cacatua galerita, 148*; *leadbeateri*, 148*
Caciques, 287;
Cairina moschata, 68*
Calcarius lapponicus, 298*; *ornatus*, 298*
Calidris tenuirostris 121*
Callaeidae, 227
Callaeus cinerea, 227*
Calypte helenae, 171*
Calyptomena viridis, 196*
Camarhynchus pallidus, 297*
Campephaga phoenicea, 219*
Campephagidae, 219
Campephilus principalis, 192*
Campylopterus hemileucus, 170*
Campyloramphus trochilirostris,
197*
Campylorhynchus brunneicapillus, 248*
Canachites canadensis, 89*
Canary, 303
Capella gallinago, 122*
Capercaillie, 88*
Capitonidae, 185
Caprimulgidae, 162
Caprimulgiformes, 159
Caprimulgus vociferus, 164*
Caracaras, 83*
Cardinals, *295*, 296*; Crested,
299; Dominican, 299
Carduelis carduelis, 301*; *spinus*, 301*
Cariama cristata, 112*
Cariamidae, 112
Carinatae, 11
Carpodacus mexicanus, 301*
Casarca ferruginea, 69*
Casmerodius alba, 51*
Cassidix mexicanus, 290*
Cassowaries, 18; Australian,
19*; Bennett's, 19*
Casuariiformes, 18
Casuarius bennetti, 19*; *casuarius*, 19*
Catamblyrhynchus diadema,
292*
Catbirds, 230, *249*, 250; Black,
250; Green, 230, 231*; White-throated, 230
Catharacta skua, 129*
Cathartes aura, 72*
Cathartidae, 73
Catharus aurantiirostris, 251*
Centrocercus urophasianus, 88*
Centropus grilli, 152*
Centurus aurifrons, 193*;
radiolatus, 192*
Cephalopterus ornatus, 205*
Cepphus grylle, 138*
Cereopsis novae-hollandiae, 64*
Certhia familiaris, 238*
Certhiidae, 237
Cettia diphone, 257*
Ceyx erithacus, 177*
Chachalaca, Rufous-bellied, 87*
Chaetorhynchus, 221
Chaetura gigantea, 165*; *pelagica*, 165*, 166
Chaffinch, 299
Chalcomitris senegalensis, 278*
Chalcostigma herrani, 171*
Chamaeidae, 243

Charadriidae, 118
Charadriiformes, 115
Charadrius semipalmatus, 120*;
vociferus, 120*
Chat, Palm, 266*; Rose-breasted, 285*; Yellow-breasted,
285
Chauna chavaria, 63*
Chen hyperborea, 66*
Chenopis atrata, 67*
Chickadee, Black-capped, 236
Chicken, Domestic, 97; Mother
Carey's, 37; Pharaoh's, 75;
Prairie, 89, 90*
Chiffchaff, 256
Chionididae, 127
Chionis alba, 128*
Chlamydera maculata, 231*
Chloephaga leucoptera, 66*
Chloroceryle amazona, 176*
Chlorophonia occipitalis, 293*
Chloropseidae, 245
Chloropsis aurifrons, 245*
Chordeiles minor, 164*
Choriotis kori, 114*
Chough, 223*; Alpine, 226;
Common, 226; White-winged,
228*
Chrysococcyx cupreus, 152*
Chrysocolaptes lucidus, 193*
Chrysoenas victor, 143*
Chrysolampis mosquitus, 171*
Chrysolophus amherstiae, 92*;
pictus, 92*
Chuck-will's-widow, 163
Chunga, 112
Cicinnurus regius, 232*
Ciconia ciconia, 57*; *nigra*, 57*
Ciconiidae, 56
Ciconiiformes, 50
Cinclidae, 246
Cinclosoma cinnamomeum,
240*
Cinclus cinclus, 246*; *mexicanus*, 246*
Cinnyricinclus leucogaster, 273*
Cinnyris asiaticus, 278*; *regius*,
278*; *venustus*, 278*
Circus cyaneus, 69*
Ciridops anna, 284
Cissa chinensis, 225*; *ornata*,
225*
Cisticola juncides, 256*
Cistothorus platensis 247*
Cladorhynchus leucocephalus,
120*
Clamator coromandus, 152*
Clangula hyemalis, 69*
Climacteris erythrops, 239*
Cnemophilus macgregorii, 230*
Coccyzus americanus, 152*
Cochleariidae, 55
Cochlearius cochlearius, 55*
Cochoas, 251
Cockatoos, Great Black, 148*;
Leadbeater's, 148*; Palm,
148*; Sulphur-crested, 148*;
White, 148
Cocks-of-the-rock, 203, 204,
205*; Peruvian, 205*
Coeligena torquata, 170*
Coereba flaveola, 286*
Coerebidae, 284
Colaptes auratus, 192*
Colies, 174
Coliiformes, 174
Colinus virginianus, 91*
Colius macrourus, 174*
Collocalia inexpectata, 167*
Columba livia, 144*

Columbiformes, 140
Columbigallina passerina, 144*
Condor, Andean, 72*, 73; California, 72*, 73
Conebills, 284
Conopophaga melanops, 201*;
melanogaster, 201*
Conopophagidae, 201
Contopus virens, 207*
Conure, Golden, 146*
Coots, *22*, 107, *124*; American,
110*; Common, 108; Horned,
108
Coppersmith, 185
Coraciidae, 179
Coraciiformes, 175
Coracina lineata, 219*
Coragyps atratus, 72*
Corcorax melanorhamphus,
228*
Cordon-bleu, Red-cheeked, 303*
Cormorants, *38*, 43; Brandt's,
44; Cape, 43; Common, 40*,
43; Double-crested, 40*, 44,
132; Flightless, 44; Great,
40*, 43, 44; Guanay, 40*, 43,
44; King, 44; Pallas's, 44;
Pied, 44; Pygmy, 44; Red-faced, 44*; Sea, 43; Spectacled, 44; Spotted, 44; White-breasted, 44
Corvidae, 223
Corvus brachyrhynchos, 224*;
corax, 224*; *cornix*, 224*
Cosmopsarus regius, 274*
Cotinga amabilis, 204*
Cotingas, *195*, 203, *210*; Black-necked, Red, 204*; Lovely,
204; Pompadour, 203, 205*;
Snowy, 203
Cotingidae, 203
Coturnix coturnix, 95, 96*
Coucals, 154; Black, 152*
Coursers, Cream-coloured, 126*;
Indian, 126*
Cowbirds, *151*, 248, 289, 307;
Baywinged, 289, 291; Bronze,
291; Brown-headed, 291;
Giant, 289, 291; Redeyed,
291; Screaming, 291; Shiny,
290*, 291
Cracidae, 87
Cracticidae, 228
Cracticus torquatus, 229*
Crakes, 107; Black, 107; Corn,
107; Ruddy, 107*; Sora,
107; Spotted, 107*; Yellow,
107
Cranes, 101, 102; Black-necked,
105; Common, 105; Crowned,
103*, 105; Demoiselle, 103*,
105; Japanese, 105; Sandhill,
103*, 105; Sarus, 104*, 105;
Wattled, 105; White, 105;
White-headed, 105; White-naped, 104*, 105; Whooping,
14, 103*, 105
Craspedophora magnifica, 233*
Crax rubra, 86*
Creepers, *196*, 237, 239; Brown,
237; Plain-headed, 239; Red-browed, 239*; Red-fronted,
239; Spotted, 239*; Striped-headed, 239*; Tree, 237,
238*; Wall, 238*; Wood,
196
Crossbills, 302, 303; Red, 302,
303; White-winged, 301*,
302
Crossoptilon mantchuricum, 93*
Crotophaginae, 153

Crows, *152, 195, 223*; Bald, 241*, 243; Black, 223; Carrion, 223, 225; Common, 223, 224*; Hooded, 224*; House, 223; Jungle, 223; King, 220*, 221; Wattled, 227*

Crowtits, 242; Vinous-throated, 241*, 242

Crypturellus variegatus, 21*

Cuckoos, 150, 151, *182, 307*; Black-billed, 153; Common, 151; 152*; Drongo-, 152, 221; Emerald, 152*; Great Spotted, 152; Guira, 153; Malayan Ground, 154; Peacock, 154; Pheasant, 154; Red-winged Indian, 152*; Shining, 152, 153; Striped, 154; Yellow-billed, 152*, 153

Cuckoo-shrikes, 219, Barred, 219*; Ground, 220; Oriole, 220; Red-shouldered, 219*; Wattled, 220

Cuculidae, 151

Cuculiformes, 150

Cuculus canorus, 152*

Curassows, 87; Great, 86*; Great Razor-billed, 86*

Curlews, 120; Bristle-thighed, 121; Eskimo, 120; Eurasian, 120; Hudsonian, 120; Long-billed, 120, 121*; Madagascar, 120; Stone, 125*, 126

Cursorius coromandelicus, 126*; *cursor*, 126*

Cyanerpes cyaneus, 294*

Cyanocitta cristata, 225*

Cyanolyca turcosa, 225*

Cyanopica cyanus, 225*

Cyanoptila cyanomelana, 260*

Cyclarhis gujanensis, 282*

Cygnus buccinator, 67*; *melancoryphus*, 67*; *olor*, 67*

Cypseloides, 166

Cypsiurus parvus, 166*

Dacelo gigas, 176*

Dacninae, 293

Daphoenositta, 239

Daption capensis, 31*

Darters, *see* Anhingas

Dendrocolaptes certhia, 197*

Dendrocolaptidae, 196

Dendrocopos, 191

Dendroica caerulescens, 285*; *magnolia*, 286*

Dendrocygna autumnalis, 70*; *viduata*, 68*

Dendronanthus indicus, 264*

Diamondbirds, Red-tipped, 280; Spotted, 280; Yellow-tailed, 280*

Diatryma, 13, 112

Dicaeidae, 279

Dicaeum cruentatum, 279*; *hirundinaceum*, 280*

Dichromanassa rufescens, 51*

Dickcissel, 295

Dicruridae, 220

Dicrurus macrocercus, 220*

Diglossa baritula, 292*

Dinemellia dinemelli, 304*

Dinornis maximus, 14

Diomedea exulans, 30*, 33*; *immutabilis*, 30*; *nigripes*, 30*

Diomedeidae, 32

Diphyllodes magnificus, 233*; *respublica*, 232*

Dippers, Asiatic, 246; Common,

Dippers (*continued*) 246*; North American, 246*; White-headed, 246

Divers, Black-throated, 25*; Great Northern, 25*; Red-throated, 25*; White-throated, 25

Diving Petrels, Common, 38*; Georgian, 38; Magellan, 38; Peruvian, 38

Dodos, 140, 141*

Dolichonyx oryzivorus, 290*

Dollar Bird, 180

Domicella domicella, 146*

Dotterel, *see* Plovers

Dovekie, 138*, 139

Doves, 141; Collared Turtle, 145; Ground, 144*; Inca, 144*; Java, Turtle, 143*; Mourning, 144*, 145; Orange, 143*; Rock, 142, 144*; Turtle, 145; White-winged, 144*

Dowitchers, 122; Short-billed, 121*

Drepanididae, 283

Dromadidae, 125

Dromas ardeola, 125*

Dromiceidae, 20

Dromiceius novae-hollandiae, 19*

Dromococcyx, 154

Drongo-cuckoo, 152, *221*

Drongos, 220; Black, 220*, 221; Crested, 221; Grey, 220; Great Racquet-tailed, 220; Mountain, 221; Velvet-mantled, 221

Dryocopus, 194

Ducks, 64; Black, 68; Black-headed, 71; Bufflehead, 71; Canvas-back, 68, 69*; Dipping, 68; Diving, 69; Eiders, (Common, 70, 71*, King, 70, Spectacled, 70, 71*, Steller's, 69*, 70); Gadwall, 68, Goldeneye, 71, (Barrow's, 69*, 71); Goosander, 70; Harlequin, 69*, 71; Labrador, *14*, 71; Longtailed, 71; Mallard, 68*; Mandarin, 69, 70*; Mergansers, Hooded, 69*, 70, (Redbreasted, 70, 71*); Muscovy, 68*, 69; Musk, 71; Old Squaw, 69, 71; Perching, 69; Pink-headed, 65; Pintail, 68*; Pochard, 69; Red-head, 69; Ruddy, 69*, 71; Scaup, Greater, 69*; Scoters, (Black, 71; Surf, 69*, 71, Velvet, 71, White-winged, 71); Shelducks, (Common, 69, Crested, *14*, 68, Ruddy, 69*); Shoveler, 68*; Smew, 69*, 70; Steamer, 69, (Flightless, 68*); Stiff-tailed, 71; Teals, (Baical, 68*, Cinnamon, 68*, Cotton, 70, Garganey, 68*, Green-winged, 68*); Torrent, 68*; Tree, (Black-bellied, 70*, Fulvous, 68, White-faced, 68*); Whistling, 68; White-headed, 71; Wigeon, Eurasian, 68*; Wood, 69, 70*

Ducula concinna, 143*

Dulus dominicus, 266*

Dumetella carolinensis, 249*

Dunlin, 120*, 122

Dunnock, 263

Dupetor, 52

Eagles, 75, 80, 81; Bald, 79*, 81, *82*; Bateleur, 79*, 81; Golden, 78*, 80, 81; Harpy, 79*, 81; Ornate Hawk-, 80*; Serpent, 81; White-tailed Sea, 81

Earth-creeper, Striated, 199*

Eclectus, 147

Ectopistes migratorius, 145*

Egg, illustrations—*see* endpapers; text—*see* individual birds

Egrets, Cattle, 51*, 54; Common, 51*, 54; Intermediate, 54; Large, 51*, 54; Little, 54; Reddish, 51*, 54; Snowy, 51*, 54

Egretta thula, 51*

Elanoides forficatus, 76*

Elephant Birds, 14

Elopteryx, 38

Emberiza cioides, 300*; *hortulana*, 300*; *melanacephala*, 300*

Empidonax, 209; *virescens*, 207*, 209

Emus, 19*, 20

Ensifera ensifera, 171*

Ephippiorhynchus senegalensis, 57*

Eremophila alpestris, 215*

Erithacus rubecula, 253*

Erolia alpina, 120*; *minutilla*, 121*

Erythrura trichroa, 302*; *amandava*, 302*; *formosa*, 303*; *locustella*, 303*; *melanotis*, 303*; *nitidula*, 303*

Eudocimus albus, 59*; *ruber*, 59*

Eudromia elegans, 21*

Eudyptes crestatus, 29*

Eudyptula minor, 28*

Eumomota superciliosa, 180*

Euphonia, Yellow-crowned, 291*, 293

Eurylaimidae, 195

Eurypyga helias, 112*

Eutoxeres aquila, 171*

Excalfactoria chinensis, 91*

Fairy Bluebirds, *222*, 245*

Falco peregrinus, 84*; *sparverius*, 84*

Falconet, Red-thighed, 84*

Falconidae, 83

Falconiformes, 72

Falcons, 83; Laughing, 83; Peregrine, 83, 84*; Pygmy, 83

Fantails, *152*, 262

Ferminia cerverai, 248*

Ficedula narcissina, 261*

Figbird, Yellow, 222*

Finches, Blue-faced Parrot, 302*, 304; Cardinal, 295; Darwin's, 295, 297; American-European, 302, Galapagos, 295; Gold-, 301*, 302; Gouldian, 303*, 304; Green Tiger, 303*; Haw-, 303; House, 301*, 302; Large Ground, 297*; Locust, 303*; Melba, 303*; Mexican House, 302; Painted, 304; Parrot-, 302*, 304; Plush-capped, 294; Purple, 302; Purple-breasted, 304; Saffron, 299*; Scarlet, 302; Snow, 306;

Finches (*continued*) Weaver, 301, 306; Woodpecker, 297*; Zebra, 304

Finfoots, 22, 111, *124*; African, 112*

Firecrest, 257

Flamingos, Andean, 62; Greater, 61*, 62; James's, 62; Lesser, 62

Flickers, Red-shafted, 193; Yellow-shafted, 192*, 193

Florisuga mellivora, 170*

Flowerpeckers, 279; Midget, 280; Scarlet-backed, 279*

Flowerpiercer, 294; Cinnamon-bellied, 292*

Flycatchers, 207; Acadian, 207*, 209; Alder, 209; Boat-billed, 208; Broad-billed, 260; Derby, 207*, 208, 209; Great Crested, 208*, 209; Japanese Blue, 260*; Kiskadee, 207*, 209; Least, 209; Monarch, Black-naped, blue, 260, 261*; Narcissus, 260, 261*; Northern Royal, 207*, 208; Old World, 259; Paradise, 261*, (Black, 261*); Scissortailed, 208*, 209; Silky, spotted, 260, 261*, 265; Traill's, 209; Tyrant, 207*; Vermilion, 208*, 209

Formicariidae, 199

Fowl, Rock, 243; Bare-headed, 241*; Jungle, 97*; Maleo, 86; Mallee, 85*, 86; Scrub, 85

Fowl-like Birds, 85

Francolin, Chinese, 91*

Francolinus pintadeanus, 91*

Fratercula arctica, 139*

Fregata magnificens, 48*; *minor*, 48*

Fregatidae, 48

Friarbird, Noisy, 276* ·

Frigate-birds, 48; Ascension, 49; Christmas Island, 49; Great, 48*, 49; Lesser, 49; Magnificent, 48*, 49

Fringilla montifringilla, 300*

Fringillidae, 295

Frogmouths, 160; Grey Owlet, 161*; Tawny, 157*, 160

Fruitcrows, Crimson, 203; Purple-throated, 203

Fulica americana, 110*

Fulmar, 31*; Silver-grey, 36

Fulmarus glacialis, 31*

Furnariidae, 198

Furnarius rufus, 198*

Galbula dea, 188*

Galbulidae, 187

Gallicolumba luzonica, 143*, 145

Galliformes, 85

Gallinula chloropus, 109*

Gallinules, American, 109; Common, 109*; Purple, 108*, 109

Gallirallus australis, 110, 111*

Gallito, Brown, 202; Grey, 202*

Gallus gallus, 97*

Gannets, Australian, 46; Cape, 46; Northern, 46, 47*

Garrulax leucolophus, 240*

Garrulus glandarius, 225*

Gavia arctica, 25*; *immer*, 25*; *stellata*, 25*

Gaviformes, 24
Geese, 65; Abyssinian Blue-winged, 68; Andean, 68; Bar-headed, 66*, 67; Barnacle, 66*, 67; Bean, 65; Blue, 66; Brant, 67; Canada, 66*; Cape Barren, 64*, 65; Emperor, 66*; Egyptian, 66*, 68; Grey-lag, 65, 66*; Hawaiian, 67; Kelp, 68; Magellan, 66*; Orinoco, 68; Pied, 67; Pink-footed, 65; Pygmy, (Green, 70, Indian, 70); Red-breasted, 66*, 67; Ross's, 66; Snow, 66*, (Lesser, 66); Spur-wing, 64*, 65; Swan, 65; White-fronted, 64*, 65, (Lesser, 65)
Geisiloceros, 184
Gennaeus nycthemerus, 92*; *swinhoii*, 93*
Geococcyx californianus, 153*
Geospiza magnirostris, 297*
Glareola pratincola, 125*
Glareolidae, 126
Glaucidium brasilianum, 157*
Gnatcatcher, Blue-grey, 258*
Gnateaters, Black-breasted, 201*; Black-cheeked, 201*
Gnatwrens, 258
Goatsuckers, 159
Godwit, Bar-tailed, 121*
Goldcrest, 257
Goldfinch, American, 302; European, 301*, 302
Gonolek, Black-headed, 268*, 270
Goosander, 70
Gorsachius, 53
Goshawk, 76*, 77
Goura cristata, 143*
Grackles, 287; Boat-tailed, 288, 290*
Gracula religiosa, 271, 273*
Grallaria guatemalensis, 200*; *perspicillata*, 200*
Grallina cyanoleuca, 228*
Grallinidae, 227
Granatellus pelzelni, 285*
Grassquit, Yellow-faced, 299*
Grebes, 22, 108, 111, 124; Eared, 22; Great Crested, 22*; Horned, 22*, Little, 23*; Pied-billed, 23*; Red-necked, 22*; Sun, 111; Titicaca, 23
Greenbul, Yellow-streaked, 244*
Greenlet, Grey-headed, 282*
Greenshank, 119
Grenadiers, 303
Grosbeak, Black-headed, 296; Blue, 296*; Blue-black, 296; Evening, 302; Japanese, 303; Pine, 302; Rose-breasted, 296; Ultramarine, 296
Grouse, 88; Black, 88*, 89; Blue, 90; Hazel, 91; Red, 91; Ruffed, 88*, 90; Sage, 88*; Sharp-tailed, 89; Spruce, 89*, 90; Willow, 90*, 91
Gruidae, 102
Gruiformes, 101
Grus americana, 103*; *antigone*, 104*; *canadensis*, 103*; *vipio*, 104*
Guacharo, 160
Guanay, 40*, 43, 44
Guan, White-crested, 87*
Guillemot, Black, 137, 138*; Brünnich's, 138*; Common, 138, 139*
Guineafowls, Black, 98; Hel-

Guineafowls (*continued*) meted, 98; Vulturine, 98, 99*; White-breasted, 98
Guiraca caerulea, 296*
Gulls, 130; Black-headed, 131*, 132; Brown-headed, 132; Buller's, 132, 133; Burgomaster, 132; California, 130*, 132; Franklin's, 132; Glaucous, 132; Great Black-backed, 131*, 132; Heermann's, 131*; Herring, 131*, 132; Iceland, 132; Kittiwake, 130, 132; Laughing, 131*, 132; Little, 131; Ring-billed, 133; Ross's, 134; Saunders, 132; Silver, 133
Gygis alba, 130*
Gymnogyps californianus, 72*
Gymnostinops montezuma, 288*
Gyps fulvus, 75*
Gyrfalcon, 83

Habia rubica, 291*
Haematopodidae, 118
Haematopus palliatus, 121*
Halcyon chloris, 177*; *leucocephala*, 176*; *smyrnensis*, 176*
Haliaeetus leucocephalus, 79*
Haliastur indus, 76*
Hammerhead, 55, 56*
Harpactes oreskios, 172*
Harpia harpyja, 79*
Harriers, Hen, 81; Marsh, 81*
Hawfinch, 303
Hawk-eagle, Ornate, 80*
Hawks, 75, 154, 182; Broad-winged, 79; Cooper's, 78; Duck, 84; Fish, 82*; Marsh, 81*; Red-shouldered, 73, 79; Red-tailed, 73, 77*, 79; Sharp-shinned, 78; Sparrow, (American, 84*, European, 78); Swainson's, 79
Heath Hen, 14, 89
Heliornithidae, 111
Helmet Bird, 268
Helmet-shrikes, 270*
Hemipode, Collared, 102*
Hemiprocne longipennis, 165*
Hemiprocnidae, 167
Hen Harrier, 81*
Herons, 50; Agami, 54*; Black, 51*, 54; Blue, (Great, 50*, 54, Little, 51*, 54); Boatbilled, 55*; Buff-backed, 54; Chestnut-backed, 54; Goliath, 54; Grey, 54; Great White, 54; Green, 50*, 53; Imperial, 54; Louisiana, 54; Night, (Black-crowned, 51*, 53, Japanese, 53, Rufous, 53, Yellow-crowned, 51*, 53); Pied, 54; Pond, 53, 54; Purple, 51*, 54; Reef, 54; Squacco, 53; Sumatra, 54; Tiger, Lined, 52*, 53
Hesperornis, 12
Heteralocha acutirostris, 227*
Himantopus mexicanus, 120*
Hirundinidae, 216
Hirundo rustica, 216*
Histrionicus histrionicus, 69*
Hoatzin, 100*, 182
Honeycreepers, Blue, 294; Green, 284; Hawaiian, 283*; Red-legged, 294*; Thick-skinned, 284

Honeyeaters, 275; Cardinal, 277*; Helmeted, 275, 277*; White-eared, 275
Honeyguides, 151, 186, 289; Black-throated, 186; Greater, 185*, 186
Hoopoes, 181*, 182
Hoplopterus armatus, 120*
Hornbills, 182; Casqued, 183; Great, 181*, 183; Ground, 183; Helmeted, 182
Huia, 227*
Hummingbirds, 164, 168; Anna's, 169; Allen's, 169; Andean Rainbow, 168; Bee, 168, 171*; Broad-tailed, 169; Collared Inca, 170*; Coquettes, (Adorable, 170*, Frilled, 170*, Guiana, 170*); Crimson Topaz, 170*; Geoffroy's Wedgebill, 170*; Giant, 168, 171*; Goldthroat, 170*; Green-tailed Sylph, 171*; Loddiges' Racquet-tail, 168, 170*; Ruby and Topaz, 171*; Ruby-throated, 168, 171*; Sappho Comet, 171*; Streamertail, 171*; Thornbill, (Herran's, 171*, Popelaire's, 170*); Train-bearing Hermit, 171*; Violet Sabrewing, 170*; Violet-eared, 170, (Gould's, 170*), Whitenecked Jacobin, 170*; Whitetipped Sicklebill, 171*
Hydranassa caerulea, 51*, 54
Hydrobates pelagicus, 31*
Hydrobatidae, 37
Hydrophasianus chirurgus, 116*
Hylocichla guttata, 252*, 253; *mustelina*, 252*, 253
Hylophilus decurtatus, 282*
Hylophylax naevioides, 200*
Hyphanturgus ocularis, 305*
Hypocolius ampelinus, 266*
Hypositta corallirostris, 239*
Hypothymis azurea, 261*
Hypsipetes, 244

Ibisbill, 123, 124
Ibises, Glossy, 59, (White-faced, 59); Sacred, 59*; Scarlet, 59*; White, 59*; Wood, 57*
Icteridae, 287
Icterus icterus, 288*; *pectoralis*, 288*
Ichthyornis, 12
Iiwi, 284
Indicator indicator, 185*
Indicatoridae, 186
Iora, Common, 245*
Irena puella, 245*
Iridoprocne bicolor, 216*
Ixobrychus exilis, 50*; *minutus*, 52*

Jabiru mycteria, 57*, 58
Jacamars, 187; Great, 188*; Paradise, 188*
Jacamerops aurea, 188*
Jacana spinosa, 116*
Jaçanas, African, 116*; American, 116*; Pheasant-tailed, 116*
Jackdaw, 225
Jaegers, Long-tailed, 128*; Parasitic, 128*; Pomarine, 129*

Jays, Blue, 225*, 226; Canada, 226; Common, 226; Eurasian, 225*; Scrub, 226; Siberian, 226; Turquoise, 225*
Jumper, Grey, 228
Junco oreganus, 298*
Jynx torquilla, 194*

Kagu, 111, 112*, 113
Kaka, 149
Kakapo, 148
Kea, 149*
Kestrel, 84
Killdeer, 118
Kingbird, Eastern, 208*
Kingfishers, 175; Amazon, 176*; Belted, 175, 176*; Common, 175, 176*; Grey-hooded, 176*; Indian Three-toed, 177*; Pied, 176; Ruddy, 177; Sacred, 177; White-collared, 177*; White-throated, 176*
Kinglets, Formosan, 257, 258*; Golden-crowned, 257; Ruby-crowned, 257, 258*
Kinkimavo, 222
Kiskadee, Great, 207*, 209
Kites, Bat-eating, 76; Black, 77; Brahminy, 76*, 77; Everglade, 76*; Hook-billed, 77; Mississippi, 77; Plumbeous, 77; Swallow-tailed, 76*, 77; White-tailed, 76
Kittacincla malabarica, 253*
Kittiwake, 132
Kiwis, North Island, 15*; Stewart Island, 15*
Knot, 122; Great, 121*
Kokako, 227
Kookaburra, Laughing, 176*, 177

Lagopus lagopus, 90*
Lalage sueurii, 219*
Lammergeyer, 77
Lamprotornis, 272
Laniarius barbarus, 268*
Laniidae, 269
Lanius collurio, 268*; *excubitor*, 268*; *schach*, 268*
Lapwings, 119, 120*; 182; Red-wattled, 120*
Laridae, 130
Larks, Black, 215; Bush, 215; Horned, 215*; Meadow, 289; Shore, 215*; Sky, 215*
Larosterna inca, 134*
Larus argentatus, 131*; *atricilla*, 131*; *californicus*, 130*; *heermanni*, 131*; *marinus*, 131*; *ridibundus*, 131*
Laughing Thrushes, 242; White-crested, 240*
Laurillardia, 271
Leafbird, Golden-fronted, 245*
Leiothrix argentauris, 240*; *lutea*, 240*
Leipoa ocellata, 85*
Leistes militaris, 290*
Leptopterus madagascarinus, 268*
Leptoptilos crumeniferus, 57*
Leucotreron cincta, 143*
Limnodromus griseus, 121*
Limosa lapponica, 121*
Limpkin, 106*, 109*
Linnet, 302
Little Auk, 138*, 139

Lobivanellus indica, 120*
Lobotos, 220
Locustella certhiola, 256*
Locust-finch, 303*
Loddigesia mirabilis, 170*
Logrunners, 241
Lonchura ferruginosa, 302*
Longclaw, Yellow-throated, 264*
Longspurs, Chestnut-collared, 298*; Lapland, 298*, 299
Loons, *see* Divers
Lophodytes cucculatus, 69*
Lophophorus impejanus, 92*
Lophorina superba, 232*
Lophornis magnifica, 170*; *pavonis*, 170*
Lophortyx californica, 91*
Lophura diardi, 93*
Lorikeets, Painted, 148; Rainbow, 146*
Lory, Black-capped, 146*
Lovebirds, 147; Masked, 146*
Loxia leucoptera, 301*
Loxigilla, 299
Lunda cirrhata, 139*
Luscinia megarhynchos, 252*; *svecica*, 254*
Lybius torquatus, 185*
Lyrebirds, 213, *223*; Albert's, 213; Superb, 213*
Lyrurus tetrix, 88*

Macaws, Gold and Blue, 147, 149*; Hyacinth, 147, 149*; Military, 147, 149*; Red and Green, 147; Scarlet, 147, 149*
Macgregoria, 235
Macronyx croceus, 264*
Magpie-larks, 227, 228*
Magpies, Azure-winged, 225*; Ceylon Blue, 225*, 226; Common, 225*, 226; Green, 225*, 226; Yellow-billed, 226
Malcohas, 153
Mallard, 68*
Malurus lamberti, 258*
Mamo, 284
Manakins, 205, 229; Black and White, 206; Cirrhate, 206*; Gould's, 206; Pearl-headed, 206*; Thrush-like, 206; Yellow-thighed, 206*
Mannikins, Bronze, 304; Chestnut, 302*, 304
Manucodes, 232
Martins, African River, 218; Brown-backed, 218; Brown-chested, 217*; Grey-breasted, 217*; House, 218; Purple, 217*; Sand, 218
Meadowlarks, Eastern, 289; Western, 289, 290*
Megaceryle alcyon, 176*
Megalaima franklini, 185*
Megaloprepia magnifica, 143*
Megapodiidae, 85
Melanerpes erythrocephalus, 192*
Melanitta perspicillata, 69*
Melanophoyx ardesiaca, 51*
Melanotis caerulescens, 249*
Meleagrididae, 98
Meleagris gallopavo, 99*
Meliphaga cassidix, 277*
Meliphagidae, 275
Melitophagus bulocki, 180*
Melopsittacus undulatus, 147*
Menura novaehollandiae, 213*
Menuridae, 213

Merganetta armata, 68*
Mergansers, 70*
Mergellus albellus, 69*
Mergus serrator, 71*
Merlin, 83
Meropidae, 179
Merops apiaster, 180*; *nubicus*, 180*
Mesembriornis, 112
Mesia, Silver-eared, 240*
Mesites, Brown, 101*
Mesitornithidae, 101
Mesoenas unicolor, 101*
Micrathene whitneyi, 156*
Microbates, 258
Microgoura, 145
Microhierax caerulescens, 84*
Mimidae, 249
Mimus polyglottos, 249*
Miners, 199
Minivets, Flamed, 219*; Rosy, 219*
Mino coronatus, 272, 273*
Mirafra, 215
Mistletoe Bird, 280*
Mitu mitu, 86*
Moas, 14, *15*
Mockingbird, 249*; Blue, 249*
Moho braccatus, 275; *nobilis*, 276*
Molothrus bonariensis, 290*
Momotidae, 178
Monal, 96
Monias benschi, 101
Monticola solitaria, 253*
Montifringilla, 306
Moorhen, 109*
Morus bassana, 47*
Motacilla alba, 264*; *cinerea*, 264*
Motacillidae, 263
Motmots, 178; Turquoise-browed, 180*
Mound-builders, 85
Mousebird, Blue-naped, 174*
Mudlarks, Australian, 227
Mudnest Builders, 227
Munias, 303, 304
Murrelets, Ancient, 139*; Craveri's, 139; Crested, 139; Kittlitz's, 139; Marbled, 139; Xantus', 139
Murres, Common, 139*; Thick-billed, 138*
Muscicapa striata, 261*
Muscicapidae, *251*, 259
Muscivora forficata, 208*
Musophagidae, 150
Mutton-bird, Australian, 35*
Myadestes townsendi, 251*, 254
Mycteria americana, 57*
Myiarchus crinitis, 208*
Myioborus torquatus, 285*
Mynahs, Common, 271, 273*, 274; Golden-crested, 273*; Hill, 271, 273*; Papuan, 272
Myrmeciza exsul, 200*
Myrmotherula axillaris, 200*
Myzomela cardinalis, 277*

Nectarinia reichenowi, 278*
Nectariniidae, 278
Nene, 67
Neodrepanis coruscans, 212*
Neogaeornis, 23
Neomixis, 242
Neophron percnopterus, 75*
Neositta, 239
Nesoctites micromegas, 194*

Nesomimus, 250
Nestor notabilis, 149*
New Zealand Wrens, 212
Nighthawk, Common, 162, 164*
Nightingale, 252*, 255
Nightjars, European, 162; Pennant-winged, 163, 164*; Standard-winged, 163
Ninox, 159
Noddy, Brown, 130*, 133, 134, 136
Notharchus Macrorhynchos, 188*
Notornis, 110
Nucifraga columbiana, 225*
Numenius americanus, 121*
Numididae, 98
Nutcracker, Clark's, 225*, 226
Nuthatches, Azure, 238; Brown-headed, 238; Coral-billed, 239*; Eurasian, 238; Pygmy, 238*; Red-breasted, 238*; Rock, 238; Velvet-fronted, 238*; White-breasted, 238*
Nyctanassa violacea, 51*
Nyctea scandiaca, 156*
Nyctibiidae, 161
Nyctibius griseus, 161*
Nycticorax nycticorax, 51*, 53

Oceanites oceanicus, 31*
Oceanodroma leucorhoa, 31*
Oenanthe oenanthe, 254*
Oilbird, 157*, 160
Onychorhynchus mexicanus, 207*
O-o, 275, 276*
Opisthocomus hoazin, 100*
Oreortyx pictus, 91*
Orioles, Baltimore, 287; Black-headed, 221; Black-naped, 221, 222*; Bullock's, 287; Golden, 221; Maroon, 222*; Old World, 221; Orchard, 287; Scott's, 287; Spot-breasted, 288*
Oriolidae, 221
Oriolus chinensis, 222*; *traillii*, 222*
Ornithosis, 147
Oropendolas, Chestnut-headed, 288*; Green, 288*; Montezuma, 288*; Wagler's, 287
Ortalis wagleri, 87*
Orthonyx, 241
Orthotomus sutorius, 255*
Ortolan, 300*
Ortyxelos, 102
Oscines, 195
Osprey, 82*
Ostrich, 11, 16, 17*, *182*
Otidae, 113
Otis tarda, 114*
Otus asio, 157*
Ouzel, Ring, 252
Ovenbirds, 198, 285; Rufous, 198*
Owlet Frogmouths, 161, Grey, 161*
Owls, 72, 154; Barn, 154, 156*; Barred, 157*, 159; Bay, 154; Burrowing, 155*, 159; Eagle, (Milky, 155*, Spotted, 158, Verreaux's, 159); Elf, 156*, 159; Fishing, Pell's, 158*; Great Grey, 159; Hawk-, 159; Horned, 158, (Great, 156*); Pygmy, 159, (Ferruginous, 157*); Scops, 158; Screech,

Owls (*continued*)
155, 157*, 158; Short-eared, 159; Snowy, 155, 156*, 158; Spectacled, 156*, 150; Tawny, 158; Wood, 159
Oxpeckers, Red-billed, 275; Yellow-billed, 274*, 275
Oxyruncus cristatus, 210*
Oxyruncidae, 210
Oxyura jamaicensis, 69*
Oystercatchers, 118; American, 121*

Pachycephala pectoralis, 259*
Padda oryzivora, 304
Palaeudyptes, 27
Palm Chat, 266*
Pandion haliaetus, 82*
Pandionidae, 82
Panyptila sancti-hieronymi, 165*
Paphosia adorabilis, 170*
Paradigalla, 235
Paradisaea apoda, 233*; *regia*, 232; *respublica*, 234; *rudolphi*, 233*; *wilsoni*, 234
Paradisaeidae, 232
Paradoxornis webbiana, 241
Parakeets, Carolina, *14,* 147; Grey-breasted, 149; Hanging, 147; Slaty-headed, 146*
Pardalotus punctatus, 280*
Paridae, 235
Parrotbills, 242
Parrotfinch, Blue-faced, 302*
Parrots, 146, *150*; African Grey, 146*; Owl, 148; Pygmy, 146
Partridges, Grey, 95; Red-legged, 91*, 95
Parulidae, 284
Parus coeruleus, 235*; *major*, 235*; *varius*, 235*
Passer domesticus, 304*; *montanus*, 304*
Passeres, 195
Passeriformes, 195
Passerina ciris, 296*
Pastor, Rosy, 271, 272, 274*
Patagona gigas, 171*
Pavo cristatus, 94*
Peacock, Congo, 95, 96
Peafowl, Common, 94*, 96; Javanese, 97
Pedionomus torquatus, 102*
Pelecanidae, 40
Pelecaniformes, 38
Pelecanoides urinatrix, 38*
Pelecanoididae, 38
Pelecanus occidentalis, 41*, 42*; *onocrotalis*, 40*
Pelicans, 40, *49, 63, 132*; Brown, 41*, 42*; White, 40*
Pellorneum ruficeps, 240*
Penguins, 26, *129, 137*; Adélie, 29*; Chinstrap, 28*; Crested, 28; Emperor, 26*; 29; Galapagos, 28; Gentoo, 28*; Humboldt, 28; Jackass, 28*; King, 26*, 29; Little (Blue), 28*, 29; Macaroni, 28; Magellan, 28*; Rockhopper, 29*; Yellow-eyed, 29
Peppershrike, Rufous-browed, 282*
Perching Birds, 195
Peregrine, 83
Pericrocotus flammeus, 219*; *roseus*, 219*
Perisoreus, 226
Petrels, Antarctic, 36; Diving,

Petrels (continued)
38*; Fork-tailed, 37; Frigate, 37; Gadfly, 34; Giant, 27, 36; Gould, 31*; Leach's, 31*, 37; Pintado, 31*, 36; Snowy, 36; Storm, 31*, 37; White-winged, 31*; Wilson's, 31*, 37
Petrochelidon pyrrhonata, 216*
Petroica, 260
Petronia, 306
Pewee, Wood, 207*, 209
Phaëthon aethereus, 39*; lepturus, 39*; rubricauda, 39*
Phaëthontidae, 39
Phaethornis syrmatophorus, 171*
Phainopepla nitens, 265, 266*
Phalacrocoracidae, 43
Phalacrocorax auritus, 40*; bougainvillei, 40*; carbo, 40*; carunculatus, 40*; urile, 44*
Phalaropes, 22, 124; Grey, 124*; Northern, 124*; Red, 124*; Wilson's, 124*
Phalaropodidae, 124
Phalaropus fulicarius, 124*; lobatus, 124*
Pharomachrus mocino, 172*
Phasianidae, 92
Phasianus colchicus, 92*
Pheasants, Argus, 92, 95*, (Great, 96, Reinhart's, 96); Brown Eared, 93*; Common, 96; Copper, 93*, 96; English, 95; Fireback, 93*; Golden, 92*, 96; Impeyan, 92*; Lady Amherst, 92*; Mikado, 96; Mongolian, 95; Reeve's, 93*; Ring-necked, 92*, 95; Silver, 92*; Swinhoe's, 93*
Philacte canagica, 66*
Philemon corniculatus, 276*
Philepitta castanea, 212*
Philepittidae, 212
Philesturnus carunculatus, 227*
Philetairus socius, 305
Philomachus pugnax, 122*
Philydor, 199
Phlegopsis nigro-maculata, 200*
Phoebe, Eastern, 208*, 209
Phoenicircus nigricollis, 204*
Phoenicopteridae, 61
Phoenicopterus ruber, 61*
Phoenicurus phoenicurus, 253*
Phoenix, 96
Phororhacos, 13
Phyllastrephus flavostriatus, 244*
Phylloscopus trochilus, 257*
Phytotoma rutila, 210*
Phytotomidae, 210
Pica pica, 225*
Picathartes gymnocephalus, 241*
Piculet, Antillian, 194*
Picus canus, 194*; flavinucha, 193*
Pigeons, 141, 295; Bleeding Heart, 143*, 145; Blue-crowned, 143*; Cape, 31*, 36; Carrier, 142; Fruit, 142, (Imperial, 142, 143*, Magnificent, 143*, Yellow-bellied, 143*); Large Green, 143*; Nutmeg, 142, (Green, 142; Pied, 142); Passenger, 14, 143, 145*; Puerto Rican Blue, 145; Rock, 142, 144*; Tooth-billed, 142; Wood, 145
Pinguinus impennis, 137*
Pipile cumanensis, 87*

Pipits, Meadow, 263; Pechora, 263; Red-throated, 263; Richard's, 263; Rock, 263; Sprague's, 263; Tawny, 263; Water, 263, 264*
Pipra iris, 206*; mentalis, 206*
Pipridae, 205, 206
Piranga olivacea, 293*
Pitangus sulphuratus, 207*
Pithys albifrons, 200*
Pitta granatina, 211*; steerii, 211*
Pittas, Blue-winged, 211; Fairy, 211; Garnet, 211*; Noisy, 211; Steere's, 211*
Pittidae, 211
Plantcutters, Chilean, 210; Peruvian, 210; Reddish, 210*
Platalea leucorodia, 60*
Plautus alle, 138*
Plectrophenax nivalis, 298
Plectropterus gambensis, 64*
Plegadis falcinellus, 59*
Ploceidae, 295, 301
Ploceus cucullatus, 305*; philippinus, 304*
Plovers, 118; Black-bellied, 118, 120*; Blacksmith, 119, 129*; Crab, 125*; Dotterel, 118; Egyptian, 126; Golden, 118, 120*; Killdeer, 118, 129*; Masked, 119; Piping, 118; Ringed, 118; Semipalmated, 120*; Snowy, 118; Swallow, 125*, 126; Upland, 121; Wrybill, 119
Pluvialis dominica, 120*
Pochard, 69
Podargidae, 160
Podargus strigoides, 157*
Podica senegalensis, 112*
Podicipediformes, 22
Podiceps auritus, 22*; cristatus, 22*; griseigena, 22*; ruficollis, 23*
Podilymbus podiceps, 23*
Poephila gouldiae, 303*
Polioptila caerulea, 258*
Polysticta stelleri, 69*
Polytmus guainumbi, 170*
Pomatostomus temporalis, 240*
Poor-me-one, 161
Poor-will, 163
Popelaria popelairii, 170*
Porphyrula martinica, 108*
Porzana carolina, 110*; fusca, 107*; porzana 107*
Potoos, Common 161*; Giant, 161; Mexican, 161
Prairie Chicken, 89, 90*
Pratincoles, 125*, 126
Prions, 36
Prionops plumata, 270*
Proboscíger aterrimus, 148*
Procellariidae, 34
Procellariiformes, 31
Procnias tricarunculata, 204*
Progne chalybea, 217*; subis, 217*; tapera, 217*
Promerops cafer, 277*
Prosthemadera novaeseelandiae, 276*
Protonotaria citrea, 285*
Prunella collaris, 262*; modularis, 262*
Prunellidae, 262
Psarisomus dalhousiae, 196*
Psarocolius viridis, 288*
Psittaciformes, 146
Psittacosis, 147
Psittacula himalayana, 146*

Psittacus erithacus, 146*
Psittirostra, 284
Ptarmigans, Rock, 91; White-tailed, 91; Willow, 90*, 91
Pteridophora alberti, 233*
Pterocles alchata, 140*
Pteroclidae, 140
Pterodroma, 34; leucoptera, 31*
Pteroglossus, bitorquatus, 189*; viridis, 189*
Pteruthius erythopterus, 240*
Ptilonorhynchidae, 229
Ptilonorhynchus violaceus, 230*
Ptiloris victoriae, 234
Puffbirds, 187; Collared, 188*; White-necked, 188*
Puffins, Common, 139*; Horned, 139; Tufted, 139*
Puffinus puffinus, 34*; tenuirostris, 35*
Pulsatrix perspicillata, 156*
Pycnonotidae, 243
Pycnonotus jocosus, 243*
Pygoscelis adeliae, 29*; antarctica, 28*; papua, 28*
Pyrocephalus rubinus, 208*
Pyromelana orix, 305*
Pyrrhocorax pyrrhocorax, 223*, 226
Pyrrhula pyrrhula, 301*
Pyrruloxia sinuata, 296*
Pytelia melba, 303*

Quails, 92; Bobwhite, 91*, 93, 94; Bustard, 102*; California, 91*, 93, 94; Chinese Button, 102; Coturnix, 95, 96*; Gamble's, 94; Harlequin, 94, 95; Mountain, 91*, 94; New World, 93; Old World, 93, 94; Painted, 91*, 92, 94; Plumed, 94
Quail-thrush, Cinnamon, 240*
Quelea quelea, 304*
Quelea, Red-billed, 304*, 307
Quetzal, 172*

Rails, 101, 107, 141; Bensch's, 101; Black, 107; Clapper, 107; King, 107; Laysan, 109; Sora, 107, 110*; Virginia, 107, 110*; Wake Island, 109; Water, 107; Wood, Ypecaha, 107*; Yellow, 107
Rallidae, 107
Rallus limicola, 110*
Ramphastidae, 188
Ramphastos cuvierii, 188*; sulfuratus, 189*; toco, 189*
Ramphocaenus, 258
Ramphocelus passerinii, 293*
Raphidae, 141
Raphus cucullatus, 141*
Ratites, 12, 15-20
Raven, 195, 223, 224*
Razorbill, 138*
Recurvirostra americana, 120*
Recurvirostridae, 123
Redpoll, 302*
Redshank, 119
Redstarts, 285; Collared, 285*; European, 253*; Painted, 285*
Redwing, 253
Regulus calendula, 258*; goodfellowi, 258*
Remiz pendulinus, 236*
Rhabdornis mystacalis, 239*
Rhea americana, 19*

Rheas, Common, 19*; Darwin's, 18
Rheiformes, 18
Rhinocrypta lanceolata, 202*
Rhinocryptidae, 202
Rhipidura leucophrys, 259*
Rhodinocichla rosea, 292*
Rhodonessa, 65
Rhynochetidae, 111
Rhynochetos jubatus, 112*
Richmondena cardinalis, 296*
Riflebird, Magnificent, 233*
Rifleman, 212
Roadrunner, 153*
Robins, American, 119, 253*; European, 253*, 255; Pekin, 240*, 242; Red-capped, 260; Scarlet, 260
Rollers, Abyssinian, 180; Broad-billed, 180; Cuckoo-, 181; European, 180; Ground-, 181; Indian, 180; Lilac-breasted, 180*; Racquet-tailed, 180
Rook, 225
Rostratula benghalensis, 117*
Rostratulidae, 117
Rostrhamus sociabilis, 76*
Ruff, 122*, 123
Rupicola peruviana, 205*; rupicola, 205*
Rynchopidae, 137
Rynchops nigra, 130*

Saddleback, 227*
Sagittariidae, 74
Sagittarius serpentarius, 74*
Salpornis spilonotus, 239
Saltator atriceps, 297*
Saltator, Black-headed, 297*; Buff-throated, 297
Sanderling, 119, 123
Sandgrouse, Pallas's, 140; Pintailed, 140*
Sandpipers, 119; Bartramian, 121; Common, 120; Green, 119; Greenshank, 119; Least, 121*, 122; Red-backed, 122; Redshank, 119; Semipalmated, 122; Solitary, 119; Spotted, 120, 121*; Western, 122; Wood, 119; Yellowlegs, 119, (Greater, 121*, Lesser, 119)
Sappho sparganurus, 171*
Sapsuckers, Williamson's, 193; Yellow-bellied, 192*, 193
Sarcorhamphus papa, 72*
Saxicola torquata, 254*
Sayornis phoebe, 208*
Scaniornis, 61
Scardafella inca, 144*
Schistes geoffroyi, 170*
Schoeniophylax phryganophila, 198*
Scolopacidae, 119
Scolopax rusticola, 122*
Scopidae, 55
Scopus umbretta, 56*
Scotopelia peli, 158*
Screamers, Black-necked, 63*; Crested, 63; Horned, 63*
Scrub-birds, Noisy, 214; Rufous, 214*
Scythebill, Red-billed, 197*
Secretary Bird, 74*
Seedeaters, 195, 295, 299, 301; Black, 299; New World, 295, 301; Old World, 295, 301; Variable, 299*
Seedsnipe, Patagonian, 127*

Seleucides ignotus, 233*
Semeiophorus vexillarius, 164*
Semioptera wallaceii, 233
Semnornis ramphastinus, 185
Sericulus aureus, 231*; *chrysocephalus*, 230*
Seriemas, Burmeister's, 112; Crested, 112*
Setophaga picta, 285*
Shags, 43; King, 40*
Shama, White-rumped, 253*
Sharpbill, Crested, 210*
Shearwaters, Greater, 35; Manx, 34*; Short-tailed, 35; Slender-billed, 35*; Sooty, 35
Sheathbills, 27, 127, 128*
Shiffornis, 206
Shoveller, 68
Shrikes, 269; Black-headed, 268*; Bull-headed, 269; Caterpillar, 219; Great Grey, 268*; Gorgeous Bush, 268*; Helmet, 270, (Spectacled, 270, Straight-crested, 270*); Lesser Grey, 269; Loggerhead, 269; Northern, 268*, 270; Red-backed, 268*; Swallow-, 267; Vanga, 268*
Shrike-vireo, Chestnut-sided, 282*
Sialia sialis, 253*
Sicalis flaveola, 299*
Sicklebill, 268
Silky Flycatchers, 265
Siskin, 301*, 302
Sitellas, 241
Sitta canadensis, 238*; *carolinensis*, 238*; *frontalis*, 238*; *pygmaea*, 238*
Sittasomus griseicapillus, 197*
Sittidae, 237
Skimmers, African, 137; Black, 130*, 137; Indian, 137
Skuas, Arctic, 128*; Great, 129*; Long-tailed, 128*; Pomatorhine, 129*
Skylark, 215*
Smew, 69*
Snipes, Australian, 122; Common, 122*; Painted, 117*
Solitaires, Reunion, 141; Rodriguez, 141; Townsend's, 251*, 254
Somateria mollissima, 71*; *fischeri*, 71*
Sparrows, 295; Black-chinned, 299; Brewer's, 298; Chipping, 298; Claycoloured, 298; Field, 298; Goldencrowned, 298; Grasshopper, 298; Greenbacked, 299; Harris, 298; Hedge, 262*; House, 248, 304*, 306; Java, 304; Lark, 298; Lincoln's, 298; Olive, 299; Orange-billed, 299; Rock, 306; Sage, 299; Savannah, 298; Seaside, 299; Sharp-tailed, 299; Song, 298; Swamp, 298; Tree, 298; (Eurasian, 304*, 306); Vesper, 298; White-crowned, 298; White-throated, 298*
Speotyto cunicularia, 155*
Sphecotheres flaviventris, 222*
Sphenisciformes, 26
Spheniscus demersus, 28*; *magellanicus*, 28*
Sphyrapicus varius, 192*
Spiderhunter, Little, 278*, 279
Spinetail, Pale-breasted, 198*; White-cheeked, 198*

Spizaëtus ornatus, 80*
Spizella arborea, 298*
Spoonbills, Eurasian, 60*; Roseate, 60*
Sporophila aurita, 299*
Spreo superbus, 274*
Squatarola squatarola, 120*
Starlings, Amethyst, 273*; Common, 271, 272, 274*; Glossy, 272; Golden-breasted, 272, 274*; Grey, 271; Superb, 272, 274*; Wattled, 271, 272
Steatornis caripensis, 157*
Steatornithidae, 160
Steganopodes, 38
Steganopus tricolor, 124*
Steganura paradisea, 305*
Stelgidopteryx ruficollis, 216*
Stercorariidae, 128
Stercorarius longicaudus, 129*; *parasiticus*, 128*; *pomarinus*, 129*
Sterna dougalli, 134*; *fuscata*, 134*; *hirundo*, 130*; *paradisaea*, 134*
Stilts, Banded, 120*, 123; Black-necked, 120*, 123; Pied, 123
Stipiturus malachurus, 258*
Stitchbird, 277
Stonechat, 254*
Stone Curlews, 125*, 126
Storks, Adjutant, 57*, 58; Black, 57*, 58; Marabou, 57*, 58; Saddlebilled, 57*; Shoebill, 55, 56*; Whalehead, 55; White, 57*; Wood, 57*
Streptopelia bitorquata, 143*
Strigidae, 155
Strigiformes, 154
Strix varia, 157*
Struthidea, 228
Struthio camelus, 17*
Struthioniformes, 16
Sturnella neglecta, 290*
Sturnidae, 271
Sturnus roseus, 274*; *vulgaris*, 274*
Sugarbird, Cape, 277*
Sula dactylatra, 47*; *leucogaster*, 47*; *nebouxii*, 47*; *sula*, 47*
Sulidae, 46
Sunbirds, False, Wattled, 212*; Golden-winged, 278*; Purple, 278*; Regal, 278*; Variable, 278*; White-breasted, 279
Sunbittern, 112*, 113
Sun Grebes, 111
Surfbird, 123
Surniculus, 221
Swallow-plover, 126
Swallows, 165, 216; Bank, 218; Barn, 216*; Chimney, 217; Cliff, 216*; Mosque, 218; Red-rumped, 218; Rough-winged, 216*; Tree, 216*; Welcome, 217; Wood, 265
Swallow-shrike, Ashy, 267
Swallow Tanager, 292*, 294
Swans, Bewick's, 65; Black, 65, 67*; Black-necked, 65, 67*; Mute, 65, 67*; Trumpeter, 65, 67*; Whistling, 65; Whooper, 65
Swiftlet, Cave, 167; Edible-nest, 167*; Grey, 167; Grey-rumped, 167
Swifts, Alpine, 166; Black, 166; Chimney, 165*, 166; Common, 166; Crested, 167, (Indian, 165*); Palm, 166,

Swifts (*continued*)
(African, 166*); Scissor-tailed, 165*, 166; Spinetailed, 166, (Brown-throated, 165*, 166); White-rumped, 165*
Sylvia atricapilla, 256*; *curruca*, 152*
Sylviidae, 251, 255
Synallaxis albescens, 198*
Synthliboramphus antiquum, 139*
Syrmaticus reevesii, 93*; *soemmerringii*, 93*

Tachyeres pteneres, 68*
Tadorna tadorna, 69*
Tailorbirds, Long-tailed, 255*, 257
Takahe, 110
Talegallus, 86
Tanagers, Arnault's, 293; Azure-rumped, 293; Black-eared, 293*; Blue, 292; Blue-grey, 292, 293*; Cabanis's, 293; Golden-masked, 292; Gould's, 293; Hepatic, 292; Masked, 293*; Paradise, 293*; Plush-capped, 292*, 294; Red-crowned Ant, 291*; Rose-breasted Thrush-, 292*, 294; Scarlet, 292, 293*; Scarlet-rumped, 293*; Summer, 292; Swallow, 292*, 294; Velvet, 292; Western, 292
Tanagra luteicapilla, 291*
Tangara chilensis, 293*; *nigrocincta*, 293*; *parzudakii*, 293*
Tapaculos, Ocellated, 202*; Silver-fronted, 202
Tapera, 154
Taraba major, 200*
Taurac corythaix, 150*
Teals, 68
Teleonema filicauda, 206*
Telophorus quadricolor, 268*
Terathopius ecaudatus, 79*
Teratornis incredibilis, 73
Teratornix merriami, 73
Terns, 130, 133; Arctic, 133, 134*, 135; Black, 134; Brown Noddy, 130*, 133, 134, 136; Caspian, 134; Common, 130*, 134; Crested, 134; Fairy, 130*, 134; Forster's, 134; Inca, 134*; Least, 136; Roseate, 134*, 136; Royal, 130*, 134; Sooty, 133, 136
Terpsiphone atrocaudata, 261*; *paradisi*, 261
Tersinia viridis, 292*
Tetrao urogallus, 88*
Tetraonidae, 88
Thalasseus maximus, 130*
Thamnophilus doliatus, 200*
Thick-heads, 262
Thick-knees, 125, 126
Thinocoridae, 127
Thinocorus rumicivorus, 127*
Thornbill, Red-fronted, 199
Thrashers, Brown, 249*; California, 250; Crissal, 250; LeConte's, 250; Pearly-eyed, 250; Sage, 250; Scaly-breasted, 250; White-breasted, 250
Thraupidae, 291
Thraupis virens, 293*
Threskiornis aethiopica, 59*
Threskiornithidae, 59

Thrushes, 251; Black-throated, 253; Bonin Island, 251; Chat-, 254; Dusky, 253; Eyebrowed, 253; Fieldfare, 255; Grey-cheeked, 253; Gray's, 252; Hermit, 252*, 253; Laughing-, 242, (White-crested, 240*); Mistle, 253; Naumann's, 253; Nightingale, 252*, 253, 255; Orange-billed Nightingale, 251*; Red-throated, 253*; Redwing, 253; Rock-, 254, (Blue, 253*, 254, Red-bellied, 253*, 254); Shama, White-rumped, 253*; Song, 251, 253; Swainson's, 253; Veery, 253; White-chinned, 252; Wood, 251, 252*; Wren-, 254*
Tiaris olivacea, 299*
Tichodroma muraria, 238*
Tieke, 227
Tigrisoma lineatum, 52*
Timalia pileata, 240*
Timaliidae, 240
Tinamiformes, 21
Tinamous, 21; Crested, 21*; Variegated, 21*
Titmice, 235; Tufted, 236
Tits, Bearded, 242; Blue, 235*; Bush, 236; Crested, 236; Crow-, 242; Great, 235*, 236; Long-tailed, 236*, (Red-headed, 236*); Penduline, 236*; Pygmy, 236; Sultan, 236; Varied, 235*; Willow, 236
Tityra, masked, 204*
Todidae, 178
Todies, 178; Jamaican, 180*
Todus todus, 180*
Topaza pella, 170*
Torgos tracheliotus, 75*
Totanus melanoleucus, 121*
Totipalmate Swimmers, 38
Toucanet, Emerald, 189*, 190
Toucans, Cuvier's, 188*; Keel-billed, 190; Laminated Hill, 188*; Sulphur-breasted, 189*; Toco, 189*, 190
Touraco, Knysna, 150*
Towhee, 298
Toxostoma rufum, 249*
Tragopan temmincki, 92*
Treecreeper, Red-browed, 239*
Trembler, 250
Treron capellei, 143*
Trichoglossus haematodus, 146*
Trigonoceps occipitalis, 75*
Triller, White-winged, 219*, 220
Trochilidae, 168
Trochilus polytmus, 171*
Troglodytes aëdon, 248*; *troglodytes*, 247*
Troglodytidae, 247
Trogon collaris, 172*; *viridis*, 172*
Trogoniformes, 172
Trogons, Bar-tailed, 172*; Gartered, 173; Narina, 173; Orange-breasted, 172*; White-tailed, 172*
Tropic-birds, Red-billed, 39*; Red-tailed, 39*; White-tailed, 39*
Troupial, 287, 288*
Trumpeter, White-winged, 106*
Tubinares, 31
Tui, 276*
Turdidae, 251
Turdoidinae, 242
Turdus merula, 252*; *migratorius*, 253*

Turkeys, Brush, 85*; Ocellated, 99*; Wild, 99*
Turko, Chilean, 202
Turnicidae, 102
Turnis suscitator, 102*
Turnstones, Black, 123; Ruddy, 120*
Twite, 302
Tylas, 222
Tympanuchus cupido, 90*
Tyranni, 195, 196
Tyrannidae, 207
Tyrannus tyrannus, 208*
Tyrant Flycatchers, 207
Tyto alba, 156*
Tytonidae, 154

Ula-ai-hawane, 284
Umbrellabird, Ornate, 203, 205*
Upucerthia serrana, 199*
Upupa epops, 181*
Upupidae, 182
Uraeginthus bengalensis, 303*
Uria aalge, 139*; *lomvia*, 138*

Vanellus vanellus, 120*
Vanga-shrikes, Blue, 268*; Hook-billed, 268; La Fresnaye's, 268; Red-tailed, 268; Rufous, 268
Veery, 253
Verdin, 237
Vermivora, 285
Vestiaria coccinea, 283*
Vireo flavifrons, 281*; *olivaceus*, 281*
Vireolanius melitophrys, 282*
Vireonidae, 281
Vireos, Black-capped, 282; Blue-headed, 282; Philadelphia, 283; Red-eyed, 281*; White-eyed, 282; Yellow-green, 282; Yellow-throated, 281*

Vultur gryphus, 72*
Vultures, American, 73; Bearded, 77; Black, 72*; Eared, 75*; Egyptian, 75*; Griffon, 75*, 76; Hooded, 76; King, 72*; Old World, 75; Turkey, 72*; White-headed, 75*, 76; Yellow-headed, 74

Waders, 115
Wagtails, 263; Forest, 264*; Grey, 264*; Pied, 264*; Willie-, 259*, 262; Yellow, 264
Wallcreeper, 238*
Warblers, Blackburnian, 286; Blackpoll, 285; Black-throated Blue, 285*; Blue-winged, 285; Bonin White-eyed, 241; Brewster's, 285; Bush, 257*; Cape May, 285; Cerulean, 286; Chestnut-sided, 285; Connecticut, 285; Fantail, 256*, 257; Garden, 255; Golden-winged, 285; Grass, 257; Grasshopper, 256, (Pallas's, 256*); Greenish, 256; Hooded, 285*; Kentucky, 285; Kirtland's, 285; Lawrence's, 285; Leaf, 256; Magnolia, 286*; Myrtle, 285; Nashville, 285; New World, 284; Old World, 255; Ovenbird, 285, 286; Palm, 285; Parula, 285; Pine, 285; Prairie, 285; Prothonotary, 285*, 286; Red, 285; Reed, 256, (Great, 256*); Sutton's, 285; Tennessee, 285; White-throat, 255, (Lesser 152*); Willow, 257*, (Arctic, 256); Wood, 256, 284; Wren-, 259; Yellow-throat, 285
Waterfowl, 63
Wattlebirds, 227, 276
Wattle-eye, Black-throated, 260

Waxbills, Common, 303; Orange-cheeked, 303; Yellow-bellied, 303*
Waxwings, Bohemian, 265*; Cedar, 265; Japanese, 265
Weaverbirds, 304
Weaverfinches, *152*, 304
Weavers, Baya, 304*, 306; Bishop, 307, (Red, 307); Black-headed, 305*; Paradise, 307; Social, 305*, 306; Sparrow, 304, 306; Spectacled, 305*; Village, 305*, 306; Whidah, 307; White-headed Buffalo, 304*, 305; Widow, 304, 307
Weka, 110, 111*
Whalehead, 55
Wheatear, 254*
Whidah, Long-tailed, 307
Whimbrel, 120
Whinchat, 254
Whip-poor-will, 163, 164*
Whistlers, 262; Golden, 259*
White-eyes, 280; Common, 281; Oriental, 281*
Whitethroat, Lesser, 152*
Widowbird, Paradise, 305*, 307
Wigeon, 68
Willet, 121
Wilsonia citrina, 285*
Woodcocks, American, 122, *163*; Eurasian, 122*
Woodcreepers, 196, *237*; Barred, 197*; Olivaceous, 197*; Ruddy, 197
Woodhoopoes, 182
Woodpeckers, 191; Acorn, 193; Crimson-backed, 193*, 194; Downy, 192; Golden-fronted, 193*; Great Black, 194; Green, 191; Grey-headed, 194*; Ground, 194; Hairy, 192; Ivory-billed, *14*, 192*, 194, (Imperial, 194, Magellanic, 194); Jamaica, 192*, 193; Pileated, 194; Red-bellied, 193; Red-headed,

Woodpeckers (*continued*) 192*, 193; Spotted, Great, 192, (Lesser, 192); Three-toed, (Black-backed, 193, Northern, 192); Yellow-naped, 193*
Wood Pewee, 207*
Wood-swallows, Little, 267; White-browed, 267*
Wren-babbler, 242
Wrens, Bewick's, 247; Bush, 212*; Cactus, 247, 248*; Carolina, 248; Emu, 258*; House, 248*; Marsh, 247, (Longbilled, 247, Short-billed, 247*); New Zealand, 212; Purple-backed, 254; Rock, 212; Stephen Island, 212; Variegated, 258*, 259; Winter, 247*, 248; Wood, 248, (Grey-breasted, 247, White-breasted, 247); Zapata, 247, 248*
Wren-thrush, 254*
Wren-tit, 241, 243
Wren-warbler, 259
Wrynecks, 191, 194*

Xanthocephalus xanthocephalus, 290*
Xenicus longipes, 212*
Xenops minutus, 198*
Xenops, Plain, 198*, 199
Xipholena punicea, 203*

Yellowlegs, 119, 121*

Zarhynchus wagleri, 288*
Zeledonia coronata, 254*
Zenaida asiatica, 144*
Zenaidura macroura, 144*
Zonotrichia albicollis, 298*
Zosteropidae, 280
Zosterops palpebrosa, 281*

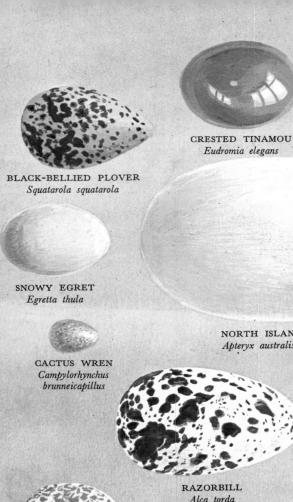

BLACK-BELLIED PLOVER
Squatarola squatarola

CRESTED TINAMOU
Eudromia elegans

GUANAY CORMORANT
Phalacrocorax bougainvillei

PEREGRINE FALCON
Falco peregrinus

AMERICAN JACANA
Jacana spinosa

COMMON NIGHTHAWK
Chordeiles minor

BLACK SKIMMER
Rynchops nigra

SWALLOW-TAILED KITE
Elanoides forficatus

SNOWY EGRET
Egretta thula

GREAT HORNED OWL
Bubo virginianus

AMERICAN ROBIN
Turdus migratorius

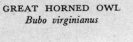

CACTUS WREN
Campylorhynchus brunneicapillus

NORTH ISLAND KIWI
Apteryx australis mantelli

RUFF
Philomachus pugnax

SLATY-BACKED GULL
Larus schistisagus

EARED GREBE
Podiceps caspicus

BELTED KINGFISHER
Megaceryle alcyon

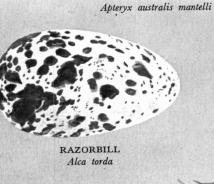
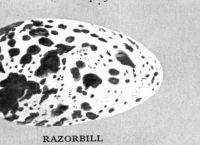

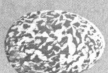

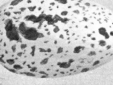

RAZORBILL
Alca torda

CANADA GOOSE
Branta canadensis

INCA TERN
Larosterna inca

GUIRA CUCKOO
Guira guira

GREAT CRESTED FLYCATCHER
Myiarchus crinitus

SCARLET IBIS
Eudocimus ruber

OLD WORLD BITTERN
Botaurus stellaris

MADAGASCAR BULBUL
Ixocincla madagascariensis

RED-BREASTED MERGANSER
Mergus serrator

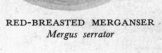

PRITCHARD'S MEGAPODE
Megapodius pritchardi

LONG-TAILED JAEGER
Stercorarius longicaudus

HOUSE WREN
Troglodytes aëdon

TURKEY VULTURE
Cathartes aura

WILLOW GROUSE
Lagopus lagopus

SCARLET MACAW
Ara macao

EUROPEAN BLACKBIRD
Turdus merula

BROWN BOOBY
Sula leucogaster

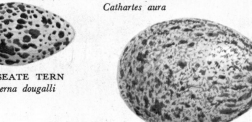
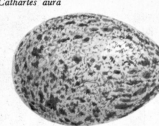

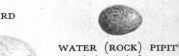

WOOD THRUSH
Hylocichla mustelina

ROSEATE TERN
Sterna dougalli

REDDISH PLANTCUTTER
Phytotoma rutila

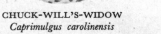

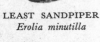

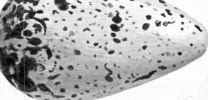

LEAST SANDPIPER
Erolia minutilla

THICK-BILLED MURRE
Uria lomvia

YELLOW-SHAFTED FLICKER
Colaptes auratus

CHUCK-WILL'S-WIDOW
Caprimulgus carolinensis

RED-TAILED TROPIC-BIRD
Phaëthon rubricauda

PAURAQUE
Nyctidromus albicollis

WATER (ROCK) PIPIT
Anthus spinoletta